CLYMER

EVINRUDE/JOHNSON

FOUR-STROKE OUTBOARD SHOP MANUAL

5-70 HP • 1995-2001

The World's Finest Publisher of Mechanical How-to Manuals

PRIMEDIA
Business Magazines & Media

P.O. Box 12901, Overland Park, KS 66282-2901

FIRST EDITION
First Printing November, 2002

Printed in U.S.A.

CLYMER and colophon are registered trademarks of PRIMEDIA Business Magazines & Media Inc.

This book was printed at Von Hoffmann an ISO certified company.

ISBN: 0-89287-804-5

Library of Congress: 2002114587

AUTHOR: Clymer Staff.

ILLUSTRATIONS: Mike Rose.

WIRING DIAGRAMS: Bob Caldwell.

EDITOR: Jason Beaver.

PRODUCTION: Susan Hartington.

COVER: Photo courtesy of Bombardier.

CLYMER PUBLICATIONS
PRIMEDIA Business Magazines & Media

Chief Executive Officer Timothy M. Andrews
President Ron Wall

The following product lines are published by PRIMEDIA Business Directories & Books.

More information available at *primediabooks.com*

Contents

Quick Reference Data

MAINTENANCE SCHEDULE

Frequency	Task
Before each use	Visually inspect the boat hull for damage
	Check fuel level in gas tank
	Check for signs of fuel or oil leakage
	Check engine crankcase oil level and condition
	Check the propeller for wear or damage
	Check the water intake for debris
	Check that the battery cables are clean and tight
	Check the engine mounting fasteners for tightness
	Check the remote steering cable operation and visually inspect for wear or damage
	Check all controls for proper operation (especially emergency stop switch/clip/lanyard)
After each use	Visually inspect the boat hull for damage
	Check for signs of fuel or oil leakage
	Check engine crankcase oil level and condition
	Check the propeller for wear or damage
	Check the water intake for debris
	Visually inspect the anode(s) for wear or damage
	Check the engine mounting fasteners for tightness
	Rinse exterior of engine, hull and propeller with fresh water (if used in salt, polluted or brackish water). Coat motor casing with wax, as necessary
	Flush cooling system once engine has cooled (if used in salt, polluted or brackish water)
	Shut off the battery switch (fuel injected models) to prevent battery drain
	Check the fishing line trap (every 15-20 hours) on 8-15 hp models
	(continued)

Frequency	Task
Lubrication service at least every 60 days in freshwater service or 30 days in salt, brackish or polluted water service	Choke and carburetor linkage greasing (except fuel injected engines) Electric starter pinion lubrication Check power trim/tilt reservoir fluid level and condition (40-70 hp models) Shift lever shaft and detent greasing Swivel bracket, tilt/run lever, tilt shaft and clamp screw (as applicable) greasing Throttle linkage greasing Change the gearcase oil (40-70 hp models)
Initial 20 hour break-in service (also perform after 20 hour break-in, following a major overhaul including new rings)	Lubricate the remote steering cable ram Check cylinder head bolt torque (5-15 hp models) Remove and inspect the spark plugs, clean or replace as necessary Check all electrical wires and connectors for damage, corrosion and proper fitting Check any linkage adjustments Check the engine mounting fasteners for tightness Lubricate all grease fittings Replace the inline fuel filter and/or fuel filter canister, as applicable Thoroughly check the boat and motor fuel tank and hoses for leaks or damage Check all engine systems for signs of deterioration or damage Change the engine crankcase oil and change or clean the filter (to drain the break-in oil from the engine) Change the gearcase oil Check valve lash clearance adjustment Check and adjust the steering friction (5-15 hp models) Check power trim reservoir fluid level and condition (40-70 hp models) Perform bypass air screw adjustment (40-50 hp models)
Every 50 hours/6 months	Perform all applicable lubrication services Thoroughly check all hoses and fittings for deterioration and leaks Check gearcase oil level and condition Check the battery condition, electrolyte level, and charge Check all anodes and ground wires Check for loose fasteners If OMC carbon guard is not used consistently in fuel supply, decarbon combustion chambers using OMC Engine Tuner
Every 100 hours/annually	Perform all lubrication services Perform all 50 hour/6 month checks or services Change the engine crankcase oil* (always change crankcase oil immediately prior to storage regardless of number of hours used that season) Change the gearcase oil (always change case oil immediately prior to storage) Grease the propeller shaft and tighten the retaining nut (or check the drive pin) Inspect the propeller shaft seals for leakage, replace if necessary Inspect the battery cables for wear or damage, clean, tighten and replace, as necessary Lubricate the remote steering cable ram

(continued)

MAINTENANCE SCHEDULE (continued)

Frequency	Task

Every 100 hours/annually (continued)	Inspect the timing belt (except 40-50 hp models)
	Perform a pre-season tune-up:
	Check engine compression
	Inspect, clean and regap or replace the spark plugs
	Apply a light coat of electric grease to the spark plugs and
	    interior of the leads
	Check all electrical wires and connectors for damage, corrosion
	    and proper fitting
	Visually inspect ignition components, test and replace components,
	    as necessary
	Replace the inline fuel filter and/or fuel filter canister,
	    as applicable
	Check and adjust engine idle speed and control linkage
	    (5-15 hp models)
	Check the steering friction and adjust, if necessary (5-15 hp models)
	Check cylinder head bolt torque (5-15 hp models)
	Check and retorque fasteners, as necessary
	Decarbon the combustion chambers using OMC Engine Tuner
	Verify proper engine and cooling system operation (take a test run)

Every 200 hours/annually	Perform all 100 hour/annual services Perform idle bypass air screw adjustment (40-70 hp models) Check valve clearance and adjust, as necessary
Every 800 hours/4 years	Replace the timing belt (except 40-50 hp models)

*The manufacturer recommends the use of Evinrude or Johnson Ultra four-stroke engine oil. When using this oil the manufacturer extends the oil change interval to 200 hours, but still should be done at least annually and immediately prior to storage, regardless of the number of hours used that season.

FUEL RECOMMENDATIONS

Model	Fuel type – minimum octane No.
All models*	Regular unleaded / 87 octane AKI (RON + MON/2) or 90 octane RON

*Do not use fuels with more than 10% ethanol or 5% methanol with 5% cosolvents. Carbureted models that are not equipped with an emissions port/tube may use leaded gasoline of the same minimum specified octane. Use of leaded gasoline in fuel injected models or in carbureted models with emission tube/port may cause engine damage.

OIL AND LUBRICANT RECOMMENDATIONS*

Item	Lubricant type
Choke and carburetor linkage	OMC Triple-Guard grease
Electrical contacts/connectors	Dielectric grease
Electric starter pinion	OMC starter pinion lube
Engine crankcase oil	
Preferred for all models	Evinrude or Johnson Ultra four-stroke engine oil
or for 5-15 hp models	SAE 10W-30 SG or SH motor oil
or for 40-70 hp models	SAE 10W-40 SG or SH motor oil
Gearcase oil	OMC Ultra-HPF gearcase lube
Power trim/tilt reservoir	OMC Power trim/tilt and power steering fluid

(continued)

OIL AND LUBRICANT RECOMMENDATIONS* (continued)

Item	Lubricant type
Propeller shaft splines	OMC Triple-Guard grease
Shift lever shaft and detent	OMC Triple-Guard grease
Swivel bracket	OMC Triple-Guard grease
Throttle linkage	OMC Triple-Guard grease
Tilt/run lever shaft, tilt shaft and clamp screws	OMC Triple-Guard grease

*Be certain that replacement fluids meet OMC specifications before substituting another fluid for the original designated fluid type.

CAPACITIES

Engine model	Engine size cu. in. (cc)	Engine oil U.S. (metric)	Gearcase oil U.S. (metric)
5 and 6 hp	7.8 (128)	27.0 fl. oz. (800 ml)	11 fl. oz. (325 ml)
8 and 9.9 hp	12.87 (211)	33.8 fl. oz. (1000 ml)	9.0 fl. oz. (266 ml)
9.9 and 15 hp	18.61 (305)	43.0 fl. oz. (1272 ml)	9.0 fl. oz. (266 ml)
40 and 50 hp	49.7 (815)	2.5 qt. (2.4 L)	21 fl. oz. (620 ml)
70 hp	79.2 (1298)	4.8 qt. (4.5 L)	19 fl. oz. (562 ml)

SPARK PLUG TYPE AND GAP

Engine model	Engine size cu. in. (cc)	Plug make and type	Gap in. (mm)
5 and 6 hp	7.8 (128)	Champion P10Y	0.027 (0.7)
8 and 9.9 hp	12.87 (211)	Champion P10Y	0.027 (0.7)
9.9 and 15 hp	18.61 (305)	Champion RA8HC	0.030-0.040 (0.8-1.0)
40 and 50 hp	49.7 (815)	NGK DCPR6E	0.035-0.039 (0.9-1.0)
70 hp	79.2 (1298)	NGK BPR6ES	0.030 (0.8)

VALVE CLEARANCE SPECIFICATIONS

Engine model	Engine size cu. in. (cc)	Intake in. (mm)	Exhaust in. (mm)
5 and 6 hp	7.8 (128)	0.003 (0.08)	0.005 (0.13)
8 and 9.9 hp	12.87 (211)	0.003 (0.08)	0.005 (0.13)
9.9 and 15 hp	18.61 (305)	0.004 (0.10)	0.006 (0.15)
40 and 50 hp	49.7 (815)	0.007-0.009 (0.18-0.23)	0.007-0.009 (0.18-0.23)
70 hp	79.2 (1298)	0.005 (0.13)	0.006 (0.15)

CARBURETOR SCREW ADJUSTMENT SPECIFICATIONS

Engine model	Engine size cu. in. (cc)	Initial low speed setting	Float level OMC gauge No.	Float drop setting in. (mm)
5 hp	7.8 (128)			
1997		6 turns	324891	1-1 3/8 (25-35)
1998-2001		1 5/8 turns	324891	1-1 3/8 (25-35)
6 hp	7.8 (128)			
1997		6 turns	324891	1-1 3/8 (25-35)
1998-2001		4 turns	324891	1-1 3/8 (25-35)

(continued)

CARBURETOR SCREW ADJUSTMENT SPECIFICATIONS (continued)

Engine model	Engine size cu. in. (cc)	Initial low speed setting	Float level OMC gauge No.	Float drop setting in. (mm)
8 and 9.9 hp	12.87 (211)	5 turns	324891	1-1 3/8 (25-35)
9.9 and 15 hp	18.61 (305)	4 turns	324891	1-1 3/8 (25-35)

IDLE SPEED AND MINIMUM TEST RPM SPECIFICATIONS

Engine model	Engine size cu. in. (cc)	Idle rpm in gear	Test propeller OMC part No.	Minimum test rpm
5 and 6 hp	7.8 (128)			
1997-1998		850-950	390239	4700
1999-2001		1150-1250	444508	5500
8 and 9.9 hp[1,2]	12.87 (211)			
1995-1998		850-950	386537	4700
1999-2001		950-1050	386537	4800
9.9 and 15 hp[3]	18.61 (305)			
1995-1997		800-900	340177	3500-5000[1]
1998		950-1050	340177	3500-5000[1]
1999		750-850	340177	3500-5000[1]
2000-2001		850-950	340177	3500-5000[1]
40 and 50 hp	49.7 (815)	800-900	N/A	N/A
70 hp	79.2 (1298)	700	386665	5000

1. 9.9 hp rope start – 3500 rpm
2. 9.9 electric start – 4000 rpm
3. 15 hp – 5000 rpm

Chapter One

General Information

This detailed and comprehensive manual covers Johnson and Evinrude four-stroke outboard motors (5-70 hp) from their introduction in 1995 to 2001.

This manual can be used by anyone from a first time do-it-yourselfer to a professional mechanic. The text provides step-by-step information on maintenance, tune-up, repair and overhaul. Hundreds of illustrations guide the reader through every job.

A shop manual is a reference that should be used to find information quickly. Clymer manuals are designed with that in mind. All chapters are thumb tabbed and important items are indexed at the end of the manual. All procedures, tables, photos and instructions in this manual are designed for the reader who may be working on the machine or using the manual for the first time.

Keep the manual in a handy place such as a toolbox or boat. It will help to better understand how the boat runs, lower repair and maintenance costs and generally increase enjoyment of the boat.

Frequently used specifications and capacities from individual chapters are summarized in the *Quick Reference Data* at the front of the book. Specifications concerning specific systems are at the end of each chapter.

Tables 1-4 are at the end of this chapter.

Table 1 lists the engines covered in this manual.

Table 2 lists technical abbreviations.

Table 3 lists metric tap and drill sizes.

Table 4 lists conversion formulas.

MANUAL ORGANIZATION

All dimensions and capacities are expressed in U.S. standard and metric units of measurement.

This chapter provides general information on shop safety, tool use, service fundamentals and shop supplies. The tables at the end of the chapter include general engine information.

Chapter Two provides methods and suggestions for quick and accurate diagnosis and repair of problems. Troubleshooting procedures discuss typical symptoms and logical methods to pinpoint the trouble.

Chapter Three explains all periodic lubrication and routine maintenance necessary to keep the outboard operating well. Chapter Three also includes recommended tune-up procedures, eliminating the need to constantly consult other chapters on the various assemblies.

Subsequent chapters describe specific systems, providing disassembly, repair, assembly and adjustment procedures in simple step-by-step form.

Some of the procedures in this manual specify special tools. When possible, the tool is illustrated in use. Well-equipped mechanics may be able to substitute similar tools or fabricate a suitable replacement. However, in some cases, the specialized equipment or expertise may make it impractical for the home mechanic to attempt the procedure. When necessary, such operations are identified in the text with the recommendation to have a dealership or specialist perform the task. It may be less expensive to have them perform these jobs, especially when considering the cost of the equipment. This is true with machine work for power head rebuilds, as machinists spend years perfecting their trade and even professional mechanics will often rely upon their services.

WARNINGS, CAUTIONS AND NOTES

The terms WARNING, CAUTION and NOTE have specific meanings in this manual.

A WARNING emphasizes areas where injury or even death could result from negligence. Mechanical damage may also occur. WARNINGS *are to be taken seriously.*

A CAUTION emphasizes areas where equipment damage could result. Disregarding a CAUTION could cause permanent mechanical damage, though injury is unlikely.

A NOTE provides additional information to clarify or make a procedure easier. Disregarding a NOTE could cause inconvenience, but would not cause equipment damage or injury.

SAFETY

Professional mechanics can work for years and never sustain a serious injury or mishap. Follow these guidelines and practice common sense to safely service the motor.

1. Do not operate the motor in an enclosed area. The exhaust gasses contain carbon monoxide, an odorless, colorless, and tasteless poisonous gas. Carbon monoxide levels build quickly in small enclosed areas and can cause unconsciousness and death in a short time. Make sure the work area is properly ventilated or operate the motor outside.

2. *Never* use gasoline or any extremely flammable liquid to clean parts. Refer to *Handling Gasoline Safely* and *Cleaning Parts* in this chapter.

3. *Never* smoke or use a torch in the vicinity of flammable liquids, such as gasoline or cleaning solvent.

4. After removing the engine cover, allow the engine to air out before performing any service work. Review *Fuel System Service Precautions* at the beginning of Chapter Five or Chapter Six.

5. Use the correct tool type and size to avoid damaging fasteners.

6. Keep tools clean and in good condition. Replace or repair worn or damaged equipment.

7. When loosening a tight or stuck fastener, always ask yourself what would happen if the wrench should slip. In most cases, it is safer to pull on a wrench or a ratchet than

it would be to push on it. Be careful; protect yourself accordingly.

8. When replacing a fastener, make sure to use one with the same measurements and strength as the old one. Refer to *Fasteners* in this chapter for additional information.

9. Keep your work area clean and uncluttered. Keep all hand and power tools in good condition. Wipe greasy and oily tools after using them. They are difficult to hold and can cause injury. Replace or repair worn or damaged tools. Do not leave tools, shop rags or anything that does not belong in the hull.

10. Wear safety goggles during all operations involving drilling, grinding, the use of a cold chisel or *any* time the safety of your eyes is in question (when debris may spray or scatter). **Always** wear safety goggles when using solvent and compressed air.

11. Do not carry sharp tools in clothing pockets.

12. Always have an approved fire extinguisher available. Make sure it is rated for gasoline (Class B) and electrical (Class C) fires.

13. Do not use compressed air to clean clothes, the boat/motor or the work area. Debris may be blown into eyes or skin. *Never* direct compressed air at yourself or someone else. Do not allow children to use or play with any compressed air equipment.

14. When using compressed air to dry rotating parts, hold the part so it cannot rotate. Do not allow the force of the air to spin the part. The air jet is capable of rotating parts at extreme speed. The part may become damaged or disintegrate, causing serious injury.

Handling Gasoline Safely

Gasoline is a volatile flammable liquid and is one of the most dangerous items in the shop.

Because gasoline is used so often, many people forget that it is hazardous. Only use gasoline as fuel for gasoline internal combustion engines. Do not use it as a cleaner or degreaser. Keep in mind, when working, gasoline is always present in the fuel tank, fuel lines and carburetor or fuel rail. To avoid a disastrous accident when working around the fuel system, carefully observe the following precautions:

1. *Never* use gasoline to clean parts. See *Cleaning Parts* in this chapter.

2. When working on the fuel system, work outside or in a well-ventilated area.

3. Do not add fuel to the fuel tank or service the fuel system while the boat is near an open flame, sparks or where someone is smoking. Gasoline vapor is heavier than air. It collects in low areas and is much more easily ignited than liquid gasoline.

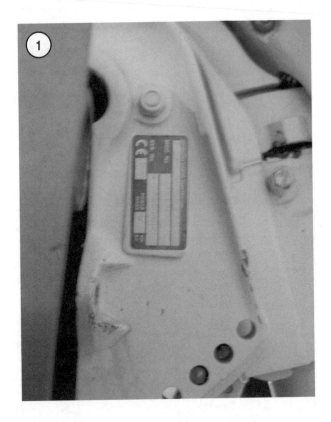

for shop use. Most are poisonous and extremely flammable. To prevent chemical exposure, vapor buildup, fire and serious injury, observe each product warning label and note the following:

1. Read and observe the entire product label before using any chemical. Always know what type of chemical is being used and whether it is poisonous and/or flammable.

2. Do not use more than one type of cleaning solvent at a time. If mixing chemicals is called for, measure the proper amounts according to the manufacturer.

3. Work in a well-ventilated area.

4. Wear chemical-resistant gloves.

5. Wear safety glasses.

6. Wear a vapor respirator if the instructions call for it.

7. Wash hands and arms thoroughly after cleaning parts.

8. Keep chemical products away from children and pets.

9. Thoroughly clean all oil, grease and cleaner residue from any part that must be heated.

10. Use a nylon brush when cleaning parts. Metal brushes may cause a spark.

11. When using a parts washer, only use the solvent recommended by the equipment manufacturer. Make sure the parts washer is equipped with a metal lid that will lower in case of fire.

SERIAL NUMBER AND MODEL IDENTIFICATION

Serial number/model tags are affixed to the engine (**Figure 1**), usually on the engine clamp bracket. Record these numbers in the *Quick Reference Data* section at the front of the manual. Have these numbers available when ordering parts.

Model numbers designate the make, type, horsepower and options used on the engine. The first letter (J or E) designates whether the model was produced for sale under the Johnson or Evinrude marks. The next designation is a number (one or two digit) representing the horsepower rating of the motor a 5, 6, 8, 10 (for the 9.9), 15, 40, 50 or 70. For 1995-1998 a letter designator F (representing four-stroke) follows the horsepower rating. On 1999 and later models the F is replaced by 4, and it no longer directly follows the horsepower rating. The remaining letters (either following the F or before and after the 4) designate design features such as rope start, electric start, electric tiller, remote, etc.

One potentially confusing point when trying to identify these four-stroke models comes from the fact that Johnson/Evinrude produced two different engines both with the 9.9 hp rating. One model, only produced for 1997 and 1998, was based on the same 12.87 cu. in. (211 cc) motor as the 8 hp models, and will most often be listed with those

4. Allow the engine to cool completely before working on any fuel system component.

5. When draining a carburetor or fuel fitting, catch the fuel in a plastic container and then pour it into an approved gasoline storage device.

6. Do not store gasoline in glass containers. If the glass breaks, a serious explosion or fire may occur.

7. Immediately wipe up spilled gasoline with rags. Store the rags in a metal container with a lid until they can be properly disposed of, or place them outside in a safe place for the fuel to evaporate.

8. Do not pour water onto a gasoline fire. Water spreads the fire and makes it more difficult to extinguish. Use a class B, BC or ABC fire extinguisher to extinguish the fire.

9. Always turn off the engine before refueling. Do not spill fuel onto the engine components. Do not overfill the fuel tank. Leave an air space at the top of the tank to allow room for the fuel to expand because of temperature fluctuations.

Cleaning Parts

Cleaning parts is one of the more tedious and difficult service jobs performed in the home garage. There are many types of chemical cleaners and solvents available models throughout this manual. They may be referred to as the 8/9.9 or the 211 cc motor in the text. More prevalent is another 9.9 hp model, produced from 1995-2001, which was based on the same 18.91 cu. in. (305 cc) motor as the 15 hp models. Throughout this manual procedures will reference this version of the 9.9 as either the 9.9/15 or the 305 cc engine. Unfortunately for the owner/mechanic, the engine cases of all these models bear the 9.9 designator and the model code on the engine tag list them both as E10 or J10 motors. The design feature codes can be used to tell the difference between the two. For 8/9.9 or 211 cc models the E10 or J10 is immediately followed by FA, FC, FEL, FO, FT or FW (and additional letters designating other design features). Any other combination of letters following E10 or J10 (including other combinations of FE, such as FEX) means the motor is part of the 9.9/15 or 305 cc family.

In addition to the model tag, most motors are equipped with a unique serial number on the power head. For 40-70 hp models the number is stamped into a welch plug affixed to the power head (**Figure 2**).

On 5-15 hp models, the serial/model number tag is affixed to the port side clamp bracket.

On 40 and 50 hp models, the serial/model number tag is affixed to the starboard side clamp bracket. The welch plug is located on the port side of the power head below the flywheel cover (**Figure 3**).

On 70 hp models, the serial/model number tag is affixed to the port side clamp bracket (**Figure 4**). The welch plug is located on the port side of the power head above the bottom intake runner (**Figure 5**).

ENGINE OPERATION

All engines covered by this manual work on the Otto cycle of intake, compression, power and exhaust phase operation. The four-stroke engine is named such because it accomplishes each one of these four phases with a different stroke (movement upward or downward) of the piston. (In contrast, two-stroke motors combine these functions performing two of them with any given movement of the piston). Refer to **Figure 6** and the accompanying text to help understand the power cycle of a four-stroke motor. The large arrows in **Figure 6** represent the direction of piston movement during each stroke.

The complete four-stroke engine power cycle begins with the intake stroke (A, **Figure 6**), during which the piston moves downward creating a vacuum in the combustion chamber. The vacuum draws the air/fuel mixture into the chamber through the intake valve (which is opened by the camshaft). The intake valve closes at some point be-

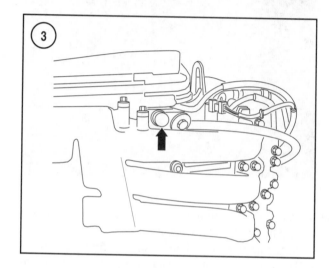

fore the piston begins moving upward significantly on the next stroke.

The compression stroke (B, **Figure 6**) follows the intake stroke. During this phase, the piston moves upward applying pressure (compressing) the air/fuel mixture. The term top dead center (TDC) refers to the point at which the piston is physically at the top of the compression stroke. The spark plug is normally fired at some point before the piston reaches TDC (measured in degrees of crankshaft rotation) giving the spark ample time to ignite the fuel mixture before the piston must reverse direction and travel downward on the power stroke.

Correct ignition timing is critical to the combustion process. If the spark occurs too soon (too advanced before TDC), the engine will knock and the piston, still traveling upward, will fight the force of the combustion attempting to force the piston downward. Likewise, if the spark occurs too late (retarded, after TDC) the piston will have already traveled part way down without the additional force of the combustion (wasting some of the combustion energy).

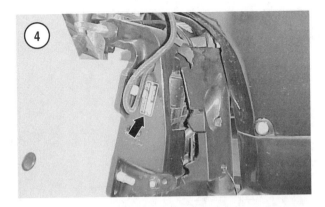

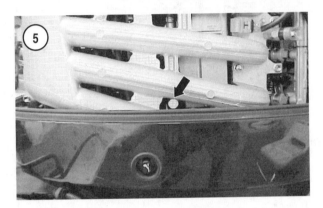

The power stroke (C, **Figure 6**) occurs as the piston passes TDC and begins to travel downward in the cylinder. This is the point where the piston drives the crankshaft (and the gear shafts and eventually the propeller) with force. On multi-cylinder motors, the other piston(s) will each be on a different portion of the cycle.

Once the piston reaches the bottom of its travel, the exhaust stroke (D, **Figure 6**) begins as crankshaft rotation once again causes the piston to begin traveling upward. This time, the camshaft will open the exhaust valve, allowing the piston to force any unburned gasses or byproducts from combustion out through the exhaust manifold. As the piston reaches the top of this stroke, the camshaft begins opening the intake valve and the cycle repeats.

Understanding the mechanical operation of a four-stroke motor is useful during service or overhaul. For instance, one easy way to find TDC on any given piston is to observe the camshaft and valves as the engine is slowly rotated by hand via the flywheel. If the exhaust valve opens then closes, followed by the intake valve, the piston will soon approach top dead center. When the piston reaches the top of its travel (as determined by observation through the spark plug port or by a timing reference mark) with both of the valves closed, it is at TDC.

FASTENERS

Proper fastener selection and installation is important to ensure that the engine operates as designed and can be serviced efficiently. The choice of original equipment fasteners is not arrived at by chance. Make sure replacement fasteners meet all the same requirements as the originals.

Threaded Fasteners

Threaded fasteners secure most of the components on the boat and motor. Most are tightened by turning them clockwise (right-hand threads). If the normal rotation of the fastener being tightened loosens, the fastener may have left-hand threads. If a left-hand threaded fastener is expected, it is noted in the text.

Nuts, bolts and screws are manufactured in a wide range of thread patterns. To join a nut and bolt, the diameter of the bolt and the diameter of the hole in the nut must be the same and the threads must be properly matched.

The best way to tell if the threads on two fasteners match is to turn the nut on the bolt (or the bolt into the threaded hole in a piece of equipment) with fingers only. Make sure both pieces are clean; remove Loctite or other sealer residue from threads if present. If force is required, check the thread condition on each fastener. If the thread condition is good but the fasteners jam, the threads are not compatible. A thread pitch gauge (**Figure 7**) can also be used to determine pitch.

> *NOTE*
> *To ensure the fastener threads are not mismatched or cross-threaded, start all fasteners by hand. If a fastener is hard to start or turn, determine the cause before tightening with a wrench.*

Two dimensions are required to match the thread size of the fastener: the number of threads in a given distance and the outside diameter of the threads.

Two systems are currently used to specify threaded fastener dimensions: the U.S. Standard system and the metric system. Although fasteners may appear similar, close inspection shows that the thread designs are not the same (**Figure 8**). Pay particular attention when working with unidentified fasteners; mismatching thread types can damage threads.

> *NOTE*
> *Most Johnson and Evinrude motors (especially the 40 hp and larger four-stroke models) are manufactured with predominantly International Organization for Standardiza-*

⑥

FOUR-STROKE PRINCIPLES

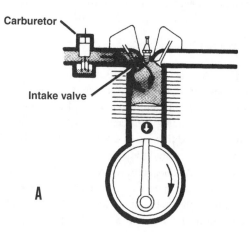

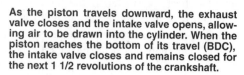

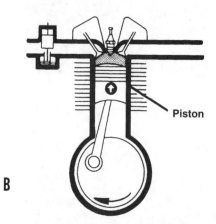

A

As the piston travels downward, the exhaust valve closes and the intake valve opens, allowing air to be drawn into the cylinder. When the piston reaches the bottom of its travel (BDC), the intake valve closes and remains closed for the next 1 1/2 revolutions of the crankshaft.

B

When the crankshaft continues to rotate, the piston moves upward, compressing the air.

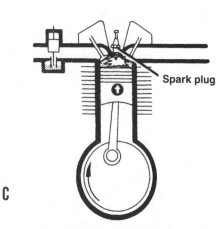

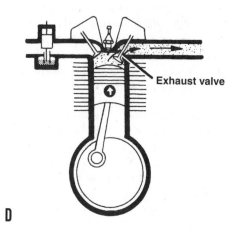

C

As the piston almost reaches the top of its travel, the injector sprays fuel into the combustion chamber. The fuel is ignited by the heat of compression. The piston continues to top dead center (TDC) and is pushed downward by the expanding gases.

D

When the piston almost reaches BDC, the exhaust valve opens and remains open until the piston is near TDC. The upward travel of the piston forces the exhaust gases out of the cylinder. After the piston has reached TDC, the exhaust valve closes and the cycle repeats.

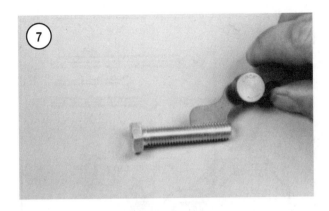

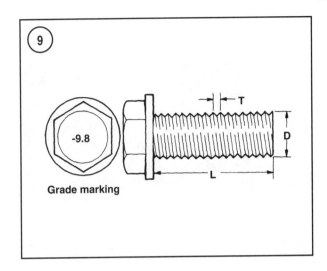

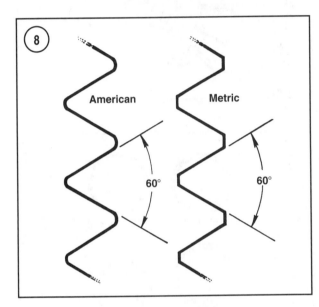

tion (ISO) metric fasteners, though some models may be equipped with components using U.S. Standard fasteners depending on the model and application.

U.S. Standard fasteners are sorted by grades (hardness/strength). Bolt heads are marked to represent different grades, no marks means the bolt is grade zero, two marks equal grade two, three marks equal grade five, four equal grade six, five equal grade seven and six marks equal grade eight. It is important when replacing fasteners to make sure the replacements are of equal or greater strength than the original.

U.S. standard fasteners generally come in two pitches, coarse and fine (the coarse bolts/screws have fewer threads per inch than the fine). They are normally referred to by size such as 1/2-16 or 3/8-24. In these names the first number, 1/2 or 3/8 in the example, represent the measurement of the bolt diameter from the top of the threads to the top of the other side. The second number represents the

number of threads per inch (16 or 24 in the case of the examples).

International Organization for Standardization (ISO) metric threads come in three standard thread sizes: coarse, fine and constant pitch. The ISO coarse pitch is used for most common fastener applications. The fine pitch thread is used on certain precision tools and instruments. The constant pitch thread is used mainly on machine parts and not for fasteners. The constant pitch thread, however, is used on all metric thread spark plugs.

The length (L, **Figure 9**), diameter (D) and distance between thread crests (pitch) (T) classify metric screws and bolts. The numbers 8—1.25 × 130, identify a typical bolt. This indicates the bolt has diameter of 8 mm. The distance between thread crests is 1.25 mm and the length is 130 mm.

NOTE
*When purchasing a bolt from a dealership or parts store, it is important to know how to specify bolt length. The correct way to measure bolt length is to measure the length, starting from underneath the bolt head to the end of the bolt (**Figure 10**). Always measure bolt length in this manner to avoid purchasing or installing bolts that are too long.*

The grade marking located on the top of the fastener (**Figure 9**) indicate the strength of metric screws and bolts. The higher the number, the stronger the fastener. Unnumbered fasteners are the weakest.

Many screws, bolts and studs are combined with nuts to secure particular components. To indicate the size of a nut, manufacturers specify the internal diameter and the thread pitch.

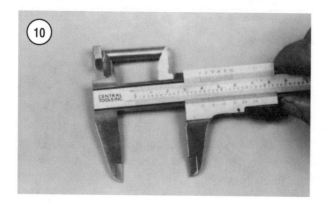

The measurement across two flats on a nut or bolt indicates the wrench size.

WARNING
Do not install fasteners with a strength classification lower than what was originally installed by the manufacturer. Doing so may cause equipment failure and/or damage.

Torque Specifications

The materials used during the manufacturing of the engine may be subjected to uneven stresses if the fasteners of the various subassemblies are not installed and tightened correctly. Fasteners that are improperly installed or work loose can cause extensive damage. It is essential to use an accurate torque wrench, described in this chapter, with the torque specifications in this manual. Torque specifications are listed at the end of each chapter. If a torque is not listed, use the General Torque Specifications in **Table 5** of this chapter.

Specifications for torque are provided in Newton-meters (N·m), foot-pounds (ft.-lb.) and inch-pounds (in.-lb.). Torque specifications for specific components (including all critical torque figures) are at the end of the appropriate chapters. Torque wrenches are covered in the *Basic Tools* section.

Self-Locking Fasteners

Several types of bolts, screws and nuts incorporate a system that creates interference between the two fasteners. Interference is achieved in various ways. The most common type is the nylon insert nut and a dry adhesive coating on the threads of a bolt.

Self-locking fasteners offer greater holding strength than standard fasteners, which improves their resistance to vibration. Most self-locking fasteners cannot be reused.

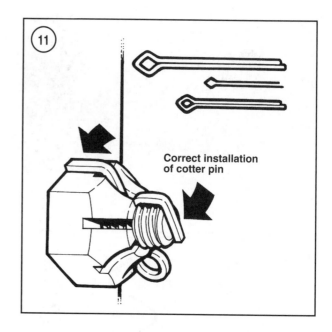

Correct installation of cotter pin

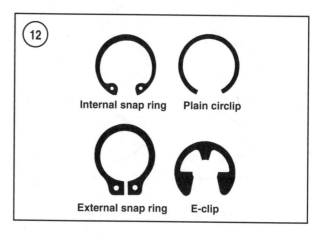

Internal snap ring   Plain circlip

External snap ring   E-clip

The materials used to form the lock become distorted after the initial installation and removal. It is a good practice to discard and replace self-locking fasteners after their removal. Do not replace self-locking fasteners with standard fasteners.

Washers

There are two basic types of washers: flat washers and lockwashers. Flat washers are simple discs with a hole to fit a screw or bolt. Lockwashers prevent a fastener from working loose. Washers can be used as spacers and seals, or to help distribute fastener load and to prevent the fastener from damaging the component.

As with fasteners, when replacing washers make sure the replacement washers are the same design and quality.

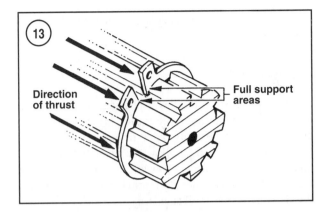

Direction of thrust

Full support areas

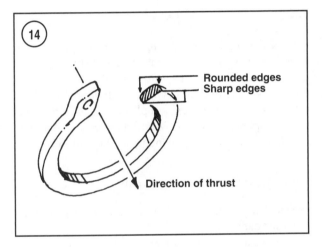

Rounded edges
Sharp edges

Direction of thrust

NOTE
Give as much care to the selection and purchase of washers as given to bolts, nuts and other fasteners. Avoid washers that are made of thin and weak materials. These will deform and crush the first time they are used in a high torque application, allowing the nut or bolt to loosen.

Cotter Pins

A cotter pin is a split metal pin inserted into a hole or slot to prevent a fastener from loosening. In certain applications, the fastener must be secured in this way. For these applications, a cotter pin and castellated (slotted) nut are used.

To use a cotter pin, first make sure the diameter is correct for the hole in the fastener. After correctly tightening the fastener and aligning the holes, insert the cotter pin through the hole and bend the ends over the fastener (**Figure 11**). Cut the arms to a suitable length to prevent them from snagging on clothing, or worse, skin; remember that

exposed ends of the pin cut flesh easily. When the cotter pin is bent and its arms cut to length, it must be tight. If it can be wiggled, it is improperly installed.

Unless instructed to do so, never loosen a torqued fastener to align the holes. If the holes do not align, tighten the fastener just enough to achieve alignment.

Cotter pins are available in various diameters and lengths. Measure length from the bottom of the head to the tip of the shortest pin.

Do not reuse cotter pins as their ends may break causing the pin to fall out, allowing the fastener to loosen.

Snap Rings

Snap rings (**Figure 12**) are circular-shaped metal retaining clips. They help secure parts and gears in place such as shafts, pins or rods. External type snap rings retain items on shafts. Internal type snaap rings secure parts within housing bores. In some applications, in addition to securing the component(s), snap rings of varying thickness also determine endplay. These are usually called selective snap rings.

There are two basic types of snap rings: machined and stamped snap rings. Machined snap rings (**Figure 13**) can be installed in either direction, since both faces have sharp edges. Stamped snap rings (**Figure 14**) have a sharp edge and a round edge. When installing a stamped snap ring in a thrust application, install the sharp edge facing away from the part producing the thrust.

Observe the following when installing snap rings:
1. Remove and install snap rings with snap ring pliers. See *Snap Ring Pliers* in this chapter.
2. In some applications, it may be necessary to replace snap rings after removing them.
3. Compress or expand snap rings only enough to install them. If overly expanded, they lose their retaining ability.
4. After installing a snap ring, make sure it seats completely.
5. Wear eye protection when removing and installing snap rings.

E-rings and circlips are used when it is not practical to use a snap ring. Remove E-rings with a flat blade screwdriver by prying between the shaft and E-ring. To install an E-ring, center it over the shaft groove and push or tap it into place.

SHOP SUPPLIES

Lubricants and Fluids

Periodic lubrication helps ensure long life for any type of equipment. The *type* of lubricant used is just as important as the lubrication service itself, although in an emergency the wrong type of lubricant is usually better than no lubricant at all. The following information describes the types of lubricants most often used on marine equipment. Make sure to follow the manufacturer's recommendations for lubricant types.

> *NOTE*
> *For more information on Johnson and Evinrude recommended lubricants, please refer to the **Quick Reference Data** at the beginning of this manual or the information and tables in Chapter Three.*

Generally, all liquid lubricants are called *oil*. They may be mineral-based (including petroleum bases), natural-based (vegetable and animal bases), synthetic-based or emulsions (mixtures). *Grease* is oil to which a thickening base was added so that the end product is semi-solid. Grease is often classified by the type of thickener added; lithium soap is commonly used.

Engine oil

Engine oil is classified by two standards: the American Petroleum Institute (API) service classification and the Society of Automotive Engineers (SAE) viscosity rating. This information is on the oil container label. Two letters indicate the API service classification. The number or sequence of numbers and letter (10W-40 for example) is the oil's viscosity rating. The API service classification and the SAE viscosity index are not indications of oil quality.

The service classification indicates that the oil meets specific lubrication standards. The first letter in the classification (**S**) indicates that the oil is for gasoline engines. The second letter indicates the standard the oil satisfies. The classification started with the letter (**A**) and is currently at the letter (**J**).

Always use an oil with a classification recommended by the manufacturer. Using an oil with a classification different than that recommended can cause engine damage.

Viscosity is an indication of the oil's thickness. Thin oils have a lower number while thick oils have a higher number. Engine oils fall into the 5- to 50-weight range for single-grade oils.

Most manufacturers recommend multigrade oil. These oils perform efficiently across a wide range of operating conditions. Multigrade oils are identified by a (**W**) after the first number, which indicates the low-temperature viscosity.

Engine oils are most commonly mineral (petroleum) based; however synthetic and semi-synthetic types are used more frequently. When selecting engine oil, follow the manufacturer's recommendation for type, classification and viscosity.

Gear oil

Gear oil is used in the lower housing to lubricate the gear shafts. As with engine oils, gear oils receive a service classification and viscosity rating from the American Petroleum Institute (API). Follow the manufacturer's recommendations when choosing gear oil. Most manufacturers recommend a marine gear oil that meets the GL-5 hypoid gear oil standard.

Greases

Grease is lubricating oil with thickening agents added to it. The National Lubricating Grease Institute (NLGI) grades grease. Grades range from No. 000 to No. 6, with No. 6 being the thickest. Typical multipurpose grease is NLGI No. 2. For specific applications, manufacturers may recommend water-resistant type grease or one with an additive such as molybdenum disulfide (MoS2).

Cleaners, Degreasers and Solvents

Many chemicals are available to remove oil, grease and other residue.

Before using cleaning solvents, consider how they will be used and disposed of, particularly if they are not water-soluble. Local ordinances may require special procedures for the disposal of many types of cleaning chemicals. Refer to *Safety and Cleaning Parts* in this chapter for more information on their use.

Use electrical contact cleaner to clean wiring connections and components without leaving any residue. Carburetor cleaner is a powerful solvent used to remove fuel deposits and varnish from fuel system components. Use this cleaner carefully, as it may damage finishes.

Generally, degreasers are strong cleaners used to remove heavy accumulations of grease from engine and frame components.

Most solvents are used in a parts washing cabinet for individual component cleaning. For safety, use only non-flammable or high flash point solvents.

Gasket Sealant

Sealants are used in combination with a gasket or seal and are occasionally alone. Follow the manufacturer's recommendation when using sealants. Use extreme care when choosing a sealant different from the type originally recommended. Choose sealants based on their resistance to heat, various fluids and their sealing capabilities.

One of the most common sealants is RTV, or room temperature vulcanizing sealant. This sealant cures at room temperature over a specific time period. This allows the repositioning of components without damaging gaskets.

Moisture in the air causes the RTV sealant to cure. Always install the tube cap as soon as possible after applying RTV sealant. RTV sealant has a limited shelf life and does not cure properly if the shelf life has expired. Keep partial tubes sealed and discard them if they have surpassed the expiration date.

Applying RTV sealant

Clean all old gasket residue from the mating surfaces. Remove all gasket material from blind threaded holes; it can cause inaccurate bolt torque. Spray the mating surfaces with aerosol parts cleaner and then wipe with a lint-free cloth. The area must be clean for the sealant to adhere.

Apply RTV sealant in a continuous bead 2-3 mm (0.08-0.12 in.) thick. Circle all the fastener holes unless otherwise specified. Do not allow any sealant to enter these holes. Assemble and tighten the fasteners to the specified torque within the time frame recommended by the RTV sealant manufacturer (usually within 10-15 minutes).

Gasket Remover

Aerosol gasket remover can help remove stubborn gaskets. This product can speed up the removal process and prevent damage to the mating surface that may be caused by using a scraping tool. Most of these types of products are very caustic. Follow the gasket remover manufacturer's instructions for use.

Threadlocking Compound

A threadlocking compound is a fluid applied to the threads of fasteners. After tightening the fastener, the fluid dries and becomes a solid filler between the threads. This makes it difficult for the fastener to work loose from vibration, or heat expansion and contraction. Some threadlocking compounds also provide a seal against fluid leakage.

Before applying threadlocking compound remove any old compound from both thread areas and clean them with aerosol parts cleaner. Use the compound sparingly. Excess fluid can run into adjoining parts.

Threadlocking compounds come in different strengths. Follow the particular manufacturer's recommendations regarding compound selection. Two manufacturers of threadlocking compound are ThreeBond and Loctite, which offer a wide range of compounds for various strength, temperature and repair applications.

Applying threadlock

Make sure surfaces are clean. If a threadlock was previously applied to the component, remove this residue.

Shake the container thoroughly and apply to both parts, then assemble the parts and/or tighten the fasteners.

GALVANIC CORROSION

A chemical reaction occurs whenever two different types of metal are joined by an electrical conductor and immersed in an electrolytic solution such as water. Electrons transfer from one metal to the other through the electrolyte and return through the conductor.

The hardware on a boat is made of many different types of metal. The boat hull acts as a conductor between the metals. Even if the hull is wooden or fiberglass, the slightest film of water on the hull provides conductivity (by acting as electrolyte). This combination creates a good environment for electron flow. Unfortunately, this electron flow results in galvanic corrosion of the metal involved, causing one of the metals to be corroded or eroded away. The amount of electron flow, and therefore the amount of corrosion, depends on several factors:

1. The types of metal involved.
2. The efficiency of the conductor.
3. The strength of the electrolyte.

Metals

The chemical composition of the metal used in marine equipment has a significant effect on the amount and speed of galvanic corrosion. Certain metals are more resistant to corrosion than others. These electrically negative metals are commonly called *noble*; they act as the cathode in any reaction. Metals that are more subject to corrosion are electrically positive; they act as the anode in a reaction. The more *noble* metals include titanium, 18-8 stainless steel and nickel. Less *noble* metals include zinc, aluminum and magnesium. Galvanic corrosion becomes more excessive as the difference in electrical potential between the two metals increases.

In some cases, galvanic corrosion can occur within a single piece of metal. For example, brass is a mixture of zinc and copper, and, when immersed in an electrolyte, the zinc portion of the mixture will corrode away as a galvanic reaction occurs between the zinc and copper particles.

Conductors

The hull of the boat often acts as the conductor between different types of metal. Marine equipment, such as the engine/gearcase of the outboard can act as the conductor. Large masses of metal, firmly connected together, are more efficient conductors than water. Rubber mountings and vinyl-based paint can act as insulators between pieces of metal.

Electrolyte

The water in which a boat operates acts as the electrolyte for the corrosion process. The more efficient a conductor is, the more excessive and rapid the corrosion will be.

Cold, clean freshwater is the poorest electrolyte. Pollutants increase conductivity; therefore, brackish or saltwater is an efficient electrolyte. This is one of the reasons that most manufacturers recommend a freshwater flush after operating in polluted, brackish or saltwater.

Protection from Galvanic Corrosion

Because of the environment in which marine equipment must operate, it is practically impossible to totally prevent galvanic corrosion. However, there are several ways in which the process can be slowed. After taking these precautions, the next step is to *fool* the process into occurring only in certain places. This is the role of sacrificial anodes and impressed current systems.

Slowing Corrosion

Some simple precautions can help reduce the amount of corrosion taking place outside the hull. These precautions are not substitutes for the corrosion protection methods discussed under *Sacrificial Anodes* and *Impressed Current Systems* in this chapter, but they can help these methods reduce corrosion.

Use fasteners made of metal more noble than the parts they secure. If corrosion occurs, the parts they secure may suffer but the fasteners are protected. The larger secured parts are more able to withstand the loss of material. Also major problems could arise if the fasteners corrode to the point of failure.

Keep all painted surfaces in good condition. If paint is scraped off and bare metal exposed, corrosion rapidly increases. Use a vinyl- or plastic-based paint, which acts as an electrical insulator.

Be careful when applying metal-based antifouling paint to the boat. Do not apply antifouling paint to metal parts of the boat or the outboard engine/gearcase. If applied to metal surfaces, this type of paint reacts with the metal and results in corrosion between the metal and the layer of paint. Maintain a minimum 1 in. (25 mm) border between the painted surface and any metal parts. Organic-based paints are available for use on metal surfaces.

Where a corrosion protection device is used, remember that it must be immersed in the electrolyte along with the boat to provide any protection. If you raise the outboard out of the water with the boat docked, any anodes on the engine will be removed from the corrosion process rendering them ineffective. (Of course, when raised out of the water/electrolyte the engine requires less protection.) Never paint or apply any coating to anodes or other protection devices. Paint or other coatings insulate them from the corrosion process.

Any change in the boat's equipment, such as the installation of a new stainless steel propeller, changes the electrical potential and may cause increased corrosion. Always consider this fact when adding equipment or changing exposed materials. Install additional anodes or other protection equipment as required ensuring the corrosion protection system is up to the task. The expense to repair corrosion damage usually far exceeds that of additional corrosion protection.

Sacrificial Anodes

Sacrificial anodes are specially designed to do nothing but corrode. Properly fastening such pieces to the boat causes them to act as the anode in any galvanic reaction that occurs; any other metal in the reaction acts as the cathode and is not damaged.

Anodes are usually made of zinc, a less noble material. Some anodes are manufactured of an aluminum and indium alloy. This alloy is less noble than the aluminum alloy in drive system components, providing the desired sacrificial properties. The aluminum and indium alloy is more resistant to oxide coating than zinc anodes. Oxide coating occurs as the anode material reacts with oxygen in the water. An oxide coating insulates the anode, dramatically reducing corrosion protection.

Anodes must be used properly to be effective. Simply fastening anodes to the boat in random locations does not do the job.

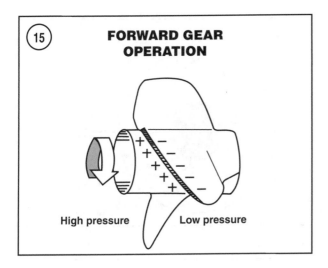

FORWARD GEAR OPERATION

High pressure   Low pressure

First determine how much anode surface is required to adequately protect the equipment's surface area. A good starting point is provided by the Military Specification MIL-A-818001, which states that one square inch of new anode protects either:

1. 800 sq. in. of freshly painted steel.
2. 250 sq. in. of bare steel or bare aluminum alloy.
3. 100 sq. in. of copper or copper alloy.

This rule is valid for a boat at rest. If underway, additional anode areas are required to protect the same surface area.

The anode must be in good electrical contact with the metal that it protects. If possible, attach an anode to all metal surfaces requiring protection.

Quality anodes have inserts around the fastener holes that are made of a more noble material. Otherwise, the anode could erode away around the fastener hole, allowing the anode to loosen or possibly fall off, thereby losing needed protection.

Impressed Current System

An impressed current system can be added to any boat. The system generally consists of the anode, controller and reference electrode. The anode in this system is coated with a very noble metal, such as platinum, so that it is almost corrosion-free and can last almost indefinitely. The reference electrode, under the boat's waterline, allows the control module to monitor the potential for corrosion. If the module senses that corrosion is occurring, it applies positive battery voltage to the anode. Current then flows from the anode to all other metal components, regardless of how noble or non-noble these components may be. Essentially, the electrical current from the battery counter-acts the galvanic reaction to dramatically reduce corrosion damage.

Only a small amount of current is needed to counteract corrosion. Using input from the sensor, the control module provides only the amount of current needed to suppress galvanic corrosion. Most systems consume a maximum of 0.2 Ah at full demand. Under normal conditions, these systems can provide protection for 8-12 weeks without recharging the battery. Remember that this system must have constant connection to the battery. Often the battery supply to the system is connected to a battery switching device causing the operator to inadvertently shut off the system while docked.

An impressed current system is more expensive to install than sacrificial anodes, but considering the low maintenance requirements and the superior protection it provides, the long term cost may be lower.

PROPELLERS

The propeller is the final link between the boat's drive system and the water. A perfectly maintained engine and hull are useless if the propeller is the wrong type, damaged or deteriorated. Although propeller selection for a specific application is beyond the scope of this manual, the following provides the basic information needed to make an informed decision. A professional at a reputable marine dealership is the best source for a propeller recommendation.

How a Propeller Works

As the curved blades of a propeller rotate through the water, a high-pressure area forms on one side of the blade and a low-pressure area forms on the other side of the blade (**Figure 15**). The propeller moves toward the low-pressure area, carrying the boat with it.

Propeller Parts

Although a propeller is usually a one-piece unit, it is made of several different parts (**Figure 16**). Variations in the design of these parts make different propellers suitable for different applications.

The blade tip is the point of the blade furthest from the center of the propeller hub or propeller shaft bore. The blade tip separates the leading edge from the trailing edge.

The leading edge is the edge of the blade nearest the boat. During forward operation, this is the area of the blade that first cuts through the water.

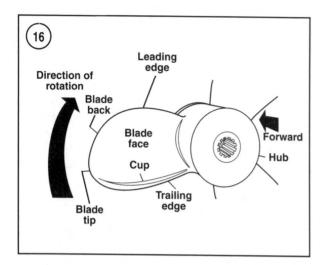

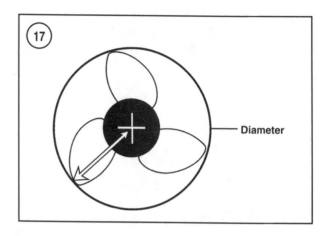

The trailing edge is the surface of the blade furthest from the boat. During reverse operation, this is the area of the blade that first cuts through the water.

The blade face is the surface of the blade that faces away from the boat. During forward operation, high-pressure forms on this side of the blade.

The blade back is the surface of the blade that faces toward the boat. During forward gear operation, low-pressure forms on this side of the blade.

The cup is a small curve or lip on the trailing edge of the blade. Cupped propeller blades generally perform better than non-cupped propeller blades.

The hub is the center portion of the propeller. It connects the blades to the propeller shaft. On most drive systems, engine exhaust is routed through the hub; in this case, the hub is made up of an outer and inner portion, connected by ribs.

A diffuser ring is used on through-hub exhaust models to prevent exhaust gasses from entering the blade area.

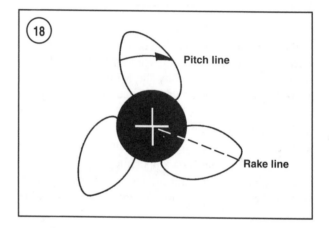

Propeller Design

Changes in length, angle, thickness and material of propeller parts make different propellers suitable for different applications.

Diameter

Propeller diameter is the distance from the center of the hub to the blade tip, multiplied by two. Essentially it is the diameter of the circle formed by the blade tips during propeller rotation (**Figure 17**).

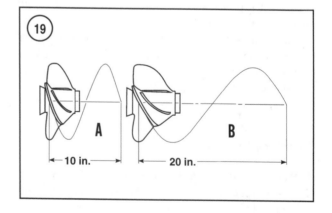

Pitch and rake

Propeller pitch and rake describe the placement of the blades in relation to the hub (**Figure 18**).

Pitch describes the theoretical distance the propeller would travel in one revolution. In A, **Figure 19**, the propeller would travel 10 in. in one revolution. In B, **Figure 19**, the propeller would travel 20 in. in one revolution.

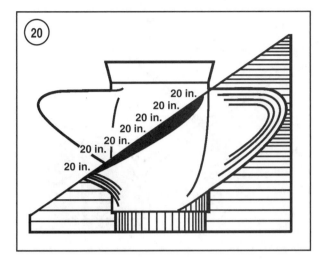

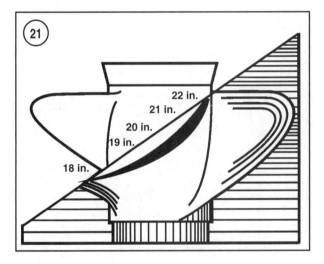

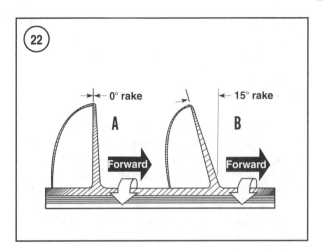

This distance is only theoretical; during typical operation, the propeller achieves only 75-85% of its pitch. Slip rate describes the difference in actual travel relative to the pitch. Lighter, faster boats typically achieve a lower slip rate than heavier, slower boats.

Propeller blades can be constructed with constant pitch (**Figure 20**) or progressive pitch (**Figure 21**). On a progressive propeller, the pitch starts low at the leading edge and increases toward the trailing edge. The propeller pitch specification is the average of the pitch across the entire blade. Propellers with progressive pitch usually provide better overall performance than constant pitch propellers.

Blade rake is specified in degrees and is measured along a line from the center of the hub to the blade tip. A blade that is perpendicular to the hub (A, **Figure 22**) has 0° rake. A blade that is angled from perpendicular (B, **Figure 22**) has a rake expressed by its difference from perpendicular. Most propellers have rakes ranging from

0-20°. Lighter, faster boats generally perform better using a propeller with a greater amount of rake. Heavier, slower boats generally perform better using a propeller with less rake.

Blade thickness

Blade thickness is not uniform at all points along the blade. For efficiency, blades are as thin as possible at all points while retaining enough strength to move the boat. Blades are thicker where they meet the hub and thinner at the blade tips. This construction is necessary to support the heavier loads at the hub section of the blade. Overall blade thickness is dependent on the strength of the material used.

When cut along a line from the leading edge to the trailing edge in the central portion of the blade, the propeller blade resembles an airplane wing. The blade face, where high-pressure exists during forward rotation, is almost flat. The blade back, where low-pressure exists during forward rotation, is curved, with the thinnest portions at the edges and the thickest portion at the center.

Propellers that run only partially submerged, as in racing applications, may have a wedge shaped cross-section (**Figure 23**). The leading edge is very thin and the blade thickness increases toward the trailing edge, where it is thickest. If a propeller such as this type is run totally submerged, it is very inefficient.

Number of blades

The number of blades on a propeller is a compromise between efficiency and vibration. A one-bladed propeller would be the most efficient, but it would create an unacceptable amount of vibration. As blades are added, efficiency decreases, but so does vibration. Most propellers have three or four blades, representing the most practical trade-off between efficiency and vibration.

Material

Propeller materials are chosen for strength, corrosion resistance and economy. Stainless steel, aluminum, plastic and bronze are the most commonly used materials. Bronze is quite strong but rather expensive. Stainless steel is more common than bronze because of its combination of strength and lower cost. Aluminum alloy and plastic materials are the least expensive but usually lack the strength of stainless steel. Plastic propellers are more suited for lower horsepower applications.

Direction of rotation

Propellers are made for both right-hand and left-hand rotations although right-hand is the most commonly used. As viewed from the rear of the boat while in forward gear, a right-hand propeller turns clockwise and a left-hand propeller turns counterclockwise. Off the boat, the direction of rotation is determined by observing the angle of the blades (**Figure 24**). A right-hand propeller's blade slant from the upper left to the lower right; a left-hand propeller's blades are opposite.

Cavitation and Ventilation

Cavitation and ventilation are *not* interchangeable terms; they refer to two distinct problems encountered during propeller operation.

To help understand cavitation, consider the relationship between pressure and the boiling point of water. At sea level, water boils at 212° F (100° C). As pressure increases, such as within an engine cooling system, the boiling point of the water increases—it boils at a temperature higher than 212° F (100° C). The opposite is also true. As pressure decreases, water boils at a temperature lower than 212° F (100° C). If the pressure drops low enough, water will boil at normal room temperature.

During normal propeller operation, low pressure forms on the blade back. Normally the pressure does not drop low enough for boiling to occur. However, poor propeller design, damaged blades or using the wrong propeller can cause unusually low pressure on the blade surface (**Figure 25**). If the pressure drops low enough, boiling occurs and bubbles form on the blade surfaces. As the boiling water moves to a higher pressure area of the blade, the boiling ceases and the bubbles collapse. The collapsing bubbles

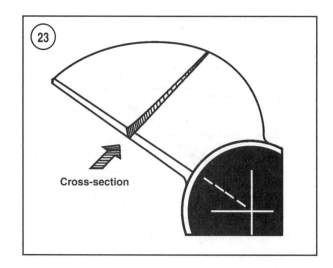

Cross-section

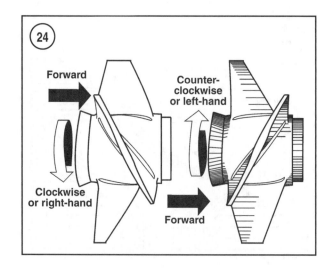

Forward

Counter-clockwise or left-hand

Clockwise or right-hand

Forward

release energy that erodes the surface of the propeller blade.

Corroded surfaces, physical damage or even marine growth combined with high-speed operation can cause low pressure and cavitation on outboard gearcase surfaces. In such cases, low pressure forms as water flows over a protrusion or rough surface. The boiling water forms bubbles that collapse as they move to a higher pressure area toward the rear of the surface imperfection.

This entire process of pressure drop, boiling and bubble collapse is called *cavitation*. The ensuing damage is called *cavitation burn*. Cavitation is caused by a decrease in pressure, not an increase in temperature.

Ventilation is not as complex a process as cavitation. Ventilation refers to air entering the blade area, either from above the water surface or from a through-hub exhaust system. As the blades meet the air, the propeller momentarily loses its bite with the water and subsequently

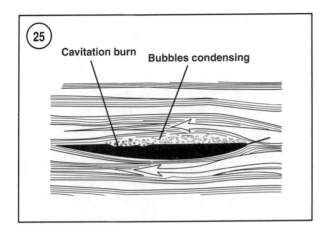

25

Cavitation burn   Bubbles condensing

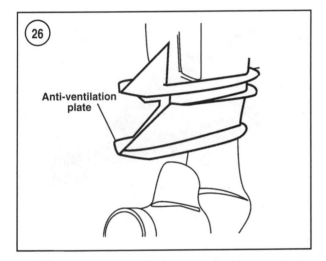

26

Anti-ventilation plate

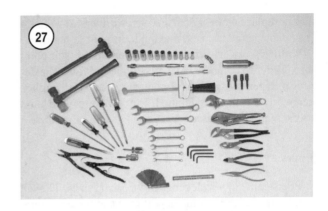

27

BASIC TOOLS

Most of the procedures in this manual can be carried out with simple hand tools and test equipment familiar to the home mechanic. Always use the correct tools for the job at hand. Keep tools organized and clean. Store them in a tool chest with related tools organized together.

After using a tool, wipe off dirt and grease with a clean cloth and return the tool to its correct place. Wiping tools off is especially important when servicing the craft in areas where they can come in contact with sand. Sand is very abrasive and causes premature wear to engine parts.

Quality tools are essential. The best are constructed of high-strength alloy steel. These tools are light, easy to use and resistant to wear. Their working surface is devoid of sharp edges and the tool is carefully polished. They have an easy-to-clean finish and are comfortable to use. Quality tools are a good investment.

When purchasing tools to perform the procedures covered in this manual, consider the potential frequency of use. If starting a tool kit, consider purchasing a basic tool set (**Figure 27**) from a large tool supplier. These sets are available in many tool combinations and offer substantial savings when compared to individually purchased tools. As work experience grows and tasks become more complicated, specialized tools can be added.

Screwdrivers

Screwdrivers of various lengths and types are mandatory for the simplest tool kit. The two basic types are the slotted tip (flat blade) and the Phillips tip. These are available in sets that often include an assortment of tip sizes and shaft lengths.

As with all tools, use a screwdriver designed for the job. Make sure the size of the tip conforms to the size and shape of the fastener. Use them only for driving screws. Never use a screwdriver for prying or chiseling metal. Re-

loses most of its thrust. An added complication is that the propeller and engine over-rev, causing very low pressure on the blade back and massive cavitation.

Most marine drive systems have a plate (**Figure 26**) above the propeller designed to prevent surface air from entering the blade area. This plate is an *anti-ventilation plate*, although it is often incorrectly called an *anticavitation plate*.

Most propellers have a flared section at the rear of the propeller called a diffuser ring. This feature forms a barrier, and extends the exhaust passage far enough aft to prevent the exhaust gases from ventilating the propeller.

A close fit of the propeller to the gearcase is necessary to keep exhaust gasses from exiting and ventilating the propeller. Using the wrong propeller attaching hardware can position the propeller too far aft, preventing a close fit. The wrong hardware can also allow the propeller to rub heavily against the gearcase, causing rapid wear to both components. Wear or damage to these surfaces allows the propeller to ventilate.

pair or replace worn or damaged screwdrivers. A worn tip may damage the fastener, making it difficult to remove.

Phillips screwdrivers are sized according to their point size. They are numbered one, two, three and four. The degree of taper determines the point size; the No. 1 Phillips screwdriver is the most pointed. The points are more blunt as the number increases.

Pliers

Pliers come in a wide range of types and sizes. Though pliers are useful for holding, cutting, bending and crimping, they should never be used to turn bolts or nuts.

Each design has a specialized function. Slip-joint pliers are general-purpose pliers used for gripping and bending. Diagonal cutting pliers are needed to cut wire and can be used to remove cotter pins. Needlenose pliers are used to hold or bend small objects. Locking pliers (**Figure 28**), sometimes called vise-grips, are used to hold objects very tightly. They have many uses ranging from holding two parts together to gripping the end of a broken stud. Use caution when using locking pliers, as the sharp jaws damage the objects they hold.

Snap Ring Pliers

Snap ring pliers (**Figure 29**) are specialized pliers with tips that fit into the ends of snap rings to remove and install them.

Snap ring pliers are available with fixed action (either internal or external) or convertible (one tool works on both internal and external snap rings). They may have fixed tips or interchangeable ones of various sizes and angles. For general use, select convertible type pliers with interchangeable tips.

> *WARNING*
> *Snap rings can slip and fly off when removing and installing them. Also, the snap ring plier tips may break. Always wear eye protection when using snap ring pliers.*

Hammers

Various types of hammers are available to fit a number of applications. A ball-peen hammer is used to strike another tool, such as a punch or chisel. Soft-faced hammers are required when a metal object must be struck without damaging it. *Never* use a metal-faced hammer on engine components, as damage does occur in most cases.

Always wear eye protection when using hammers. Make sure the hammer face is in good condition and the

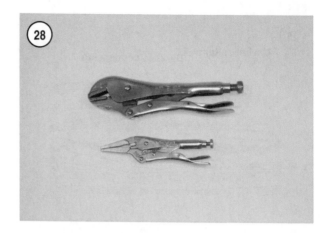

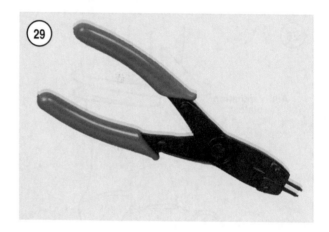

handle is not cracked. Select the correct hammer for the job and make sure to strike the object squarely. Do not use the handle or the side of the hammer to strike an object.

When striking a hammer against a punch, cold chisel or similar tool, the face of the hammer should be at least 1/2 in. larger than the head of the tool. When it is necessary to strike hard against a steel part without damaging it, use a brass hammer. Brass will give when used on a harder object.

Wrenches

Box-end, open-end and combination wrenches (**Figure 30**) come in a variety of types and sizes.

The number stamped on the wrench refers to the distance between the work areas. This size must match the size of the fastener head.

The box-end wrench is an excellent tool because it grips the fastener on all sides. This factor reduces the chance of the tool slipping. The box-end wrench is designed with either a six or 12-point opening. For stubborn or damaged

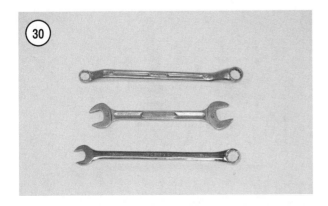

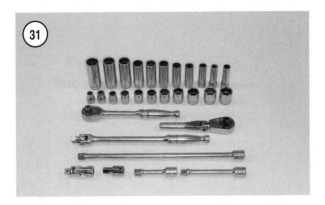

fasteners, the six-point provides superior holding ability by contacting the fastener across a wider area at all six edges. For general use, the 12-point works well. It allows the wrench to be removed and reinstalled without moving the handle over such a wide arc.

An open-end wrench is fast and works best in areas with limited overhead access. It contacts the fastener at only two points, and can slip under heavy force, or if the tool or fastener is worn. A box-end wrench is preferred in most instances, especially when breaking loose and applying the final tightness to a fastener.

The combination wrench has a box-end on one end, and an open-end on the other. This combination makes it a very convenient tool.

Adjustable Wrenches

An adjustable wrench or Crescent wrench can fit nearly any nut or bolt head that has clear access around its entire perimeter. Adjustable wrenches are best used as a backup wrench to keep a large nut or bolt from turning while the other end is being loosened or tightened with a box-end or socket wrench.

Adjustable wrenches contact the fastener at only two points, which makes them more subject to slipping off the fastener. The fact that one jaw is adjustable and may loosen only aggravates this shortcoming. Make certain the solid jaw is the one transmitting the force.

Socket Wrenches, Ratchets and Handles

Sockets that attach to a ratchet handle (**Figure 31**) are available with six-point or 12-point openings and different drive sizes. The drive size (1/4, 3/8, 1/2 and 3/4 in.) indicates the size of the square hole that accepts the ratchet handle. The number stamped on the socket is the size of the work area and must match the fastener head.

As with wrenches, a six-point socket provides superior-holding ability, while a 12-point socket needs to be moved only half as far to reposition it on the fastener.

Sockets are designated for either hand or impact use. Impact sockets are made of thicker material for more durability. Compare the size and wall thickness of two sockets, say a 19-mm hand socket and a 19-mm impact socket. Use impact sockets when using an impact driver or air tools. Use hand sockets with hand-driven attachments.

> *WARNING*
> *Do not use hand sockets with air or impact tools, as they may shatter and cause injury. Always wear eye protection when using impact or air tools.*

Various handles are available for sockets. The speed handle is used for fast operation. Flexible ratchet heads in varying lengths allow the socket to be turned with varying force, and at odd angles. Extension bars allow the socket setup to reach difficult areas. The ratchet is the most versatile. It allows the user to install or remove the nut without removing the socket.

Sockets combined with any number of drivers make them undoubtedly the fastest, safest and most convenient tool for fastener removal and installation.

Impact Driver

An impact driver provides extra force for removing fasteners, by converting the impact of a hammer into a turning motion. This makes it possible to remove stubborn fasteners without damaging them. Impact drivers and interchangeable bits (**Figure 32**) are available from most tool suppliers. When using a socket with an impact driver make sure the socket is designed for impact use. Refer to *Socket Wrenches, Ratchets and Handles* in this chapter.

> *WARNING*
> *Do not use hand sockets with air or impact tools as they may shatter and cause injury.*

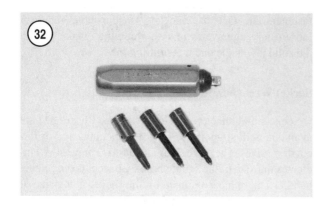

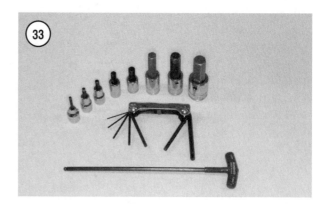

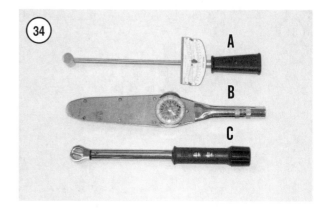

Always wear eye protection when using impact or air tools.

Impact drivers are great for the home mechanic as they offer many of the advantages of air tools without the need for a costly air compressor to run them.

Allen Wrenches

Allen or setscrew wrenches (**Figure 33**) are used on fasteners with hexagonal recesses in the fastener head. These wrenches come in L-shaped bar, socket and T-handle types. Allen bolts are sometimes called socket bolts.

Torque Wrenches

A torque wrench is used with a socket, torque adapter or similar extension to measure torque while tightening a fastener. Torque wrenches come in several drive sizes (1/4, 3/8, 1/2 and 3/4) and have various methods of reading the torque value. The drive size is the size of the square drive that accepts the socket, adapter or extension. Common types of torque wrenches include the deflecting beam (A, **Figure 34**) the dial indicator (B) and the audible click (C).

When choosing a torque wrench, consider the torque range, drive size and accuracy. The torque specifications in this manual provide an indication of the range required.

A torque wrench is a precision tool that must be properly cared for to remain accurate. Store torque wrenches in cases or separate padded drawers within a toolbox. Follow the manufacturer's instructions for their care and calibration.

Torque Adapters

Torque adapters or extensions extend or reduce the reach of a torque wrench. The torque adapter shown on the top of **Figure 35** is used to tighten a fastener that cannot be reached because of the size of the torque wrench head, drive, and socket. If a torque adapter changes the effective lever length the torque reading on the wrench will not equal the actual torque applied to the fastener. It is necessary to recalibrate the torque setting on the wrench to compensate for the change of lever length. When using a torque adapter at a right angle to the drive head, calibration is not required, since the effective length has not changed.

To recalculate a torque reading when using a torque adapter, use the following formula, and refer to **Figure 35**.

$$TW = \frac{TA \times L}{L + A}$$

TW is the torque setting or dial reading on the wrench.

TA is the torque specification (the actual amount of torque that should be applied to the fastener).

A is the amount that the adapter increases (or in some cases reduces) the effective lever length as measured along the centerline of the torque wrench (**Figure 35**).

L is the lever length of the wrench as measured from the center of the drive to the center of the grip.

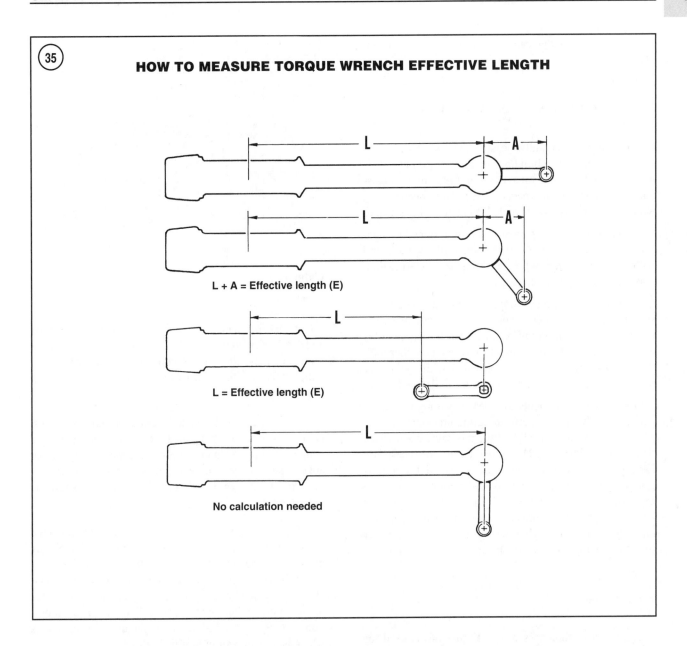

HOW TO MEASURE TORQUE WRENCH EFFECTIVE LENGTH

L + A = Effective length (E)

L = Effective length (E)

No calculation needed

The effective length of the torque wrench measured along the centerline of the torque wrench is the sum of **L** and **A** (**Figure 35**).

Example:

TA = 20 ft.-lb.

A = 3 in.

L = 14 in.

$$TW = \frac{20 \times 14}{14 + 3} = \frac{280}{17} = 16.5 \text{ ft. lb.}$$

In this example, the torque wrench would be set to the recalculated torque value (TW = 16.5 ft.-lb.). When using a beam-type wrench, tighten the fastener until the pointer aligns with 16.5 ft.-lb. In this example, although the torque wrench is pre-set to 16.5 ft.-lb., the actual torque is 20 ft.-lb.

SPECIAL TOOLS

Some of the procedures in this manual require special tools. These are described in the appropriate chapter and are available from either the manufacturer or a tool supplier.

In many cases, an acceptable substitute may be found in an existing tool kit. Another alternative is to make the tool. Many schools with a machine shop curriculum welcome outside work that can be used as practical shop applications for students.

PRECISION MEASURING TOOLS

The ability to accurately measure components is essential to successfully rebuilding an engine. Equipment is manufactured to close tolerances, and obtaining consistently accurate measurements is essential to determining which components require replacement or further service.

Each type of measuring instrument is designed to measure a dimension with a certain degree of accuracy and within a certain range. When selecting the measuring tool, make sure it is applicable to the task.

As with all tools, measuring tools provide the best results if cared for properly. Improper use can damage the tool and result in inaccurate results. If any measurement is questionable, verify the measurement using another tool. A standard gauge is usually provided with measuring tools to check accuracy and calibrate the tool if necessary.

Precision measurements can vary according to the experience of the person performing the procedure. Accurate results are only possible if the mechanic possesses a feel for using the tool. Heavy-handed use of measuring tools produces less accurate results than if the tool is grasped gently by the fingertips so the point at which the tool contacts the object is easily felt. This feel for the equipment produces more accurate measurements and reduces the risk of damaging the tool or component. Refer to the following sections for specific measuring tools.

Feeler Gauge

The feeler or thickness gauge (**Figure 36**) is used for measuring the distance between two surfaces.

A feeler gauge set consists of an assortment of steel strips of graduated thickness. Each blade is marked with its thickness. Blades can be of various lengths and angles for different procedures.

A common use for a feeler gauge is to measure valve clearance. Wire (round) type gauges are used to measure spark plug gap.

To obtain a proper measurement using a feeler gap, make sure the proper-sized blade passes through the gap with some slight drag. The blade should not need to be forced through, and should not have any play up-and-down between the surfaces being measured.

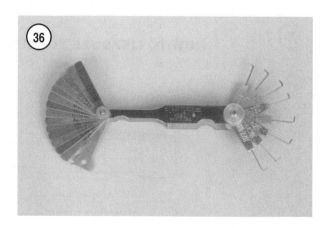

Calipers

Calipers are excellent tools for obtaining inside, outside and depth measurements. Although not as precise as a micrometer, they allow reasonable precision, typically to within 0.05 mm (0.001 in.). Most calipers have a range up to 150 mm (6 in.).

Calipers are available in dial, vernier or digital versions. Dial calipers have a dial gauge readout that provides convenient reading. Vernier calipers have marked scales that are compared to determine the measurement. Most convenient of all, the digital caliper uses an LCD to show the measurement.

To help ensure accurate readings, properly maintain the measuring surfaces of the caliper. There must not be any dirt or burrs between the tool and the object being measured. Never force the caliper closed around an object; close the caliper around the highest point so it can be removed with a slight drag. Some calipers require calibration. Always refer to the manufacturer's instructions when using a new or unfamiliar caliper.

To read a vernier caliper refer to **Figure 37**. The fixed scale is marked in 1 mm increments. Ten individual lines on the fixed scale equal 1 cm. The movable scale is marked in 0.05 mm (hundredth) increments. To obtain a reading, establish the first number by the location of the 0 line on the movable scale in relation to the first line to the left on the fixed scale. In this example, the number is 10 mm. To determine the next number, note which of the lines on the movable scale align with a mark on the fixed scale. A number of lines will seem close, but only one aligns exactly. In this case, 0.50 mm is the reading to add to the first number. The result of adding 10 mm and 0.50 mm is a measurement of 10.50 mm.

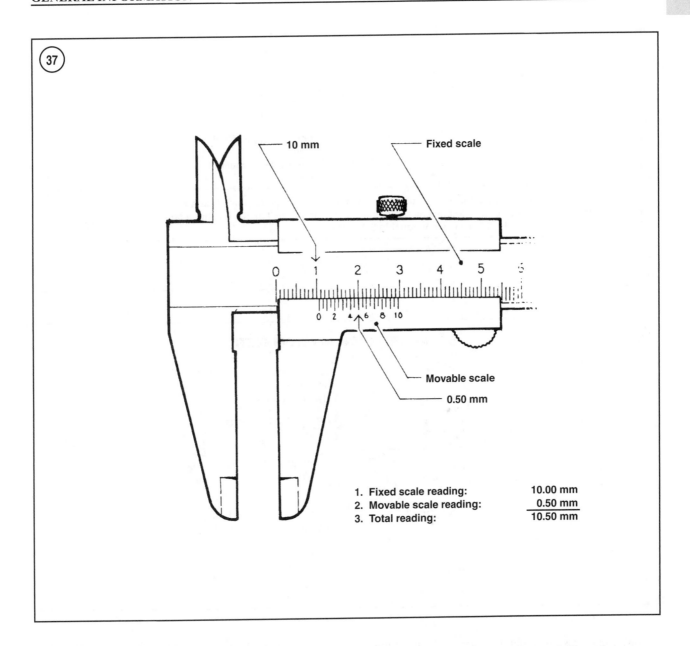

1. Fixed scale reading: 10.00 mm
2. Movable scale reading: 0.50 mm
3. Total reading: 10.50 mm

Micrometers

A micrometer is an instrument designed for linear measurement using the decimal divisions of the inch or meter (**Figure 38**). While there are many types and styles of micrometers, most of the procedures in this manual call for an outside micrometer. The outside micrometer is used to measure the outside diameter of cylindrical forms and the thickness of materials.

A micrometer's size indicates the minimum and maximum size of a part that it can measure. The usual sizes are 0-1 in. (0-25 mm), 1-2 in. (25-50 mm), 2-3 in. (50-75 mm) and 3-4 in. (75-100 mm).

Micrometers covering a wider range of measurement are available, using a large frame with interchangeable anvils of various lengths. This type of micrometer offers a cost savings; however, its overall size may make it less convenient.

Reading a Micrometer

When reading a micrometer, numbers are taken from different scales and added together. The following sections describe how to take measurements with various types of outside micrometers.

DECIMAL PLACE VALUES*

0.1	Indicates 1/10 (one tenth of an inch or millimeter)
0.010	Indicates 1/100 (one one-hundreth of an inch or millimeter)
0.001	Indicates 1/1000 (one one-thousandth of an inch or millimeter)

*This chart represents the values of figures placed to the right of the decimal point. Use it when reading decimals from one-tenth to one one-thousandth of an inch or millimeter. It is not a conversion chart (for example: 0.001 in. is not equal to 0.001 mm).

STANDARD INCH MICROMETER

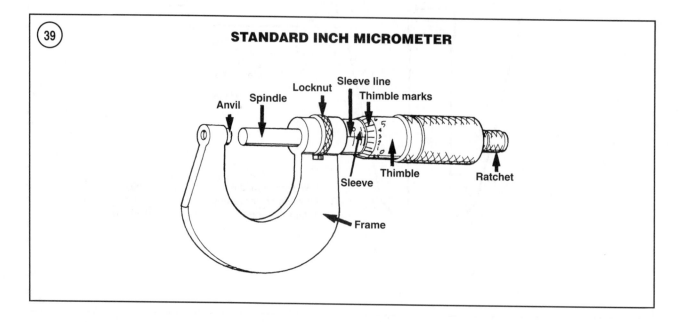

For accurate results, properly maintain the measuring surfaces of the micrometer. There cannot be any dirt or burrs between the tool and the measured object. Never force the micrometer closed around an object. Close the micrometer around the highest point so it can be removed with a slight drag. **Figure 39** shows the markings and parts of a standard inch micrometer. Be familiar with these terms before using a micrometer in the following sections.

Standard inch micrometer

The standard inch micrometer is accurate to one-thousandth of an inch or 0.001. The sleeve is marked in 0.025 in. increments. Every fourth sleeve mark is numbered 1, 2, 3, 4, 5, 6, 7, 8, 9. These numbers indicate 0.100 in., 0.200 in., 0.300 in., and so on.

The tapered end of the thimble has twenty-five lines marked around it. Each mark equals 0.001 in. One complete turn of the thimble will align its zero mark with the first mark on the sleeve or 0.025 in.

When reading a standard inch micrometer, perform the following steps while referring to **Figure 40**.

1. Read the sleeve and find the largest number visible. Each sleeve number equals 0.100 in.

2. Count the number of lines between the numbered sleeve mark and the edge of the thimble. Each sleeve mark equals 0.025 in.

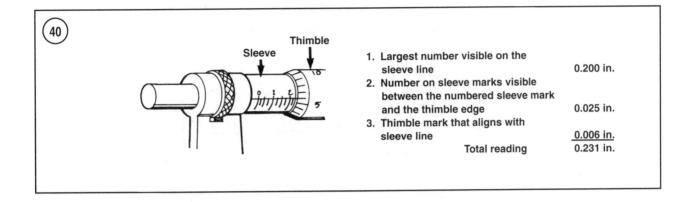

40

Thimble

Sleeve

1. Largest number visible on the
   sleeve line   0.200 in.
2. Number on sleeve marks visible
   between the numbered sleeve mark
   and the thimble edge   0.025 in.
3. Thimble mark that aligns with
   sleeve line   <u>0.006 in.</u>
                        Total reading   0.231 in.

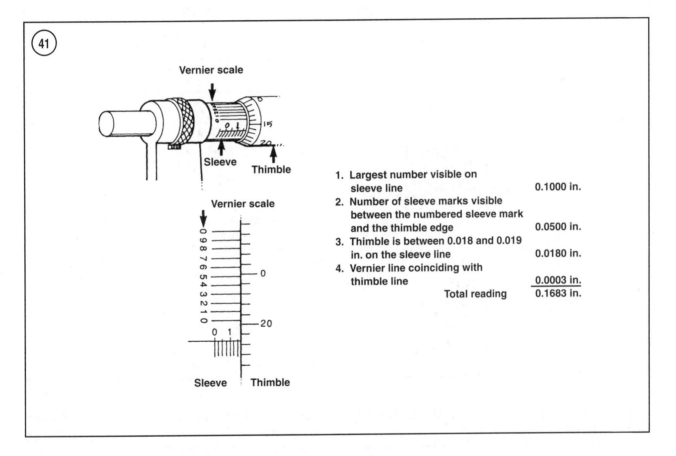

41

Vernier scale

Sleeve

Thimble

Vernier scale

Sleeve   Thimble

1. Largest number visible on
   sleeve line   0.1000 in.
2. Number of sleeve marks visible
   between the numbered sleeve mark
   and the thimble edge   0.0500 in.
3. Thimble is between 0.018 and 0.019
   in. on the sleeve line   0.0180 in.
4. Vernier line coinciding with
   thimble line   <u>0.0003 in.</u>
                        Total reading   0.1683 in.

3. Read the thimble mark that aligns with the sleeve line. Each thimble mark equals 0.001 in.

> *NOTE*
> *If a thimble mark does not align exactly with the sleeve line, estimate the amount between the lines. For accurate readings in ten-thousandths of an inch (0.0001 in.), use a vernier inch micrometer.*

4. Add the readings from Steps 1-3.

Vernier inch micrometer

A vernier inch micrometer is accurate to one ten-thousandth of an inch or 0.0001 in. It has the same marking as a standard inch micrometer with an additional vernier scale on the sleeve (**Figure 41**).

The vernier scale consists of 11 lines marked 1-9 with a 0 on each end. These lines run parallel to the thimble lines and represent 0.0001 in. increments.

When reading a vernier inch micrometer, perform the following steps while referring to **Figure 41**.

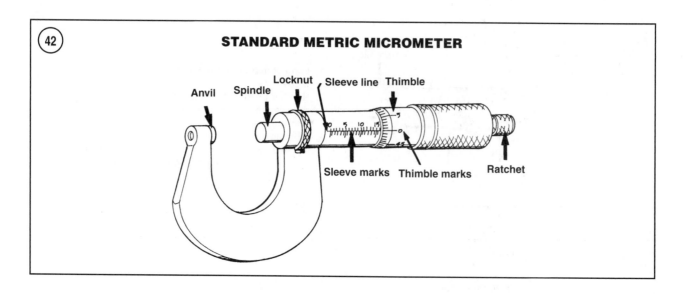

(42)

STANDARD METRIC MICROMETER

Anvil Spindle Locknut Sleeve line Thimble

Sleeve marks Thimble marks Ratchet

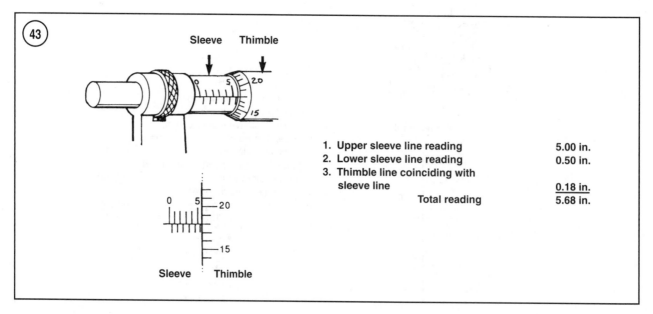

(43)

Sleeve Thimble

1. Upper sleeve line reading	5.00 in.
2. Lower sleeve line reading	0.50 in.
3. Thimble line coinciding with sleeve line	0.18 in.
Total reading	**5.68 in.**

Sleeve Thimble

1. Read the micrometer in the same way as a standard micrometer. This is the initial reading.

2. If a thimble mark aligns exactly with the sleeve line, reading the vernier scale is not necessary. If they do not align, read the vernier scale in Step 3.

3. Determine which vernier scale mark aligns with one thimble mark. The vernier scale number is the amount in ten-thousandths of an inch to add to the initial reading from Step 1.

Metric micrometer

The standard metric micrometer (**Figure 42**) is accurate to one one-hundredth of a millimeter (0.01 mm). The sleeve line is graduated in millimeter and half millimeter increments. The marks on the upper half of the sleeve line equal 1.00 mm. Every fifth mark above the sleeve line is identified with a number. The number sequence depends on the size of the micrometer. A 0-25 mm micrometer, for example, has sleeve marks numbered 0 through 25 in 5 mm increments. This numbering sequence continues with larger micrometers. On all metric micrometers, each mark on the lower half of the sleeve equals 0.50 mm.

The tapered end of the thimble has fifty lines marked around it. Each mark equals 0.01 mm.

One complete turn of the thimble aligns its 0 mark with the first line on the lower half of the sleeve line or 0.50 mm.

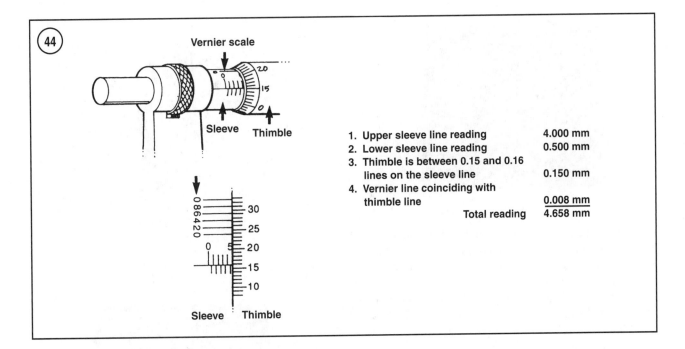

1. Upper sleeve line reading   4.000 mm
2. Lower sleeve line reading   0.500 mm
3. Thimble is between 0.15 and 0.16 lines on the sleeve line   0.150 mm
4. Vernier line coinciding with thimble line   <u>0.008 mm</u>

             Total reading   4.658 mm

When reading a metric micrometer, add the number of millimeters and half-millimeters on the sleeve line to the number of one one-hundredth millimeters on the thimble. Perform the following steps while referring to **Figure 43**.

1. Read the upper half of the sleeve line and count the number of lines visible. Each upper line equals 1 mm.
2. See if the half-millimeter line is visible on the lower sleeve line. If so, add 0.50 to the reading in Step 1.
3. Read the thimble mark that aligns with the sleeve line. Each thimble mark equals 0.01 mm.

NOTE
If a thimble mark does not align exactly with the sleeve line, estimate the amount between the lines. For accurate readings in two-thousandths of a millimeter (0.002 mm), use a metric vernier micrometer.

4. Add the readings from Steps 1-3.

Metric vernier micrometer

A metric vernier micrometer (**Figure 44**) is accurate to two-thousandths of a millimeter (0.002 mm). It has the same markings as a standard metric micrometer with the addition of a vernier scale on the sleeve. The vernier scale consists of five lines marked 0, 2, 4, 6, and 8. These lines run parallel to the thimble lines and represent 0.002-mm increments.

When reading a metric vernier micrometer, refer to **Figure 44** and perform the following steps.

1. Read the micrometer in the same way as a standard metric micrometer. This is the initial reading.
2. If a thimble mark aligns exactly with the sleeve line, reading the vernier scale is not necessary. If they do not align, read the vernier scale in Step 3.
3. Determine which vernier scale mark aligns exactly with one thimble mark. The vernier scale number is the amount in two-thousandths of a millimeter to add to the initial reading from Step 1.

Micrometer Adjustment

Before using a micrometer, check its adjustment as follows.

1. Clean the anvil and spindle faces.
2A. To check a 0-1 in. or 0-25 mm micrometer:
    a. Turn the thimble until the spindle contacts the anvil. If the micrometer has a ratchet stop, use it to ensure the proper amount of pressure is applied.
    b. If the adjustment is correct, the 0 mark on the thimble will align exactly with the 0 mark on the sleeve line. If the marks do not align, the micrometer is out of adjustment.
    c. Follow the manufacturer's instructions to adjust the micrometer.
2B. To check a micrometer larger than 1 in. or 25 mm use the standard gauge supplied by the manufacturer. A standard gauge is a steel block, disc or rod that is machined to an exact size.

a. Place the standard gauge between the spindle and anvil, and measure the outside diameter or length. If the micrometer has a ratchet stop, use it to ensure the proper amount of pressure is applied.

b. If the adjustment is correct, the 0 mark on the thimble will align exactly with the 0 mark on the sleeve line. If the marks do not align, the micrometer is out of adjustment.

c. Follow the manufacturer's instructions to adjust the micrometer.

Micrometer Care

Micrometers are precision instruments. Use and maintain them with great care.

Note the following:

1. Store micrometers in protective cases or separate padded drawers in a toolbox.

2. When in storage, make sure the spindle and anvil faces do not contact each other or another object. If they do, temperature changes and corrosion may damage the contact faces.

3. Do not clean a micrometer with compressed air. Dirt forced into the tool causes wear.

4. Lubricate micrometers with WD-40 to prevent corrosion.

Telescoping and Small Bore Gauges

Use telescoping gauges (**Figure 45**) and small hole gauges to measure bores. Neither gauge has a scale for direct readings. Use an outside micrometer to determine the reading.

To use a telescoping gauge, select the correct size gauge for the bore. Compress the movable post and carefully insert the gauge into the bore. Carefully move the gauge in the bore to make sure it is centered. Tighten the knurled end of the gauge to hold the movable post in position. Re-

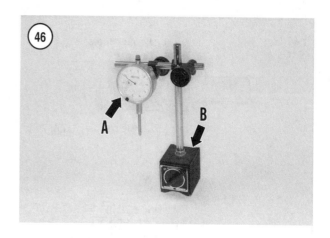

move the gauge and measure the length of the posts. Telescoping gauges are typically used to measure cylinder bores.

To use a small-bore gauge, select the correct size gauge for the bore. Carefully insert the gauge into the bore. Tighten the knurled end of the gauge to carefully expand the gauge fingers to the limit within the bore. Do not overtighten the gauge, as there is no built-in release. Excessive tightening can damage the bore surface and the tool. Remove the gauge and measure the outside dimension. Small hole gauges are typically used to measure valve guides.

Dial Indicator

A dial indicator (**Figure 46**) is a gauge with a dial face and needle used to measure variations in dimensions and movements, such as crankshaft and gear shaft runout limits.

Dial indicators are available in various ranges and graduations and with three basic types of mounting bases: magnetic, clamp, or screw-in stud. When purchasing a

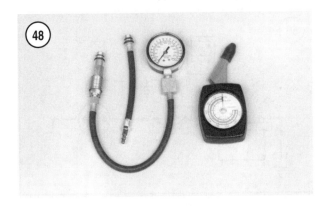

dial indicator, select the magnetic stand type (B, **Figure 46)** with a continuous dial (A).

Cylinder Bore Gauge

The cylinder bore gauge is a very specialized precision tool that is only needed for major engine repairs or rebuilds. The gauge set shown in **Figure 47** is comprised of a dial indicator, handle and a number of different length adapters (anvils) used to fit the gauge to various bore sizes. The bore gauge can be used to measure bore size, taper and out-of-round. When using a bore gauge, follow the manufacturer's instructions.

Compression Gauge

A compression gauge (**Figure 48**) measures the combustion chamber (cylinder) pressure, usually in psi or kg/cm2. An engine is capable of mechanically generating on the compression stroke. The gauge adapter is either inserted or screwed into the spark plug hole to obtain the reading. Disable the engine so it does not start and hold the throttle in the wide-open position when performing a

compression test. An engine that does not have adequate compression cannot be properly tuned.

Multimeter

A multimeter (**Figure 49**) is an essential tool for electrical system diagnosis. The voltage function indicates the voltage applied or available to various electrical components. The ohmmeter function tests circuits for continuity, or lack of continuity, and measures the resistance of a circuit.

Some less expensive models contain a needle gauge and are known as analog meters. Most high-quality (but not necessarily expensive) meters available today contain digital readout screens. Digital multimeters are often known as DVOMs. When using an analog ohmmeter, the needle must be zeroed or calibrated according to the meter manufacturer's instructions. Some analog and almost all digital meters are self-zeroing and no manual adjustment is necessary.

Some manufacturers' specifications for electrical components are based on results using a specific test meter. Results may vary if using a meter not recommended by the manufacturer is used.

ELECTRICAL SYSTEM FUNDAMENTALS

A thorough study of the many types of electrical systems used in today's engines is beyond the scope of this manual. However, a basic understanding of electrical basics is necessary to perform simple diagnostic tests.

Voltage

Voltage is the electrical potential or pressure in an electrical circuit and is expressed in volts. The more pressure (voltage) in a circuit, the more work that can be performed.

Direct current (DC) voltage means the electricity flows in one direction. All circuits powered by a battery are DC circuits.

Alternating current (AC) means the electricity flows in one direction momentarily then switches to the opposite direction. Alternator output is an example of AC voltage. This voltage must be changed or rectified to direct current to operate in a 12-volt battery powered system.

Measuring voltage

Unless otherwise specified, perform all voltage tests with the electrical connectors attached.

When measuring voltage, select a meter range one scale higher than the expected voltage of the circuit to prevent damage to the meter. To determine the actual voltage in a circuit, use a voltmeter. To simply check if voltage is present, use a test light.

NOTE
When using a test light, either lead can be attached to ground.

1. Attach the negative meter test lead to a good ground (bare metal). Make sure the ground is not insulated with a rubber gasket or grommet.
2. Attach the positive meter test lead to the point being checked for voltage (**Figure 50**).
3. If necessary for the circuit being checked, turn on the ignition switch. This will be necessary if the point being checked only has power applied when the ignition switch is turned ON, but the example in **Figure 50** shows a measurement at the positive battery terminal, which should always have voltage if the battery is charged. The test light should light or the meter should display a reading. The reading should be within one volt of battery voltage. If the voltage is less, there is a problem in the circuit.

Voltage drop test

Resistance causes voltage to drop. This resistance can be measured in an active circuit by using a voltmeter to perform a voltage drop test. A voltage drop test compares the difference between the voltage available at the start of a circuit to the voltage at the end of the circuit. But it does so while the circuit is operational. If the circuit has no resistance, there will be no voltage drop. The greater the resistance, the greater the voltage drop will be. A voltage drop of one volt or more usually indicates excessive resistance in the circuit.

1. Connect the positive meter test lead to the electrical source (where electricity is coming from).
2. Connect the negative meter test lead to the electrical load (where electricity is going). See **Figure 51**.
3. If necessary, activate the component(s) in the circuit.
4. A voltage reading of 1 volt or more indicates excessive resistance in the circuit. A reading equal to battery voltage indicates an open circuit.

Resistance

Resistance is the opposition to the flow of electricity within a circuit or component and is measured in ohms. Resistance causes a reduction in available current and voltage.

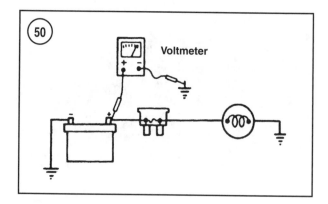

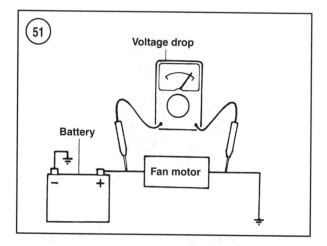

Resistance is measured in an inactive circuit with an ohmmeter. The ohmmeter sends a small amount of current into the circuit and measures how difficult it is to push the current through the circuit.

An ohmmeter, although useful, is not always a good indicator of a circuit's actual ability under operating conditions. This fact is due to the low voltage (6-9 volts) that the meter uses to test the circuit. The voltage in an ignition coil secondary winding can be several thousand volts. Such high voltage can cause the coil to malfunction, even though it tests acceptable during a resistance test.

Resistance generally increases with temperature. Perform all testing with the component or circuit at room temperature. Resistance tests performed at high temperatures may indicate high resistance readings and result in the unnecessary replacement of a component.

Resistance and continuity testing

CAUTION
Only use an ohmmeter on a circuit that has no voltage present. The meter will be damaged if it is connected to a live circuit. Re-

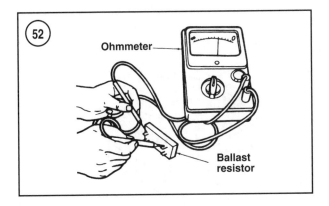

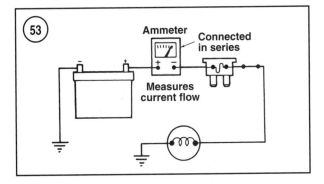

member, if using an analog meter, it must normally be calibrated each time it is used or the scale is changed.

A continuity test can determine if the circuit is complete. This type of test is performed with an ohmmeter or a self-powered test lamp.

1. Disconnect the negative battery cable.

2. Attach one test lead (ohmmeter or test light) to one end of the component or circuit.

3. Attach the other test lead to the opposite end of the component or circuit (**Figure 52**).

4. A self-powered test light will come on if the circuit has continuity or is complete. An ohmmeter will indicate either low or no resistance if the circuit has continuity. An open circuit is indicated if the meter displays infinite resistance.

Amperage

Amperage is the unit of measure for the amount of current within a circuit. Current is the actual flow of electricity. The higher the current, the more work that can be performed up to a given point. If the current flow exceeds the circuit or component capacity, the system will be damaged.

Measuring amps

An ammeter measures the current flow or amps of a circuit (**Figure 53**). Amperage measurement requires that the circuit be disconnected and the ammeter be connected in series to the circuit. Always use an ammeter that can read higher than the anticipated current flow to prevent damage to the meter. Connect the red test lead to the electrical source and the black test lead to the electrical load.

BASIC MECHANICAL SKILLS

Most of the service procedures covered are straightforward and can be performed by anyone reasonably handy with tools. It is suggested, however, to consider your own capabilities carefully before attempting any operation involving major disassembly.

1. *Front*, as used in this manual, refers to the front of the engine or the side of the engine facing the boat; the front of any component is the end closest to the front of the engine or boat. The *left* and *right* sides refer to the position of the parts as viewed by the boat operator sitting and facing forward. These rules are simple, but confusion can cause a major inconvenience during service.

2. When disassembling engine or drive components, mark the parts for location and mark all parts that mate together. Small parts, such as bolts, can be identified by placing them in plastic sandwich bags. Because many types of ink fade when applied to tape, use a permanent ink pen. Seal the bags and label them with masking tape and a marking pen. If reassembly will take place immediately, place nuts and bolts in a cupcake tin or egg carton in the order of disassembly.

3. Protect finished surfaces from physical damage or corrosion. Keep gasoline off painted surfaces.

4. Use penetrating oil to free frozen or tight bolts, then strike the bolt head a few times with a hammer and punch. (Use a screwdriver on screws.) Avoid the use of heat where possible, as it can warp, melt or affect the temper of parts. Heat also ruins finishes, especially paint and plastics.

5. Unless otherwise noted, no parts removed or installed (other than bushings and bearings) in the procedures given in this manual should require unusual force during disassembly or assembly. If a part is difficult to remove or install, find out why before proceeding.

6. Cover all openings after removing parts or components to prevent things like dirt or small tools from falling in.

7. Read each procedure *completely* while looking at the actual parts before starting a job. Make sure you *thor-*

oughly understand what is to be done and then carefully follow the procedure, step by step.

8. For the Do-it-Yourselfer, recommendations are occasionally made to refer service or maintenance to a dealership or a specialist in a particular field. In these cases, the work will be done more quickly and economically than performing the job yourself.

9. In procedural steps, the term *replace* means to discard a defective part and replace it with a new or exchange unit. *Overhaul* means to remove, disassemble, inspect, measure, repair or replace defective parts, reassemble and install major systems or parts.

10. Some operations require the use of a hydraulic press. If a suitable press is not available, it would be wiser to have these operations performed by a shop equipped for such work, rather than to try to do the job yourself with makeshift equipment that may damage the engine.

11. Repairs go much faster and easier if the machine is clean before beginning work.

12. If special tools are required, make arrangements to get them before starting. It is frustrating and time-consuming to start a job and then be unable to complete it.

13. Make diagrams or take a picture wherever similar-appearing parts are found. For instance, crankcase bolts often are not the same length. You may think you can remember where everything came from—but mistakes are costly. You may also get sidetracked and not return to work for days or even weeks—in which time, carefully laid out parts may have become disturbed.

14. When assembling parts, be sure all shims and washers are put exactly where they came out.

15. Whenever a rotating part butts against a stationary part, look for a shim or washer. Use new gaskets if there is any doubt about the condition of the old ones. A thin coating of silicone sealant on non-pressure type gaskets may help them seal more effectively.

16. If it becomes necessary to purchase gasket material to make a gasket for the engine, measure the thickness of the old gasket (at an uncompressed point) and purchase gasket material with the same approximate thickness.

17. Heavy grease can be used to hold small parts in place if they tend to fall out during assembly. However, keep grease and oil away from electrical components, unless otherwise directed.

18. Never use wire to clean out jets and air passages. They are easily damaged. Use compressed air to blow out the carburetor only if the diaphragm is removed first.

19. Take your time and do the job right. Do not forget that a newly rebuilt engine must be broken in just like a new one.

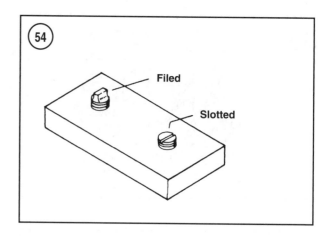

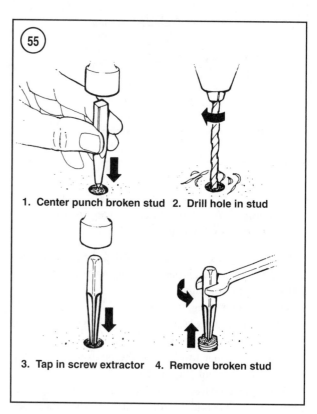

1. Center punch broken stud   2. Drill hole in stud

3. Tap in screw extractor   4. Remove broken stud

Removing Frozen Fasteners

If a fastener cannot be removed, several methods may be used to loosen it. First, apply penetrating oil such as Liquid Wrench, WD-40 or PB Blaster. Apply it liberally and let it penetrate for 10-15 minutes. Rap the fastener several times with a small hammer. Do not hit it hard enough to cause damage. Reapply the penetrating oil if necessary.

For frozen screws, apply penetrating oil as described, then insert a screwdriver in the slot and rap the top of the

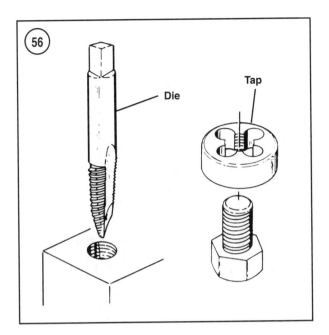

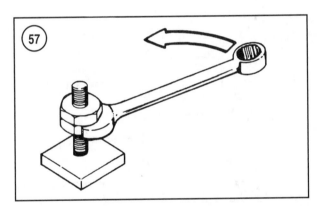

If the head breaks off flush (which too often happens in this situation), use a screw extractor. To do this, centerpunch the exact center of the remaining portion of the screw or bolt. Drill a small hole in the screw and tap the extractor into the hole. Back the screw out with a wrench on the extractor (**Figure 55**).

> *NOTE*
> *Broken screw extraction sometimes fails to remove the fastener from the bore. If this occurs, or if the screw is drilled off-center and the threads are damaged, a threaded-insert will be necessary to repair the bore. Check for one at a local dealership or supply store and follow the manufacturer's instructions for installation.*

Repairing Damaged Threads

Occasionally, threads are stripped through carelessness or impact damage. Often the threads can be repaired by running a tap (for internal threads on nuts) or die (for external threads on bolts) through the threads (**Figure 56**). Use only a specially designed spark plug tap to clean or repair spark plug threads.

If an internal thread is damaged, it may be necessary to install a Helicoil or some other type of thread insert. Follow the manufacturer's instructions when installing the insert.

If it is necessary to drill and tap a hole, refer to **Table 3** for metric tap drill sizes.

Stud Removal/Installation

A stud removal tool that makes the removal and installation of studs easier is available from most tool suppliers. If one is not available, thread two nuts onto the stud and tighten them against each other to lock them in place, then remove the stud by turning the lower nut (**Figure 57**).

> *NOTE*
> *If the threads on the damaged stud do not allow installation of the two nuts, it is necessary to remove the stud with a pair of locking pliers or a stud remover.*

Removing Hoses

When removing stubborn hoses, do not exert excessive force on the hose or fitting. Remove the hose clamp and carefully insert a small screwdriver or pick tool between the fitting and hose. Apply a spray lubricant under the hose and carefully twist the hose off the fitting. Clean the

screwdriver with a hammer. This loosens the corrosion so the screw can be removed in the normal way. If the screw head is too damaged to use this method, grip the head with locking pliers and twist the screw out.

Avoid applying heat unless specifically instructed, as it may melt, warp or remove the temper from parts.

Removing Broken Fasteners

If the head breaks off a screw or bolt, several methods are available for removing the remaining portion. If a large portion of the remainder projects out, try gripping it with locking pliers. If the projecting portion is too small or a sufficient grip cannot be obtained on the protruding piece, file it to fit a wrench or cut a slot in it to fit a screwdriver (**Figure 54**).

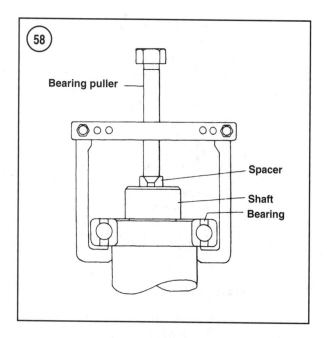

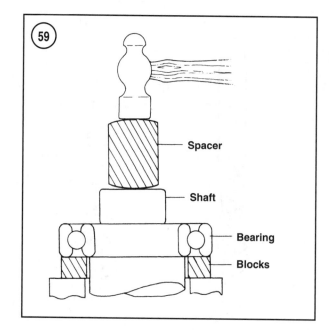

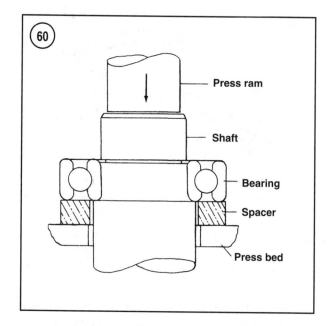

fitting of any corrosion or rubber hose material with a wire brush. Clean the inside of the hose thoroughly. Do not use any lubricant when installing the hose (new or old). The lubricant may allow the hose to come off the fitting, even with the clamp secure.

Bearings

Bearings are used in the engine and gearcase assembly to reduce power loss, heat and noise resulting from friction. Because bearings are precision parts, it is necessary to maintain them with proper lubrication and maintenance. If a bearing is damaged, replace it immediately. When installing a new bearing, try not to damage it. Bearing replacement procedures are included in the individual chapters where applicable; however, use the following sections as a guideline.

NOTE
Unless otherwise specified, install bearings with the manufacturer's mark or number facing outward.

Removal

While bearings are normally removed only when damaged, there may be times when it is necessary to remove a bearing that is in good condition. However, improper bearing removal will damage the bearing, shaft, and/or case half. Note the following when removing bearings.

1. When using a puller (**Figure 58**) to remove a bearing from a shaft, take care not to damage the shaft. Always place a piece of metal between the end of the shaft and the puller screw. In addition, place the puller arms next to the inner (**not outer**) bearing race.

2. When using a hammer to remove a bearing from a shaft, do not strike the hammer directly against the shaft. Instead, use a brass or aluminum spacer between the hammer and shaft (**Figure 59**) and make sure to support both bearing races with wooden blocks as shown.

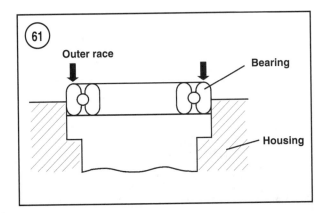

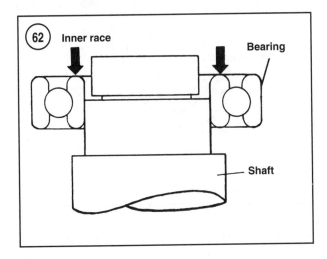

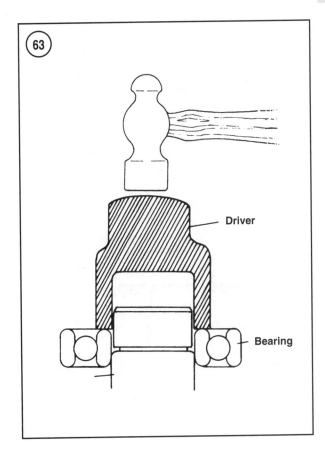

3. The ideal method of bearing removal is with a hydraulic press. In order to prevent damage to the bearing and shaft or case, note the following when using a press:

    a. Always support the inner and outer bearing races with a suitable size wooden or aluminum spacer ring (**Figure 60**). If only the outer race is supported, pressure applied against the balls and/or the inner race will damage them.

    b. Always make sure the press ram (**Figure 60**) aligns with the center of the shaft. If the ram is not centered, it may damage the bearing and/or shaft.

    c. The moment the shaft is free of the bearing, it will drop to the floor. Secure or hold the shaft to prevent it from falling.

Installation

1. When installing a bearing in a housing, apply pressure to the *outer* bearing race (**Figure 61**). When installing a bearing on a shaft, apply pressure to the *inner* bearing race (**Figure 62**).

2. When installing a bearing as described in Step 1, use some type of driver. Never strike the bearing directly with a hammer or the bearing will be damaged. When installing a bearing, use a driver, a piece of pipe or a socket with a diameter that matches the bearing race. **Figure 63** shows the correct way to use a socket and hammer to install a bearing on a shaft.

3. Step 1 describes how to install a bearing in a case half or over a shaft. However, when installing a bearing over a shaft *and* into a housing at the same time, a tight fit is required for both outer and inner bearing races. In this situation, install a spacer underneath the driver tool so that pressure is applied evenly across both races. See **Figure 64**. If the outer race is not supported as shown, the balls or rollers will push against the outer bearing race and damage it.

Installing an interference fit bearing over a shaft

When a tight fit is required, the bearing inside diameter will be smaller than the shaft. In this case, driving the bearing on the shaft using normal methods may cause bearing damage. Instead, heat the bearing before installation. Note the following:

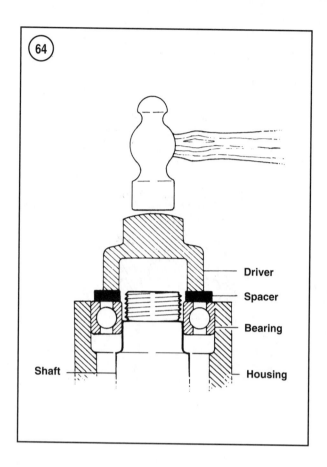

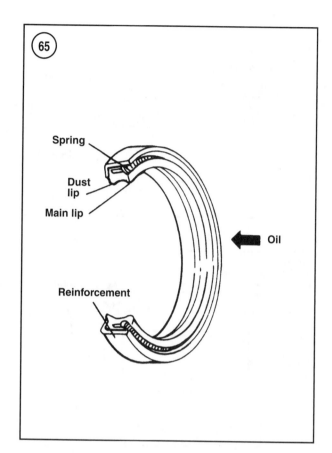

1. Secure the shaft so that it is ready for bearing installation. Also, take this opportunity (while the parts are cold) to size and gather the appropriate spacers and drivers for installation.

2. Clean the bearing surface on the shaft of all residue. Remove burrs with a file or sandpaper.

3. Fill a suitable pot or beaker with clean mineral oil. Place a thermometer rated higher than 120° C (248° F) in the oil. Support the thermometer so it does not rest on the bottom or side of the pot.

4. Remove the bearing from its wrapper and secure it with a piece of heavy wire bent to hold it in the pot. Hang the bearing so it does not touch the bottom or sides of the pot.

5. Turn the heat on and monitor the thermometer. When the oil temperature rises to approximately 120° C (248° F), remove the bearing from the pot and quickly install it. If necessary, place a socket on the inner bearing race and tap the bearing into place. As the bearing chills, it will tighten on the shaft so work quickly when installing it. Make sure the bearing is installed completely.

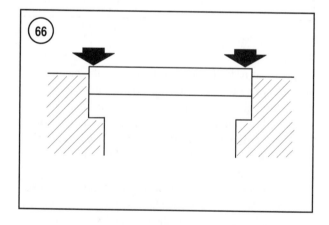

Replacing an interference fit bearing in a housing

Bearings are generally installed in a housing with a slight interference fit. Driving the bearing into the housing using normal methods may damage the housing or bearing. Instead, heat the housing (to make the inner diameter of the bore larger) and chill the bearing (in order to make the outer diameter slightly smaller) before installation. This makes bearing installation much easier.

CAUTION
Before heating the crankcases in this proce-
dure to remove the bearings, wash the cases
thoroughly with detergent and water. In or-
der to prevent a possible fire hazard, rinse
and rewash the cases as required to remove
all traces of oil and other chemical deposits.

1. While the parts are still cold, determine the proper size and gather all necessary spacers and drivers for installation.
2. Place the new bearing in a freezer to chill it and slightly reduce the outside diameter.
3. While the bearing is chilling, heat the housing to a temperature of about 100° C (212° F) in an oven or on a hot plate. An easy way to check if the housing is hot enough is to drop tiny drops of water on the case; if they sizzle and evaporate immediately, the temperature is correct. Heat only one housing at a time.

CAUTION
Do not heat the housing with a propane or
acetylene torch. Never bring a flame into
contact with the bearing or housing. The di-
rect heat will destroy the case hardening of
the bearing and will likely warp the hous-
ing.

4. Remove the housing from the oven or hot plate using a thick kitchen potholder, heavy protective gloves or heavy shop cloths.

NOTE
A suitable size socket and extension works
well for removing and installing bearings.

5. Hold the housing with the bearing side down and tap the bearing out. Repeat for all bearings in the housing.

NOTE
Always install bearings with the manufac-
turer's mark or number facing outward.

6. While the housing is still hot, install the chilled new bearing(s) into the housing. Install the bearings by hand, if possible. If necessary, lightly tap the bearing(s) into the housing with a socket placed on the outer bearing race. *Do not* install new bearings by driving on the inner bearing race. Drive each bearing into the bore until it seats completely.

Seal Replacement

Seals (**Figure 65**) are used to contain oil, water, grease or combustion gasses in a housing or shaft. Improper removal of a seal can damage the components. Improper installation of the seal can damage the seal. Note the following:
1. Prying is generally the easiest and most effective method of removing a seal from a housing. However, always place a rag underneath the pry tool to prevent damage to the housing.
2. Pack waterproof grease in the seal lips before installing the seal.
3. In most cases, install seals with the manufacturer's numbers or marks facing out.
4. Install seals with a socket placed on the outside of the seal as shown in **Figure 66**. Drive the seal squarely into the housing. Never install a seal by hitting directly against the top of the seal with a hammer.

Table 1 GENERAL ENGINE SPECIFICATIONS

Engine hp (cu in./cc)	Year	No. of cyl.	Camshaft type/valves per cyl.	Fuel system	Approximate weight lb. (kg)	Shaft length in. (mm)
5 hp (7.8/128)						
Short/rope start	1997-2001	1	OHC/2	Single carb	68 (31)	15 (381)
Long/rope start	1997-2001	1	OHC/2	Single carb	72 (33)	20 (508)
6 hp (7.8/128)						
Short/rope start	1997-2001	1	OHC/2	Single carb	68 (31)	15 (381)
Long/rope start	1997-2001	1	OHC/2	Single carb	72 (33)	20 (508)
8 hp (12.87/211)						
Short/rope start	1995-1996	2	OHC/2	Single carb	85 (39)	15 (381)
Short/rope start	1997-2001	2	OHC/2	Single carb	82 (37)	15 (381)
Long/rope start	1995-1996	2	OHC/2	Single carb	88 (40)	20 (508)
Long/rope start	1997-2001	2	OHC/2	Single carb	87 (39)	20 (508)
Extra long	1995-1996	2	OHC/2	Single carb	91 (41)	25 (635)
Extra long	1997	2	OHC/2	Single carb	91 (41)	25 (635)

(continued)

Table 1 GENERAL ENGINE SPECIFICATIONS (continued)

Engine hp (cu in./cc)	Year	No. of cyl.	Camshaft type/ valves per cyl.	Fuel system	Approximate weight lb. (kg)	Shaft length in. (mm)
9.9 hp (12.87/211)						
Short/rope start	1997	2	OHC/2	Single carb	93 (42)	15 (381)
Short/rope start	1998	2	OHC/2	Single carb	82 (37)	15 (381)
Long/rope start	1997	2	OHC/2	Single carb	96 (43)	20 (508)
Long/rope start	1998	2	OHC/2	Single carb	87 (39)	20 (508)
Extra long	1997-1998	2	OHC/2	Single carb	101 (46)	25 (635)
9.9 hp (18.61/305)						
Short/rope start	1995-2001	2	OHC/2	Single carb	99 (45)	15 (381)
Long/rope start	1995-2001	2	OHC/2	Single carb	104 (47)	20 (508)
Long/electric remote	1995-2001	2	OHC/2	Single carb	114 (52)	20 (508)
Extra long	1995-2001	2	OHC/2	Single carb	119 (54)	25 (635)
15 hp (18.61/305)						
Short/rope start	1995-2001	2	OHC/2	Single carb*	99 (45)	15 (381)
Long/rope start	1995-2001	2	OHC/2	Single carb*	104 (47)	20 (508)
Long/electric remote	1995-2001	2	OHC/2	Single carb*	114 (52)	20 (508)
40 hp (49.7/815)	1999-2001	3	DOHC/4	MPEFI	238 (108)	20 (508)
50 hp (49.7/815)	1999-2001	3	DOHC/4	MPEFI	238 (108)	20 (508)
70 hp (79.2/1298)	1999-2001	4	SOHC/2	MPEFI	343 (156)	20 (508)

*Equipped with accelerator pump.

Table 2 TECHNICAL ABBREVIATIONS

ABDC	After bottom dead center
ATDC	After top dead center
BBDC	Before bottom dead center
BDC	Bottom dead center
BTDC	Before top dead center
C	Celsius (Centigrade)
cc	Cubic centimeters
CDI	Capacitor discharge ignition
CKP	Crankshaft position
CMP	Camshaft positioin
CT	Cylinder temperature
CTP	Closed throttle position
cu. in.	Cubic inches
DOHC	Dual-overhead camshafts
ECU	Electronic control unit
EFI	Electronic fuel injection
EM	Exhaust manifold
F	Fahrenheit
ft.-lb.	Foot-pounds
g	Gram
gal.	Gallons
hp	Horsepower
IAC	Idle air control
IAT	Intake air temperature
in.	Inches
kg	Kilogram
kg/cm^2	Kilograms per square centimeter
kgm	Kilogram meters
km	Kilometer
L	Liter
m	Meter
MAG	Magneto
MAP	Manifold absolute pressure

(continued)

Table 2 TECHNICAL ABBREVIATIONS (continued)

mm	Millimeter
MPEFI	Multi-Port Sequential Electronic Fuel Injection
N.A.	Not available
N•m	Newton-meters
oz.	Ounce
OHC	Overhead camshaft
psi	Pounds per square inch
pto	Power take off
pts.	Pints
qt.	Quarts
rpm	Revolutions per minute
WOT	Wide open throttle

Table 3 METRIC TAP AND DRILL SIZES

Metric tap (mm)	Drill size	Decimal equivalent	Nearest fraction
3 × 0.50	No. 39	0.0995	3/32
3 × 0.60	3/32	0.0937	3/32
4 × 0.70	No. 30	0.1285	1/8
4 × 0.75	1/8	0.125	1/8
5 × 0.80	No. 19	0.166	11/64
5 × 0.90	No. 20	0.161	5/32
6 × 1.00	No. 9	0.196	13/64
7 × 1.00	16/64	0.234	15/64
8 × 1.00	J	0.277	9/32
8 × 1.25	17/64	0.265	17/64
9 × 1.00	5/16	0.3125	5/16
9 × 1.25	5/16	0.3125	5/16
10 × 1.25	11/32	0.3437	11/32
10 × 1.50	R	0.339	11/32
11 × 1.50	3/8	0.375	3/8
12 × 1.50	13/32	0.406	13/32
12 × 1.75	13/32	0.406	13/32

Table 4 CONVERSION TABLES

Multiply	By	To get equivalent of
Length		
Inches	25.4	Millimeter
Inches	2.54	Centimeter
Miles	1.609	Kilometer
Feet	0.3048	Meter
Millimeter	0.03937	Inches
Centimeter	0.3937	Inches
Kilometer	0.6214	Mile
Meter	3.281	Mile
Fluid volume		
U.S. quarts	0.9463	Liters
U.S. gallons	3.785	Liters
U.S. ounces	29.573529	Milliliters
Imperial gallons	4.54609	Liters
Imperial quarts	1.1365	Liters
Liters	0.2641721	U.S. gallons
Liters	1.0566882	U.S. quarts
Liters	33.814023	U.S. ounces
Liters	0.22	Imperial gallons
Liters	0.8799	Imperial quarts

(continued)

Table 4 CONVERSION TABLES (continued)

Multiply	By	To get equivalent of
Fluid volume (continued)		
Milliliters	0.033814	U.S. ounces
Milliliters	1.0	Cubic centimeters
Milliliters	0.001	Liters
Torque		
Foot-pounds	1.3558	Newton-meters
Foot-pounds	0.138255	Meter-kilograms
Inch-pounds	0.11299	Newton-meters
Newton-meters	0.7375622	Foot-pounds
Newton-meters	8.8507	Inch-pounds
Meters-kilograms	7.2330139	Foot-pounds
Volume		
Cubic inches	16.387064	Cubic centimeters
Cubic centimeters	0.0610237	Cubic inches
Temperature		
Fahrenheit	(F − 32) 0.556	Centigrade
Centigrade	(C × 1.8) + 32	Fahrenheit
Weight		
Ounces	28.3495	Grams
Pounds	0.4535924	Kilograms
Grams	0.035274	Ounces
Kilograms	2.2046224	Pounds
Pressure		
Pounds per square inch	0.070307	Kilograms per square centimeter
Kilograms per square centimeter	14.223343	Pounds per square inch
Kilopascals	0.1450	Pounds per square inch
Pounds per square inch	6.895	Kilopascals
Speed		
Miles per hour	1.609344	Kilometers per hour
Kilometers per hour	0.6213712	Miles per hour

Table 5 GENERAL TORQUE SPECIFICATIONS

Screw or nut size	in.-lb.	ft.-lb.	N•m
U.S. Standard			
6-32	9	–	1.0
8-32	20	–	2.3
10-24	30	–	3.4
10-32	35	–	4.0
12-24	45	–	5.1
1/4-20	70	–	7.9
1/4-28	84	–	9.5
5/16-18	160	13	18
5/16-24	168	14	19
3/8-16	–	23	31
3/8-24	–	25	34
7/16-14	–	36	49
7/16-20	–	40	54
1/2-13	–	50	68
1/2-20	–	60	81
Metric			
M5	36	–	4
M6	70	–	8
M8	156	13	18
M10	–	26	35
M12	–	35	48
M14	–	60	81

Chapter Two

Troubleshooting

This chapter concentrates on the actual troubleshooting procedure. Once the defective component is identified, refer to the appropriate chapter for removal and replacement procedures. Refer to the *Quick Reference Data* section at the front of the manual for tables containing common engine specifications, and spark plug recommendations. Refer to Chapter One for information regarding tools and test equipment.

Tables 1-14 are at the end of the chapter. Use **Tables 1-3** (along with the procedures in this chapter) for troubleshooting. They list possible causes and components or systems to check when troubleshooting various engine symptoms. Many of the tests referred to by the charts are found in this chapter. The repair procedures, as well as some of the tests are found in the chapters covering the specific systems being checked. The remaining tables give specifications that are used during the various testing procedures in this chapter.

Troubleshooting is the process of testing individual systems with the express purpose of isolating good systems from the defective or nonfunctional system(s). When a system is identified as defective, troubleshooting consists of testing the individual components from the suspect system. It is very important to perform only one test procedure at a time, otherwise it will be difficult, if not impossible, to determine the condition of each individual component. Occasionally a component in a system cannot be stand-alone tested. In this case, other components are tested and eliminated until the suspect component is identified as defective by the process of elimination.

The two most important rules of troubleshooting are to test systems before components and to be methodical. Testing systems before components allows the troubleshooter to narrow down the search for the problem by eliminating all the components within systems that check out. Working methodically prevents time wasted by testing systems or components that are unrelated to the problem or that do not build upon knowledge gained by previous tests to narrow down the possible culprit. Haphazardly jumping from one system or component to another may eventually solve the problem, but time and effort will be wasted. Use the various system descriptions and diagrams provided in this manual to identify all components in a system. Test each component in a rational order to determine which component has caused the system's failure.

The troubleshooting process generally begins when an unusual symptom (decrease in performance or unsatisfactory operating characteristic) is noticed. The next step is to define the symptom as accurately as possible. Key points to consider are:

1. Did the problem occur suddenly or gradually?

2. Is there a specific engine speed or load at which the problem occurs?

3. Does the weather (extreme hot or cold) or engine temperature affect the symptom?

4. Has any service work been performed recently that could affect the symptom (or during which a mistake could have caused the symptom)?

5. Has the unit recently come out of storage?

6. Has the fuel supplier or fuel grade been recently changed?

7. Is the manufacturer's recommended oil being used?

8. Have any accessories been added to the boat or engine?

Once the symptom is adequately defined, attempt to duplicate the problem. Check the easy, simple areas first. Never assume anything. Do not overlook the obvious. If the engine does not start, first check the possible simple causes such as a failure to prime the fuel system, attaching the safety lanyard or an incorrect starting procedure. If the engine suddenly quits, check the easiest, most accessible problem first. Make sure there is gasoline in the tank. Check the fuses. If nothing obvious turns up in a quick check, look a little further.

Before beginning any troubleshooting procedure, perform a thorough visual inspection of the unit. Pay special attention to the condition of the battery cable connections (at both ends), all electrical harness connectors and terminals, fuel quantity, quality and supply. Look for engine overheating, leaks (fuel, oil and water) and mechanical integrity (loose fasteners, cracked or broken castings). Learning to recognize visual defects is a skill that comes from self-discipline and patience. Take your time and look closely. Use your hands to touch, feel and wiggle components.

Be realistic about your capabilities, especially if working in a home garage or driveway. Avoid situations where major disassembly is required if it is beyond your qualifications. Service departments tend to charge heavily to reassemble an engine that comes into the shop in several boxes, while some refuse to even take on such a job.

Proper lubrication, maintenance and engine tune-up as described in Chapter Three will reduce the necessity for troubleshooting. However, because of the harsh and demanding environment in which the outboard motor operates, troubleshooting is inevitable at some point.

TEST WHEELS (PROPELLERS)

Use a test wheel (propeller) for test procedures that require the engine to be run under load. The correct test wheel will suitably load the engine while producing a minimal amount of thrust. A test wheel can be used in a test tank, with the boat on a trailer (backed into the water) or with the boat launched and tied to a dock.

Test wheels are available from OMC Genuine Parts and are listed in the *Quick Reference Data* section at the front of this manual. The test wheel is also used to determine if the engine is producing its rated power. A minimum test speed is listed for each engine in the *Quick Reference Data* section. If the engine can reach or exceed the specified minimum test speed with the specified test wheel installed, the engine is producing its rated power. The gearcase must be submerged in water to at least its normal operating depth, and it must be shifted into FORWARD gear for this test.

A suitable test propeller can also be made by modifying (turning down) the diameter of a standard low pitch aluminum propeller until the recommended wide-open throttle speed can be obtained with the motor in a test tank (smaller motors) or on a trailer, backed into the water (larger engines). Because this type of test propeller produces considerable thrust, be careful when tying the boat to a dock. Some docks may not be able to withstand the load.

Propeller repair stations can provide the modification service. Normally, approximately 1/3 to 1/2 of the blades will be removed. However, it is far better to remove too little, than too much. It may take several tries to achieve the correct full throttle speed, but once achieved, no further modifications are required. Many propeller repair stations have experience with this type of modification and may be able to recommend a starting point.

Test wheels and/or propellers allow simple tracking of engine performance. The full-throttle test speed of an engine fitted with the correct test wheel or correctly modified propeller can be tracked (recorded) from season to season. It is not unusual for a new or rebuilt engine to show a slight increase in test propeller speed as complete break-in is achieved. The engine will generally hold this speed over its normal service life. As the engine begins to wear out, the test wheel (propeller) speed will show a gradual decrease.

EPA COMPLIANCE

The Environmental Protection Agency (EPA) certifies emission output for all 1998 and later models. Certified models have an EPA certification plate mounted near the model identification plate on the engine midsection.

All repairs or service procedures must be performed exactly as specified to ensure the engine continues to comply with EPA requirements. For the same reason, all replacement parts must meet or exceed the manufacturer's specifications.

If in doubt as to whether a repair or service procedure to the engine will adversely affect the ability to maintain

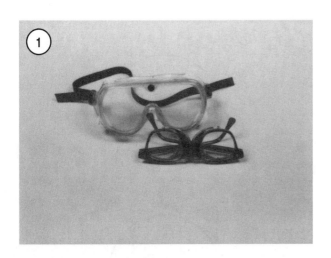

EPA compliance, contact an Evinrude or Johnson dealership, before beginning the repair or procedure.

SAFETY PRECAUTIONS

Wear approved eye protection (**Figure 1**) at all times. Especially when machinery is in operation and hammers are being used. Wear approved ear protection during all running tests and in the presence of noisy machinery. Keep loose clothing tucked in and long hair tied back and secured. Refer to the *Safety* section in Chapter One for additional safety guidelines.

When making or breaking any electrical connection, always disconnect the negative battery cable. When performing tests that require cranking the engine without starting, disconnect and ground the spark plug leads to prevent accidental starting and sparks.

Securely cap or plug all disconnected fuel lines to prevent fuel discharge when the motor is cranked or the primer bulb is squeezed.

Thoroughly read the relevant testing and repair procedures covered by this manual and note all test equipment and special tools that are required. Also, make sure to read carefully all tool or part manufacturer's instructions and safety sheets. Do not substitute parts unless they meet or exceed the original manufacturer's specifications.

Never run an outboard engine without an adequate water supply. Never run an outboard engine at wide-open throttle without an adequate load. Do not exceed 3000 rpm in neutral (no load).

Safely performing on-water tests requires two people—one person to operate the boat, the other to monitor the gauges or test instruments. All personnel must remain seated inside the boat at all times. It is not acceptable to lean over the transom while the boat is under way. Use extensions to allow all gauges and meters to be located in the normal seating area.

PRELIMINARY TROUBLESHOOTING

Before testing any system or component always perform a preliminary inspection on the engine. Most operational problems are simple in nature and easy to remedy.

The first part of this section lists the basic operating requirements for the engine. The second section lists instructions for performing a preliminary inspection on the engine.

To ensure safe and accurate testing always read the test procedures thoroughly. If experience or equipment is lacking, have the procedure performed by an experience marine repair shop.

Operating Requirements

An engine needs three basic elements to run properly: correct fuel/air mixture, compression and spark at the right time (**Figure 2**). If one element is missing, the engine will not run. Four-stroke engine operating principles are described in Chapter One under *Engine Operation*. The ignition system is typically the weakest link of the three basic elements. More problems result from ignition breakdowns than from any other source. Keep that in mind before tampering with carburetor adjustments or the fuel injection system, as applicable.

If the engine has been sitting for any length of time and refuses to start, check and clean the spark plugs. Then check the condition of the battery (if used) to make sure it has an adequate charge. If these are good, look at the gasoline delivery system. This includes the fuel tank, fuel pump, carburetor or fuel injectors, fuel filter and fuel line. Gasoline deposits may have gummed up the fuel injectors or the carburetor jets and air passages. Gasoline tends to lose its potency after standing for long periods. Condensation may contaminate it with water. Drain the old gas and try starting with a fresh tankful.

Preliminary Inspection

Most engine malfunctions can be corrected by performing a preliminary inspection. Check all items listed in this section. If the problems persist after checking or correcting these items refer to **Tables 1-3** and check, test or adjust the components listed under the applicable symptom. Check the following:

1. Make sure the fuel tank vent is opened.

2. Make sure the engine has an adequate supply of fresh fuel.

3. Inspect the engine for loose, disconnected, dirty or corroded wires.

4. Check the position of the lanyard engine stop switch if so equipped.

5. Check the battery and cable connections for tight and clean connections (Chapter Seven).

6. Make sure the battery is fully charged (Chapter Seven).

7. Check the condition of the spark plugs and regap as necessary (Chapter Three).

8. Test for spark at each cylinder. See *Spark Test* in this chapter.

9. Make sure the boat hull is clean and in good condition.

10. Make sure the condition of the propeller and that a suitable propeller is installed.

TESTING AND REPAIRING ELECTRICAL COMPONENTS

Most dealerships and parts houses do not accept returns on electrical parts. When testing electrical components, make sure to perform the test procedures as described in this chapter and that the test equipment is working properly. If a test result shows that the component is defective but the reading is close to the service limit, have the component tested by a Johnson or Evinrude dealership to verify the test result before purchasing a new component.

Resistance testing can be especially tricky. Keep in mind that resistance, as a property, normally will fluctuate with temperature. Also, meters vary with quality and therefore readings on the same component vary also. The specifications on all tests, unless noted, were performed with a digital multimeter and a component test temperature of approximately 20° C (68° F).

Normally, the given resistance value of a component or wire will rise or increase as temperature increases. This is true for most resistor and windings. However, some manufacturers use negative temperature coefficient sensors for certain functions. Negative temperature coefficient sensors work in the opposite manner of most other electrical components. This means that as temperature **increases** while testing a negative temperature coefficient sensor, the resistance of the temperature sensor will **decrease**. For this reason, pay close attention to both resistance testing specifications and test conditions whenever troubleshooting electrical components.

For more information on troubleshooting and test equipment, refer to *Electrical System Fundamentals* and to *Multimeter* in Chapter One.

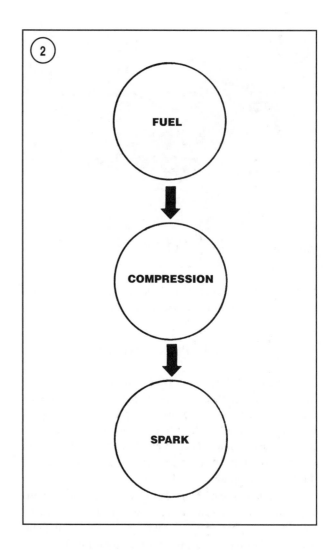

Electrical Repairs

Check all electrical connections for corrosion, mechanical damage, heat damage and loose connections. Clean and repair all connections as necessary. All wire splices or connector repairs must be made with waterproof marine grade connectors and heat shrink tubing. Marine and industrial suppliers are good sources for quality electrical repair equipment.

Four distinct types of connectors are commonly found on Johnson/Evinrude outboard engines.

1. *Bullet connectors*—The bullet connector (**Figure 3**) is a common connector used widely in the industry. The bullet connectors used on Evinrude/Johnson engines use vinyl sleeves with several internal sealing ribs to seal the sleeve to the lead as tightly as possible. Replacement male and female connectors, and their appropriate sleeves are listed in the manufacturer's parts catalog. The connectors are crimped in place using standard crimping pliers. Make

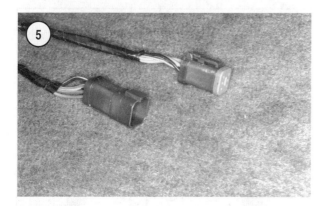

sure the correct vinyl sleeve (male or female) is slid in place over the lead before crimping the connector in place.

2. *Amphenol connectors*—Amphenol connectors have been widely used on Evinrude/Johnson engines since 1978. Amphenol connectors are identified by their round, dark, rubber connector bodies. Often a wire locking-clip (or wire bail) is used to keep the connector from vibrating apart. A disconnected Amphenol connector and its wire bail are shown in **Figure 4**. Replacement connector body part numbers are listed in the manufacturer's parts cata-

log. Special tools are available from dealerships for crimping, pin insertion and pin removal on these connectors.

> *CAUTION*
> *Always lubricate Amphenol connectors with isopropyl alcohol when connecting or disconnecting the bodies and/or replacing pins. The water-resistant molded seals in the bodies can be irreparably damaged if no lubricant is used.*

3. *Deutsch connectors*—OMC began using Deutsch connectors (**Figure 5**) when the modular wiring system (MWS) was introduced on remote control models beginning with the 1996 model year. The modular wiring harness is designed to allow flexible, uncomplicated rigging with exceptional durability. These connectors are considered totally waterproof when correctly installed and serviced. Their hard plastic bodies, orange locking wedges and orange silicone elastomer seals easily identify Deutsch style connectors. An external locking tab prevents the connectors from vibrating apart and must be manually released before the connectors can be separated. Each terminal pin is locked into the connector body with its own individual internal locking tab. Connector bodies are available in two, four, six and eight pin configurations, with all configurations using the same male and female terminal pins. Replacement connector body, locking wedge and seal part numbers are listed in the manufacturers parts catalog. Two service tools (a connector service tool and crimping pliers) and a connector repair kit are available from dealerships.

> *CAUTION*
> *Always lubricate the seals of Deutsch connectors with OMC Electrical Grease when reconnecting the bodies and/or replacing the pins. If the locking wedge has been removed, the connector body cavity (for the wedge) must be filled with OMC Electrical Grease to within 1/32 in. (0.8 mm) of the wedge to the connector body mating surface.*

4. *Packard connectors*—While the Packard connector (**Figure 6**, typical) is used extensively in the automotive industry, its use is somewhat limited on Evinrude/Johnson engines. This connector is only used to connect an engine harness directly to an electrical or ignition component and is not used to connect one harness to another.

> *CAUTION*
> *Always lubricate the seals of Packard connectors with OMC Electrical Grease when*

reconnecting the bodies or replacing the pin(s), body or seal(s).

There are two styles of Packard connectors (**Figure 6**) used on engines covered in this manual. The first style is easily identified by a flat arrangement of the terminal pins (in a straight row), the large U-shaped locking tab and the ribbed replaceable seals (one sealing leads to the body and the other sealing leads the body to the component). This connector is used in four and five-pin configurations on the engine shown in.

To replace the body or the wire-to-body seal, remove and cut all terminal pins from their wires. Unlock the pins individually by inserting a suitable terminal tool (from an automotive tool supplier) into the rear of the body after sliding out the wire-to-body seal and sliding it away from the body. Make sure the wires are routed through the new seal and/or connector body before crimping new terminal pins to the leads. After crimping, pull the wires (and pins) into the connector body until they lock in place. This is a *pull-to-lock* connector.

The second style of Packard connector is a six-pin configuration. This connector is easily identified by the two stacked rows of terminal pins (three each row). Each pin has its own individual rear seal, while a common ribbed seal is used to seal the connector body to the component.

To replace the body (or the wire-to-body seals), individually unlock the terminal pins by inserting a suitable terminal tool (such as a paper clip) into the front of the body and depressing the locking tab. The pin and lead may then be pulled out the rear of the body. Before reinserting the pin, lead and seal into the body, make sure to bend each pin locking tab up slightly to ensure a positive lock. Then push each lead (and pin) into the body until it locks in to place. This is a *push-to-lock* connector.

Wiring Harnesses

While many variations of wiring harnesses, switches, warning systems and controls are available, many engines are equipped with the OMC modular wiring system (MWS). The MWS system was designed to be used with an OMC System Check engine-monitoring gauge. The system check gauge (**Figure 7**) has four light emitting diodes (LEDs) that allow the operator to easily identify whether:

1. The engine is overheating.
2. The engine oil pressure is below specification.
3. The electronic engine control system on fuel injected engines is malfunctioning (check engine). Several styles of OMC tachometers are also available with the System Check gauge integrated into the tachometer. If a System

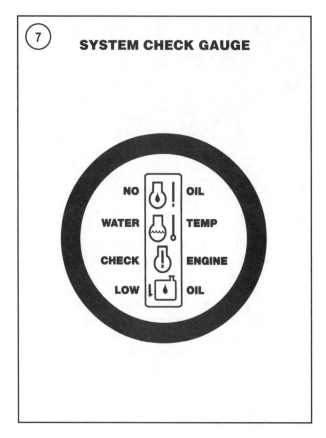

SYSTEM CHECK GAUGE

NO — OIL
WATER — TEMP
CHECK — ENGINE
LOW — OIL

2

MODULAR WIRING SYSTEM (MWS) HARNESS

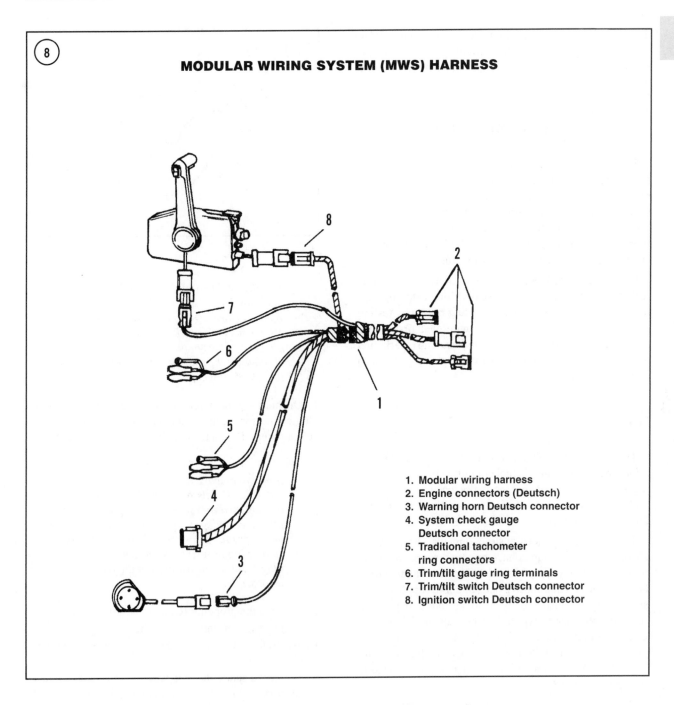

8

1. **Modular wiring harness**
2. **Engine connectors (Deutsch)**
3. **Warning horn Deutsch connector**
4. **System check gauge Deutsch connector**
5. **Traditional tachometer ring connectors**
6. **Trim/tilt gauge ring terminals**
7. **Trim/tilt switch Deutsch connector**
8. **Ignition switch Deutsch connector**

Check gauge is not used, an audible driver module must be installed in its place. The module will sound the warning horn if any of the previously mentioned problems arise, but will not differentiate the exact cause of the warning signal.

NOTE
*If the Check Engine light on the OMC System Check gauge is illuminated, refer to **Diagnostic System**, under the **Electronic Fuel***

Injection section in this chapter for details concerning reading and diagnosing trouble codes.

The MWS main harness (**Figure 8**) typically uses three Deutsch connectors to connect the boat (remote control) harness to the engine harness. At the remote control end, a series of Deutsch connectors is used to connect the boat harness to the remote control (or ignition switch) harness, the warning horn, the system check gauge (or audible driver module) and a trim/tilt switch (if equipped). Ring terminals are provided for the trim/tilt gauge, a conventional tachometer, switched battery positive (B+) and a black ground lead.

STARTING DIFFICULTY

Slow starting or an inability to start the engine is usually related to an engine malfunction. First verify that the proper starting procedures are followed. Starting procedures vary by model and optional equipment. Review the owner's manual for starting procedures. Then, perform a thorough *Preliminary Inspection* to eliminate any obvious causes, such as a weak battery or low fuel level.

If no obvious cause is found, this section provides information to help pinpoint the cause of difficult starting. Remember that organized troubleshooting begins by testing and eliminating at the highest system level first. Since three things are necessary for the engine to run (spark, fuel and engine compression), start by narrowing it down to one of these three areas.

Spark Test

The first step in isolating a starting problem is to determine whether the cause is fuel or ignition related (as compression problems do not normally occur suddenly or without other obvious warning signs, like severe engine knocking/rattling).

This section provides instructions for checking the spark at the spark plug connector. Use a spark gap tester for this test. Many types of spark testers are available from both marine and automotive parts and tool suppliers. The simplest type consists of what looks like a spark plug (usually with a screw-type adjustable gap) and a large alligator clip that is used to fasten the device to an engine ground. In all cases, follow the tool manufacturer's instructions closely to avoid injury or possible damage to the ignition system.

Refer to *Checking the Fuel System* in this chapter if adequate spark is present yet starting difficulty persists.

WARNING
Electric shock can cause serious injury or death. High voltages are generated by the ignition system. Never touch wires or wire connections while the engine is running. Never perform ignition system testing in wet conditions. Never perform electrical testing when fuel or fuel vapors are present.

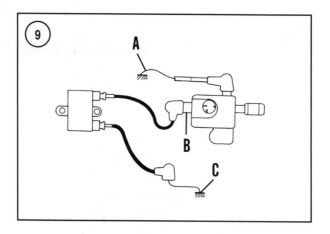

NOTE
The 40 and 50 hp models use an ignition coil integrated into the spark plug connector. When performing a spark test on these models, connect the spark gap tester to the spark plug end of the connector. On all other models connect the spark gap tester to the end of the spark plug cap.

1. On multi-cylinder motors, make a note of the spark plug connector locations and lead routing before disconnecting them. Disconnect all spark plug connectors.

WARNING
If possible, leave the spark plugs in the cylinder head. This prevents the possibility of air/fuel mixture escaping through the spark plug bore and igniting during the test. If it is necessary to remove the plugs, position the spark plug tester(s) and/or grounded spark plug leads as far away from the open bores as possible.

2. Remove the propeller (Chapter Nine) for safety.
3. Connect the ground lead of the spark gap tester (A, **Figure 9**) to a suitable engine ground such as the cylinder head bolt.
4. Connect a spark plug connector to the spark gap tester (B, **Figure 9**). On adjustable spark gap testers, adjust the gap to approximately 3/8 in. (9 mm) for carbureted motors or to 7/16 in. (11 mm) for fuel injected motors.
5. Connect all remaining spark plug leads to a suitable engine ground (C, **Figure 9**). Shift the engine into NEUTRAL. Make sure the ignition switch or key is ON.
6. Observe the spark gap tester while operating the electric or manual starter. Correct ignition system operation produces a strong blue spark as the engine cranks.
7. On multi-cylinder motors, repeat Steps 3-6 for the remaining cylinders.

8. Install the propeller.

9. Clean and install the spark plugs and connect the spark plug connectors to the correct spark plug.

10. Refer to *Ignition System* in this chapter if a no spark or weak spark condition is indicated on any of the cylinders.

NOTE
For carbureted models, if a spark test shows good spark, but a problem is still suspected with the ignition system, perform a running output test on the **Ignition Module/Power Pack** *as detailed in this chapter. If one cylinder shows good spark, but not another, test the ignition coil. If no spark is found, check the ignition system starting with stop circuit testing.*

Checking the Fuel System

Fuels have a relatively short shelf life. Even if stored under ideal conditions, fuel starts to deteriorate within a few months.

Marine engines may sit idle for several weeks at a time making them far more susceptible to fuel problems. Starting difficulty, performance problems and potential engine damage can result from using stale fuel.

As fuel evaporates, a gummy deposit may form in the carburetor or other fuel system components. These deposits clog fuel filters, fuel lines, fuel pumps and small passages within the carburetor.

Fuel stored in a vented tank tends to absorb water vapor over time. The water separates from the fuel, and then settles to the bottom of the tank leading to the formation of rust or deposits in the fuel tank. Rust, water or deposits eventually contaminate the fuel system. Inspect the fuel in the fuel tank if the engine refuses to start and the ignition system is not at fault. An unpleasant or unusual odor indicates the fuel has exceeded its shelf life and must be re-

placed. Refer to *Inspecting the Fuel* for additional information.

WARNING
Use extreme caution when working with the fuel system. Fuel is extremely flammable and if ignited can result in serious injury or death. Never smoke or allow sparks around fuel or fuel vapors. Wipe up any spilled fuel with a shop towel, then dispose of the shop towel in a responsible manner. Check all fuel hoses, connections and fittings for leaks after any fuel system repair. Correct all fuel system leaks before returning the engine to service.

NOTE
Contact a local waste pickup service, automotive repair facility or marine dealership to properly dispose the fuel. If fuel is not too badly contaminated by water or too stale, it may be mixed with fresh fuel and used to power lawn mowers, power yard equipment or even an automobile (when diluted sufficiently to prevent misfiring or unstable idle).

Inspecting the Fuel

Most carbureted models covered by this manual are equipped with a float bowl drain screw (**Figure 10**, typical) and a drain nipple on the bottom of the float bowl to which a small plastic hose can be attached to facility draining.

On models equipped with electronic fuel injection, a dedicated fuel system drain is provided in the vapor separator tank. But, access to the fuel drain may require removal of the intake manifold and other components. In many cases, it is easier to drain a sample of fuel from the hoses connected to the low pressure fuel filter (**Figure 11**). Removal and installation instructions for the low pressure fuel filter used on fuel injected engines are provided in Chapter Six.

In either case, inspect the fuel as follows:

WARNING
Step one ensures that fuel is not sprayed from an open hose or fitting because of an accidental cranking of the engine or activation of the fuel pump during repair.

1. Disconnect and secure the negative battery cable so it does not contact the battery terminal.

2A. On carbureted models, perform the following:

a. Locate the float bowl drain screw (**Figure 10**, typical) on the bottom of the float bowl cover.

b. If present, attach a small plastic drain hose to the float bowl drain nipple (direct the other end of the fuel into a container suitable for holding fuel), otherwise position a small drain pan or a shop rag to catch fuel escaping from the bore.

c. Carefully open the bowl drain screw or remove the screw, as applicable. If necessary, squeeze the primer bulb (**Figure 12**) a few times to refill the bowl. Continue until an adequate fuel sample is obtained.

d. Securely close the bowl drain screw. If used, drain any residual fuel from the drain hose then pull the hose from the drain fitting.

2B. On fuel injected models perform the following:

a. Disconnect the hoses from the fuel filter as described in Chapter Six.

b. Place a suitable container under the disconnected hoses.

c. Slowly squeeze the primer bulb (**Figure 12**) while capturing the fuel flowing from the hoses. Continue until an adequate fuel sample is obtained.

d. Reconnect the hoses as described in Chapter Six.

3. An inability to obtain a fuel sample indicates a faulty fuel tank, primer bulb, fuel hose, fuel pump, fitting or inlet needle on carbureted models. Inspect these components following the instructions provided in Chapter Five or Chapter Six (as applicable).

4. Clean up any spilled fuel at once. Dispose of fuel-contaminated shop towels in a responsible manner.

5. Carefully pour the fuel sample into a suitable see-through container.

6. Visually inspect and carefully smell the fuel. An unusual odor, debris, cloudy appearance or the presence of water is an indication of a problem with the fuel. If any of these conditions are noted perform the following:

a. Drain the fuel system and dispose of the fuel in a responsible manner.

b. Clean and inspect the entire fuel system if water is found. Refer to Chapter Five or Chapter Six for fuel system repair instructions, as applicable.

c. Thoroughly clean or replace all fuel filters.

7. Clean up spilled fuel. Gently squeeze the primer bulb while checking for signs of fuel leakage. Correct the cause of fuel leakage at once.

8. Reconnect the negative battery cable.

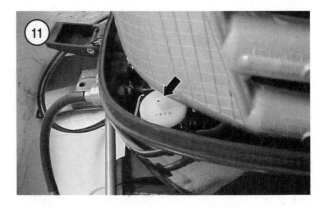

FUEL SYSTEM

WARNING
Use extreme caution when working on the fuel system. Fuel presents a serious fire risk. Never smoke or allow sparks to occur around fuel or fuel vapors. Wipe up spilled fuel with a shop towel and dispose of the towel in a responsible manner. Check all fuel hoses, connections and fittings for leaks after any fuel system repair. Correct any fuel system leakage before returning the engine to service.

This section provides instructions for inspecting and testing the following:

1. Fuel tank, hoses and fittings.

2. Primer bulb.

3. Low pressure fuel filter.

4. Fuel pump.

5. Carburetor and choke valve (5-15 hp models).

Refer to *Electronic Fuel Injection* (EFI) in this chapter to test specific EFI components.

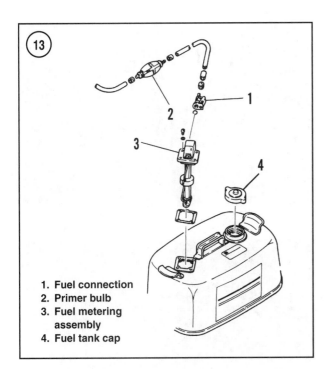

1. Fuel connection
2. Primer bulb
3. Fuel metering assembly
4. Fuel tank cap

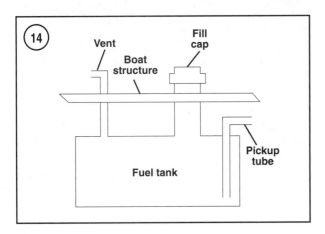

Fuel Tank, Hoses and Fittings

A fault with the fuel tank, hoses or fittings can cause stalling, rough idle or poor performance at higher engine speeds.

Many fuel tank related problems are the result of inadequate fuel tank venting. Inadequate fuel tank venting causes a vacuum to form within the tank as fuel is drawn from it. Rough engine operation, poor performance or stalling occurs when the engine mounted fuel pump is unable to overcome the vacuum. Temporarily remove the fuel tank cap when suspecting inadequate venting. A closed or faulty vent is likely when the engine performs correctly with the cap removed. On portable fuel tanks a screw type vent is normally integrated into the fuel tank. This feature allows closing of the vent when transporting the fuel tank. Always open the vent screw before starting the engine. A hull mounted vent fitting and hose is used with built-in fuel tanks. Inspect this fitting for debris blockage.

Loose clamps, worn quick connectors or leaking hoses allow air to enter the fuel system. Air intrusion may result in inadequate fuel flow at higher engine speeds. Higher engine speeds require a greater amount of fuel. The air displaces the fuel required for the engine. Typical symptoms include poor performance, rough running conditions or misfiring at higher engine speeds. Under normal circumstances small amounts of vapor or air are purged from the fuel system. Air entering the system combined with slower fuel pump speed at idle prevents the air from being adequately purged. Typically, the engine stalls after running at idle speed for a few minutes.

Collapsed hoses, faulty connectors or blocked passages restrict fuel flow to the engine. Typically, fuel restriction problems surface only at higher engine speeds. The restriction usually allows adequate fuel flow at lower engine speeds. Often times the primer bulb collapses at higher engine speeds. This condition indicates the restriction is located between the primer bulb and the fuel tank pickup. Be aware that improper primer bulb installation or a faulty check valve can cause a collapsed primer bulb. Fuel restrictions typically cause a rough running condition, poor performance or misfiring at higher engine speeds.

Small outboards are usually equipped with a portable fuel tank (**Figure 13**). They are easily removed for filling, cleaning and inspection. Larger boats with larger outboards are equipped with built-in fuel tanks (**Figure 14**). Access panels in the boat usually allow access to the serviceable electric sending unit and fuel pickup tube. Removal of built-in fuel tanks can be quite difficult. In many cases the boat structure must be disassembled to access the tank. Remove the tank for cleaning and inspection when leakage, rust or excessive amounts of contaminants are found in the fuel sample. Built-in fuel tanks are usually equipped with an antisiphon valve. This valve is mounted to the pickup tube fitting. It prevents fuel from flowing from the tank should a leak occur in the fuel supply hose. Be aware that a blocked or faulty antisiphon valve can cause a fuel restriction. Always replace the valve if it is blocked or corroded.

WARNING
Automotive type replacement fuel hoses may not meet outboard requirements. Fuel leakage may occur and result in a fire or explo-

sion. Always use marine specific hoses sold by the tank or engine manufacturer.

NOTE
Always check to ensure the fuel tank vent is open before testing the fuel tank. The vent is integrated into the fill cap on most portable fuel tanks. A boat mounted fuel tank uses a boat mounted vent hose and hull fitting.

Checking for air or fuel leakage

Leakage can occur at any point along the fuel supply hose (**Figure 15**). Disconnect the quick connector from the engine. Gently squeeze the primer bulb while inspecting the section from the primer bulb to the check valve portion of the quick connector (**Figure 16**). Tighten or replace hose clamps when leakage is detected at hose connection points. Replace the hose, primer bulb and quick connectors if they are leaking.

Carefully connect the fuel supply hose to the engine. Again gently squeeze the primer bulb while inspecting the quick connectors. Replace both the fuel hose and engine mounted quick connectors if there is fuel leakage. The condition causing the leakage usually affects both connectors.

Inspect the section of hose from the primer bulb to the fuel tank connection. Tighten or replace hose clamps when there is leakage at hose connection points. Pump the primer bulb until it firms up. A spongy feel or inability to firm up the bulb indicates possible air leakage. The leakage point is at the fuel tank connection, fuel hoses or fuel tank pickup. First test the primer bulb as described in this chapter. A faulty connection, fuel hose or fuel tank pickup is indicated if the primer bulb tests correctly.

Disassemble and inspect these components as described in Chapter Five or Chapter Six, as applicable.

Checking for a fuel restriction

NOTE
Run the engine at full throttle for several minutes to verify a faulty fuel tank or fuel supply hose. Do this procedure in a test tank or on the boat (in the water).

The most effective method for checking the fuel supply is to temporarily run the engine on a known good portable fuel tank and fuel supply hose. Make sure the inside diameter of the fuel hose and fuel fittings is 5/16 in. (8 mm) or larger. Using hoses or fittings that are too small can cause a fuel restriction at higher engine speeds. Fill the portable tank with fresh fuel then connect the fuel hose to the en-

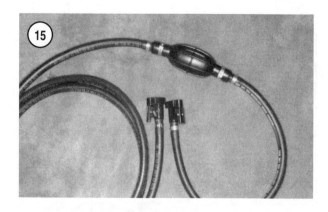

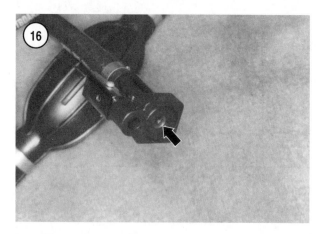

gine. Run the engine under actual operating conditions. A faulty fuel supply hose or fuel tank is indicated when the engine performs properly with the known good fuel tank. On applications with a built-in fuel tank, inspect the antisiphon valve for defects before condemning other fuel system components.

CAUTION
Avoid using excessive force when pumping the primer bulb. The pressure in the line may exceed the normal fuel system pressures and lead to fuel leakage or a flooding condition within the fuel system.

If the engine malfunctions, pump the primer bulb while an assistant operates the boat. There is a faulty engine mounted fuel pump or partially blocked fuel filter when the engine performs properly only when the primer bulb is pumped. Inspect the fuel pump and filter as described in Chapter Five or Chapter Six, as applicable. A flooding carburetor or faulty vapor separator tank on EFI models is indicated when the problem worsens when the primer bulb is pumped. Check these components as described in this chapter.

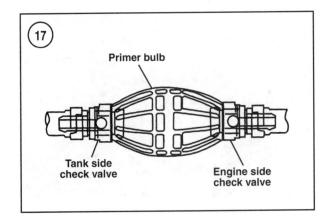

17

Primer bulb

Tank side
check valve

Engine side
check valve

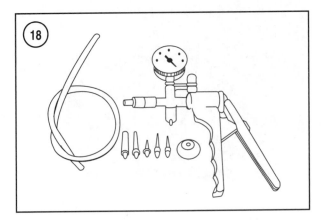

18

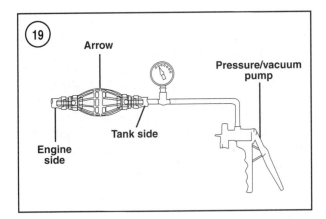

19

Arrow

Pressure/vacuum
pump

Tank side

Engine
side

Primer Bulb

The primer bulb (**Figure 17**) is essentially a hand operated fuel pump integrated into the fuel supply hose. It fills the fuel hoses and carburetor fuel bowl or vapor separator tank on EFI models with fuel before starting the engine.

This pump is necessary in most applications, as fuel tends to evaporate from the fuel system during periods of

non-use. Considerable cranking would be required before the engine-mounted pump could provide enough fuel for starting. A faulty primer bulb can prevent priming of the fuel system or cause a fuel restriction.

Pump the primer bulb only if the engine has been off for several hours. Never use excessive force when pumping the primer bulb. Excessive force can cause the fuel system to flood. Gently squeeze the primer bulb until it becomes firm. A firm primer bulb indicates that the carburetor fuel bowl or vapor separator tank on EFI models is full.

Additives in the fuel can cause deterioration of some rubber and composite fuel system components including the primer bulb. This deterioration occurs on the inner surfaces of the primer bulb. Squeeze the primer bulb until fully compressed then quickly release it. Replace the primer bulb if it sticks together on the internal surfaces or remains collapsed. Thoroughly inspect the fuel hoses and other fuel system components when this condition happens. They also may have deteriorated surfaces.

The primer bulb system (**Figure 17**) consists of the bulb, tank side check valve and engine side check valve. Testing for leakage and correct check valve operation requires a pressure/vacuum pump (**Figure 18**). These are available from most automotive parts stores and tool suppliers. Pressure test the primer bulb as follows:

1. Disconnect the fuel supply hose from the engine and fuel tank connection. Place the primer bulb over a container suitable for holding fuel. Remove and discard the hose clamps at both fuel hose connections to the primer bulb. Carefully pull both fuel lines from the primer bulb. Drain all fuel from the disconnected hoses.

2. The arrow marking on the primer bulb body points to the engine side check valve. Direct the engine side check valve into a suitable container then carefully squeeze the primer bulb until all fuel is removed.

3. Connect the *pressure* fitting of a hand operated pressure/vacuum pump to the check valve fitting on the tank side (**Figure 19**). Clamp the pump hose securely to the fitting. Gently operate the pump. Air must exit the engine side check valve fitting when the pump is operated. Replace the primer bulb if there are incorrect test results.

4. Connect the *pressure* fitting of a hand operated pressure/vacuum pump to the check valve fitting on the engine side (**Figure 20**). Clamp the pump hose securely to the check hose fitting. Gently operate the pump. Air must not exit the tank side check valve fitting when the pump is operated. Replace the primer bulb if there are incorrect test results.

5. Connect the pressure/vacuum pump to the primer bulb as described in Step 4. Submerge the primer bulb in a container of water. Gently operate the pump to pressurize the line from the engine to the primer bulb (and the chambers

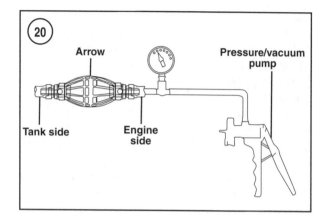

within the bulb itself). Replace the primer bulb if it is leaking. Thoroughly dry the primer bulb.

6. Noting the *arrow* on the primer bulb for correct orientation, install the fuel hoses onto the valve fittings. The arrow must point to the hose leading to the engine. Install new hose clamps onto both fuel hose connections. Make sure the clamps fit securely. Pump the primer bulb while checking for correct operation and fuel leakage. Correct any fuel leakage before operating the engine.

Low-Pressure Fuel Filter

A blocked low-pressure fuel filter causes hard starting, stalling, misfiring or poor performance. Typically the engine malfunction worsens with increased engine speed. This filter prevents contaminants from reaching the low-pressure fuel pump.

Carbureted models may be equipped with an inline filter or, on 9.9/15 hp motors a filter element located under the fuel pump cover. Still other carbureted models may not have a filter at all.

Fuel injected models are equipped with a canister fuel filter (**Figure 21**). For 40 and 50 hp models the filter is mounted on the rear starboard side of the power head. On 70 hp models the filter is mounted on the front port side of the power head.

With the exception of the filter mounted under the pump cover on the 9.9/15 hp motors, these fuel filters allow visual inspection for contamination and are nonserviceable. Replace the inline filter when an inspection reveals dark staining or visible contaminants (refer to Chapter Five or Chapter Six, as applicable). If a clogged element is suspected on 9.9/15 hp motors, refer to Chapter Five for instructions on removal, inspection and cleaning.

Fuel Pump

A camshaft driven mechanical fuel pump delivers fuel from the fuel tank to the carburetor or vapor separator tank on EFI engines. For 5/6 hp (128 cc) and 8/9.9 hp (211 cc) engines the pump is mounted to the valve cover on the rear center of the engine (**Figure 22**). For 9.9/15 hp (305 cc) motors, the pump (**Figure 23**) is mounted on the aft, port side of the motor, slightly aft and between the spark plugs. On all EFI motors, the mechanical fuel pump (**Figure 24**) is mounted on the cylinder head cover, found at the rear of the power head.

The most common fuel pump problem is inadequate fuel pressure/delivery. However, the pump may leak (internally or externally) or provide, in rare cases, excessive fuel pressure.

Inadequate fuel delivery may cause rough operation, misfiring or stalling at idle speed. However, in most cases inadequate fuel delivery surfaces only at higher engine speeds because the fuel pump is able to supply the fuel needed at lower engine speeds. Typical fuel pump testing requires a gauge installed to the outlet side of the fuel pump. Fuel pump pressure testing is time consuming and can be potentially dangerous if fuel leakage is present. A practical method is to use the hand operated primer bulb

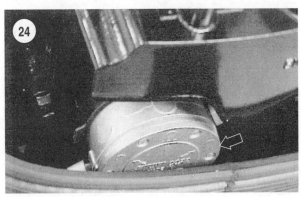

as an auxiliary fuel pump. If a fault occurs, vigorously pump the primer bulb, while an assistant operates the boat. Stop pumping the bulb and note if the fault again surfaces. A faulty fuel pump is likely if the engine performs correctly only when the primer bulb is pumped.

External fuel leakage results from loose fuel pump screws or leaking gaskets. Internal fuel leakage allows fuel into the rocker arm or camshaft cover. The fuel dilutes the engine oil. Operating the engine with diluted oil will cause increased wear and power head failure if not corrected. For this reason it is imperative to always check the oil level and condition as described in Chapter Three before operating the outboard. Internal leakage causes a strong fuel smell in the oil and a rising oil level. Correct this condition immediately.

Excessive fuel pump pressure causes a flooding condition within the carburetor(s), or vapor separator tank on EFI models. High fuel pump pressure is usually caused by a mechanically damaged fuel pump. Suspect a fault with the fuel pump when flooding carburetor symptoms exist only when the engine is running and the static check, see *Flooding Carburetor* in this chapter, reveals no faults. Repair the fuel pump as described in Chapter Five or Chapter Six if inadequate fuel delivery, fuel leakage or high fuel pump pressure is indicated.

CAUTION
Never run an outboard without first providing cooling water. Use either a test tank or flush/test device. Always remove the propeller before running the engine on a flush/test device. Install a test propeller to run the engine in a test tank.

NOTE
*Always inspect all fuel filters **before** testing the fuel pump.*

Carburetor

This section provides typical carburetor (**Figure 25**) related symptoms and possible causes. All 5-15 hp models are equipped with a single carburetor. The 40-70 hp models are EFI equipped.

Rough idle or stalling at idle

1. Choke valve or fuel primer solenoid malfunction.
2. Flooding carburetor.
3. Improper carburetor adjustments.
4. Plugged carburetor passages.
5. Air leakage at the carburetor mount.

Shaking at various engine speeds

1. Improper carburetor adjustments.
2. Choke valve malfunction.
3. Plugged carburetor passages.
4. Improper float level adjustment.
5. Air leakage at the carburetor mount.

Bogging or sagging on acceleration

1. Improper carburetor adjustments.
2. Faulty accelerator pump.
3. Plugged carburetor passages.
4. Improper float level adjustment.
5. Flooding carburetor.
6. Incorrect propeller.

Spark plug fouling

1. Choke valve or fuel primer solenoid malfunction.
2. Improper carburetor adjustments.
3. Flooding carburetor.
4. Improper float level adjustment.
5. Plugged carburetor passages.

Poor performance at higher engine speed

1. Plugged carburetor passages.
2. Choke valve or fuel primer solenoid malfunction.
3. Improper float level adjustment.
4. Improper carburetor adjustments.
5. Air leakage at the carburetor mount.

Flooding carburetor

A flooding condition allows excessive amount of fuel into the engine. This condition may cause rough idling, stalling, excessive exhaust smoke and spark plug fouling.

Flooding may be caused by debris in the inlet needle and seat, a worn inlet needle and seat, or a misadjusted or damaged float.

It is not necessary to run the engine to verify a flooding condition. A visual inspection of the carburetor opening indicates a flooding condition. Position the engine in the vertical or normal running position before checking for a flooding condition. Inaccurate test results are likely if the engine is tilted during testing.

1. Disconnect the negative battery cable, then disconnect and ground the spark plug leads for safety.

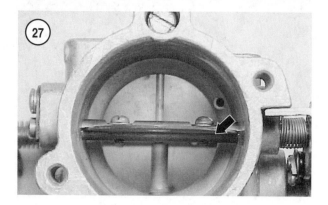

2. Remove the air intake silencer (**Figure 26**, 9.9/15 hp model shown, others similar) for access to the carburetor throttle bore.

3. Open the choke valve fully (**Figure 27**) using the choke valve knob and cable.

4. Look into the front of the carburetor (**Figure 28**) while gently pumping the primer bulb. Fuel flowing from the opening or into the throat indicates a flooding condition. Repair the carburetor as described in Chapter Five if there is flooding.

5. Install the air intake silencer, spark plug leads and the negative battery cable.

Choke valve malfunction

Carbureted models are either equipped with a manual choke or fuel primer solenoid to ease in cold start situations. Typically, the manual choke is found on tiller control models, while the primer solenoid is found on remote models. On models equipped with a manually operated choke plate (**Figure 27**), the system operates by mechanically restricting air flow (thereby enriching air/fuel mixture) during cold starts. The valve is closed (**Figure 29**) mechanically when the choke knob is pulled outward thereby actuating the choke cable and linkage. Incorrect

choke valve operation can cause hard starting, rough engine operation, stalling or spark plug fouling.

Operate the choke valve only if starting a cold engine. Operating the choke on a warm engine causes hard starting, rough engine operation, excessive exhaust smoke and spark plug fouling. As a general rule, refrain from operating the choke unless the engine has been off for two hours or more.

Testing requires visual inspection of the choke valve plate while actuating the choke knob. On most models, the air intake silencer must be removed in order to obtain a clear, unobstructed view of the choke valve plate.

1. Disconnect the negative battery cable, then remove the spark plug leads and connect the leads to an engine ground, for safety.

2. Remove the air intake silencer (**Figure 26**, 9.9/15 hp motor shown, others similar) for access to the carburetor throttle bore.

3. Pull the choke knob outward and observe if the choke valve closes fully (**Figure 29**). If it does not close fully, check for a threaded adjustment on the knob end of the cable that will correct this condition. Also, visually check for bent or damaged linkage. If necessary, disconnect the cable from the carburetor linkage and manually operate the

the choke linkage to make sure the valve is not binding. A choke that does not close properly can cause hard starting and stalling during cold engine operation. Repair or replace choke valve components as necessary.

4. Push the choke knob back in toward the engine case and observe if the valve opens fully (**Figure 27**). If it does not open fully, check for a threaded adjustment on the knob end of the cable that will correct this condition. Also, visually check for bent or damaged linkage. If necessary, disconnect the cable from the carburetor linkage and manually operate the choke linkage to make sure the valve is not binding. A choke that does not open properly can cause spark plug fouling, rough engine operation, racing idle speeds and stalling once the engine warms up. Repair or replace choke valve components as necessary.

5. Install the air intake silencer, spark plug leads and the negative battery cable.

Improper carburetor adjustments

Improper carburetor adjustment can cause hard starting, rough idling, stalling or hesitation on acceleration. Each model is equipped with an idle speed adjustment screw and a low speed idle (pilot screw). The pilot screw adjustment affects the fuel mixture at lower engine speeds. If a poor running condition occurs at medium-to-high speeds the pilot screw adjustment is not the cause.

Carburetor overhaul and initial set-up is covered in Chapter Five, while the idle speed and mixture adjustments are in Chapter Four.

Improper float level adjustment

The carburetor fuel level has a significant effect on engine performance. A higher than specified fuel level will result in a rich mixture, while a lower one results in a lean mixture. These conditions could cause hard starting, rough idling, poor performance, or excessive exhaust smoke. If the setting is considerably off, the carburetor could flood or run out of fuel.

The float level adjustment controls the fuel level. Check and adjust the float level as described in Chapter Five.

Plugged carburetor passages

Plugged carburetor passages and jets cause hard starting or operational problems at any engine speed. Problems caused by plugged passages and jets usually surface after the engine has been stored for several months or longer. Contamination often forms in the fuel bowl as the fuel evaporates. When fresh fuel enters the bowl, contamination plugs the carburetor passages.

Plugged jets or passages can cause hard starting, stalling or rough operation at various engine speeds. Typically the engine starts then dies as the choke is opened. This condition occurs because the choke valve is compensating for the lean mixture.

Eliminate all other potential problems (*Preliminary Inspection* in this chapter) before assuming the carburetor is at fault. If fuel contamination is found, repair the carburetor as described in Chapter Five and inspect the entire fuel system for similar contamination to prevent future carburetor problems.

Faulty accelerator pump

The carburetors on 5/6 hp models as well as 1998 and later 15 hp models are equipped with an accelerator pump to provide additional fuel to the engine during rapid acceleration. The additional fuel is necessary to prevent a lean condition until high speed fuel delivery occurs. A fault with the accelerator pump causes a popping noise, bogging or stalling upon rapid acceleration. Typically, the engine performs correctly if the throttle is advanced slowly. Slow throttle advancement allows gradual high speed fuel delivery. The accelerator pump is integrated into the carburetor. Repair the carburetor as described in Chapter Five if these symptoms are noted on 5/6 hp, as well as 1998 and later 15 hp models.

Air leaks at the carburetor mount

Air leakage at the carburetor to the intake manifold mounting surfaces (**Figure 30**, typical) causes a lean air/fuel mixture. Common air leak symptoms include:

1. A hissing or squealing noise from the engine.
2. Rough idle.
3. Hesitation on acceleration.
4. Poor high speed performance.
5. Spark plug overheating (Chapter Three).

One common method for locating a leakage point involves using a typical spray lubricant such as WD-40. Run the engine, using a flush test adapter or in a test tank. Run the engine at idle speed then spray the lubricant onto the perimeter of the carburetor-to-intake mating surface (**Figure 30**). Engine vacuum will draw the lubricant into the engine at the point of leakage. An increase in idle speed or any change in the idle characteristic when the lubricant is sprayed indicates a leak is present. Direct the spray type lubricant to specific areas to pinpoint the leakage. Remove the carburetor as directed in Chapter Five

then inspect the suspected surfaces for damage. Always replace any gaskets when the carburetor is removed.

> *CAUTION*
> *Continued lean operating conditions can lead to power head damage.*

Fuel Primer Solenoid

Some 8/9.9 and 9.9/15 hp using an electric fuel primer solenoid (**Figure 31**) in place of a traditional choke valve to enrich the air/fuel mixture and help with cold engine

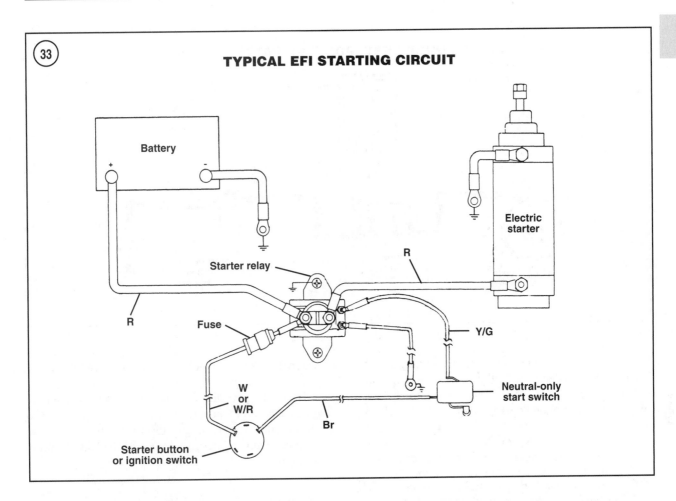

TYPICAL EFI STARTING CIRCUIT

③

Battery

Starter relay

Fuse

R

W or W/R

Starter button or ignition switch

Br

Electric starter

R

Y/G

Neutral-only start switch

starts. This feature is usually found on remote electric start models. Instead of restricting the air flow to increase the ratio of fuel in the air/fuel mixture, the solenoid injects pressurized fuel directly into the carburetor (on the vacuum or intake manifold side of the throttle plate) or to the intake manifold.

The fuel primer solenoid is an electric valve. As such, it does not pump fuel itself, but opens or closes a passage that allows a pressurized fuel supply to flow. A fuel line from the pump supplies pressurized fuel to the valve. When power is applied to the circuit, the solenoid energizes, opening the valve. An internal spring forces the valve closed when the circuit is deactivated.

The primer is also equipped with a manual valve lever that is used to prime the engine in the event of circuit failure. If the circuit is not working, rotate the valve lever by hand to the open position (which allows fuel to flow continuously from the valve to the engine until the valve is closed again) and crank the engine. Do not leave the valve open for extended periods or the engine may experience flooding or extreme rich operation. Return the valve to the

closed position after the engine has cranked a few times or immediately upon start up.

A schrader valve is located under a removable cap on one end of the manual valve. The valve is provided as a convenient way to inject fogging oil or OMC Engine Tuner to the engine during storage or tune-up services, respectively.

Fuel Primer Solenoid Removal and Installation or *Function Testing* procedures are in Chapter Five.

ELECTRIC STARTING SYSTEM

This section provides test instructions for the electric starting system and related components.

The carbureted models are all equipped with a rewind type manual starter (A, **Figure 32**). The 9.9 hp (both 211 and 305 cc) models as well as 15 hp models may also be equipped with an optional electric starting system (B, **Figure 32**). All EFI models are equipped with electric starting (**Figure 33**, typical EFI shown, carbureted similiar).

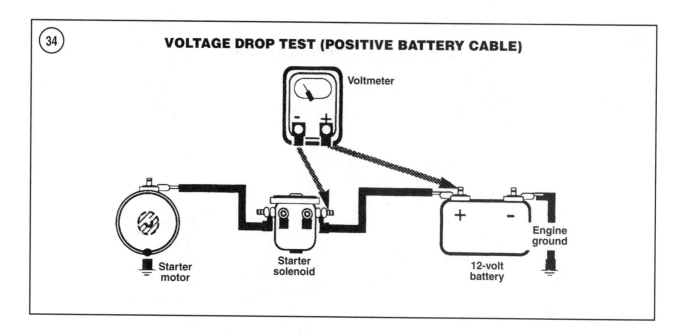

34 **VOLTAGE DROP TEST (POSITIVE BATTERY CABLE)**

Voltmeter

Starter motor

Starter solenoid

12-volt battery

Engine ground

The major components of the electric starting system (**Figure 33**) include the battery, starter button or ignition switch, starter motor, starter relay, neutral-only start switch (on remote models) and wiring.

> *WARNING*
> *Use extreme caution when working around batteries. Never smoke or allow sparks to occur around batteries. Batteries produce explosive hydrogen gas that can explode resulting in injury or death. Never make the final connection of a circuit to the battery terminal as an arc may occur and lead to fire or explosion.*

On electric start models, battery power is supplied to the starter motor through remote mounted relay or solenoid. An engine mounted start switch (tiller models) or a boat mounted remote key switch (remote models) activates the relay/solenoid when the circuit is closed allowing fused battery power to the actuator switch side of the relay. On remote models, a neutral safety switch is also incorporated into the key side of the starter circuit. For safety, the switch remains open (preventing the key switch from activating the relay) unless the gearcase is placed in neutral before starting the engine.

The starter motor (B, **Figure 32**) is capable of producing a large amount of torque for a short period of time. Generating the torque necessary to start the engine consumes a large amount of current and in doing so produces a fair amount of heat. Prolonged operation is the most common cause of starter failure. Never operate the elec-

tric starter for more than 20 seconds without allowing it to cool for at least two minutes.

The starting system requires a fully charged battery to provide the large amount of electrical current necessary to operate the starter motor. Electric start models are equipped with an alternator to charge the battery during operation.

Troubleshooting Preparation

If the following procedures do not locate the problem, refer to **Table 1** for additional information. Before troubleshooting the starting circuit, make sure of the following:

1. The battery is fully charged.
2. The shift control lever is in the NEUTRAL position.
3. All electrical connections are clean and tight. The battery cable connections must be secured with hex nuts and corrosion resistant lock washers. Do not use wing nuts to secure the battery cables to the battery.
4. The wiring harness is in good condition, with no worn or frayed insulation.
5. The fuse protecting the starter switch is not blown.
6. The power head and gearcase are not the problem (mechanical failure).

> *CAUTION*
> *Unless otherwise noted, perform all voltmeter or test lamp tests with the leads connected and the connection or terminals exposed to accommodate test lead connection.*

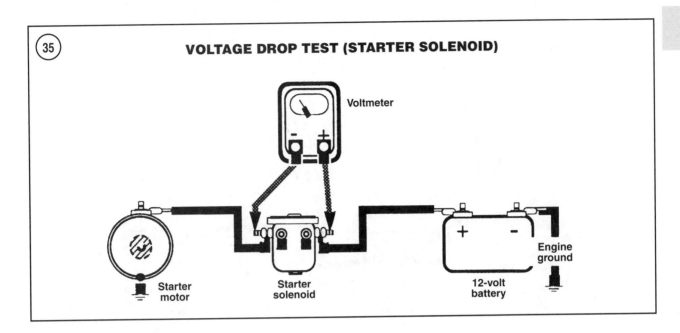

VOLTAGE DROP TEST (STARTER SOLENOID)

Voltmeter

Starter motor

Starter solenoid

12-volt battery

Engine ground

2

Testing the Electric Starting System (Carbureted Models)

Starter motor turns slowly

1. Make sure the battery is in acceptable condition and fully charged.

2. Inspect all electrical connections for looseness or corrosion. Clean and tighten as necessary.

3. Check for the proper size and length of battery cables, especially if they were just replaced or, if they have been in service for a long time (as resistance will build over time as the cables fray under the insulation). Refer to **Table 2** for recommended minimum cable gauge sizes and lengths. Replace cables that are undersized or relocate the battery to shorten the distance between the battery and starter solenoid.

4. Disconnect and ground the spark plug leads to the engine to prevent accidental starting. Turn the flywheel clockwise by hand and check for mechanical binding. If mechanical binding is evident, remove the lower gearcase to determine if the binding is in the power head or the lower gearcase. If no binding is evident, continue to Step 5.

5. Perform the starting system voltage drop test as described in this chapter.

6. Check the starter motor no-load current draw and no-load speed as described in this chapter.

7. Reconnect the spark plug leads when finished with the troubleshooting procedure.

Starting system voltage drop test

As described under *Voltage Drop Test*, in the *Electrical System Fundamentals* of Chapter One, resistance causes voltage to drop. Excessive resistance in the battery cables, starter solenoid and starter cable can restrict the voltage to the starter, causing the starter motor to turn slowly. Slow cranking speeds cause low ignition system output and subsequent hard starting.

Use the following procedure to determine if any of the cables or the starter solenoid is the source of an excessive voltage drop. If the problem is intermittent, try gently pulling, bending and flexing the cables and connections during the test. Sudden voltmeter fluctuations indicate a poor connection.

Remember that a voltage drop test is measuring the difference in voltage from the beginning of a circuit or component to the end of the circuit or component. If there is resistance in the circuit, the voltage at the end of the circuit will be less than the voltage at the beginning. The circuit must be active to take a voltage drop reading (in this case the starter must be engaged). A voltmeter reading of 0 (zero) means that no resistance is present in the test circuit. A reading of battery voltage means that the circuit is completely open (battery voltage going in and nothing coming out).

Refer to **Figures 34-37** for this procedure. Clean, tighten, repair or replace any cable or solenoid with excessive voltage drop.

1. Disconnect and ground the spark plug leads to the engine to prevent accidental starting.

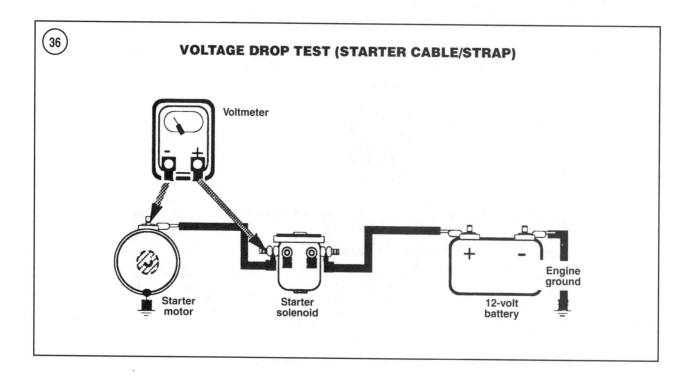

2. Connect the positive (red) voltmeter lead to the positive battery terminal and the negative voltmeter lead to the positive solenoid terminal as shown in **Figure 34**.

3. Engage the electric starter and observe the meter. If the meter indicates more than 0.3 volt, the positive battery cable has excessive resistance. Clean the connections, repair the terminal ends or replace the positive battery cable.

CAUTION
If using an older analog voltmeter, do not connect the positive voltmeter lead in Step 4 until after the engine begins cranking. The open solenoid will read battery voltage and could damage the voltmeter if set to a very low volt scale. In addition, disconnect the voltmeter before cranking stops.

4. Connect the negative voltmeter lead to the starter side of the solenoid as shown in **Figure 35**. Engage the electric starter. While the engine is cranking, touch the positive voltmeter lead to the battery cable positive solenoid terminal as shown in **Figure 35**. Note the meter reading, then remove the positive voltmeter lead and discontinue cranking. If the meter indicates more than 0.2 volt, the starter solenoid has excessive internal resistance and must be replaced.

5. Connect the positive voltmeter lead to the starter side of the solenoid and the negative voltmeter lead to the starter motor terminal as shown in **Figure 36**. Engage the electric starter and observe the meter. If the meter indi-

cates more than 0.2 volt, there is excessive resistance in the starter motor cable (or strap). Clean the connections, repair the terminal ends or replace the starter motor cable (or strap).

6. Connect the positive voltmeter lead to the engine end of the negative battery cable and the negative voltmeter lead to the negative battery terminal as shown in **Figure 37**. Engage the electric starter and observe the meter. If the meter indicates more than 0.3 volt, there is excessive resistance in the battery negative cable. Clean the connections, repair the terminal ends or replace the negative battery cable.

7. Reconnect the spark plug leads when finished.

Starter motor does not turn (tiller control models)

A test lamp or voltmeter are both acceptable tools for troubleshooting the starter circuit, but a voltmeter is more accurate and easier to use. If using a voltmeter, all test readings must be within 1 volt of battery voltage. A reading of 1 volt or more below battery voltage indicates excessive resistance with the circuit being tested. If using a test lamp, first connect the test lamp directly to the battery and observe the brightness of the bulb. It is necessary to reference the rest of your readings against this test (by remembering how brightly the bulb was illuminated or by repeating this check for comparison to the current test). If the bulb does not glow as brightly as when it was connected directly to the battery, there is excessive resistance.

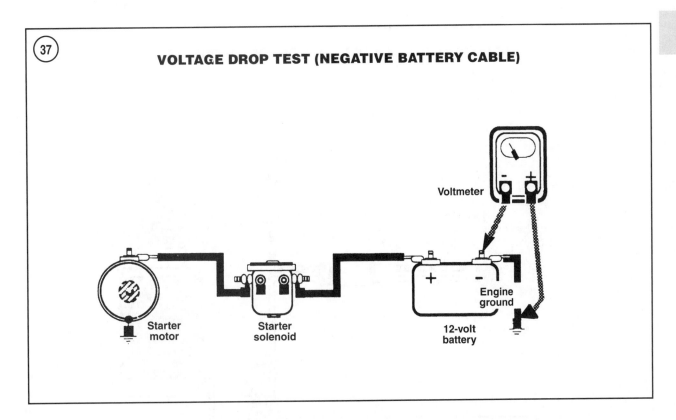

VOLTAGE DROP TEST (NEGATIVE BATTERY CABLE)

Voltmeter

Starter motor

Starter solenoid

12-volt battery

Engine ground

Refer to **Figure 38** for this procedure. Refer to the back of the manual for specific model wiring diagrams.

CAUTION
Disconnect and ground the spark plug leads to the engine to prevent accidental starting during all test procedures. Make sure the shift lever is in the NEUTRAL position.

1. Connect the test lamp or voltmeter lead to the positive terminal of the battery and touch the test lamp probe to metal anywhere on the engine block. The test lamp must light. If the lamp does not light or is dim, the battery ground cable connections are loose or corroded, or there is an open circuit in the battery ground cable. Clean and tighten the connections or replace the battery cable as required. If using a test lamp, note the brightness of the lamp at this point. If using a voltmeter, note battery voltage (remember that the battery should be in good condition and fully charged when testing).

2. Connect the test lamp lead or voltmeter negative lead to a good engine ground and connect the test lamp probe or voltmeter positive lead to the starter power input terminal (1, **Figure 38**). Press the start button and observe the lamp or voltmeter. The test lamp must light or the voltmeter must show battery voltage. If the lamp does not light or is very dim, the battery cable connections are loose or cor-

roded, or there is an open circuit in the cable between the battery and the solenoid. Clean and tighten the connections or replace the battery cable as required or continue testing the circuit with Step 3. If the lamp is bright or the voltmeter shows battery voltage, repair or replace the starter as described in Chapter Seven.

3. Connect the test lamp or voltmeter between a good engine ground and the battery input terminal of the starter solenoid (2, **Figure 38**). There should be battery voltage present at all times, if not, check the battery and cables. If sufficient voltage is present, proceed with Step 4.

4. Connect the test lamp or voltmeter between the start button input terminal on the solenoid (3, **Figure 38**) and a good engine ground. Press the start button and observe the test lamp or voltmeter. There should be battery voltage present with the start button depressed. If not, check the fuse, start button and wiring. If sufficient voltage was present, proceed with Step 5.

5. Connect the test lamp or voltmeter between the starter power output terminal of the solenoid (4, **Figure 38**) and a good engine ground. Press the start button and observe the test lamp or voltmeter. There should be battery voltage present. If not, check the solenoid. If sufficient voltage was present, but the starter still does not receive sufficient voltage at the input terminal, replace the solenoid-to-starter cable.

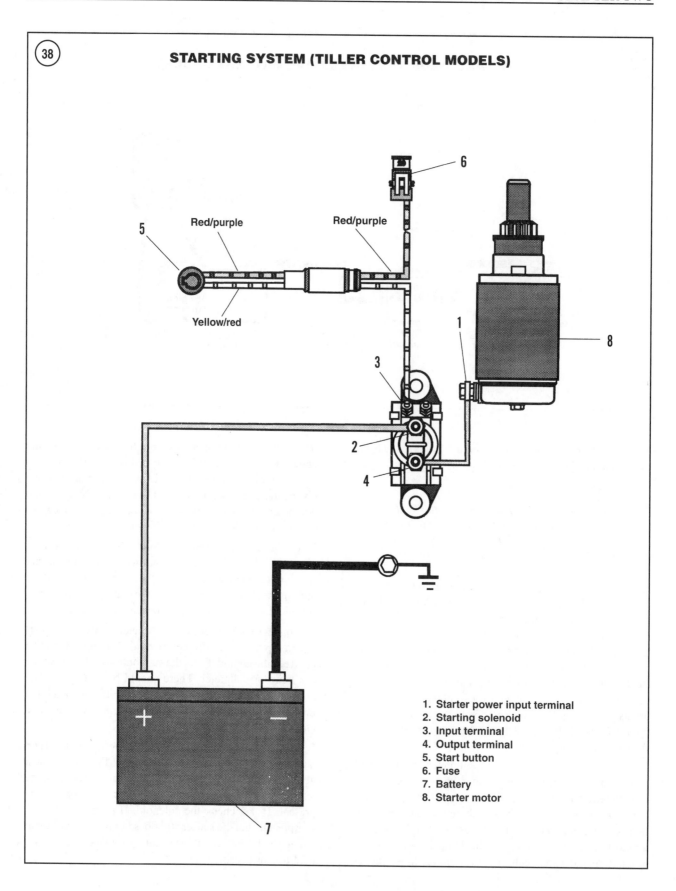

STARTING SYSTEM (TILLER CONTROL MODELS)

Red/purple

Red/purple

Yellow/red

1. Starter power input terminal
2. Starting solenoid
3. Input terminal
4. Output terminal
5. Start button
6. Fuse
7. Battery
8. Starter motor

6. If the circuit checks out properly, yet the starter does not operate properly, remove the starter and inspect for paint or corrosion on the mounting bolts and bosses. If paint or corrosion is found, clean the mounting bolts and bosses. Reinstall the starter and test the starter engagement. If the starter still does not engage, repair or replace the starter, as necessary (Chapter Seven).

7. Reconnect the spark plug leads.

Starter motor does not turn (remote control models)

A test lamp or voltmeter are both acceptable tools for troubleshooting the starter circuit, but a voltmeter is more accurate and easier to use. If using a voltmeter, all test readings must be within 1 volt of battery voltage. A reading of 1 volt or more below battery voltage indicates excessive resistance with the circuit being tested. If using a test lamp, first connect the test lamp directly to the battery and observe the brightness of the bulb. It is necessary to reference the rest of your readings against this test (by remembering how brightly the bulb was illuminated or by repeating this check for comparison to the current test). If the bulb does not glow as brightly as when it was connected directly to the battery, there is excessive resistance.

CAUTION
Disconnect and ground the spark plug leads to the engine to prevent accidental starting during all test procedures. Make sure the shift control lever is in the NEUTRAL position.

Refer to **Figure 39** for this procedure. Refer to the back of the manual for specific model wiring diagrams.

1. Connect the test lamp or voltmeter lead to the positive terminal of the battery and touch the test lamp probe to metal anywhere on the engine block. The test lamp must light. If the lamp does not light or is dim, the battery ground cable connections are loose or corroded, or there is an open circuit in the battery ground cable. Clean and tighten the connections or replace the battery cable as required. If using a test lamp, note the brightness of the lamp at this point. If using a voltmeter, note battery voltage. Remember that the battery should be in good condition and fully charged when testing.

2. To keep the starter from engaging during testing, disconnect the red cable from the solenoid (7, **Figure 39**) to the starter (8) at one end and leave it disconnected for Steps 3-9. Cover the cable end with a small plastic bag or piece of tape to prevent accidentally completing the circuit during testing.

3. Check the starter activation side of the circuit (key switch, neutral switch and wiring to solenoid) by disconnecting the black solenoid wire (1, **Figure 39**) and connecting a test light or voltmeter between it from the engine ground and a good engine ground. Turn the key to START and observe the test light or voltmeter. Battery voltage should be present. If voltage is not present, turn the key switch OFF and proceed with Step 4. If sufficient battery voltage is present, turn the key switch OFF and proceed to Step 9.

4. Make sure the problem is not with the solenoid ground wire by repeating the previous test, but this time connecting the test light or voltmeter between the ground terminal on the solenoid (2, **Figure 39**) and a good engine ground. Turn the key to START and observe the test light or voltmeter. Voltage should be present. If voltage is not present, turn the key switch OFF and proceed with Step 5. If sufficient battery voltage was present, the open circuit is between the solenoid ground terminal and the engine ground. Clean and tighten the connections or replace the ground lead, as applicable.

5. Continue to follow the activation circuit back to the next connection/component. Connect the test light or voltmeter between the activation circuit input terminal (wire from the neutral safety switch) on the solenoid (3, **Figure 39**) and a good engine ground. Turn the key to START and observe the test light or voltmeter. Voltage should be present. If voltage is not present, turn the key switch OFF and proceed with Step 6. If sufficient voltage is present, the problem is with the solenoid, replace it following the procedure in Chapter Seven.

6. Continue to follow the activation circuit back to the next connection/component. Connect the test light or voltmeter between the key switch terminal for the neutral safety switch (4, **Figure 39**, yellow/red wire) and a good ground. Turn the key to START and observe the test light or voltmeter. Battery voltage should be present. If voltage is not present, turn the key switch OFF and proceed with Step 7. If sufficient battery voltage is present, the open circuit is between test points 3 and 4 from **Figure 39**. Check first that the plunger on the neutral safety switch is working properly (opening the circuit in one position and closing it in the other). Adjust or replace the switch, as necessary. Also, check the continuity of wires from the key switch to the neutral switch and from the neutral switch to the solenoid.

7. Continue to follow the activation circuit back to the other side of the key switch. Connect the test light or voltmeter between the key switch terminal for power (5, **Figure 39**) from the fuse and a good ground. Check with the key switch OFF. If battery voltage is present, check the key switch and replace, as necessary. If sufficient voltage is not present, recheck the condition of the fuse and/or check for an open circuit in the wiring between the sole-

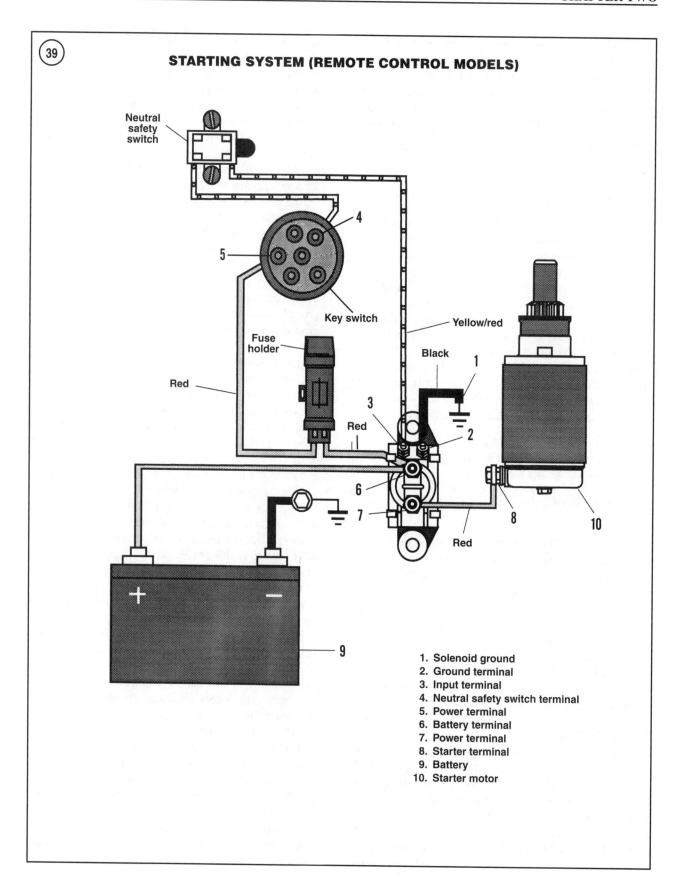

STARTING SYSTEM (REMOTE CONTROL MODELS)

Neutral safety switch

4

5

Key switch

Yellow/red

Fuse holder

Black

Red

Red

3

2

1

6

7

8

10

Red

9

1. Solenoid ground
2. Ground terminal
3. Input terminal
4. Neutral safety switch terminal
5. Power terminal
6. Battery terminal
7. Power terminal
8. Starter terminal
9. Battery
10. Starter motor

noid battery terminal (6, **Figure 39**) and the key switch (5, **Figure 39**).

8. Connect the test light or voltmeter between the solenoid battery terminal (6, **Figure 39**) and a good engine ground. Battery voltage should always be present. If no voltage is present, check for an open circuit between the solenoid battery terminal and the positive terminal of the battery. If sufficient voltage is present, proceed with Step 9.

9. Connect the test light or voltmeter between the solenoid starter output terminal (7, **Figure 39**) and a good engine ground. Turn the key switch to START and observe the test lamp or voltmeter. If no voltage is present, the solenoid is faulty. Replace it as directed in Chapter Seven. If the solenoid clicks and the meter reads voltage, proceed with Step 10.

10. Connect the test light or voltmeter between the starter power terminal (8, **Figure 39**) and a good engine ground. Turn the key switch to START and observe the test lamp or voltmeter. If no voltage is present, check the solenoid-to-starter cable and connections (tighten the connections or replace the cable, as applicable). If sufficient battery voltage is present, overhaul or replace the starter.

11. Reconnect the spark plug leads.

Push buttons starter switch test (tiller handle models)

Refer to the back of the manual for wiring diagrams, as necessary and use an ohmmeter to perform this test.

1. Disconnect the negative battery cable from the battery.

2. Disconnect the 2-pin Amphenol connector for the start switch (yellow/red and red/purple wires). The connector is normally found on the front of the motor, near the starter motor.

3. Connect an ohmmeter across the two wires for the start switch (yellow/red and red/purple wires). The meter must read no continuity (infinite resistance). Replace the start button if any other reading is noted.

4. Depress the start button. The meter must now show continuity (low resistance). Replace the start button if any other reading is noted.

5. Reconnect all wires when finished. Connect the negative battery cable last.

Ignition (key) switch circuit test

The following procedure tests the ignition switch on remote control electric start models from the engine wiring harness. Use an ohmmeter calibrated on the resistance scale to test the key switch circuits. Refer to **Figure 40** for connector positions during this procedure.

1. Disconnect the negative battery cable from the battery, then install the stop/start switch clip and lanyard.

2. Locate and disconnect the 6-pin remote wiring traditional harness at the engine.

3. Turn the key switch to the OFF position.

4. On the control side of the harness, connect the leads of an ohmmeter to terminals 4 and 6 as shown in **Figure 40**. The ohmmeter should show continuity.

5. With the leads of an ohmmeter still connected to terminals 4 and 6, turn the key switch to ON. The ohmmeter must now show continuity with the key switch in the ON position.

6. Move the ohmmeter leads to terminals 1 and 2 (**Figure 40**). Push in on the key while the switch is in the ON and START positions. The ohmmeter should show continuity while pressing and no continuity when the key is released.

7. Place the control handle in NEUTRAL and connect the ohmmeter leads to terminals 2 and 5 as shown in **Figure 40**. Turn the key to the START position. The meter should show continuity. Release the key. The meter should show no continuity.

8. If the results vary, check the instrument and key switch harnesses and connectors for opens, corrosion or damage. If no problems are found with the harness, test the key switch as detailed in this section.

Ignition (key) switch test

The following procedure tests the ignition key switch on models equipped with an OMC key switch assembly. On models equipped with the modular wiring system (MWS) and Deutsch connectors, the color codes of the wires and their corresponding pin location in the connector body are self-evident.

Use an ohmmeter calibrated on the resistance scale to test the key switch circuits. Refer to **Figure 40** for this procedure.

1. Disconnect the negative battery cable from the battery.

2. Gain access to the key switch and disconnect the wires from the key switch terminals. Note the color code and terminal markings.

3. Connect one lead of the ohmmeter to the ignition switch B terminal (red/purple wire) and the other ohmmeter lead to the A terminal (purple wire). When the switch is in the OFF position, there should be no continuity.

4. Turn the switch to the ON or RUN position. The ohmmeter should indicate continuity.

5. Turn the switch to the START or CRANK position. The ohmmeter should indicate continuity.

6. Connect one lead of the ohmmeter to the B terminal (red/purple wire) and the other ohmmeter lead to the S terminal (yellow/red wire). When the switch is in the OFF position, there should be no continuity.

7. Turn the switch to the START or CRANK position. The ohmmeter should indicate continuity.

8. Turn the switch to the OFF or STOP position. Connect one ohmmeter lead to an M terminal (black/yellow wire) and the other ohmmeter lead to the other M terminal (black wire). The ohmmeter should indicate continuity. Turn the switch to the ON (RUN) and START (CRANK) positions. The ohmmeter must read no continuity in both positions.

9. Turn the switch to the OFF or STOP position. Connect one ohmmeter lead to the B terminal (red/purple wire) and the other ohmmeter lead to the C terminal (purple/white wire). The ohmmeter shold read no continuity.

10. Turn the switch to the ON or RUN position. The ohmmeter must read no continuity. Press in on the key to engage the CHOKE or PRIME position. The ohmmeter should read continuity in the CHOKE or PRIME position.

11. Turn the switch to the START or CRANK position. The ohmmeter should read no continuity. Press in on the key to engage the CHOKE or PRIME position. The ohmmeter should read continuity in the CHOKE or PRIME position.

12. Replace the ignition (key) switch if it does not perform as specified.

13. Reconnect all wires when finished. Connect the negative battery cable last.

Neutral safety switch testing

The purpose of the neutral safety switch is to allow starter engagement *only* when the shift lever (gearcase) is in the NEUTRAL position. The starter must not engage when the shift lever (gearcase) is in either the FORWARD or REVERSE positions.

Tiller handle models equipped with a neutral safety switch require adjustment of the switch to ensure proper operation. The switch must be adjusted any time it has been removed or replaced, or if improper operation is noted.

Remote control models require remote control shift cable adjustment to ensure proper operation. See Chapter Four for shift cable adjustments and Chapter Twelve for remote control component servicing. The shift cable must be adjusted anytime it, the gearcase or the control box has been removed, repaired or replaced, or if improper operation is noted.

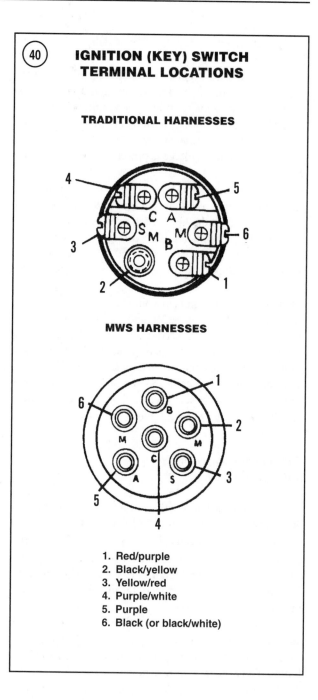

40 **IGNITION (KEY) SWITCH TERMINAL LOCATIONS**

TRADITIONAL HARNESSES

MWS HARNESSES

1. Red/purple
2. Black/yellow
3. Yellow/red
4. Purple/white
5. Purple
6. Black (or black/white)

CAUTION
Moving the shift lever into FORWARD or REVERSE gear with the engine not running can damage the control box, shift cable and gearcase. Have an assistant rotate the propeller when it is necessary to shift the gearcase with the engine not running.

Refer to **Figure 40** for connector positions during this procedure. To quickly test the switch and boat harness using an ohmmeter, proceed as follows:

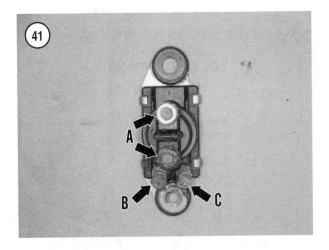

1. Disconnect the negative battery cable from the battery and position the remote control shift lever into the NEUTRAL position.

2. Locate and disconnect the 6-pin remote wiring harness at the engine.

3. Connect the leads of an ohmmeter to terminals 2 and 5 from **Figure 40**. Turn the key to the START position. The meter should show continuity.

4. While an assistant is rotating the propeller, position the shift lever in the FORWARD gear position.

5. Turn the ignition (key) switch to the START position while noting the meter reading. The meter should indicate no continuity.

6. While an assistant is rotating the propeller, position the shift lever in the REVERSE gear position.

7. Turn the ignition (key) switch to the START position while noting the meter reading. The meter should indicate no continuity.

8. If the test results are not as specified, either the boat wiring harness or the neutral safety switch is defective. Test the isolated neutral safety switch as described in Step 9. If the switch tests are satisfactory, there is an open circuit or high resistance in the boat harness yellow/red or red/purple wires. Repair or replace the harness as necessary.

9. To test only the neutral safety switch, proceed as follows:

   a. Open the control box to gain access to the switch (refer to Chapter Twelve for procedures on OMC remote controls).

   b. Disconnect both yellow/red wires from the switch.

   c. Connect an ohmmeter to the switch terminals.

NOTE
The switch must be depressed in NEUTRAL and extended in FORWARD and REVERSE.

   d. Depress the switch while noting the meter reading. The ohmmeter should indicate continuity.

   e. Release (extend) the switch while noting the meter reading. The ohmmeter should indicate no continuity.

   f. Replace the switch if it does not perform as specified.

10. Reconnect all wires when finished. Connect the negative battery cable last.

Starter solenoid bench test

NOTE
All engine wiring harness leads must be disconnected from the solenoid for this test.

Solenoid style varies, but all solenoids have two large terminal studs and two small terminal studs. Refer to **Figure 41** for this procedure.

1. Disconnect the negative battery cable from the battery.

2. Tag and disconnect all wires from the solenoid terminal studs. If necessary, remove the solenoid from the engine.

3. Connect an ohmmeter across the two large terminal studs (A, **Figure 41**). The ohmmeter should indicate no continuity. Replace the solenoid if any other reading is noted.

4. Attach a 12-volt battery (with suitable jumper leads) to the two small terminal studs Refer to **Figure 41** and connect the positive side of the battery to (B) and the negative side of the battery to C). An audible click should be heard as if the solenoid engages. The ohmmeter across the two large terminal studs should now indicate continuity. Replace the solenoid if any other reading is noted.

5. Reconnect all wires when finished. Connect the negative battery cable last.

Starter motor no-load current draw test

If starter system troubleshooting indicates that additional starter motor tests are necessary, use the starter no-load current draw test as an indicator of internal starter condition. A clamp-on or inductive ammeter, if available, is the simplest to use, as no electrical connections are required.

The starter motor speed must be measured during the no-load current draw test. A vibration tachometer, such as the Frahm Reed Tachometer can be used for this test. Simply hold the tachometer against the starter frame while the starter is running to measure its speed. A stroboscopic tachometer may also be used, but remember to make a reference mark on the starter drive (pinion gear) before beginning the test. Another option is to use a tachometer designed for model airplane engines, available from most hobby shops. This type of tachometer is simply held against the end of the starter drive to measure the speed.

1. Remove the starter motor assembly from the power head (Chapter Seven). Securely fasten the starter motor in a vise or other suitable holding fixture. Do not damage the starter motor by over tightening the vise.

2. Obtain a fully charged battery with a minimum rating of at least 350 cold cranking amps (CCA). The battery must be in good condition for the test results to be accurate.

3. Connect a suitable voltmeter to the battery as shown in **Figure 42**.

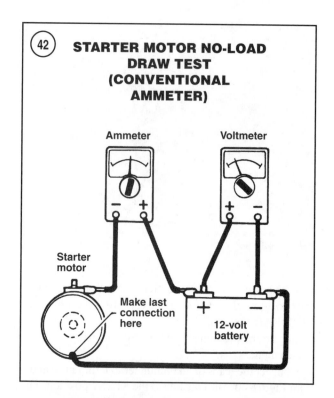

CAUTION
Make sure the ammeter used in the next step has sufficient capacity to measure the expected amperage draw (30 amps) with an adequate safety margin. For example, if the expected amperage draw is 30 amps, use a 50 amp or larger ammeter.

4A. *Conventional ammeter*—Using heavy gauge battery cables or jumper cables, connect a conventional ammeter in series with the positive battery cable and the starter motor terminal (**Figure 42**). Then connect another heavy gauge battery cable or jumper cable to the negative battery terminal, but do not connect this cable to the starter at this time.

4B. *Inductive or clamp-on ammeter*—Using heavy gauge battery cables or jumper cables, connect the positive battery terminal to the starter motor terminal. Then install the clamp-on or inductive ammeter over this cable. Then connect another heavy gauge battery cable or jumper cable to the negative battery terminal, but do not connect this cable to the starter at this time.

WARNING
*Make the last battery connection to the starter frame in Step 5. **Do not** create any sparks at or near the battery or a serious explosion could occur.*

NOTE
The battery must maintain at least 12.0-12.4 volts during the test. If the voltage falls below this range, yet the current draw does not exceed of 30 amps, the battery is defective or not of sufficient capacity for the test.

5. When ready to perform the no-load test, prepare a tachometer for the rpm measurement, then quickly and firmly connect the remaining cable to the starter motor frame (**Figure 42**). Note the amperage, voltage and rpm

readings, and then disconnect the jumper cable from the starter motor frame.

6. If the motor exceeds 30 amps of current draw during cranking to obtain 6500-7500 rpm, or cannot achieve the specified rpm, repair or replace the motor. See Chapter Seven.

Testing the Electric Starting System (EFI Models)

Failure to operate or slow rotation of the starter can be caused from numerous sources. Check the battery as de-

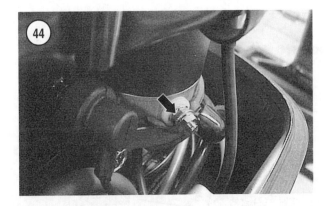

2

4. Shift the engine into NEUTRAL. Have an assistant operate the starter button or ignition switch while reading the voltage measurement. A voltage reading of 9.5-11.5 volts is normal.

5. Repeat Step 3 and Step 4 with the negative meter test lead connected to a suitable engine ground. A dirty or faulty starter ground wire connection is indicated if a different voltage reading is measured in Step 5 than in Step 4. Clean or repair faulty wire connections as required.

6A. A defective fuse, starter relay, neutral-only start switch, starter button, ignition switch or wiring is indicated if no voltage is noted in Step 4 and Step 5. Perform the *Voltage at the starter relay* test as described in this chapter.

6B. A defective starter motor is indicated if correct voltage is indicated in Step 4 yet the starter fails to operate or operates slowly. Repair the starter as described in Chapter Seven.

6C. A defective battery, battery terminal, wire terminal or starter relay is indicated if less than 9.5 VDC is measured in Step 4. Test, replace or repair these components as required.

7. Position the insulating cover over the starter wire terminal (**Figure 44**). Reconnect the spark plug leads.

Voltage at the starter relay

The mounting location for the starter relay varies by model. On 40 and 50 hp models the starter relay is located on the starboard side of the power head and next to the electric starter (**Figure 46**). On 70 hp models the starter relay is located on the starboard side of the power head and just to the rear of the silencer cover (**Figure 47**).

1. Disconnect the spark plug leads and connect them to an engine ground. Shift the engine into NEUTRAL.

2. Select the 20 or 40 VDC scale on the multimeter. Connect the negative meter test lead to a suitable engine ground. Connect the positive meter lead to the battery cable side of the relay. A measurement of 12 VDC or higher should be noted. Low or no voltage indicates a faulty battery, battery cable or terminal. Clean, repair or replace these components as required.

3. Connect the negative meter test lead to a suitable engine ground. Connect the positive meter lead to the starter cable side of the relay. Do not select the cable leading to the battery for this test. Have an assistant operate the starter button or ignition switch while observing the voltage reading. There should be a reading of 9.5 VDC or greater.

4. Carefully disconnect the yellow/green wire from the relay. Connect the positive meter test lead to the disconnected wire. Connect the negative meter test lead to the

scribed in Chapter Seven before testing the starting system. Perform the tests in the following order:

1. Voltage at the starter.
2. Voltage at the starter relay.
3. Voltage to the ignition switch.
4. Testing the neutral only start switch.
5. Testing the starter relay.
6. Testing the ignition switch.

Voltage at the starter

1. Disconnect and ground the leads from each spark plug.

2. Locate the large red wire connecting the starter relay to the starter (**Figure 43**). Carefully pull the insulating cover away to access the starter cable terminal near the bottom of the starter (**Figure 44**).

3. Select the 20 or 40 VDC scale on the multimeter. Connect the positive meter test lead to the starter wire terminal (**Figure 44**). Connect the negative meter test lead to the engine ground terminal at the top of the starter (**Figure 45**).

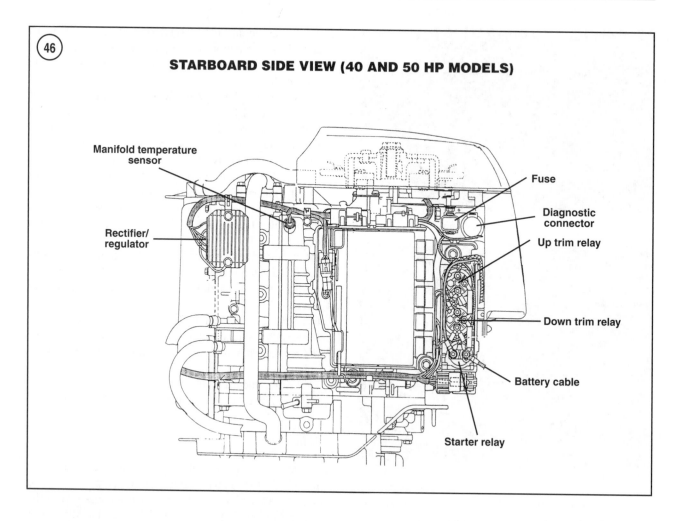

46

STARBOARD SIDE VIEW (40 AND 50 HP MODELS)

Manifold temperature sensor

Fuse

Diagnostic connector

Up trim relay

Rectifier/regulator

Down trim relay

Battery cable

Starter relay

wire terminal for the small black wire leading to the starter relay. Have an assistant operate the starter button or ignition switch while observing the voltage reading. There should be a reading of 12 VDC or higher.

5. Repeat Step 4 with the negative meter test lead connected to a suitable engine ground. The meter should read 12 VDC or higher. A faulty connection or defective small black wire is indicated if the correct voltage is noted in this step but not in Step 4. Clean, repair or replace the black wire or terminals as required.

6. There is a faulty starter relay if incorrect voltage is noted in Step 3 only. Low voltage readings in both Steps 3 and Step 4 indicate a faulty fuse, neutral–only start switch, starter button/ignition switch or wire. Test these components as described in this chapter.

7. Reconnect the spark plug leads.

Voltage at the ignition switch

A dash or remote control mounted ignition switch is used on all remote control models. Long jumper leads may be required to test remote control models. Some 40-70 hp motors may be equipped with accessory tiller controls, if so, use the ignition switch mounted to the tiller control. This is the same type of switch used on remote control models.

Access to the ignition switch wire connector is required for testing. This may require partial disassembly of the remote control or tiller control housing. Blown fuses and corroded terminals and disconnected wires are the primary cause for no or low voltage at the starter button or ignition switch. Check for and correct these conditions before disassembling any other components. On remote control models, cycle the ignition switch to the ON position while observing the dash mounted instruments. The instruments receive voltage from the ignition switch. A blown fuse or faulty wiring is not likely if the instruments come on with the ignition switch.

1. Disconnect the negative battery cable.

2. Access the voltage supply wire for the selected model as follows:

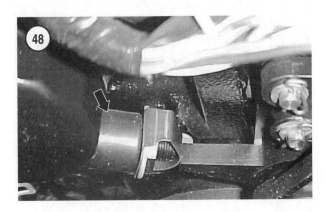

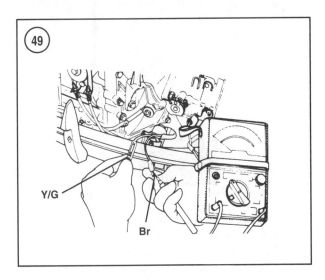

a. *Tiller control models*—Remove the lower cover from the tiller control as described in Chapter Eleven. Trace the white ignition switch wire to the tiller control harness. Disconnect the white wire from the harness.

b. *Ignition switch mounted in the remote control*—Disassemble the remote control as described

in Chapter Twelve to access the ignition switch wires. Trace the white ignition switch wire to the remote control harness. Disconnect the white wire from the harness.

c. *Dash mounted ignition switch*—Locate the ignition switch wires beneath the dashboard. Trace the white ignition switch wire to the instrument harness. Disconnect the wire from the instrument harness.

3. Select the 20 or 40 VDC scale on the multimeter. Connect the positive meter test lead to the harness side of the white wire. Connect the negative meter test lead to a suitable engine ground.

4. Connect the negative battery cable. The correct voltage reading is 12 volts or greater. No or low voltage indicates a faulty battery, fuse, wire or connection. Inspect these components for defects as described in this chapter.

5. Test the ignition switch, neutral-only start switch and starter relay if the voltage reading is correct.

6. Disconnect the negative battery cable. Disconnect the test leads. Connect the starter switch or white ignition switch wire to the engine wire harness, remote control harness, tiller control harness or instrument harness. Route all wires to prevent interference.

7. Reassemble the remote control or tiller control bracket as described in Chapter 11 or Chapter 12. Connect the negative battery cables.

Neutral-only start switch test

All EFI models use an engine mounted neutral-only start switch (**Figure 48**). This switch opens the circuit leading to the starter relay if the engine is shifted into FORWARD or REVERSE. The switch is mounted to allow direct contact with the shift linkage.

1. Disconnect the negative battery cable. Trace the yellow/green wire from the starter relay to the neutral-only start switch. Disconnect both the yellow/green and brown wires from the neutral-only start switch.

2. Set the multimeter to check resistance. Connect the positive meter test lead to the yellow/green wire (**Figure 49**). Connect the negative meter test lead to the brown wire.

3. Shift the engine into NEUTRAL and note the meter reading. The switch should have continuity.

4. Shift the engine into FORWARD and REVERSE while noting the meter readings. The switch should have no continuity with the engine shifted into forward and reverse gear. Repeat Step 3 and Step 4 several times to check for intermittent faults.

5. Replace the neutral–only start switch if the switch operation is incorrect in Step 3 or Step 4.

6. Disconnect the test leads. Connect the yellow/green and brown wires. Route all wires to prevent interference.

7. Connect the negative battery cable.

Starter relay test

Testing requires a multimeter, fully charged cranking battery and jumper leads. The first section tests the resistance of the winding within the starter relay. The second provides a functional test to verify correct switching within the relay. Perform both the resistance and functional test. Replace the relay if it fails either test.

1. Remove the starter relay from the power head as described in Chapter Seven.

2. Test the resistance of the internal winding as follows:
   a. Set the multimeter to read resistance.
   b. Connect the positive meter test lead to the yellow/green starter relay wire (**Figure 50**).
   c. Connect the negative meter test lead to the relay ground (40-50 hp motors) or to the black wire (70 hp motors).
   d. Note the resistance reading. Replace the relay if the resistance measurement is not with the specification in **Table 7**.

3. Perform the starter relay functional test as follows:
   a. Set the multimeter to read resistance.
   b. Connect the positive meter test lead to one of the large diameter wire terminals of the relay (**Figure 51**). Connect the negative meter test lead to the other large wire terminal.
   c. The meter must indicate no continuity.
   d. Using suitable jumper leads connect the yellow/green relay wire to the positive terminal of a fully charged battery (**Figure 51**). Observe the meter reading while connecting the negative battery terminal to the black wire or ground of the relay.
   e. As the connection to the battery is made the relay should have continuity. If not, replace the relay.

4. Disconnect all meter and battery terminal connections. Install the relay as described in Chapter Seven.

Ignition switch test

The ignition switch provides current for the gauges, starting circuit, choke solenoid and engine control circuits on EFI models. This switch also controls the ignition stop circuit. Access to the ignition switch wires is required for testing. Partial disassembly of the remote control or tiller control bracket is required for most models.

1. Disconnect the negative battery cable. Set the multimeter to read resistance.

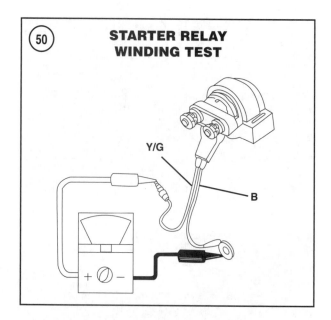

50   STARTER RELAY WINDING TEST

Y/G

B

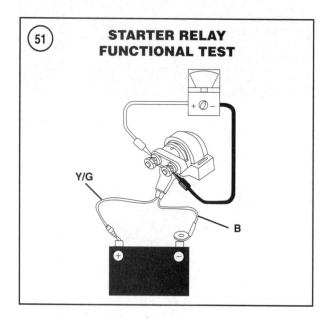

51   STARTER RELAY FUNCTIONAL TEST

Y/G

B

2. Access the ignition switch wires as follows:
   a. *Tiller control models*—Remove the lower cover from the tiller control as described in Chapter Eleven.
   b. *Ignition switch mounted in the remote control*—Disassemble the remote control as described in Chapter Twelve until the ignition switch wires are accessible.
   c. *Dash mounted ignition switch*—Locate the ignition switch wires beneath the dashboard. Remove the ignition switch from the dash if necessary for wire access.

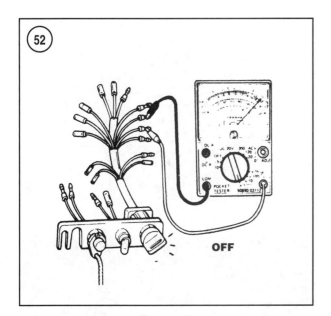

OFF

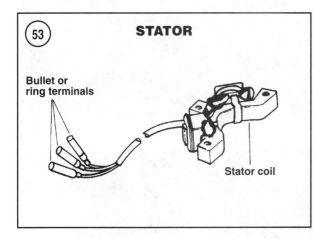

STATOR

Bullet or
ring terminals

Stator coil

3. Carefully disconnect all ignition switch wire connectors from the remote control, tiller control on the instrument harness.

4A. Turn the ignition switch OFF (**Figure 52**). Connect the positive meter test lead to the black switch wire. Connect the negative meter test lead to the green switch wire. The meter should indicate continuity.

4B. Turn the ignition switch ON and note the meter reading. The meter should indicate no continuity.

5A. Turn the ignition switch OFF. Connect the positive meter test lead to the white switch wire. Connect the negative meter test lead to the gray switch wire then note the meter reading. The meter should indicate no continuity.

5B. Note the meter reading while cycling the ignition switch from ON to START. The meter should indicate continuity.

6A. Turn the ignition switch OFF. Connect the positive meter test lead to the white switch wire. Connect the negative meter test lead to the brown switch wire then note the meter reading. The meter should indicate no continuity.

6B. Turn the ignition switch ON and note the meter reading. The meter should indicate no continuity.

6C. Turn the ignition switch to the START position. The meter should indicate continuity.

7A. Turn the ignition switch OFF. Connect the positive meter test lead to the white switch wire. Connect the negative meter test lead to the orange switch lead, and then note the meter reading. The meter should indicate no continuity.

7B. Turn the ignition switch ON, and then note the meter reading. The meter should indicate no continuity.

7C. Turn the ignition switch ON. Note the meter reading while repeatedly pushing, then releasing the ignition switch. The meter should indicate continuity with the key depressed and a no continuity reading when released.

8. Disconnect all test leads. Replace the ignition switch if any operation is incorrect.

9. Carefully connect all ignition switch wire connectors to their respective connections to the remote control, tiller control or instruments harness. Route all wires to prevent them from contacting any moving components.

10. Connect the negative battery cable.

CHARGING SYSTEM

An alternator type charging system is standard on all electric start models and optional on most rope start models. The charging system provides electric current to charge the cranking battery (electric start motors) and/or to operate other engine or boat mounted electric components. The systems used on these motors can be broken into two basic categories, non-regulated and regulated systems. The regulated systems are further broken down into the types used by carbureted motors and those used by fuel injected models. However, all types operate in a similar fashion.

All charging systems covered in this manual use a stator (**Figure 53**, non-regulated system shown, regulated system similar, but the component is completely round on other systems) mounted beneath a flywheel (**Figure 54**, typical) equipped with permanent magnets. A rectifier is used on the 4- or 6-amp, non-regulated charging system found on most carbureted engines covered in this manual, while a rectifier/regulator is used on models that are equipped with a 12- or 17-amp charging system. The 12-amp system is found on a few carbureted engines, such as the 9.9 High Thrust model, while the 17-amp system is used on fuel-injected motors.

This section provides a brief description of charging system operation followed by component test instructions.

WARNING
Use extreme caution when working around batteries. Never smoke or allow sparks to occur around batteries. Batteries produce explosive hydrogen gas that can explode resulting in injury or death. Never make the final connection of a circuit to the battery terminal as an arc may occur and lead to fire or an explosion.

System Operation

Alternating current is produced in the stator (battery charge coil) as the flywheel magnets pass near the charge coil. The rectifier converts this current to direct current capable of charging the battery. If the flywheel is removed, make sure that the magnets have not attracted any metal debris. Any metal objects attached to the flywheel may contact and damage the electrical system coils.

NOTE
Because output is non-regulated on models equipped with a 4- or 6-amp regulated charging system, using a maintenance free battery is typically not recommended. Using standard vented batteries, which allow checking and refilling of electrolyte that has evaporated because of charging, allows for a longer service life.

Models with a rectifier (**Figure 55**, typical) are non-regulated. The low current output on these models generally does not provide sufficient current to overcharge the battery. However, output is directly proportional to engine speed and continued high speed operation with a small battery or low electrical needs may result in overcharging. Check the battery electrolyte level often in such applications (Chapter Seven).

Models with a regulator (**Figure 56**, typical) rectify and regulate the charging current to the battery and accessory demands. A regulated system reduces, but does not eliminate the need to add water to the battery.

If overcharging is suspected, test the regulator by performing the charging system output test in this chapter. In most cases overcharging is the result of a defective regulator. However, in rare cases the battery may be at fault.

A defective charging system usually causes a weak or discharged battery. However, in situations where numerous electrical accessories are used, the current demands may exceed the capability of a correctly operating charg-

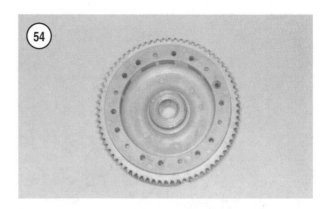

ing system. The installation of an auxiliary battery, or batteries and a battery isolator (**Figure 57**) may be required to handle the accessory load and prevent the cranking battery from being discharged.

On carbureted models with a remote control the tachometer is powered by the charging system. In most

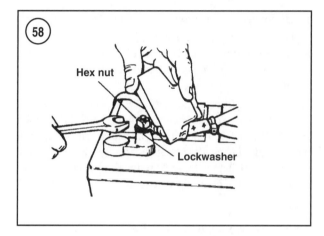

2. Check for loose or corroded connections. A terminal strip or bullet connectors are used on most charging system connections, clean, tighten, repair or replace as necessary. Replace battery wing nuts with corrosion resistant hex nuts and lockwashers. Place a lockwasher under the battery cable as shown in **Figure 58**. Loose battery cable connections will cause a charging system failure.

3. Check the rectifier or rectifier/regulator (**Figure 55** or **Figure 56**, typical) mounting hardware for corrosion, evidence of electrical arcing and loose fasteners. These components are grounded through their mounting hardware. The mounting screws and bosses must be free of paint and corrosion and the screws must be securely tightened. Loose mounting screws cause erratic operation and premature failure.

4. Check the battery condition. Charge or replace the battery as necessary.

5. Check the wiring harness between the stator and battery for cut, chafed or deteriorated insulation and corroded, loose or broken connections. Repair or replace the wiring harness as necessary.

6. Visually inspect the stator windings for discoloration and burned windings. Replace any stator that is overheating.

CAUTION
Unless otherwise noted, perform all voltage tests with the leads connected and the terminals exposed to accommodate test lead connection. All electrical components must be securely grounded to the power head any time the engine is cranked or started or the components will be damaged.

cases, if the tachometer is inoperative, the charging system is defective.

On fuel injected models the engine control module or CDI unit controls the tachometer. On these models the tachometer is not affected by a defective charging system.

CAUTION
Never remove or disconnect the battery cables or any lead of the charging system while the engine is running. Permanent damage to the charging system components will occur. Make sure any switching device installed does not break or open the charging system connection to the battery during engine operation.

System Inspection (All Models)

Before troubleshooting the charging system, check the following:

1. Make sure the battery is properly connected. If the battery polarity is reversed, the rectifier or rectifier/regulator will be damaged.

Charging System Output Test

This test requires a digital multimeter, shop tachometer and a flush/test device or suitable test tank. Perform the *System Inspection* as detailed in this chapter before proceeding. Failure of charging system components is usually caused by faulty wiring/connections or improper battery connections. Correct all faulty wiring or connections before replacing any electrical component, as an open or short in the system could damage the replacement part when installed and operated.

WARNING
Stay clear of the propeller shaft while running an outboard on a flush/test device. Remove the propeller before running the engine to help avoid injury or death. Disconnect all spark plug leads and the battery

cables before removing or installing the propeller.

CAUTION
Never run an outboard without first providing cooling water. Use either a test tank or flush/test device. Remove the propeller before running the engine on a flush/test device. Use a suitable test propeller to run the engine in a test tank.

1. Select the 20 or 40 VDC voltage scale on the multimeter. Connect the tachometer to the engine following the manufacturer's instructions. Switch all electrical accessories OFF.

2. With the engine switched OFF, connect the positive meter test lead to the positive battery terminal. Touch the negative meter test lead to a suitable engine ground such as a clean cylinder head bolt. Use jumper leads if necessary. Record the voltage displayed on the meter.

3. Start the engine and run it at idle speed. Connect the meter test lead as indicated in Step 2. Record the voltage reading.

4. Raise the engine speed to approximately 2000 rpm. Record the voltage reading.

5. Turn OFF the engine and all accessories. Disconnect the meter test leads.

6. Compare the idle and 2000 rpm voltage readings with the results in Step 2. The voltage should increase 0.3 volt or more. Test the stator (battery charge coil), rectifier or regulator if a voltage increase of less than 0.3 volt is observed.

NOTE
Regulated systems are designed to keep system voltage output at approximately 14.5 volts in order to maintain battery charge near 13 volts. Output below 12 volts or above 15 volts usually indicates a problem with the regulator/rectifier, but confirm through testing before replacement.

7. Repeat Steps 2-4 with all electrical accessories switched ON. Compare the idle and 2000 rpm voltage readings with the results in Step 2. The voltage should increase 0.3 volts or more. Test the stator (battery charge coil), rectifier or regulator if a voltage increase of less than 0.3 volt is observed. If these items test well, the charging system is not capable of meeting the accessory load. A 0.3 volt or more increase indicates that the accessory load is within the charging system capacity.

Current Draw Test

Use this test to determine if the total load of the engine electrical system and boat accessories exceeds the capacity of the charging system.

NOTE
If using a clamp-on or inductive ammeter, install the probe on the positive battery cable (near the battery) and go directly to Step 3. If using a conventional ammeter, make sure the ammeter is rated for at least 20 amps.

1. Disconnect the negative battery cable from the battery.

2. Disconnect the positive battery cable from the battery. Securely connect a suitable ammeter between the positive battery post and the positive battery cable. Reconnect the negative battery cable.

3. Turn the ignition switch ON (RUN) and turn on all accessories. Note the ammeter reading. Turn the ignition switch OFF (STOP) and turn off all accessories. If the ammeter reading exceeds the rated capacity of the charging system (see Chapter Seven), reduce the accessory load connected to the charging system.

Stator (Battery Charge Coil) Test

This test requires a digital multimeter as all test specifications are near or below 1 ohm. Stator (battery charge coil) appearance and wire colors vary by model. If necessary, refer to the wire diagrams at the end of the manual to identify the wire colors. Trace the indicated wires to the wires leading beneath the flywheel. Stator removal is not required for testing. Remove the coil only when necessary to access the wire connectors. Stator resistance specifications are in **Table 8**.

1. Disconnect the negative battery cable. Disconnect and ground the spark plug leads. If applicable on fuel injected models, carefully unwrap the spiral wrap from the stator coil wires.

2. Connection points for the stator coil wires vary by model and charging system components.

   a. On carbureted models, disconnect the yellow and yellow/gray wires to the stator.

   b. On 40 and 50 hp models disconnect the three white coil wires from the three yellow wires leading to the regulator.

   c. On 70 hp models disconnect the three yellow coil wires from the three yellow wires leading to the regulator.

3. Set the multimeter to the resistance scale. Inspect the battery charge coil wire terminals for dirty or damaged terminals. Clean and repair them as required.

4. Connect the meter test leads to the stator wires. For fuel injected models, connect the meter in all combinations across the three different connector terminals/wires. Record the meter readings.

5. Compare the meter readings with the stator resistance specifications in **Table 8**. Replace the stator (Chapter Seven) if the measurements are out of specification.

6. Carefully route and reconnect the stator wires. Route the wires to prevent interference and, if applicable, carefully wrap the spiral wrap around them.

7. Reconnect the spark plug leads and negative battery cable.

Rectifier Test

A rectifier (**Figure 55**) is used on carbureted models equipped with a non-regulated charging system. This component is either mounted directly to the side of the engine next to the starter motor on 9.9/15 hp (305 cc) models or underneath the rope start assembly, on the front of the same side as the electric starter on 9.9 (211 cc) models.

1. Disconnect the negative battery cable. Disconnect and ground the spark plug leads.

2. Note the wire routing and connection points then carefully disconnect all the rectifier leads from the engine harness.

3. Set the multimeter to the resistance scale, then connect one of the meter probes to a good engine ground and the other to the yellow/gray wire. Note the reading on the meter, then reverse the leads (or press the reverse polarity button on the meter, if equipped) and note the reading. The readings should be high in one direction and low in the other, indicating the diode is good. If readings are the same (high or low) in both directions, the diode is damaged and the rectifier should be replaced.

4. Repeat Step 3, but using the yellow wire this time. Results are determined the same way as in Step 3.

5. Repeat Step 3, but using the gray wire this time. Results are determined the same way as in Step 3.

6. Connect one of the multimeter probes to the red wire and the other to each of the three wires tested in Steps 3-6 (yellow/gray, yellow and then gray) each in turn. Results should be similar to Step 3 across each combination of red wire and one of the three other wires.

7. Replace the rectifier as described in Chapter Seven if test results are incorrect or, if problems are still suspected, perform the *Regulator/Rectifier Load Test* in this chapter.

8. Carefully route and reconnect the battery charge coil wires. Route all wires to prevent interference.

9. Reconnect the spark plug leads and negative battery cable.

Regulator/Rectifier Load Test

A regulator/rectifier is used on some carbureted and all fuel injected models. In all cases, this component is used on motors equipped with a regulated 12- or 17-amp charging system. The purpose of the regulator is to control output of the charging system to prevent over or under-charging the battery.

The appearance and mounting location of the regulator varies by model. On carbureted models, it is mounted to the front of the engine, just below the rope starter (**Figure 56**, typical). Its appearance is box-shaped and finned for cooling, which differs greatly from the cylindrical metal cylinder shape of the rectifier used on other carbureted models.

For fuel injected models the rectifier/regulator is mounted on the starboard side of the engine. On 40 and 50 hp models, it is mounted to the rear starboard side of the power head directly above the low pressure fuel filter. On 70 hp models it is mounted to the starboard side of the power head beneath the electrical component cover. Remove the cover on these models to access the regulator wire terminals.

Refer to the wire diagrams at the end of the manual to identify the regulator wire colors, as necessary. Trace the wires from the stator (battery charge coil) to the regulator.

Because the regulator/rectifier is a solid state component, no reliable resistance tests are available to ensure the condition of the regulator. Instead, a carbon pile tester and ammeter are used to test the regulator under normal engine operating conditions involving a discharged battery. Use a test tank during this procedure because the engine must be run under load at 3000-5000 rpm depending on the model.

Refer to **Figure 59** when conducting tests on a carbureted motor or to **Figure 60** when conducting tests on a fuel injected model.

1. Before proceeding, use a multimeter to verify that the battery power feed circuit to the regulator is intact (since the regulator requires battery voltage to operate correctly.) by checking for battery power at the proper wire with the key ON, but the engine not running:

    a. On carbureted models, check the purple wire bullet connector for the regulator.

    b. On fuel injected models, check the regulator white wire (10, **Figure 60**).

2. Disconnect the cables from the battery, then connect an ammeter (of minimum 0-40 amp capacity) in series as follows:

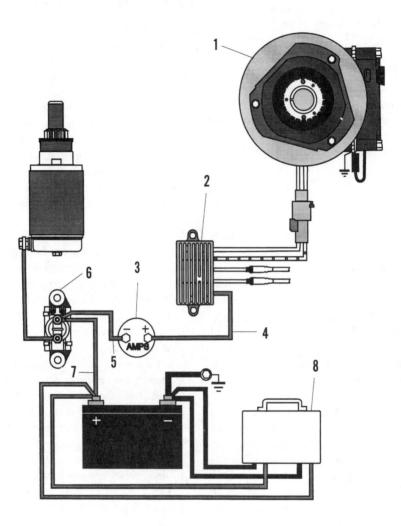

⑤⁹ REGULATOR/RECTIFIER (CARBURETED MODELS)

1. Stator (battery charge coil)
2. Regulator/rectifier
3. Ammeter (0-40 amp charge)
4. Red wire
5. Jumper wire
6. Starter solenoid
7. Red battery cable
8. Carbon pile tester

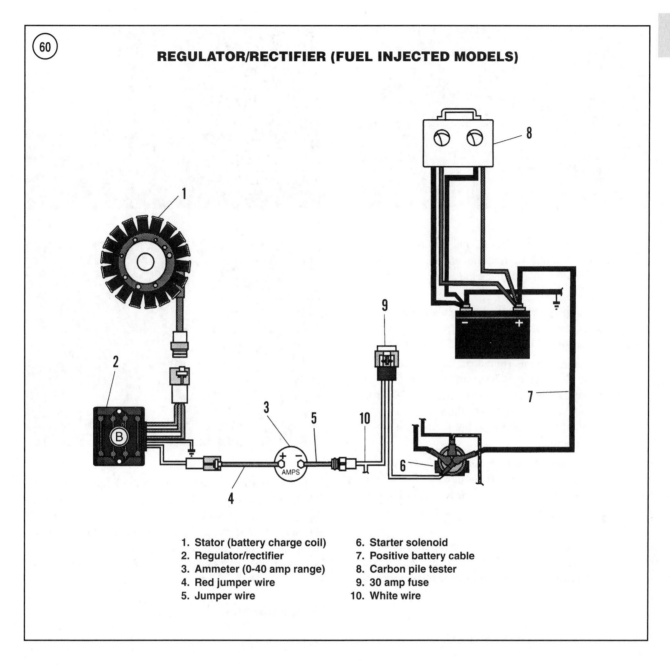

REGULATOR/RECTIFIER (FUEL INJECTED MODELS)

1. Stator (battery charge coil)
2. Regulator/rectifier
3. Ammeter (0-40 amp range)
4. Red jumper wire
5. Jumper wire
6. Starter solenoid
7. Positive battery cable
8. Carbon pile tester
9. 30 amp fuse
10. White wire

a. On carbureted motors, install the ammeter in series between the regulator red wire (4, **Figure 59**) and the battery side of the starter solenoid/relay (6) using a jumper wire (5).

b. On fuel injected motors, install the ammeter in series between the male and female connectors of the regulator white wire (10, **Figure 60**) using jumper wires (4 and 5).

3. Connect the battery cables and connect a carbon pile tester to the battery terminals according to the tool manufacturer's instructions.

WARNING
*Excessive battery discharge rates will release explosive hydrogen gas from the battery electrolyte. Avoid **all** possible ignition sources from sparks to any open flame or severe injury or death could occur.*

4. Start and warm the engine to normal operating temperature then run the engine at the specified rpm while using the variable carbon pile tester to draw the battery down at a rate equivalent to the stator's full output while performing the following:

a. On 4- or 6-amp systems (found on non-regulated carbureted models), run the engine at approximately 3000 rpm and check the ammeter for full or nearly full 4- or 6-amp output.

b. On 12-amp systems (found on regulated carbureted models), run the engine at 5000 rpm and check the ammeter for full or nearly full 12-amp output.

c. On 17-amp systems (found on fuel injected models), run the engine at 700 rpm and check for approximately 10 amps output, then at 1200 rpm check for approximately 16 amps and finally, at about 5000 rpm, look for output to drop slightly to about 13 amps.

5. Slowly decrease the battery load toward zero amps while watching the ammeter. It should show slowly reduced amperage output. Check the battery voltage as the current draw decreases, voltage should stabilize at approximately 14.5 volts.

6. If test results vary and the stator has already passed a static ohmmeter check, and all other system wiring/connections are verified as proper, replace the regulator/rectifier.

IGNITION SYSTEM

This section provides a description of the various ignition systems and test instructions for the ignition system components.

Refer to the *Troubleshooting Preparation* in this chapter and **Table 3** at the end of the chapter before performing any test. Avoid unnecessary parts replacement and wasted effort by using systematic and logical troubleshooting procedures. Make sure to eliminate the possibility of a poor connection or damaged wiring before replacing an ignition component. Refer to the wiring diagrams at the end of the manual and confirm that the correct wire color/connections are used when performing tests.

Before starting ignition subsystem or component troubleshooting, determine if there is an ignition system fault by conducting a *Spark Test* as detailed in this chapter. If the spark test points to an ignition system fault, proceed with the various circuit and component tests given in this section, in the order they are given until the fault is found.

System Operation

5-15 hp models

The ignition system on 5-15 hp carbureted models is a solid state condenser discharge system (CDI). The ignition module/power pack CDI unit determines ignition timing based on engine speed, which makes it very efficient. For 9.9/15 hp (305 cc) models, the module (**Figure 61**) is mounted under the flywheel (at the front of the engine directly underneath the rope start handle). On 5/6 hp (128 cc) and 8/9.9 hp (211 cc) models, the power pack (**Figure 62**) is mounted at the front, starboard side of the engine. The timing (static and dynamic) is not adjustable. The system is very reliable and maintenance is limited to spark plug cleaning and replacement. In most cases prob-

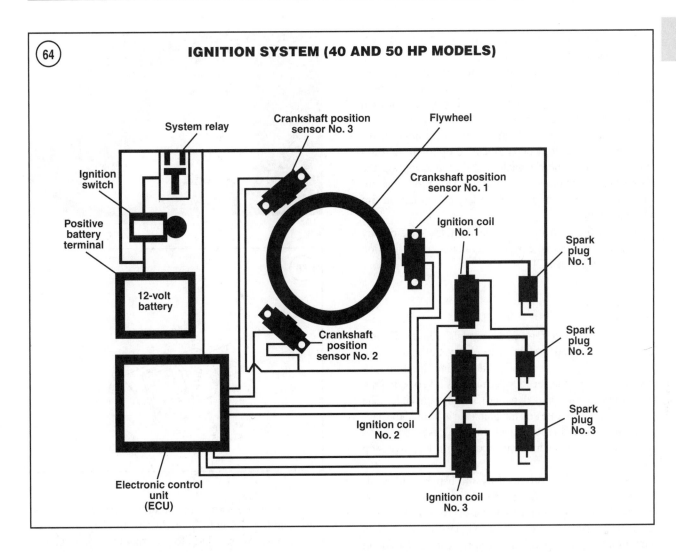

IGNITION SYSTEM (40 AND 50 HP MODELS)

64

lems are related to poor wire connections or a defective stop switch.

This system generates voltage using an ignition power coil and charge coil mounted under the flywheel on top of the power head. The charge coil supplies voltage to the ignition module, while the power coil supplies voltage to the speed limiting operating warning system (SLOW), the timing sensor on 9.9/15 hp (305 cc) models and other ignition functions. Both the ignition power and charge coils are part of the stator assembly, but can be replaced separately on 5/6 hp (128 cc) and 8/9.9 hp (211 cc) models. A separate timing sensor or pulser coil (**Figure 63**) is also used on these 5/6 hp (128 cc) and 8/9.9 hp (211 cc) models to provide a timing signal to the ignition module (power pack). The timing sensor on other models is integrated into the stator assembly and is not serviceable separately.

The ignition module/power pack serves multiple functions. It stores and distributes voltage generated by the charge coil and, in response to signals from the timing

sensor energizes the ignition coil primary circuit winding. The module has a built-in rpm limiter to protect the engine by preventing over-revving and also controls the SLOW system functions which protects the engine from low oil condition or, on remote models, engine overheating temperature operating conditions.

The stop switch or ignition switch turns off the ignition system by sending a ground signal to the ignition module/power pack.

40 and 50 hp models

The ignition system on 40 and 50 hp models (**Figure 64**) is a fully transistorized direct ignition system. The electronic control unit (ECU) (also known as an ECM) determines ignition timing based on engine speed, which makes it very efficient. The timing (static and dynamic) is not adjustable. The system is very reliable and maintenance is limited to spark plug cleaning and replacement.

In most cases, problems are related to poor wire connections or a defective stop circuit.

System current is provided by the battery and is directed to the ECU via the system relay and ignition switch. A crankshaft position sensor (**Figure 65**) for each cylinder signals the ECU as to engine speed and piston position based on when the raised flywheel boss passes the sensors. The ECU determines the optimum ignition timing by using these signals and then interrupting the current to the primary coil winding. This procedure induces a high voltage in the secondary coil circuit to fire the spark plugs.

When the ignition switch is turned off, the system relay is de-energized and no current is available to the ignition coil (**Figure 66**) or ECU.

70 hp models

The ignition system on 70 hp models (**Figure 67**) is a fully transistorized system. The electronic control unit (ECU) (also known as an ECM) determines ignition timing based on engine speed, which makes it very efficient. The timing (static and dynamic) is not adjustable. The system is very reliable and maintenance is limited to spark plug cleaning and replacement. In most cases, problems are related to poor wire connections or a defective stop circuit.

System current is provided by the battery and is directed to the ECU via the system relay and ignition switch. Two crankshaft position sensors (**Figure 65**) and a camshaft position sensor provide signals to the ECU to determine engine speed and piston position based on when the raised boss passes the sensors. The ECU determines the optimum ignition timing by using these signals and then interrupting the current to the primary coil winding. This induces a high voltage in the secondary coil circuit to fire the spark plugs.

This system has two ignition coils, one for cylinders 1 and 4, and one for cylinders 2 and 3. When an individual coil fires, it fires both spark plugs simultaneously, even though only one cylinder is at TDC.

When the ignition switch is turned off, the system relay is de-energized and no current is available to the ignition coil or ECU.

Stop Circuit Testing

This section provides test instructions for the stop circuit wiring to help determine if an ignition fault is due to the stop circuit and ignition or stop switch or if it concerns the ignition module and coil side of the circuit.

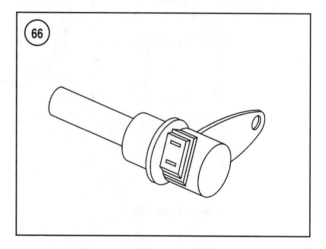

A malfunction in the stop circuit usually results in a no start condition. Refer to *Spark Test* in this chapter to determine if spark is present before testing the stop circuit. If the system produces a strong spark, it is unlikely that the stop circuit is defective. However, testing may discover that there is an intermittent fault. Perform the tests with the engine off.

5-15 hp tiller control models

1. If not already done to determine if there is an ignition fault, prepare the engine for a *Spark Test* as detailed in this chapter.
2. Disconnect the stop button wiring as follows:
    a. On 5/6 hp (128 cc) and 8/9.9 hp (211 cc) models, disconnect the single-pin *Amphenol* connector located between the stop switch and ignition module (black wire). The other wire from the stop switch is also black, but it ends at a ground terminal one of the lower mounting bolts of the ignition module.
    b. On 9.9/15 hp (305 cc) models, disconnect the three-pin *Amphenol* connector located between the

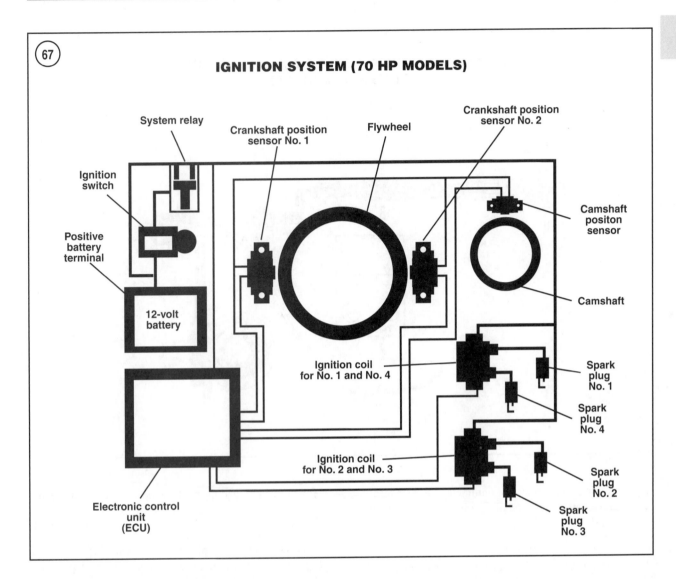

(67)

IGNITION SYSTEM (70 HP MODELS)

System relay

Ignition switch

Positive battery terminal

12-volt battery

Electronic control unit (ECU)

Crankshaft position sensor No. 1

Flywheel

Crankshaft position sensor No. 2

Camshaft positon sensor

Camshaft

Ignition coil for No. 1 and No. 4

Spark plug No. 1

Spark plug No. 4

Ignition coil for No. 2 and No. 3

Spark plug No. 2

Spark plug No. 3

stop switch and ignition module. (Terminal B and C are bridged on the other side of the connector. Wiring on the engine side of the connector runs to both the ignition module and the stop switch.)

3. Crank the engine and observe the spark tester as follows:

a. If spark jumps at all gaps, but did not in a preliminary test, the problem is the stop circuit.

b. On 5-6 hp models, if there is no spark, check the secondary ignition coil and the ignition power coil.

c. On 8-15 hp models, if there is no spark at one gap, test the secondary ignition coil for that spark plug. If there is no spark at both gaps, test the ignition power coil.

5-15 hp remote control models

Determine if there is an ignition system fault by conducting a *Spark Test* as detailed in this chapter. If the spark test reveals a problem with the ignition circuit, use the following procedure to eliminate/test the key switch. Refer to **Figure 68** during the following procedure:

NOTE
Do not run the engine while conducting the following test.

1. Disconnect the battery cables.
2. Trace the ignition module wiring from the module (located at the front of the engine, under the rope start handle) back to the first connector (a two-wire connector on the module side of the circuit and a wire connector on the key switch side of the circuit). Disconnect the ignition

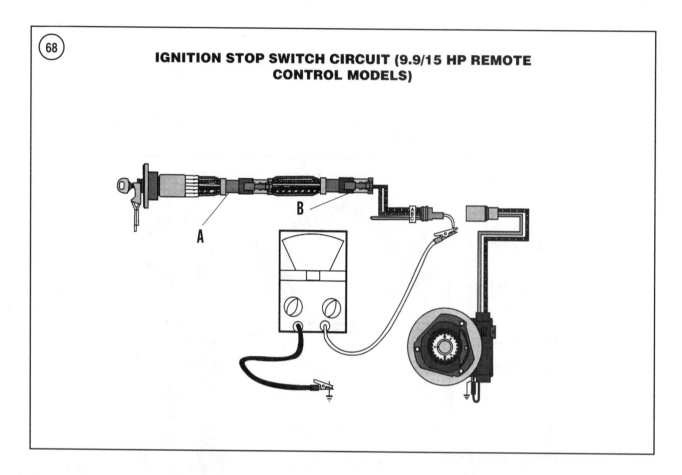

IGNITION STOP SWITCH CIRCUIT (9.9/15 HP REMOTE CONTROL MODELS)

module wiring and connect an ohmmeter between terminal B on the key switch side of the circuit and a good engine ground.

NOTE
Refer to the wiring diagrams at the end of this manual to confirm the position and color of the wire for terminal B of the ignition module connector, but on most models it should be the center terminal with the black/yellow wire to the key switch.

3. With the ohmmeter connected as described in Step 2, observe the reading in the key OFF and ON positions. The meter must show continuity (with 0 or low resistance) with the key OFF, but must show high or infinite resistance (no continuity) with the key ON. If resistance is low with the switch ON, proceed with Step 4.

4. If the key on resistance from Step 3 is low, disconnect the harness black/yellow wire from the key switch *M* terminal. Refer to Chapter Twelve, as necessary to disassemble the remote to access the switch and to *Ignition (Key) Switch Circuit Test* in the *Starting System* section of this chapter for more information on switch terminal locations. If the ohmmeter connection in Step 3 now shows a

high or infinite reading, replace the key switch. If the meter connection now shows a low resistance, proceed to Step 5.

5. Disconnect the six-pin connector at the key switch (A, **Figure 68**). If the meter connection from Step 3 now shows a high reading, repair or replace the key switch wiring harness between the switch and the connector. If the meter now reads a low resistance, proceed to Step 6.

6. Disconnect the 6-pin key switch connector at the engine (B, **Figure 68**) that contains the black/yellow wire. If the meter connection from Step 3 now shows a high reading, repair or replace the instrument/key switch wiring harness between the key switch connector and the engine connector. If the meter now shows a low resistance, repair or replace the engine harness.

7. Reconnect all wiring harnesses connections removed for testing, then connect the battery cables and check for proper ignition system and stop circuit operation.

8. If the engine fails to shut off when testing before or after repairs, test for an open in the black/yellow wire or black/white wire and/or for damaged key switch or faulty ignition module.

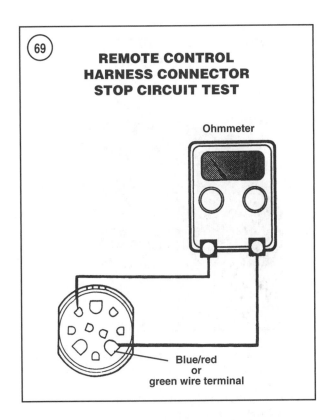

2

NOTE
The green wire connects to a blue/red engine harness wire.

4. Observe the meter reading. There should be continuity.

5. Observe the meter reading while placing the ignition switch in the ON position. There should be no continuity.

6. Observe the meter reading while placing the ignition switch in the START position. There should be no continuity. Return the switch to the ON position.

7. Observe the meter reading while activating the lanyard switch. Continuity should be present with the lanyard switch activated.

8. Check all wire connections, then test the ignition and lanyard switch if there is an incorrect test result. Test all other ignition system components if no spark is present yet the stop circuit tested correctly.

9. Connect the remote control wire harness to the engine wire harness, then install the spark plug leads. Route all wires and hoses carefully to prevent interference. Connect the negative battery cable.

Stop Switch Test (5-15 hp Tiller Control Models)

The stop switch/lanyard switch on 5-15 hp tiller control models is mounted either at the base of the tiller grip (**Figure 70**) or along the side of the tiller handle (**Figure 71**). The stop switch is a combination stop button and emergency stop device (lanyard switch).

With the clip and lanyard removed, the switch is in the *stop* position (the circuit is closed to ground).

With the clip and lanyard installed, the switch is in the *run* position (the circuit is open).

NOTE
Do not run the engine while conducting the following test.

1. Install the clip and lanyard.

2. Disconnect the stop button wiring as follows:

40-70 hp models

1. Disconnect the negative battery cable. Disconnect and ground the spark plug leads.

2. Disconnect the remote or tiller control wire harness connector from the engine wire harness.

3. Set the multimeter to the resistance scale. Connect the positive meter test lead to the green wire terminal of the remote or tiller control harness (**Figure 69**). Connect the negative meter test lead to the black wire terminal of the harness. Place the ignition switch in the OFF position.

a. On 5/6 hp (128 cc) and 8/9.9 hp (211 cc) models, disconnect the single-pin *Amphenol* connector located between the stop switch and ignition module (black wire). The other wire from the stop switch is also black, but it ends at a ground terminal on one of the lower mounting bolts of the ignition module.

b. On 9.9/15 hp (305 cc) models, disconnect the 3-pin *Amphenol* connector located between the stop switch and ignition module, and locate terminal C (black wire on the stop button side of the connector).

3. Set an ohmmeter to the resistance scale, and then connect the ohmmeter between the stop button side of the connector (terminal C on 9.9/15 hp models) and a good engine ground. The reading must show high or infinite resistance. This indicates the circuit is open.

4. Momentarily press inward on the stop button while watching the ohmmeter. The meter must show 0 or low resistance when the button is depressed, closing the circuit to ground.

5. Remove the safety lanyard and check the meter. The meter must show 0 or low resistance once the lanyard is removed, closing the circuit to ground.

6. Replace the switch for safety if test results vary.

7. Reconnect the switch wiring when repairs and/or tests are completed.

Ignition/Key Switch Test

Refer to *Starting System* in this chapter for ignition key switch test instructions.

System Relay Test (40-70 hp Models)

The system relay supplies electrical current to the ignition coils and fuel injection system. A fault with the system relay generally prevents the engine from starting. Intermittent faults usually cause engine stalling after running the engine for a few minutes. Typically the engine will not restart unless the ignition is switched off long enough to allow the relay to cool.

The system relay is mounted on the upper starboard side of the power head near the engine control module. Removal of the electrical component cover is required to access the relay.

A multimeter, fully charged battery and jumper leads are required for this test.

1. Refer to **Figure 72** for terminal identification:
   a. **B+** – 12 volt positive solenoid, white wire.
   b. **B-** – 12 volt negative ECU (ground), pink/black wire.

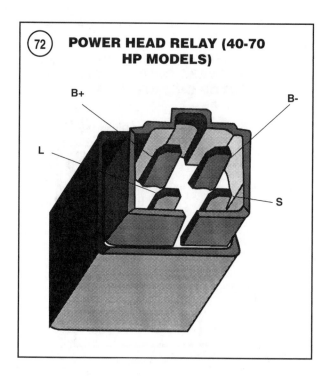

POWER HEAD RELAY (40-70 HP MODELS)

c. **L** – Load, 12 volt, large gray wire.

d. **S** – Key switch, small gray wire.

2. Disconnect the negative battery cable.

3. Carefully pull the relay away from the power head. Disconnect the relay from the engine wire harness and place it on a clean work surface with the connector retainer facing up as indicated in (**Figure 72**).

4. Set the multimeter to the resistance scale. Connect the positive meter test lead to the B+ relay terminal. Connect the negative meter test lead to the L relay. Observe the meter reading. There should be no continuity.

5. Connect the ohmmeter leads to the B- and S terminals. The meter must show 80-120 ohms resistance.

6. Using an appropriate jumper lead, connect the relay terminal S to the positive terminal of a fully charged 12-volt battery. Connect another jumper lead to the negative terminal of the battery.

7. With the meter connected across B+ and L, touch the other jumper (the one connected to the negative terminal of the battery) to relay terminal B-. Observe the meter reading while touching the jumper lead to relay terminal B-. Continuity should be noted across B+ and L with power applied to B- and S. Test the wire harness capacitor as described in this section if the EFI components fail to switch on yet the relay tests correctly.

8. Replace the system relay if a test result is incorrect.

9. Clean the terminals, then carefully plug the relay to the engine wire harness connector. Secure the relay to the mounting location behind the electrical components

cover. Route all wires to prevent interference. Install the electrical component cover.

10. Connect the negative battery cable.

Wire Harness Capacitor Test (40-70 hp Models)

The wire harness capacitor reduces electrical interference from the system relay. A fault with this component generally prevents the relay from switching on. Perform a spark test as described in this chapter. The system relay and capacitor are operating correctly if spark is present on any of the spark plug leads. The manufacturer does not provide test instructions for the capacitor. An internally shorted capacitor allows current from the ignition circuit to flow to ground instead of activating the system relay. A shorted capacitor is easily detected with a multimeter. A meter with capacitor testing capability is required to test the capacitance. Test the relay as follows:

1. Disconnect the negative battery cable. Remove and ground the spark plug leads.

2. Disconnect the remote control or tiller control harness from the engine wire harness. Remove the system relay from the engine wire harness as described in this chapter (see *System Relay Test*).

3. Locate the diagnostic connector (**Figure 73**) at the lower starboard side of the power head. Remove the cover from the connector.

4. Set the multimeter to the resistance scale. Connect the positive meter test lead to the gray wire terminal within the connector. Connect the negative meter test lead to an engine ground.

5. Observe the meter readings. There should be no continuity. Replace the engine wire harness if continuity is noted.

6. Test the capacitance of the capacitor as follows:

    a. Connect the test leads of a meter capable of testing capacitors as noted in Step 4.

    b. Note the meter reading. The capacitance should be approximately 470 microfarad.

    c. Replace the engine wire harness if there is a significant variation in capacitance. In almost all cases the capacitor fails Step 5 if incorrect capacitance is indicated.

7. Install the cover onto the diagnostic connector. Install the system relay. Connect the spark plug leads and the negative battery cable.

Power Coil Test (5-15 hp Models)

A fault with the power coil generally prevents the engine from starting. An intermittent short of the pulser coil winding can cause hard starting and/or an ignition misfire. Removing the power coil is not required for testing. Testing can occur using various steps of the following procedure. The dynamic tests in Step 2 and Step 3 are the most reliable, since they indicate voltage under use, as opposed to the static resistance tests found in Step 4 and Step 5 using an ohmmeter. But, the dynamic tests require a digital multimeter capable of reading/displaying peak voltage values. If one is not available, proceed with Step 4 and Step 5, making sure to eliminate all other possible causes of system problems before replacing the coil based only on a slightly out of specification resistance check. Also, keep in mind that resistance readings for this component vary with temperature. To ensure accurate results, test the coil at 68° F (20° C).

1. Trace the ignition power coil wires from beneath the flywheel to the connections between the stator and the ignition module/power pack:

    a. On 5/6 hp (128 cc) and 8/9.9 hp (211 cc) models, disconnect the orange wire bullet connectors between the stator and power pack.

    b. On 9.9/15 hp (305 cc) models, disconnect the four-pin Packard connector between the stator and ignition module (it contains two orange stator leads).

2. To check for a grounded power coil, set a peak-reading multimeter to indicate a max positive voltage value (a range of 500 volts should be sufficient), then connect the black meter lead to a good engine ground and the red lead to one of the orange stator wires. Crank the engine and observe the reading. Repeat this step with the other orange wire. A reading (of any value) at each of the orange wires indicates that the power coil is grounded. Either locate and repair the ground or replace the power coil or stator assembly, as applicable.

3. If there is no reading in Step 2 check the peak output during cranking. Attach the black lead from the meter to one orange stator wire and the red meter lead to the other.

Crank the engine and again observe the peak voltage as compared with the power coil cranking voltage in **Table 9**:

   a. If the peak cranking voltage is at or above the specification, test the charge coil if problems are still suspected.

   b. If the peak cranking voltage is below the specification, check the condition of the wiring and connectors. If the wiring and connectors are good, proceed with Step 4.

4. Check the power coil condition using an ohmmeter. With the negative battery cable disconnected for safety (and to protect the meter), take a power coil resistance reading by setting the multimeter to the resistance scale and connecting the meter probes across the two orange stator leads. Compare the reading with the specification in **Table 9**. If readings are out of range (with the ambient temperature at or near specification), replace the stator assembly or power coil, as applicable.

5. Check the power coil for a grounded condition using an ohmmeter. Repeat Step 1, but without cranking the engine and with the multimeter set to the resistance scale. Any reading other than very high or infinite resistance across either of the orange wires and a good engine ground indicates the power coil or wires are grounded. Repair or replace, as necessary.

6. Reconnect the wiring and the negative battery cable when repairs and/or tests are completed.

Ignition Charge Coil Test (5-15 hp Models)

A fault with the ignition charge coil generally prevents the engine from starting. A partial short of the coil winding can cause hard starting and/or an ignition misfire. Removing the ignition charge coil is not required for testing. Testing can occur using various steps of the following procedure. The dynamic tests in Step 2 and Step 3 are the most reliable, since they indicate voltage under use, as opposed to the static resistance tests found in Step 4 and Step 5 using an ohmmeter. But, the dynamic tests require a digital multimeter capable of reading/displaying peak voltage values. If one is not available, proceed with Step 4 and Step 5, making sure to eliminate all other possible causes of system problems before replacing the coil based only on a slightly out of specification resistance check. Also, keep in mind that resistance readings for this component vary with temperature. To ensure accurate results, test the coil at 68° F (20° C).

1. Trace the ignition charge coil wires from beneath the flywheel to the connections between the stator and the ignition module/power pack:

   a. On 5/6 hp (128 cc) and 8/9.9 hp (211 cc) models, disconnect the two brown wire bullet connectors between the stator and power pack.

   b. On 9.9/15 hp (305 cc) models, disconnect the four-pin Packard connector between the stator and ignition module (it contains two brown stator leads).

2. To check for a grounded charge coil, set a peak-reading multimeter to indicate a max positive voltage value (a range of 500 volts should be sufficient), then connect the black meter lead to a good engine ground and the red lead to one of the brown stator wires. Crank the engine and observe the reading. Repeat this step with the other brown stator wire. A reading (of any value) at each of the brown wires indicates that the charge coil is grounded. Either locate and repair the ground or replace the charge coil or stator assembly, as applicable.

3. If there is no reading in Step 2 check the peak output during cranking. Attach the black lead from the meter to one brown stator wire and the red meter lead to the other wire. Crank the engine and again observe the peak voltage as compared with the charge coil cranking voltage in **Table 9**:

   a. If the peak cranking voltage is at or above the specification, test the ignition module/power pack if problems are still suspected.

   b. If the peak cranking voltage is below the specification, check the condition of the wiring and connectors. If the wiring and connectors are good, proceed with Step 4.

4. Check the charge coil condition using an ohmmeter. With the negative battery cable disconnected for safety (and to protect the meter), take a charge coil resistance reading by setting the multimeter to the resistance scale and connecting the meter probes across the two brown stator wires. Compare the reading with the specification in **Table 9**. Replace the stator assembly or charge coil, as applicable, if readings are out of range (with the ambient temperature at or near specification).

5. Check the charge coil for a grounded condition using an ohmmeter. Repeat Step 1, but without cranking the engine and with the meter set to the resistance scale. Any reading other than very high or infinite resistance across either of the brown wires and a good engine ground indicates the charge coil or wires are grounded. Repair or replace, as necessary.

6. Reconnect the wiring and the negative battery cable when repairs and/or tests are completed.

Timing Sensor (5/6 hp and 8/9.9 hp Models)

The 5/6 hp (128 cc) and 8/9.9 hp (211 cc) models use a timing sensor (also known as a pulser coil) to signal the ignition module/power pack for proper ignition timing. The timing sensor (**Figure 63**) is located on the top of the power head, just in front of the flywheel. Testing can occur dynamically, with a peak-reading voltmeter, or statically with an ohmmeter, but the dynamic tests are preferred, when possible. If a peak-reading voltmeter is not available, proceed with Step 4 and Step 5, making sure to eliminate all other possible causes of system problems before replacing the coil based only on a slightly out of specification resistance check. Also, keep in mind that resistance readings for this component vary with temperature. To ensure accurate results, test the coil at 68° F (20° C).

1. Trace the sensor wiring as necessary to disconnect the black wire between the starter mount plate and the sensor, as well as the white/black wire bullet connector.

2. To check for a grounded timing sensor, set a peak-reading multimeter to indicate a max negative voltage value (a low-voltage range of 5 volts is necessary). Connect the negative meter lead to a good engine ground and the positive lead to the sensor end of the white/black bullet connector. Crank the engine and observe the reading. A reading of any value indicates that the charge coil is grounded. Either locate and repair the ground or replace the timing sensor assembly, as applicable.

3. If there is no reading in Step 2, check the timing sensor output during engine cranking. Reconnect the black sensor wire to the starter mount plate, then attach the black lead from the meter to the black sensor wire connection. Connect the meter positive lead to the sensor end of the white/black bullet connector. Crank the engine and observe the peak voltage:

    a. If the peak cranking voltage is 0.2 volt or higher test the ignition module/power pack.

    b. If the peak cranking voltage is below 0.2 volt, check the condition of the wiring and connectors. If the wiring and connectors are good, proceed with Step 4.

4. Check the timing sensor condition using an ohmmeter. With the negative battery cable disconnected for safety (and to protect the meter), take a timing sensor coil resistance reading. Set the multimeter to the resistance scale, then connect the negative meter probe to the black sensor wire and the positive meter probe to the sensor end of the white/black bullet connector. Compare the reading with the timing sensor specification in **Table 10**. Replace the timing sensor if readings are out of range.

5. Check the sensor coil for a grounded condition using an ohmmeter. Disconnect the negative sensor wire from the starter mounting plate, then connect the negative lead of the ohmmeter to a good engine ground and the positive meter lead to the sensor end of the white/black bullet connector. Any reading other than very high or infinite resistance indicates the timing sensor coil or are grounded. Repair or replace, as necessary.

6. Reconnect the wiring and the negative battery cable when repairs and/or tests are completed.

Ignition Module Test
(5-15 hp Models)

The ignition module or power pack used on carbureted engines is a solid state component, no static resistance (ohmmeter) tests are available for diagnostics. A peak-reading voltmeter must be used with the engine cranking or running.

During the dynamic engine cranking output portion of this test, use a load adapter, such as the Stevens load adapter (part No. PL-88). If this tool is not available, make an adapter using a 10-ohm, 10-watt resistor.

During the dynamic engine running output portion of this test, a terminal extender must be installed on the primary side of the ignition coil allowing the circuit to be completed while operating. If the terminal extender is not available, use an old primary side ignition wire (installed between the module and coil) instead. Cut a small section of the insulation away from the old wire. Be careful not to nick or break any strands of the wire beneath the insulation (which would increase resistance in the circuit if sufficient amounts were damaged). The voltmeter probe could then be clipped onto or carefully pressed against the exposed portion of the wire.

1. For safety and preventing accidental starting during the cranking test in Step 2, twist and remove all secondary ignition lead(s) from the spark plug(s), then connect them (it) to a good engine ground.

2. To perform an ignition module/power pack output test, proceed as follows:

    a. Disconnect the small primary wire between the ignition module and the primary terminal on the ignition coil. Connect one end of the load adapter to the primary wire. If using the Stevens load adapter, connect the red lead to the primary wire. Connect the other end of the load adapter or resistor to a good engine ground.

    b. Set a peak-reading voltmeter to the positive voltage scale with a range up to 500 volts, then connect the positive meter lead to the primary wire (alongside

the load adapter) and the negative lead to a good engine ground.

c. Crank the engine while observing the voltmeter. It
should be equal to or greater than the ignition module cranking voltage listed in **Table 10**. If the primary wire has proper output, but there is a spark
problem, test the ignition coil as directed in this
chapter. If the primary wire shows no or insufficient
output and all other components in the ignition system have tested good up to this point, replace the ignition module.

3. To perform an ignition module running output test,
proceed as follows:

a. If Step 1 and Step 2 were followed, reconnect the
spark plug secondary wire(s) from the ignition coil
to the plug(s).

b. Install a terminal extender, or an equivalent, between the ignition module primary wire and the ignition coil. Check that no wires or testing
equipment will interfere with moving engine components.

c. Set a peak-reading voltmeter to the positive voltage
scale with a range up to 500 volts, then connect the
positive meter lead to the terminal extender (or the
exposed portion of the extra module primary wire)
and the black lead to a good engine ground.

d. Start the engine and allow it to run under load in a
test tank at the rpm where the problem was noted.
Observe the voltmeter, it should be equal to or
greater than the ignition module running voltage
listed in **Table 10**. If the primary wire has proper
output, but there is a spark problem, test the ignition
coil as directed in this section. If the primary wire
shows insufficient output, check the charge coil as
directed in this section. If the wire shows no output,
double-check the connections and retry. If the test
still shows no output, repeat Step 2.

4. After completing the tests in Step 2 or Step 3, make
sure to remove the load adapter or terminal extender. If
Step 3 was not performed, reconnect the spark plug leads.
Reconnect the primary wire from the ignition module to
the ignition coil.

Crankshaft Position (CKP) Sensor Test
(40-70 hp Models)

The crankshaft position sensor (**Figure 74**) is mounted
to the top of the power head and next to the flywheel. Two
crankshaft position sensors are used on 70 hp models,
while three crankshaft position sensors are used on 40 and
50 hp models.

If there is a problem with the crankshaft position sensor
the symptoms will vary depending on the model.

On 40 and 50 hp models a fault with sensor No. 1, 2 or 3
results in no spark at the corresponding cylinder. A fault
with more than one sensor results in no spark to all three
cylinders.

On 70 hp models a fault with one sensor causes the engine control unit (ECU) to rely on the signal from the
other sensor. Normal operation continues. A fault with
both sensors causes no spark to all cylinders.

Removing the crankshaft position sensor is not required
for testing. Resistance readings for this component vary
with temperature. To ensure accurate results, test the coil
at 20° C (68° F).

1. For safety and protecting the test equipment, disconnect the negative battery cable.

2. Locate and unplug the appropriate ECU connectors
and corresponding terminals in order to connect an ohmmeter to conduct a resistance check, as follows:

a. For 40 and 50 hp models, refer to **Table 13** to determine the proper connector numbers, terminal numbers, wire colors and resistance specifications.

NOTE
Connector views and pinouts can be found
*for these motors under **Electronic Engine***
Component Testing Through the ECU
Harness** in the **Electronic Fuel Injection
section of this chapter.

b. Disconnect the small four-wire connector *E* from
the end of the ECU. Identify terminals No. 1 (black
wire) and No. 4 (red/blue wire) for the port side
CKP sensor or terminals No. 1 (black wire) and No.
3 (white/black wire) for the starboard sensor.

3. Set the multimeter to the resistance scale.

4. Connect the meter test leads to the sensor wire terminals indicated in Step 2. Record the meter reading.

5. Compare the meter readings with the specification
provided in **Table 13** for 40 and 50 hp models or in **Table
11** for 70 hp models. Replace the crankshaft position sensors as described in Chapter Six if the reading is incorrect.

6. Connect the wiring harness and route the wires to
avoid interference.

7. Connect the negative battery cable.

Camshaft Position (CMP) Sensor Test (40-70 hp Models)

A fault with the camshaft position sensor causes the engine control unit (ECU) to base fuel and ignition timing
on the crankshaft position sensors. If this problem occurs
the engine will run normally but the ECU will display EFI
failure code No. 24.

Sensor mounting location varies.

On 40 and 50 hp models the sensor is mounted at the upper rear of the valve cover near the No. 1 coil.

On 70 hp models the sensor is mounted on top of the
cylinder head next to the camshaft pulley. The sensor
wires pass under the starboard side of the timing belt.

Removing the camshaft position sensor is not required
for testing. Resistance readings for this component vary
with temperature. To ensure accurate results, test the coil
at 20° C (68° F).

1. Disconnect the negative battery cable for safety and
protecting the testing equipment.

2. Trace the camshaft position sensor wires from either
sensor to the sensor connector (40-50 hp models) or to the
four-pin connector at the ECU. (Refer to the wiring diagrams at the back of this manual.) Carefully disconnect
the sensor harness from the sensor or the ECU, as applicable.

NOTE
*On 70 hp models, the sensor is wired to the
ECU E connector (the four-pin connector
found at one end of the ECU). For these
models, check terminals No. 1 (black wire)
and No. 2 (orange/green wire). Connector
views and pinouts can be found under **Electronic Engine Component Testing
Through the ECU Harness** in the **Electronic Fuel Injection** section of this chapter.*

3. Set the multimeter to the resistance scale.

4. Connect the meter test leads to the sensor wire terminals or the ECU terminals for the sensor and record the
meter reading.

5. Compare the meter readings with the specification
provided in **Table 11**. Replace the camshaft position sensor as described in Chapter Six if the reading is incorrect.

6. Connect the sensor wire harness to the engine control
module. Route the wires to avoid interference.

7. Connect the spark plug leads and the negative battery
cable.

Ignition Coil Tests

A fault with the ignition coil generally causes no spark
at the affected cylinder. A partial short within the coil can
cause an ignition misfire. Generally this type of fault occurs at higher engine speeds. A common cause of ignition
coil failure is due to an internal short. Internal shorts cause
arcing within the coil housing that prevents a strong blue
spark at the plug. A clicking noise emanating from the coil
is common with this type of failure. Resistance testing
may not detect this type of internal short. Replace the coil
if a clicking noise is detected along with other symptoms
of ignition trouble.

This section provides resistance test instructions for the
primary and secondary winding. Test both coil windings if
the coil is suspect. Resistance testing requires an accurate,
high-quality multimeter. Because of the low resistance
readings, use a digital multimeter if testing the primary
coil winding. Although a digital meter is still preferred
when testing the secondary winding, a quality analog meter will usually perform sufficiently.

Removing of the ignition coil is not required for testing
providing the coil wire connectors are accessible. For 40
and 50 hp models, the primary and secondary coil circuits
may be tested through the appropriate terminals of the
ECU wiring harness. For more details on this type of testing refer to *Electronic Engine Component Testing
Through the ECU Harness* in the *Electronic Fuel Injection* section of this chapter. Also, refer to **Table 13** for
connectors, terminals, wire colors and resistance specifications on 40 and 50 hp models.

Ignition coil removal and installation instructions are
provided in Chapter Seven.

The number of coils and mounting locations vary by
model.

The 5-15 hp models are equipped with a single coil
(**Figure 75**) located on the rear, starboard side of the
power head.

The 40 and 50 hp models are equipped with three coils
integrated into the spark plug cap. This design eliminates
the spark plug lead.

The 70 hp model is equipped with two coils. Each coil
fires two cylinders.

Primary coil winding test

1. Disconnect the negative battery cable (if so equipped) for safety and protecting the test equipment. Note the routing and connection points, then disconnect the ignition coil wires (if so equipped).

2. Set the meter to the resistance scale.

3. For 5-15 hp models, test the primary side of the coil as follows:

    a. Connect the negative meter test lead to a good ground tab on the coil and the positive lead to the primary terminal (the small terminal where the ignition module wire attaches).

    b. Compare the result to the ignition coil primary resistance specification in **Table 10**.

    c. Leave the negative meter lead connected to the ground tab, then connect the positive lead to a/the coil secondary spark plug tower. Resistance should be very high or infinite. For 8-15 hp motors, repeat this test with the other coil secondary tower. Again, resistance should be very high or infinite.

4. For 40 and 50 hp models touch the positive meter test lead to the ignition coil terminals of the ECU connector *A* that connects to the orange, blue or green engine harness wires. Touch the negative meter test lead to the coil terminals of ECU connector *B* that connects to the gray engine harness wires. Make sure the leads touch the ignition coil terminals and not the wire harness terminals. Refer to **Table 13** for more information on terminal pin numbers. Compare the readings to the specifications in **Table 13**.

5. For 70 hp models the test can either be conducted through the ECU wiring harness or at the coil connector terminals.

    a. To test through the ECU harness, refer to the wiring diagrams at the back of the manual. Touch the positive meter test lead to ECU harness terminal that connects to the orange or blue engine harness wires. Touch the negative meter test lead to the harness terminal that connects to the gray engine harness wire.

    b. To test directly at the coil, connect the meter leads directly to the two coil terminals that connect to the blue/gray or orange/gray wire engine harnesses.

    c. In either case, compare the results with the primary circuit specifications in **Table 11**.

6. If tests are out of specification, verify that the proper connectors and wires were checked. Unless testing directly at the coil, trace the wires and verify that there are no damaged sections of wire or loose, corroded or damaged terminals. Replace the ignition coil(s) as described in Chapter Seven if no other causes of an incorrect reading are found.

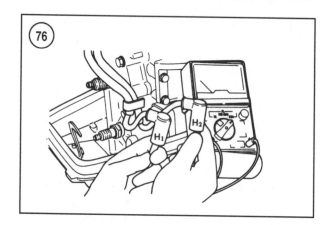

7. Connect the wire harness to the ECU, ignition coil wires or terminals, as applicable. Route the wires to avoid interference.

8. Connect the negative battery cable (if so equipped).

Secondary coil winding test

Accurate testing requires removing the spark plug leads on carbureted models. On 40 and 50 hp fuel injected models there are no leads. 70 hp model specifications include lead resistance.

1. Disconnect the negative battery cable (if so equipped) for safety and protecting the test equipment. Note the routing and connection points, then disconnect all ignition coil wires (except for the leads on 70 hp motors).

2. Set the meter to the appropriate resistance scale.

3. Connect the meter test leads to the coil as indicated:

    a. On 5/6 hp models, connect the positive meter test lead to the spark plug lead terminal on the ignition coil and the negative meter lead to the small ignition module primary coil terminal. Compare the results with the ignition coil secondary resistance specification in **Table 10**.

b. On 8-15 hp models, connect the positive meter test lead to one of the spark plug lead terminals on the ignition coil and the negative meter lead to the other spark plug lead terminal. Compare the results with the ignition coil secondary resistance specification in **Table 10**.

c. On 40 and 50 hp models touch the positive meter test lead to the ignition coil terminal that connects to the gray engine harness wire. Touch the negative meter test lead to the coil terminal that connects to the spark plug. This can be done through the appropriate ECU harness connector if the coil is still connected to the wiring, or directly at the coil if the coil is completely removed from the engine. Compare the results with the secondary circuit specifications in **Table 11** or **Table 13**.

d. On 70 hp models connect the positive meter test lead to the contact within the spark plug cap (**Figure 76**). Connect the negative meter test lead to the contact within the other spark plug cap for the same coil. Compare the readings with the specification in **Table 11**.

4. Replace the ignition coil(s) as described in Chapter Seven if the reading is incorrect.

5. Install the coil and/or reconnect the wiring, as applicable. Route the wires to avoid interference.

6. If equipped, connect the negative battery cable.

Spark Plug Leads (5-15 and 70 hp Models)

All engines except the 40 and 50 hp models (that use individual coils mounted on top of each spark plug) use a spark plug lead to connect the secondary ignition side of the coil to the spark plug. These spark plug high tension leads wear with age and may cause excessively high resistance in the secondary ignition circuit over time. A quick check of a lead is possible by removing the lead from the spark plug and the ignition coil, and then connecting ohm-

meter test probes to either end of the lead and noting the resistance specification. For 5-15 hp models, the reading should be very low, near zero. For 70 hp models, compare the reading with the specification for the high tension leads in **Table 11**.

Even if leads test within specification for resistance, it does not mean that the insulation is not cracked or perforated, allowing misfiring under load or when wet. If in doubt, the engine can be run in a test tank, while spraying a light coating of water from a spray bottle onto the leads and listening for engine stumble.

Electronic Control Unit (ECU) Test (40-70 hp Models)

All fuel injected models covered by this manual use an ECU. It controls the operation of the ignition and electronic fuel injection systems. A faulty ECU can cause a failure to start, irregular idle, ignition misfire or incorrect speed limiting. A faulty ECU can cause a malfunction of the electronic fuel injection system as well. Refer to *Electronic Fuel Injection* in this chapter if an ECU fault is suspected.

Because the ECU is a solid state component, testing the ECU involves a process of elimination rather than a direct testing procedure. Test all other components of the ignition system as described in this chapter, then replace the ECU *only* if an ignition misfire is verified and faulty wiring, connectors or ignition system components are ruled out. Faulty wires or connectors cause far more ignition problems than a fault with the ECU.

In some instances a faulty ECU causes incorrect operation of the warning system. Refer to *Warning System* in this chapter for additional information. Replace the ECU if all warning system components test correctly yet incorrect warning system operation persists.

Flywheel

A faulty flywheel can cause a constant or intermittent ignition misfire. In some rare instances a faulty flywheel causes erratic ignition timing. This problem occurs because of a buildup of grease or other contaminants on the flywheel magnets. A cracked or damaged flywheel magnet (**Figure 77**) can cause similar symptoms.

Remove and inspect the flywheel as described in Chapter Eight if an ignition misfire occurs and other causes are ruled out. Weak flywheel magnets can cause inadequate current to operate the ignition system components. Touch the tip of a screwdriver to the inner and outer flywheel magnets. Always compare inner flywheel magnets with other inner magnets. Compare outer magnets to other outer magnets. Replace the flywheel if there is a weak flywheel magnet.

Clean debris or contaminants from the flywheel using a mild solvent. Using strong solvents can damage the adhesive that bonds the magnets to the flywheel. Make sure all metallic debris is removed.

WARNING SYSTEMS

CAUTION
Avoid operating the engine if the warning system activates. Continued operation can lead to serious engine damage.

The warning system provides a means to alert the operator in the event of overheating (remote models), low oil pressure, and on fuel injected engines, of excessive engine speed or a fault with the fuel injection system. Circuits within the *System Check* monitor the gauge (carbureted models) or the ECU (fuel injected models) and switch on warning lights or a buzzer if a fault is detected. Additional circuits then initiate an ignition misfire or reduced timing to limit engine speed. This section provides a brief description of the systems followed by component test instructions.

System Operation

Warning system components and mode of operation varies by model. Use the wire diagrams at the back of the manual to assist with component and wire color identification. Refer to the following sections for the various models.

5-15 hp models

These models are equipped with a water pump indicator stream (**Figure 78**, typical) and an oil pressure warning system. Remote control models are also equipped with a cylinder head mounted temperature switch.

Always make sure that a strong stream of water exits the fitting at the lower rear area of the engine cover while operating the engine. Thoroughly inspect the cooling system if the water stream is weak or absent. Check the stream more frequently if the engine is operated in sand or debris-laden water.

The oil pressure warning system consists of the oil pressure switch (**Figure 79**), warning light (remote models) and warning horn. The oil pressure switch controls the operation of the warning buzzer and light by providing a ground circuit. When the ignition switch is turned on, bat-

tery voltage is applied to the buzzer and the circuit is completed through the closed oil pressure switch. The buzzer should sound to verify that the system is operational. When the engine is started and if oil pressure is sufficient to open the switch, the circuit is open and the buzzer ceases.

If the ignition module detects low oil pressure, it reduces the ignition timing to limit engine speed to 2000 rpm and initiates an ignition misfire. Normal operation resumes after switching the engine off and correcting the cause of the oil pressure warning. The CDI unit also initiates an ignition misfire if the engine speed exceeds a predetermined limit to prevent potential power head damage. Normal operation resumes when the engine speed falls once again into an acceptable operating range.

If the oil pressure warning light and/or buzzer comes on, stop the engine immediately and check the oil level as described in Chapter Three. Check the oil pressure as described in this chapter if the oil level is correct and the warning continues. Test all components of the warning system if the oil pressure is correct and the warning persists.

Some models are also equipped with a temperature switch mounted in the cylinder head. The switch functions in much the same way as the oil pressure switch. If

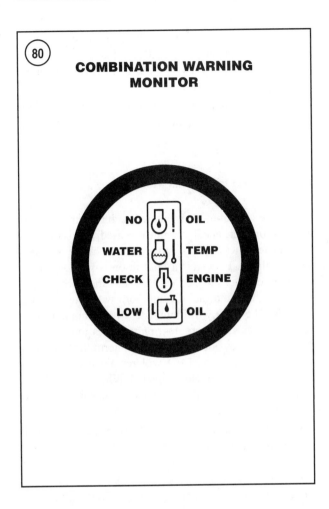

80

COMBINATION WARNING MONITOR

NO · OIL

WATER · TEMP

CHECK · ENGINE

LOW · OIL

during engine operation the switch temperature exceeds approximately 240° F (116° C), the switch will close the circuit activating the warning system.

40-70 hp models

These models are equipped with a low oil pressure, engine overheat and overspeed warning system. When a warning is detected by the oil pressure switch, engine temperature sensor or exhaust manifold temperature sensor, the electronic control unit (ECU) illuminates the combination warning monitor (**Figure 80**) or combination tachometer/warning monitor and sounds the warning buzzer.

The warning buzzer is normally located within the remote control, tiller control housing or behind the dash. The warning buzzer is activated by the ECU providing a ground circuit. When the ignition switch is turned on, battery voltage is applied to the buzzer and if the circuit is completed through the ECU, the buzzer sounds.

The oil pressure warning system consists of the oil pressure switch, a oil warning light (**Figure 80**), buzzer and the ECU. The oil pressure switch closes and sends a ground signal to the ECU if the pressure falls below approximately 10-19 psi (70-130 kPa). If low oil pressure is detected, the ECU illuminates the oil light and sounds the warning buzzer in an on-off tone.

The overheat warning system consists of an engine temperature sensor and exhaust manifold temperature sensor. An overheat warning occurs if the ECU detects excessive temperature from either sensor. On 40 and 50 hp models this occurs at 250° F (121° C) or higher. On 70 hp models this occurs at 234° F (111° C) or higher. If there is overheating the ECU illuminates the *water temp* light (**Figure 80**) and sounds the warning buzzer.

The ECU can also initiate an overheat warning if it detects a rapid temperature increase after starting a cold engine or excessive engine speed before the engine reaches normal operating temperature. Allow the engine to reach normal operating temperature before operating at higher speeds.

In addition to activating the *oil* and *temp* lights, the ECU limits engine speed to 3000 rpm by intermittently switching off the fuel injectors. If the warning system is activated by low oil pressure, normal operation resumes after switching the engine off and correcting the cause of low oil pressure. If the warning is due to overheating, the temperature must drop below the activation temperatures.

If the *oil* or *temp* warning indicators are activated, stop the engine immediately and check the oil level as described in Chapter Three. Start the engine and check the water indicator stream (**Figure 78**) at the back of the lower engine cover. Thoroughly inspect the cooling system if the stream is weak or absent. Check the oil pressure as described in this chapter if the oil level is correct and a strong water stream is present. Test all components of the warning system if the oil pressure is correct and the cooling system is functioning.

If a check engine warning occurs, check the battery condition as described in Chapter Seven. If the battery tests correctly, the ECU may have detected a fault within the electronic engine control system (and stored a diagnostic trouble code). Refer to the diagnostic information on the fuel injection system in this chapter.

Check Gauge Self-Test Mode

The self-test function activates each time the key is turned to the on or run position. The electronics in the gauge or the ECU sound the warning horn for 1/2 second and illuminate all four gauge LEDs, then turn off each LED in sequence. Each self-test makes sure the warning

2

horn and all LEDs are functioning, and the electronic control circuits in the gauge or ECU are operating correctly.

NOTE
If the battery voltage at the gauge drops below 7 volts, the gauge may re-enter self-test mode.

If the gauge does not self-test correctly, proceed as follows:

1. *LED(s) does not illuminate*—If one, two or three of the LEDs do not illuminate, the gauge or ECU may be at fault and, if so, must be replaced (but check the circuits for those gauges first just to make sure). If all four LEDs do not illuminate, proceed as follows:

   a. Test the purple wire at the gauge eight-pin connector for battery voltage with the ignition switch in the ON or RUN position. (Use a voltmeter with the positive lead attached to the terminal for the purple wire and the negative lead connected to the terminal for the black wire). Repair or replace the purple wire, 20 amp fuse and/or ignition key switch as necessary.

   b. Test the black wire at the gauge's eight-pin connector for continuity back to the negative battery terminal. Repair or replace the black wire as necessary.

   c. If the purple wire indicates battery voltage and the black wire indicates continuity, replace the system check gauge.

2. *Warning horn does not sound for 1/2 second*—If the LEDs also do not illuminate, go back and complete Step 1 before proceeding. If the LEDs illuminate, but the horn does not sound, proceed as follows:

   a. If a known good horn is available, substitute it. If the replacement horn sounds, the problem is the horn. If a known good horn is not available, proceed with substep b.

   b. Disconnect the eight-pin connector at the system check gauge. Turn the ignition switch to the ON or RUN position. Using a suitable jumper lead, ground the connector tan/blue wire to the black lead. If the warning horn sounds, replace the system check gauge. If the warning horn does not sound, leave the gauge disconnected and proceed.

   c. Disconnect the warning horn from its two-pin connector. Test the tan/blue wire for continuity between the warning horn (two-pin) and gauge (eight-pin) connectors. If continuity is not noted, repair or replace the tan/blue wire (and/or connectors) as necessary. When finished, reconnect the eight-pin connector to the gauge.

   d. Test the two-pin connector's purple wire (on the wiring harness side) for battery voltage with the ig-

nition switch in the ON or RUN position. Repair or replace the purple wire, 20 amp fuse and/or ignition switch as necessary. Reconnect the two-pin connector when finished.

   e. If at this point, the warning horn will not sound for 1/2 second during the self-test, replace the warning horn.

Check Gauge Operational Mode

The operational mode is entered each time the self-test mode is complete and the engine is started. In this mode, if a sensor activates (switched to ground on switch type sensors) or the ECU detects a fault in one of the signals it monitors on fuel injected engines, the appropriate LED will illuminate and the warning horn will sound for ten seconds. The LED will illuminate for a minimum of 30 seconds, even if the problem only occurs momentarily. This allows easy identification of intermittent warning signals. However, the LED will remain illuminated as long as the sensor remains activated. When the sensor deactivates (not grounded on switch type sensors), the LED will remain illuminated for an additional 30 seconds.

If an additional sensor activates, the warning horn will again sound for ten seconds and the appropriate LED will illuminate.

If the warning system activates under operation, identify which LED is illuminated and refer to the following:

1. *Water temp*—If the overheat signal occurs during operation, reduce the engine speed to idle and check the water discharge (tell-tale) indicator for a steady stream of water, indicating that the water pump is operating correctly. If there is not an adequate water discharge at the tell-tale indicator, stop the boat, then shift the gearcase into reverse and briefly apply the throttle to clear any debris that may be covering the water intake screens. If the water temp LED is still illuminated, and/or water discharge is not noted at the tell-tale indicator, the engine must be turned off, allowed the engine to cool and determine the cause of the overheating.

2. *No oil*—If the oil pressure switch in the power head detects pressure less than 10-19 psi, the switch will close the circuit illuminating the LED and sound the warning buzzer. Should this occur during engine operation, stop the engine immediately. Check the oil level according to the procedure in Chapter Three. If the level is sufficient, check the oil pressure as directed in this chapter. Do not resume engine operation until either the low pressure condition has been remedied or until diagnosis shows for certain that the switch or circuitry is faulty.

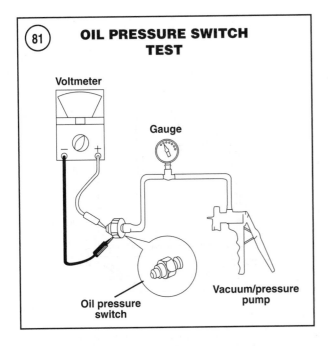

(81) **OIL PRESSURE SWITCH TEST**

Voltmeter

Gauge

Oil pressure switch

Vacuum/pressure pump

CAUTION
Operating the engine with insufficient oil pressure will damage the power head.

3. *Check engine*—If the ECU on fuel injected engines detects an improper sensor signal in the engine control system it will store a diagnostic trouble code and illuminate the gauge *Check Engine* LED as long as the fault is present. In most cases the engine continues to operate, but possibly in a safe-mode designed to get the boat back to shore with diminished performance until the sensor signal is restored. Refer to *Electronic Fuel Injection* in this chapter.

Check Gauge Diagnostic Mode (Carbureted Models)

The electronics system on carbureted models features a gauge diagnostic mode (not to be confused with the ECU diagnostic trouble code readout on EFI systems). The gauge diagnostic mode is entered by turning the ignition switch to the on or run position, but without actually starting the engine. The gauge goes through its self-test mode, then it automatically enters the diagnostic mode. In this mode, the warning horn circuits are disabled so a technician can manually activate the circuits and check the LEDs. If a sensor/switch is activated in this mode (by simulating sensor fault conditions or by manually connecting the sensor wire to ground), the appropriate LED illuminates as long as the sensor is activated.

NOTE
Do not use the diagnostic mode unless the self-test mode has satisfactorily activated.

To test the wiring harness warning circuits, turn the ignition switch to the ON or RUN position, and verify that the self-test successfully activates and completes, then proceed as follows:

1. *Water temp*—Proceed as follows:
   a. Disconnect the engine temperature switch from the engine harness connector.
   b. Using a suitable jumper wire, hold the engine harness end of the tan wire to a good engine ground.
   c. The *Water temp* LED must illuminate as long as the tan wire is held to ground. If not, repair or replace the tan wire.
2. *No oil*—Proceed as follows:
   a. Disconnect the wiring from the oil pressure switch.
   b. Connect a suitable jumper wire between the tan/yellow wire from the switch harness and a good engine ground. The *No Oil* LED must remain illuminated as long as the wire is connected to ground. If not, repair or replace the tan/yellow wire, as applicable.
3. Turn the ignition switch to the OFF position and reconnect all wires when finished.

Oil Pressure Switch Testing

The location of the oil pressure switch (**Figure 79**) varies by model.

On 5/6 hp (128 cc) models, the switch is mounted under a rubber boot on the upper port side of the power head, directly in front of the carburetor air intake.

On 8/9.9 hp (211 cc) models, the oil pressure switch is mounted under a rubber boot on the upper port side of the power head, directly behind the carburetor and just in front of the oil dipstick.

On 9.9/15 hp (305 cc) models, the switch is mounted under a rubber boot on the upper port side of the power head, directly above the oil filter and just in front of the oil fill. Use the wiring diagrams color codes to verify proper location.

On 40 and 50 hp (815 cc) models, the switch is mounted to the upper port side of the power head and just below the flywheel.

On 70 hp (1298 cc) models, the switch is mounted on the starboard side of the power head. On these models, remove the electric component holder and engine control unit to access the switch.

This test requires a multimeter and a vacuum/pressure pump (**Figure 81**). Test the switch as follows:

1. Remove the oil pressure switch from the power head following the instructions provided in Chapter Seven.

2. Locate the pressure port fitting on the vacuum/pressure pump. Carefully slide an appropriately sized hose over the fitting side of the oil pressure switch (**Figure 81**). Apply a clamp over the connection to ensure accurate test results. Do not apply pressure at this time.

3. Set the multimeter to the resistance scale.

4. Connect the positive meter test lead to the wire terminal on the oil pressure switch (**Figure 81**). Connect the negative meter test lead to the body of the oil pressure switch. Clamp the test lead to the switch if necessary to ensure a reliable test lead connection.

5. The multimeter should indicate continuity.

6. Observe the multimeter reading and the pressure gauge while slowly applying pressure to the switch. Record the pressure reading when the meter indicates no continuity and compare that to the following:

   a. On 5/6 hp (128 cc) models no continuity when the pump gauge reaches 15 psi (103 kPa).

   b. On 8/9.9 hp (211 cc) models no continuity when the pump gauge reaches 10 psi (70 kPa).

   c. On 9.9/15 hp (305 cc) models no continuity when the pump gauge reaches 20 psi (138 kPa).

   d. On 40/50 hp (815 cc) and 70 hp (1298 cc) models no continuity should occur by the time the pump gauge reaches 10-19 psi (70-130 kPa).

7. Replace the oil pressure switch if there are inconsistent or incorrect test results noted. This is especially necessary if the switch opens (no continuity) at a pressure much lower than the specification. A switch that opens prematurely could allow the engine to run with oil pressure below specification (possibly causing engine damage).

8. Install the oil pressure switch as described in Chapter Seven.

Temperature Sensor Testing

The temperature sensors (cylinder and exhaust) used on EFI models differ slightly from the switches used on carbureted models, but both are tested in a similar fashion. The sensors on EFI models are thermistors (variable resistors) that give different feedback readings to the ECU depending on the temperature measured. This allows the ECU to adjust fuel mapping to better match varying engine conditions, while also monitoring for a overheating condition. The switch on carbureted models is a simple on/off type switch and is used exclusively by the warning system to turn on the LED and/or warning buzzer. The switch is normally open, preventing the circuit from grounding. When the switch approaches a predetermined temperature, it closes and activates the system. In both

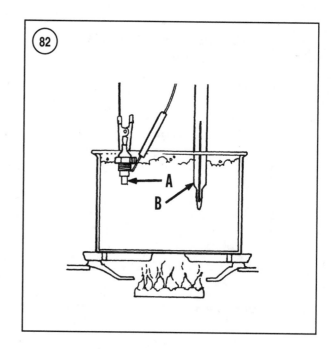

cases, the method used to test the sensor/switch is to suspend it in a warm liquid and take resistance readings as the temperature is increased.

> *NOTE*
> *The 40-70 hp EFI models use both an engine and exhaust manifold temperature sensor. Refer to the wiring diagrams and verify the color of the connecting wire to select the proper sensor.*

> *NOTE*
> *On 40-50 hp models, the switch can also be tested through the ECU wiring harness. Slightly different resistance specifications are given for these tests. Refer to **Table 13** for ECU harness connectors, terminals, wire colors and resistance values if sensor testing is conducted through the harness. Also, refer to **Electronic Engine Component Testing Through the ECU Harness** in the **Electronic Fuel Injection** section of this chapter.*

A multimeter, a thermometer (or thermosensor adapter for the multimeter), some length of mechanic's wire, a metal or laboratory grade glass container and a heat source (such as a camp stove) are necessary for this test.

> *WARNING*
> *When testing the switch on a carbureted model, avoid using an open flame to heat the*

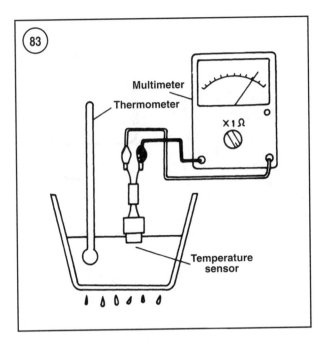

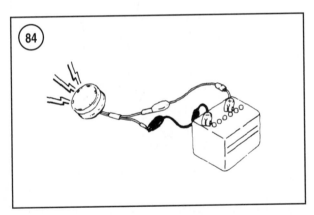

NOTE
To ensure test accuracy, do not allow the sensor/switch or thermometer to touch the bottoms or sides of the container during the test.

4. Suspend the thermometer in the container next to the sensor as shown in B, **Figure 82** or in **Figure 83**. Note the temperature after allowing a few minutes for the thermometer to stabilize.

5. Slowly raise the temperature of the liquid, while watching the readings on the multimeter as follows:

    a. On carbureted models, the switch must remain open (showing no continuity) at temperatures up to and including 192-222° F (90-104° C). The switch should close (showing continuity on the meter) once the temperature reaches 234-246° F (112-120° C) or higher.

    b. On EFI models, refer to the temperature sensor specifications in **Table 12**. Specifications are given for various temperatures. Make sure to check sensor readings across the temperature range temperatures from low to high. Do not boil the water. Record the resistance at the listed temperatures.

6. Replace the temperature sensor/switch if any readings are incorrect.

7. Install the sensor as described in Chapter Six or Seven, as applicable.

Warning Buzzer

WARNING
When performing a test using a battery, never make the final connection of a circuit at the battery terminal. Arcing may occur and ignite the explosive gasses that form near the battery.

Use a fully charged battery and jumper leads for this test. The warning buzzer location may vary with the boat and engine rigging, but it is typically mounted within the control box or behind the dash on remote control models. On tiller control models the buzzer is normally located within the tiller control housing or under the engine top cover.

Access to both buzzer wire terminals is required for testing. If applicable, on remote control models, disassemble the remote control enough to access the wires. Remote control disassembly and assembly instructions are provided in Chapter Twelve.

Connect the warning buzzer wires to the battery using jumper leads as shown in **Figure 84**. Replace the warning buzzer if it fails to emit a loud warning tone.

container, as it is filled with oil. If possible, use an electric camp stove or hot plate.

1. Remove the temperature switch as described in Chapter Seven for carbureted models, or the appropriate temperature sensor as described in Chapter Six for fuel injected models, as applicable.

2. Set a multimeter to the resistance scale.

3A. Connect one of the meter leads to the switch terminal and the other lead to the metal body of the switch (A, **Figure 82**). Suspend the sensor in a container of cool four-stroke engine oil (automotive oil is acceptable for this test).

3B. Connect the positive meter test lead to the violet or light green wire terminal of the sensor. Connect the negative meter test lead to the black wire terminal. Suspend the sensor in a container of cool water (**Figure 83**).

FUSES

Fuses are used on all electric start and battery charging models. Fuses help protect wires and electric components from shorted or overloaded circuits. Blown fuses seldom occur during normal engine operation. Worn or damaged wiring, incorrect wire routing and loose connections cause most fuse failures.

Far more electrical problems are the result of failed fuses and/or damaged wiring than the failure of electric components.

Check the fuse(s) if the electric starter fails to operate or the starter operates but the engine fails to start. On remote control models, a blown fuse may prevent the dash mounted instruments and the warning buzzer from operating when the ignition key is switched on. Visually inspect the fuse for a broken or burned element (**Figure 85**). A blown fuse is usually visually apparent. However, a fuse can still fail and not appear blown. Test the fuse to verify its condition.

Fuse Testing

Use a multimeter for this test. Refer to the wiring diagrams at the end of the manual to identify the fuse connection points. Trace the indicated wire colors to the fuse. Test the fuse as follows:

1. Disconnect the negative battery cable. Remove the fuse as follows:
   a. On push in fuses, carefully pull the fuse (**Figure 85**) from the wire harness.
   b. On glass tube fuses, pull the fuse holder (**Figure 86**) from the mounting clamp. Pull the ends of the fuse holder to release the fuse.
2. Set a multimeter to the resistance scale. Connect the meter test leads to each end or contact of the fuse. A continuity reading indicates a good fuse.
3. If there is a blown fuse, thoroughly inspect the engine wire harness and connections. Repair or replace faulty wires or connections before installing a new fuse.
4. Install the fuse, then connect the negative battery cable. Start the engine and operate the components powered by the blown fuse. A repeat failure of the fuse indicates a hidden short circuit along the circuit. Refer to the wiring diagrams at the end of the manual to identify the wires or

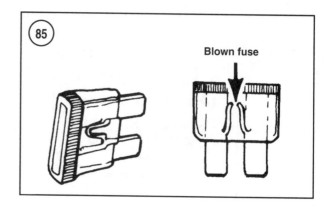

Blown fuse

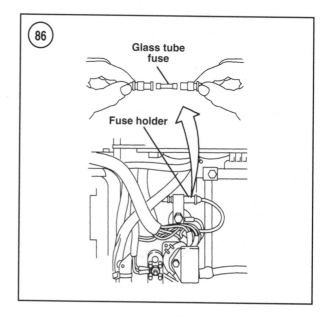

Glass tube fuse

Fuse holder

components connected to the fuse. Inspect or test all wiring or components along the affected circuit.

5. If no wiring faults are found, check for radios or other electrical accessories wired into the circuit. The amperage draw from these accessories and the engine instruments may exceed the fuse capacity. Provide an alternate connection point for accessories to prevent potential fuse failure.

6. Connect the negative battery cable.

WIRE HARNESS

Because of the harsh marine environment, wiring harness problems commonly occur. Suspect a wiring harness problem if an electrical malfunction occurs and all related components test correctly. Most wire harness problems are caused by dirty or damaged wire terminals. In some instances a broken or damaged wire within the harness

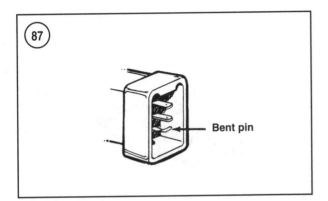

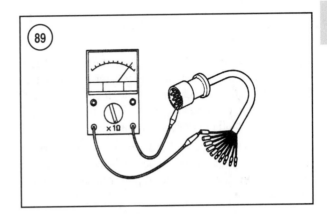

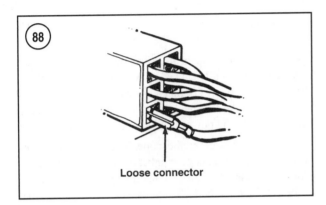

causes an intermittent open or short circuit. One method to check for this type of intermittent problem is to carefully wiggle various points on the wire harness while operating the engine and listening for the engine malfunction. Inspect the wire terminals and test the wire harness if a faulty harness seems to be at fault.

Terminal Inspection

1. Disconnect the negative battery cable (if so equipped). Remove and ground the spark plug leads.

2. Refer to the wiring diagrams at the end of the manual to identify the wire connection points. Disconnect all wire harness connectors from the electrical components.

3. Inspect the connectors for a bent pin (**Figure 87**). Pull on the wires at the back of the connector to check for a loose connector (**Figure 88**). Repair or replace the affected wire or harness if either of these conditions exist.

4. Using a small pick or screwdriver, gently clean all corrosion or contaminants from the terminals. Work carefully and avoid damaging the terminals. Clean contaminants from the wire terminals using an electrical contact cleaner.

Wire Harness Testing

Refer to the wiring diagrams at the end of the manual to identify wire harness connection points.

1. Disconnect the negative battery cable (if so equipped) to protect the test equipment and any solid state devices connected to the harness being tested. Remove and ground the spark plug leads for safety.

2. Refer to the wiring diagrams at the end of the manual to identify the wire connection points.

3A. On tiller control models, disconnect the tiller control harness from the engine wire harness.

3B. On remote control models, disconnect the remote control harness from the engine wire harness.

4. Note the wire routing and connection points then disconnect all electric components from the engine wire harness.

5. Set a multimeter to the resistance scale. Connect the meter test leads to each end of the selected wire color or circuit (**Figure 89**). The meter must indicate continuity. No continuity indicates a faulty wire or terminal.

6. With the meter test leads connected as described in Step 5, bend, twist and manipulate the entire length of the suspect wire while observing the meter. A faulty wire is indicated if the meter gives intermittent no continuity readings while the harness is wiggled. Using the meter, verify the faulty section of wire.

7. Repair or replace the wire if there is a constant or intermittent fault. Carefully connect the wire harness to the remote or tiller control harness and all electrical components. Make sure all connectors lock (**Figure 90**) to the harness or electric components.

8. Install the spark plug leads and connect the negative battery cable (if so equipped).

POWER HEAD

This section troubleshoots and tests the power head. Areas covered include engine noises, lubrication system failure, detonation and preignition, engine seizure, valve train failure, oil entering the combustion chamber and water entering the oil or combustion chamber.

Problems with the power head can be as simple as stuck piston rings, requiring only chemical additives to free them, or as advanced as a seized power head requiring a complete overhaul.

Engine Noises

Although noise occurs in the power head during normal operation, a ticking noise or heavy knocking noise that intensifies under acceleration is a reason for concern. Ignoring suspicious noise may result in increased damage to the power head. If it seems that a worn or damaged power head component is making the noise, consider having a professional technician familiar with that model listen to the engine. In many cases, the trained ear of an experienced technician who knows that model can determine if and what components have failed. Make sure the noise is the result of the power head before proceeding with an expensive and time-consuming internal inspection. The cause may be as simple as a loose bracket or fastener. Refer to the following sections that best describe the engine noise.

> *WARNING*
> *Use extreme caution when working on or around a running engine. Never wear loose fitting clothing. Keep everyone away from the flywheel, drive belts and the propeller shaft while the engine is running.*

Ticking noise

A ticking noise is common if valve adjustment is required or a valve train component has failed. Valve adjustment instructions are in Chapter Four. See *Valve Train Failure* in this chapter for additional troubleshooting tips.

A damaged piston can also cause a ticking noise. Inspect the spark plug for physical damage (**Figure 91**) or unusual deposits. Follow with a compression test as described in this chapter. Complete power head disassembly and repair is required if the compression is low or physical damage or unusual deposits are on the spark plug.

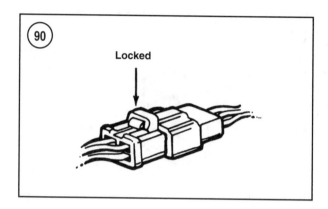

Whirring noise

A whirring noise that is more pronounced as the throttle is decreased is usually caused by worn or damaged crankshaft bearings. Be aware that a normal whirring noise can emanate from the flywheel. Noises can also transfer from the gearcase to the power head via the drive shaft.

Using a mechanic's stethoscope, listen to the noise emanating from the front or crankcase side of the cylinder block. Compare the noise emanating from the individual cylinders. This method often verifies a bearing noise and which cylinder is affected.

Low oil pressure almost always accompanies bearing failure. Check the oil level and condition as described in Chapter Three. Test the oil pressure as described in this chapter if the oil level and condition are correct. Disassemble and repair the cylinder block if low oil pressure and bearing noise are verified.

Knocking noise

A knocking noise usually indicates a failed crankshaft or connecting rod bearing. Damaged piston and cylinder head components can also cause a knocking noise.

Use a mechanic's stethoscope to determine if the noise is emanating from the crankcase or cylinder head area of the power head. If the noise is more pronounced in the crankcase area, a problem probably exists in the crankshaft and connecting rod components. If the noise is more pronounced in the cylinder head area, a problem probably exists with the piston or valve train components.

On multi-cylinder motors, remove one spark plug lead and attach it to an engine ground. Start the engine and listen for noise. Install the spark plug lead and repeat the process for the remaining cylinders. If less noise is noted with a particular lead grounded, suspect that cylinder.

CAUTION
If a spark plug lead is not grounded the electrical system may be damaged. Do not remove a spark plug lead with insulated pliers and attempt to ground it while the engine is running. If the lead is not quickly grounded the electrical system may be damaged.

Check the oil level and condition as described in Chapter Three. Correct low oil level or change diluted oil and check for knocking noise. Test the oil pressure as described in this chapter. When combined with low or unstable oil pressure, a knocking noise generally indicates a problem within the power head. Disassemble and repair the power head as described in Chapter Eight.

Lubrication System Failure

Running the engine with insufficient lubrication causes excessive wear and damage to power head components. Knocking or other types of noise are almost always present with a lubrication system failure. In some cases the only symptom is excessive wear of the valve train components. This condition usually surfaces when the components are inspected during routine valve adjustments.

Lubrication system failures can be related to a faulty lubrication system component or problems with the oil itself. Common causes of lubrication system failure include:

1. Low oil level.
2. Dirty or diluted oil.
3. Wrong type of oil.
4. A plugged oil screen or filter.
5. Worn or damaged oil pump components.
6. Damaged or dislodged oil pickup tube.

The low oil pressure warning system activates only if oil pressure drops below a set value. This value is set low enough to prevent a warning system activation at the lower pressure developed at idle speed. A fault with the lubrication system can prevent adequate oil pressure at higher engine speeds yet provide adequate oil pressure at idle speed.

Engine seizure may result from continued operation without sufficient oil pressure. Refer to *Engine Seizure* in this chapter.

Check the oil pressure as described in this chapter if the low oil pressure warning system activates or a lubrication system failure is indicated. Disassemble, inspect and repair the power head if the lubrication system is suspect or there are symptoms of lubrication failure. Power head disassembly, inspection and repair instructions are provided in Chapter Eight.

Check for thin diluted oil or the wrong type as described in Chapter Three if there is excessive valve train component wear. To prevent repeat failure or additional wear, locate and correct any oil related problems before operating the engine.

Detonation

Detonation damage is the result of the heat and pressure in the combustion chamber becoming too great for the fuel being used. Fuel normally burns at a controlled rate that causes the expanding gasses to drive the piston down. When conditions in the engine allow the heat and pressure to get too high, the fuel may explode violently. These violent explosions in the combustion chamber cause serious damage to internal engine components. Carbon deposits, inadequate cooling, lean fuel mixture, over-advanced ignition timing and lugging are some of the conditions that cause detonation. Never use a fuel with a lower than recommended octane rating. Using it may cause detonation under normal operating conditions. If detonation occurs, the engine produces a pinging noise. Continued operation with detonation results in eventual engine seizure. Detonation damage to the pistons (**Figure 92**), valves and cylinder walls reduces engine compression and causes poor

performance and a rough idle. Inspect the spark plugs for aluminum deposits (**Figure 93**) or melted electrodes (**Figure 94**). Follow with a compression test as described in this chapter. Disassemble and repair the power head as described in Chapter Eight if low compression is present or the spark plugs indicate possible engine damage. To avoid repeat failure, address the cause of detonation before returning the engine to service.

Preignition

Preignition is the result of a glowing object in the combustion chamber causing early ignition. The wrong spark plug heat range, carbon deposits and inadequate cooling are some of the causes of preignition. Preignition can lead to excessive power head component damage. Detonation damage is very similar and the early ignition can cause the increased heat and pressure that causes detonation. A hole commonly forms in the piston dome (**Figure 95**) where preignition has occurred. As with detonation damage, the engine runs poorly, particularly at idle speed. Inspect the spark plugs as described in Chapter Three and perform a compression test as described in this chapter to check for damage. Aluminum deposits (**Figure 93**) or a melted electrode (**Figure 94**) and low compression indicate piston damage. Disassemble and repair the power head as described in Chapter Eight if these conditions exist. To avoid repeat failure, address the cause of preignition before returning the engine to service.

Engine Seizure

If the engine slowed down or came to an abrupt stop and the starter is unable to turn the engine over, the engine may have seized. The engine may start after it cools and then run rough at idle and lack power at higher speeds. Continued operation causes more extensive damage.

The primary reason for seizure is an internal power head problem, such as a failed crankshaft and rod bearing or detonation/preignition damage. Typically the failed power head or gearcase components cause a gradual reduction in power and speed. The engine then seizes as the throttle is reduced to investigate the cause of reduced power. Failure of valve train components can cause an immediate engine seizure. Extensive damage is likely with an immediate seizure, especially at higher engine speeds.

Always inspect the gearcase for contaminated lubricant (as described in Chapter Three) before disassembling the power head. A gearcase failure can be easily mistaken for a power head failure.

Valve Train Failure

Failed or worn valve train components can cause an inability to start the engine, hard starting, rough running conditions, poor performance, backfiring from the exhaust or intake manifold, ticking noises or an engine seizure.

CAUTION
Internal damage to the valves and pistons
can result from attempting to start the en-

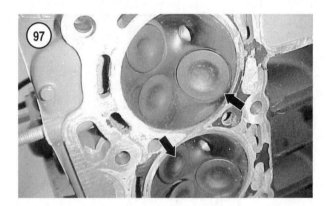

gine with incorrect valve timing or a broken timing belt.

Timing belt (5-15 hp and 70 hp models)

A damaged timing belt (**Figure 96**) can cause an inability to start the engine, sluggish performance or a rough running condition. A broken timing belt prevents camshaft operation and causes a no start condition.

If the timing belt is worn, the belt may jump over one or more of the teeth on the crankshaft pulley. This problem results in improper valve timing. Typical symptoms include rough idle, poor performance and backfiring. Check the valve timing as described in Chapter Four to determine if the belt has jumped. Replace the timing belt as described in Chapter Eight if inspection reveals excessive wear or jumped teeth. To prevent potential power head damage, inspect the timing belt at the intervals listed in Chapter Three.

Valve guides

Worn valve guides cause inconsistent or improper valve to seat contact. The resulting poor sealing causes poor idle, backfiring and in some cases high oil consumption.

Worn valve guides usually occur only on an engine with high operating hours. Worn valves guides usually accompany worn valves and seats (**Figure 97**). A compression test usually does not detect worn valve guides unless they are worn to the point where they affect the valves sealing ability. Disassembly and measurement is the only accurate method to detect worn valve guides.

Valves

Corrosion or heavy carbon deposits can cause a valve to stick open. Worn or damaged valves or valve contact surfaces (**Figure 97**) prevent the valve from sealing properly. Either condition results in lower compression, rough running or backfiring. Backfiring or popping noises coming from the intake or carburetor(s) indicate a problem with an intake valve. Likewise backfiring or other unusual noises coming from the exhaust indicates a problem with an exhaust valve.

If detecting backfiring, try running the engine with one spark plug lead at a time grounded. If the backfire ceases when spark is interrupted from a given cylinder, the problem is on that cylinder.

A valve that is stuck open can contact the top of the piston, causing a bent valve and/or damage to the piston. Stuck valves are generally the result of improper long-term storage, water entering the cylinder from a blown head gasket or submersion of the engine. Using the wrong type of oil, a lean fuel condition, overheating, or lugging the engine all contribute to increased deposits or excessive valve wear.

Perform a compression test as described in this chapter if it seems there is a valve or valve seat problem. Disassemble and inspect the valves and seats to verify this condition.

Camshaft

A damaged camshaft can cause rough idle and/or poor overall performance. The most common problem is caused by excessive wear or rounding of the camshaft lobes (**Figure 98**). A worn camshaft lobe prevents the valve from fully opening and the affected cylinder from developing full power.

Camshaft wear is caused by dirty, diluted or the wrong type of engine oil. Continuous operation (at low speed) in very cold water can contaminate the oil with fuel. Check and/or change the oil frequently if operating under these conditions.

Improper valve adjustment also contributes to camshaft wear. Adjust the valves at the recommended intervals to reduce the chance of camshaft wear. Refer to maintenance intervals and instructions in Chapter Three.

Perform a compression test to check for camshaft related problems. Low compression is usually present on the affected cylinder. Noisy valve operation almost always accompanies camshaft wear. Try running the engine with one spark plug lead at a time grounded. A worn camshaft lobe causes little difference in power output when the spark plug lead of the affected cylinder is grounded.

Visually inspect the camshaft surfaces if the indicated symptoms are present. Remove the rocker arm cover (**Figure 99**) as described in Chapter Four under *Valve Adjustment*. Inspect the camshaft surfaces as described in Chapter Eight. Replace the camshaft and other worn or damaged components if there are defects.

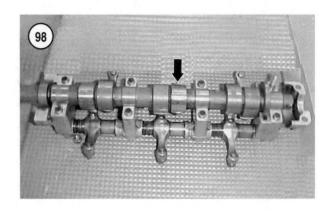

Rocker arm

Some engines covered by this manual use rocker arms to transfer camshaft lobe lift to the valve stems (opening the valves). Rocker arm wear causes a noise emanating from the cylinder head and poor performance because of a loss of compression in the corresponding cylinder. Perform a compression test as described in this chapter to verify which cylinder is affected. Remove the rocker arm cover (**Figure 99**) as described in Chapter Four under *Valve Adjustment*. Visually inspect all rocker arms for damaged or excessively worn surfaces. Replace worn or damaged components as described in Chapter Eight.

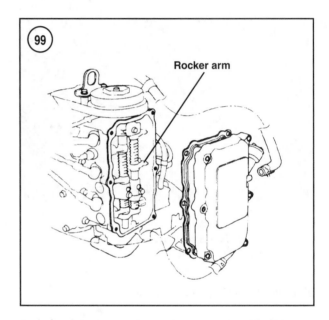

Rocker arm

Water Entering the Combustion Chamber

Water can enter the combustion chamber from a number of areas, such as water in the fuel, water entering the intake manifold, leaking exhaust covers/gaskets, leaking cylinder head or gasket, internal leakage in the cylinder block or a leak at the power head-to-drive shaft housing mating surfaces. The typical symptom of water intrusion is rough running particularly at idle. However, the engine may still run correctly at higher engine speeds. Remove and inspect the spark plugs to verify water intrusion. Rust, white deposits or water on a plug is likely with water intrusion. Compare the suspect spark plug(s) with the plugs from remaining cylinders. Water intrusion removes carbon deposits from the spark plug. Install a spark plug from an unaffected cylinder into the suspect cylinder. Run the engine, then remove and inspect the spark plug. If the carbon deposits have been removed or there is water on the plug this indicates water intrusion. If there is water intrusion remove the cylinder head as described in Chapter Eight. A cylinder with water intrusion has significantly

less carbon deposits on the piston, valves, and cylinder head surfaces. Complete power head repair is not required if the cause and damage is confined to the cylinder head. Typical causes include a failed cylinder head gasket or cracked cylinder head.

Internal leakage in the cylinder block can be difficult to find. Casting flaws, pinholes, and cracks may or may not be visible. Replace the cylinder block or cylinder head if water intrusion persists and there is no visible defect. Always inspect the exhaust cover for defects before condemning other components. Continued water intrusion eventually causes power head failure.

Water Entering the Oil

Water entering the oil causes a milky appearance and an increase in oil level. Water can enter the oil from a number of areas. Typical causes include leakage at the cylinder

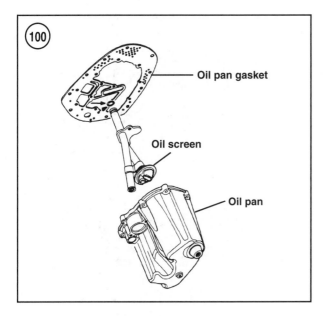

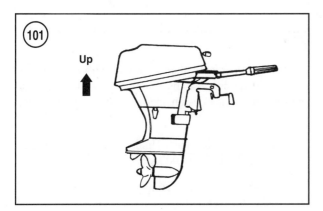

head gasket, oil pan gasket (**Figure 100**, typical) and cracks or other defects in the cylinder block or head. Continued operation at low engine speed in very cool or humid climates allows a fair amount of water condensation in the oil pan. Change the oil and filter as described in Chapter Three if there is water found in the oil. Operate the engine while stopping frequently to check for water. If no water is found, normal condensation is the likely source. Remove and inspect the power head components if water reappears in the oil. Continued operation with water entering the oil eventually causes power head failure.

Failed Cylinder Head Gasket

A failed cylinder head gasket allows compression leakage, water leakage and/or oil leakage. Leakage usually occurs internally yet it can occur externally. Typical symptoms include rough running (particularly at idle speed), water entering the cylinder(s), water entering the oil and overheating (particularly at higher engine speeds). In some instances a whistling noise occurs near the cylinder head to cylinder block mating surfaces.

Perform a compression test as described in this chapter if these symptoms exist. Typically two adjoining cylinders have lower readings than the others. Minor leakage may not be detected with a compression test. Perform a leak down test if the above symptoms occur and other causes are ruled out. A leak down test offers a more reliable means for detecting minor leakage. It may be necessary to remove and inspect the gasket and mating surfaces to verify this type of fault.

Oil Entering the Cylinders

Oil entering the cylinder(s) is almost always the result of storing the engine improperly. If positioned improperly, oil from the crankcase or oil pan can flow past the piston rings and enter the combustion chamber. If the engine does not turn over, the cylinders may be hydraulically locked. Remove the spark plugs and slowly rotate the flywheel to expel the oil. Check and correct the oil level before starting the engine. Other symptoms of oil entering the cylinders include fouled spark plugs and high oil consumption.

The preferred storage position is upright (**Figure 101**). If it is necessary to store or transport the engine on the side or top, drain the oil as described in Chapter Eight. Refill the oil before operating the engine.

External Oil Leakage

In most cases, oil leakage is easily detected and corrected. Common leakage points include the rocker arm cover (**Figure 99**), oil filter mounting surface, fuel pump mounting surface and crankcase cover mating surfaces (**Figure 102**). Carefully clean the engine surfaces with a degreasing agent. Run the engine until it reaches operating temperature. Turn the engine off, and then inspect all potential leakage points for fresh leakage. Tighten fasteners or replace gaskets for the affected surface or component.

High Oil Consumption

All engines burn some oil during normal operation because of oil that enters the combustion chamber past the piston rings and valves. There are no standard oil consumption specifications. Oil consumption rates vary by model, condition of the engine and operating conditions.

New or recently rebuilt engines generally consume more oil during the break-in period. After the break-in period oil consumption drops. Engines with worn internal components generally burn more oil. A typical symptom of excessive oil consumption is blue smoke coming from the exhaust during hard acceleration or high speed operation.

Inspecting the spark plug usually reveals oil fouling. Perform a compression test as described in this chapter if there are oil fouled spark plugs or blue exhaust smoke. Worn or damaged components generally cause low compression results. Check for external oil leakage or leakage at the oil pan gasket (**Figure 100**) if high oil consumption is noted and oil burning is ruled out.

Compression Test

CAUTION
Make sure the cranking battery is fully charged before performing a compression test. Using a weak battery may result in low compression readings.

Use a compression gauge (**Figure 103**) with a spark plug port adapter for this test. Make sure the threaded end of the gauge or adapter matches the threads of the spark plug bore.

1. Operate the engine with a flush fitting adapter or in a test tank until it reaches normal operating temperature, then stop the engine.

2. Remove the spark plugs and identify from what cylinder each was removed. Connect the spark plug leads to ground.

3. Place the throttle in the wide open position.

4. Thread the compression gauge/adapter into the No. 1 (top) spark plug opening.

5. Stand clear of the remaining spark plug openings during testing. Observe the compression gauge while operating the manual or electric starter. Make sure the engine has made a minimum of ten revolutions. Record the maximum compression reading.

6. Repeat Step 4 and Step 5 for the remaining cylinders. Record all compression readings.

7. The manufacturer does not provide standard or minimum compression specifications, but recommends that the readings be compared to the other cylinder(s). Variation between the cylinders should not exceed 15 psi (103 kPa) for engines through 15 hp. On 40-70 hp engines, the lowest cylinder reading should be within 80% of the highest cylinder reading. On single cylinder engines, record the compression figure and continue with the test.

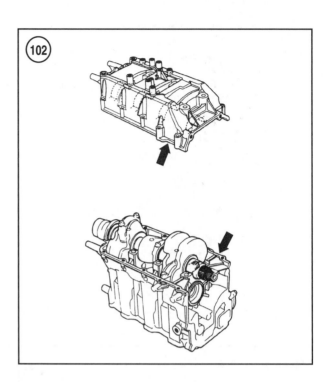

Although the manufacturer does not provide compression specifications, use the following average specifications from similar design marine engines as a general *guide:*

a. Typical single/twin cylinder carbureted engines: 115-142 psi (800-1000 kPa).

b. Typical three/four cylinder EFI engines: 185-228 psi (1300-1600 kPa).

8. Squirt approximately one teaspoon of engine oil into the spark plug opening of any cylinder suspected to have low compression. Rotate the engine several revolutions to distribute the oil in the cylinder(s). Repeat Step 4 and Step 5 for each suspected cylinder. This step is another good way to check compression on single cylinder engines to see if oil added to the cylinder changes the reading, which would indicate a compression problem.

9. Compare the second compression reading with the first compression reading. A higher second reading indicates the low compression is due to a problem with the piston, piston rings or cylinder walls. Of course, a problem with a valve or valve seat may still be possible if there is no increase in compression. Repair the power head as described in Chapter Eight.

10. Place the throttle in the idle speed position. Remove the compression gauge and adapter. Install the spark plugs and leads.

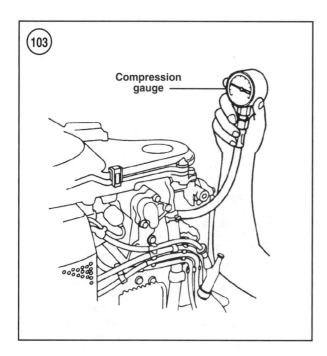

(103)

Compression gauge

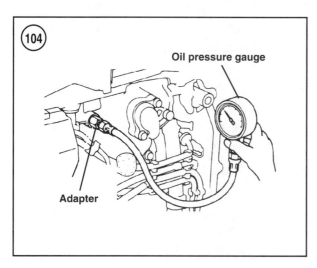

(104)

Oil pressure gauge

Adapter

Oil Pressure Test

This test requires a shop tachometer, oil pressure gauge (pressure range of 0-100 psi [0-690 kPa]) and 1/8 in NPT adapter.

Perform the test while running the engine in a suitable test tank, as engine speeds will exceed the recommended maximums for using a flush test device. Take all necessary precautions to prevent injury to yourself or others. The test is conducted by installing the pressure gauge, via the adapter, into the oil pressure switch mounting bore on carbureted models, or in the oil pressure plug port on EFI models.

For carbureted models, refer to *Oil Pressure Switch Testing* in this chapter to locate the switch or refer to the switch procedure in Chapter Seven for removal and installation instructions. For 40-50 hp EFI models, remove the port lower engine cover and locate the oil pressure port plug directly below the spin-on oil filter. On 70 hp models, remove the starboard lower engine cover to access the oil pressure port plug found directly above the spin-on oil filter.

1. Run the engine until it reaches operating temperature. This may take as much as 10 minutes. Stop the engine immediately if the oil pressure warning system on EFI models activates.

2. Switch the engine OFF. On carbureted models, remove the oil pressure switch as described in Chapter Seven. Tape back the disconnected oil pressure switch wire to prevent grounding or contact with moving components. On 40-70 hp models remove the oil pressure port plug.

3. Install the 1/8 in. NPT adapter into the threaded opening for the oil pressure switch or the port plug, as applicable, and tighten firmly, then attach the oil pressure gauge (**Figure 104**) to the adapter.

4. Following the manufacturer's instructions, connect the shop tachometer to the engine. Start the engine and watch the oil gauge. Pressure should be established within 10 seconds of start-up. Stop the engine and check for mechanical problems if pressure does not build in that time. Once pressure builds, quickly check for oil leakage at the gauge attaching points. Stop the engine and correct any leakage before proceeding.

5. Slowly advance the throttle until the tachometer reads the indicated rpm and record the oil pressure reading. Compare this to the specifications as follows:

   a. On 5/6 hp (128 cc) models, pump pressure should be at least 15 psi (103 kPa) at 900 rpm. Raise the throttle speed and watch the gauge. Pump pressure should be 35-40 psi (241-276 kPa) at 4200-5200 rpm.

   b. On 8/9.9 hp (211 cc) models, pump pressure should be at least 10 psi (70 kPa) at 900 rpm. Raise the throttle speed and watch the gauge. Pump pressure should be 35-40 psi (241-276 kPa) at 4200-5200 rpm.

   c. On 9.9/15 hp (305 cc) models, pump pressure should be at least 20 psi (140 kPa) at 2000 rpm. Raise the throttle speed and watch the gauge. Pump pressure should be 35-45 psi (241-310 kPa) at 5000-6000 rpm.

   d. On 40/50 hp (815 cc) models, pump pressure should be 42-54 psi (290-372 kPa) at 4000 rpm.

   e. On 70 hp (1298 cc) models, pump pressure should be 60-70 psi (414-483 kPa) at 3000 rpm.

2

6. Return the throttle to idle speed then switch the engine OFF. Remove the shop tachometer, oil pressure gauge and adapter. Wipe up any spilled oil.

7. On carbureted models, install the oil pressure switch as described in Chapter Seven. For EFI models, coat the threads of the port plug with a Teflon pipe sealant, then install the plug and tighten firmly.

8. Compare the oil pressure reading with the specification. A low oil pressure reading indicates low oil level, diluted oil, the wrong type of oil, a faulty oil pump or damage to the crankshaft and bearings. A high oil pressure reading indicates a faulty or blocked oil pressure relief valve, blockage at the power head mating surface or blockage in the cylinder oil passages. Inspect or repair these components as described in Chapter Eight.

COOLING SYSTEM

The cooling system used on these four-stroke outboards is relatively simple. Water is pumped by the drive shaft driven water pump (**Figure 105**) to the exhaust manifold area of the power head. This water enters the cylinder block then cylinder head. Water exits the cylinder head and block through the thermostat, pressure relief valve, water indicator stream and dedicated drain passages. Except for the water indicator stream all exiting water is directed back into the drive shaft housing.

All models are equipped with a thermostat that restricts exiting water (**Figure 106**, typical) to maintain a minimum power head temperature and improve low speed running characteristics.

The water indicator stream appears once the cooling passages are filled with water and water starts exiting the power head. The water stream fitting commonly becomes blocked with debris, which restricts water flow. This problem leads one to suspect a cooling system malfunction. Clean the opening in the fitting using a stiff piece of wire before testing or inspecting other cooling system components.

Larger models are equipped with a water pressure relief valve. This valve allows additional water flow at higher engine speeds by providing an additional exit passage. Increased water pump flow and pressure at higher engine speeds causes the valve to open.

As water flows through the power head it absorbs then removes excess heat. If the engine is overheating, the problem is that water is not flowing through the power head in sufficient volume or it is not absorbing the heat. In most cases the cause of overheating is related to insufficient waterflow. However, salt or other deposits in the cooling passages not only restrict water flow, they insulate the components and prevent heat transfer to the water.

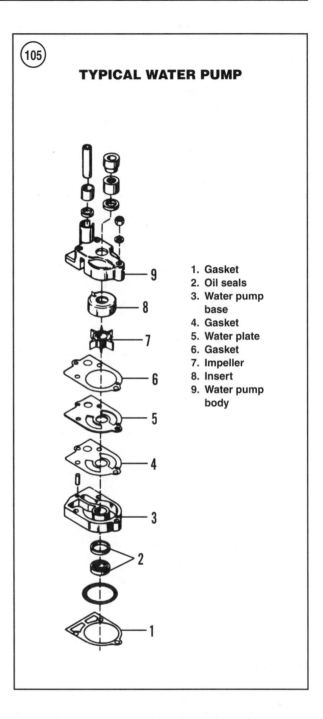

(105)

TYPICAL WATER PUMP

1. Gasket
2. Oil seals
3. Water pump base
4. Gasket
5. Water plate
6. Gasket
7. Impeller
8. Insert
9. Water pump body

NOTE
If possible, check for overheating under actual running conditions on the water or in a test tank. When testing engines, using a pressurized flush test device may mask problems with the water pump and other cooling system components by providing more pressurized water than the system would otherwise be capable of providing the engine by itself.

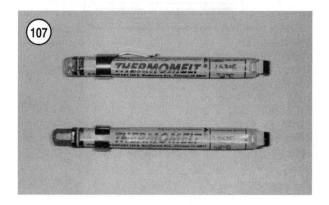

Cooling System Test

Inspect the water pump as described in Chapter Nine if the indicator stream fails to appear within a few seconds of starting the engine or the overheat warning system activates.

Verify overheating using Thermomelt Stiks (**Figure 107**) or an equivalent temperature reacting substance. Thermomelt Stiks are designed to melt at a given temperature. Make a mark on the cylinder head, near the cylinder temperature gauge with two different test sticks, one with a 125° F (52° C) stick and one with a 163° F (73° C) stick. On models not equipped with an engine temperature sensor, make the marks next to the spark plug opening. Stop the engine if the temperature exceeds 194° F (90° C) to avoid engine damage. When using Thermomelt Stiks, the mark for the 125° F (52° C) stick should melt, while the mark for the163° F (73° C) stick should remain chalky. If the cooler mark remains chalky, check for possible causes of overcooling, like a stuck open thermostat. If the warmer mark melts, check for causes of overheating, including a damaged water pump/impeller or a stuck closed thermostat.

NOTE
When testing the cooling system, make sure the water supplied to the engine is not excessively hot or cold. Ideally, water supplied to the flush fitting should be 60-80° F (16-27° C).

If the temperature exceed 194° F (90° C), inspect or test the thermostat as described in this chapter. The thermostat is far easier to access than the water pressure relief valve. Inspect the water pressure relief valve on EFI models if overheating occurs primarily at higher engine speeds and a faulty water pump and thermostat are ruled out. Remove the cylinder head and exhaust cover as described in Chapter Eight for water passage inspection if overheating persists and no faults are found with the water pressure relief valve. Water pressure relief valve, exhaust cover and thermostat removal and installation instructions are in Chapter Eight.

Thermostat Testing

WARNING
To avoid serious injury, remove the propeller before running the engine on a flush test device. Disconnect the negative battery cable and spark plug leads before removing or installing the propeller.

CAUTION
Never run an outboard without providing cooling water. Use either a test tank or flush test device.

A fault with the thermostat can cause overheating or prevent the engine from reaching normal operating temperature. Use a thermometer, piece of string and a container of water that can be heated for this test.

The thermostat components on carbureted engines are assembled in the thermostat bore of the power head. In some cases, changes of the thermostat (vernatherm) may not be obvious in this test. On those engines, it may make more sense to run the engine to check the motor by temporarily removing the thermostat. If an engine has trouble coming up to temperature, and shows no difference in the amount of time necessary to come up to temperature once the thermostat is removed, try installing a new thermostat first, as that is the most likely cause. If an engine is suffering from overheating problems, try removing the thermostat to see if that solves the problem. Again install a new thermostat if the engine does not overheat once the old one was removed. In either case, operating the engine without the thermostat is for testing purposes only. Failure to maintain the thermostat and cooling system in proper working order will lead to other engine performance problems.

1. Remove the thermostat as described in Chapter Eight. Suspend the thermostat in a container of water (**Figure 108**).

2. Place a thermometer in the container and begin heating the water. Continue to heat the water while observing the thermostat for valve opening. Stop the test if the water begins boiling before the thermostat opens.

NOTE
To ensure accurate testing, make sure that neither the thermostat nor the thermometer touch the bottom or sides of the container. This step ensures that both items are at the same temperature as the water at all times.

3. Record the temperature when the thermostat just starts to open. Stop heating the water and again observe the thermostat as the water cools. Record the temperature when the thermostat just starts to close.

4. Compare the opening temperature with the following specifications:

    a. On carbureted models, the thermostat should open at approximately 136-144° F (58-62° C).

    b. On EFI models, the thermostat should open at approximately 126-134° F (52-57° C).

5. Although closing temperature specifications are not provided by the manufacture, typically a thermostat should close within about 10° F (-12° C) of the opening temperature.

6. Replace the thermostat if an opening or closing temperature is much different than indicated.

7. Install the thermostat as described in Chapter Eight.

GEARCASE

Problems with the gearcase can include water or lubricant leakage, a slipping propeller hub, failed internal components, noisy operation, or shifting difficulty. The keys to preventing gearcase problems are to avoid contact with underwater objects, shift the engine at idle speed only and perform regular maintenance. Maintenance instructions for the gearcase are provided in Chapter Three.

Water or Lubricant Leakage

A small amount of water may be present in the lubricant if the gearcase has not received regular maintenance and is stored while submerged in water. Even with near perfect seals and sealing surfaces, small amounts of water seep into the gearcase with use. A small amount of water

is usually not visibly apparent as it is held in suspension by the gearcase lubricant. Small amounts of suspended water cause very little harm to the gearcase components. Changing the gearcase lubricant at regular intervals removes the water and other contaminants before it leads to damaged components.

NOTE
Storing the motor out of the water does not help forgo the need for regular maintenance as water may still contaminate the gearcase oil as a result of condensation.

Worn or damaged seals and/or shafts allow excessive amounts of water into the gearcase. As the amount of water increases, the gearcase lubricant takes on a milky appearance. Continued water intrusion causes the water to separate from the lubricant and settle to the bottom of the gearcase housing. Unless promptly removed, the non-suspended water causes corrosion damage to gears, bearings and shafts. Check the gearcase lubricant level and condition at the recommended intervals (Chapter Three) to detect water intrusion before it leads to damaged components. Pressure test the gearcase as described in this chapter if the oil has a milky appearance or water is found in the gearcase.

The presence of gearcase lubricant on or around the gearcase indicates a leak and the need to pressure test the gearcase. Failure to correct leakage causes eventual gear, bearing and shaft damage. Gearcase repair instructions are in Chapter Nine.

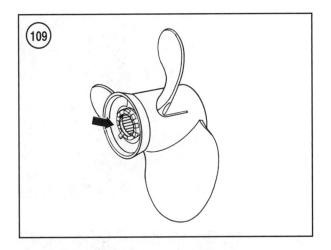

Metal Contamination in the Lubricant

Fine metal particles form in the gearcase during normal use. The gearcase lubricant may have metal flake appearance when inspected during routine maintenance. Touch the end of the drain plug, then rub some of the metal particles between your fingers. If many of the particles are large enough to feel, inspect the gearcase and repair it as needed (Chapter Nine).

Propeller Hub Slippage

Most four-stroke outboards (except the smallest that use a shear-pin propeller) use a shock hub type propeller. The shock absorbing hub is integrated into the splined section of the propeller (**Figure 109**). The hub connects the splined section of the propeller shaft to the propeller. It is constructed of a rubber material that provides a cushioning effect to the gearcase components during shifting. This material reduces the wear that occurs during normal operation. It cannot prevent damage because of high speed shifting. The hub provides some protection to the gearcase components should the propeller strike an underwater object at lower boat and engine speeds. Again, it cannot provide any guarantee against damage at higher speeds.

With use, weathering and age the propeller hub material deteriorates. A deteriorated hub spins within its bore instead of turning the propeller. Typically the hub is able to spin the propeller at lower throttle settings. Increased throttle setting causes spinning that causes increased engine speed with no or very little increase in boat speed. In most cases the boat does not reach planing speed. Check for hub spinning by making reference marks on the propeller shaft and propeller. Operate the engine until the suspected slipping occurs. Compare the marks after removing the engine from the water. Repair the propeller if the reference marks do not align after running the engine.

Gearcase Vibration or Noise

Normal gearcase noise is barely noticeable over normal engine noise. A rough growling noise or loud high pitched whine may be reason for concern. These noises are usually caused by faulty internal components. On occasion, a knocking noise may emanate from the gearcase, leading one to believe a problem is present in the power head. Inspect the gearcase lubricant for metal contamination if abnormal noises are heard. Contamination indicates gearcase component failure.

A knocking or grinding noise from the gearcase is likely caused by damaged gears or other components. Damaged gears typically create a substantial amount of large metal particles. The gears may be damaged from underwater impact or high speed shifting. This type of failure usually damages most internal components and necessitates complete repair. Refer to Chapter Nine for instructions.

Squealing or a high pitched whine usually indicates a bearing problem or, in some cases, gear misalignment. The only way to verify that a problem exists is to disassemble and inspect the gearcase components. Refer to Chapter Nine for instructions.

Vibration in the engine can and often does originate in the gearcase. In most cases, the vibration is due to a bent propeller shaft or damaged propeller. The propeller may appear to be in perfect condition, yet be out of balance. The best way to solve propeller-caused vibration is to have the propeller examined by a propeller shop. Another option is to try a different propeller. Have the propeller balanced and trued if there is a significant reduction in vibration.

Always check for a bent propeller shaft if vibration is present. Check the propeller shaft following the instructions provided in Chapter Nine. Hitting an underwater object(s) usually bends the propeller shaft. In many cases, other damage occurs to the gearcase. Inspect the gearcase lubricant as described in this chapter.

Never operate the engine if it vibrates excessively. Vibrating components place added stress on the gears, bearings and other components.

Shifting Difficulty

Difficult or hard shifting is usually caused by improperly adjusted shift cables or linkage. Adjust the shift cables or linkage as described in Chapter Four. Check for

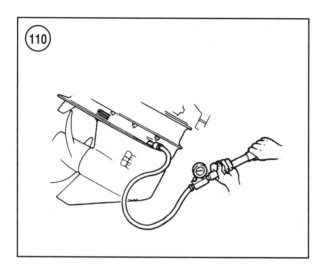

worn, stiff or improperly routed shift cables or linkage if the adjustment is correct. Inspect the shifting components within the gearcase if difficult shifting persists. Refer to Chapter Nine for gearcase repair instructions.

Pressure Testing

Use a gearcase pressure tester for this test. A container of water large enough for gearcase submersion may also be required.

1. Thoroughly drain the gearcase following the instructions in Chapter Three. Refer to Chapter Nine to remove the gearcase from the engine.

2. Install the pressure tester fitting into the oil level plug opening. Install the drain plug into the drain/fill opening. Securely tighten the drain plug and pressure tester fitting.

3. Slowly apply pressure to the gearcase. Push, pull and turn all shafts while observing the gauge and increasing the pressure. Stop increasing pressure when it reaches 3-6 psi (21-42 kPa). If the unit does not hold pressure for at least 10 seconds, submerge the gearcase and look for bubbles to find the leak.

NOTE
On some models (such as the gearcases for the 8-15 hp models), hold the driveshaft down in position to keep it from becoming partially dislodged while pressure is increased.

4. If no leakage was evident in Step 3, slowly increase the pressure to 16-18 psi (110-124 kPa). Again, if the pressure does not hold, submerge the gearcase and look for bubbles to find the leak.

5. Slowly release the air pressure from the gearcase. Replace the defective seal(s) or other components as described in Chapter Nine.

6. Refer to Chapter Nine to install the gearcase. Refill the gearcase with lubricant as described in Chapter Three.

TRIM SYSTEM

The type of trim and tilt system varies by model and optional equipment. Refer to the appropriate section.

5-15 hp Models

These models are equipped with a tilt pin (**Figure 111**) and mechanical reverse lock mechanism. The tilt pin can be adjusted to the angle of the boat transom by moving the pin to a different clamp bracket hole (**Figure 111**). The mechanical reverse lock mechanism prevents the engine from tilting up when operated in reverse gear.

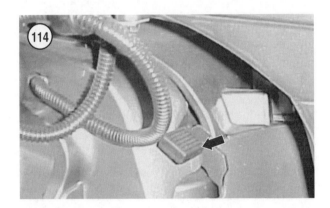

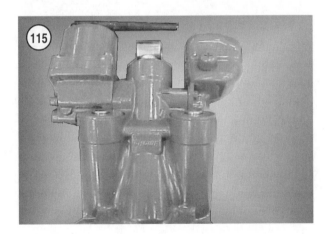

40 and 50 hp Models

These models are equipped with either a gas assist tilt system (**Figure 112**) or a single hydraulic cylinder power trim system (**Figure 113**).

The gas assist tilt system uses pressurized nitrogen gas to assist with tilting the engine for trailering or beaching the boat. The gas assist hydraulic cylinder holds the engine in the selected running position, holds the engine down in reverse and provides shock absorbing capability

during impact with underwater objects. Moving the tilt lock lever (**Figure 114**) opens or closes the valves that release or lock the engine in position.

The optional single cylinder hydraulic trim system is mounted (except for the switches and relays) between the clamp brackets. An electric motor driven hydraulic pump delivers the pressurized fluid required by the system. The hydraulic cylinder provides shock absorbing capability during impact with underwater objects. This self-contained system requires no external hydraulic lines that may corrode or leak.

Selecting the up position on the trim switch causes the electric motor and pump to rotate and direct pressurized fluid to the up side of the hydraulic cylinder. The working force created by the pressurized fluid is strong enough to move the engine against the propeller thrust while underway. Stopping the hydraulic pump closes valves that lock the fluid within the cylinder to hold the engine in position.

Selecting the down position on the trim switch causes the electric motor and pump to reverse direction and direct fluid to the down side of the cylinder and move the engine down.

A manual relief valve is located within an opening in the port clamp bracket. When opened it releases the fluid from the hydraulic cylinders, allowing manual engine tilting.

70 hp Models

These models are equipped with a three cylinder hydraulic trim system (**Figure 115**). Except for the switches and relays, the entire system is positioned between the clamp brackets. This system requires no external hydraulic lines that may corrode or leak. Engine mounted relays control the rotation direction of the electric motor and hydraulic pump.

Selecting the up position on the trim switch causes the pump to rotate in a direction that directs fluid to the up side of the trim and tilt cylinders (3 and 4, **Figure 116**). The working force created by the cylinders is strong enough to tilt the engine out against propeller thrust. Stopping the hydraulic pump closes valves that lock the fluid within the cylinder to hold the engine in position. The tilt cylinder (4, **Figure 116**) provides shock absorbing capability during impact with underwater objects.

When the trim cylinders (3, **Figure 116**) fully extend, the tilt cylinder becomes the only means to move the engine up or out. The engine tilts quicker as all the fluid is directed to the tilt cylinder. However the system develops less force as only one cylinder drives the system. The reduced force effectively limits the trim range while running at higher throttle settings. At lower throttle settings

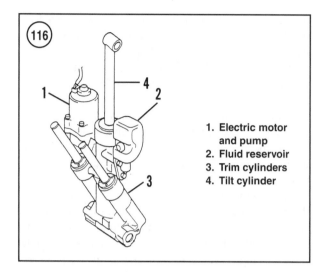

1. Electric motor and pump
2. Fluid reservoir
3. Trim cylinders
4. Tilt cylinder

the single cylinder provides enough force to tilt the engine up for shallow water operation.

Selecting the down position on the switch causes the electric motor and pump to reverse direction. Fluid is then directed to the down side of the tilt cylinder causing the engine to move downward.

A manual relief valve is located within an opening in the port clamp bracket (**Figure 117**). When opened, it releases the fluid from the hydraulic cylinders, allowing manual engine tilting.

NOTE
A fault with the gas assist tilt system causes a leak down or a loss of assist when tilting the engine. This system is non-serviceable. Replace the system as described in Chapter Eleven if there is a fault.

Hydraulic Trim System Testing

Diagnose hydraulic trim problems by comparing the symptoms in the following section with the possible causes listed under each symptom. Refer to Chapter Eleven when performing any of the following:

Will not move up or down

1. Check the electric trim motor operation.
2. Check the fluid level.
3. Check the position of the manual relief valve.
4. Inspect the manual relief valve O-ring.
5. Replace the hydraulic pump.

Leaks down from the full tilt position

1. Check the position of the manual relief valve.
2. Check the fluid level.
3. Remove and inspect the manual relief valve.
4. Have a professional replace all system seals and O-rings.
5. Replace the hydraulic pump if the symptoms persist.

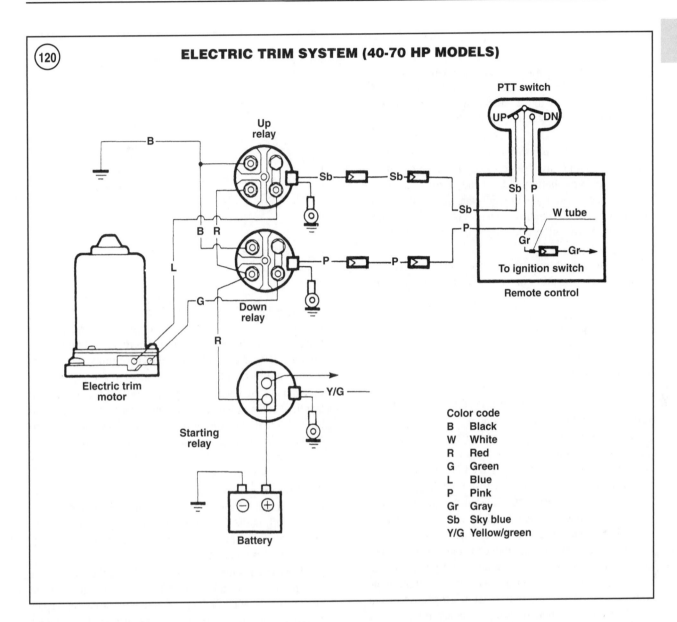

(120) **ELECTRIC TRIM SYSTEM (40-70 HP MODELS)**

Color code
B   Black
W   White
R   Red
G   Green
L   Blue
P   Pink
Gr Gray
Sb Sky blue
Y/G Yellow/green

Engine will not move against propeller thrust yet holds tilt position

1. Have a professional replace all system seals and O-rings.
2. Replace the hydraulic pump.

Engine tilts up in reverse or while slowing down

1. Check the position of the manual relief valve.
2. Check the fluid level.
3. Remove and inspect the manual relief valve.
4. Have a professional replace all system seals and O-rings.

5. Replace the hydraulic pump.

Electrical Trim System

The major electrical components of the trim system include the electric motor, trim relays (**Figure 118**) and the trim switches (**Figure 119**, typical). The 40-70 hp models may be equipped with an optional trim position sender and dash mounted trim gauge. The relays control current flow to the electric trim motor (**Figure 120**).

The main wire harness is connected to the battery with a fuse. A defective fuse prevents battery voltage from reaching the trim switches. Refer to *Fuse Test* in this chapter for instructions if the trim system will not operate in either direction. If the fuse is blown, the starter and gauges will also be inoperative.

Selecting the up position on the trim switch directs current to the up reply (**Figure 120**). The relay connects the blue trim motor wire to the battery side of the starting relay. The motor then rotates in the direction that causes the engine to trim up.

Selecting the down position on the switch directs current to the down relay. The relay connects the green trim motor wire to the battery side of the starting relay. The motor then rotates in the direction that causes the engine to trim down. When the trim system is not activated the relays connect the blue and green trim motor wires to ground.

The system monitors the trim position with a variable resistance trim position sender and dash mounted trim gauge.

Test the trim system as described in the following sections if the pump fails to operate.

Relay switching test

Use a multimeter for this test. Perform this test before testing other trim system components.

1. Using the wiring diagrams at the end of the manual, identify the wire colors used for the trim switches (**Figure 119**, typical) and trim relays (**Figure 121**). Trace the wires to their connection points at the trim relays.

2. Select the 20 or 40 VDC scale on the meter. Connect the negative meter test lead to the black wire at the up relay and the positive lead to the red wire at the up relay. Note the meter reading then move the meter negative lead to the black wire on the down relay. Battery voltage must be present at both connections. If battery voltage is not present, first inspect the battery cables for loose or corroded terminals, Then inspect the black relay ground wires for loose, damaged or corroded terminals. Repair faulty connections as required.

3. Connect the negative meter test lead to the black wire terminal at the up relay. Connect the positive lead to the red wire terminal at the up relay. Note the meter reading then move the positive lead to the red wire on the down relay. Battery voltage must be present at both connections. If not, check for a loose, damaged or corroded wire terminal. Repair faulty wires and terminals as required.

4. Connect the negative meter test lead to the black wire terminal at the up relay and the positive test lead to the sky blue (sb) terminal on the relay. Toggle the trim switches in the UP direction while observing the meter. There should be battery voltage. If not, test the trim switches as described in this chapter.

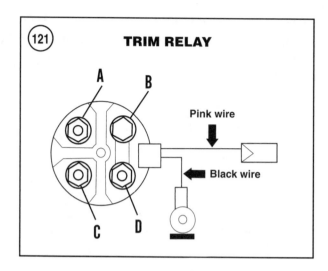

5. Move the positive meter test lead to the blue (L) wire at the up relay. Note the meter reading while toggling the trim switch in the UP direction. There should be battery voltage. If not, perform the relay continuity test as described in this chapter.

6. Connect the negative meter test lead to the black wire terminal at the down relay and the positive test lead to the pink terminal at the relay. Toggle the trim switches in the DOWN direction while observing the meter. There should be battery voltage. If not, test the trim switches as described in this chapter.

7. Move the positive meter test lead to the green wire on the down relay. Note the meter reading while toggling the trim switch in the down direction. Battery voltage should be noted. If not, perform the relay continuity test as described in this chapter.

8. If the test results are as specified, but the trim motor fails to operate, check for damaged blue and green wires and terminals. If no faults are found with the wires, repair or replace the electric trim motor as described in Chapter Eleven.

Relay continuity test

This test requires a multimeter, jumper leads and a fully charged 12 volt battery.

1. Disconnect the negative battery cable. Disconnect all cables from the relays.

2. Set the multimeter to the resistance scale. Connect the meter to the relay terminals (**Figure 121**) as follows:

   a. Connect the test leads to the C and D relay terminals. There should be no continuity.

   b. Connect the test leads to the A and B relay terminals. There should be continuity.

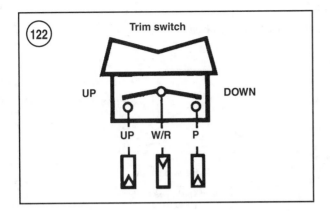

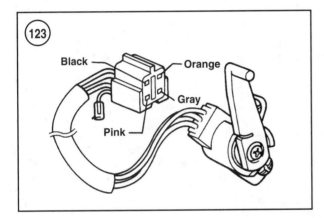

remote control disassembly instructions. Disassemble the remote control to the point necessary to access the trim switch wire connectors.

2. Carefully disconnect the three trim switch wires from the remote control or engine wire harness.

3. Set the multimeter to the resistance scale. Connect the positive meter test lead to the white/red or gray wire terminal. Connect the negative lead to the sky blue (sb) wire terminal. In the off position, the switch should have no continuity.

4. With the leads connected as described in Step 3, toggle the switch to the UP position. The switch should have continuity in the up position.

5. Connect the positive meter test lead to the white/red or gray wire terminal. Connect the negative lead to the pink wire terminal. The switch should have no continuity in the off position.

6. With the leads connected as described in Step 5, toggle the switch to the DOWN position. The switch should have continuity. Note the meter reading while toggling the switch to the UP position. The switch should have no continuity.

7. Replace the trim switch if the test results are incorrect. Clean the wire terminals and carefully connect the switch wires to the remote control or engine wire harness. Route the wires to avoid interference.

8. Reconnect all wires. Connect the negative battery cables.

Trim position sender

NOTE
Avoid attempting to repair damaged wire insulation on trim motor and trim position sender wires. It is almost impossible to totally seal worn, cracked or damaged wire insulation. Even a pin-sized hole allows water into the component. Also note that increased engine corrosion is likely if active circuits are in contact with water.

A faulty sender is generally the result of deteriorated or corroded wiring. Place the engine in the full tilt position and inspect the sensor wires for worn or damaged insulation. Replace the sender as described in Chapter Eleven if there is defective wiring. Adjust the trim position sender as described in Chapter Eleven if the gauge fails to reach the full up and down positions.

1. Remove the trim position sender as described in Chapter Eleven. Set a multimeter to the R × 100 scale.

2. Connect the negative meter test lead to the black sender wire (**Figure 123**) and the positive lead to the pink sender wire. Allow the spring on the sender to move the

c. Connect the test leads to the B and C terminals. There should be continuity.

3. Connect the test leads to the C and D relay terminals. Using jumper wires, connect the positive terminal of the battery to the sky blue (sb) or pink relay wire (**Figure 121**). Note the meter reading while connecting the black relay wire to the negative battery terminal. There should be continuity.

4. Repeat Step 2 and Step 3 for the remaining relay. Replace the relay if it does not function as specified.

Trim switch test

The trim system is controlled by a three-position switch (**Figure 122**) mounted to the remote control, dash panel, tiller handle or lower engine cover (**Figure 119**, typical).

Testing instructions are similar regardless of the switch location. Battery voltage is applied to the switch by a wire connection to the ignition switch or the engine wire harness. Check the fuse or wire harness if voltage is not present on the wire.

1. Disconnect the negative battery cable. If testing the remote control mounted switch, refer to Chapter Twelve for

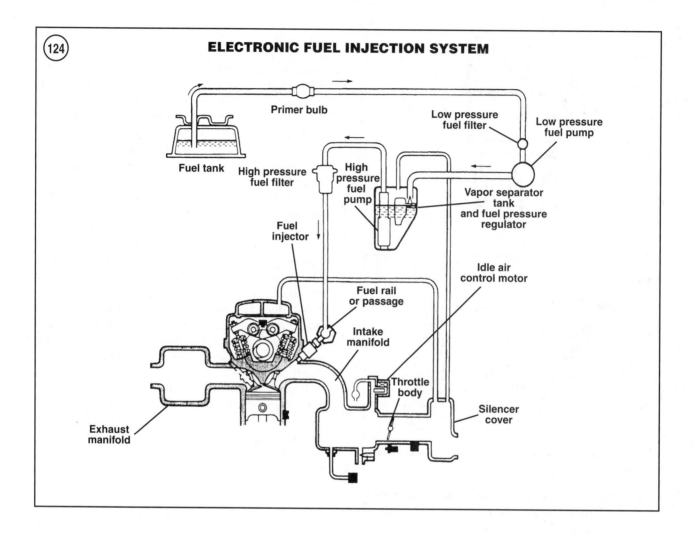

124

ELECTRONIC FUEL INJECTION SYSTEM

Primer bulb

Low pressure
fuel filter

Low pressure
fuel pump

Fuel tank

High pressure
fuel filter

High
pressure
fuel
pump

Vapor separator
tank
and fuel pressure
regulator

Fuel
injector

Idle air
control motor

Fuel rail
or passage

Intake
manifold

Throttle
body

Silencer
cover

Exhaust
manifold

---

lever to the full tilt position. The meter readings should indicate 360-540 ohms.

3. Note the meter readings while slowly moving the sender lever toward the full down position (against spring tension). The meter should indicate 800-1200 ohms with the sender in the full down position.

4. Replace the sender if it fails to operate as described. Replace the sender if there are abrupt changes in the resistance while moving the lever. The resistance must change smoothly while moving the lever.

5. Install the trim position sender as described in Chapter Eleven.

6. Check all wiring from the sender to the gauge for worn or damaged wires and faulty connectors if the gauge fails to operate but the sender tests correctly. Replace the gauge if it fails to operate properly and no faults exist with the sender and wiring.

ELECTRONIC FUEL INJECTION

This section contains procedures for testing and troubleshooting the EFI system on all 40-70 hp models.

Before troubleshooting the fuel injection system, make sure that potential problems with other systems are eliminated as described in the *Preliminary Inspection* section of this chapter. After potential problems unrelated to the fuel system have been eliminated, check the EFI system diagnostic codes *before* disconnecting the battery. If no codes are present, yet the problem(s) persist, verify the operation of the fuel supply system, then test the electronic control system.

A haphazard approach may eventually determine the cause of problems, however, only a systematic approach can avoid wasted time and the possibility of unnecessary parts replacement. Before purchasing parts in an attempt to repair a problem, remember that most parts suppliers do not accept returns on electrical components.

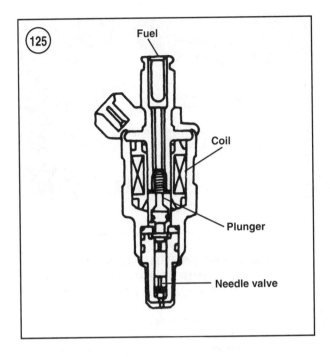

Figure 125

Fuel

Coil

Plunger

Needle valve

switch. Signals from these sensors combined with information on engine speed allow the ECU to compute the amount of fuel injected on-time for maximum performance and economy.

Incorporated into the fuel injection system is a self-diagnostic capability. A dash mounted warning light blinks if it detects a malfunction with the system. See *Diagnostic System* in this chapter for test procedures.

The fuel injectors (**Figure 125**) discharge fuel into the intake manifold runners and are basically solenoid-activated fuel valves that open when the ECU provides electric current.

Injector opening time or duration varies depending on engine and ambient conditions. For warm-up and high load conditions the injectors remain open longer. When the engine reaches operating temperature and when cruising with light loads, the injector opening-time is reduced.

When compared to carburetor-equipped engines, EFI systems provide improved fuel economy, warm-up, throttle response, performance, reduced emissions and automatic altitude compensation.

System Operation

The fuel injection system consists of the following subsystems:

1. The low-pressure fuel delivery system.
2. The high-pressure fuel delivery system.
3. The engine control system.

The low-pressure system consists of the cam driven low-pressure fuel pump, the low-pressure fuel filter and the vapor separator tank (**Figure 124**). The fuel level is regulated in the separator by a float and needle valve. The system delivers fuel to the separator from the fuel tank. If a flooding condition should occur in the separator the excess fuel is routed to the throttle body.

These components and their operation is similar to those found on carbureted engines. Inspect them as described under *Fuel System* in this chapter.

The high-pressure system consists of the vapor separator tank, high-pressure electric fuel pump (**Figure 124**), which is located in the separator, high-pressure fuel filter, fuel pressure regulator (also incorporated into the separator tank) and the fuel injectors. The system delivers fuel to the injectors from the vapor separator tank. Pressure is controlled by the regulator, which is connected to the fuel supply line via a T-fitting. Fuel pressure is regulated by venting excess fuel pressure back into the vapor separator.

The engine control system consists of the electronic control unit (ECU), manifold absolute pressure (MAP) sensor, intake air temperature (IAT) sensor, cylinder temperature sensor and the closed throttle position (CTP)

Fuel Supply System (High-Pressure)

Test procedures for the low pressure fuel system are explained earlier in this chapter under *Fuel System*.

Check the operation of the electric fuel pump as described in this section if the engine refuses to start. Follow with the fuel pressure test to determine if the high-pressure fuel system is operating properly. Test the remaining fuel supply system components if the fuel pressure is incorrect.

> *WARNING*
> *Use extreme caution when working with the fuel system. Fuel can spray out under high pressure. Always use required safety gear. Never smoke or perform any test around an open flame or other source of ignition. Fuel and/or fuel vapor represent a serious fire and explosive hazard.*

Electric Fuel Pump Test

This test checks for fuel pump operation and the voltage supply to the pump.

1. Locate the vapor separator tank behind the intake manifold (**Figure 126**). Place a stethoscope or wooden dowel to the body of the vapor separator to listen for fuel pump operation.
2. Have an assistant switch the ignition key switch to the ON position while listening for pump operation. Do not

start the engine. Switch the ignition OFF for 30 seconds and repeat the test.

3. The fuel pump must operate for 2-3 seconds then cease each time the ignition key switch is cycled to the ON position. Place the switch in the OFF position for 30 seconds between each cycle.

4. Check the voltage supply to the pump if it fails to operate as follows:

    a. Disconnect the topside wire harness from the vapor separator tank.

    b. Select the 20 VDC scale on the multimeter. Connect the positive meter test lead to the pink wire terminal in the engine wire harness connector. Connect the negative meter test lead to the black/white wire terminal of the connector.

    c. Observe the meter while an assistant cycles the ignition key switch to the ON position. The meter should indicate 6-12 volts for 2-3 seconds. If not perform substep d.

    d. Move the positive meter test lead to the battery terminal of the starter relay and repeat substep c. Check the 15 amp fuse if the voltage reading is as described in substep c. Check all wiring and connections before replacing a blown fuse.

    e. Test the 30 amp fuse, system relay, neutral switch, ignition key switch and all wiring if no voltage is found in substep c and the 15 amp fuse is in working order. If all other components test correctly, suspect a defective ECU.

5. Connect the wire harness connector to the vapor separator tank.

Fuel Pressure Test

This test verifies that fuel is being supplied to the fuel injectors at the required pressure. Make sure the fuel pump is operating before testing the pressure. While this test can verify that the fuel pump and regulator are operating under controlled conditions, it cannot verify that fuel pressure is adequate at all engine operating speeds. If fuel delivery problems are suspected at certain engine speeds, operate the engine with the gauge attached to the fuel system. Leaking fuel lines, restricted passages and blocked filters can restrict fuel flow and reduce fuel pressure in the low-pressure and high-pressure systems. If a fuel restriction is present, the fuel pressure may be correct at slow engine speeds, but decline dramatically at higher throttle settings. If this symptom is the case, check the filters, antisiphon valve, fuel tank pickup and low-pressure fuel pump as described in this chapter.

A fuel pressure gauge capable of measuring pressures up to 46 psi (317 kPa) and a special adapter and hose

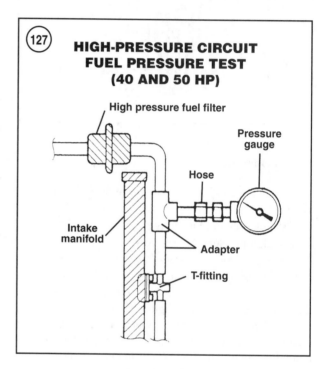

HIGH-PRESSURE CIRCUIT FUEL PRESSURE TEST (40 AND 50 HP)

High pressure fuel filter

Pressure gauge

Hose

Intake manifold

Adapter

T-fitting

(OMC part No. 5000900 or equivalent) are required. A dangerous fuel leak can occur if the gauge does not seal properly to the fuel test hose.

1. Properly relieve the fuel system pressure as detailed in Chapter Six, and then disconnect the negative battery cable for safety while installing the fuel pressure gauge.

2A. On 40 and 50 hp models, disconnect the harness connector from all three ignition coils.

2B. On 70 hp models, disconnect the spark plug leads and connect them to an engine ground.

3A. On 40 and 50 hp models, install the fuel pressure gauge as follows:

    a. Loosen the clamps and carefully remove the hose connecting the high pressure fuel filter to the T-fitting (**Figure 127**). Wipe up any spilled fuel.

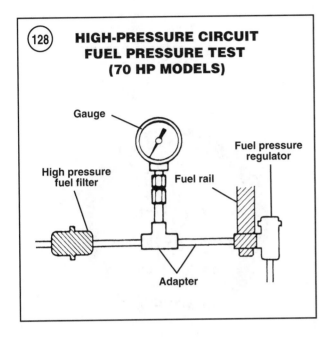

HIGH-PRESSURE CIRCUIT FUEL PRESSURE TEST (70 HP MODELS)

Gauge

Fuel pressure regulator

High pressure fuel filter

Fuel rail

Adapter

b. Connect the adapter, hoses and pressure gauge to the T-fitting and high pressure fuel filter as shown in **Figure 127**.

3B. On 70 hp models, install the fuel pressure gauge as follows:

a. Remove the lower engine cover as described in *Replacing the Oil Filter* in Chapter Three.

b. Loosen the clamps and carefully remove the hose connecting the high pressure fuel filter to the fitting at the bottom of the fuel rail (**Figure 128**). Wipe up any spilled fuel.

c. Connect the adapter, hoses and pressure gauge to the fuel rail fitting and the high pressure fuel filter as shown in **Figure 128**. Install the lower engine covers.

4. Connect the negative battery cable. Squeeze the primer bulb to fill the vapor separator tank with fuel. Observe the pressure gauge while switching the ignition key switch to the ON position. The gauge must indicate 34 psi (234 kPa) of fuel pressure.

a. Test the fuel pressure regulator as described in this chapter if the pressure is less than the specification. Inspect or check all filters and the vapor separator tank if the regulator tested correctly.

b. Replace the high pressure fuel pump if all other components test or check correctly.

5. Reconnect the harness connectors to the coils (40 and 50 hp models) or the spark plug leads (70 hp models). Install the lower engine cover as described in Chapter Three if removed. Start the engine using a flush/test adapter, test

tank or with the boat in water. Check for and correct fuel leakage before proceeding.

6. Observe the pressure readings while operating the engine at various speeds. The pressure gauge must indicate approximately 34 psi (234 kPa).

a. Test the fuel pressure regulator and the vapor separator tank if the fuel pressure remains below the specification at all speeds.

b. Check the fuel supply tank, low pressure pump and all filters if the fuel pressure remains below the specification only at higher engine speeds.

c. A faulty vapor separator tank or fuel pump is indicated if low fuel pressure occurs and all other components test or check correctly. Inspect or replace these components as described in Chapter Six.

7. Relieve the fuel system pressure as described in Chapter Six, then disconnect the negative battery cable again for safety.

8. Remove the pressure gauge, adapters and fittings. Wipe up any spilled fuel.

a. On 40 and 50 hp models install the hose connecting the high pressure fuel filter to the T-fitting and secure with clamps.

b. On 70 hp models install the hose connecting the high pressure fuel filter to the fitting at the bottom of the fuel rail and secure with clamps.

9. Connect the negative battery cable. Check for and correct fuel leakage before operating the engine.

WARNING
Remove the propeller before running the engine to avoid injury. Disconnect the spark plug leads and negative battery cable before removing and installing the propeller. Stay clear of the propeller shaft while running an outboard on a flush/test device.

CAUTION
Never run an outboard without providing cooling water. Use either a test tank or flush/test device. Use a test propeller to run the engine in a test tank.

Fuel Pressure Regulator Test

Use a regulated pressure pump, pressure gauge and a length of fuel supply hose or equivalent to test the operation of the fuel pressure regulator.

1. Refer to Chapter Six as necessary for information on the vapor separator tank.

2. Properly relieve the fuel system pressure as detailed in Chapter Six.

3. Remove the fuel supply line from the regulator pressure nipple at the bottom of the vapor separator tank assembly. Use a small drain pan to catch any escaping fuel.

4. Connect the regulated pressure pump to the regulator pressure nipple using the length of fuel supply hose.

5. Apply 45 psi (310 kPa) of air pressure to the pressure regulator nipple and shut the pump off. The pressure should be 34 psi (234 kPa) or more.

6. Stop operating the pump and observe the gauge to check for a pressure drop.

7. Replace the fuel pressure regulator (Chapter Six) if it fails to operate as described and there are no fuel leaks.

Diagnostic System

> *NOTE*
> *High-power electrical equipment such as stereos and communication radios may interfere with the electronic fuel injection system. Switch these devices off if trouble is detected with the engine. Reroute the wiring for these devices in order to prevent interference.*

If the ECU detects a malfunction, the dash-mounted check engine light (**Figure 129**) blinks and the warning horn sounds. The ECU provides a substitute value for the defective component. This feature allows the engine to continue to operate, although at a reduced capacity. It is possible that the substitute value may match the actual operating conditions, allowing the engine to run normally when the conditions equal the substitute value.

After a malfunction has been corrected the warning system operation returns to normal.

The check engine light is also used to read the diagnostic trouble codes (**Table 14**). Identify codes by observing the flashing light sequence. Refer to the following example and **Figure 130** (the example is not a valid code for these models) for a description of how to interpret the flashing signals.

A short duration light ON followed by a short duration light OFF then a short duration ON indicates a 2 for the first digit of the code. The second digit of the code is displayed after a short OFF period. Continuing with the example in **Figure 130**, a short light ON indicates a 1, or a code of 21. A longer duration light OFF period separates individual stored codes, if there are any. Otherwise the first code repeats. If more than one code is stored, they are repeated in numerical order.

Read the diagnostic codes as follows:

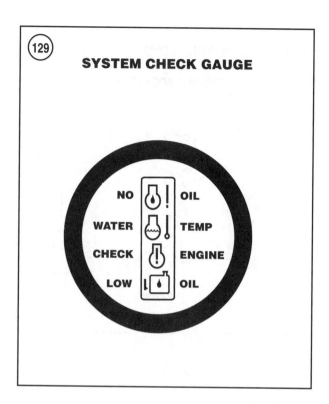

SYSTEM CHECK GAUGE

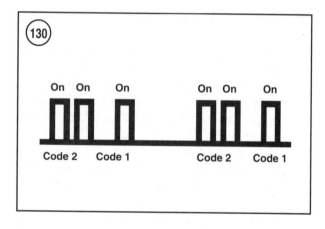

1. Turn the key switch to the ON position. Do not start the engine. At this point all four LEDs illuminate and then go out, one at a time.

2. If a trouble code is present, the *Check Engine* LED begins to flash. Count the flashing lights to determine the codes. Record all codes. Switch the ignition OFF.

3. Refer to **Table 14** to determine the defective circuit. The problem may be with the component, wiring or a system that would make the component read out of specification.

4. Test the indicated sensor or system components as described in this chapter. Do not overlook the possibility that the wiring/connectors may be the source of a malfunction.

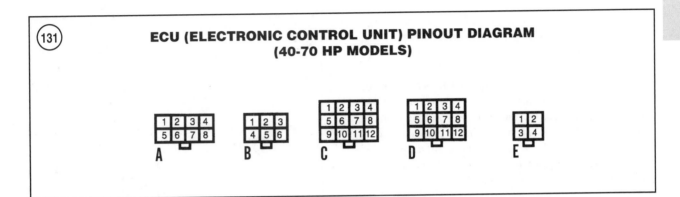

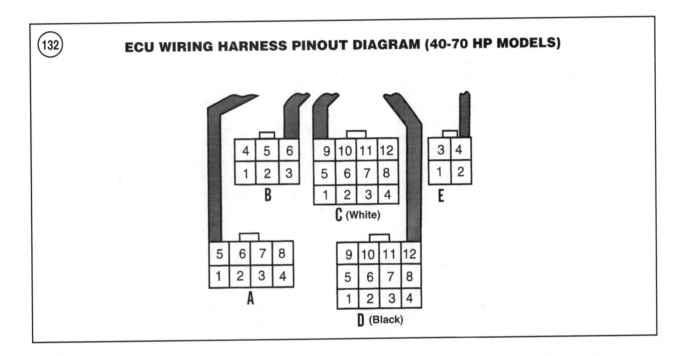

Always start with the simple and work to the more difficult. Presence of a code does *not* necessarily mean that the component corresponding to the code is defective. It means that the ECU sees an electrical signal that is out of the normal operating range.

5. Disconnect the battery for 3 minutes or longer to clear the trouble codes from the engine control unit.

6. Repeat this test sequence after repairing or replacing the faulty component to ensure a correct diagnosis.

Electronic Engine Component Testing Through the ECU Harness

On fuel injected models, most engine control sensors can be tested through the ECU wiring harness by disconnecting the proper connector and checking the appropriate terminals. **Figure 131** provides a pinout diagram for the ECU. Connectors and pins in **Figure 131** are shown from the perspective of looking at the back of the ECU. **Figure 132** provides a pinout diagram for the wiring harness connectors that attach to the back of the ECU, so they are a mirror image of the ECU pinouts. Component and harness testing should occur on the connectors pictured in **Figure 132**.

For 40 and 50 hp models, refer to **Figure 132** for connector views in order to help identify the proper connector and terminal location. Connector numbers, terminal locations, corresponding wire colors and resistance values are in **Table 13**.

NOTE
Keep in mind that resistance readings for most components vary with temperature. To

ensure accurate results, unless specified otherwise, test the components at 68° F (20° C).

For 70 hp models, refer to **Figure 132** for connector views in order to help identify the proper connector and terminal location. Use the connector views along with the terminal and wire colors provided in the individual component testing procedures to verify proper terminal locations. Resistance values for component tests on 70 hp models are in **Table 11** and **Table 12**.

NOTE
Table 13 *lists resistance values for component testing through the ECU harness. They differ slightly from the direct test values listed in* ***Table 12****. The manufacturer provides both sets of values on 40 and 50 hp models, with no specific explanation as to the variance. The differences are slight and further testing should be conducted before condemning a component based solely on a test where the result is out of spec only by the difference in the two sets of values. The manufacturer does not provide a second set of values for testing the 70 hp models.*

Fuel Injector Operation Test

Check fuel injector operation using a mechanic's stethoscope or long screwdriver to amplify or feel the noise produced by each injector. The injectors are mounted to the intake manifold or fuel rail on the rear and port side of the power head.

1. Place the outboard motor in a test tank, in the water or attach a flush device.

2. Start the engine and run it at idle speed.

3. Place a stethoscope or long screwdriver against the body of each fuel injector (**Figure 133**). If using a screwdriver, place the handle to your ear or hold the driver lightly and feel for a slight tapping.

4. A clicking noise should be heard or felt from each injector indicating that it is opening. If no clicking noise is heard or if a noticeably different noise is heard from an individual injector, test the injector resistance as described in this chapter and the wiring connections between the injector and ECU. If the resistance is within specification, and the connections are in good condition, install a known good injector. If the replacement injector fails to operate, then there is a defective wiring harness between the injector and ECU or a defective ECU.

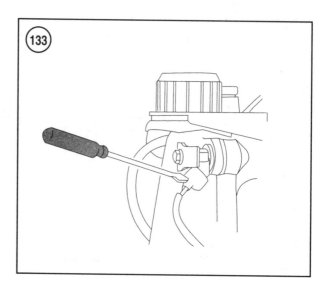

Fuel Injector Resistance Test

This test measures the resistance of the winding within the injector. A correct resistance reading does not indicate the injector is functional. An internal mechanical defect, foreign material or deposits can prevent the injector from operating. Injector removal is not required for this test.

1. Disconnect the negative battery cable to protect the test equipment. Refer to the wiring diagrams at the end of the manual to identify the wires leading to the injectors. Trace the wires to the injectors on the rear and port side of the power head.

2. Push in on the wire clip and carefully pull the wire harness connector from the top injector.

3. Set the multimeter to the resistance scale. Touch the meter test leads to the individual terminals on the injector (**Figure 134**).

4. Replace the injector if the measured resistance exceeds the specification in **Table 12**.

5. Align the tabs on the connector with the slot while connecting the harness to the injector. Repeat the resistance test for the remaining injectors.

Manifold Absolute Pressure (MAP) Sensor Test

The main signal to the ECU for determining injector opening time is the intake manifold pressure signal from the MAP sensor. For the sensor to function correctly, the vacuum hose from the manifold to the sensor must be securely attached and not leaking pressure. Make sure the hose is in good condition.

Excessive exhaust smoke, spark plug fouling and general poor performance can result from the incorrect air/fuel mixture caused by a defective MAP sensor signal.

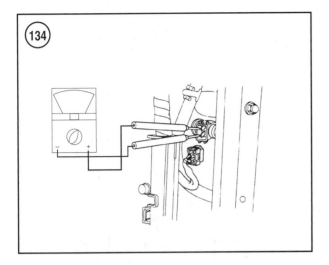

Check the operation of the MAP sensor by reading the diagnostic codes as described in *Diagnostic System*. A code 32 refers to a possible problem with the hose, since the ECU is detecting an unchanging signal regardless of engine speed. A code 34 refers to a probable electrical problem with the circuit as the ECU detects either no signal or a signal that is significantly out of range. Use the voltage output change test to check the sensor circuit. Make sure the wiring and connections are in good condition before replacing the sensor.

Because the circuit must be completed during testing, even though the instructions call for testing the ECU wiring harness, the harness must be installed. When installed, the harness connector view is a mirror image; therefore refer to the ECU pinout diagram (**Figure 131**) to help identify the proper position of the terminal for testing during this procedure. Confirm the proper position using the wiring color.

1. Set a digital multimeter to the low voltage DC scale.

2. Insert a small voltmeter probe (such as from OMC *Test Probe Kit* part No. 342677) through the back of the ECU wiring harness connector for ECU connector D terminal 7 (**Figure 131**). D7 should have a white wire. Connect the other voltmeter probe to a good engine ground.

3. Disconnect the vacuum hose from the MAP sensor and install a hand vacuum pump.

4. Turn the ignition key ON and apply vacuum according to the values in **Table 12**. Watch the voltmeter for the proper result and each vacuum reading.

5. Replace the MAP sensor if the voltage does not change according to specification with the appropriate vacuum changes.

Intake Air Temperature (IAT) Sensor Test

The IAT sensor provides a signal to the ECU indicating the temperature of the incoming air. The ECU then adjusts the injector opening time to match the fuel requirements to the conditions.

Excessive exhaust smoke, spark plug fouling and general poor performance can result from the incorrect air/fuel mixture caused by a defective IAT signal.

Check the operation of the IAT sensor by reading the diagnostic codes as described in *Diagnostic System*. If a trouble code is present, test the sensor. Since the sensor is identical in function to the other temperature sensors used by the EFI system, refer to the cylinder and exhaust manifold temperature sensor test instructions in the *Warning System* section of this chapter.

Cylinder Temperature Sensor Test

The cylinder temperature sensor provides a signal to the ECU indicating engine temperature.

The ECU then adjusts the injector opening time to match the fuel requirement to the conditions.

Excessive exhaust smoke, spark plug fouling and general poor performance can result from the incorrect air/fuel mixture caused by a defective cylinder temperature sensor signal.

Check the operation of the cylinder temperature sensor by reading the diagnostic codes as described in *Diagnostic System*. The sensor is similar to the sensor on carburetor equipped models. Refer to the cylinder and exhaust manifold temperature sensor test instructions in the *Warning System* section of this chapter.

Closed Throttle Position (CTP) Switch

The closed throttle position switch provides a signal to the ECU indicating if the throttle is in the closed position. With the throttle in the closed position, the ECU stabilizes the engine speed by actuating the idle air control (IAC) motor and altering the ignition timing. Advancing the throttle causes the ECU to increase fuel delivery and spark advancement. This feature dramatically improves throttle response.

A faulty CTP position switch generally causes hesitation during rapid throttle advancement. Other symptoms include a rough or unstable idle or high idle speed.

1. Disconnect the negative battery cable. Locate the throttle body (**Figure 135**) on the front and port side of the power head. Trace the light green/red wire to the switch location on the throttle body.

a. On 40 and 50 hp models the switch is mounted to the topside of the throttle body. Trace the indicated wire colors the to wire harness connection to the switch.

b. On 70 hp models the switch is mounted to the bottom side of the throttle body.

2. Disconnect the harness from the switch. Calibrate a multimeter to the resistance scale. Connect the positive meter test lead to an engine ground (**Figure 135**). Connect the negative meter test lead to the wire terminal on the switch.

3. Observe the meter while alternately opening and closing the throttle. The switch should have continuity with the throttle closed (switch button depressed) and no continuity when the throttle is just opened (switch button extended). Replace the throttle body (Chapter Six) if the switch does not operate as described.

4. Connect the wire harness to the switch. Route all wires to avoid interference. Connect the negative battery cable.

Neutral Switch Test

The neutral switch provides input to the engine control module as the engine is shifted into or out of neutral gear. Fuel injectors and ignition system operation is interrupted by the engine control module during attempts to start the engine if in gear.

A fault with this switch can cause a no-start condition if in neutral or allow the engine to start in gear.

1. Disconnect the negative battery cable.

2. Remove the lower engine cover as described in *Replacing the Oil Filter* in Chapter Three. Locate the neutral switch (**Figure 136**) on the lower starboard side of the power head and next to the shift linkage.

3. Set the multimeter to the resistance scale. Carefully disconnect the neutral switch wire harness from the engine wire harness. Connect the positive meter test lead to the yellow/green wire terminal of the switch. Connect the negative meter test lead to the brown wire terminal.

4. Place the remote control handle in neutral. The switch should have continuity.

5. Place the remote control in the *forward* then *reverse* gear positions while observing the meter readings. The switch should have no continuity with the engine shifted to either forward or reverse.

6. Replace the neutral switch if incorrect operation is indicated.

7. Connect the engine wire harness to the neutral switch harness connector. Route the wires to avoid interference. Install the lower engine covers. Connect the negative battery cable.

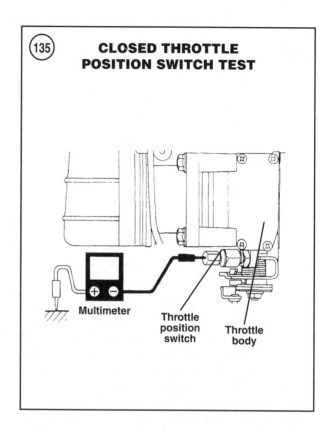

CLOSED THROTTLE POSITION SWITCH TEST

Multimeter

Throttle position switch

Throttle body

Idle Air Control (IAC) Valve

The ECU controls the idle speed using the idle air control valve. The IAC valve motor varies air flowing into a dedicated passage in the intake manifold.

Symptoms of a faulty IAC valve include stalling when the engine is shifted into gear, too slow or rough idle or excessively high idle speed. The engine usually performs correctly at higher speeds.

Check the operation of the motor by reading the diagnostic codes as described in *Diagnostic System*. If a trouble code is present, test the resistance of the motor as follows:

1. Disconnect the negative battery cable.

2. Refer to the wiring diagrams at the back of the manual to identify the wire colors used for the IAC valve. Trace the indicated wires to the IAC valve at the front and starboard side of the intake manifold. Carefully disconnect the engine wire harness from the IAC valve.

3. Set the digital multimeter to the ohm scale indicated in **Table 12**.

4. Connect the meter test leads to the individual terminals of the idle air control motor. Replace the IAC valve (Chapter Six) if the measured resistance is not within the specification in **Table 12**.

5. Connect the engine wire harness to the IAC valve. Route the wires to avoid interference. Connect the negative battery cable.

Table 1 STARTING SYSTEM TROUBLESHOOTING

Symptom	Possible causes	Corrective action
Starter does not energize	Engine not in neutral gear	Shift into neutral gear
	Weak or discharged battery	Fully charge and test the battery
	Dirty or corroded battery termimals	Thoroughly clean battery terminals
	Faulty neutral only start switch	Test neutral only start switch
	Faulty electric starter switch	Test electric starter switch
	Faulty ignition switch	Test ignition switch
	Faulty starter relay	Test starter relay
	Loose or dirty wire connection	Clean and tighten starter wire connections
	Faulty electric starter	Repair the electric starter
Starter engages flywheel (flywheel rotates slowly)	Weak or discharged battery	Fully charge and test the battery
	Dirty or corroded battery termimals	Thoroughly clean battery terminals
	Loose or dirty wire connections	Clean and tighten starter wire connections
	Engine is in gear	Correct improper linkage adjustment
	Faulty electric starter	Repair the electric starter
	Internal power head damage	Inspect power head for damage
	Internal gearcase damage	Inspect gearcase lubricant for debris
Electric starter engages (flywheel does not rotate)	Weak or discharged battery	Fully charge and test the battery
	Dirty or corroded battery terminals	Thoroughly clean battery terminals
	Loose or dirty wire connections	Clean and tighten starter wire connections
	Engine is in gear	Correct improper linkage adjustment
	Water in the cylinder(s)	Inspect spark plug(s) for water contamination
	Oil in the cylinder(s)	Inspect spark plugs for oil contamination
	Damaged starter drive gear	Inspect starter drive gear
	Damaged flywheel gear teeth	Inspect flywheel gear teeth
	Faulty electric starter	Repair the electric starter
	Seized power head	Inspect power head for damage
	Seized gearcase	Inspect gearcase lubricant fordebris
	Improper valve timing or adjustment	Check valve timing and adjustment

(continued)

Table 1 STARTING SYSTEM TROUBLESHOOTING (continued)

Symptom	Possible causes	Corrective action
Electric starter (noisy operation)	Dirty or dry starter drive gear	Clean and lubricate starter drive gear
	Damaged starter drive gear teeth	Inspect starter drive gear
	Damaged or corroded flywheel gear	Inspect flywheel drive gear teeth
	Loose starter mounting bolt(s)	Tighten starter mounting bolt(s)
	Worn or dry starter bushing(s)	Repair electric starter
Rewind starter (does not engage flywheel)	Worn or damaged drive pawl	Replace the drive pawl
	Broken or damaged friction spring	Repair the friction spring
	Dry or binding rewind mechanism	Repair the rewind starter
Rewind starter (engages the flywheel but does not rotate)	Engine is in gear	Shift engine into neutral
	Misadjusted neutral only start mechanism	Adjust the mechanism
	Damaged neutral only start mechanism	Repair the rewind starter
	Worn or damaged rewind mechanism	Repair the rewind starter
	Frayed starter rope	Replace the starter rope
	Corroded or binding starter sheave	Repair the rewind starter
	Water in the cylinders	Inspect the spark plug(s) for water contamination
	Oil in the cylinders	Inspect the spark plug(s) for oil contamination
	Improper valve timing or adjustment	Check valve timing and adjustment
	Seized or damaged power head	Inspect power head for damage
	Seized or damaged gearcase	Inspect gearcase lubricant for debris
Rewind starter (rope does not rewind)	Worn or frayed starter rope	Replace starter rope
	Broken or damaged rewind spring	Replace rewind spring
	Dry, corroded or damaged rewind mechanism	Repair rewind starter

Table 2 FUEL SYSTEM TROUBLESHOOTING

Symptom	Possible causes	Corrective action
Engine does not start	Closed fuel tank vent	Open the fuel tank vent
	Old or contaminated fuel	Provide the engine with fresh fuel
	Disconnected fuel hose	Connect fuel hose
	Faulty primer bulb	Check the primer bulb
	Choke valve not operating	Check choke valve operation
	Air or fuel leaks in hose fittings	Inspect hose fittings for leakage
	Blocked fuel filter	Inspect the filter for contaminants
	Stuck carburetor inlet needle	Repair the carburetor(s)
	Improper float level adjustment	Repair the carburetor(s)
	Blocked carburetor passages	Repair the carburetor(s)
	Faulty low pressure fuel pump	Check low pressure pump

(continued)

Table 2 FUEL SYSTEM TROUBLESHOOTING (continued)

Symptom	Possible causes	Corrective action
Engine does not start (continued)	Low battery voltage (EFI models)	Check battery and charging system
	Faulty system relay (EFI models)	Check the system relay
	Open fuel pump fuse (EFI models)	Check fuel pump fuse
	Faulty electric fuel pump (EFI models)	Check fuel system pressure
	Faulty fuel pressure regulator (EFI models)	Check fuel pressure regulator
	Faulty idle air control valve (EFI models)	Check idle air control valve
	Faulty engine temperature sensor (EFI models)	Check the engine temperature
	Faulty air temperature sensor (EFI models)	Check air temperature sensor
	Faulty MAP sensor (EFI models)	Check MAP sensor
	Faulty throttle position switch (EFI models)	Check throttle position switch
	Faulty fuel injector (EFI models)	Check fuel injector(s)
	Faulty electronic control unit (EFI models)	Check electronic control unit
Stalls or runs rough at idle	Old or contaminated fuel	Provide the engine with fresh fuel
	Improper idle speed adjustment	Adjust idle speed
	Closed or blocked fuel tank vent	Open or clear vent
	Blocked carburetor passages	Repair carburetor(s)
	Flooding carburetor	Check for carburetor flooding
	Faulty primer bulb	Check the primer bulb
	Air or fuel leaks at hose fittings	Inspect hose fittings for leakage
	Blocked fuel filter	Inspect the filter for contaminants
	Faulty low pressure fuel pump	Check low pressure pump
	Sticking choke valve	Check choke valve operation
	Low battery voltage (EFI models)	Check battery and charging system
	Flooding vapor separator tank (EFI models)	Check vapor separator tank
	Faulty idle air control valve (EFI models)	Check idle air control valve
	Faulty system relay (EFI models)	Check the system relay
	Faulty throttle position switch (EFI models)	Check throttle position switch
	Faulty engine temperature sensor (EFI models)	Check the sensor
	Faulty air temperature sensor (EFI models)	Check air temperature sensor
	Faulty MAP sensor (EFI models)	Check MAP sensor
	Faulty fuel pressure regulator (EFI models)	Check fuel pressure regulator
	Faulty electric fuel pump (EFI models)	Check fuel system pressure
	Faulty fuel injector (EFI models)	Check fuel injector(s)
	Faulty engine control module (EFI models)	Check engine control module
Idle speed too high	Improper idle speed adjustment	Adjust idle speed
	Improper throttle linkage adjustment	Adjust throttle linkages
	Binding throttle linkage	Check linkage

(continued)

Table 2 FUEL SYSTEM TROUBLESHOOTING (continued)

Symptom	Possible causes	Corrective action
Idle speed too high (continued)	Faulty idle air control valve (EFI models)	Check idle air control valve
	Faulty engine temperature sensor	Check sensor
Hesitation during acceleration	Old or contaminated fuel	Supply the engine with fresh fuel
	Faulty low pressure fuel pump	Check low pressure fuel pump
	Sticking choke valve	Check choke valve operation
	Blocked carburetor passages	Repair carburetor(s)
	Faulty accelerator pump	Repair carburetor(s)
	Blocked fuel filter	Inspect the filter(s) for contaminants
	Air or fuel leaks at hose fittings	Inspect hose fittings for leakage
	Closed or blocked fuel tank vent	Open or clear tank vent
	Flooding carburetor	Check for carburetor flooding
	Improper valve timing	Check valve timing
	Low battery voltage (EFI models)	Check battery and charging system
	Flooding vapor separator tank (EFI models)	Check vapor separator tank
	Faulty throttle position switch (EFI models)	Check throttle position switch
	Faulty engine temperature sensor (EFI models)	Check the sensor
	Faulty air temperature sensor (EFI models)	Check air temperature sensor
	Faulty MAP sensor (EFI models)	Check MAP sensor
	Faulty fuel pressure regulator (EFI models)	Check fuel pressure regulator
	Electric fuel pump failure (EFI models)	Check fuel system pressure
	Faulty fuel injector (EFI models)	Check fuel injector(s)
	Faulty electronic control unit (EFI models)	Check electronic control unit
Misfire or poor high speed performance	Old or contaminated fuel	Supply the engine with fresh fuel
	Faulty low pressure fuel pump	Check low pressure fuel pump
	Sticking choke valve	Check choke valve operation
	Misadjusted throttle linkage	Adjust throttle linkage
	Blocked carburetor passages	Repair carburetor(s)
	Blocked fuel filter(s)	Inspect the filter(s) for contaminants
	Air or fuel leaks at hose fittings	Inspect hose fittings for leakage
	Closed or blocked fuel tank vent	Open or clear vent
	Improper valve timing	Check valve timing
	Low battery voltage (EFI models)	Check battery and charging system
	Faulty engine temperature sensor (EFI models)	Check the sensor
	Faulty air temperature sensor (EFI models)	Check air temperature sensor
	Faulty MAP sensor (EFI models)	Check MAP sensor
	Faulty fuel pressure regulator (EFI models)	Check fuel pressure regulator
	Electric fuel pump failure (EFI models)	Check fuel system pressure
	Faulty fuel injector (EFI models)	Check fuel injector(s)
	Faulty electronic control unit (EFI models)	Check electronic control unit

(continued)

Table 2 FUEL SYSTEM TROUBLESHOOTING (continued)

Symptom	Possible causes	Corrective action
Excessive exhaust smoke	Flooding carburetor	Check for carburetor flooding
	Blocked carburetor passages	Repair carburetor(s)
	Improper float level	Repair carburetor(s)
	Leaking accelerator pump	Repair carburetor(s)
	Sticking choke valve	Check choke valve operation
	Flooding vapor separator tank (EFI models)	Check vapor separator tank
	Faulty engine temperature sensor (EFI models)	Check the sensor
	Faulty air temperature sensor (EFI models)	Check air temperature sensor
	Faulty MAP sensor (EFI models)	Check MAP sensor
	Faulty fuel pressure regulator (EFI models)	Check fuel pressure regulator
	Faulty fuel injector (EFI models)	Check fuel injector(s)
	Faulty electronic control unit (EFI models)	Check electronic control unit

Table 3 IGNITION SYSTEM TROUBLESHOOTING

Symptom	Possible causes	Corrective action
Engine does not start	Lanyard switch activated	Check lanyard switch
	Faulty neutral only start switch	Test neutral only start switch
	Fouled spark plug(s)	Check or replace spark plug(s)
	Faulty spark plug lead	Test spark plug lead
	Faulty spark plug cap	Test spark plug cap
	Shorted stop circuit	Test for shorted stop circuit
	Low battery voltage (EFI models)	Check battery and charging system
	Faulty system relay (EFI models)	Test the system relay
	Failed harness capacitor (EFI models)	Test the harness capacitor
	Faulty ignition charge coil	Test ignition charge coil
	Faulty pulser coil	Test pulser coil
	Faulty crankshaft position sensor(s)	Test crankshaft position sensor(s)
	Faulty camshaft position sensor	Test camshaft position sensor
	Faulty ignition coil	Test ignition coil
	Faulty CDI unit	Check CDI unit
	Faulty electronic control unit (EFI models)	Check electronci control unit
Stalls or runs rough at idle	Fouled spark plug(s)	Check or replace spark plug(s)
	Faulty spark plug lead	Test spark plug lead
	Faulty spark plug cap	Test spark plug cap
	Partially shorted stop circuit	Test for shorted stop circuit
	Low battery voltage (EFI models)	Check battery and charging system
	Faulty system relay (EFI models)	Test the system relay
	Failed harness capacitor (EFI models)	Test the harness capacitor
	Faulty ignition charge coil	Test ignition charge coil
	Faulty pulser coil	Test pulser coil
	Faulty crankshaft position sensor(s)	Test crankshaft position sensor(s)

(continued)

Table 3 IGNITION SYSTEM TROUBLESHOOTING (continued)

Symptom	Possible causes	Corrective action
Stalls or runs rough at idle (continued)	Faulty camshaft position sensor	Test camshaft position sensor
	Faulty ignition coil	Test ignition coil
	Faulty CDI unit	Check CDI unit
	Faulty electronic control unit (EFI models)	Check electronic control unit
Idle speed too high	Faulty engine temperature sensor	Test engine temperature sensor
	Faulty pulser coil	Test pulser coil
	Faulty crankshaft position sensor	Test crankshaft position sensor
	Faulty CDI unit	Check low speed timing (Chapter Four)
	Faulty electronic control unit (EFI models)	Check low speed timing (Chapter Four)
Misfire or poor high speed performance	Engine reaching rev limit	Check full speed engine rpm
	Fouled spark plug(s)	Check or replace spark plug(s)
	Faulty spark plug lead	Test spark plug lead
	Faulty spark plug cap	Test spark plug cap
	Partially shorted stop circuit	Test for shorted stop circuit
	Faulty ignition charge coil	Test ignition charge coil
	Faulty pulser coil	Test pulser coil
	Faulty crankshaft position sensor(s)	Test crankshaft position sensor(s)
	Faulty camshaft position sensor	Test camshaft position sensor
	Faulty ignition coil	Test ignition coil
	Faulty CDI unit	Check CDI unit
	Faulty electronic control unit (EFI models)	Check electronic control unit

Table 4 MINIMUM BATTERY CABLE SIZES (AWG)

Cable length	9.9-15 hp models (211-305 cc)	40-70 hp models (815-1298 cc)
1-10 ft. (0.3-3 m)	10 gauge	4 gauge
11-15 ft. (3.4-4.6 m)	8 gauge	2 gauge
16-20 ft. (4.9-6.1 m)	6 gauge	1 gauge

Table 5 CARBURETED FUEL PUMP SPECIFICATIONS

Engine rpm	Pump pressure psi (kPa)
600	1 (7)
2500-3000	1.5 (10)
4500	2.5 (17)

Table 6 FUEL INJECTION SPECIFICATIONS

Component	Specification
Fuel injector resistance	11.0-16.6 ohms
High pressure fuel pump (minimum system pressure)	34 psi (234 kPa)

2

Table 7 STARTING SYSTEM COMPONENT SPECIFICATIONS (FUEL INJECTED ENGINES)*

Component	Specification
Engine neutral switch	
Button extended (in FORWARD or REVERSE)	Infinite resistance (no continuity)
Button depressed (in NEUTRAL)	Continuity (0 or very low resistance)
Starter relay	3.5-5.1 ohms
Starter	
Armature coil	
Between commutator segments	Continuity (0 or very low resistance)
Between commutator and core	Infinite resistance (no continuity)
Between commutator and shaft	Infinite resistance (no continuity)
Brush holder	
Between positive and negative	Infinite resistance (no continuity)
Between positive and base plate ground	Infinite resistance (no continuity)
Brush length	
Standard	0.49 in. (12.5 mm)
Minimum service limit	0.35 in. (9.0 mm)
Commutator diameter	
Standard	1.30 in. (33 mm)
Minimum service limit	1.26 in. (32 mm)
Commutator mica depth	
Standard	0.02-0.03 in. (0.5-0.8 mm)
Minimum service limit	0.008 in. (0.2mm)
Stop switch	
Key ON	Continuity (0 or very low resistance)
Key OFF	Infinite resistance (no continuity)

*Resistance specifications are based upon tests conducted at an ambient/component temperature of 68° F (20° C).

Table 8 CHARGING SYSTEM COMPONENT SPECIFICATIONS*

Component	Resistance (ohms)
20 amp main power relay (fuel injected engines)	
Between B+ and L terminals (no power applied)	Infinite (no continuity)
Between B+ and L terminals (12 volts across B- and S terminals)	Continuity (0 or very low resistance)
Between B- and S terminals	80-120
Stator (battery charge coil)	
Carbureted models (6 amp winding)	1.38-1.68
Carbureted models (12 amp winding)	0.45-0.54
Fuel injected models (12 volt winding)	0.56-0.84

*Resistance specifications are based upon tests conducted at an ambient/component temperature of 68° F (20° C).

Table 9 IGNITION POWER AND CHARGE COIL SPECIFICATIONS (CARBURETED ENGINES)*

Engine model	Engine size cu. in. (cc)	Power coil ohms	Cranking voltage	Charge coil ohms	Cranking voltage
5 and 6 hp	7.8 (128)	82-102	100	800-1000	200
8 and 9.9 hp	12.87 (211)	82-102	100	800-1000	200
9.9 and 15 hp	18.61 (305)				
1995-1996					
rope start		76-92	100	1010-1230	300
1995-1996					
electric start		52-62	100	720-880	300

(continued)

Table 9 IGNITION POWER AND CHARGE COIL SPECIFICATIONS (CARBURETED ENGINES)* (continued)

Engine model	Engine size cu. in. (cc)	Power coil ohms	Cranking voltage	Charge coil ohms	Cranking voltage
9.9 and 15 hp (continued)					
1997 rope start		76-92	70	1010-1230	220
1997 electric					
start		52-62	70	720-880	220
1998 all		52-62	70	720-880	220
1999-2001 all		52-62	30	720-880	220

*Resistance specifications are based upon tests conducted at an ambient/component temperature of 68° F (20° C).

Table 10 IGNITION SYSTEM COMPONENT SPECIFICATIONS (CARBURETED ENGINES)*

Engine model	Engine size cu. in. (cc)	Ignition coil primary ohms	secondary ohms	Ignition module cranking volt./running volt.	Timing sensor ohms
5 and 6 hp	7.8 (128)	0.23-0.33	225-325	50/220	132-162
8 and 9.9 hp	12.87 (211)				
1995-1996		0.23-0.33	2000-2600	100/240	132-162
1997-2001		0.23-0.33	2000-2600	50/240	132-162
9.9 and 15 hp	18.61 (305)	0.23-0.33	2000-2600	100/240	–

*Resistance specifications are based upon tests conducted at an ambient/component temperature of 68° F (20° C).

Table 11 IGNITION SYSTEM COMPONENT SPECIFICATIONS (FUEL INJECTED ENGINES)*

Component	Resistance (ohms)
Crankshaft position (CKP) and camshaft position (CMP) sensors	168-252
Ignition coil primary circuit	1.9-2.5
Ignition coil secondary circuit	
40 and 50 hp models (tested without leads)	8100-11,100
70 hp models (tested with leads connected)	15,000-28,000
High tension leads (70 hp models only)	2500-4100

*Resistance specifications are based upon tests conducted at an ambient/component temperature of 68° F (20° C).

Table 12 ENGINE SENSOR AND SWITCH SPECIFICATIONS (FUEL INJECTED ENGINES)*

Component	Specification
Closed throttle position (CTP) switch	
Button extended	Infinite resistance (no continuity)
Button depressed	Continuity (0 or very low resistance)
Fuel injector resistance	11.0-16.6 ohms
Intake air control (IAC) valve	
40 and 50 hp models	21.5-32.3 ohms
70 hp models	4.8-7.2 ohms
Manifold absolute pressure (MAP) sensor	
0 in. hg. (0 kPa) vacuum applied to hose	4.0 volts
11.8 in. hg. (40 kPa) vacuum applied to hose	2.42 volts
24 in. hg. (80 kPa) vacuum applied to hose	0.84 volts

(continued)

Table 12 ENGINE SENSOR AND SWITCH SPECIFICATIONS (FUEL INJECTED ENGINES)* (continued)

Component	Specification
Oil pressure switch	
Less than 10-19 psi (70-131 kPa) oil pressure	Continuity (0 or very low resistance)
10-19 psi (70-131 kPa) or more oil pressure	Infinite resistance (no continuity)
Temperature sensors	
Cylinder (CT) and intake air (IAT)	
At 32° F (0° C)	5100-6000 ohms
At 77° F (25° C)	1900-2100 ohms
At 122° F (50° C)	760-900 ohms
At 135° F (57° C)	340-420 ohms
Exhaust manifold (EM)	
40 and 50 hp models	See CT and IAT specifications
70 hp models	2318-2562 ohms

*Except for temperature sensors, resistance specifications are based upon tests conducted at an ambient/component temperature of 68° F (20° C).

Table 13 ENGINE COMPONENT TESTING THROUGH ECU HARNESS (40 AND 50 HP MODELS)*

Component	ECU harness terminals connectors and terminals (wire colors)	Resistance (ohms)
CKP sensor		
No. 1	E4 (R/B) and D1 (B/W)	168-252
No. 2	E3 (W/B) and D1 (B/W)	168-252
No. 3	E1 (R/W) and D1 (B/W)	168-252
CT sensor	D3 (Lg/W) to D1 (B/W)	See temperature sensors
EM temperature sensor	C9 (V/W) to D1 (B/W)	See temperature sensors
Fuel injector		
No. 1	A4 (O/B) and B5 (Gr)	11.0-16.5
No. 2	A7 (B/Y) and B5 (Gr)	11.0-16.5
No. 3	A8 (R/W) and B5 (Gr)	11.0-16.5
IAC valve	B4 (B/R) and B5 (Gr)	21.5-32.3 ohms
IAT sensor	D6 (Lg/B) to D1 (B/W)	See temperature sensors
Ignition coil primary circuit		
No. 1	A5 (O) and B5 (Gr)	1.9-2.5
No. 2	A1 (Bl) and B5 (Gr)	1.9-2.5
No. 3	A3 (G) and B5 (Gr)	1.9-2.5
Ignition coil secondary circuit		
No. 1	B5 (Gr) to No. 1 spark plug cap	8,100-11,100
No. 2	B5 (Gr) to No. 2 spark plug cap	8,100-11,100
No. 3	B5 (Gr) to No. 3 spark plug cap	8,100-11,100
Starter relay	D11 (Y/G) to ground	3.5-5.1
Temperature sensors circuit values		
At 32° F (0° C)	refer to CT, IAT or EM	5300-6600 ohms
At 77° F (25° C)	refer to CT, IAT or EM	1800-2300 ohms
At 122° F (50° C)	refer to CT, IAT or EM	730-960 ohms
At 135° F (57° C)	refer to CT, IAT or EM	330-450 ohms

*Except for temperature sensors, resistance specifications are based upon tests conducted at an ambient/component temperature of 68° F (20° C).

Table 14 EFI DIAGNOSTIC CODES

Code	Failure
11	Charging system malfunction
14	Cylinder temperature sensor
15	Exhaust manifold temperature sensor
22	Closed throttle position switch
	(continued)

Table 14 EFI DIAGNOSTIC CODES (continued)

Code	Failure
23	Intake air temperature sensor
24	Camshaft position sensor
31	Idle air control valve
32	MAP sensor hose
34	MAP sensor
42	Crankshaft position sensor

Chapter Three

Lubrication, Maintenance and Tune-up

This chapter covers lubrication, maintenance and tune-up procedures. **Table 1** at the end of the chapter lists the maintenance items and recommended intervals for service. When operating in harsh conditions (saltwater, brackish or polluted waters, or extreme low or high temperatures) it may be necessary to perform many of the service intervals more often. **Tables 2-5** provide capacities and specifications. Refer to **Table 6** for torque specifications.

Regular maintenance is critical to trouble free operation, engine longevity and performance. Pay particular attention to the procedures covered in *Before and After Each Use* in this chapter. Frequent attention to these items may prevent significant engine damage.

This chapter is divided into the following sections:
1. Before and after each use.
2. Lubrication service.
3. Power head maintenance.
4. Midsection maintenance.
5. Gearcase maintenance.
6. Storage (preparation and re-commissioning).
7. Pre-season tune-up.
8. Clearing a submerged motor.
9. Tune-up.

BEFORE AND AFTER EACH USE

Table 1 lists the checks, inspection and maintenance required before and after operating the outboard. Refer to the specific instructions provided in this section.

Inspecting the Boat Hull for Damage

Before and after each use, make sure to visually inspect the boat hull for damage that could adversely affect boat handling, lead to structural safety concerns or place an undue burden on the engine by causing excessive drag.

Checking the Fuel Level

Always make sure the fuel tank is full when leaving the dock or ramp. Make sure to check the fuel level after each use and compare it with the amount of time spent on the water underway. Sudden increases in fuel consumption that are not linked to a change in use (wide-open throttle operation versus idling or low speed trolling) may indicate a need for engine service such as a tune-up or it might be the first sign of problems with the drive system, such as propeller damage.

Checking for Signs of Fuel or Oil Leakage

A visual inspection of all accessible hoses, fittings and seals will help uncover a damaged or weeping hose or seal before it fails completely (possibly stranding the boat and passengers). Immediately investigate fuel vapors for the possibility of a fuel leak.

WARNING
Use extreme caution if working with or around fuel. Never smoke around fuel or fuel vapors. Make sure no sparks, flame or ignition source is present in the work area. Flame or sparks can ignite fuel or fuel vapors and result in a fire or an explosion.

To perform a quick visual inspection, pump the primer bulb to fill the fuel system hoses on carbureted engines or turn the ignition switch on to energize the fuel pump for a few seconds. Inspect the fuel hoses from the fuel tank to the carburetor or vapor separator tank. Refer to Chapter Six or Chapter Seven, as applicable, to determine the fuel system hose routing and connection points. If there is fuel leakage, tighten clamps or replace defective hoses.

Visually inspect the power head and the inner part of the lower engine cover for the presence of oil residue. Wipe

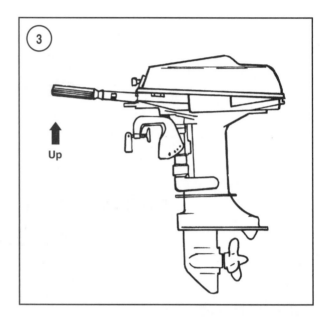

the power head with a clean white shop towel to help identify the leakage point. Most oil leakage occurs at the rocker arm cover (**Figure 1**) or oil filter mounting area (**Figure 2**). Tighten loose fasteners/filters or replace hoses and gaskets as required to correct the oil leakage before operating the engine.

Checking the Engine Crankcase Oil Level and Condition

CAUTION
Never start the engine with a low or high oil level. Low oil level or overfilling can cause inadequate power head lubrication.

Always check the oil level before and after each use. Accurate oil level measurements are only possible if the engine is switched off for 30 minutes or more and the engine is placed in a completely vertical position (**Figure 3**).

3

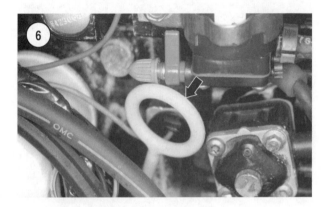

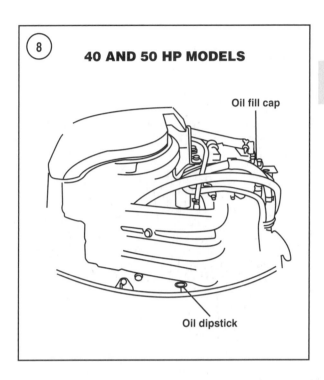

on the top, starboard side of the engine, on the flat portion of the engine, just above the ignition coil.

On 9.9 and 15 hp (305 cc) models, the oil dipstick (**Figure 6**) is located on the port side of the power head, just behind the spin-on oil filter. The oil fill cap (**Figure 7**) is located on the top, port side of the engine, on the flat portion of the engine above the oil filter.

On 40 and 50 hp (815 cc) models, the oil dipstick (**Figure 8**) is located on the lower port side of the power head. The oil fill cap is located at the rear of the engine, on top of the rocker arm cover.

On 70 hp (1298 cc) models, the oil dipstick is located on the lower rear and port side of the power head (**Figure 9**). The oil fill cap is located on the rear of the engine, toward the bottom of the rocker arm cover.

1. Position the engine vertically (**Figure 3**) with the ignition switched OFF.

NOTE
To ensure the most accurate measurement, when possible, check the oil after the engine has sat overnight. If the engine was run recently, allow at least 30 minutes for the oil to flow down into the crankcase and to begin cooling off.

2. Remove the upper engine cover and locate the dipstick on the port side of the engine.

3. Carefully pull the oil dipstick from the engine and wipe it clean.

Oil dipstick and oil fill cap locations vary by model. Refer to the following information to locate these components.

On 5 and 6 hp (128 cc) models, the oil dipstick (**Figure 4**) is located on the port side of the power head protruding from between the carburetor and the manual starter housing. The oil fill cap (**Figure 5**) is located on the top, starboard side of the engine, on the flat portion of the engine, just above the ignition coil.

On 8 and 9.9 hp (211 cc) models, the oil dipstick is located on the port side of the power head, between the carburetor and the intake manifold. The oil fill cap is located

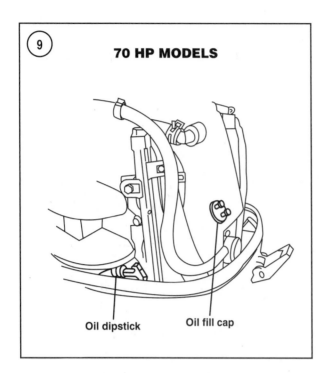

70 HP MODELS

Oil dipstick   Oil fill cap

4. Insert and fully seat the dipstick back into its opening.

5. Once again, carefully pull the dipstick from the engine, holding it vertically with the bottom downward and note the oil level line (**Figure 10**). On all models the oil level is correct when it is at or slightly below the top or *full* marking on the dipstick. The markings vary slightly from model to model:

    a. For 5/6 hp (128 cc) models and 8/9.9 hp (211 cc) models, the dipstick contains two markings, *L* for low and *F* for full.

    b. For 9.9/15 hp (305 cc) models, the dipstick contains *add* and *full* marks.

    c. For 40/50 hp models, the dipstick contains add and full marks (lines) with a crosshatched area between the two marks representing an acceptable oil level area for engine operation.

    d. For 70 hp models, the dipstick contains two dots, the bottom one is the *add* mark and the top (closest to the handle) is the *full* mark.

6. Inspect the oil on the dipstick for water, a milky appearance (which results from moisture contamination) or significant fuel odor. Refer to Chapter Two if any of these conditions occur.

7. Remove the oil fill cap if there is a low oil level. Add a small amount of four-stroke engine oil and recheck the oil level. Continue until the oil level just reaches or is slightly below the full level line. Do not overfill the engine with oil. Drain excess oil from the engine as described in this chapter during the oil change procedure.

8. Insert the oil dipstick fully into its opening. Install the oil fill cap. Rotate the oil fill cap until it is locked into position.

Propeller Inspection

> *WARNING*
> *Never operate the engine with significant propeller damage. Damage to the propeller can cause a significant decrease in performance, increased wear from excessive vibration, unusual handling characteristics and/or excessive engine speed.*

Inspect the propeller for bent, dinged or missing blade sections before and after operating the engine. Dress small imperfections using a suitable file. Avoid removing too much material or an imbalance can occur. Straighten small bends with locking type pliers. Have the propeller repaired at a reputable propeller repair shop if there is significant damage (**Figure 11**).

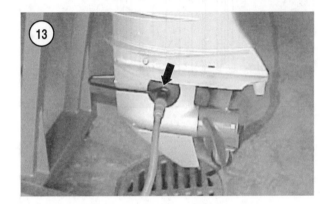

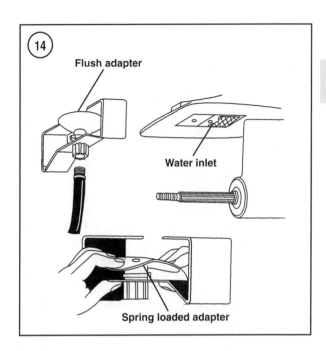

Checking the Water Intakes for Debris

Visually inspect the water intakes on the lower side of the gearcase for debris or obstructions. Clean any water vegetation or other debris from the intakes. Blockage reduces cooling water flow, and if there is a lot of blockage, it could lead to engine overheating and damage.

Engine Mounting Hardware Inspection

The 5-15 hp models are equipped with screw type clamps (**Figure 12**) for the upper engine mounting bolts, however these engines may also be bolted in place instead of using the screw clamps. Securely tighten both clamp screws before operating the engine. All other models use bolts and nuts on both the upper and lower ends of the clamp brackets. Make sure all mounting hardware is tight before operating the engine.

Cooling System Flushing

Flush the cooling system periodically with fresh, clean water to help prevent possible damage to the engine cooling system from blockage due to corrosion or debris. Flush the system immediately (dockside or on the trailer)

following use in salt, brackish or polluted water. Avoid possible engine damage due to thermal shock from flushing a very hot engine with very cold water. If necessary, allow the engine to cool for 10-15 minutes, then proceed with the flushing procedure. The system should also be flushed anytime any dirt or contaminants may have been pulled though the water intake, such as operation through churned-up silt, sand or other debris.

> *CAUTION*
> *Inspect the cooling system for proper operation every time the engine is run. On all models a stream of water exiting from the rear of the lower engine cover indicates that the water pump is operating. Never run the engine if it overheats or if the water stream is absent.*

> *NOTE*
> *All models from 8-70 hp are equipped with a freshwater flush port, though an adapter it is necessary to use this port on most models (it is included on some). Follow the directions given below when using the flush port, as conditions (such as engine running or not running) vary slightly from model to model. Clamp-type adapters (Figure 13) or a test tank may also be used on these models. For 5/6 (128 cc) models, no separate flushing port is provided, so a test tank or special water flush adapter (Figure 14) must be used.*

Some engine maintenance, testing or tune-up procedures require that the engine be run for some length of time when using a flush cooling system to prevent engine damage. On all models, a clamp-type flush adapter (refer to **Figure 13** or **Figure 14**) may be used; though the flushing port is preferred on 70 hp models. Also, on 8-15 hp models, the flushing port can be used. For 40 and 50 hp models, the clamp-type adapter is preferred, as the flushing port does not provide adequate cooling water to the power head during engine operation. In all cases, a test tank may also be used.

1. If using a test tank perform the following:
  a. Make sure the test tank is of sturdy material (strong enough to hold the engine). For 5/6 hp (128 cc) models, a sturdy 30 gal. (113 L) garbage can is sufficient, but larger models may require more capacity and a stronger tank. If necessary, use a wooden plank positioned between the engine clamp bracket and the test tank (**Figure 15**).
  b. Place the engine into the test tank. Make sure the water level is above the gearcase water inlet (above the anti-ventilation plate on the 5/6 hp (128 cc) models, since the water inlet is on the underside of the plate).
  c. Securely tighten the engine mounting bolts before starting the engine.

2. If using a flush test adapter (clamp-type or flush port-type) perform the following:
  a. Position the outboard vertically (recommended on most models, but mandatory on the 8-15 hp and 70 hp models if flushing is to occur with the engine running).
  b. Remove the propeller for safety.
  c. Attach the water hose to the flush test adapter.
  d. Route the water hose to avoid contact with moving parts. Secure the hose with tie straps as required.

3. If using a clamp-type flush test adapter, connect it to the proper location as follows:
  a. For 5/6 hp (128 cc) models, use a spring-loaded clamp-type adapter (**Figure 14**) on the anti-ventilation plate (directly over the water inlet).
  b. For 8-70 hp models, if using a clamp-type adapter, position the adapter cup directly over the water inlet(s) on the side of the gearcase, below the anti-ventilation plate. For 40/50 hp (815 cc) models, cover the other water inlet, located on the underside of the anti-ventilation plate using a piece of tape.

4. If using a port-type flush adapter, connect it to the proper location as follows:
  a. For 8/9.9 hp (211 cc) models, remove the top engine case for access, then remove the flush port plug (slotted-head) from the center of the intake mani-

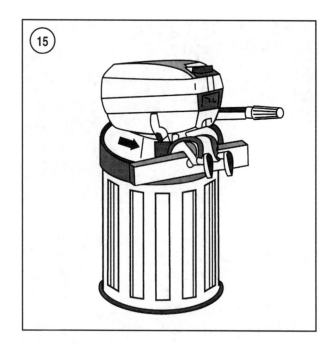

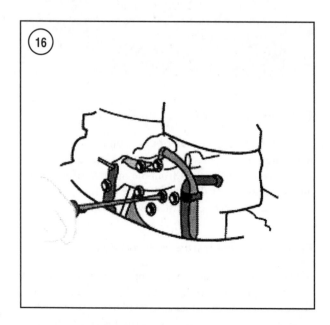

fold on the rear, port side of the motor (**Figure 16**). Connect the hose and adapter.

  b. For 9.9/15 hp (305 cc) models, remove the top engine case for access, and then remove the flush port plug (slotted-head) from the port side of the engine case (**Figure 17**), just above and slightly behind the spin-on oil filter. Connect the hose and adapter.

  c. For 40/50 hp (815 cc) models, remove the flushing port plug located at the center of the starboard side of the gearcase (**Figure 18**), immediately above the

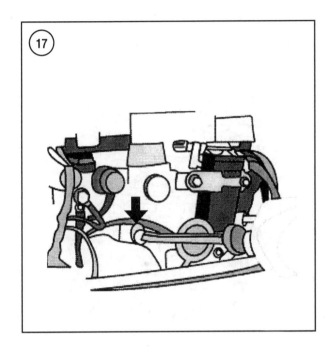

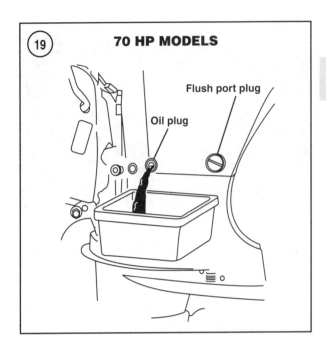

70 HP MODELS

Flush port plug

Oil plug

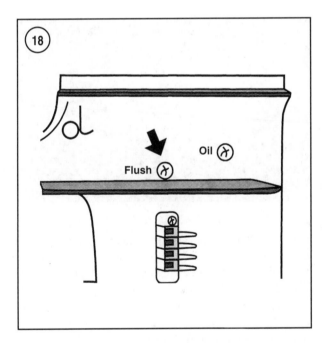

Oil

Flush

6. If using a test tank or if running the engine is desired for other reasons, turn the engine on and run it in neutral until the engine reaches normal operating temperature. For 5-15 hp engines, run the engine at fast idle. For 40 and 50 hp models, the engine speed should be about 1000 rpm. For 70 hp models, the engine idle speed should be at or below 1500 rpm. Verify that the same cooling system indicator stream is present while running the engine, if not, stop the engine and investigate before proceeding.

CAUTION
*The 8-15 hp and 70 hp models **must not** be running if flushing the engine in the tilted position. In this position the oil pump pickup is exposed to air in the tilted position and the lack of oiling can cause power head damage. The 40/50 hp (815 cc) models **must not** be running if flushing the engine while using the flushing port because this port will restrict water supply to the engine.*

anti-ventilation plate and behind the gearcase oil level plug.

d. For 70 hp (1298 cc) models, remove the flushing port plug located at the rear, port side of the engine case (**Figure 19**).

5. When using a flush adapter, turn the water source on, making sure the water pressure does not exceed 45 psi (310 kPa). Ideally the water pressure should be somewhere between 20-45 psi (140-300 kPa).

7. Continue to flush the engine or run the engine for a minimum of 10 minutes or until the water exiting the engine is clear. If running the engine, monitor the engine temperature and stop the engine immediately if steam or overheating starts to occur.

8. For carbureted models, slow the engine idle for a few minutes.

9. Stop the engine, if running.

10. Shut the water off and remove the flush adapter or remove the engine from the test tank, as applicable.

11. If not done already, place the engine in the vertical position (**Figure 3**) allowing the water to thoroughly drain from the cooling system. If the engine is going to be placed in storage where there may be freezing temperatures, make sure the water drains completely to prevent engine damage should the water freeze.

Shutting the Battery Switch Off

The ECU on fuel injected models constantly draws a small amount of electric current. If the engine is to be run at least every three to four weeks, this small draw is not a concern. If the boat is equipped with a battery switch, shutting it off will isolate the battery from the engine, thus preventing this slow, parasitic drain. If the engine sits idle for at least three or more weeks and no battery switch is installed, consider pulling the green 30 amp fuse from the fuse holder located on the side of the engine. To prevent confusion the next time the engine is started, tape a note to the key or key switch as a reminder.

LUBRICATION SERVICE

There are many internal and external moving parts of an outboard engine that will wear slightly during normal use. Lubricants, whether they are internal engine crankcase or gearcase oils or external greases and other oils, are used to minimize wear due to normal use. They minimize friction between sliding or rotating surfaces. As a secondary purpose, lubricants provide a coating that protects against the corrosive affects of moisture, salt or pollutants. Regular lubrication services are the most important maintenance performed.

Corrosion Maintenance

Reducing corrosion damage is an effective way to ensure maximum performance, reliability and durability of

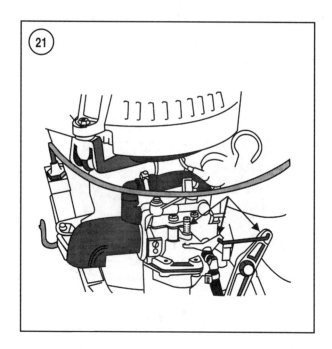

the engine. One simple and very important way to reduce corrosion in the cooling system passages is to always flush the system after running the engine. Refer to *Cooling System Flushing* in this chapter.

Visually inspect the anodes each time the engine is operated to make sure no sudden damage has occurred or that one has come loose. Also, make sure to clean and carefully inspect or replace the anodes at the interval specified in **Table 1**. The anode material is more corrosively active than other exposed engine components. Essentially, the anodes sacrifice themselves to protect the engine from corrosion damage. Corrosion protection is drastically reduced if the anodes are dirty, deteriorated or not grounded. Inspect the anodes as described in this chapter.

Using a corrosion preventative spray on the exterior engine components can substantially reduce corrosion dam-

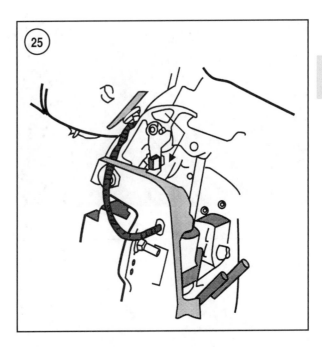

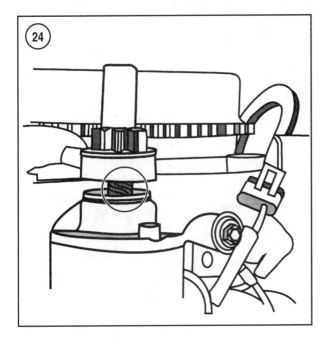

age to engine wiring, terminals, exposed fasteners and other components. Regular use is highly recommended if the engine is operated in salt, brackish or polluted water. Corrosion preventative sprays are available from most marine dealerships and marine supply stores. Follow the instructions on the container for proper use.

Choke and Carburetor Linkage
Lubrication (5-15 hp Models)

On carbureted models, remove the top engine case for access, then grease the carburetor and choke linkage using OMC Triple-Guard or an equivalent water resistant marine grease at the intervals in **Table 1**. Refer to **Figures 20-23** for appropriate lubrication points.

Electric Starter Pinion Lubrication

On models equipped with an electrical starter, apply a small amount of OMC brand or equivalent starter pinion lube on the sliding surfaces of the starter pinion (**Figure 24** shows a 9.9/15 hp [305 cc] model, others similar). If necessary, remove the manual starter cover for better access.

Power Trim/Tilt Reservoir Fluid Check

On 40-70 hp models, the correct fluid level in the power trim/tilt reservoir ensures proper system operation. During regular lubrication services, tilt the engine up and engage the tilt support for access to the reservoir cap. For safety, support the engine in this position. Remove the fluid reservoir cap (**Figure 25**, 70 hp models shown, 40/50 hp models similar) from the power trim/tilt reservoir located on the engine support bracket. If necessary, add OMC Power Trim/Tilt and Power Steering fluid to bring the level even with the bottom of the filler cap bore when the unit is at full tilt. Refer to *Fluid Level Inspection in Chapter Eleven*.

Shift Lever Shaft/Detent and Throttle Greasing

Lubricate the shift and throttle linkage using OMC Triple-Guard or an equivalent water resistant marine grease at the intervals in **Table 1**. Regular lubrication prevents corrosion and helps ensure smooth operation. Apply a

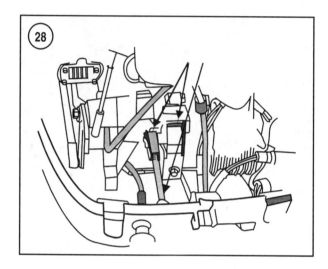

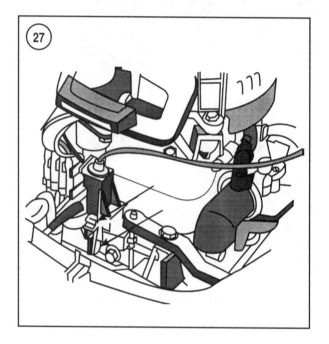

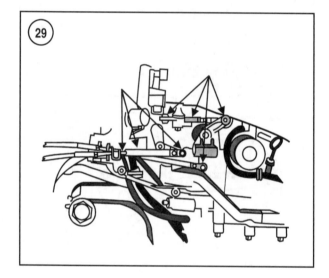

small amount of grease to all pivot points, throttle roller and throttle cam surfaces. Excessive lubrication provides no additional benefit and may attract dirt and debris. Use a small amount of penetrating oil if difficult access prevents the application of grease to a particular point.

Refer to **Figures 26-30** for appropriate lubrication points:

1. **Figure 26** shows the 5/6 hp (128 cc) shift lever shaft and detent.

2. **Figure 27** shows the 8/9.9 hp (211 cc) shift lever shaft and detent.

3. **Figure 28** shows the 9.9/15 hp (305 cc) shift lever shaft and detent.

4. **Figure 29** shows the 40/50 hp (815 cc) shift lever shaft and throttle cable.

5. **Figure 30** shows the 70 hp (1298 cc) shift lever shaft and throttle cable.

Swivel, Tilt Pin/Shaft and Clamp Screw Lubrication

During normal lubrication services (at intervals recommended in **Table 1**), apply OMC Triple-Guard or an equivalent high quality water resistant grease to all accessible tilt pivot points (**Figure 31**) on the midsection. Grease fittings are provided on most models for the tilt (**Figure 32**) and/or pivot pins. Pump grease into the fitting until the old or contaminated grease is expelled from the pivot point.

Refer to **Figures 33-40** for appropriate lubrication points:

1. **Figure 33** shows the 5/6 hp (128 cc) tilt pivot grease fittings and clamp screw threads. **Figure 34** shows the tilt linkage slider and steering grease fittings. **Figure 35** shows the tilt pivot pin.

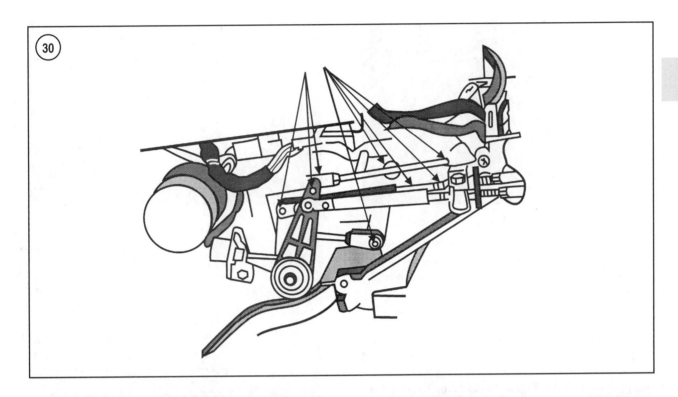

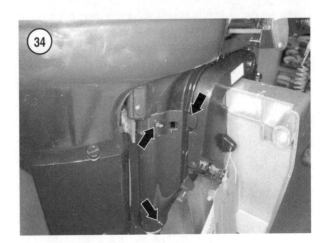

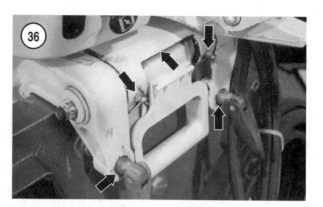

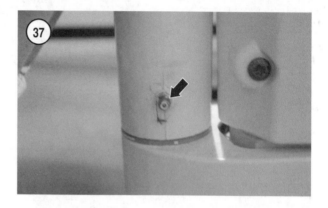

2. **Figure 36** shows the 8/9.9 hp (211 cc) and 9.9 hp (305 cc) with the clamp screw threads, along with tilt grease fittings (one arrow points to a grease fitting found under the handle). Also, be sure to check the steering shaft for a grease fitting(s) (**Figure 37**) and use a grease gun to lubricate the fitting(s).

3. **Figure 38** shows the 70 hp (305 cc) model swivel bracket and tilt support grease fittings and lubrication points. 40/50 hp (815 cc) swivel and tilt support lubrication points are similar. **Figure 39** shows the 40/50 hp (815 cc) steering system and tilt tube lubrication points and fittings. **Figure 40** shows the 70 hp (1298 cc) steering system and tilt tube lubrication points and fittings.

Steering Cable Lubrication

> *CAUTION*
> *The steering cable must be in the retracted position before grease is injected into the grease fitting. The cable can become hydraulically locked if grease is injected with the cable extended. Refer to the cable manufacturer's instructions for the type and frequency of lubrication.*

During periodic lubrication service, make sure to coat the steering cable ram (cable-to-engine contact linkage) with high quality, water resistant marine grease. Some aftermarket steering cables have a grease fitting. Regular lubrication of the cable dramatically increases its life. Lubricate the cable with the grease recommended by the cable manufacturer or marine all-purpose grease. Inject the grease into the fitting until a slight resistance is felt. Do not overfill the cable.

POWER HEAD MAINTENANCE

Maintenance to the power head involves changing the engine oil and filter, as well as inspecting various power

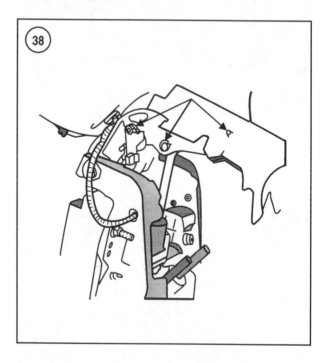

head components and systems, including the fuel system, electrical system and valve train. It also involves some of the procedures described in *Lubrication Service*.

3

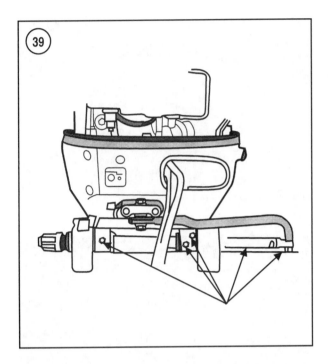

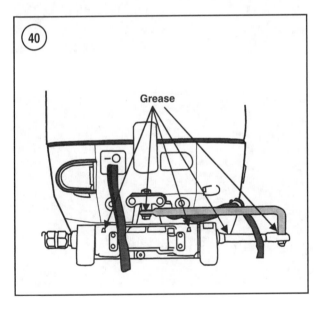

Grease

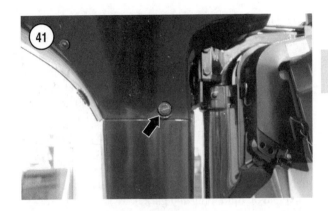

Changing the Engine Oil

Performing regular oil changes is the most effective way to ensure engine durability. The manufacturer recommends Johnson or Evinrude Ultra 4-Stroke Crankcase Oil be used. Change the oil and filter (change or clean the filter, as applicable) every 200 hours or annually (immediately before storage). If Johnson/Evinrude oil is not available the manufacturer advises the use of a high-detergent SG or SH oil of the proper viscosity, but in such cases

the oil change interval is reduced to 100 hours (or still annually). If using a substitute four-stroke oil, use SAE 10W-30 for 5-15 hp models, or SAE 10W-40 for 40-70 hp models.

WARNING
Never use two-stroke outboard engine oil in a 4-stroke outboard. Using the wrong type of oil will cause significant engine wear and possibly power head failure.

CAUTION
Infrequent oil change intervals may contribute to camshaft wear. Excessive valve clearance found during annual service could be an indication to make sure the recommended fluid is used.

CAUTION
On 5-15 hp models used under severe operating conditions such as sea-water temperatures exceeding 68° F (20° C) or under constant heavy load operation, use SAE 10W-40 or SAE 10W-50 for increased protection. Also, if there is high oil consumption under normal conditions try SAE 10W-50 to slow oil use.

It is recommended that the engine oil be changed when the oil is hot. This allows the oil to drain faster and more thoroughly, removing more contaminants from the engine.

Provide a source of cooling water as described in *Cooling System Flushing* and operate the engine before and after the oil change.

1. Place the engine in the vertical position (**Figure 3**).

2. Refer to the oil drain plug location for the selected model:

   a. On 5/6 hp (128 cc) and 8/9.9 hp (211 cc) models, the plug is located on the starboard side lower engine cover (**Figure 41**) just above the gearcase.

b. On 9.9/15 hp (305 cc) models, the plug is located at the base of the starboard side of the engine, at the gearcase split line.

c. On 40-70 hp models, the plug is located on the forward, port side of the lower engine cover (**Figure 19** shows the 70 hp model, the 40 and 50 hp models are similar).

3. Remove the oil fill cap to provide better oil flow and place a large drain pan below the drain plug.

4. Using a screwdriver (5-15 hp models) or an appropriately sized Allen wrench (40-70 hp models), carefully remove the oil drain plug and gasket.

5. When most of the oil is drained, tilt the engine upward slightly and pivot it toward the drain plug side to ensure thorough drainage. Clean contaminants from the plug and plug opening. Place a *new* gasket onto the drain plug then carefully thread the plug into the opening. Tighten the plug securely.

6. Remove and inspect (clean or replace, as applicable) the oil filter. Refer to *Oil Filter Replacement* in this chapter.

7. Refer to *Checking the Engine Oil Level and Condition* as described in this chapter to determine the oil fill cap locations and instructions. Add the oil gradually, checking the oil level often. Continue to add oil until the level reaches the upper mark on the dipstick.

8. Start the engine and allow it to idle until it reaches normal operating temperature. Check for leakage.

> *CAUTION*
> *If placing the engine into storage, **do not** run the engine, (even briefly) as combustion byproducts will form in the engine oil.*

9. Recheck the oil level once the engine is cooled and the oil has settled back into the crankcase.

Oil Filter Cleaning or Replacement

Change the engine oil and replace the oil filter (or inspect and clean the reusable filter element on 5/6 hp [128 cc] or 8/9.9 hp [211 cc] models) at the intervals in **Table 1**. The 305 cc and larger models are equipped with disposable spin-on oil filters. The easiest method to remove these filters is to use a cap-style filter wrench (**Figure 42**).

1. Drain the engine oil as described in this chapter.

2. Remove the upper engine cover and locate the oil filter, as follows:

a. For the 5/6 hp (128 cc) models, the reusable filter element (**Figure 43**) is mounted under a large hex-head cap located in a bore toward the rear, starboard side of the power head (directly in front of the

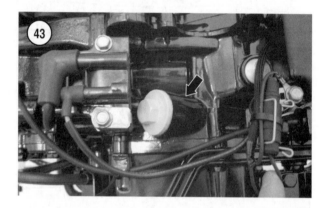

ignition coil). Remove the starboard lower engine cover in order to access the filter.

b. For the 8/9.9 hp (211 cc) models, the reusable filter element is mounted under a large hex-head cap located in a bore on the stern, port side, bottom of the power head (directly below the rear of the intake manifold). It looks similar to the type used on the 5/6 hp engine (**Figure 43**). Dislodge or completely remove the port lower engine cover in order to access the filter.

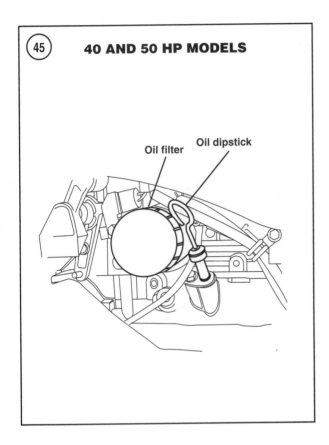

45   **40 AND 50 HP MODELS**

Oil filter   Oil dipstick

c. For the 9.9/15 hp (305 cc) models, the disposable spin-on oil filter (**Figure 44**) is located on center of the port side of the power head, just above the point where the oil dipstick enters the power head.

d. For the 40/50 hp (815 cc) models, the disposable spin-on oil filter (**Figure 45**) is located on the lower center, port side of the power head. It is directly below the manifold, and just in behind the shift lever shaft and throttle cable.

e. For the 70 hp (1298 cc) models, the disposable spin-on oil filter (**Figure 46**) is located on the lower center, starbard side of the power head. It is directly below the electronic control unit (ECU) and just behind the shift lever shaft and throttle cable.

3. Based on the location, determine if it is necessary to remove the lower side engine cover. Though it is possible on some models to remove the spin-on filter (such as some tiller control 9.9/15 hp models) without first removing this cover, it is much easier and much less likely to make a mess if the cover is removed from the engine as follows:

a. Carefully pull the seal (1, **Figure 47**, 70 hp model shown, others similar though bolt locations vary) from the top halves of the lower cover.

CAUTION
Never force the covers off. If they are stuck after removing the screws, double-check to make sure that there are no an additional screws bolted to the covers.

b. Remove the cover screws (**Figure 48**, 9.9/15 hp model shown, others similar). On most larger models, the cover screws are visible around the perimeter of the engine, but on smaller models, such as the 5/6 hp and 8/9.9 hp engines, the screws are all accessed on the inside of the case. On 8/9.9 hp models, the filter can be removed if the cover is simply dislodged. If choosing to do it this way, loosen but do not completely remove the cover retainers. In the case of the aft retainer, remove the nut and washer, but do not withdraw the bolt on these models.

NOTE
The externally mounted screws on some models are Torx type fasteners. Make sure to use the proper type and size Torx driver to prevent damage.

NOTE
When removing the lower engine covers on 5/6 hp and 8/9.9 hp models, the screws are located inside the cover and must be accessed in various ways. There are two screws located at the front of the engine

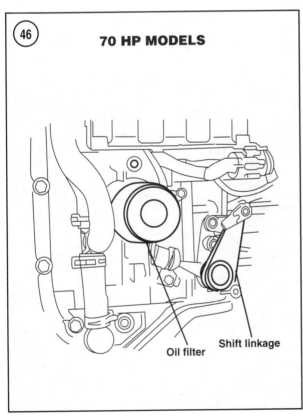

46   **70 HP MODELS**

Oil filter   Shift linkage

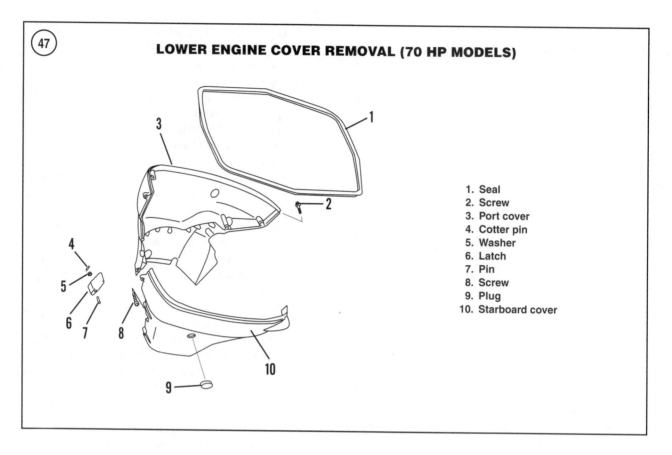

47 LOWER ENGINE COVER REMOVAL (70 HP MODELS)

1. Seal
2. Screw
3. Port cover
4. Cotter pin
5. Washer
6. Latch
7. Pin
8. Screw
9. Plug
10. Starboard cover

(Figure 49). *The lower of these two screws can be accessed either using a stubby screwdriver or by using a long screwdriver inserted through the choke knob opening in the front of the cover (after loosening the choke knob bracket from the cover). There are also two screws located at the back of the engine. The upper screw (Figure 50) is easy to access, but reach through the cooling system indicator to get the lower screw (Figure 51). To remove the lower, aft cover screw, pull the cooling system indicator from the hose, and push the hose back into the cover, then use a long-shaft screwdriver through the hole in the cover.*

NOTE
When removing the lower engine cover screws on the 9.9/15 hp models, look for two screws on the top of the lower cover, five around the lower sides and one in the rear starboard side of the cover, behind the water indicator hose. It is usually necessary to disconnect the water indicator hose to access the bolt at the rear starboard side of the cover.

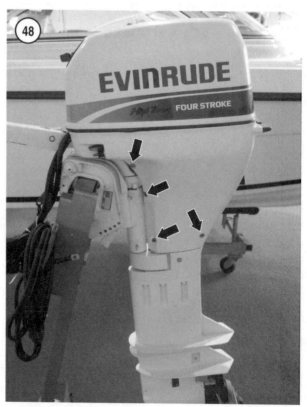

3

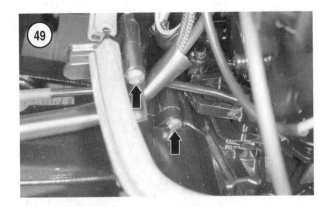

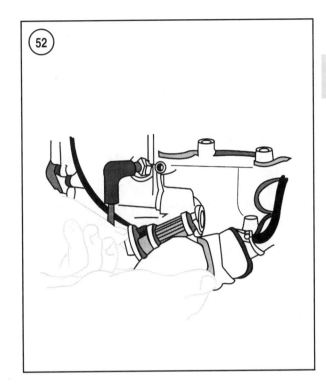

c. If necessary, remove the aft cover latch (6, **Figure 47**). On 8/9.9 hp models, the cover latch should be left alone if the cover is just being dislodged and not completely removed.

d. Carefully pull the port (8-50 hp models) or starboard (5/6 or 70 hp models) cover from the engine. It is not necessary to disconnect the choke or control linkage if the covers are supported out of the way while working. If removing the covers completely, make sure to carefully disconnect all hoses, choke and/or control cables.

4. For the 5/6 hp (128 cc) and 8/9.9 hp (211 cc) models, remove and service the filter as follows:

a. For 5/6 hp (128 cc) models, remove the ignition coil and position aside with the wiring still connected. Be careful not to drop and lose the spacer(s) behind the coil, the retaining bolts or the star washers. Note the screw, washer, ground strap and spacer orientation. Failure to install these components properly may cause damage to the coil during operation. Refer to Chapter Seven for more details regarding coil removal.

b. Place a rag under the oil filter element nut, then use a wrench or socket and ratchet to loosen and remove the nut along with the filter element (**Figure 52**).

c. Carefully rinse the element using solvent, then dry it using low pressure compressed air or at least 15 minutes to dry if compressed air is not available.

d. Inspect the element for excessive clogging or damage and replace, if necessary.

e. Coat the filter element and O-rings with fresh four-stroke engine oil, then install the element into the bore and thread the nut.

f. Tighten the filter nut 1/4 turn after the O-ring contacts the base.

5. For 9.9/15 hp (305 cc), 40/50 hp (815 cc) and 70 hp (1298 cc) models, replace the oil filter as follows:

a. Place a shop towel under the oil filter.

b. Engage the oil filter wrench or adapter (**Figure 42**) onto the oil filter.

c. Unscrew and remove the filter from the power head. Wipe up any spilled oil.

d. Make sure the sealing ring is not stuck to the oil filter mounting surface (**Figure 53**). Use a clean lint free shop towel to clean all oil or debris from the mounting surface.

e. Apply a thin coating of engine oil to the sealing ring (**Figure 54**) of the new oil filter.

f. Thread the new filter onto the oil filter adapter until the sealing washer just contacts the filter mounting surface. Tighten the filter by hand an additional 1/4 to 2/3 turn.

6. Wipe up any spilled oil, and then install the lower engine cover by carefully aligning the screw holes in the two covers, while also aligning the lower cover mating surfaces. Install and securely tighten the screws. Install the after cover latch (if removed) and the cover seal.

NOTE
When installing the engine covers, make sure there are no hoses, cables or other engine components pinched between the covers.

7. Fill the engine with oil as described in this chapter.

8. Provide a temporary cooling system to the engine (as described in the *Cooling System Flushing* procedure in this chapter), then start the engine and check for leakage.

Timing Belt Inspection

All models, except the 40/50 hp (815 cc), are equipped with a timing belt (**Figure 55**). The 40/50 hp models use a timing chain. Inspect the timing belt every year and to replace it every four years or 800 hours of operation, whichever comes first. A belt that breaks or jumps a tooth may disable the engine and strand the boat. Models equipped with a timing chain do not require regular inspection.

On some models, such as some versions of the 9.9/15 hp (305 cc) model, the timing belt is visible once the engine cover is removed. On others, such as the 8/9.9 hp (211 cc) and the 5/6 hp (128 cc) motors, although the belt is partially visible, thorough inspection is much easier once the manual starter cover and/or assembly is removed. For 70 hp (1298 cc) models, remove the flywheel cover to inspect the belt.

1. Disconnect the negative battery cable for safety while working around the flywheel.

2. Remove the spark plugs to make it easier to turn the engine over and ground the spark plug leads.

3A. On manual start models, if necessary for better access, remove the manual starter as described in Chapter Ten.

3B. On electric start only models, if necessary for better access, remove the flywheel cover as described in Chapter Eight.

4. Use compressed air to blow debris from the camshaft pulley, flywheel and timing belt.

5. Inspect the belt surfaces for worn, cracked or oil soaked surfaces.

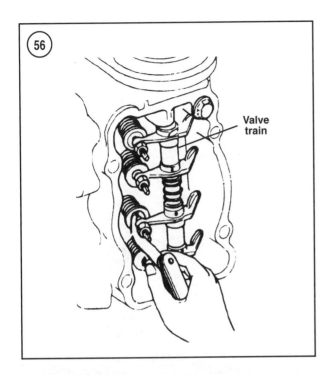

Valve train

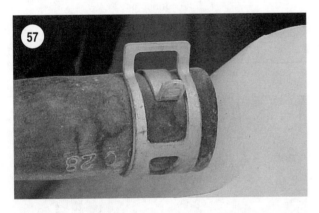

6. Manually rotate the flywheel while inspecting all of the timing belt cogs.

7. Inspect the flywheel and camshaft pulley teeth for worn or damaged surfaces.

8. Replace the timing belt and related components as described in Chapter Eight if there are any defects.

9. If removed, install the manual starter or flywheel, as applicable, onto the power head.

10. Install the spark plugs and leads, then connect the negative battery cable and install the engine cover.

Valve Adjustment

Running the engine with incorrect valve clearances can cause rough engine operation, excessive valve train noise and excessive wear to the valve train components (**Figure 56**). Normal engine wear gradually causes the valve clearances to change. It is important that this wear be compensated for by periodic valve clearance adjustments. Infrequent maintenance can also cause valve train wear.

Check the valve adjustment at the intervals listed in **Table 1**. Valve adjustment procedures are covered in Chapter Four. Infrequent oil changes or using the incorrect type of oil may contribute to camshaft wear. If excessive valve clearance is noted during inspection, this could be an indication to change the engine oil more frequently or to make sure the recommended oil is used.

Hose and Clamp Inspection

> *WARNING*
> *Use caution if working with the fuel system. Never smoke around fuel or fuel vapors. Make sure no flame or source of ignition is present in the work area. Flame or sparks can ignite fuel or fuel vapors resulting in a fire or an explosion.*

Inspect the entire fuel system and oil breather system for leaking hoses or connections at the intervals specified in **Table 1**. Replace any plastic tie clamps if they are brittle or damaged.

Carefully tug all fuel and oil breather hoses to check for a tight fit at all connections. Inspect spring type hose clamps (**Figure 57**) for corrosion or lack of spring tension. Replace any hose clamps that are in questionable condition.

Replace fuel hoses that are hard, brittle, leaking or feel spongy. Use only original equipment replacement hoses. Other types of hoses may not meet Coast Guard requirements. Refer to Chapter Five or Chapter Six for hose routing and connection points.

Inspect the portable fuel tank and related components, as follows:

1. Inspect the primer bulb (2, **Figure 58** shows a typical tank assembly) and fuel hoses for cracked, weathered, sticky or damaged surfaces. Replace any defective or suspect components as described in Chapter Five or Chapter Six, as applicable.

2. Squeeze the primer bulb while checking the hoses, primer bulb and connectors for fuel leakage. Replace any leaking components.

3. Remove the fuel tank cap (4, **Figure 58**) and inspect the inside of the fuel tank. If debris or deposits are found within the tank, disassemble and clean the fuel tank as described in Chapter Five or Chapter Six, as applicable.

4. Install the fuel tank cap and shut the cap mounted vent. Tilt the fuel tank enough to apply fuel to the mounting gasket for the fuel metering assembly. Repair any leakage at the mounting gasket as described in Chapter Five or Chapter Six, as applicable.

Fastener Inspection

Loose fasteners causing power head mounted components to vibrate and produce noise is often confused with internal engine noise. Be on the lookout for loose fasteners whenever operating or servicing the engine. Inspect the nuts and bolts that attach the fuel filter (if applicable), the electric or manual starter, wire and cable clamps and other power head mounted components.

Tighten loose fasteners to the specification provided in the appropriate chapter. If a torque specification is not available, tighten the fasteners to the general torque specifications in Chapter One.

Tighten the power head mounting, flywheel, intake manifold, cylinder head (on 5-15 hp models), water jacket and rocker arm cover fasteners at the initial 20 hours and annually or after each 100 hours of service, whichever comes first. Refer to the appropriate chapter for tightening sequence, tightening torque and specific instructions.

Battery Inspection

Check the battery condition and fluid level at the intervals listed in **Table 1**. Unlike automobiles, boats may sit idle for weeks without running. Without proper maintenance, the battery loses its charge and begins to deteriorate. Marine engines are exposed to a great deal more moisture than automobiles, resulting in more corrosion forming on the battery terminals. Clean the terminals and charge the battery at 30-day intervals during storage (or keep the battery on an automatically regulated charger.) Refer to Chapter Seven for complete battery testing, maintenance and charging instructions.

CAUTION
Allowing a battery to discharge excessively and electrolyte levels to drop allows corrosion to form on the internal plates. The freezing point of electrolyte in a discharged battery is much lower than that of a properly charged battery.

Power Head Anode Inspection

A power head mounted anode is used on the 9.9/15 hp (305 cc) models, on an aft facing boss (**Figure 59**) found

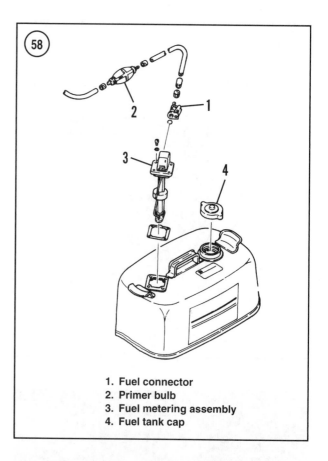

1. Fuel connector
2. Primer bulb
3. Fuel metering assembly
4. Fuel tank cap

on the manifold at the rear starboard side of the engine. A power head anode is also used on 40-70 hp models (**Figure 60**) bolted to the exhaust manifold/exhaust cover. It can be inspected visually and with an ohmmeter once the top engine case is removed. To visually check the anode, compare it with a replacement part (or take a measurement when the anode is new). Replace the anode once it is reduced in size by 1/3.

An ohmmeter can be used to verify proper conductivity of the anode. Refer to Chapter One for more information

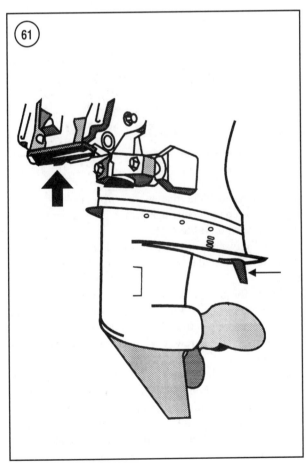

on *Galvanic Corrosion*. Connect one lead from the ohmmeter to a good ground on the power head and the other to the anode. If necessary, clean the contact surface of the anode slightly to ensure good contact between the anode and the meter lead. There should be little or no resistance across the leads. If not, remove the anode and carefully clean the contact surfaces of the anode and power head of all corrosion, dirt, oil, debris or other residue. Clean the anode mounting screw threads and the threads in the power head to ensure proper conductivity.

CAUTION
Never paint or coat the anode or the engine surface where the anode mounts. Any paint or foreign matter could isolate the anode electrically from the engine, preventing it from protecting the engine.

MIDSECTION MAINTENANCE

Midsection maintenance involves inspecting the sacrificial anodes, checking for loose nuts and bolts and checking/adjusting the steering friction. It also involves some of the lubrication procedures found earlier in this chapter under *Lubrication Service*. These maintenance items reduce corrosion damage, reduce wear to bushings and pins and help ensure smooth tilting and steering movement.

Anode Inspection

Some models are equipped with a midsection mounted anode. For 40-70 hp models, the midsection anode is mounted on the base of the engine mount clamp assembly (top arrow, **Figure 61** shows the 70 hp model, 40 and 50 hp models use two anodes, one on each half of the split clamp). When used, clean and inspect the midsection mounted anode (**Figure 62**) at the intervals listed in **Table 1**. Inspect the anodes more frequently if the engine is normally operated or stored in salt, brackish or polluted water. Anodes can be inspected visually and with an ohmmeter.

To visually check the anode, use a stiff brush to clean deposits and other material from the exposed anode surfaces. Compare it with a replacement part (or take a measurement when the anode is new). Replace the anode if it loses 1/3 or more of its material or contains deep pitting.

An ohmmeter can be used to verify proper conductivity of the anode (refer to Chapter One for more information on *Galvanic Corrosion*). Connect one lead from the ohmmeter to a good ground on the engine mount and the other to the anode. Make sure the contact surface of the anode is clean to ensure good contact between the anode and the meter lead. There should be little or no resistance across the leads. If not, remove the anode and carefully clean the contact surfaces of the anode and engine of all corrosion, dirt, oil, debris or other residue. Clean the anode mounting screw threads and the threads in the engine to ensure proper conductivity.

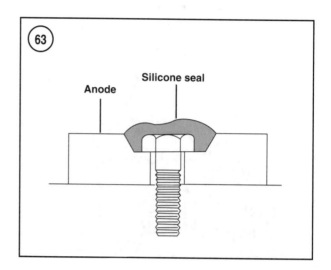

CAUTION
Never paint or coat the anode or the engine surface where the anode mounts. Any paint or foreign matter could isolate the anode electrically from the engine, preventing it from protecting the engine.

If necessary, remove and replace the anode as follows:
1. Remove the anode mounting bolt(s) and carefully pry the anode from the mounting surface.
2. Use a stiff brush to thoroughly clean the mounting bolts, bolt holes and the anode mounting surface. Continue cleaning until the surface is shiny. Use a tap and die set or thread chaser to ensure the threads of both the mounting bolts and the bolt holes are clean and free of corrosion or other insulating coatings. Do not apply any paint or other material to the anode mounting surface.
3. Use a stiff brush and file to clean all contaminants or casting slag from the mounting surfaces of the anode. The anode mounting surfaces must be clean and true to ensure proper grounding and a flush fit to the midsection.
4. Install the anode and mounting bolt(s). Securely tighten the bolt(s).
5. Cover the mounting bolt heads with a coating of silicone seal as indicated in **Figure 63**. Allow adequate time for curing of the sealant before placing the engine in the water.

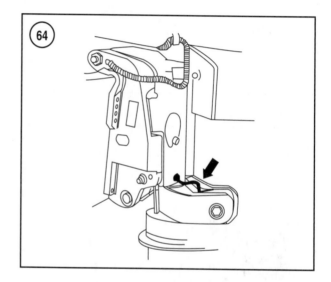

Anode ground wire inspection

Ground wires (**Figure 64**) are used on some models to maintain electrical continuity to the engine for movable midsection components. Broken, corroded or damaged ground wires prevent the anodes from protecting the ungrounded components. Inspect the ground wires at the intervals listed in **Table 1**.

1. Visually inspect the wires for broken, frayed or corroded surfaces. Replace defective or questionable ground wires.
2. Check for the presence of corrosion in or around ground wire terminals (**Figure 65**). If corrosion is present, disconnect and clean the wire terminals as follows:
   a. Remove the screw, wire and washer from the engine.
   b. Use a stiff brush and/or file to clean all corrosion, paint or other contaminants from the wire terminal, screw and insulating washer.
   c. Use an appropriate thread chaser to clean corrosion, paint or other contaminants from the threaded screw opening.

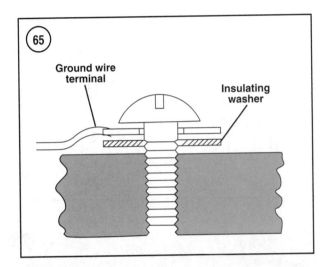

Ground wire terminal

Insulating washer

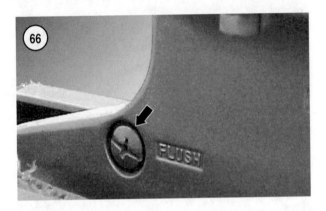

d. Install the wire terminal then insulating washer to the screw. Position the components as indicated in **Figure 65**. Install and securely tighten the screw. Make sure the wire terminal is positioned so it does not bind or stretch when tilting or steering the engine.

Fastener Inspection

Tighten all accessible midsection bolts and nuts at the intervals listed in **Table 1**. On 5-15 hp models, check and snug all fasteners securely. If the same fastener appears loose at multiple inspections, remove it and check the thread conditions. If necessary, apply a light coating of OMC Nut Lock or an equivalent threadlocking compound, then reinstall and snug the fastener. For 40-70 hp models, refer to Chapter Eleven to determine the location and torque specification for all fasteners used in the midsection. If a specific torque specification is not provided, tighten the fasteners to the general torque specification in Chapter One.

Steering Friction

The 5-15 hp models covered by this manual are equipped with a steering friction screw. The screw should be set so that a slight drag is felt when turning the engine. Refer to the *Steering Friction Adjustment* in Chapter Four.

GEARCASE MAINTENANCE

Maintenance to the gearcase involves checking and changing the gearcase lubricant, lubricating the propeller shaft, tightening the propeller nut, checking the fish line trap (8-15 hp models), inspecting gearcase mounted anodes and checking for loose fasteners. Refer to **Table 1** for gearcase maintenance requirements and intervals.

Checking the gearcase lubricant at periodic intervals may make it possible to detect potential gearcase problems and correct the cause before more extensive damage occurs. Normal gearcase operation contaminates the lubricant with small metal shavings from the gears and from small amounts of moisture from condensation; by changing the lubricant at the specified intervals, additional wear caused by the contamination can be eliminated.

CAUTION
Never use automotive gear lubricant in the gearcase. It is not suitable for marine applications, and its use can lead to increased wear and corrosion of internal components.

CAUTION
Make sure that the correct gearcase plugs are removed when checking or changing the gearcase lubricant. Some models have a flush plug (Figure 66) located on the same side of the gearcase as the gearcase fill/level plugs. The flush plug is used with a special adapter to flush contaminants from the cooling system. On models so equipped, the word FLUSH is cast into the gearcase housing next to the plug.

CAUTION
Inspect the sealing washers anytime the gearcase plugs are removed. Replace missing or damaged sealing washers to prevent leakage.

Gearcase Lubricant Inspection

Check the gearcase lubricant level and condition at the intervals specified in **Table 1**. Refer to *Gearcase Lubricant Replacement* for the recommended gearcase lubricant.

3

1. Position the engine in the upright position for at least one hour before checking the lubricant.

2. Disconnect the negative battery cable for safety, to ensure no accidental attempt to start the engine occurs while working around the propeller.

3. Position a suitable container under the gearcase. Slowly remove the fill/drain plug (**Figure 67**) and allow a small sample (a teaspoon or less) to drain from the gearcase. Quickly install the fill/drain plug and tighten it securely. Refer to Chapter Two if water or a milky appearance is in the fluid sample.

4. Rub a small amount of the fluid sample between your finger and thumb. Refer to Chapter Two if the lubricant feels gritty or if metal particles are present.

5. Slowly remove the level/vent plug (**Figure 68**, 9.9/15 hp model shown, others similar). Make sure the lubricant level is even with the bottom of the level/vent plug opening. If necessary, slowly pump lubricant into the fill/drain plug opening until fluid flows from the level/vent opening. Suspect a leak if more than 1 oz. (29 ml) is required to fill the gearcase. Refer to Chapter Two if a leak is suspected. Install the level/vent then drain/fill plugs. Securely tighten both plugs.

NOTE
When adding lubricant to the gearcase, installing the level/vent plug before removing the pump fitting from the fill/drain plug opening will help prevent fluid from draining rapidly while attempting to reinstall the fill/drain plug.

6. Allow the gearcase to remain undisturbed in a shaded area for one hour, and then recheck the fluid level. Add more lubricant if necessary.

7. Connect the negative battery cable.

Gearcase Lubricant Replacement

Use only OMC Ultra-HPF or equivalent marine gearcase lubricant marine that meets GL5 specifications. If necessary, OMC Hi-Vis gearcase lube may be used as a substitute. **Table 4** lists the approximate gearcase capacity for all models.

1. Disconnect the negative battery cable for safety.

2. Place a suitable container under the gearcase. Remove the level/vent plug (**Figure 67**) to provide the necessary ventilation to drain the gearcase, and then slowly remove the fill/drain plug (**Figure 69**, 9.9/15 hp model shown, others similar), allowing the lubricant to flow into the drain pan.

3. Inspect the gearcase lubricant as described in *Gearcase Lubricant Inspection*.

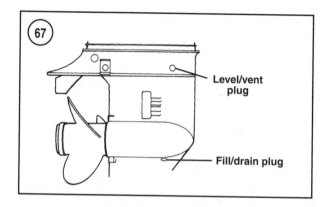

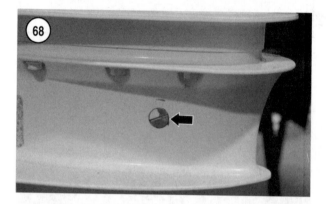

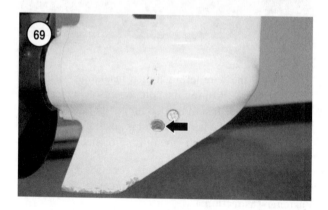

4. Once most of the lubricant is drained, tilt the engine slightly and allow the gearcase to drain completely.

5. Use a pump dispenser or squeeze tube to *slowly* pump lubricant into the drain/fill opening (**Figure 70**). Continue to fill the gearcase until lubricant flows from the level/vent opening. Without removing the pump or tube from the drain/fill opening, install and securely tighten the level/vent plug.

NOTE
When adding lubricant to the gearcase, installing the level/vent plug before removing

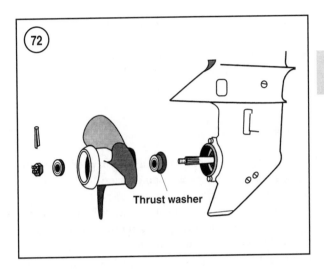

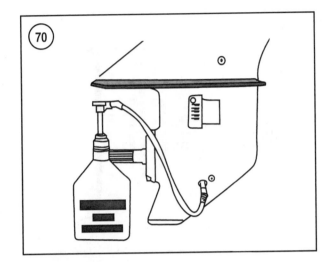

Thrust washer

the pump fitting from the fill/drain plug opening will help prevent fluid from draining rapidly while attempting to reinstall the fill/drain plug.

6. Remove the pump or tube from the drain/fill opening and *quickly* install the fill/drain plug to prevent excessive fluid leakage. Tighten the fill/drain plug and level/vent plugs to the specification in **Table 6**.

7. Allow the gearcase to remain undisturbed in a shaded area for one hour, then recheck the fluid level. Add more lubricant if necessary.

8. Connect the negative battery cable. Properly dispose of the old lubricant.

Propeller Shaft and Nut Lubrication

Remove the propeller in order to clean and lubricate the propeller shaft and tighten the propeller nut (**Figure 71**) or install the drive pin at the intervals specified in **Table 1**. Regular lubrication with marine grade all purpose grease such as OMC Triple-Guard grease prevents corrosion and

potential propeller shaft seizure. Perform this maintenance more frequently as necessary when operating in salt, brackish or polluted water.

1. Disconnect the negative battery cable for safety, to ensure no accidental attempt to start the engine occurs while working around the propeller.

2. Remove the propeller as described in Chapter Nine.

NOTE
The 8-15 hp models are equipped with a fish line trap to protect the propeller shaft seals. If equipped, make sure to check and clean the trap of any fishing line and to face it the proper direction (with the groove facing forward). Note the proper orientation during removal to prevent confusion during assembly.

3. Clean all corrosion and old grease from the propeller shaft and splined section of the propeller. Apply a coating of grease to the propeller shaft splines.

4. Install the propeller and secure it by installing the drive pin (5/6 hp models) or by tightening the propeller nut to specification and installing a new cotter pin (8-70 hp models), as described in Chapter Nine.

Checking the Fish Line Trap

The 8-15 hp models are equipped with a special propeller shaft thrust washer (**Figure 72**). The washer contains an integral fishing line trap designed to keep entangled fishing line from cutting the propeller shaft seal. On these models, the manufacturer recommends removing the propeller every 15-20 hours (or anytime fishing line may become entangled) in order to check the trap and free it of any remaining debris. During installation the washer must be positioned with the proper side facing out and a line trap groove facing forward (**Figure 73**) in order to perform its job. Make sure to note the direction of the trap groove during removal. Refer to *Propeller* in Chapter Nine for removal and installation instructions.

Anode Inspection

Models covered by this manual are equipped with various engine and gearcase mounted sacrificial anodes to help inhibit corrosion. Clean and inspect the gearcase mounted anode(s) at the intervals listed in **Table 1**. Inspect the anodes more frequently if operating the engine in salt, brackish or polluted water.

The 5-15 hp models use a small rectangular anode or anodes. The 5/6 hp (128 cc) models use an anode mounted under the anti-ventilation plate (**Figure 74**) just in front of the water inlet. Other models that are 15 hp and below in size use one or more anodes attached to the aft, starboard and/or port side of the case (**Figure 75**), immediately above the anti-ventilation plate. A second anode may be mounted on the port side as well. If the anode is not located where described on 5 or 6 hp models, check underneath the anti-ventilation plate for a possible alternate location. Other engines, such as the 40-70 hp models, use a dual-purpose anode that also serves the purpose of a trim tab (lower arrow, **Figure 61**) located on the aft, underside of the anti-ventilation plate, located just above the propeller. The trim tab (**Figure 76**) can be pivoted on its mount to reduce steering torque. Trim tab adjustment instructions are in Chapter Four. Adjustment is not usually required if the trim tab is reinstalled in the original position. Use a felt tip marker or tape and make reference marks prior to removing or loosening the trim tab mounting bolt.

Anodes can be inspected visually and by using an ohmmeter. To visually check the anode, use a stiff brush to clean deposits and other material from the exposed anode surfaces. Compare it with a replacement part (or take a measurement when the anode is new). Replace the anode if it loses 1/3 or more of its material or contains deep pitting.

An ohmmeter can be used to verify proper conductivity of the anode (refer to Chapter One for more information on *Galvanic Corrosion*). Connect one lead from the ohmmeter to a good ground on the gearcase and the other to the anode. Make sure the contact surface of the anode is clean to ensure good contact between the anode and the meter lead. There should be little or no resistance across the leads. If not, remove the anode and carefully clean the contact surfaces of the anode and case of all corrosion, dirt, oil, debris or other residue. Clean the anode mounting

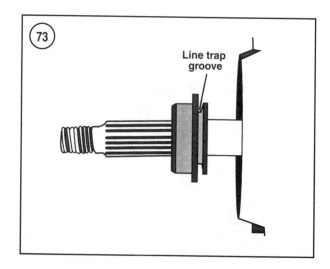

Line trap groove

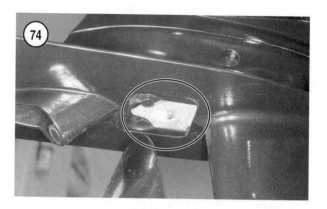

screw threads and the threads in the engine to ensure proper conductivity.

CAUTION
Never paint or coat the anode or the engine surface where the anode mounts. Any paint or foreign matter could isolate the anode electrically from the engine, preventing it from protecting the engine.

If necessary, remove and replace the anode as follows:

1. Remove the anode or trim tab mounting bolt and carefully pry it from the mounting surface.

2. Use a stiff brush to thoroughly clean the mounting bolt(s), bolt hole(s) and mounting surfaces. Clean the surfaces until they are shiny. Do not apply any paint or other material to the mounting surface.

3. Use a stiff brush and file to clean all contaminants or casting slag from the mounting surfaces of the anode or trim tab. The anode mounting surfaces must be clean and true to ensure a good ground connection and a flush fit to the gearcase.

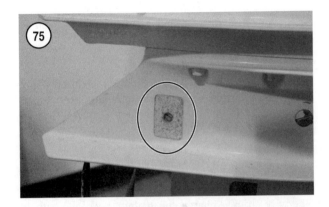

4. Install the anode or trim tab and mounting bolt. For trim tabs, align the reference marks. Tighten the mounting bolt.

5. Cover the mounting bolt head with a coating of silicone seal as indicated in **Figure 63**. Allow adequate time for curing of the sealant before placing the engine in the water.

Fastener Inspection

Tighten the gearcase fasteners at the intervals listed in **Table 1**. Refer to Chapter Nine to determine the fastener locations and torque specifications. If a torque specification is not available, tighten the fastener to the general torque specifications in Chapter One.

STORAGE (PREPARATION AND RE-COMMISSIONING)

Except for some commercial applications, outboard engines seldom operate year round. Special preparation is required if the engine requires either short- or long-term storage.

Several months of non-use can cause a general deterioration of the boat and engine. This is especially true in areas of extreme temperature variations. This deterioration can be minimized with careful preparation for storage. Proper storage can help prevent fuel, ignition and power head malfunctions after re-commissioning.

Storage Area Selection

When selecting a storage area, consider the following:

1. It is best if the storage area is dry. A heated area is even better, but not necessary. If possible, insulate the storage area to minimize extreme temperature variations.

2. If the building contains large windows, mask them to keep sunlight off the boat and motor.

3. Avoid buildings in industrial areas where corrosive emissions may be present. If possible, avoid areas close to saltwater.

4. Consider risk of fire, theft or vandalism. Check with an insurer regarding insurance coverage while in storage.

Preparing the Boat and Engine for Storage

The amount of preparation a boat and engine should undergo before storage depends on the expected length of non-use, storage area conditions and personal preference. Consider the following list the minimum requirement:

1. Wash the boat hull and motor thoroughly. Make sure all marine life, dirt or debris is removed. Inspect the water stream fitting on the lower engine cover for debris. Inspect the speedometer opening at the leading edge of the gearcase or any other gearcase drains for debris. If present, clean the debris with a piece of wire and/or compressed air.

2. For all engines, stabilize the fuel supply using fuel stabilizer.

NOTE
Use OMC 2+4 Fuel Conditioner when treating the fuel systems. OMC 2+4 is normally used in a ratio of 1.0 oz. (30 ml) for each gallon (3.8 L), but follow the directions on the bottle if they differ.

3. For 40-70 hp models, use a 6.0 gal. (23 L) gas tank to mix 5.0 gal. (19 L) of gas, 2.0 qt. (1.9 L) of OMC Storage Fogging Oil and 2.5 oz. (74 ml) of OMC 2+4 Fuel Conditioner or equivalent storage fluids. This tank is used during the procedure as a storage fuel mixture. Connect the tank to the engine.

4. Attach a flushing attachment as a cooling water/flushing source (refer to *Cooling System Flushing* in this chapter).

5. Start and run the engine at 1500 rpm for approximately five minutes on 5-15 hp models or 10 minutes on 40-70 hp models. This step ensures the entire fuel supply system contains the mixtures.

CAUTION
Do not keep the outboard tilted when storing in below-freezing temperatures as residual water in the cooling system could freeze, possibly causing engine damage.

6. Stop the engine and remove the flushing source, while keeping the outboard vertical. Allow the cooling system to drain completely.

7. Drain the engine crankcase and gearcase oils while they are still warm. Replace the oil filter. Refill the crankcase and gearcase with fresh oil. For details, refer to the procedures in this chapter.

CAUTION
***Do not** leave the engine filled with used oil. It likely contains moisture and, in the case of the crankcase oil, acids and other damaging byproducts of combustion that will damage engine bearings.*

8. Tag the leads, then remove the spark plugs as described in this Chapter. Spray a generous amount of fogging oil into the spark plug ports. Turn the flywheel slowly by hand (clockwise, in the normal direction of rotation) to distribute the fogging oil evenly across the cylinder walls. For 40-70 hp models, the starter can be used to crank the engine over in short bursts, but make sure the spark plugs and leads remain disconnected to prevent accidental starting. If necessary, re-spray into each cylinder when that piston reaches the bottom of its travel.

NOTE
Engines with a rope start can be slowly and carefully turned using the rope starter. For other models, turn the flywheel by hand or use a suitable tool. On 40-70 hp models, make sure to turn the flywheel clockwise.

9. For carbureted models (5-15 hp) spray fogging oil into the carburetor air intake (down the throttle bore).

10. Reinstall and tighten the spark plugs, but leave the leads disconnected to prevent starting until the engine is ready for recommissioning.

11. For models equipped with portable fuel tanks, disconnect and relocate them to a well ventilated storage area, away from the engine. Drain any fuel lines that remain attached to the tank.

CAUTION
The electrolyte in a discharged battery has a much lower freezing point and is more likely to freeze and crack the battery case when stored in areas that will experience freezing temperatures.

12. Remove the battery and store in a cool, dry place. If possible, place the battery on a smart charger or tender, otherwise, trickle charge the battery once a month to maintain proper charge.

13. For 40-70 hp models, disconnect the speedometer hose from the upper most connector and blow all water from the gearcase speedometer pickup. If compressed air is available, use **no more** than 25 psi (172 kPa) of air pressure in order to prevent possible system damage.

14. Remove the propeller and check thoroughly for damage. Clean the propeller shaft and apply a protective coating of grease.

15. Clean all components under the engine cover and apply a corrosion preventative spray.

16. Do not forget the boat and trailer. Coat the boat and outside painted surfaces of the trailer with a fresh coating of wax and cover it with a breathable cover. If possible, place the trailer on stands or blocks so the wheels are supported off the ground. Check the air pressure in the tires. If necessary, service the wheel bearings.

NOTE
*Always store a Johnson/Evinrude four-stroke engine vertically on the boat or on a suitable engine stand. Do **not** lay it down for any length of time, as engine oil will seep past the rings causing extreme smoking upon startup.*

Returning the Boat and Engine to Service

The amount of service required when returning a boat and engine to service after storage depends on the length of non-use and storage conditions. At the very least, perform a complete pre-season tune-up and lubrication service, along with all annual maintenance not performed when the engine was placed into storage. If the engine is stored for more than one winter, pay particular attention to the inspection procedures especially regarding hoses and fittings. Check the engine crankcase and gear oils for excessive moisture contamination. If necessary, change the engine oils. Refer to **Table 1** to evaluate the service intervals and to determine which additional items require service.

Install the battery (Chapter Seven) if so equipped. If the fuel tank was emptied, or if it must be emptied because the fuel is stale, fill the tank with fresh fuel. Pump the primer bulb and check for fuel leakage or flooding at the carburetor or vapor separator tank. For fuel injected engines, pressurize the fuel system by turning the ignition on and listening to verify the fuel pump does run for a few seconds. Inspect the fuel rail and fittings under the engine top case for leaks.

Attach a flush device or place the outboard in a test tank and start the engine. Run the engine at idle speed and warm it to normal operating temperature. Check for proper operation of the cooling, electrical and warning systems. Refer to Chapter Two for troubleshooting procedures, if necessary.

CLEARING A SUBMERGED MOTOR

In order to prevent engine damage, recover an engine that is dropped overboard or otherwise completely submerged as soon as possible. Once a submerged engine is recovered exposure to the atmosphere allows corrosion to begin etching highly polished bearing surfaces of the crankshaft, connecting rods and bearings. For this reason, service the recovered engine within three hours of initial submersion.

If the engine cannot be started or serviced immediately, re-submerge it in a tank of freshwater to minimize exposure to the atmosphere and slow the corrosion process. Do not delay any more than absolutely necessary and service the engine as soon as possible. This is especially important if the engine was submerged in salt, brackish or polluted water. This procedure does not preserve the engine indefinitely. Service the engine within a few days of protective submersion.

Once recovered, vigorously wash all debris from the engine with freshwater upon retrieval.

If the engine was submerged while running, internal damage such as a bent connecting rod is likely, so the power head should be disassembled and inspected. Refer to Chapter Eight for power head repair instructions.

CAUTION
*Do **not** start a recovered engine until at least Steps 1-5 are performed to ensure that the engine is not hydro-locked and is properly lubricated. Starting a hydro-locked engine could cause major damage to the power head, including bending or breaking a connecting rod.*

If an engine is submerged for any length of time it should be thoroughly disassembled and cleaned (both the power head and gearcases do not necessarily have to be disassembled; it depends on whether water intruded, to determine this check the crankcase and gearcase oil for contamination). Electrical components should be dried and cleaned or replaced, as necessary.

The amount of cleaning and disassembly that must take place also depends on the type of water in which the engine was submerged. Engines submerged, even for shorter lengths of time, in salt, brackish or polluted water require more thorough servicing than ones submerged in freshwater for the same length of time. Complete power head disassembly and inspection is required when sand, silt or other gritty material is found inside the engine cover.

Many components of the engine suffer the corrosive effects of submersion in salt, brackish or polluted water. The symptoms may not occur for some time after the event. Salt crystals form in many areas of the engine and start intense corrosion. The wire harness and connections are usually affected in a short period of time. Since it is difficult to remove the salt crystals from the harness connectors, it is best to replace the wire harness and clean all electrical component connections. The starter motor, relays and switches on the engine usually fail if not thoroughly cleaned or replaced.

To service the engine, proceed as follows:

1. Remove the engine cover and *vigorously* wash all material from the engine with freshwater. Completely disassemble and inspect the power head if sand, silt or gritty material is present inside the engine cover.

2. Grasp the spark plug leads (by the cap, not the wire) and remove them by twisting side-to-side while pulling upward away from the plug. Remove the spark plugs as described in this Chapter. Inspect the spark plugs, clean and re-gap or replace, as necessary.

3. Disconnect the fuel supply line from the engine. Drain and clean all fuel lines. Depending on the circumstances surrounding the submersion, inspect the fuel tank for contamination and drain, if necessary.

4. Support the engine horizontally with the spark plug ports facing downward to allow water drainage. Help force the water out by slowly rotating the flywheel by hand approximately 20 times or until there is no water. If there are signs of water present, spray some fogging oil into the spark plug ports before turning the flywheel to help dislodge moisture and lubricate the cylinder walls.

CAUTION
Turn the flywheel slowly, feeling for sticking or binding that could indicate internal damage from hydro-lock. This problem could

*occur, especially if the engine was sub-
merged while running or cranked in an attempt to start before water was drained.*

5. For 5-15 hp models, drain the carburetor. The best
method to thoroughly drain/clean the carburetor is to remove and disassemble it. For details refer to the carburetor procedures in Chapter Five.

6. Support the engine in the normal upright position.
Check the engine crankcase and gearcase oils for contamination. Refer to the procedures in this chapter.

7. Drain the crankcase engine oil and change the filter.
Refer to the procedures in this chapter. If contaminated oil
drains from the crankcase, flush the crankcase using a
quart or two of fresh four-stroke engine oil by pouring it
into the engine and allowing it to drain from the crankcase.

8. The gearcase is sealed and, if the seals are in good condition, should have survived the submersion without contamination. If contamination was found in Step 6, look for
possible leaks in the seals, then drain the gearcase and
make the necessary repairs before refilling it. Refer to
Chapter Nine for gearcase service.

9. Remove all external electrical components for disassembly and cleaning. Spray all electrical connectors with
electrical contact cleaner and apply a small amount of dielectric grease prior to reconnecting to prevent corrosion.
For electric start models, remove, disassemble and clean
the starter components. For details on the electrical system components, refer to Chapter Seven.

10. Inject or pour a small amount of four-stroke engine
oil into each of the spark plug holes.

11. Reassemble all removed components and remount
the engine or place it in a test tank. Start and run the engine
for a half hour.

NOTE
*If the engine fails to start, remove the spark
plugs again and check for moisture on the
tips. If necessary, use compressed air to
clean moisture from the electrodes or replace the plugs. Refer to Chapter Two for
troubleshooting instructions if the engine
still does not start.*

12. Stop the engine, then recheck the engine and gearcase
oils. Perform all other lubrication services.

TUNE-UP

A complete tune-up involves a series of adjustments,
tests, inspections and component replacement procedures
designed to return the engine to original performance

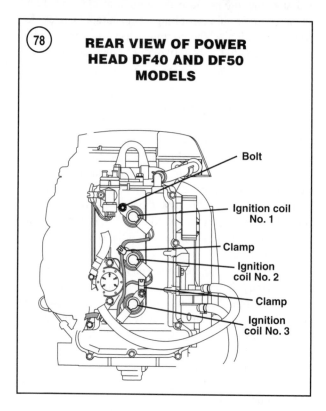

specifications. Only a complete tune-up delivers the expected performance, economy and durability. To perform
a complete tune-up, follow all of the applicable instructions listed in this section.

Spark Plugs

No other component effects engine performance more
than the spark plugs. Although it is possible to clean and
re-gap spark plugs that are not excessively worn or fouled,
it is always best to replace spark plugs when performing a
complete tune-up. Cleaned and re-gapped plugs do not
provide the performance of new spark plugs.

The first step of a tune-up is to remove and inspect the spark plugs. The condition of the plugs can be used as an indication of engine operating conditions. Inspect used plugs as described in *Spark Plug Reading*. Correct any abnormal condition before proceeding with the tune-up. Refer to **Table 5** for the recommended spark plugs and gap.

Since the second step of a tune-up is to perform a compression test (for which the plugs must be removed from the engine), combine the two procedures to save time. If doing it this way, before removing the spark plugs, connect a water cooling source, then start and run the engine to normal operating temperature to get proper readings for the compression test. In this way the spark plugs do not have to be reinstalled before the compression test only to be re-removed again in order to conduct the compression test itself.

Spark Plug Removal

Remove and inspect the spark plugs during each tune-up at the intervals specified in **Table 1** or more often if there is a drop in engine performance. A careful inspection of the spark plugs can provide an indication of potential engine problems. Correcting the problem can prevent potential damage to power head components.

The spark plugs can also be removed for other purposes during engine service, such as to relieve engine compression, making it easier to turn the engine over by hand. This is useful when performing major repairs such as installing a new timing belt or chain, when finding top dead center of a cylinder or even when distributing engine or fogging oil evenly along the cylinder walls prior to storage.

CAUTION
If possible, disconnect spark plug leads by hand. If necessary, use special insulated pliers to remove the spark plug cap from the spark plugs. The caps are easily perforated by the gripping surfaces of standard pliers.

A damaged cap may cause an ignition misfire.

1. Disconnect the negative battery cable for safety.
2. For 5-15 hp and 70 hp models, tag and disconnect each spark plug lead by carefully twisting the spark plug caps (**Figure 77**) by hand to free them from the spark plugs. Pull the lead from each plug.
3. On 40 and 50 hp models there are no secondary spark plug leads as each ignition coil is mounted directly on top of each spark plug. To remove the coils:
   a. Carefully bend the clamps (**Figure 78**) to expose the bolts retaining ignition coils No. 2 and No. 3.
   b. Tag each of the coils.
   c. For each coil, remove the bolt and carefully pull the coil from the spark plug and power head.
   d. If necessary, squeeze the connector and disengage the wiring from the coil, freeing the coil completely from the engine.
4. Clean all corrosion or contaminants from the spark plug lead or coil cap. Inspect the cap for torn, weathered or perforated surfaces. Replace the coil or lead cap, if defective.
5. Using compressed air, blow all debris from the spark plug–to–cylinder head mating surfaces. If compressed air is not available, use a stiff bristled brush to clean as much debris from the area as possible.
6. Using an appropriate spark plug socket, remove each spark plug and either tagged or arranged them to identify them by cylinder.
7. Inspect the spark plugs as detailed under *Spark Plugs Reading* in this chapter.

Spark Plug Gap and Installation

CAUTION
In order to prevent possible engine damage always install a spark plug into a cool cylinder head and never overtighten.

A new spark plug must be carefully gapped to ensure a reliable, consistent spark. Use a special spark plug gapping tool and a wire feeler gauge.

1. If necessary, clean carbon, corrosion or other contaminants from the spark plug openings in the power head using an appropriate sized spark plug bore thread chaser (**Figure 79**).
2. Check and correct the spark plug gap (**Table 5**) as follows:
   a. Use a wire feeler gauge and measure the spark plug gap between the center and side electrode as shown in **Figure 80**. If the gap (**Figure 81**) is correct the

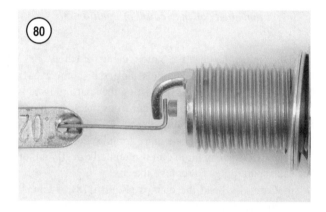

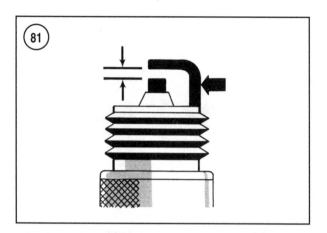

gauge with the specified diameter (**Table 5**) will pass between the electrodes with a slight drag.

b. If there is no drag, or if the gauge will not pass through, bend the side electrode with a gapping tool (**Figure 82**) to set the proper gap. Never tap the spark plug against a hard object to close the gap. Doing so can damage the spark plug insulator.

3. Apply a *small* amount of antiseize compound to the threads of the spark plug. Do not use oil.

4. Thread the spark plug into the cylinder head by hand until it seats. Very little effort is required. If force is necessary, carefully back the plug out again and make sure that it was not being cross-threaded.

NOTE
On 40 and 50 hp models, use a small section of hose with an inner diameter slightly smaller than the spark plug insulator to hold the spark plug as a tool reduces the possibility of cross-threading the plug.

5. Using an appropriate spark plug socket, tighten the spark plugs to the specification in **Table 6**.

6. Apply a light coating of dielectric grease or OMC Triple-Guard grease to the ribbed section of the spark plug insulator in order to prevent corrosion between the plug and the spring terminal.

7. Connect the spark plug leads as follows:

a. On 40 and 50 hp models, carefully guide the spark plug connector end of the ignition coil onto the spark plug. Rotate the ignition coil to align the retaining bolt holes. Install and securely tighten the coil retaining bolts. Make sure the ignition coil wires are correctly routed as shown in **Figure 78**, then bend the clamps down to retain the wires.

b. On all other models, route the leads to the correct plug and away from any moving components. Carefully slide the cap over the spark plug and push the cap until it snaps onto the spark plug.

8. Connect the negative battery cable.

Spark Plug Reading

Because the firing end of a spark plug operates in the combustion chamber, its condition reflects the operating conditions of the engine. Important information about engine performance and/or the specific condition of a given cylinder can be determined by careful examination of the spark plug. During a tune-up, compare the plugs removed from each cylinder to **Figure 83**, noting the following information.

Normal condition

A light tan- or gray-colored deposit and no abnormal gap wear or erosion indicates proper engine, fuel system and ignition operating conditions. It also indicates that plug in use is matched properly to previous motor use. In most cases, the plug may be regapped and returned to service.

SPARK PLUG CONDITIONS

NORMAL

GAP BRIDGED

CARBON FOULED

OVERHEATED

OIL FOULED

SUSTAINED PREIGNITION

3

Carbon fouled

Soft, dry, sooty deposits covering the entire firing end of the plug are evidence of incomplete combustion. Even though the firing end of the plug is dry, the plug insulation is decreased. An electrical path is formed that lowers the voltage from the ignition system. Engine misfiring is a possible sign of carbon fouling. One or more of the following can cause carbon fouling:

1. Too rich of a fuel mixture (incorrect jetting or improperly operating fuel injection system).
2. Spark plug heat range is too cold for use.
3. Overly retarded ignition timing.
4. Ignition component failure.
5. Low engine compression.

Oil fouled

The tip of an oil fouled plug has a black insulator tip, a damp oily film over the firing end and a carbon layer over the entire nose. The electrodes are usually not worn. Common causes for this condition are:

1. Wrong type of oil.
2. Ignition component failure.
3. Spark plug heat range too cold.
4. Engine still undergoing break-in.

Oil fouled spark plugs may be cleaned in an emergency, but it is better to replace them. It is important to correct the cause of fouling before returning the engine to service.

Gap bridging

Plugs with this condition have gaps shorted out by combustion deposits between the electrodes. If encountered, check for an improper oil type, excessive carbon in the combustion chamber or a clogged exhaust port and pipe. Make sure to correct the cause of this condition, as continued build-up leads to ignition system failure.

Overheating

Badly worn electrodes and premature gap wear are signs of overheating, along with a gray or white blistered porcelain insulator surface. The most common cause for this condition is using a spark plug of the wrong heat range (too hot). If the engine is not modified and the plug is of the recommended heat range, check the following possible causes:

1. Lean fuel mixture (incorrect main jet/improperly operating fuel injection system).
2. Ignition timing too advanced.
3. Cooling system malfunction.
4. Engine air leak.
5. Improper spark plug installation (overtightening).
6. No spark plug gasket.

Worn out

Corrosive gasses formed by combustion and high voltage sparks have eroded the electrodes. Spark plugs in this condition require more voltage to fire under hard acceleration. Replace the spark plug.

Preignition

If the electrodes are melted or damaged, preignition is almost certainly the cause. Check for carburetor/throttle body mounting or intake manifold leaks and overly advanced ignition timing. It is also possible that a plug of the wrong heat range (too hot) is being used. Find the cause of the preignition before returning the engine into service.

Spark Plug Heat Range

Plugs with heat ranges that are either hotter or colder than the original plugs are available. However, in most cases the heat range of the spark plugs originally installed by the manufacturer (**Table 5**) should perform adequately under most conditions. Do not change the spark plug heat range to compensate for adverse engine or carburetion conditions. Doing so only compound the problem.

In general, use a hot plug for low speeds and low temperatures. Use a cold plug for high speeds and high temperatures. The plugs should operate hot enough to burn off unwanted deposits, but not so hot that it becomes damaged or causes preignition. Determine if plug heat range is correct by examining the insulator as described in *Spark Plug Reading*.

When replacing plugs with another type, make sure the reach or thread length is correct. The thread length of any replacement spark plug must be the same as the original, which matches the length of the threads in the cylinder head spark plug hole. A longer than standard plug could interfere with the piston, causing engine damage. A short plug provides poor ignition.

Compression Test

Refer to Chapter Two for compression testing procedures. Correct any mechanical condition causing low compression before proceeding with the tune-up.

Ignition Component Inspection

Perform a visual inspection on the ignition system components such as the spark plug leads, ignition coil(s) and wiring. Check for deteriorated or damaged parts. Cracks in insulation can produce sparks or even arching that might prevent the system from working properly. Replace any component with deteriorated or damaged parts. If any component looks good, but is suspect due to poor performance, refer to Chapter Two for information on Troubleshooting and Chapter Seven for information on the Electrical and Ignition Systems.

Fuel Filter Inspection and Replacement

> *WARNING*
> *Use caution if working with the fuel system. Never smoke around fuel or fuel vapors. Make sure no flame or source of ignition is present in the work area. Flame or sparks can ignite fuel or fuel vapors causing a fire or explosion.*

Eventually dirt, fuel deposits and other contaminants form from condensation and evaporation or enter the fuel system. These contaminants are trapped by the fuel filter(s). Regular inspection and filter replacement helps prevent eventual filter blockage and fuel starvation problems. Clean, inspect or change the fuel filter at the intervals listed in **Table 1**.

Carburetor equipped models may be equipped with a single low pressure inline fuel filter (**Figure 84**, typical). But some models, such as the 9.9/15 hp (305 cc), are equipped with a removable filter element, mounted under the fuel pump inlet cover (**Figure 85**). Fuel injected models use both low and high pressure fuel filters. The low pressure filter can normally be visually inspected. The EFI high pressure filter (**Figure 86**) cannot be visually inspected. With the exception of the pump mounted filter element (which can be removed, cleaned and reinstalled), these filters are non-serviceable and must be replaced if contaminated.

Replace the inline and canister filters at the interval listed in **Table 1** or more often if there are fuel starvation/fuel pressure problems. Fuel filter replacement instructions are provided in Chapter Five or Chapter Six, as applicable. If problems are suspected, low pressure inline filters may be visually checked as follows:

1. Disconnect the negative battery cable.
2. Locate the low pressure fuel filter as follows:
   a. On 5-15 hp models, follow the fuel line back from the fuel pump to locate the low pressure, inline filter (if used).
   b. On 40-70 hp models, the low pressure fuel filter is located at the lower port, front side of the power head, just below the intake manifold.
3. Inspect the filter housing with a flashlight for sediment or contamination. Replace the filter if dark staining or if there is a significant amount of sediment within the filter housing. Inspect the fuel tank, hoses and fittings for contamination if rust colored deposits are detected inside the filter.
4. Inspect the fuel hose connections and hose clamps for leakage, split hoses, corroded clamps or other defects. Replace defective hoses and clamps as required.

5. Inspect the filter body for cracked, softened or leaking surfaces. Replace the filter as described in Chapter Five or Chapter Six if these or other defects.

6. Connect the negative battery cable.

Ignition Timing

All Johnson/Evinrude four-stroke outboards are equipped with electronic ignition timing control. The ignition timing is non-adjustable. On fuel-injected models, ignition timing control can be verified using a timing light.

Checking timing on fuel injected models

The electronic control unit (ECU) on fuel injected models controls both the fuel delivery/injection system, as well as the ignition system. Based on input from various sensors the ECU adjusts ignition timing to optimize engine operation.

During engine cranking, all ignition coils will fire simultaneously whenever a piston reaches 7° (40 and 50 hp models) or 5° (70 hp models) before top dead center (BTDC). Once the engine speed exceeds 440 rpm, the ECU begins ignition timing based on programmed mapping.

Once the engine starts and runs at fast idle, ignition timing remains fixed. For 40 and 50 hp models, the ECU will fix timing at 9° BTDC with the engine running in neutral above 1200 rpm. For 70 hp models, the ECU will fix timing at 5° BTDC with the engine running in neutral above 1000 rpm.

During idling/trolling operation, the ECU varies ignition timing to help stabilize idle speed. For 40 and 50 hp models the ECU controls ignition timing at 5-13° BTDC with the engine speed between 800-900 rpm. For 70 hp models, the ECU maintains ignition timing at 6-14° BTDC with a stable engine speed of 700 rpm.

For normal operation including acceleration, deceleration and engine speeds in gear, above idle, the ECU follows various ignition timing mapping programs. For 40 hp models, the ECU maintains timing between 0-32° BTDC. For 50 hp models the ECU maintains ignition timing of 0-25° BTDC. On 70 hp models, the ECU maintains timing between 10-36° BTDC.

To check ignition timing, connect the timing light according to the tool manufacturer's instructions, then run the engine either at idle in neutral using a cooling water supply or mounted on a boat or in a test tank and under the various conditions noted above. Timing marks on the flywheel cover at the top of the engine (**Figure 87**). If proper

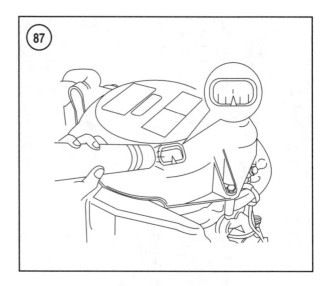

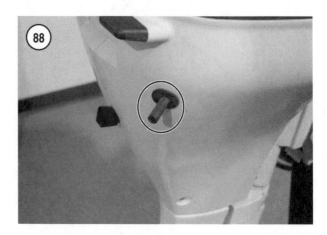

fixed timing is noted during fast idle operation, the ECU is controlling engine timing.

Fuel System Adjustments

The initial low-speed setting is adjustable on 5-15 hp carbureted models. No periodic adjustment is necessary. Adjustment is only necessary if the carburetor is rebuilt or a replacement is installed. Carburetor idle speed adjustment is described in Chapter Four.

Adjustments to EFI models are limited to an annual check/adjustment of the air bypass screw setting. Refer to Chapter Four.

It is possible to adjust the air/fuel mixture through electronic recalibration. However, this adjustment must be performed by a dealership and is seldom necessary.

Engine Idle Speed and Linkage Adjustments (5-15 hp Models Only)

The engine shift lever detent (remote models) and idle speed adjustments are performed at each pre-season tune-up. For details on these procedures, refer to Chapter Four. No carburetor air/fuel mixture adjustments are necessary unless a carburetor is rebuilt or replaced. In the case of carburetor service, the initial carburetor adjustments must be performed before the engine synchronization and linkage adjustments.

Decarbon the Combustion Chambers

During normal engine operation carbon can build up on components in the combustion chamber. Over time the carbon may cause sticking piston rings, leading to blow-by or excessive engine oil consumption. Johnson/Evinrude recommends using OMC Carbon Guard fuel additive with every fuel fill-up. If not using OMC Carbon Guard on a regular basis, the manufacturer recommends using OMC Engine Tuner at regular intervals to remove carbon deposits.

When using OMC Engine Tuner, run the engine on a water supply or in a test tank at fast idle, then spraying the entire contents of the can into the carburetor or throttle body, and keeping the engine from stalling as it is sprayed. For severe cases of carbon build-up, remove the spark plugs and spray directly onto the pistons/valves, allowing it to soak for at least an hour. Once it has soaked, turn the engine over a couple of times to remove excess cleaner,

reinstall the spark plugs and pour the remainder of the bottle into the intake. After application, allow the engine to soak for at least 15 minutes, then start and run the engine above 1/2 throttle for 3-5 minutes.

NOTE
If OMC Engine Tuner is used immediately before storage, the engine should be properly fogged after the full de-carbon procedure is followed.

Verify Proper Engine and Cooling System Operation (Test Run)

The final step in a tune-up is the test run. Operate the engine on a flush/test device or in a test tank to verify correct starting and idle speed prior to running the engine under actual running conditions. Verify that cooling water is circulating by checking for spray at the cooling system indicator (**Figure 51** or **Figure 88**, typical). Connect a shop tachometer then start the engine. Allow the engine to reach operating temperature before advancing the throttle. Check the full throttle engine speed with a normal passenger and fuel load. Adjust the trim position on power trim models to achieve the highest boat speed then note the tachometer reading. Record the maximum engine speed and refer to Chapter Four to determine the correct engine operating speed. Check the propeller for damage or correct pitch if the maximum engine speed is below or above the recommended range. If the engine speed is too low, check the fuel and ignition system for faults as described in Chapter Two.

Table 1 MAINTENANCE SCHEDULE

Frequency	Task
Before each use	Visually inspect the boat hull for damage
	Check fuel level in gas tank
	Check for signs of fuel or oil leakage
	Check engine crankcase oil level and condition
	Check the propeller for wear or damage
	Check the water intake for debris
	Check that the battery cables are clean and tight
	Check the engine mounting fasteners for tightness
	Check the remote steering cable operation and visually inspect for wear or damage
	Check all controls for proper operation (especially emergency stop switch/clip/lanyard)
	(continued)

Table 1 MAINTENANCE SCHEDULE (continued)

Frequency	Task
After each use	Visually inspect the boat hull for damage
	Check for signs of fuel or oil leakage
	Check engine crankcase oil level and condition
	Check the propeller for wear or damage
	Check the water intake for debris
	Visually inspect the anode(s) for wear or damage
	Check the engine mounting fasteners for tightness
	Rinse exterior of engine, hull and propeller with fresh water (if used in salt, polluted or brackish water). Coat motor casing with wax, as necessary
	Flush cooling system once engine has cooled (if used in salt, polluted or brackish water)
	Shut off the battery switch (fuel injected models) to prevent battery drain
	Check the fishing line trap on 8-15 hp models
Lubrication service At least every 60 days in freshwater service or 30 days in salt, brackish or polluted water service	
	Choke and carburetor linkage greasing (except fuel injected engines)
	Electric starter pinion lubrication
	Check power trim/tilt reservoir fluid level and condition (40-70 hp models)
	Shift lever shaft and detent greasing
	Swivel bracket, tilt/run lever, tilt shaft and clamp screw (as applicable) greasing
	Throttle linkage greasing
	Change the gearcase oil (40-70 hp models)
Initial 20 hour break-in service (also perform after 20 hour break-in, following a major overhaul including new rings)	
	Lubricate the remote steering cable ram
	Check cylinder head bolt torque (5-15 hp models)
	Remove and inspect the spark plugs, clean or replace as necessary
	Check all electrical wires and connectors for damage, corrosion and proper fitting
	Check any linkage adjustments
	Check the engine mounting fasteners for tightness
	Lubricate all grease fittings
	Replace the inline fuel filter and/or fuel filter canister, as applicable
	Thoroughly check the boat and motor fuel tank and hoses for leaks or damage
	Check all engine systems for signs of deterioration or damage
	Change the engine crankcase oil and change or clean the filter (to drain the break-in oil from the engine)
	Change the gearcase oil
	Check valve lash clearance adjustment
	Check and adjust the steering friction (5-15 hp models)
	Check power trim reservoir fluid level and condition (40-70 hp models)
	Perform bypass air screw adjustment (40-50 hp models)
Every 50 hours/6 months	Perform all applicable lubrication services
	Thoroughly check all hoses and fittings for deterioration and leaks
	Check gearcase oil level and condition

(continued)

Table 1 MAINTENANCE SCHEDULE (continued)

Frequency	Task
Every 50 hours/6 months (continued)	Check the battery condition, electrolyte level, and charge Check all anodes and ground wires Check for loose fasteners If OMC carbon guard is not used consistently in fuel supply, decarbon combustion chambers using OMC Engine Tuner

Every 100 hours/annually	Perform all lubrication services
	Perform all 50 hour/6 month checks or services
	Change the engine crankcase oil* (always change crankcase oil immediately prior to storage regardless of number of hours used that season)
	Change the gearcase oil (always change case oil immediately prior to storage)
	Grease the propeller shaft and tighten the retaining nut (or check the drive pin)
	Inspect the propeller shaft seals for leakage, replace if necessary
	Inspect the battery cables for wear or damage, clean, tighten and replace, as necessary
	Lubricate the remote steering cable ram
	Inspect the timing belt (except 40-50 hp models)
	Perform a pre-season tune-up:
	  Check engine compression
	  Inspect, clean and regap or replace the spark plugs
	  Apply a light coat of electric grease to the spark plugs and interior of the leads
	  Check all electrical wires and connectors for damage, corrosion and proper fitting
	  Visually inspect ignition components, test and replace components, as necessary
	  Replace the inline fuel filter and/or fuel filter canister, as applicable
	  Check and adjust engine idle speed and control linkage (5-15 hp models)
	  Check the steering friction and adjust, if necessary (5-15 hp models)
	  Check cylinder head bolt torque (5-15 hp models)
	  Check and retorque fasteners, as necessary
	  Decarbon the combustion chambers using OMC Engine Tuner
	  Verify proper engine and cooling system operation (take a test run)

Every 200 hours/annually	Perform all 100 hour/annual services Perform idle bypass air screw adjustment (40-70 hp models) Check valve clearance and adjust, as necessary
Every 800 hours/4 years	Replace the timing belt (except 40-50 hp models)

*The manufacturer recommends the use of Evinrude or Johnson Ultra four-stroke engine oil. When using this oil the manufacturer extends the oil change interval to 200 hours, but still should be done at least annually and immediately prior to storage, regardless of the number of hours used that season.

Table 2 FUEL RECOMMENDATIONS

Model	Fuel type – minimum octane No.
All models*	Regular unleaded / 87 octane AKI (RON + MON/2) or 90 octane RON

*Do not use fuels with more than 10% ethanol or 5% methanol with 5% cosolvents. Carbureted models that are not equipped with an emissions port/tube may use leaded gasoline of the same minimum specified octane. Use of leaded gasoline in fuel injected models or in carbureted models with emission tube/port may cause engine damage.

Table 3 OIL AND LUBRICANT RECOMMENDATIONS*

Item	Lubricant type
Choke and carburetor linkage	OMC Triple-Guard grease
Electrical contacts/connectors	Dielectric grease
Electric starter pinion	OMC starter pinion lube
Engine crankcase oil	
Preferred for all models	Evinrude or Johnson Ultra four-stroke engine oil
or for 5-15 hp models	SAE 10W-30 SG or SH motor oil
or for 40-70 hp models	SAE 10W-40 SG or SH motor oil
Gearcase oil	OMC Ultra-HPF gearcase lube
Power trim/tilt reservoir	OMC Power trim/tilt and power steering fluid
Propeller shaft splines	OMC Triple-Guard grease
Shift lever shaft and detent	OMC Triple-Guard grease
Swivel bracket	OMC Triple-Guard grease
Throttle linkage	OMC Triple-Guard grease
Tilt/run lever shaft, tilt shaft and clamp screws	OMC Triple-Guard grease

*Be certain that replacement fluids meet OMC specifications before substituting another fluid for the original designated fluid type.

Table 4 CAPACITIES

Engine model	Engine size cu. in. (cc)	Engine oil U.S. (Metric)	Gearcase oil U.S. (Metric)
5 and 6 hp	7.8 (128)	27.0 fl. oz. (800 ml)	11 fl. oz. (325 ml)
8 and 9.9 hp	12.87 (211)	33.8 fl. oz. (1000 ml)	9.0 fl. oz. (266 ml)
9.9 and 15 hp	18.61 (305)	43.0 fl. oz. (1272 ml)	9.0 fl. oz. (266 ml)
40 and 50 hp	49.7 (815)	2.5 qt. (2.4 L)	21 fl. oz. (620 ml)
70 hp	79.2 (1298)	4.8 qt. (4.5 L)	19 fl. oz. (562 ml)

Table 5 SPARK PLUG TYPE AND GAP

Engine model	Engine size cu. in. (cc)	Plug make and type	Gap in. (mm)
5 and 6 hp	7.8 (128)	Champion P10Y	0.027 (0.7)
8 and 9.9 hp	12.87 (211)	Champion P10Y	0.027 (0.7)
9.9 and 15 hp	18.61 (305)	Champion RA8HC	0.040 (1.0)
40 and 50 hp	49.7 (815)	NGK DCPR6E	0.035-0.039 (0.9-1.0)
70 hp	79.2 (1298)	NGK BPR6ES	0.030 (0.8)

Table 6 MAINTENANCE TORQUE SPECIFICATIONS

Component	in.-lb.	ft.-lb.	N•m
Gearcase oil fill/drain and level/vent plugs			
5-15 hp models	84-86	–	9-10
40-50 hp models	115	–	13
70 hp models	–	11-15	15-20
Propeller nut			
5-6 hp models	not applicable – drive pin retained	–	–
8-70 hp models	120	–	14
Spark plugs			
5-15 hp models	–	14-18	19-24
40-50 hp models	–	11-14	15-19
70 hp models	–	18-21	24-28
Trim tab anode			
40-50 hp models	–	11-15	15-20
70 hp models	–	14	19

Chapter Four

Synchronization and Adjustment

This chapter provides complete synchronization and adjustment instructions for all Johnson/Evinrude four-stroke outboards. **Tables 1-3**, located at the end of the chapter, provide valve clearance, carburetor settings and idle speed specifications. Refer to **Table 4** for torque specifications.

Synchronization and adjustment are critical to maintaining optimum engine operation.

Each model requires some form of periodic adjustment. However, the electronic fuel and ignition systems on some models eliminate many of the traditional adjustment procedures. And models still utilizing a carbureted fuel system rely upon a single carburetor with a mixture screw requiring adjustment only if the carburetor is rebuilt or replaced. On multi-cylinder models, the use of fuel injection eliminates complicated multi-carburetor synchronization.

Refer to the maintenance intervals in Chapter Three to determine when adjustments are required. Some adjustments described in this chapter are only necessary when a component has been removed, rebuilt or replaced.

VALVE ADJUSTMENT

Correct valve clearance is critical to proper engine performance and longevity. Too little clearance may hold the valve open slightly and possibly damage the valve due to overheating. While excessive clearance may prevent the valve from opening completely, which will reduce engine performance.

For all models, a set of flat feeler gauges is necessary to check valve clearance. For 5-15 hp models, adjustment is easier with a tappet adjustment tool (OMC part No. 341444 or an equivalent). The 40-50 hp models utilize replaceable shims to adjust valve clearance. The adjustment procedure requires a micrometer for shim measurement, an assortment of shims and a tappet holder tool (OMC part No. 345832 or an equivalent).

Valve specifications are for a cold engine (preferably one that has been allowed to sit overnight) with the power head at approximately 20° C (68° F).

5-15 hp Models

1. Disconnect the negative battery cable.

2. Remove the spark plug(s) and ground the spark plug lead(s).

NOTE
On all but the 5/6 hp models, tag the spark plug leads before disconnecting them to ensure installation to the proper plugs upon assembly.

3. If necessary for additional clearance, remove the lower engine covers as described in Chapter Three under *Oil Filter Replacement*.

4. Remove the manual starter as described in Chapter Ten.

5. On 5/6 hp (128 cc) and 8/9.9 hp (211 cc) models, tag and disconnect the three hoses from the rocker arm cover. Two of the hoses are connected to the fuel pump cover near the center of the rocker cover and will likely contain fuel. Use a rag to catch all spilled fuel.

6. On 9.9/15 hp (305 cc) models, disconnect the hose from the side of the rocker arm cover and, if necessary, remove the spark plug wires from the retaining clips at the top of the cover.

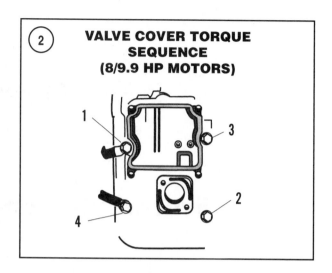

NOTE
On some models, other engine hoses that run near the cover may interfere slightly with removal. Either carefully pull these hoses out of the way (while they are still attached) or, if necessary, tag and disconnect the hoses before proceeding.

7. Support the rocker arm cover while removing the four (5/6 and 8/9.9 hp) or eight (9.9/15 hp) cover bolts using the reverse of the rocker arm cover torque sequence. Refer to **Figures 1-3**. Carefully pull the rocker arm cover from the cylinder head. Inspect the gasket for damage.

8. Rotate the flywheel clockwise to properly align the timing mark(s) for valves being checked, as follows:

a. For 5/6 hp (128 cc) and 8/9.9 hp (211 cc) models, turn the flywheel slowly until the triangular mark on the flywheel aligns with the raised mark on the manual starter boss and the mark on the camshaft pulley aligns with the protrusion on the cylinder head. At this point both valves should be closed on 5/6 hp models, confirming that the cylinder is TDC. For 8/9.9 hp models, both valves for cylinder No. 1

should be closed, confirming that No. 1 is at TDC (conversely, the exhaust valve should be open on cylinder No. 2). Proceed with Step 9 and check the valves (only the valves for cylinder No. 1 on 8/9.9 hp models at this time).

b. For 9.9/15 hp models, turn the flywheel slowly until the pointer on the cam pulley aligns with the protrusion on the manual starter boss and the white mark on the lower belt guide aligns with the crankcase–to–cylinder block split line (on the port side). In this position the valves for the No. 2 piston should both be closed, confirming that the No. 2 piston is TDC of the compression stroke. If so, proceed with Step 9 and check the valves for the No. 2 cylinder only. If the exhaust valve is open, the flywheel is one full turn off from having the No. 2 piston at TDC.

9. Measure the clearances of the intake and exhaust valves (**Figure 4**). Insert feeler gauges of various sizes between the rocker arm and the valve stem (**Figure 5**) for

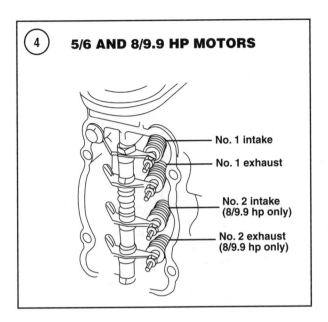

④ 5/6 AND 8/9.9 HP MOTORS

- No. 1 intake
- No. 1 exhaust
- No. 2 intake (8/9.9 hp only)
- No. 2 exhaust (8/9.9 hp only)

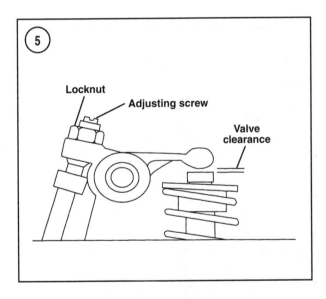

⑤

- Locknut
- Adjusting screw
- Valve clearance

both valves. The size that passes between the arm and stem with a slight drag indicates the valve clearance. Compare the clearance measured with the specification in **Table 1**. In all cases, the intake valves are adjacent to the ports for the intake manifold and the exhaust valves are adjacent to the exhaust ports or manifold. The intake and exhaust valves may be further identified as follows:

   a. On 5/6 hp (128 cc) and 8/9.9 hp (211 cc) models, the intake valve is the upper rocker while the exhaust valve is the lower rocker (**Figure 4**).

   b. On 9.9/15 hp (305 cc) models the intake valve is on the bottom of each cylinder while the exhaust valve rocker is on the top.

10. If necessary, adjust the valve clearance as follows:

   a. Loosen the locknut (**Figure 5**).

   b. Turn the adjusting screw until the clearance is correct.

   c. Hold the screw while tightening the locknut to the specification in **Table 4**.

   d. Recheck the valve clearance and readjust if necessary.

11. For 8-15 hp models, rotate the flywheel clockwise one full revolution (360°). This step turns the camshaft pulley one half of a revolution (180°) so the pointer faces opposite the timing mark on the starter boss. In this position the opposite cylinder from Step 8 will be at TDC as follows:

   a. For 8/9.9 hp (211 cc) models, the valves for the No. 2 cylinder should now be closed. Repeat Step 9 and Step 10 for the No. 2 cylinder.

   b. For 9.9/15 hp (305 cc) models, the valves for the No. 1 cylinder should now be closed. Repeat Step 9 and Step 10 for the No. 1 cylinder.

12. Install a new rocker arm cover gasket. Coat the gasket of 5/6 hp (128 cc) models with OMC Triple-Guard or equivalent grease or the gasket of 8/9.9 hp (211 cc) models with OMC Gasket Sealing Compound. Leave the gasket on 9.9/15 hp (305 cc models dry). For all models, cover the cover screw threads with a light coating of OMC Gasket Sealing Compound. Install the rocker arm cover and tighten the bolts using the proper crossing pattern (**Figures 1-3**) to the specification in **Table 4**.

13. Connect the hoses removed in Step 5 or Step 6, as applicable.

14. Install the lower engine covers.

15. Install the manual starter as described in Chapter Ten.

16. Install the spark plug(s) and lead(s). Connect the negative battery cable.

17. Provide a cooling water source, then start the engine and check for oil leakage at the rocker arm cover mating surfaces.

18. Install the upper engine cover.

40 and 50 hp Models

1. Disconnect the negative battery cable.

2. Remove the spark plugs (Chapter Three).

3. Remove the lower engine covers as described in Chapter Three under *Oil Filter Replacement*.

4. Remove the flywheel cover as described in Chapter Eight.

5. Rotate the engine clockwise to bring the No. 1 cylinder to TDC of the compression stroke (relieving mechanical pressure from the fuel pump arm), and then remove the

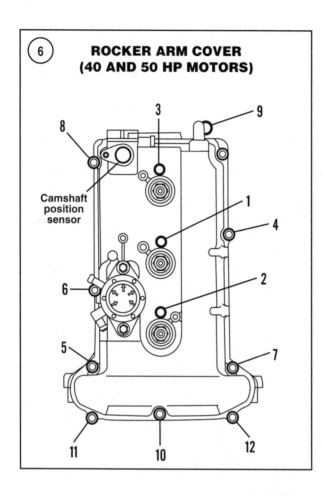

⑥ **ROCKER ARM COVER (40 AND 50 HP MOTORS)**

Camshaft position sensor

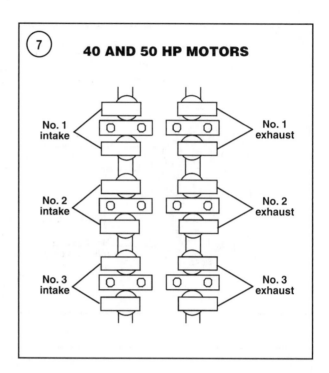

⑦ **40 AND 50 HP MOTORS**

No. 1 intake — No. 1 exhaust

No. 2 intake — No. 2 exhaust

No. 3 intake — No. 3 exhaust

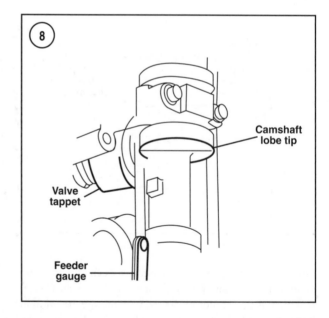

⑧

Camshaft lobe tip

Valve tappet

Feeder gauge

low pressure fuel pump from the cylinder head cover as described in Chapter Six.

NOTE
The No. 1 cylinder is at TDC of the compression stroke when the mark on the crankshaft aligns with the mark on the crankcase and the marks on the camshaft sprockets align with the protrusions on the cylinder head. At TDC of a compression stroke, the base of the camshaft lobe is directly above the valve tappet shim. (The raised portion of the lobe will face away from the valve tappet/shim.)

6. Remove the breather hose and ignition coils from the cylinder head cover.

7. Carefully remove the harness connector from the camshaft position sensor (**Figure 6**).

8. Loosen and remove the cylinder head cover bolts in the opposite of the tightening sequence in **Figure 6**. Carefully remove the cover (along with the gasket and O-rings) from the power head. Inspect the gasket for damaged surfaces and replace it as required.

9. Verify that the flywheel is still in the No. 1 TDC position from Step 5. If so, the camshaft lobes (**Figure 7**) will face out and be directly opposite the valve tappets (**Figure 8**).

10. Insert feeler gauges of various sizes between the tappet shim and the camshaft lobe (**Figure 8**). The gauge size that passes between the shim and lobe with a slight drag indicates the valve clearance. Record the clearance for each valve.

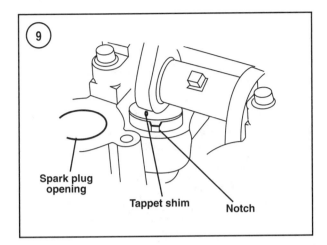

Spark plug opening

Tappet shim

Notch

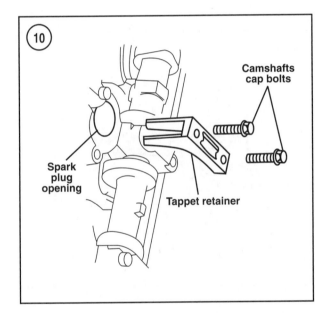

Camshafts cap bolts

Spark plug opening

Tappet retainer

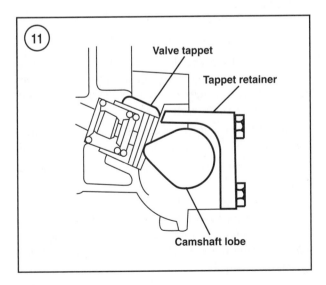

Valve tappet

Tappet retainer

Camshaft lobe

11. Rotate the flywheel clockwise until the No. 3 camshaft lobe tips (**Figure 8**) are facing out and directly opposite the valve tappets.

12. Insert feeler gauges of various sizes between the tappet shim and the camshaft lobe (**Figure 8**). The size that passes between the shim and lobe with a slight drag indicates the valve clearance. Record the valve clearance for each valve.

13. Rotate the flywheel clockwise until the No. 2 camshaft lobe tips (**Figure 8**) are facing out and directly opposite the valve tappets.

14. Insert feeler gauges of various sizes between the tappet shim and the camshaft lobe (**Figure 8**). The size that passes between the shim and lobe with a slight drag indicates the valve clearance. Record the valve clearance for each valve.

15. Compare the clearances with the specifications in **Table 1**. If there is an incorrect valve clearance, replace the tappet shim as described in Step 16. Determine the amount of change needed as follows:

    a. *Valve clearance greater than the specification*—Subtract the valve clearance specification (middle of the range) in **Table 1** from the measured clearance. Increase the shim thickness by this amount.

    b. *Valve clearance less than the specification*—Subtract the measured clearance from the valve clearance specification (middle of the range) in **Table 1**. Decrease the shim thickness by this amount.

16. Replace the tappet shim as follows:

    a. Rotate the flywheel clockwise until the camshaft lobe tip for the selected valve is opposite the tappet (**Figure 8**). Carefully rotate the tappet within its bore until the notch (**Figure 9**) is facing toward the opposite camshaft. The notch must be accessible for tappet shim removal.

    b. Rotate the flywheel clockwise one complete revolution or until the camshaft lobe tip contacts the tappet shim (opening the valve). Remove the bolts from the camshaft cap next to the selected valve.

    c. Place the tappet retainer (OMC part No. 345832 or an equivalent) over the camshaft cap as shown in **Figure 10**. Each end of the retainer is marked either *IN* (for intake) or *EX* (for exhaust) and the appropriate end should face inward toward the center of the cylinder head (the relief point on the tappet from which the shim will be removed). Thread the camshaft cap bolts through the retainer and the camshaft cap. Securely tighten the bolts. Make sure the fingers of the tool contact the barrel portion of the tappet (**Figure 11**) and not the shim itself.

d. Rotate the flywheel clockwise one-half revolution or until the camshaft lobe tip rotates 90° away from the tappet. Insert a screwdriver (with tape covering the blade to prevent scoring or damage) into the tappet notch and carefully pry the shim from the tappet (**Figure 12**). Use a magnet to pull the shim from the tappet. Do not use fingers.

e. Measure the shim thickness (**Figure 13**). Shims are available in sizes from 0.086-0.118 in. (2.18-3.0 mm) in 0.001 in. (0.025 mm) increments. Select the correct shim thickness as described in Step 15.

> *NOTE*
> *The shim thickness is identified by the number on the face of the shim, divided by 100 (moving the decimal point two places to the left). For example, a shim with the number 256 on the face is 2.56 mm thick. Shims removed from the engine must be measured since wear may have changed the thickness.*

f. Place the selected shim into the tappet with the numbered side facing down. Make sure the shim fully seats against the step within the tappet.

g. Rotate the flywheel counterclockwise one-half revolution or until the camshaft lobe tip contacts the tappet shim (**Figure 11**). Remove the bolts from the camshaft cap and tappet retainer. Carefully pull the retainer from the cap. Install and evenly tighten the camshaft cap bolts to specifications in **Table 4**.

h. Repeat Step 16 for all valves with incorrect clearance. Recheck the valve clearance (Steps 9-15) and correct if necessary.

17. Apply a light coating of GM Silicone Rubber Sealer (or equivalent RTV gasket sealant) to the cylinder head cover mating surfaces of the cylinder head (O-rings and gasket). Install the cover to the cylinder head. Tighten the cover bolts in the sequence indicated in **Figure 6** to the specification in **Table 4**.

18. Carefully connect the harness connector to the camshaft position sensor (**Figure 6**).

19. Connect the breather hose, then install the spark plugs and the ignition coils.

20. Install the fuel pump to the cylinder head cover as described in Chapter Six.

21. Install the flywheel cover as described in Chapter Eight.

22. Install the lower engine covers.

23. Connect the negative battery cable.

24. Provide a cooling water source, then start the engine and check for oil leakage at the rocker arm cover mating surfaces.

25. Install the engine top case.

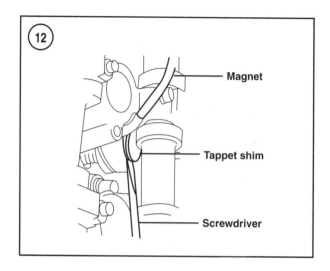

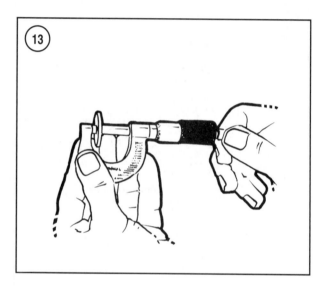

70 hp Models

1. Disconnect the negative battery cable.

2. Label and disconnect the spark plug wires. Ground the plugs to prevent potential damage if the engine is cranked while they are disconnected. Remove the spark plugs. Refer to Chapter Three, as necessary.

3. Remove the lower engine covers as described in Chapter Three under *Oil Filter Replacement*.

4. Remove the flywheel cover as described in Chapter Eight.

5. Rotate the engine clockwise to bring the No. 1 cylinder to TDC (**Figure 14**) on the compression stroke (relieving mechanical pressure from the fuel pump arm), and then remove the low pressure fuel pump from the cylinder head cover as described in Chapter Six.

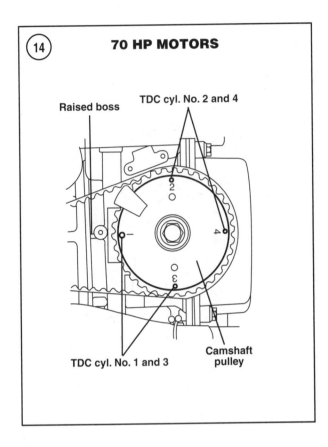

70 HP MOTORS

Raised boss

TDC cyl. No. 2 and 4

2

4

3

TDC cyl. No. 1 and 3

Camshaft pulley

4

The No. 1 cylinder is at TDC of the compression stroke when the holes in the crankshaft pulley belt guides align with the protrusion on the cylinder block and the No. 1 mark on the camshaft pulley aligns with the raised boss on the cylinder head. At TDC of a compression stroke, the base of the camshaft lobe will be touching the rocker arm (the raised portion of the lobe will face away from the rocker).

6. Disconnect the breather hose from the cylinder head cover.

7. Remove the ignition coils from the cylinder head. Refer to Chapter Seven.

8. Support the rocker arm cover while removing the six cover bolts using a crossing pattern. Pull the rocker arm cover from the cylinder head. Remove the cover gasket.

9. Verify that the flywheel is still in the No. 1 TDC position. If so, the raised portion of the camshaft lobes face away from the valve tappets (not be in contact with the rockers) and both the valves for the No. 1 cylinder are closed.

10. Measure the clearance of the No. 1 cylinder intake and exhaust valves, the No. 2 cylinder intake valve and the No. 3 cylinder exhaust valve (**Figure 15**). Insert feeler gauges of various sizes between the rocker arm and the valve stem (**Figure 16**) for each valve. The size that passes between the arm and stem with a slight drag indicates the valve clearance. Compare the clearance measured with the specification in **Table 1**.

11. If necessary, adjust the valve clearance as follows:

    a. Loosen the locknut (**Figure 16**).

    b. Turn the adjusting screw until the clearance is correct.

    c. Hold the screw while tightening the locknut to the specification in **Table 4**.

    d. Recheck the valve clearance and readjust if necessary.

12. Rotate the flywheel clockwise one full revolution (360°) until the No. 4 TDC mark aligns with the raised boss on the cylinder head (**Figure 14**).

NOTE
The camshaft turns at half the rate of the crankshaft/flywheel. Therefore, rotating the flywheel as directed in Step 12 will turn the camshaft sprocket only 180°, placing the No. 1 TDC mark exactly 1/2 a turn away from the previous location. At this point, both valves for the No. 4 cylinder should be closed.

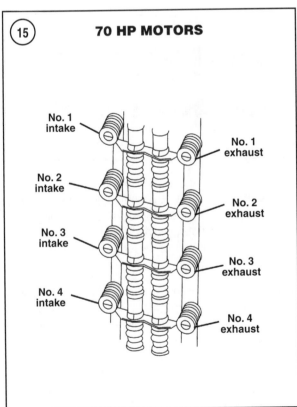

70 HP MOTORS

No. 1 intake

No. 1 exhaust

No. 2 intake

No. 2 exhaust

No. 3 intake

No. 3 exhaust

No. 4 intake

No. 4 exhaust

13. Measure the clearance of the No. 4 cylinder intake and exhaust valves, the No. 2 exhaust valve and the No. 3 intake valve (**Figure 15**). Insert feeler gauges of various sizes between the rocker arm and the valve stem (**Figure 16**) for each valve. The size that passes between the arm and stem with a slight drag indicates the valve clearance. Compare the clearance measured with the specification in **Table 1**.

14. If necessary, adjust the valve clearance as described in Step 11.

15. Rotate the flywheel clockwise one full revolution (360°), until the No. 1 TDC mark again aligns with the raised boss on the cylinder head (**Figure 14**).

16. Install a new gasket and the rocker arm cover. Tighten the cover bolts in a crossing pattern to the specification in **Table 4**.

17. Install the fuel pump to the cylinder head cover as described in Chapter Six.

18. Install the ignition coils as described in Chapter Seven.

19. Connect the breather hose to the cylinder head cover.

20. Install the flywheel cover as described in Chapter Eight.

21. Install the lower engine covers.

22. Install the spark plugs and leads.

23. Connect the negative battery cable and provide a cooling water supply, then start the engine and check for oil leakage at the rocker arm cover mating surfaces. Correct any oil leakage before returning the engine to service.

REMOTE THROTTLE LINKAGE AND CABLE ADJUSTMENT

This section provides the procedures to properly adjust the remote throttle linkage and cables. Adjust the cables during initial engine rigging, anytime the linkage is disturbed or if improper adjustment is suspected of causing engine malfunction. Periodic adjustments to the throttle cable and linkage should **not** be necessary as normal engine maintenance, though verifying proper operation is part of each tune-up.

8 and 9.9 hp (211 cc) Models

For more details on carburetor linkage, please refer to the *Idle Speed* adjustment procedure in this chapter or the carburetor information in Chapter Five.

1. Disconnect the negative battery cable to prevent accidental engine starting.

2. Identify the shift and throttle control cables as follows:

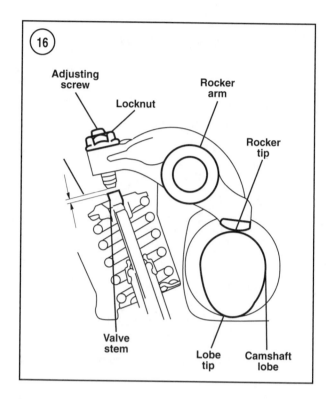

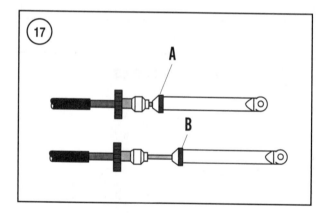

a. Shift the control handle into NEUTRAL while watching the cables (**Figure 17**). The casing guide for the throttle cable (A, **Figure 17**) will contract, while the shift cable casing (B) will move to the center of its travel.

b. Slowly shift the control handle into the FORWARD position while verifying that the throttle cable (A, **Figure 17**) begins to extend and the shift cable (B) begins to retract.

NOTE
If the control handle is moved into reverse, both casing guides should extend.

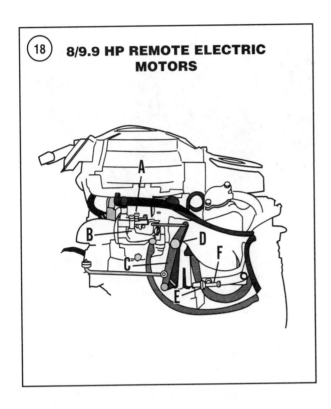

18 **8/9.9 HP REMOTE ELECTRIC MOTORS**

a. A loose throttle cable adjustment may cause high or inconsistent idle speed.

b. A tight throttle cable adjustment may cause binding or excessive pressure on the control lever throughout the shifting range.

11. Once the adjustment is completed, tighten the retainer cover screws and make sure the rubber grommet covers the control cables where they enter the lower engine cover.

12. Connect the negative battery cable.

13. Adjust the idle speed as described in this chapter.

9.9 and 15 hp (305 cc) Models

For more details on carburetor linkage, refer to the *Idle Speed* adjustment procedure in this chapter or the carburetor information in Chapter Five.

1. Disconnect the negative battery cable to prevent accidental engine starting.

2. Identify the shift and throttle control cables as follows:

   a. Shift the control handle into NEUTRAL while watching the cables (**Figure 17**). The casing guide for the throttle cable (A, **Figure 17**) will contract, while the shift cable casing (B) will move to the center of its travel.

   b. Slowly shift the control handle into the FORWARD position while verifying that the throttle cable (A, **Figure 17**) begins to extend and the shift cable (B) begins to retract.

NOTE
If the control handle is moved into reverse, both casing guides should extend.

3. If necessary, grease the cable and anchor block plates by applying a liberal amount of OMC Triple-Guard, or equivalent marine grease, to both anchor block pockets, then fully extend and grease the throttle cable as well.

4. Rotate the idle speed screw (A, **Figure 19**) until a gap exists between the screw and the throttle shaft lever (B).

5. With the remote throttle in neutral, check the fast idle lever on the carburetor to make sure it is down in the RUN position. If removed, connect the cable casing guide to the throttle lever pin and secure it using the retainer.

6. Remove all backlash from the throttle cable by pulling outward, then install the trunnion nut in the anchor pocket. Tighten the trunnion nut until a 1/32 in. (0.8 mm) gap exists between the throttle cam and the cam follower roller.

7. Move the throttle and shift control through the complete range of operation. Correct the cause of any binding or improper operation before starting the engine:

3. If necessary, grease the cable and anchor block plates by applying a liberal amount of OMC Triple-Guard, or equivalent marine grease, to both anchor block pockets, then fully extend and grease the throttle cable as well.

4. Rotate the idle speed screw (A, **Figure 18**) until a gap exists between the screw and the throttle shaft lever (B).

5. With the remote throttle in neutral, check the fast idle lever on the carburetor to make sure it is down in the run position. If removed, connect the cable casing guide to the throttle lever pin and secure it using the clip.

6. If removed, connect the throttle lever (C, **Figure 18**) and the shift support lever using the washers and retaining screw (D).

7. Remove backlash from the cables by pulling firmly, then secure it by installing the trunnion nut in the anchor pocket. Install the anchor pocket cover and finger-tighten the retaining screws.

8. Adjust the trunnion nut, as necessary, until the carburetor throttle lever closes completely to the idle stop screw.

9. Using the remote control, advance the throttle to wide-open throttle (WOT). Loosen the nut (E, **Figure 18**) and adjust the throttle stop screw (F) against the cable to hold the throttle plate in WOT. Tighten the nut once this adjustment is correct.

10. Move the throttle and shift control through the complete range of operation. Correct any binding or improper operation before starting the engine:

a. A loose throttle cable adjustment may cause high or inconsistent idle speed.

b. A tight throttle cable adjustment may cause binding or excessive pressure on the control lever throughout the shifting range.

8. If necessary, check and adjust the shift linkage, as described in this chapter.

9. Connect the negative battery cable.

10. Adjust the idle speed as described in this chapter.

40 and 50 hp Models

1. Disconnect the negative battery cable.

2. Shift the remote control from NEUTRAL to FORWARD and then, half the distance back to NEUTRAL again.

3. Remove the locking pin from the throttle arm post (10, **Figure 20**) and pull the throttle cable (2) away from the throttle arm (9).

4. Rotate the throttle arm (9, **Figure 20**) until the throttle shaft lever (11) contacts and fully depresses the protrusion on the throttle position switch (12).

5. Loosen the jam nut (4, **Figure 20**) and push in on the cable connector (5) to remove slack from the cable. With the throttle arm positioned as described in Step 4, rotate the cable connector until it fits over the throttle arm post (10, **Figure 20**). Adjust the cable to remove all slack without excessive preload (allow the throttle spring to produce preload). The flat side of the cable connector must face the throttle arm and the connector must thread onto the cable a minimum of 0.314 in. (8 mm).

6. Securely tighten the jam nut. Install the cable to the post and install the locking pin.

7. Cycle the controls from closed to full throttle several times. Return the throttle to the closed position. Make sure the throttle shaft lever (11, **Figure 20**) fully depresses the protrusion on the throttle position switch (12) without excessive cable preload. Move the controls to the fully FORWARD position and verify that the throttle lever contacts the throttle stop. Readjust the cable if there is improper adjustment or excessive cable preload.

70 hp Models

1. Disconnect the negative battery cable.

2. Identify the shift and throttle control cables as follows:

a. Shift the control handle into NEUTRAL while watching the cables (**Figure 17**). The casing guide for the throttle cable (A, **Figure 17**) will contract, while the shift cable casing (B) will move to the center of its travel.

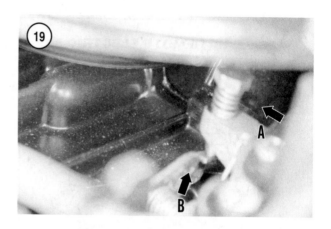

b. Slowly shift the control handle into the FORWARD position while verifying that the throttle cable (A, **Figure 17**) begins to extend and the shift cable (B) begins to retract.

NOTE
If the control handle is moved into reverse, both casing guides should extend.

3. Shift the remote control from NEUTRAL to FORWARD and then, half the distance back to NEUTRAL again.

4. Remove the locking pin from the throttle arm post (8, **Figure 21**) and pull the throttle cable (4) away from the throttle arm (12).

5. Rotate the throttle arm (12, **Figure 21**) until the throttle shaft lever (on the bottom of the throttle body) contacts and fully depresses the protrusion on the throttle position switch (1).

6. Loosen the jam nut (6, **Figure 21**) and push in on the cable connector (7) to remove slack from the cable. With the throttle arm positioned as described in Step 3, rotate the cable connector (7, **Figure 21**) until it fits over the throttle arm post (8). Adjust the cable to remove all slack without excessive preload (using throttle spring pressure to hold the throttle closed). The flat side of the cable connector must face the throttle arm and the connector must thread onto the cable a minimum of 0.314 in. (8 mm).

7. Securely tighten the jam nut. Install the cable to the post and install the locking pin.

8. Cycle the controls from closed to full throttle several times. Return the throttle to the closed position. Make sure the throttle arm lever fully depresses the protrusion on the throttle position switch (1, **Figure 21**) without excessive cable preload. Move the controls to the fully FORWARD position and verify that the throttle lever contacts the throttle stop. Readjust the cable if improper adjustment or excessive cable preload occurs.

4

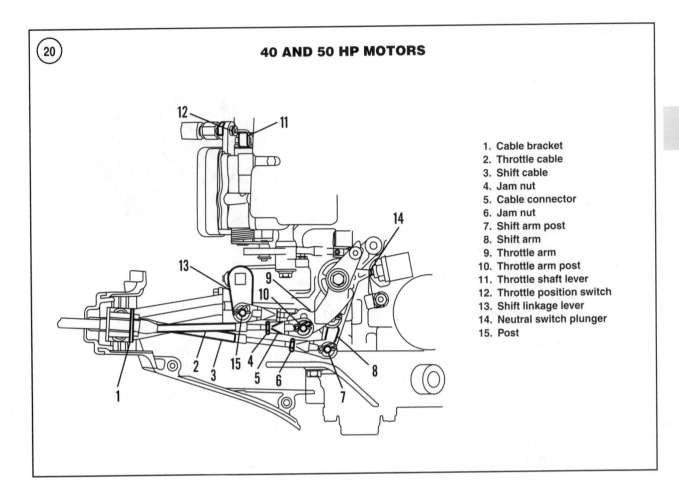

20

40 AND 50 HP MOTORS

1. Cable bracket
2. Throttle cable
3. Shift cable
4. Jam nut
5. Cable connector
6. Jam nut
7. Shift arm post
8. Shift arm
9. Throttle arm
10. Throttle arm post
11. Throttle shaft lever
12. Throttle position switch
13. Shift linkage lever
14. Neutral switch plunger
15. Post

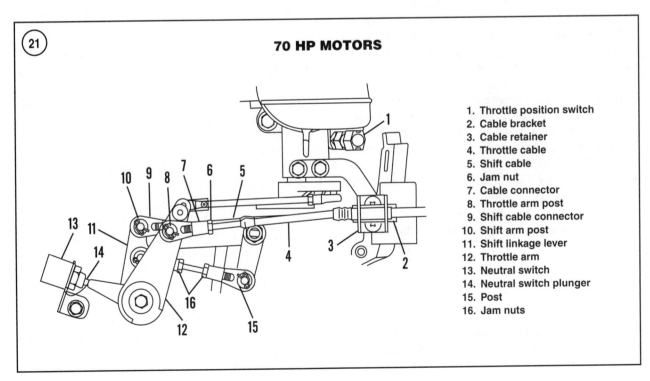

21

70 HP MOTORS

1. Throttle position switch
2. Cable bracket
3. Cable retainer
4. Throttle cable
5. Shift cable
6. Jam nut
7. Cable connector
8. Throttle arm post
9. Shift cable connector
10. Shift arm post
11. Shift linkage lever
12. Throttle arm
13. Neutral switch
14. Neutral switch plunger
15. Post
16. Jam nuts

SHIFT CABLE AND LINKAGE ADJUSTMENT

Adjust the shift cable/linkage during initial engine rigging, anytime the gearcase or shift linkage is disturbed or if incorrect adjustment is suspected of causing an engine malfunction. Refer to the instructions for the selected model. Periodic adjustments to the shift cable and linkage should **not** be necessary as normal engine maintenance, though verifying proper operation is part of each tune-up.

9.9 and 15 hp (305 cc) Models

1. Disconnect the negative battery cable and remove the propeller from the gear case for safety. Refer to Chapter Nine for details on propeller removal.
2. While slowly rotating the propeller shaft, move the shifter to the NEUTRAL position.
3. For remote models, remove the shift cable trunnion nut from the anchor pocket.
4. Locate the detent spring adjustment screw (A, **Figure 22**) on the lower front of the motor, below and inline with the hand starter. Loosen the adjustment screw, and then disconnect the neutral lockout link (B, **Figure 22**) from the shift lever.
5. Make sure the gearcase is in neutral, then move the detent sprint until it fully engages the notch of the shift lever detent, then secure it by tightening the adjustment screw.
6. Using the neutral lockout link (B, **Figure 22**), move the starter lockout plunger (C) into a horizontal position.
7. Adjust the neutral lockout link connector so the lockout plunger remains in a horizontal position once the connector is attached to the shift lever, then fasten the connector to the shift lever.
8. For remote models, remove any remaining cable backlash by pulling on the casing, and then use the cable trunnion nut to locate it properly in the anchor pocket. Secure the cable to the anchor retainer and tighten the screw to the specifications in **Table 4**.
9. Refer to Chapter Nine for instructions, then install the propeller.
10. Connect the negative battery cable.
11. Operate the engine and check for proper shift engagement. Make any corrections before returning the engine to service.

40 and 50 hp Models

1. Disconnect the negative battery cable and remove the propeller from the gearcase for safety. For details, refer to Chapter Nine for propeller procedures.

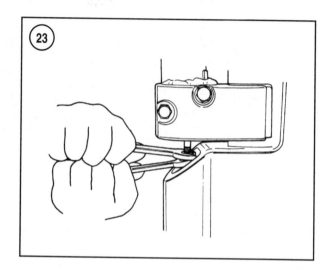

2. Remove the locking pin and carefully pull the shift linkage from the post (15, **Figure 20**) on the shift linkage lever (13).

3. Move the shift linkage lever toward the front and rear of the engine to locate the neutral detent. The propeller shaft rotates freely in both directions in neutral gear. Place a piece of tape on the power head that is directly in line with the shift linkage lever. Make a mark that aligns with the shift linkage lever when in neutral.

4. Move the shift linkage lever toward the front of the engine until the bump or detent is felt when the forward gear engages. Rotate the propeller shaft counterclockwise as viewed from the rear to engage the clutch to the forward gear. Place a piece of tape on the power head that is directly in line with the shift linkage lever. Make a mark that aligns with the shift linkage lever when in forward.

5. Move the shift linkage lever (13, **Figure 20**) toward the rear of the engine until the bump or detent is felt when the reverse gear engages. Rotate the propeller shaft clockwise as viewed from the rear to fully engage the clutch to

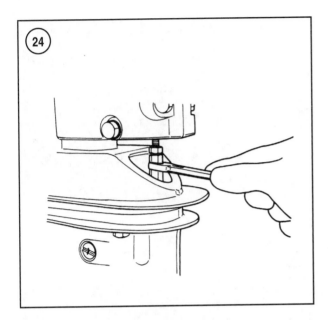

the reverse gear. Place a piece of tape on the power head that is directly in line with the shift linkage lever. Make a mark that aligns with the shift linkage lever when in reverse.

6. Place the shift linkage lever (13, **Figure 20**) into neutral. Measure the distance from the neutral–to–forward and neutral–to–reverse marks to determine the amount of shift selector movement. The amount of movement required to engage forward or reverse from neutral must be equal. Perform Steps 7-10 if there is unequal lever movement.

7. Locate the lower–to–upper shift shaft connector on the front edge of the drive shaft housing.

8. Loosen the jam nut (**Figure 23**) and rotate the shift connector (**Figure 24**) until equal shift selector movement is achieved.

9. Thread the connector onto the lower shift shaft a minimum of six threads. Securely tighten the jam nut (**Figure 23**).

10. Check the shift linkage lever for equal movement. Several adjustments may be required before equal movement occurs. Verify proper gear engagement and readjust as required.

11. Place the shift linkage lever in neutral. Rotate the propeller shaft to verify neutral gear. Install the linkage to the post (15, **Figure 20**) of the shift linkage lever (13). Slip the locking pin into the hole in the post.

12. Remove the locking pin and pull the shift cable connector from the shift arm post (7, **Figure 20**).

13. Inspect the alignment of the tip on the shift arm (8, **Figure 20**) to the neutral switch plunger (14). The tip on

the shift lever must align with the plunger of the switch. Correct misalignment as follows:

   a. Remove the locking pin and pull the linkage from the shift lever post (15, **Figure 20**).

   b. Loosen the jam nut at the lever end of the linkage. Rotate the linkage connector until the lever and plunger align.

   c. Make sure the linkage connector threads onto the linkage a minimum of 0.314 in. (8 mm). Securely tighten the jam nut.

   d. Install the linkage to the post and install the locking pin. Verify correct adjustment.

14. Place the remote control shift selector in NEUTRAL. To remove excessive slack, push in lightly on the shift cable during adjustment. Loosen the jam nut (6, **Figure 20**) and rotate the cable connector until it aligns with the shift arm post (7) on the shift arm. Make sure the cable end threads onto the shift cable a minimum of 0.314 in. (8 mm). Securely tighten the jam nut. Install the shift cable to the shift arm and install the locking pin. Verify correct alignment of the shift lever and neutral switch. Readjust the shift cable as necessary. Securely tighten all fasteners.

15. Install the propeller and connect the negative battery cable.

16. Operate the engine and check for proper shift engagement. Verify proper operation of the neutral switch. The engine must not start if in gear. Make any corrections before returning the engine to service.

70 hp Models

1. Disconnect the negative battery cable and remove the propeller from the gearcase for safety. For details, refer to Chapter Nine for propeller procedures.

2. Remove the locking pin and carefully pull the shift linkage from the shift arm post (10, **Figure 21**) on the shift linkage lever (11).

3. Move the shift linkage lever toward the front and rear of the engine to locate the neutral detent. The propeller shaft rotates freely in both directions in neutral gear. Place a piece of tape on the power head that is directly in line with the shift linkage lever. Make a marking that aligns with the shift linkage arm.

4. Move the shift linkage lever (11, **Figure 21**) toward the front of the engine until the bump or detent indicating forward gear engagement is felt. Rotate the propeller shaft counterclockwise as viewed from the rear to fully engage the clutch to the forward gear. Place a piece of tape on the power head that is directly in line with the shift linkage lever. Make a mark that aligns with the shift linkage lever.

5. Move the shift linkage lever (11, **Figure 21**) toward the rear of the engine until the bump or detent indicating

reverse gear engagement is felt. Rotate the propeller shaft clockwise as viewed from the rear to fully engage the clutch to the reverse gear. Place a piece of tape on the power head that is directly in line with the shift linkage arm. Make a mark that aligns with the shift linkage arm.

6. Place the shift linkage lever (11, **Figure 21**) in neutral. Measure the distance from the neutral–to–forward and neutral–to–reverse marks to determine the amount of shift selector movement. Position the shift lever at the mid-point between the forward and reverse gear marks. Verify the gearcase is in reverse gear.

7. The tip of the shift lever must align with the neutral switch plunger (14, **Figure 21**) in neutral gear. Correct misalignment as follows:

   a. Remove the locking pins and remove the shift linkage from its post (15, **Figure 21**) on the shift linkage and shift arm lever (11).

   b. Loosen the jam nuts (16, **Figure 21**) and evenly rotate the shift linkage connectors until the tip and plunger align with the linkage installed. Make sure the linkage connectors thread onto the linkage a minimum of 0.314 in.(8 mm).

   c. Verify correct alignment and install the locking pins.

8. Position the shift linkage lever (11, **Figure 21**) in neutral during shift cable adjustment. Verify free propeller shaft rotation and correct neutral switch plunger alignment. Adjust the shift cable as follows:

   a. Place the remote control shift lever in neutral gear. To remove excessive slack, push in lightly on the shift cable during adjustments.

   b. Loosen the jam nut and rotate the shift cable connector (9, **Figure 21**) until it aligns with the shift arm post (10). Make sure the cable connector threads onto the cable a minimum of 0.314 in. (8 mm) and securely tighten the jam nut.

   c. Install the cable connector onto the shift arm post and install the locking pin.

9. Cycle the remote or tiller control shift lever to check for equal movement from neutral to engage forward and reverse gears. Readjust the shift cable connector until equal movement occurs. Verify proper gear engagement and alignment of the neutral switch plunger tip and shift lever.

10. Install the propeller and connect the negative battery cable.

11. Operate the engine and check for proper shift engagement. Verify proper operation of the neutral switch. The engine must not start if in gear. Make any corrections before returning the engine to service.

TILLER CONTROL ADJUSTMENTS

Though some of the carbureted models covered by this manual are set up for use with a remote, most of the 5-15 hp models produced are equipped with tiller controls. Adjustments to the tiller controls on these models include idle speed, throttle friction and tilt friction. Perform these adjustments at the intervals in the maintenance chart in Chapter Three, or whenever performance dictates they are necessary.

Tiller Control Idle Speed Adjustment

The tiller control on 5-15 hp motors includes a throttle grip on the end of the tiller arm. The knob protruding from the end of the tiller grip is used to adjust idle speed (**Figure 25**) above or below the carburetor setting, based on need during varying operating conditions. The idle speed is set with the engine warmed to normal operating temperature.

1. Provide a source of cooling water as detailed under *Cooling System Flushing* in Chapter Three.

2. Start and run the engine at idle until it reaches normal operating temperature. Make sure the engine runs at SLOW idle once normal temperature is reached. If not,

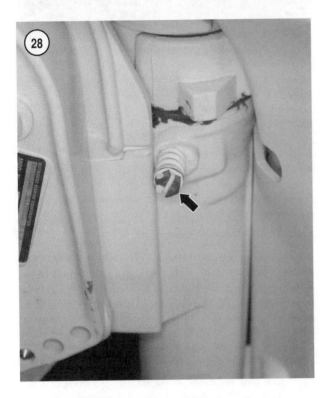

throttle grip (on the tiller arm). When used, the throttle friction screw (**Figure 26**) should only be turned sufficiently to produce a slight drag during acceleration or deceleration. Never overtighten the screw.

Tilt Friction Adjustment

The tilt friction screw (**Figure 27**), located on the engine clamp bracket is used to control gearcase motion when returning to vertical from the tilt position. Do *not* tighten the screw in an attempt to lock the engine in the tilted position. If the engine drops suddenly, tighten the nut sufficiently to control the engine.

STEERING FRICTION ADJUSTMENT

A steering friction screw (**Figure 28**) is located on the engine clamp bracket. The screw itself is set by the manufacturer with the proper adjustment before delivery, but adjustment may loosen in service so check it after the initial 20 hour break-in and periodically thereafter.

The screw is tightened (turned *clockwise*) in order to increase friction or loosened (turned *counterclockwise*) to decrease friction.

> *WARNING*
> ***Never** use the steering friction screw to lock the engine in position (for hands-free steering operation). The reduced/locked steering that would result could cause serious injury during boat operation.*

CARBURETOR IDLE MIXTURE SCREW ADJUSTMENT

The carbureted models are equipped with an idle mixture adjustment screw mounted vertically in a round housing (A, **Figure 29**, 5/6 hp model shown, others similar).

> *NOTE*
> *EPA emission regulation prohibits tampering with emission related adjustment.*

No periodic adjustment of the idle mixture screw is necessary, unless the carburetor is overhauled or replaced to ensure proper engine performance.

To properly adjust the idle speed mixture, run the engine with the propeller installed and under load, either in a test tank or on a boat.

> *CAUTION*
> *Use extreme caution when seating the idle mixture screw. The tapered seat is easily*

troubleshoot possible mechanical problems such as a stuck throttle cable/linkage, intake vacuum leak (allowing more air into the engine for a higher idle speed) or improper base carburetor adjustments.

3. Once the engine is running at slow idle, turn the knob (**Figure 25**) *clockwise* to *increase* or *counterclockwise* to *decrease* idle speed.

Throttle Friction Adjustment

Most tiller control carbureted models are equipped with a throttle friction adjustment knob on the end side of the *damaged if using excessive force. Turn the screw lightly and stop when resistance is felt.*

NOTE
This procedure assumes that the idle mixture screw was set to the proper initial number of turns back from a lightly seated position as directed during carburetor overhaul in Chapter Five. Refer to the procedures in Chapter Five and the specifications in **Table 2** *at the end of this chapter for initial mixture screw adjustment.*

1. Locate the carburetor idle mixture screw (**Figure 30**, 9.9/15 hp model shown) in the cylindrical housing on top of the carburetor.

2. If not done already during overhaul, refer to **Table 2** to determine the adjustment specification.

3. Lightly rotate the pilot screw clockwise until it just contacts the internal seat. Do not use excessive force. Then back the screw out the number of turns indicated in **Table 2**.

4. Place a shop tachometer in the four-cycle setting. Then connect it to the primary lead for the ignition coil.

5. Start and run the engine, using 1/2 throttle until it warms to normal operating temperature.

6. For tiller models, turn the idle speed adjustment knob counterclockwise (when facing the tiller handle) to allow the slowest possible idle speed position.

7. While allowing the engine to run at slow speed, adjust the idle mixture screw (using OMC part No. 910245 or an equivalent female slotted adjustment tool) until the highest consistent rpm is attained.

NOTE
Each time the idle mixture screw is turned, allow at least 15 seconds for the engine to respond to the new setting before making a further adjustment.

8. Turn the idle mixture screw counterclockwise 1/8 of a turn in order to prevent a potentially damaging lean condition. This condition is especially possible while adjusting the screw with the engine in neutral.

9. If possible, reduce engine speed using the spring-wound idle speed screw (not the mixture screw), then shift the gearcase to FORWARD. With the engine running in gear, use the idle speed screw to achieve an idle rpm that is equal to or more than the minimum idle rpm in gear specification in **Table 3**.

10. Run the engine, in gear, near full throttle for one minute, then quickly reduce speed to slow and shift into

NEUTRAL. If the mixture screw adjustment is correct the engine will continue to run smoothly.

11. If the engine pops or stalls in Step 10, the idle mixture screw is set too lean. Turn the screw counterclockwise 1/16 of a turn and allow at least 15 seconds for the engine to respond. Then repeat Step 10 to check the new adjustment.

NOTE
If the idle mixture screw cannot be properly set, look for other problems. Make sure the fuel supply is good and there is no stale or water contaminated fuel in the tank. Check the carburetor to verify there are no problems with the overhauled or replacement unit. For more information on engine performance troubleshooting, refer to Chapter Two.

12. Repeat Step 10 and Step 11 until the mixture is correct. Once the idle mixture screw is set, verify the engine idle speed and adjust the idle speed screw further, as necessary.

13. After adjusting the idle speed, shut the engine down and seal the idle mixture screw cavity using RTV silicone.

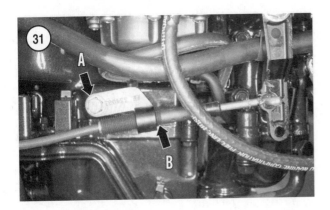

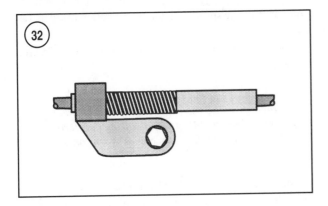

IDLE SPEED ADJUSTMENT

To properly adjust the idle speed, run the engine with the propeller installed and under load. the engine must operate normally on a boat that is unrestrained and not secured to a dock, mooring or trailer. Use an assistant so that one person is free to navigate while the other can perform the idle speed adjustment.

Always adjust the idle speed with the correct propeller installed. Idle speed specifications are in **Table 3**.

5-15 hp Models (Idle Stop Screw)

On carbureted models, a spring wound idle stop screw is used to hold the carburetor throttle plate open very slightly, even when the throttle control on the tiller or remote is manually closed. Periodic checking and adjustment is part of routine maintenance.

1. Install a shop tachometer following the tool manufacturer's instructions.

NOTE
OMC recommends using the tachometer in the four-cycle setting and connecting it to the primary ignition coil wire.

2. Start the engine and allow it to reach normal operating temperature using partial throttle.

3. Reduce engine speed to the slowest setting allowed by the throttle control. For tiller models, use the idle speed adjusting knob on the end of the tiller handle to slow the engine by turning it counterclockwise (when facing the end of the handle) to the slowest position.

4. Stop the engine.

5. For remote models, free the cable from the anchor retainer and remove the throttle cable trunnion nut from the anchor pocket.

6. For tiller models, remove the screw and washer retaining the throttle cable bracket (A, **Figure 31**) to the side of the power head.

7. For 9.9/15 hp (305 cc) models, pull on the cable casing in order to move the throttle cam away from the cam follower roller.

8. Start the engine and observe the speed on the shop tachometer. Compare the speed to the specifications in **Table 3**. If adjustment is necessary, stop the engine (for safety) and turn the spring wound idle speed screw (A, **Figure 19** 9.9/15 hp shown or B, **Figure 29** 5/6 hp model shown, others similar) on the carburetor to make an adjustment. Restart the engine and recheck idle speed with the gearcase in FORWARD. Repeat this cycle until the proper setting is obtained.

WARNING
The manufacturer does not recommend adjusting the idle speed with the engine running for safety reasons.

9. Once the proper idle speed setting is confirmed, stop the engine.

10. For tiller models, twist the tiller grip to the full slow position, then properly set the throttle cable bracket position as follows:

   a. For 5/6 hp (128 cc) models, thread the throttle cable bracket on the cable until there are only two threads exposed on the rear end of the bracket (A, **Figure 31**).

   b. For 8/9.9 hp (211 cc) models, thread the throttle cable bracket on the cable until there is only one thread exposed on the front end of the bracket (**Figure 32**).

   c. For 9.9/15 hp (305 cc) models, thread the throttle cable bracket on the cable until it is 1/8 in. (3 mm) from the end of the housing threads (**Figure 33**).

11. For tiller models, pull slightly on the cable casing to remove backlash, then secure the throttle cable bracket using the screw and washer. Tighten the screw to the specifications in **Table 4**.

4

12. For all 9.9/15 hp (305 cc) models, verify that there is a 1/32 in. (0.8 mm) gap between the throttle cam and cam follower roller on the engine. If adjustment is necessary on tiller models, remove the throttle bracket screw and turn the bracket on the housing threads until the proper gap is achieved.

40 and 50 hp Models (Idle Bypass Air Screw Adjustment)

Idle speed on 40 and 50 hp models is controlled electronically through the idle air control (IAC) valve. The valve is a stepper motor that controls the amount of air entering the engine in order to produce fast idle (significant for quick engine warm up). Once the engine reaches normal operating temperature, the IAC valve normally closes and idle air is supplied strictly through the IAC bypass. During warm engine operation, the idle bypass air screw adjustment determines the amount of air circumventing the otherwise closed IAC valve.

Perform the warm engine idle speed and bypass air screw adjustment at the intervals in Chapter Three.

1. Install a shop tachometer following the manufacturer's instructions and provide a cooling water source. See *Cooling System Flushing* in Chapter Three.

2. Start the engine and run it until it reaches normal operating temperature.

NOTE
Adjust the idle speed with the engine in neutral gear.

3. Place the throttle control in the idle position.

4. Disconnect the IAC hose from the intake air silencer (**Figure 34**). Block air flow by using a plastic plug to seal the hose, or by covering it with plastic or tape.

5. If present, remove the rubber plug from the idle speed screw opening (**Figure 35**). Slowly turn the idle speed screw until the idle speed reaches 800 rpm.

NOTE
Turning the screw inward or clockwise reduces air flow (decreasing engine rpm), while turning the screw outward or counterclockwise increases air flow (increasing engine rpm).

6. Have an assistant advance the throttle to 2000 rpm, then slowly return the throttle to idle. Allow a few minutes for the idle to stabilize then note the idle speed. Readjust the idle speed as necessary.

7. Unblock the IAC valve hose and have an assistant shift the engine into FORWARD gear. Record the idle speed.

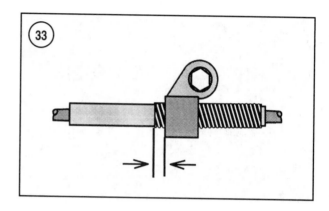

Compare the idle speed with the specification listed in **Table 3**.

8. If idle speed is incorrect in Step 7, check the IAC valve for proper operation.

NOTE
Incorrect idle air bypass screw adjustment may affect the IAC dashpot during deceleration, as well as fast-idle engine warm-up operation.

9. Shift the engine to NEUTRAL and switch the engine OFF, then remove the tachometer and reinstall the rubber idle air screw plug.

70 hp Models

The idle speed on 70 hp models is controlled electronically by the idle air control (IAC) located on the front side of the intake. The valve is a stepper motor that controls the amounts of air entering the engine in order to produce fast idle (significant for quick engine warm up). Once the engine reaches normal operating temperature, the IAC valve normally closes and idle air is supplied strictly through the IAC bypass (a small brass inlet on the intake manifold that looks like a hose connector).

During warm engine operation, the idle bypass air screw adjustment determines the amount of air circumventing the otherwise closed IAC valve. The screw, also located in the intake manifold (just downstream of the throttle body and next to the brass air inlet) is set by the manufacturer and sealed to prevent unnecessary tampering or adjustment.

Perform the warm engine idle speed and bypass air screw adjustment at the intervals in Chapter Three.

1. Install a shop tachometer following the manufacturer's instructions and provide a cooling water source. See *Cooling System Flushing* in Chapter Three.

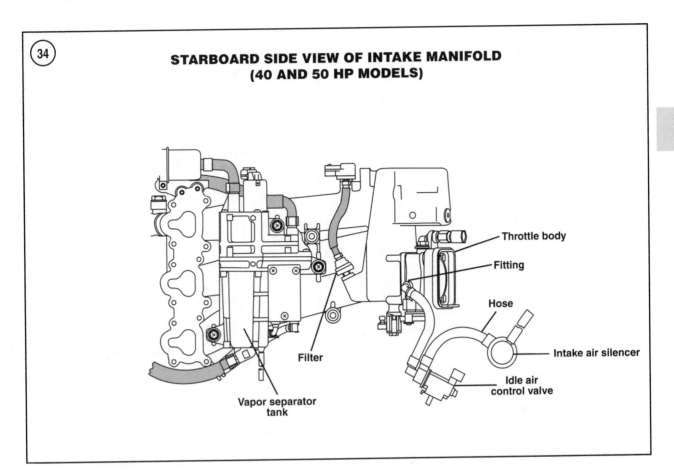

(34)

STARBOARD SIDE VIEW OF INTAKE MANIFOLD
(40 AND 50 HP MODELS)

Throttle body

Fitting

Hose

Intake air silencer

Idle air
control valve

Filter

Vapor separator
tank

4

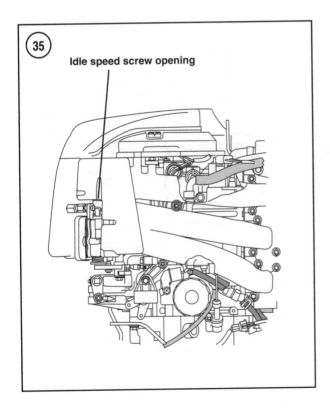

(35)

Idle speed screw opening

2. Start the engine and allow it to run until it fully reaches normal operating temperature.

NOTE
Adjust the idle speed with the engine in NEUTRAL.

3. Place the throttle control in the idle position.

4. Disconnect the IAC hose from the intake air silencer (**Figure 36**). Block air flow by using a plastic plug to seal the hose, or by covering it with plastic or tape.

5. Remove the rubber plug from the idle speed screw opening (**Figure 36**). Slowly turn the idle speed screw until the idle speed reaches 600 rpm.

NOTE
Turning the screw inward or clockwise reduces air flow (decreasing engine rpm), while turning the screw outward or counterclockwise increases air flow (increasing engine rpm).

6. Have an assistant advance the throttle to 2000 rpm, then slowly return the throttle to idle. Allow a few minutes

for the idle to stabilize then note the idle speed. Readjust the idle speed as necessary.

7. Unblock the IAC valve hose and have an assistant shift the engine into FORWARD gear. Record the idle speed. Compare the idle speed with the specification in **Table 3**.

8. If idle speed is incorrect in Step 7, check the IAC valve for proper operation.

9. Shift the engine to NEUTRAL and switch the engine OFF, then remove the tachometer and reinstall the rubber idle air screw plug.

TRIM TAB

Excessive steering torque causes the engine to pull or steer easier to one side. Some models are equipped with a removable and adjustable trim tab (often as a sacrificial anode). Proper trim tab adjustment can reduce or eliminate steering torque. Determine the direction of pull (**Figure 37**) and verify that the engine itself is not mounted or trimmed incorrectly, then adjust the trim tab as follows:

1. Shift the engine into NEUTRAL gear.

2. For safety, disconnect the negative battery cable, then either remove the spark plug coils (40-50 hp models) or disconnect and ground the spark plug leads (except 40-50 hp models).

3. Locate the trim tab just above the propeller. Loosen but do not remove the bolt located in the middle of the trim tab body. Adjust the trim tab as follows:

    a. *Boat pulls to the port side*—Move the trailing (rear) edge of the trim tab slightly to the port side.

    b. *Boat pulls to the starboard side*—Move the trailing (rear) edge of the trim table slightly to the starboard side.

4. Securely tighten the trim tab bolt (refer to **Table 4** for torque specifications on anode type trim tabs). Slowly rotate the propeller to ensure it does not contact the trim tab. Contact indicates an incorrect type or improperly installed trim tab. Replace or readjust the trim tab as needed.

5. Install the coils or connect the spark plug leads, as applicable.

6. Connect the negative battery cable (if so equipped).

7. Operate the engine and check for excess steering torque. Readjust as necessary.

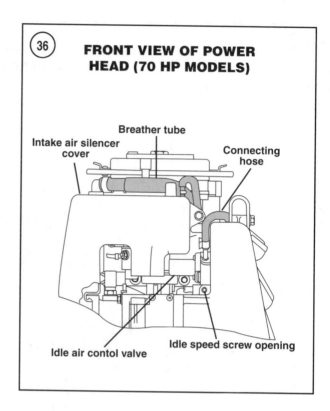

(36) FRONT VIEW OF POWER HEAD (70 HP MODELS)

Breather tube

Intake air silencer cover

Connecting hose

Idle air contol valve

Idle speed screw opening

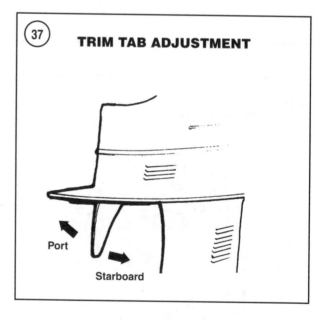

(37) TRIM TAB ADJUSTMENT

Port

Starboard

Table 1 VALVE CLEARANCE SPECIFICATIONS

Engine model	Engine size cu. in. (cc)	Intake in. (mm)	Exhaust in. (mm)
5 and 6 hp	7.8 (128)	0.003 (0.08)	0.005 (0.13)
8 and 9.9 hp	12.87 (211)	0.003 (0.08)	0.005 (0.13)
9.9 and 15 hp	18.61 (305)	0.004 (0.10)	0.006 (0.15)
40 and 50 hp	49.7 (815)	0.007-0.009 (0.18-0.23)	0.007-0.009 (0.18-0.23)
70 hp	79.2 (1298)	0.005 (0.13)	0.006 (0.15)

Table 2 CARBURETOR SCREW ADJUSTMENT SPECIFICATIONS

Engine model	Engine size cu. in. (cc)	Initial low speed setting	Float level OMC gauge No.	Float drop setting in. (mm)
5 hp	7.8 (128)			
1997		6 turns	324891	1-1 3/8 (25-35)
1998-2001		1 5/8 turns	324891	1-1 3/8 (25-35)
6 hp	7.8 (128)			
1997		6 turns	324891	1-1 3/8 (25-35)
1998-2001		4 turns	324891	1-1 3/8 (25-35)
8 and 9.9 hp	12.87 (211)	5 turns	324891	1-1 3/8 (25-35)
9.9 and 15 hp	18.61 (305)	4 turns	324891	1-1 3/8 (25-35)

Table 3 IDLE SPEED AND RPM SPECIFICATIONS

Engine model	Engine size cu. in. (cc)	Idle rpm in gear	Test propeller OMC part No.	Maximum rpm
5 and 6 hp	7.8 (128)			
1997-1998		850-950	390239	4700
1999-2001		1150-1250	444508	5500
8 and 9.9 hp[2,3]	12.87 (211)			
1995-1998		850-950	386537	4700
1999-2001		950-1050	386537	4800
9.9 and 15 hp[4]	18.61 (305)			
1995-1997		800-900	340177	3500-5000[1]
1998		950-1050	340177	3500-5000[1]
1999		750-850	340177	3500-5000[1]
2000-2001		850-950	340177	3500-5000[1]
40 and 50 hp	49.7 (815)	800-900	n/a	n/a
70 hp	79.2 (1298)	700	386665	5000

1. Minimum test rpm for 18.61 cu. in. / 305cc motors
2. 9.9 hp rope start – 3500 rpm
3. 9.9 electric start – 4000 rpm
4. 15 hp – 5000 rpm

Table 4 ADJUSTMENT TORQUE SPECIFICATIONS

Component	in.-lb.	ft.-lb.	N•m
Camshaft cap bolts			
40-50 hp models	84-90	–	9.5-10.2
Trim tab (anode type tab)			
40-50 hp models	–	11-15	15-20
70 hp models	–	14	19

(continued)

Table 4 ADJUSTMENT TORQUE SPECIFICATIONS (continued)

Component	in.-lb.	ft.-lb.	N•m
Valve adjusters			
5/6 hp (128 cc) and 8/9.9 (211 cc) models			
1995-1998	10-20		1.1-2.3
1999-2001	100-115		11-13
9.9/15 (305 cc) models	10-20		1.1-2.3
40-50 hp models	N/A, shim adjustment		
70 hp models		12-13	16-18
Valve (cylinder head or rocker arm) covers			
5-15 hp models	84-106		9-12
40-50 hp models	40-54		4.5-6.0
70 hp models	84-96		9-11
Shift cable			
9.9/15 hp (305 cc) models			
Anchor retainer screw	60-84		7-9
Throttle cable bracket			
Tiller models	48-96		5.4-10.8

Chapter Five

Carbureted Fuel System

This chapter provides instructions on removal, repair and installation of all carbureted fuel system components.

The fuel system consists of a fuel tank (portable or built in depending on the boat), a fuel supply line (normally equipped with a primer bulb), a mechanical fuel pump assembly mounted to the power head and a single carburetor.

Fuel system specifications are in **Tables 1-3** at the end of the chapter.

FUEL SYSTEM SERVICE PRECAUTIONS

Gasoline is an extremely volatile substance, as well as a known carcinogen. Observe the following precautions when working on the fuel system:

1. Always have a Coast Guard-approved fire extinguisher close at hand when working on the engine.

2. Immediately after removing the engine cover, check for the presence of raw gasoline fumes. If strong fumes can be smelled, determine their source and correct the problem.

3. Gasoline dripping onto a hot engine component may cause a fire. Always allow the engine to cool completely before working on any fuel system component.

4. Wear gloves and eye protection when working on the fuel system.

5. Wipe up spilled gasoline immediately with dry rags. Then store the rags in a suitable metal container until they can be cleaned or disposed of. Do not store gas or solvent-soaked rags in the boat hull.

6. Always disconnect the negative battery cable before working on the engine. Disconnecting the battery will help prevent the possibility of accidental sparks during service that could ignite vapors or spilled fuel and will help prevent the possibility of accidental fuel spillage if the engine is cranked for any reason while fuel hoses or fittings are disconnected during service.

7. Do not service any fuel system component in the vicinity of open flames, sparks or with anyone smoking near the work area.

8. Do not use any type of electric powered tool in the hull or on the boat until the fuel system is checked for leaks, and if found, repaired and the system retested.

9. Check the fuel system for leaks after completing repairs.

Gaskets, Seals and O-rings

To avoid potential fuel or air leakage, replace all displaced or disturbed gaskets, seals or O-rings anytime after removing a fuel system component from the engine. For convenience try to have the required gasket or repair kit on hand before removing and disassembling the components.

Whenever possible during carburetor or fuel system service, avoid making handmade gaskets. Small pieces of material from the cut edges may break free and block the fuel jets and other passages in the carburetor.

Cleaning Fuel System Components

The most important step in carburetor repair is the cleaning process. Use a good quality solvent, suitable reservoir for the solvent and a cleaning brush to remove the deposits that commonly occur in the fuel system. Spray type carburetor cleaners are available at most auto parts stores. They are effective in removing most stubborn deposits. Avoid using any solvents that are not suitable for aluminum.

Remove all plastic or rubber components from the fuel pump, carburetor or filter assembly before cleaning them with solvent (as most solvents damage plastic and rubber components). Gently scrape away gasket material with a blunt tip scraper. Never scrape away any material other than the gaskets from the component. Use a stiff cleaning brush and solvent to remove deposits from the carburetor bowl. Do not use a wire brush as delicate sealing surfaces can quickly become damaged. Blow out all passages and orifices with compressed air (**Figure 1**). A piece of straw from a broom works well to clean out small passages. Never use stiff wire for this purpose as the wire may enlarge the size of the passage, possibly altering the carburetor calibration. Soak the component in the solvent for several hours if the deposits are particularly difficult to remove.

One small particle left in the carburetor can cause a serious malfunction. Never compromise the cleaning process. Continue to clean until *all* deposits and debris are removed.

FUEL FILTER

On carbureted models, the fuel filter varies with engine type, as well as engine rigging and installation. Some applications are equipped with a single low pressure inline fuel filter (**Figure 2**, typical). Some models, specifically the 9.9/15 hp (305 cc), are equipped with a removable fuel pump (A, **Figure 3**) mounted filter element. But many 5/6 hp (128 cc) and 8/9.9 hp (211 cc) engines may not be equipped with a fuel filter at all. On these models it is a good idea to install a filter in the fuel supply line. See a marine parts dealership to determine what is available.

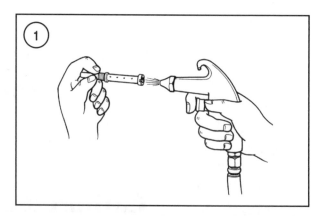

Inline filters are typically non-serviceable and must be replaced if contaminated. However, the element found under the fuel pump cover on 9.9/15 hp (305 cc) models is serviceable and may be removed, cleaned and, if not damaged reinstalled.

1. Disconnect the negative battery cable (if so equipped), for safety.

2. If equipped with an inline filter, proceed as follows:

    a. Locate the inline filter by tracing the fuel tank hose to the filter coupling.

    b. If used, cut and discard the plastic tie clamps used on some hoses or remove the spring type hose clamps (or threaded clamps, as applicable).

    c. Position a container or clean shop towel under the fuel filter. Note the orientation of the fuel hose fittings before removing the filter. Carefully pull the hoses from the fuel filter fittings. Manipulate the hose carefully to avoid bending or breaking the fuel hose fittings.

> *NOTE*
> *Replace hoses that are hard or brittle. If it is necessary to cut the hose, use care to avoid damaging the fuel hose fitting.*

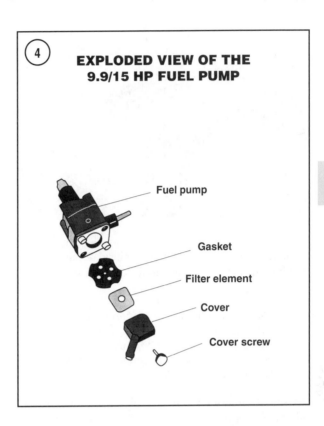

**EXPLODED VIEW OF THE
9.9/15 HP FUEL PUMP**

- Fuel pump
- Gasket
- Filter element
- Cover
- Cover screw

d. If used, inspect all metal clamps for corrosion or lack of spring tension. Replace any faulty or questionable hose clamps.

e. If equipped, remove the fasteners that retain the filter to the power head.

f. Installation is essentially the reverse of removal, but be sure to position the new filter with the fittings orientated as noted prior to removal. Many filters are directional and, if so, contain an arrow indicating the direction of fuel flow. If so, the filter must be installed with the arrow pointing away from the fuel tank line and toward the engine fuel hose. Install and securely tighten the filter mounting fasteners (if used).

3. For the 9.9/15 hp (305 cc) models that use a fuel pump filter element, proceed as follows:

a. Locate the fuel pump assembly, which is mounted to the aft, port side of the power head, just aft of and between the spark plugs.

b. With the fuel tank inlet hose still attached to the cover nipple, remove the screw (B, **Figure 3**), and then carefully separate the cover from the pump assembly. Remove the fuel filter element and gasket mounted between the cover and pump (**Figure 4**).

c. Inspect the element and clean using a suitable solvent (such as the OMC Cleaning Solvent). Replace the element if it is damaged or cannot be cleaned.

d. Inspect the gasket for tears or damage. If necessary, replace the gasket.

e. When installing the gasket, filter element and cover, take care to make sure the components are all aligned, otherwise fuel leaks could occur or fuel passages could become restricted.

4. Observe the fuel hose fittings for fuel leakage and squeeze the primer bulb. Correct any fuel leaks before operating the engine. Wipe up any spilled fuel.

5. Connect the negative battery cable (if so equipped).

6. Inspect the engine for fuel leaks.

FUEL HOSES, FITTINGS AND CONNECTORS

The carbureted fuel delivery system consists essentially of one main circuit from fuel tank to engine. The fuel tank supply line (**Figure 5**, typical) is normally equipped with a primer bulb and may also contain an inline fuel filter. Hoses are attached to fittings on the bulb and filter and are typically clamped in place to prevent leaks and to keep them from pulling loose. The fuel supply line from the tank attaches to the mechanical fuel pump that is mounted

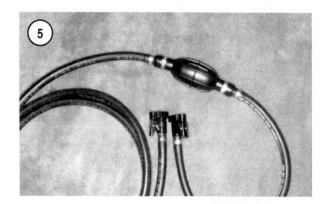

to the cover on the rear of the power head. A pump output fuel line runs from the pump to the carburetor.

NOTE
The fuel supply hose for carbureted engines must have at least a 5/16 in. (8 mm) inside diameter to ensure proper flow capacity. Do not use a larger hose if a proper seal cannot be obtained at the fittings.

Use only Johnson/Evinrude replacement fuel hoses or other fuel supply lines that meet US Coast Guard requirements for marine applications. All replacement fuel lines must be of the same inner diameter to ensure proper fit (preventing leakage) and fuel system operation. Never install a fuel hose that is smaller in diameter than the original hose.

WARNING
*The Coast Guard uses a rating system for fuel supply lines. The major differences are that A rated lines have passed a Coast Guard test regarding length of burn through time, while the B rated lines have not. The A1 and B1 lines are capable of containing liquid fuel at all times, while the A2 and B2 lines are designed to contain fuel vapor, **not** liquid. For safety reasons, do not substitute B lines for A lines.*

Inspect all fuel hoses, and replace hoses that feel sticky, spongy, are hard and brittle or have surface cracks. Replace hoses that have splits on the ends. Do not simply cut off the split end and reattach the hose. The hose likely to split again and lead to a potentially dangerous fuel leak. To avoid hose failure or interference with other components, never cut the replacement hose shorter or longer than the original. When one fuel hose on the engine requires replacement due to age or deterioration, others are likely to have similar defects. Replace all fuel hoses on the engine to ensure a reliable repair.

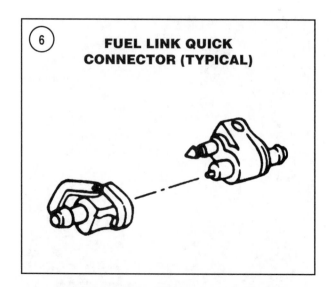

FUEL LINK QUICK CONNECTOR (TYPICAL)

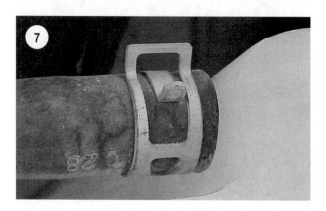

Connectors used on fuel hoses may include quick-connect types (**Figure 6**), spring type (**Figure 7**) or screw type clamps and plastic locking clamps (**Figure 8**) or wire ties. Use the same size and type of clamp that was originally on the engine. To ensure the correct clamp is used, replace it with the correct OMC part number whenever possible.

Quick connect clamps are often found on the tank side of portable fuel tanks. Like their name suggests, they are designed for easy connection/disconnection to enhance the portability of such tanks. In most cases, the quick connect fittings are retained to the hoses by clamps themselves.

Replace metal clamps if they become corroded, bent, or deformed. Replace spring-type clamps, if they have lost spring tension. When replacing a clamp at the engine end, locate any screw or tie that retains the hose or clamp to the engine cover. Remove the retainer and move the disconnected hose end over a container suitable for holding fuel. Remove and discard the hose clamp. Install a new fuel

8

9 EXPLODED VIEW OF A
TYPICAL OMC PORTABLE
GAS TANK

1. Fuel connection
2. Primer bulb
3. Fuel metering manifold
   assembly
4. Fuel tank cap

hose or clamp and tighten it securely. Make sure to secure the hose as originally noted.

Cut plastic locking or wire tie clamps to remove the hose. Some plastic locking tie clamps are not suitable for marine applications and may fail. Use only Johnson/Evinrude replacement hose clamps or equivalent marine plastic ties of the same width as the original. After placing the clamp into position, pull the end through the clamp until the hose fastens securely and does not rotate on the fitting. Avoid pulling the clamp too tight as the clamp may become damaged and loosen or fail.

5

FUEL TANKS

Two types of fuel tanks are normally used with Johnson/Evinrude 4-stroke outboards. They include the portable fuel tank (**Figure 9**, typical OMC portable tank) and built-in fuel tanks. Fuel tanks mounted onboard (portable or built-in) are commonly referred to as remote mounted fuel tanks.

Many dealerships offer portable fuel tanks constructed of steel or plastic. The types of components used, cleaning and repair instructions are similar for all brands of fuel tanks. Refer to a reputable marine repair shop or marine dealership when parts are needed for aftermarket fuel tanks.

Built-in fuel tanks may be used on all models. They are sometimes difficult to locate and access in the boat, in some cases, almost impossible. On some applications removing major boat components is required to access the tank. Fortunately, access panels are installed in most boats to provide access to fuel line fittings and the fuel level sender assembly.

NOTE
An air vent that allows air into the tank as fuel is consumed should be on all fuel tanks. A plugged or blocked air vent causes a vacuum to form in the tank, which may eventually overpower the suction created by the fuel pump, starving the engine of fuel. Check the tank vent periodically to make sure it is allowing air to enter the tank.

Portable Tanks

Portable fuel tanks require periodic inspection and cleaning. If water is found in the tank, inspect the remainder of the fuel system for potential contamination.

1. Remove the fuel tank cap (4, **Figure 9**) and gasket from the top of the tank assembly. Empty the tank into a suitable container.

2. Release the fuel hose connector (1, **Figure 9**) from the manifold and remove the screws that retain the pickup and fuel metering manifold assembly (**Figure 10**) to the fuel tank. Carefully remove the fuel meter and float (if so equipped) from the tank. Never force the assembly as damage may occur. Rotate or tilt the assembly as needed during removal. Remove the gasket between the pickup and fuel tank.

3. As equipped, check for free movement of the float or arm on the fuel pickup assembly. Replace the assembly if binding occurs.

> *NOTE*
> *On assemblies that have a float arm, binding can sometimes be corrected by bending the float arm into the correct position.*

4. Inspect the float. Replace the float if there is any physical damage or it appears to be saturated with fuel.

5. Remove and inspect the fuel screen from the bottom of the pickup tube. Inspect the screen for damage or blockage. Clean or replace this screen as required.

6. Add a small amount of solvent to the fuel tank. Block the fuel metering assembly opening with a shop towel. Install the fuel tank cap. Shake or agitate the tank for a few minutes. Empty the solvent, then dry the tank with compressed air.

7. Inspect the internal and external tank surfaces. Look for rusted or corroded surfaces or debris. Replace the tank if there is internal or external corrosion or damage. Replace the tank if there is fuel leakage. Repeat Step 6 if residual deposits or debris remain in the tank.

8. Assembly is the reverse of disassembly, noting the following:

   a. Clean all debris or contaminants from the adapter-to-fuel tank gasket surfaces.

   b. Install a *new* seal between the fuel metering manifold assembly and the fuel tank.

   c. Take care when installing float arm type models not to damage the fuel metering rod when installing the pickup assembly into the fuel tank.

9. Check for and correct any fuel leaks before returning the engine to service.

Built In Fuel Tanks

The only components that can be serviced without major disassembly of the boat normally includes the fuel pickup, fuel fill, fuel level sender and anti-siphon device. These components are available from many different suppliers. Removal and inspection instructions vary by model and brand. Contact the tank manufacturer or boat

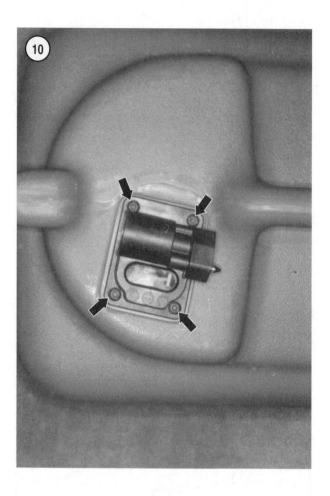

manufacturer for specific instructions. Always replace any gasket or seal if they are disturbed or suspected of leaking.

Fuel Tank Primer Bulb Replacement

The primer bulb (**Figure 11**) connects into the fuel line between the fuel tank and the engine. This section provides instructions for replacing the primer bulb. Refer to *Hose and Clamp Inspection* in Chapter Three for primer bulb testing instructions.

1. Disconnect the hose that connects the fuel tank to the engine. Drain the fuel from the hose into a suitable container. Remove and discard the fuel hose clamps at both primer bulb connections.

2. Note the arrow direction on the primer bulb, then remove the primer bulb from the fuel hoses. Drain any remaining fuel from the primer bulb into a suitable container.

3. Squeeze the primer bulb until fully collapsed. Replace the bulb if it does not freely expand or if it sticks in the col-

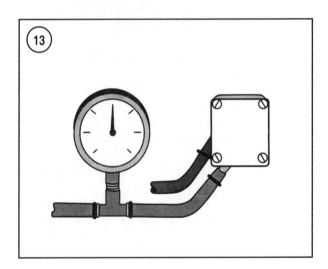

lapsed position. Replace the bulb if it appears weathered, has surface cracks or is hard to squeeze.

4. Inspect the fuel hoses for wear, damage or leaks. Replace both fuel hoses if there are defects.

5. Installation is the reverse of removal. Note the direction of flow while installing the new bulb onto the fuel hose. Arrows are present on the new bulb to aid correct installation. The arrow must align with the direction of fuel flow toward the engine. Carefully slide the fuel hoses onto the fittings on the primer bulb.

6. Install new fuel clamps at the fuel hose connections. Gently squeeze the primer bulb and check for any indications of fuel leakage. Correct any fuel leaks before returning the engine to service.

FUEL PUMP

A mechanical fuel pump is used on all carbureted models. For 5/6 hp (128 cc) and 8/9.9 hp (211 cc) models the pump is mounted to the valve cover on the rear center of the engine (A, **Figure 12**). For 9.9/15 hp (305 cc) models, the pump (A, **Figure 3**) is mounted on the aft, port side of the engine, slightly aft and between the spark plugs.

Have a shop towel and a suitable container handy because fuel will likely spill from the hoses disconnected during this procedure. Also, remember that the bottom of the carburetor contains a float bowl filled with gasoline. Be sure to drain the carburetor (for safety) before overhaul or service. To ensure correct assembly and hose routing, mark the orientation of the fuel pump and hoses before removal.

Pressure Test

Conduct this test with the engine running under load, either in a test tank or while mounted on a boat.

1. Loosen the fuel tank cap to release any pressure in the tank and then tighten the cap again.

NOTE
Check the tank location, it must not be more than 30 in. (760 mm) below the pump to ensure test accuracy.

2. Disconnect the carburetor fuel hose (from the carburetor or fuel pump, whichever is easier). Connect a fuel pressure gauge inline between the pump (**Figure 13**, typical) and the carburetor.

3. Start and run the engine in FORWARD gear at each of the rpm specifications noted in **Table 1** and note pump output.

4. If pump output is below the specification, make sure that there are no restrictions in any of the fuel lines and that any fuel filter or intank pickup screen is clean and free of debris. Retest if a clogged filter/screen or a restricted line is found and replaced.

NOTE
Use low pressure compressed air to blow through all hoses, fittings and passages to make sure they are unrestricted. Besides

5

helping to find a problem, this may remedy the cause of a restriction as well.

5. Overhaul or replace the pump if output is below specification.

Removal and Installation

1. Disconnect the negative battery cable (if so equipped).
2. On most models it is much easier to access the pump if the lower engine covers are removed. Refer to *Oil Filter Replacement* in Chapter Three.
3. Position a shop rag to catch any escaping fuel, then tag and disconnect the fuel hoses from the pump. On most models the hoses are retained by plastic wire that must be cut.
4. Loosen the mounting bolts and then pull the pump away from the rocker arm cover (5/6 and 8/9.9 hp models) or power head (9.9/15 hp models), as applicable.

NOTE
On 5/6 and 8/9.9 hp models, four screws are visible on top of the fuel pump. Two of the screws (the smaller ones on 5/6 models B, Figure 12 and the flat-head screws on 8/9.9 models) are used to retain the cover, while the other two screws are used to retain the pump to the rocker cover.

5. If necessary, remove the cover screw(s) and disassemble the fuel pump for cleaning, overhaul or inspection. Refer to the procedure in this chapter for more details.
6. Clean the mating surface of the pump and power head of any dirt, debris or, if used, any remaining gasket material. Be careful not to damage the mating surface.
7. Installation is the reverse of removal. Note the following:
   a. If a gasket was used, position the pump carefully, making sure to align the bolt holes in the gasket with the pump mounting screws. If an O-ring was used, lubricate the O-ring with a light coating of OMC Triple-Guard or an equivalent marine grease and position it on the pump base.
   b. Apply a light coating of OMC Nut Lock or an equivalent threadlocking compound to the pump mounting bolt threads.
   c. Install and tighten the fuel pump mounting screws to the specification in **Table 3**.
   d. Gently squeeze the primer bulb while checking for fuel leaks. Correct any fuel leaks before returning the engine to service.

Repair

Repair or replacement of the power head mounted fuel pump is possible without removing the carburetor or most other fuel system components. However, consider that the conditions that caused the fuel pump to fail (debris, varnish, broken or brittle gaskets) are likely present in other fuel system components. These components may also need cleaning and repair. Only repair the fuel pump if there is no doubt that the carburetor or other fuel system components are in good condition.

Replace all gaskets, diaphragms and seals during assembly. Check for proper operation and of fuel leaks after completing the repair. Correct all fuel leaks before returning the engine to service.

CAUTION
Do not apply gasket sealing compound to any fuel pump component. Small particles of compound may break free and block fuel system passages.

1. Remove the fuel pump as described in this chapter.
2. Matchmark the fuel pump front cover, housing and base to ensure proper assembly.
3. For 5/6 hp (128 cc) and 8/9.9 hp (211 cc) models, disassemble the pump as follows:
   a. Remove the O-ring from the fuel pump base.
   b. Remove the pump cover screws, then separate the pump cover, reed valve, housing and base. To ease assembly, lay out each component as it is removed in the same order and orientation.
   c. Push in the plunger and diaphragm assembly, then rotate it 90° to release the diaphragm from the base. Allow the spring pressure to gently separate the components as the plunger, spring and diaphragm are removed from the base.
4. For 9.9/15 hp (305 cc) models, disassemble the pump as follows:
   a. Remove the hex head bolt from the pump cover and then gently pry the outer cover from the fuel pump body.

NOTE
Avoid damaging the cover or body gasket surface when separating the components.

   b. Remove the remaining pump assembly screws and carefully separate the inner cover, diaphragm, housing and base components. Lay out each component as it is removed in the same order and orientation to ease assembly.
5. Inspect the surfaces of the fuel cover, body and base with a straight edge. Inspect gasket surfaces for scratches,

voids or any irregularities. Inspect the fuel pump body for cracks. Replace warped or damaged components.

6. Check the spring for damage or lack of tension.

7. Carefully inspect the diaphragm for cracks or tears.

NOTE
Whenever the pump is disassembled, it is advisable to replace the diaphragm to ensure peak performance.

8. Assembly is the reverse of disassembly, noting the following:

a. During assembly, align the matchmarks made in Step 2.

b. Always use *new* gaskets, making sure they are properly aligned as each piece is installed.

c. For 5/6 and 8/9.9 hp models, rotate the diaphragm 90° after insertion to lock it in place. Also, make sure the reed valve is in position between the cover and housing during assembly.

d. For 9.9/15 hp models, make sure the round supports located on each side of the diaphragm are positioned with the convex side (bowed side outwards) facing towards the diaphragm.

e. Apply a light coating of OMC Nut Lock or an equivalent threadlocking compound to the pump housing and cover screws (except the hex-head cover screw found on 9.9/15 hp models) and tighten to the specifications in **Table 3**.

9. Install the fuel pump as described in this chapter.

CARBURETOR

Removal and Installation

This section provides removal, repair and installation instructions for the carburetor(s). Note the routing and connection points for all hoses prior to disconnecting them. Have a shop towel and a suitable container handy as fuel will likely spill from the disconnected hoses. Inspect all fuel hoses for defects. Replace brittle, leaking, or weathered hoses.

1. Disconnect the negative battery cable or disconnect the spark plug leads for safety.

2. If necessary, remove the manual starter for additional access. Refer to the procedure in Chapter Ten.

3. Tag and disconnect the hoses from the air horn, carburetor fuel fitting and carburetor water fitting. Drain any residual fuel from the carburetor fuel hose.

4. Loosen the air horn retaining screws. For 9.9/15 hp models there is one screw on top and the other is on the side. Remove the air horn from the engine.

5. Disconnect the throttle and choke linkage. On 9.9/15 hp models, remove the choke cable clamp screw first. Then disengage the cable from the link.

6. If necessary for clearance on 5-9.9 hp (128-211 cc) models, remove the oil pressure sensor wire from the sending unit.

7. Loosen the carburetor flange nuts using a suitable box-end wrench. Because access is tight on some models, it may be necessary to use a short, thin wrench or the OMC carburetor flange nut removal tool (part No. 342211).

8. Carefully remove the carburetor, gaskets and insulator.

9. As necessary, repair the carburetor as described in this chapter.

10. Installation is the reverse of removal. Note the following:

a. For 5-9.9 hp (128-211 cc) models, connect the throttle and choke linkage before positioning the carburetor.

b. Position a *new* gasket on each side of the insulator, then install the carburetor to the intake manifold and tighten the nuts securely.

c. For 9.9/15 hp (305 cc) models, install the choke cable in the link and secure it with the power head clamp. Tighten to specifications in **Table 3**.

d. Connect the hoses as tagged and, if removed, connect the oil pressure sensor wiring.

11. If removed, install the manual starter assembly as described in Chapter Ten.

12. Gently squeeze the primer bulb while checking for fuel leaks. Correct any fuel leaks before returning the engine to service.

13. If the idle mixture needle adjustment was disturbed or the carburetor was replaced, adjust the carburetor as detailed in Chapter Four.

Overhaul

To ensure success when overhauling carburetors, always work in a clean environment. Mark all hose connections during removal to ensure proper connection during installation. Following a rebuild, always perform all applicable carburetor and linkage adjustments as described in Chapter Four.

CAUTION
Never use steel wire to clean carburetor passages. Material can be removed from the inner diameter of the orifice, disturbing the fuel calibration. Carburetor replacement may be required if

passages are damaged during the cleaning process.

CAUTION
Always replace damaged carburetor components. Seemingly insignificant damage to internal components can affect fuel delivery. Adverse effects to engine performance and durability can result from using damaged or worn components.

NOTE
Never compromise the cleaning process for the carburetor(s). Residual debris or deposits in the carburetor may break free at a later time and block passages. Use compressed air and blow through all passages to ensure they are completely clear.

1. Drain the fuel from the carburetor and inspect it for contaminants. Inspect the entire fuel system if water or other debris is noted. Failure to correct the cause of contamination may cause the symptoms to reoccur after the carburetor is rebuilt.

CAUTION
When debris is found in a carburetor, there is a good chance that the source of the debris is still present in the fuel system. For this reason, inspect and clean the tank, filter(s), pump and lines under these circumstances. The reintroduction of debris to the carburetor after a rebuild will likely cause the need for a second rebuild in a short period of time.

2. Disassemble the carburetor as described in this chapter. If valve seat or needle removal is difficult, soak the carburetor in solvent first. Do not use excessive force to remove components. Replace damaged needles or valve seats.

3. Use a suitable solvent (OMC Carburetor and Choke Cleaner) and clean all deposits from the carburetor passages, orifices and float bowl. Use low pressure compressed air (25 psi [172 kPa] or less) and blow through the passages.

4. Place all components on a clean surface. Arrange the components consistent with the illustrations in this section.

5. Inspect the sealing surface of the float valve/fuel inlet needle (**Figure 14**) for grooves, nicks, scratches or other damage. Inspect the valve seat for pitting, scratches, worn or irregular surfaces. Replace worn or damaged components.

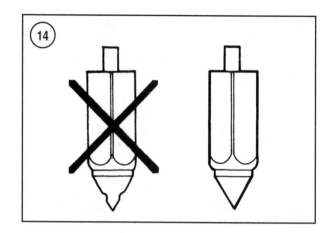

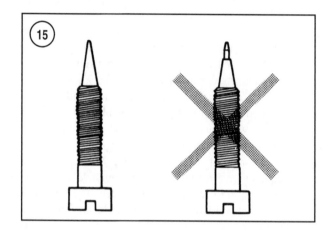

6. Inspect the pilot screw (idle mixture screw/needle) for worn or damaged surfaces (**Figure 15**). Replace as required.

7. Check the float (**Figure 16**, typical) for free movement on the carburetor body. Inspect the pin and body if the float does not move freely. If the float does not move freely, the float height will be inconsistent. Correct float height and drop setting is critical for proper carburetor/engine operation. Replace parts as required to achieve free float movement, correct float height and drop settings (**Table 2**).

8. Inspect the float for damage. Look for fuel inside translucent types. On other types, push your thumbnail gently against the surface material. A float is leaking or saturated if fuel appears at the point of contact. Replace the float if either of these conditions is noted.

9. Move the throttle lever from the closed to full open positions. If possible, remove the throttle plate and repeat this step if binding or rough operation is noted. If the throttle continues to bind a damaged throttle shaft is indicated.

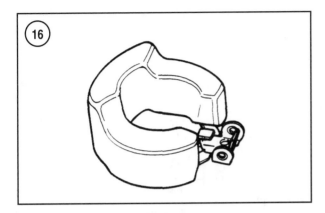

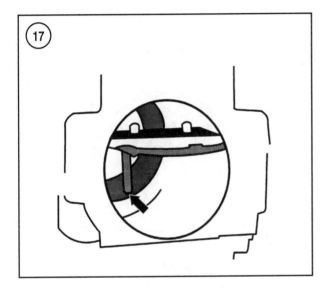

3. From the round bore on top of the carburetor, remove the idle mixture screw/needle valve (1) and spring (2).

4. Loosen and remove the seven screws holding the cover to the carburetor body, then carefully separate the two components. Remove the old gasket.

5. Turn the carburetor body over, then remove the six short screws and two long screws from the float bowl and accelerator pump housing.

6. Separate the float bowl from the carburetor body, then remove the gasket. Remove the accelerator rod (3), rod retainer (4) and the end cap (5) from the accelerator pump body on the float bowl.

7. By hand or with a pair of needlenose pliers remove the float hinge pin (6), then carefully separate the float (7) and float valve (8) from the bottom of the carburetor body.

8. Remove the inlet valve seat (9) and the gasket (10).

9. Remove the high speed jet (11) from the side of the carburetor body using OMC part No. 317002 or an equivalent orifice plug screwdriver.

10. Remove the idle speed screw (12) and spring (13).

11. Remove the air vent (14) from the side of the carburetor body.

12. Remove the accelerator pump cover from the bottom of the float bowl, then remove the spring (15), diaphragm (16) and pump rod plunger (17).

13. Thoroughly clean and inspect the carburetor components as detailed under *Overhaul*.

14. Layout the parts from the rebuild kit in the same fashion as the original components that were removed and cleaned. Compare each of the replacement components to the original components. Check with a parts supplier if there are any significant differences.

NOTE
Replace all gaskets, O-rings and sealing washers, regardless of condition.

15. Install the accelerator rod plunger (17), diaphragm (16) and spring (15) to the float bowl with the accelerator pump cover. Secure using the screw(s).

16. Carefully press the air vent (14) into the side of the carburetor body.

17. Carefully thread the high speed jet (11) into place in the carburetor body.

18. Install the fuel inlet valve seat (9) using a new gasket (10).

19. Carefully insert the float valve (8) into the valve seat (9) bore, while securing the float (7) using the hinge pin (6).

20. Check and adjust the float height and drop setting as follows:

    a. Position the carburetor body upside down (float assembly on top). In this position the weight of the

10. Check the carburetor body for leaks at the emulsion pickup tube as follows:

    a. Turn the carburetor body upside down and fill the idle circuit with isopropyl alcohol.

    b. Check in the throttle bore for alcohol leaks at the emulsion pickup tube (**Figure 17**).

    c. If leakage occurs from the tube, blow the area dry with compressed air and seal it with a drop of OMC Ultra Lock.

Disassembly/assembly 5/6 hp models

Refer to **Figure 18** for component identification.

1. Remove the carburetor from the engine, as detailed in this chapter.

2. Remove the drain plug from the bottom of the float bowl and carefully drain any remaining fuel into an approved container.

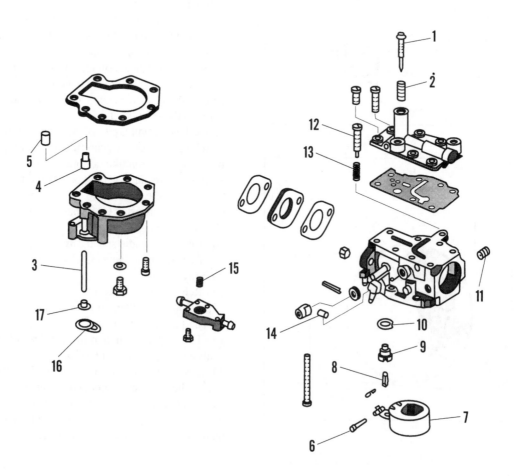

CARBURETOR (5/6 MODELS)

1. Idle mixture screw (needle valve)
2. Idle screw spring
3. Accelerator rod
4. Accelerator rod retainer
5. End cap
6. Float hinge pin
7. Float
8. Float valve (fuel inlet needle)
9. Inlet valve seat
10. Gasket
11. High speed jet (fixed orifice)
12. Idle speed screw
13. Idle screw spring
14. Air vent
15. Accelerator pump spring
16. Accelerator pump diaphragm
17. Accelerator pump rod plunger

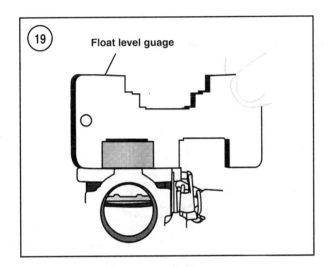

⑲ Float level guage

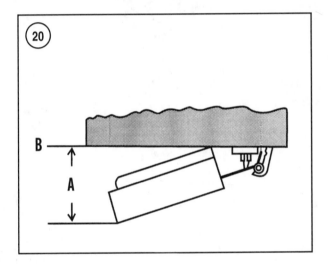

⑳

gauge labeled 2 THRU 6 HP as it is intended for two-stroke engines only.

c. If the float does not sit between the gauge notches in substep b, very carefully bend the metal arm of the float to adjust it, but **do not** force the valve down into the seat during this adjustment.

NOTE
While the float height is used to determine the point at which the inlet valve closes, the float drop setting ensures that the inlet valve opens fully when the float is in the lowest position of travel. Incorrect adjustment of the drop setting could cause fuel starvation problems.

d. With the float height set using the gauge, turn the carburetor body over and allow the float to drop down and open the inlet valve. Measure the drop setting as shown (A, **Figure 20**). Dimension A is measured from the bottom of the carburetor base (B, **Figure 20**) to the lowest point of travel on the float. Compare the measurement with the specifications in **Table 2**. If adjustment is necessary, carefully bend the tab on the float arm where the tab contacts the float seat.

21. Install the end cap (5) so it is positioned between the accelerator rod (3) and the throttle shaft cam, then install the float bowl/accelerator pump assembly to the carburetor body using the *new* gasket. Install and tighten the screws to the specification in **Table 3** using the sequence embossed on the float bowl.

22. Install the idle speed adjustment screw (12) and spring (13) into the carburetor body. Slowly thread the screw until it just contacts the idle adjustment lever.

23. Install the carburetor cover to the body using a *new* gasket. Install and tighten the screws to the specification in **Table 3** using the sequence embossed on the float bowl.

24. Install the idle mixture screw (1) and spring (2). Slowly install the screw into the bore until it *lightly* contacts the seat and then back it off the specified number of turns listed in **Table 2.** This is the initial low speed setting.

25. Install the carburetor as described in this chapter.

26. Adjust the idle mixture and speed screws as described in Chapter Four.

Disassembly/assembly 8/9.9 and 9.9/15 hp models

Refer to **Figure 21** (all 8-9.9 hp models and 1998-2001 15 hp models) and **Figure 22** (1994-1997 hp models) for component identification.

1. Remove the carburetor from the engine.

float will hold the inlet valve gently closed against the valve seat.

CAUTION
Do not force or press the inlet valve against the valve seat or the valve surfaces could be damaged.

b. Position the correct float level gauge (**Table 2**) on the carburetor body gasket surface, then carefully slide the gauge over top of the float (**Figure 19**) to ensure that the float is positioned between the notches on the gauge.

NOTE
When using the OMC float gauge on the 5/6 hp (128 cc) model, make sure to use the portion marked 9.9 and 15 HP for the correct measurement. Do not use the portion of the

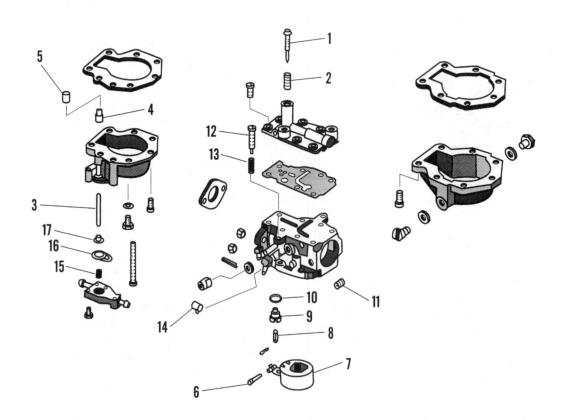

CARBURETOR (8-9.9 HP MODELS AND 1998-ON 15 HP MODELS)

1. Idle mixture screw (needle valve)
2. Idle screw spring
3. Accelerator rod
4. Accelerator rod retainer
5. End cap
6. Float hinge pin
7. Float
8. Float valve (fuel inlet needle)
9. Inlet valve seat
10. Gasket
11. High speed jet (fixed orifice)
12. Idle speed screw
13. Idle screw spring
14. Air vent
15. Accelerator pump spring
16. Accelerator pump diaphragm
17. Accelerator pump rod plunger

㉒ **CARBURETOR EXPLODED VIEW (1994-1997 15 HP MODELS)**

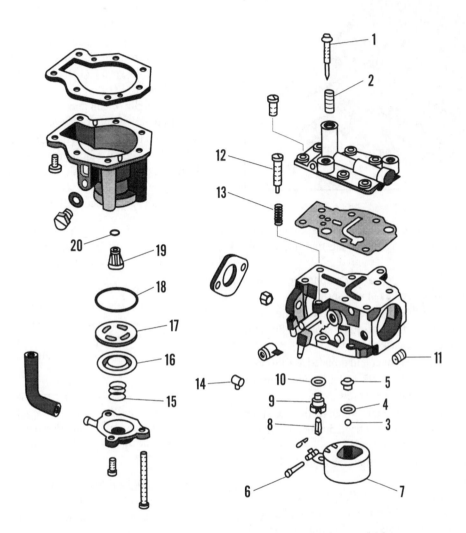

1. Idle mixture screw (needle valve)
2. Idle screw spring
3. Check ball
4. Gasket
5. Check valve cap
6. Float hinge pin
7. Float
8. Float valve (fuel inlet needle)
9. Inlet valve seat
10. Gasket
11. High speed jet (fixed orifice)
12. Idle speed screw
13. Idle screw spring
14. Air vent
15. Spring
16. Diaphragm
17. Retainer
18. Large O-ring
19. Check valve assembly
20. Small O-ring

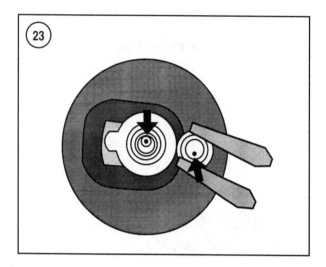

2. Remove the drain plug from the bottom of the float bowl and carefully drain any remaining fuel into an approved container.

3. From the round bore on top of the carburetor, remove the idle mixture screw/needle (1) and spring (2).

4. Loosen and remove the seven screws holding the cover to the carburetor body, then carefully separate the two components. Remove the gasket.

5. Turn the carburetor body over and proceed as follows:

   a. For 8-9.9 hp and 1994-1997 15 hp models, remove the seven float bowl cover screws.

   b. For 1998-on 15 hp models, remove the six short screws and two long screws from the float bowl and accelerator pump housing.

6. Separate the float bowl from the carburetor body, then remove the gasket.

7. For 15 hp models, proceed as follows:

   a. On 1994-1997 models, remove the check ball (3), gasket (4) and check valve cap (5) from the carburetor body.

   b. On 1998-on models, remove the accelerator rod (3), rod retainer (4) and the end cap (5) from the accelerator pump body on the float bowl.

8. By hand or with a pair of needlenose pliers, remove the float hinge pin (6), then carefully separate the float (7) and float valve (8) from the bottom of the carburetor body. Remove the inlet valve seat (9) and the gasket (10).

9. Remove the high speed jet (11) from the side of the carburetor body using OMC part No. 317002 or an equivalent orifice plug screwdriver.

10. Remove the idle speed screw (12) and spring (13).

11. On 8-9.9 hp and 1994-1997 15 hp models, remove the air vent (14) from the side of the carburetor body.

12. For 15 hp models, proceed as follows:

   a. On 1994-1997 models, loosen the bolts and remove the cover from the underside of the float bowl, then remove the spring (15), diaphragm (16), retainer (17), large O-ring (18), check valve assembly (19) and small O-ring (20).

   b. On 1998-on models, remove the accelerator pump cover from the bottom of the float bowl, and then remove the spring (15), diaphragm (16) and pump rod plunger (17).

13. Thoroughly clean and inspect the carburetor components as detailed under *Overhaul*.

14. Layout the parts from the rebuild kit in the same fashion as the original components that were removed and cleaned. Compare each of the replacement components to the original components. Check with a parts supplier if there are any significant differences.

CAUTION
Replace all gaskets, O-rings and sealing washers, regardless of condition.

15. For 15 hp models, proceed as follows:

   a. On 1994-1997 models, install the small O-ring (20), check valve assembly (19), large O-ring (18), retainer (17), diaphragm (16) and spring (15) into the bottom of the float bowl and secure using the cover.

NOTE
The retainer in Step 15, substep a is positioned with the flat side against the check valve assembly. The diaphragm is then positioned so the outer rib fits in the cover groove.

   b. On 1998-on models, install the accelerator rod plunger (17), diaphragm (16) and spring (15) to the float bowl with the accelerator pump cover. Secure using the screw(s).

16. On 8-9.9 hp and 1994-1997 models, carefully press the air vent (14) into the side of the carburetor body.

17. Carefully thread the high speed jet (11) into place in the carburetor body.

18. Install the fuel inlet valve seat (9) using a new gasket (10).

19. Carefully insert the float valve (8) into the inlet valve seat (9) bore, while securing the float (7) using the hinge pin (6).

20. Check and adjust the float height and drop setting as follows:

   a. Position the carburetor body upside down (float assembly on top). In this position the weight of the float will hold the inlet valve gently closed against the valve seat.

CAUTION
Do not force or press the inlet valve against
the valve seat or the valve surfaces could be
damaged.

b. Position the correct float level gauge (**Table 2**) on the carburetor body gasket surface, then carefully slide the gauge over the top of the float (**Figure 19**) to ensure that the float is positioned between the notches on the gauge.

NOTE
When using the OMC float gauge on all
8-15 hp models make sure to use the portion
*marked **9.9 and 15 HP** for the correct mea-*
surement.

c. If the float does not sit between the gauge notches in substep b, very carefully bend the metal arm of the float to adjust it, but **do not** force the valve down into the seat during this adjustment.

NOTE
While the float height is used to determine
the point at which the inlet valve closes, the
float drop setting ensures that the inlet valve
opens fully when the float is in the lowest
position of travel. Incorrect adjustment of
the drop setting could cause fuel starvation
problems.

d. With the float height set using the gauge, turn the carburetor body over and allow the float to drop down and open the inlet valve. Measure the drop setting as shown (A, **Figure 20**). Dimension A is measured from the bottom of the carburetor base (B, **Figure 20**) to the lowest point of travel on the float. Compare the measurement with the specifications in **Table 2**. If adjustment is necessary, care-

fully bend the tab on the float arm where the tab contacts the float seat.

21. For 15 hp models, proceed as follows:

a. On 1994-1997 models, install the check ball (3), gasket (4) and valve cap (5). The valve cap must be positioned with the orifice hole 180° apart from the idle fuel pickup tube (**Figure 23**).

b. On 1998-on models, install the end cap (5) so it is positioned between the accelerator rod (3) and the throttle shaft cam when the float bowl and accelerator pump cover assembly is installed to the carburetor body in the next step.

22. Install the float bowl (or float bowl/accelerator pump assembly, as applicable) to the carburetor body using a *new* gasket. Install and tighten the screws to the specification in **Table 3** using the sequence embossed on the float bowl.

23. Install the idle speed screw (12) and spring (13) into the carburetor body. Slowly thread the screw until it just contacts the idle adjustment lever.

24. Install the carburetor cover to the body using a *new* gasket. Install and tighten the screws to the specifications in **Table 3** using the sequence embossed on the float bowl.

25. Install the idle mixture screw (1) and spring (2). Slowly install the screw into the bore until it *lightly* contacts the seat, and then back it off the specified number of turns listed in **Table 2**. This is the initial low speed setting.

26. Install the carburetor as described in this chapter.

27. Adjust the idle mixture and speed screws as described in Chapter Four.

FUEL PRIMER SOLENOID

Some 8/9.9 and 9.9/15 hp models use an electric fuel primer solenoid (**Figure 24**) in place of a traditional choke valve to enrich the air/fuel mixture and help with cold engine starting. This feature is more often found on remote, electric start models. Instead of restricting the airflow to increase the ratio of fuel, the solenoid injects fuel under pressure directly into the carburetor or intake manifold.

A fuel line from the pump supplies pressurized fuel to the valve. When power is applied to the circuit, the solenoid energizes, opening the valve. An internal spring forces the valve closed when the circuit is deactivated.

The primer is also equipped with a manual valve lever that is used to prime the engine in the event of electrical failure. If the circuit is not working, rotate the valve lever by hand to the open position so fuel will flow continuously from the valve and crank the engine. Do not leave the valve open for extended periods or the engine may experience flooding or extreme rich operation. Return the

5

valve to the closed position after the engine has cranked a few times or immediately upon start up.

A schrader valve is located under a removable cap on one end of the manual valve. The valve is provided as a convenient way to inject fogging oil or OMC Engine Tuner to the engine during storage or tune-up services, respectively.

Functional Tests

If a problem is suspected with the fuel primer system, a quick functional test may be performed once the engine is running as follows:

1. Provide the engine with a cooling water source, then run the engine until it reaches normal operating temperature.

2. With the engine warm and running at 2000 rpm actuate the fuel primer (on electric start models this is accomplished by pushing the key in). If the circuit and primer is working properly the engine speed should drop about 1000 rpm due to overly rich operation.

3. Shut the engine OFF.

4. If a primer fitting is suspected of being clogged, remove the primer hose from that fitting and connect a 1/8 in. (3 mm) inner diameter clear vinyl hose between that fitting and a syringe filled with isopropyl alcohol. Press lightly on the syringe plunger and watch for fluid movement:

    a. If fluid moves through the fitting, there is no clog.

    b. If fluid does not move through the fitting, clean it with OMC part No. 326623 or an equivalent needle-type cleaning tool.

5. To test the solenoid valve electronically, disconnect the wiring from the valve and connect an ohmmeter across the black and purple/white wire. The meter should indicate 4-7 ohms of resistance.

6. To test the valve and seat, proceed as follows:

    a. Connect an alcohol filled syringe through a tube to the inlet fitting (1, **Figure 25**, typical, note most primers for these applications are equipped with a single discharge fitting).

    b. Pressurize the inlet fitting lightly using the syringe.

    c. No fluid should enter the fitting as long as the lever is in the *run* position. Turn the lever to the *prime* position and observe. Alcohol should flow from both discharge fittings.

    d. To check the internal components remove the four solenoid end cover screws (9, **Figure 26**, typical assembly).

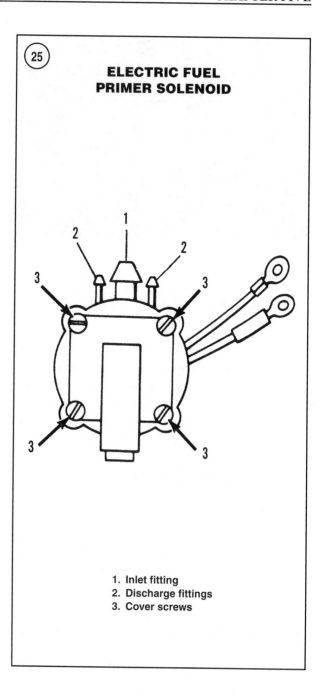

ELECTRIC FUEL PRIMER SOLENOID

1. Inlet fitting
2. Discharge fittings
3. Cover screws

Removal and Installation

1. Disconnect the negative battery cable.

2. Tag and disconnect the hoses from the primer. Wrap the end of each hose with a shop rag to catch any fuel spray when the hose is disconnected.

> *NOTE*
> *Before removing the fuel hoses, take note of any retaining straps that may have to be removed.*

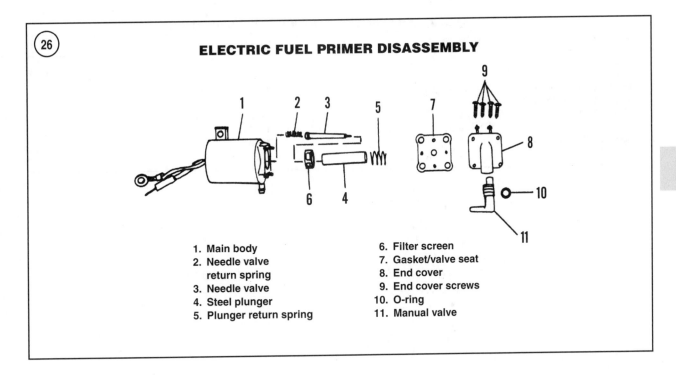

26

ELECTRIC FUEL PRIMER DISASSEMBLY

1. Main body
2. Needle valve
   return spring
3. Needle valve
4. Steel plunger
5. Plunger return spring

6. Filter screen
7. Gasket/valve seat
8. End cover
9. End cover screws
10. O-ring
11. Manual valve

5

3. Detach the solenoid bullet connector and wiring terminal.

4. Support the solenoid, then remove the bracket holding the primer to the power head.

5. Installation is the reverse of the removal steps. Note the following:

a. The hoses must be properly secured with retaining straps.

b. Pressurize the fuel system using the primer bulb and check for leaks. Make sure pressure is felt in the bulb.

Table 1 CARBURETED FUEL PUMP SPECIFICATIONS

Engine rpm	Pump pressure	
	psi	kPa
600	1	7
2500-3000	1.5	10
4500	2.5	17

Table 2 CARBURETOR SCREW ADJUSTMENT SPECIFICATIONS

Engine model	Engine size cu. in. (cc)	Initial low speed setting	Float level OMC gauge No.	Float drop setting in. (mm)
5 hp	7.8 (128)			
1997		6 turns	324891	1-1 3/8 (25-35)
1998-on		1 5/8 turns	324891	1-1 3/8 (25-35)
6 hp	7.8 (128)			
1997		6 turns	324891	1-1 3/8 (25-35)
1998-on		4 turns	324891	1-1 3/8 (25-35)
8 and 9.9 hp	12.87 (211)	5 turns	324891	1-1 3/8 (25-35)
9.9 and 15 hp	18.61 (305)	4 turns	324891	1-1 3/8 (25-35)

Table 3 CARBURETED FUEL SYSTEM TORQUE SPECIFICATIONS

Component	in.-lb.	(N•m)
Carburetor cover and float bowl screws	8-10	0.9-1.3
Fuel pump mounting screws	30-35	3.4-4.0
Fuel pump mounting screws		
5/6 and 8/9.9 hp	35-56	4.0-6.3
9.9/15 hp	30-35	3.4-4.0
Intake manifold screws	60-84	7.0-9.5
Power head clamp bolt	60-84	7.0-9.5

Chapter Six

Fuel Injection System

This chapter includes removal or repair procedures for fuel injection system components. System troubleshooting is in Chapter Two.

FUEL SYSTEM SERVICE PRECAUTIONS

Gasoline is an extremely volatile substance, as well as a known carcinogen. Observe the following precautions when working on the fuel system:

1. Always have a Coast Guard-approved fire extinguisher close at hand when working on the engine.

2. Immediately after removing the engine cover, check for the presence of raw gasoline fumes. If strong fumes can be smelled, determine their source and correct the problem.

3. Gasoline dripping onto a hot engine component may cause a fire. Always allow the engine to cool completely before working on any fuel system component.

4. Wear gloves and eye protection when working on the fuel system.

5. Wipe up spilled gasoline immediately with dry rags. Then store the rags in a suitable metal container until they can be cleaned or disposed of. Do not store gas or solvent-soaked rags in the boat hull.

6. Always disconnect the negative battery cable before working on the engine. Disconnecting the battery will help prevent the possibility of accidental sparks during service (that could ignite vapors or spilled fuel) and will help prevent the possibility of accidental fuel spillage if the engine is cranked for any reason while fuel hoses or fittings are disconnected during service.

7. Do not service any fuel system component in the vicinity of open flames, sparks or with anyone smoking near the work area.

8. Do not use any type of electric powered tool in the hull or on the boat until the fuel system is checked for leaks, and if found, repaired and the system retested.

9. Check the fuel system for leaks after completing repairs.

> *CAUTION*
> *Even minute particles of dust can contaminate the fuel injection system. Use only lint free towels to clean the fuel injection components. Work in a clean environment and take all steps necessary to prevent contamination.*

Gaskets, Seals and O-rings

To avoid potential fuel or air leakage, replace all displaced or disturbed gaskets, seals or O-rings anytime a fuel system component is removed from the engine. Have

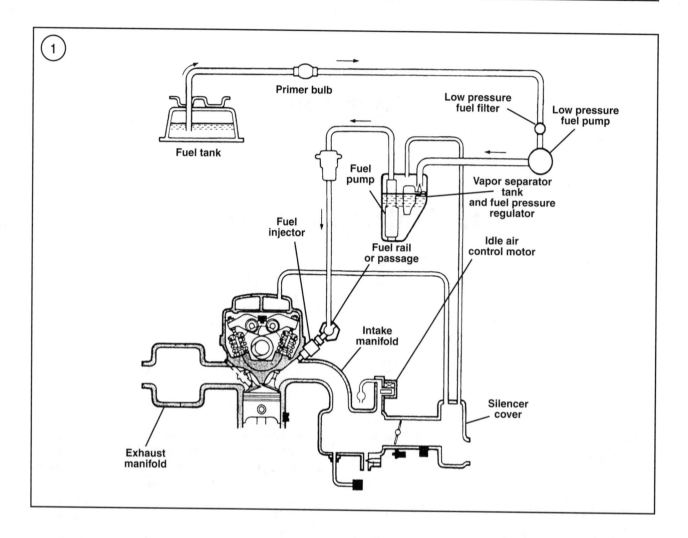

1

Primer bulb

Low pressure
fuel filter

Low pressure
fuel pump

Fuel tank

Fuel
pump

Vapor separator
tank
and fuel pressure
regulator

Fuel
injector

Fuel rail
or passage

Idle air
control motor

Intake
manifold

Silencer
cover

Exhaust
manifold

the required gasket or repair kit on hand before removing and disassembling the components.

Fuel Delivery System Description

The fuel injection system can be divided into three basic subsystems, the low pressure fuel system, the high pressure fuel system and the electronic engine controls. The low pressure system uses a mechanical pump to deliver fuel from the tank to the vapor separator. An electronic, high pressure pump mounted in the vapor separator delivers pressurized fuel to the fuel rail mounted injectors. The electronic engine control system monitors engine operation and controls operation of the high pressure pump and injectors in order to properly meter fuel delivery to match operating conditions.

The low pressure system is not unlike the fuel system used by carbureted engines. A portable or hull mounted fuel tank (that varies in design based on application and

rigging) is connected to the power head mounted fuel pump through a line containing a primer bulb and low pressure fuel filter. Refer to **Figure 1** for a schematic of the low pressure and high pressure systems.

The high pressure system, activated by the engine control system whenever the ignition is turned on, pumps fuel from the vapor separator tank through a high pressure filter to the fuel rail. When pressure rises to the controlled level, the pressure regulator relieves excess pressure by routing fuel through a fitting in the supply line, back to the vapor separator tank. Fuel injectors, controlled by the electronic control unit (ECU) are activated to open against internal spring pressure allowing fuel to spray into the intake manifold directly above the intake valve(s) for each cylinder. Injector activation occurs sequentially, immediately before the intake is ready to open.

The ECU system monitors engine operating conditions through a series of sensors. Refer to *Electronic Engine Controls, Sensors and Switches* in this chapter.

FUEL SYSTEM PRESSURIZATION

Fuel system integrity is one of the most important issues regarding engine maintenance and service. The system should be checked frequently to make sure there are no leaks that could cause an explosive condition. The high pressure system operates with fuel under pressure and must be relieved before opening fuel fittings or disconnecting fuel lines. Failure to relieve fuel system pressure properly could allow high pressure fuel spray to escape during service causing an explosive condition. Refer to the *Fuel System Service Precautions* in this chapter before performing *any* service on the fuel system.

Relieving Fuel System Pressure

40 and 50 hp models

1. Turn the key switch to the OFF position.
2. Tag and disconnect the primary wire from each of the ignition coils.
3. Push the connector lock tab down to release it and disconnect the wiring harness from the high pressure fuel pump mounted in the vapor separator.
4. Crank the engine in three second bursts 10-20 times in order to relieve the fuel pressure.

> *NOTE*
> *Squeeze the high pressure fuel line between bursts in order to check if the pressure is released. The hose should feel softer once most of the pressure is gone. Crank the engine a couple of additional times once the hose feels softer to the touch in order to ensure pressure is released.*

5. Disconnect the negative battery cable for safety during service procedures that follow the pressure relief procedure.
6. Since there may still be some fuel left in the lines, wrap a shop rag around fittings before disconnecting them.
7. Following the service procedures, pressurize the fuel system and check for leaks.

70 hp models

1. Remove the 15 amp fuse for the fuel pump circuit.
2. If the engine runs, start the engine and allow it to run until it stalls. Start or crank the engine three more times to further dissipate fuel pressure.
3. If the engine cranks, but does not run, crank the engine 5-10 times, in three second long bursts to relieve the fuel pressure.

4. If the engine neither cranks nor starts, cover the end screw on top of the fuel rail with a shop towel and slowly loosen it. Fuel will spray from the port as the screw is loosened. Keep additional shop towels handy and wipe up all spilled fuel once the pressure is relieved and then re-tighten the screw to specifications in **Table 4**.
5. Either leave the fuel pump fuse disconnected or disconnect the negative battery cable for safety during service procedures that follow the pressure relief procedure.
6. Since there may still be some fuel left in the lines, wrap a shop rag around any fitting before disconnecting.
7. Following the service procedures, pressurize the fuel system and check for leaks.

Pressurizing the System to Check for Leaks

> *WARNING*
> *Fuel injection systems operate under high pressure. A small leak may cause dangerous fuel spray that could lead to an explosive condition. Thoroughly check the fuel system prior to engine.*

Pressure check the entire fuel system after performing any type of work to the system or when parts of the system have been disconnected and then reconnected.

1. Review the *Fuel System Service Precautions* in this chapter.
2. Fill the fuel tank with gasoline.
3. Pressurize the low pressure fuel circuit using the primer bulb. Continue to squeeze the bulb until it begins to feel firm.
4. Pressurize the high pressure fuel circuit using the key switch. Turn the key ON for three seconds and then turn the key OFF again. Repeat this step 3-4 times, while listening at the vapor separator to hear the high pressure pump run each time the key is turned on. If the pump does not run, refer to Chapter Two.
5. Visually inspect all hoses and fittings in the fuel system for leaking.
6. Start the engine and idle it for a few seconds, while continuing to observe the components for leaking.
7. Shut the engine OFF and thoroughly recheck the fittings.
8. Repair or replace loose or damaged components, as required.

FUEL FILTERS

The fuel injected models use three fuel filters, two of which are inline and replaced during normal service. Each fuel system uses a replaceable inline filter, while the elec-

6

tric high pressure fuel pump inlet is also equipped with a filter screen that can be replaced, but is not done as part of routine maintenance. The pump filter screen can be replaced once the pump assembly is removed from the vapor separator assembly. Refer to the high pressure pump procedures in this chapter to replace the filter screen.

Low Pressure Filter

The low pressure fuel system is protected by a nylon canister (**Figure 2**) found in a clamp-type bracket at the port front of the power head, directly below the intake manifold. In most applications, the filter is non-serviceable and must be replaced if contaminated. But, on some models, the canister can be opened to allow inspection and cleaning the element. In both cases, check the filter annually or every 100 hours. Replace it if it cannot be cleaned.

1. Disconnect the negative battery cable.
2. Tag the hoses connected to the fittings on the top and side of the fuel filter canister. An arrow located on the canister near the top fitting indicates the fuel line that runs to the engine.
3. Squeeze the spring type hose clamps and slide them back past the raised portion of the fittings. Inspect all spring clamps for corrosion or lack of spring tension. Replace any faulty or questionable hose clamps.
4. Position a container or clean shop towel below the fuel filter. Note the orientation of the fuel hose fittings and then pull the hoses from the filter fittings. Pull each hose carefully to avoid bending or breaking the fuel hose fittings. Replace hoses that are hard or brittle.
5. Pull the filter from the power head bracket. If the filter is serviceable, clean and inspect it to determine if it can be returned to service.
6. Position the new filter on the power head with the fittings orientated as noted prior to removal.
7. Slide the inlet and outlet hoses fully onto their fittings, then secure using the hose clamps.
8. Pressurize the fuel system as described in this chapter and check for leaks. Observe the fuel hose fittings for fuel leakage and squeeze the primer bulb. Correct any fuel leaks before operating the engine. Wipe up any spilled fuel.
9. Connect the negative battery cable.

High Pressure Filter

The high pressure fuel system is protected by a metal fuel filter canister (**Figure 3**, 40/50 hp models) located inline between the high pressure pump and the fuel rail as-

sembly. The canister is attached to the middle, port side of the power head just above the fuel rail on 40 and 50 hp models or just below the intake manifold on 70 hp models.

1. Relieve the fuel system pressure as described in this chapter.
2. If necessary, remove the lower engine cover for access, as described in Chapter Three under *Oil Filter Replacement*.

> *NOTE*
> *Although the filter canister is embossed with* **IN** *and* **OUT** *markings indicating where the hose in from the fuel pump or the hose out to the fuel rail are attached, it is still a good idea to tag the hoses prior to removal. Tagging the hoses before they are disconnected helps ensure trouble-free connection during filter installation.*

3. Remove the clamps and note the orientation of the filter. Carefully pull the hoses from the fittings on each end of the filter. Drain residual fuel from the hoses.
4. Remove the bolts and the filter from the power head. Drain residual fuel from the filter.
5. Inspect the filter for rusted or damaged surfaces and replace as needed.
6. Installation is the reverse of removal. Note the following:
   a. Securely tighten the filter mounting bolts.
   b. Push the hoses fully onto the fittings and secure them with clamps. Make sure the hose coming from the fuel pump is attached to the *IN* fitting, while the

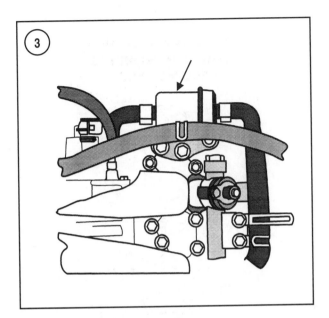

hose running out to the fuel rail is attached to the fitting marked *OUT*.

> *WARNING*
> *If the hoses were repositioned in any way during service, make sure they are routed as they were prior to removal to ensure there will be no interference with excessively hot components or components that could damage the hoses through movement and chaffing.*

c. Pressurize the fuel system as described in this chapter, then check for and correct any fuel leakage before operating the engine.

FUEL HOSES, FITTINGS AND CONNECTORS

Refer to Chapter Five.

FUEL TANK

Refer to Chapter Five.

LOW PRESSURE FUEL PUMP

A low pressure mechanical fuel pump (**Figure 4**) is mounted on the cylinder head cover, found at the rear of the power head. The pump is driven by a camshaft lobe and used to provide fuel to the reservoir (in the vapor separator) for the high pressure circuit. Have a shop towel and a suitable container handy as fuel will likely spill from the disconnected hoses. To ensure correct assembly and hose routing, mark the orientation of the fuel pump relative to the power head before removal.

Removal and Installation

1. Disconnect the negative battery cable.
2. Set the engine at TDC as described in Chapter Four under *Valve Adjustment*. Do not remove the rocker arm cover.
3. Locate the pump on the rocker arm cover at the rear of the power head.
4. Tag the hoses to ensure proper installation and note hose routing in case they are further disconnected or moved aside during service.
5. Position a small drain pan or other container to catch fuel that will drain from the fittings, then use pliers to remove spring hose clamps by squeezing the ends together. Disconnect the hoses from the fuel pump fittings. Manipulate the hoses carefully to avoid bending or breaking the fittings. Remove and replace hoses that are hard or brittle. Use care when cutting the hose to avoid damaging the fuel hose fitting. Inspect all spring clamps for corrosion or a lack of spring tension. Replace any faulty or questionable hose clamps.
6. Loosen both mounting bolts then pull the pump away from the rocker arm cover.

> *NOTE*
> *It is not necessary to remove the pump pushrod from the power head except for replacement. To replace the rod, use a pair of pliers or a magnet to pull it from the mount opening in the rocker arm cover.*

7. Remove the O-ring (10, **Figure 5**) from the fuel pump or rocker arm surface. Discard the O-ring.
8. Thoroughly clean and inspect the fuel pump mounting surfaces.
9. Installation is the reverse of removal. Note the following:

6

a. If removed, apply oil to the pushrod surfaces and carefully slide it into the mounting bore.

b. Apply a coating of oil and install a *new* O-ring (10, **Figure 5**) to the fuel pump.

c. Tighten the fuel pump mounting bolts to the specification in **Table 4**.

d. Pressurize the fuel system (as described in this chapter) and check for fuel leakage. Correct any fuel leaks before returning the engine to service.

Repair

Repair or replacement of the fuel pump is possible without removing other fuel system components. However, consider that the conditions that caused failure of the fuel pump (debris, varnish, and broken or brittle gaskets) are likely present in other fuel system components. These components may also need cleaning and repair. Repair only the fuel pump if certain that the other fuel system components are in good condition.

Replace all gaskets, diaphragms and seals during assembly. Check for proper operation and fuel leaks after completing the repair. Correct all fuel leaks before returning the engine to service.

> *CAUTION*
> *Do not apply gasket sealing compound to any fuel pump component. Small particles of compound may break free and block fuel system passages.*

Refer to **Figure 5** for component identification throughout the following procedure.

1. Remove the fuel pump as described in this chapter.

2. Matchmark the outer cover (1) to the pump body (3) and pump mounting base (11). Remove the six cover screws (6) from the fuel pump.

3. Carefully lift or pry the outer cover from the fuel pump body. Avoid damaging the gasket surface.

> *CAUTION*
> **Do not** *disturb the diaphragm attached to the outer cover unless it is going to be replaced. During installation the diaphragm surface molds to the shape of the cover and must be installed precisely in its original position.*

4. If replacement is necessary, remove the diaphragm (2) from the outer cover or pump body. Carefully pry the fuel pump body from the pump mounting base, noting orientation of the pump body so the same surface that mates the outer cover will be installed in the proper orientation during assembly.

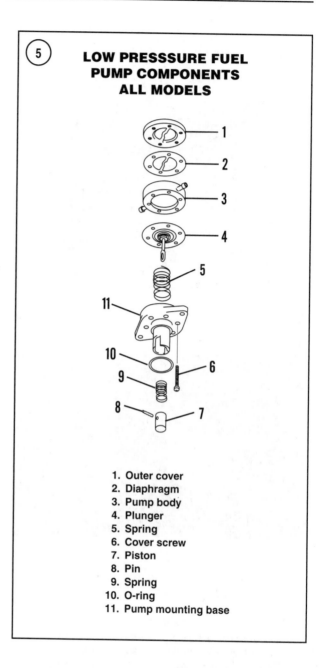

LOW PRESSSURE FUEL PUMP COMPONENTS ALL MODELS

1. Outer cover
2. Diaphragm
3. Pump body
4. Plunger
5. Spring
6. Cover screw
7. Piston
8. Pin
9. Spring
10. O-ring
11. Pump mounting base

5. Note the position of the diaphragm tab for assembly purposes, then push the plunger (4) in until the spring (5) is fully compressed. While holding the plunger fully compressed, rotate the upper portion of the plunger assembly on the pump mounting base (approximately 90°) until the pin (8) in the plunger aligns with the slot in the mounting base. Maintain pressure on the plunger.

6. Use a small magnet to pull the pin from the pump mounting base and plunger. Slowly release the pressure, allowing the plunger to push downward, then lift the plunger and spring (4 and 5) from the mounting base. Pull the piston and spring (7 and 9) from the opposite side of

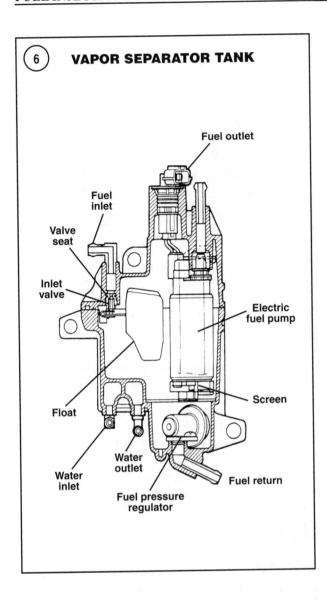

(6) VAPOR SEPARATOR TANK

Fuel outlet

Fuel inlet

Valve seat

Inlet valve

Electric fuel pump

Float

Screen

Water outlet

Water inlet

Fuel pressure regulator

Fuel return

10. Install the pin through the openings. Rotate the plunger 90° to position the pin away from the slot in the mounting base (as noted during disassembly). Slowly release the plunger and piston, making sure they do not bind in the body.

11. Install *new* gaskets and, if disturbed or if worn/damaged in any way, *new* diaphragms. Use the screw hole locations in the gaskets and diaphragms for proper orientation. All gaskets and diaphragms must be orientated as indicated in **Figure 5**.

12. Align the marks made in Step 2 and install the outer cover (1).

13. Install and securely tighten the cover screws (6). Install the fuel pump as described in this section.

6

VAPOR SEPARATOR TANK

The fuel vapor separator tank is mounted on the port side of the power head, directly behind and fastened to the intake manifold. The separator tank is primarily a fuel reservoir not unlike a cross between a large float bowl and a very small gas tank. The separator receives fuel, regulated by a float valve, from the mechanical low pressure pump. The float valve may be serviced once the cover is removed. The tank also serves as a reservoir to receive excess fuel back from the fuel rail, through the pressure regulator.

In order to reduce possible fuel related problems such as vapor lock and hot soak, the separator is water cooled during engine operation. On 70 hp models, fuel vapors are vented to the air intake silencer assembly where they are burned during normal engine operation. On 40 and 50 hp models, the fuel vapors are vented to the flywheel cover.

The high pressure fuel pump is integrated into the cover of the separator tank. Should there be any problems with the pump (other than a clogged filter screen), the cover is available only as an assembly for replacement.

The fuel pressure regulator is also integrated into the vapor separator assembly. It is mounted on the bottom of the separator tank and, on most applications, may be removed from the tank for replacement.

A drain screw for the fuel reservoir is located on the bottom of the tank assembly. The cooling water circuit is self-draining once the engine is shut off.

Refer to **Figure 6** to assist with hose connection points and component orientation.

1. Relieve the fuel system pressure, as detailed in this chapter.

2. Loosen the screw on the bottom of the separator tank and use the drain hose to empty the fuel from the tank into an approved storage container.

the base. Clean the fuel pump using a suitable solvent. Dry all components with compressed air.

7. Inspect the surfaces of the fuel cover, body and base (1, 3, and 11) with a straight edge. Inspect gasket surfaces for scratches, voids or any irregularities. Inspect the fuel pump body for cracks. Replace warped or damaged components.

8. Inspect the fuel pump check valves for bent, cracked or corroded surfaces. Replace the fuel pump body if there are defects with the check valves.

9. Insert the large spring (5) into the top of the valve body and the small spring (9) into the bottom, then align the slotted portion of the plunger (4) with the hole in the piston (7) and the slot in the mounting base. Push in on the plunger and piston to compress the springs.

3. If not done during the pressure relief procedure, press downward on the lock tab and disconnect the wiring harness from the high pressure fuel pump.

4. Remove the 15 amp fuel pump fuse holder from the retaining clip.

5. Remove the intake manifold as described in this chapter.

6. Loosen the three mounting screws and then remove the vapor separator assembly from the underside of the intake manifold.

7. Remove the five cover screws, then remove the cover and pump assembly from the top of the tank. Remove and discard the O-ring from the cover.

8. Turn the cover over and inspect the screen on the bottom end of the electric pump for contamination or damage. If necessary, replace the screen as follows:

    a. Loosen and remove the screw securing the half-moon shaped support bracket to the bottom of the pump assembly.

    b. Lift out the support bracket, then lift or carefully pry the small, round, filter screen from the bottom of the pump.

    c. Push a new filter screen into the pump, then install the support bracket and tighten the screw securely.

9. If necessary, remove the pressure regulator from the bottom of the tank as follows:

    a. Remove the plastic deflector plate from the bottom of the separator tank.

    b. Remove the screw and fuel pressure regulator from the tank.

    c. Remove the O-ring from the regulator fitting.

10. If necessary, remove and inspect or replace the float valve assembly, as follows:

    a. Remove the float pivot pin, then carefully lift the float and inlet valve needle from the cover.

    b. Remove the screw located near the inlet valve seat. Remove the plate and valve seat from the cover.

11. Clean all removed components in a suitable solvent. Blow out all passages using low pressure compressed air. Pay particular attention to the cooling passage on the side of the separator.

12. Inspect the sealing surface (**Figure 7**) of the fuel inlet valve (needle) for damage. Inspect the valve seat for pitting, worn or irregular surfaces. Replace worn or damaged components.

13. Inspect the float and pin for worn or damaged surfaces and replace if defective.

14. Assembly is the reverse of disassembly. Note the following:

    a. Install *new* O-rings in all locations during assembly. Apply a small amount of fuel to the O-ring prior to installing it to the fuel pressure regulator.

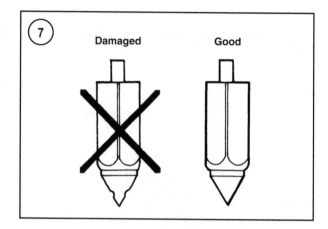

    b. Apply a light coating of OMC Adhesive M or equivalent sealant to the outer edge of the cover lip. Do not apply sealant to the O-ring, groove or inner edge of the mating surfaces.

    c. Securely tighten all screws.

    d. Upon completion, pressurize the fuel system as described in this chapter and thoroughly check for leaks.

SILENCER COVER

The air intake silencer is a plastic housing attached to the throttle body at the front of the power head.

40 and 50 hp Models

On these models, the silencer housing serves as a mounting point for the intake air temperature (IAT) sensor and the idle air control valve air hose (IAC). The silencer is equipped with a small drain valve at the bottom to allow condensation run-off.

1. If necessary for access, remove the flywheel cover as described in Chapter Eight.

2. Disconnect the air hose from the silencer cover.

3. Disconnect the wire connector from the IAT sensor.

4. Pull the silencer cover away from the throttle body. Wipe the cover clean with a shop towel and suitable solvent.

5. Align the cover and throttle body openings. Push the cover onto the throttle body. Clean the terminals and attach the connector to the air temperature sensor. Connect the air hose to the silencer cover.

6. If removed, install the flywheel cover as described in Chapter Eight.

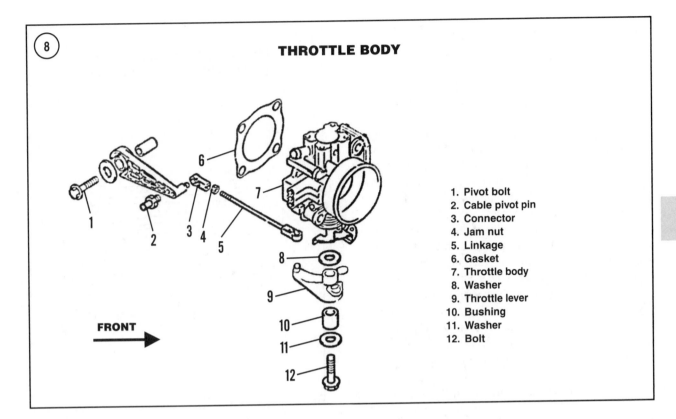

THROTTLE BODY

1. Pivot bolt
2. Cable pivot pin
3. Connector
4. Jam nut
5. Linkage
6. Gasket
7. Throttle body
8. Washer
9. Throttle lever
10. Bushing
11. Washer
12. Bolt

FRONT

6

70 hp Models

On these models, the silencer housing serves as a mounting point for the vapor separator vent hose, as well as the crankcase vent hose.

1. If necessary for access, remove the flywheel cover as described in Chapter Eight.

2. Disconnect the breather hoses from the silencer cover.

3. Remove the bolt securing the silencer cover to the intake manifold.

4. Pull the silencer cover away from the throttle body. Wipe the cover clean with a shop towel and suitable solvent.

5. Align the cover and throttle body openings. Push the cover onto the throttle body. Install the bolt into the cover and intake manifold. Securely tighten the bolt. Connect the breather hoses to the silencer cover.

6. If removed, install the flywheel cover as described in Chapter Eight.

THROTTLE BODY

The throttle body mechanically meters the amount of air that enters the engine, thus controlling engine speed. On all models, it is mounted to the front of the intake manifold, with a protective screen fitted over the air intake. A closed throttle positon (CTP) switch is mounted to the throttle body to inform the ECU when the throttle is closed.

At idle, the throttle plate closes most of the way, but is held open slightly by the CTP switch. This switch, along with the idle air control (IAC) valve and idle air bypass screw passage, provides the engine with sufficient intake air to run at idle. On 70 hp models, the intake air temperature (IAT) sensor is also mounted to the throttle body assembly.

Refer to **Figure 8** for component identification references throughout this procedure.

1. Remove the silencer cover as described in this chapter.

2. Disconnect the wire harness from its connection to the CTP switch and, on 70 hp models, from the IAT sensor.

3. Carefully pry the throttle linkage (5) from the throttle lever (9).

4. Remove the Allen bolts and carefully pull the throttle body from the intake manifold. Remove the gasket (6) from the intake manifold or throttle body.

5. Remove the bolt (12), throttle lever, washers and spacers.

6. Installation is the reverse of removal. Note the following:

   a. Install a *new* gasket during installation.

   b. Securely tighten the Allen bolts.

c. Apply a light coating of grease to all pivot points.

d. Connect the wire harness to the IAT sensor and/or CTP switch. Route the wires to avoid interference.

INTAKE MANIFOLD

The intake manifold uses a single plenum connected to a separate intake runner for each cylinder. Various components are mounted to it. On all models, the throttle body, vapor separator tank and vacuum hose for the MAP sensor are connected to it. On 70 hp models the IAC valve, IAC air silencer and the idle air bypass screw and high pressure fuel filter are also mounted to the manifold assembly, On 40 and 50 hp models, the fuel rail is a cast portion of the manifold assembly; therefore, fuel injectors and high pressure lines are attached to the manifold.

Refer to *Vapor Separator Tank* in this chapter to identify the hose connection points. Refer to the wiring diagrams at the back of the manual to assist with locating the sensors and other components attached to the manifold.

1. Relieve the fuel system pressure as described in this chapter.

2. Remove the lower engine covers as described in Chapter Three under *Oil Filter Replacement.*

3. Remove the silencer cover as described in this chapter.

4. Remove the throttle body as described in this chapter.

5. On 40 and 50 hp models loosen the clamps and remove the water inlet and outlet hoses from the vapor separator tank.

6. On 70 hp models disconnect the hoses from the low pressure fuel pump as described in this chapter.

7. Drain the fuel from the vapor separator tank as described in the *Vapor Separator Tank* procedure in this chapter.

8. Label, then disconnect all fuel hoses from the vapor separator tank. Drain the hoses while removing them. Promptly wipe up any spilled fuel.

9. On 70 hp models, unbolt the high pressure fuel filter bracket from the manifold.

10. If necessary, remove the fuel rail and/or fuel injectors as described in this chapter. For 40 and 50 hp models, the fuel rail is a cast portion of the manifold. Tag and disconnect the lines, then disconnect the injector wiring from the manifold/rail assembly.

11. Note the connection points and disconnect any remaining hoses or wire connectors from the intake manifold.

12. On 70 hp models, either remove the oil dipstick and guide tube or remove the dipstick and take great care when removing the manifold to pull it over the guide without damaging the tube.

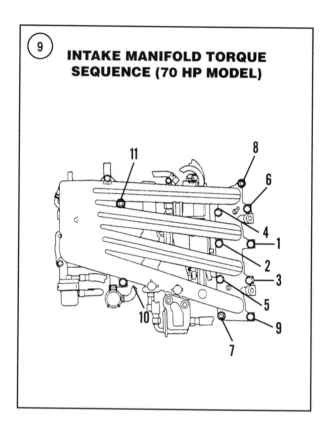

⑨ INTAKE MANIFOLD TORQUE SEQUENCE (70 HP MODEL)

13. Support the intake manifold while removing the bolts and nuts. Loosen the fasteners by gradually working at the front of the power head, then moving to the rear starting from the outside and moving inward. On 70 hp models work in the reverse of the torque sequence. Carefully pry the intake manifold from the cylinder head.

14. If necessary, remove the vapor separator tank as described in this chapter.

15. Remove the screws and lift the water jacket cover from the starboard side of the manifold.

16. Carefully scrape all gasket material from the mating surfaces.

17. Use a quick drying solvent to thoroughly clean all removed components.

18. Installation is the reverse of removal. Note the following:

a. Install *new* gaskets at all locations during assembly.

b. On 40 and 50 hp models tighten the intake mounting bolts in a crossing pattern starting at the fasteners on the cylinder head end of the runners. Then finish with the retainers at the front of the engine. Tighten all fasteners to the specification in **Table 4**.

c. On 70 hp models tighten the intake mounting bolts using the proper sequence (**Figure 9**) to the specification in **Table 4**.

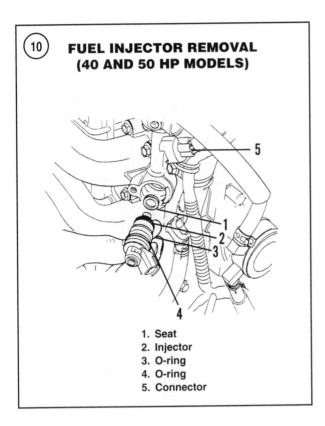

**10 FUEL INJECTOR REMOVAL
(40 AND 50 HP MODELS)**

1. Seat
2. Injector
3. O-ring
4. O-ring
5. Connector

d. Route the wires and hoses to avoid interference and connect them as noted during removal.
e. Securely tighten all fasteners.
f. Pressurize the fuel system, then check for and correct fuel leakage before operating the engine.

HIGH PRESSURE FUEL PUMP

The high pressure fuel pump is integrated into the cover of the fuel vapor separator tank. Refer to *Vapor Separator Tank* in this chapter for replacement instructions.

FUEL PRESSURE REGULATOR

The fuel pressure regulator is integrated into the cover of the fuel vapor separator tank. Refer to *Vapor Separator Tank* in this chapter for replacement instructions.

FUEL RAIL AND INJECTORS

Electronic fuel injectors deliver precisely metered amounts of fuel to the engine to match operating conditions, thus maximizing fuel economy and engine performance. The injectors are solenoid valves that open against spring pressure whenever power is applied. The internal spring quickly closes the valve as soon as the solenoid is de-energized. Because the fuel delivered to the injector through the lines by the high pressure pump is regulated to a given pressure, the amount delivered is a function of time. The longer the injector is activated, the more fuel is delivered.

The passages inside the fuel injector are quite small and easily clogged by dirt, debris or varnish in the fuel system. For this reason, the most important way to maintain the fuel injection system is through periodic filter changes and the use of fuel stabilizer when the model is in storage for more than a few weeks.

All fuel injected models covered by this manual use one injector per cylinder, mounted in a position to spray fuel behind the intake valve(s) for that cylinder. In all cases, the injectors are mounted to a fuel rail. But, on 40 and 50 hp models, the fuel rail assembly is a cast portion of the intake manifold, into which the injectors are inserted and clipped. For 70 hp models, the fuel injectors are sandwiched between a fuel rail and the intake manifold.

Install *new* O-ring seals and grommets during assembly. Note the connection points and routing of all hoses prior to removing them. Refer to the instructions for the selected model.

6

40 and 50 hp Models

1. Relieve the system pressure as described in this chapter and then disconnect the negative battery cable.
2. Remove the lower engine cover for access, as described in Chapter Three under *Oil Filter Replacement*.
3. Use compressed air to remove all debris from the injectors and intake manifold or use a soft bristled brush and/or some spray engine degreaser and rag.
4. Disconnect the wiring harness from each injector. Push in on the retaining tab and then carefully pull the wiring connector (5, **Figure 10**) from the injector (2).
5. Remove the screw(s) and retainer clip securing each injector body and intake manifold.
6. Place a shop towel below the injector to catch any remaining fuel. Then carefully pull the injector from the intake manifold. A gentle wiggle may help free an injector that is hard to remove. Remove the O-rings (3 and 4, **Figure 10**) from the injector (2).
7. Remove the injector seat (1, **Figure 10**) from the injector or the injector opening in the manifold. Repeat Steps 3-7 for the remaining injectors.
8. Clean all contaminants using a suitable solvent and lint free towels.
9. Installation is the reverse of removal. Note the following:

a. Install *new* O-rings, grommets and seals during installation.

b. Apply fresh, clean engine oil to all O-rings before installing them to the injector.

c. Carefully insert the injectors into the openings, making sure not to pinch or damage the O-rings. Rotate the injector as necessary to position the connector 180° from the retainer clip bolt.

d. Tighten the injector retainer clip screws to the specification listed in **Table 4**.

e. Pressurize the fuel system as detailed in this chapter, then check for and correct fuel leakage before operating the engine.

70 hp Models

1. Relieve the system pressure as described in this chapter and then disconnect the negative battery cable.

2. Remove the lower engine cover for access, as described in Chapter Three under *Oil Filter Replacement*.

3. Use compressed air to remove all debris from the injectors and intake manifold or use a soft bristled brush and/or some spray engine degreaser and rag.

4. Disconnect the wiring harness from each injector. Push in on the retaining tab and then carefully pull the wiring connector from the injector.

5. If the fuel rail is being completely removed from the engine (and not just pulled away to remove the injectors), remove the bolt at the bottom of the rail and remove the fuel supply hose connector. Use a shop rag to catch any remaining fuel.

6. While supporting the fuel rail (C, **Figure 11**) remove the two retaining bolts and spacers. Carefully pull the fuel rail and injectors (B) from the engine.

7. Pull the fuel injectors from the fuel rail.

8. Remove the O-rings/seals (A, **Figure 11**) from the fuel injectors and/or the injector openings in the fuel rail and engine.

9. Clean all removed components using a suitable solvent and lint free towels.

10. Installation is the reverse of removal. Note the following:

a. Install *new* seals, O-rings and sealing washers.

b. Apply a light coating of fresh, clean engine oil to the O-rings before installing them.

c. Do not pinch or damage the O-rings while installing the injectors.

d. If the fuel supply fitting connector was removed, make sure to position it so the fuel line does not become pinched or kinked. Secure the fuel rail to the engine before tightening the supply line connector to be ensured of proper orientation.

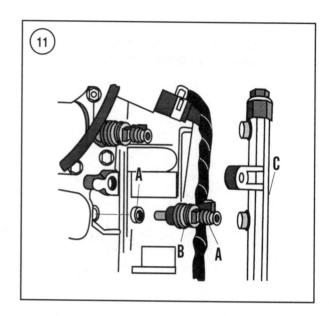

e. Tighten the fuel mounting screws and the supply line end screws to the specifications in **Table 4**.

f. Pressurize the fuel system as detailed in this chapter, then check for and correct fuel leakage before operating the engine.

ELECTRONIC ENGINE CONTROLS, SENSORS AND SWITCHES

The ECU monitors input from various engine sensors. Based on those signals, the ECU varies the amount of the fuel injected to the engine by activating the fuel injectors for longer or shorter duration during a given engine stroke.

The system uses the following sensors to meter and control various aspects of engine operation:

1. Camshaft position (CMP) sensor.

2. Crankshaft position (CKP) sensor.

3. Cylinder temperature (CT) sensor.

4. Exhaust manifold (EM) temperature sensor.

5. Intake air temperature (IAT) sensor.

6. Closed throttle position (CTP) switch.

7. Manifold air pressure (MAP) sensor.

The ECU also controls the ignition system based on inputs from the CMP sensor. The ECU uses the idle air control (IAC) valve to regulate engine speed at idle. The temperature sensors (IAT/CT) are used both for the fuel injection system and for the engine overheat warning and S.L.O.W. engine protections systems.

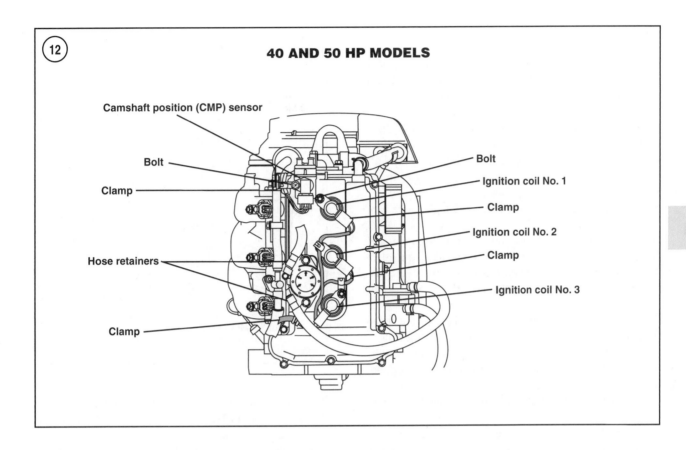

(12)   **40 AND 50 HP MODELS**

Camshaft position (CMP) sensor

Bolt

Clamp

Hose retainers

Clamp

Bolt

Ignition coil No. 1

Clamp

Ignition coil No. 2

Clamp

Ignition coil No. 3

6

NOTE
Electronic components are rarely returnable. Make certain the component is defective before replacing it. Refer to Chapter Two for Troubleshooting procedures.

Camshaft Position (CMP) Sensor Replacement

The CMP sensor signals the ECU as to where each cylinder is at any given moment. Along with the CKP sensor signal, this information is used by the ECU to determine fuel injection timing/duration, fuel pump operation, ignition timing, tachometer operation and IAC valve operation.

The sensor is a Hall-effect type, designed to generate an electrical signal to the ECU based upon a magnetic force passed through its field. For 40 and 50 hp motors, the sensor works with a reluctor bar that is pressed into the top end of the intake camshaft (port side camshaft). For 70 hp models, a reluctor bar is fitted to the top edge of the camshaft pulley generates the signal.

Prior to removal, make a sketch or take a photograph of the wire routing for reference during installation. During installation, route all wires to prevent interference with

moving parts. Use a feeler gauge to set the air gap on 70 hp models. Refer to the instructions for the selected model.

40 and 50 hp models

The CMP sensor (**Figure 12**) is mounted on the rocker arm cover. Air gap adjustment is not required on these models.

1. Disconnect the negative battery cable.

2. Carefully bend the clamp away from the sensor wire and unplug the connector from the sensor.

3. Remove the bolt (**Figure 12**) then lift the sensor and clamp from the rocker arm cover.

4. Use suitable solvent to clean all contaminants from the sensor and its mounting surface.

5. Place the tip of the sensor into the opening and seat the sensor against the rocker arm cover. Install the bolt and clamp. Securely tighten the bolt.

6. Clean the terminals and plug the wire harness connector onto the sensor. Retain the wire harness with the clamp as indicated in **Figure 12**.

7. Connect the negative battery cable.

8. Check for proper ignition system operation as described in Chapter Two.

70 hp models

The CMP sensor is mounted to the top of the cylinder head and next to the camshaft pulley (**Figure 13**). Use a feeler gauge to set the air gap on these models.

1. Disconnect the negative battery cable for safety.
2. Remove the flywheel as described in Chapter Eight.
3. Remove the CKP sensors as described in this chapter.
4. Remove both mounting screws (17, **Figure 14**) and lift the CMP sensor (16) and mounting block (15) from the cylinder head.
5. Clean the sensor mounting location and the threads of the mounting screws.
6. Place the mounting block and sensor onto the cylinder head. Apply a coating of OMC Nut Lock or an equivalent threadlocking compound to the threads and install the sensor mounting screws. Do not tighten the screws at this time.
7. Manually rotate the flywheel clockwise until the raised reactor plate on the camshaft pulley aligns with the sensor.
8. Slip a 0.030 in. (0.76 mm) feeler gauge between the sensor and the reactor plate. Lightly push the sensor toward the camshaft pulley to set the air gap. Hold the sensor in position and securely tighten both mounting screws (**Figure 13**).
9. Recheck the air gap (**Figure 13**). If the gap is correct the feeler gauge will pass between the pulley and sensor with a slight drag. Loosen the mounting screws and correct the gap as needed. Securely tighten the screws after adjustment.
10. Install the CKP sensors as described in this chapter.
11. Connect the negative battery cable.
12. Check for proper ignition system operation as described in Chapter Two.

Crankshaft Position (CKP) Sensor Replacement

Similar in both design and function to the CMP sensor, the CKP sensor is used by the ECU to determine where the piston is in the engine cycle. One difference between the CMP and CKP is the fact that the crankshaft completes two full revolutions for each single revolution of the camshaft.

The 40 and 50 hp models use three CKP sensors, each positioned to determine piston travel for one individual cylinder. Should one of the sensors fail, the engine will remain operational, but fuel and ignition will not be provided to the cylinder corresponding to the failed sensor. The sensors are mounted directly under the flywheel, evenly spaced apart around the top of the engine.

On 70 hp models, two CKP sensors are provided, one that provides piston position for the No. 1 and No. 4 cylin-

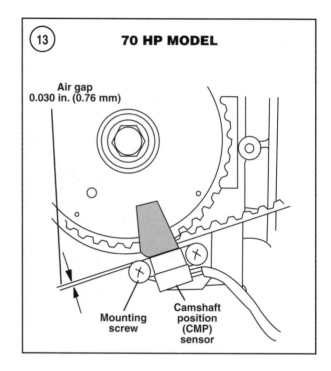

ders, and another that provides piston position for the No. 2 and No. 3 cylinders. The signals from the CKP sensors are redundant in that the ECU programming can determine rough positioning for two pistons if either sensor fails, based on the signal from the remaining CKP (as well as using input from the CMP). Should one sensor fail, the tachometer will read only half of the actual engine rpm.

Refer to **Figure 15** for 40 and 50 hp models and **Figure 14** for 70 hp models.

Replace all CKP sensors if any of them are faulty. They are incorporated into a single wire harness. The CKP and CMP sensors are incorporated into a single harness on 70 hp models.

Prior to removal, make a sketch or a photograph of the wire routing for reference during installation. During installation, route all wires to prevent interference with moving parts. Air gap adjustment is not required for the CKP sensor on 40 and 50 hp models, but a feeler gauge is required to properly set the gap on 70 hp models.

1. Disconnect the negative battery cable.
2. Remove the flywheel as described in Chapter Eight. Use compressed air to blow debris from the sensor mounting areas.
3A. On 40 and 50 hp models carefully unplug the connector (12, **Figure 15**) from the engine wire harness. Remove the six mounting screws (9, **Figure 15**) and lift the CKP sensors (7, 8 and 11) from the power head.
3B. On 70 hp models carefully unplug the connector (12, **Figure 14**) from the ECU. Release the sensor wires from

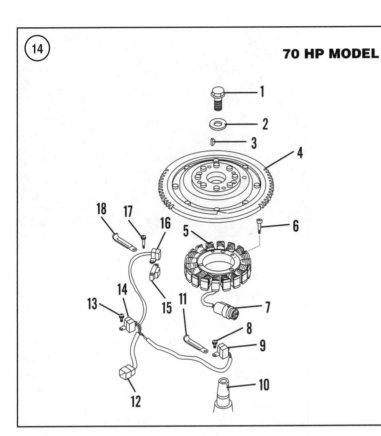

70 HP MODEL

1. Flywheel bolt
2. Washer
3. Key
4. Flywheel
5. Battery/ignition charge coil
6. Screw
7. Connector
8. Screw
9. Crankshaft position (CKP) sensor
10. Crankshaft taper
11. Clamp
12. Connector
13. Screw
14. Crankshaft position (CKP) sensor
15. Mounting block
16. Camshaft position (CMP) sensor
17. Screw
18. Clamp

6

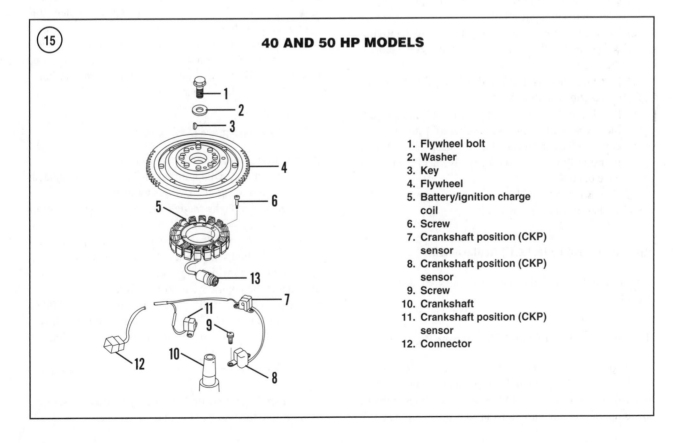

40 AND 50 HP MODELS

1. Flywheel bolt
2. Washer
3. Key
4. Flywheel
5. Battery/ignition charge coil
6. Screw
7. Crankshaft position (CKP) sensor
8. Crankshaft position (CKP) sensor
9. Screw
10. Crankshaft
11. Crankshaft position (CKP) sensor
12. Connector

the clamps (11 and 18, **Figure 14**). Remove the CMP sensor (16, **Figure 14**) as described in this chapter. Lift the CKP and CMP sensors (9, 14 and 16, **Figure 14**) from the power head.

4. Clean the sensor mounting location and the threads of the mounting screws.

5. Carefully route the sensor wires into position and place the sensors onto the power head. Arrange the sensors as noted prior to removal. Fully seat the sensor on the mounting base with the protrusions facing the flywheel.

6. Complete installation by reversing the removal procedure and noting the following:

   a. Apply OMC Nut Lock or an equivalent threadlocking compound to the mounting screws.

   b. For 70 hp models, slip a 0.030 in. (0.76 mm) feeler gauge between the sensor and the raised reactor plate section of the flywheel. Lightly push the sensor toward the flywheel to set the air gap. Hold the sensor in position and securely tighten both mounting screws. Recheck the air gap. It is correct if the feeler gauge passes between the pulley and sensor with a slight drag. Loosen the mounting screws and correct the gap as needed. Securely tighten the screws after adjustment.

   c. For 40 and 50 hp models, securely tighten the screws. Retain the wires by bending the clamp(s) over them (if applicable).

   d. Route all wires to prevent interference with moving components. Plug the sensor harness connector to the engine wire harness.

   e. On 70 hp models install and adjust the CMP sensor as described in this chapter.

   f. Install the flywheel as described in Chapter Eight. Slowly rotate the flywheel to check for interference between the sensors and the flywheel. Check for an improperly installed sensor or flywheel if interference occurs.

   g. Check for proper ignition system operation as described in Chapter Two.

Engine Control Unit (ECU) Replacement

ECU removal and installation is covered in Chapter Seven.

Temperature (CT, EM and IAT) Sensor Replacement

Sensors are used by the ECU to keep track of the intake air (IAT), cylinder (CT) and exhaust manifold (EM, **Figure 16**) temperatures. The IAT sensor determines ambient air temperatures for variations in fuel mapping. The CT

and EM are primarily used to warn of possible engine overheating and to activate the Johnson/Evinrude S.L.O.W. engine operation system that slows the engine speed in the event of overheating.

In all cases, the temperature sensors used by Johnson/Evinrude are thermistors of the negative temperature coefficient type. A thermistor is essentially a variable resistor, or a resistor that changes its resistance value according to temperature. The resistance of a negative temperature coefficient thermistor reacts opposite to temperature, meaning that resistance decreases as temperature increases (or resistance increases when the temperature decreases).

The CT is located on the top center of power head (just behind the flywheel) on 40 and 50 hp motors. For 70 hp motors, the CT is found just below the thermostat housing, behind the electric parts holder.

Intake air temperature (IAT) sensor

1. Disconnect the negative battery cable.

2. Refer to the wire diagrams at the back of the manual as necessary and locate the IAT sensor as follows:

   a. On 40 and 50 hp models the sensor is on the bottom starboard side of the silencer cover.

   b. On 70 hp models the sensor is on the topside of the throttle body (just behind the flame arrestor screen).

3. Note the routing and connection points, then carefully disconnect the engine wire harness from the sensor.

4. If equipped, carefully remove the mounting screw(s), then remove the sensor from the cover or throttle body.

5. Clean the sensor and cover or throttle body mating surfaces.

6. Installation is the reverse of removal. Note the following:

   a. If applicable, securely tighten the mounting screws.

   b. Route the wires to avoid interference.

Cylinder temperature (CT) sensor

1. Disconnect the negative battery cable for safety.
2. Refer to the wire diagrams at the back of the manual as necessary and locate the CT sensor as follows:
   a. On 40 and 50 hp models the sensor is on top of the power head, immediately behind the flywheel and in front of the thermostat housing.
   b. On 70 hp models the sensor is on the starboard side of the motor, just below the thermostat housing and behind the ECU/electric parts holder.
3. Note the routing and connection points, then carefully disconnect the engine wire harness from the sensor.
4. Carefully unthread and remove the sensor from the power head.
5. Clean the threads on the sensor and in the power head.
6. Installation is the reverse of removal.

Exhaust manifold (EM) temperature sensor

1. Disconnect the negative battery cable for safety.

WARNING
Make sure the engine has cooled thoroughly before working on or around the exhaust manifold.

2. Refer to the wire diagrams at the back of the manual as necessary and locate the EM (**Figure 16**) on the top of the exhaust manifold at the rear, starboard side of the engine.
3. Note the routing and connection points and carefully disconnect the engine wire harness from the sensor.
4. Carefully unthread and remove the sensor from the exhaust manifold.

CAUTION
The sensor may be difficult to remove, use care not to break it off in the manifold. The repeated heating and cooling cycles of the exhaust manifold may cause the sensor to seize in the manifold. If the sensor is difficult to remove, apply a penetrating lubricant such as WD-40 or PB Blaster and allow it a to penetrate before attempting to loosen the sensor.

5. Clean the threads on the sensor and in the manifold.
6. Installation is the reverse of removal.

Closed Throttle Position (CTP) Switch Replacement

The CTP switch is on the throttle body. During idle, the tip of the switch contacts the throttle lever, holding the throttle plate open slightly. The ECU uses the switch to determine when to activate trolling mode fuel mapping. The throttle position switch is calibrated to the throttle body and set at the manufacturer. Do not disturb the CTP switch positioning. Replace the throttle body assembly if the switch is faulty.

System Relay Replacement

A system relay provides power to the ECU, injectors, coil, IAC valve, diagnostic connector, and the CMP on the 40 and 50 hp models, each time the key switch is turned on. Removal, testing and installation are covered in Chapter Two.

Manifold Absolute Pressure (MAP) Sensor Replacement

The MAP sensor detects atmospheric pressure when the key is turned on (such as during engine starting) or by cranking. But, once the engine starts the sensor provides intake manifold air pressure.

A rubber hose connects the sensor to a pulse limiter mounted just behind the throttle body. The limiter is used to dampen vacuum signal changes.

1. Disconnect the negative battery cable.
2. Refer to the wire diagrams at the back of the manual and locate the MAP sensor as follows:
   a. On 40 and 50 models the sensor is on the top of the intake manifold on the port side of the power head.
   b. On 70 hp models the sensor is on the starter bracket at the front and port side of the power head above the throttle body.
3. Note the routing and connection points and carefully disconnect the engine wire harness and hoses from the sensor.
4. Carefully remove the mounting screw(s) and the sensor from the intake manifold or power head.
5. Clean the sensor and power head or manifold mating surfaces.
6. Installation is the reverse of removal. Note the following:
   a. Securely tighten the mounting screw(s).
   b. Route the wires to avoid interference.

Idle Air Control (IAC) Valve and Air Silencer Replacement

The ECU uses the IAC valve to supply additional air for increases in idle speed (over and above what is provided by the idle air bypass screw and the effect that the CTP switch has by holding the throttle plate open slightly).

1. Remove the air intake Silencer Cover as described in this chapter.

2. Refer to the wire diagrams at the back of the manual as necessary, and locate the IAC valve as follows:

    a. On 40 and 50 models the valve is on the front of the engine, just to the starboard side of the throttle body.

    b. On 70 hp models the valve is mounted to the intake manifold just above and slightly port of the throttle body. It is visible from the front of the engine, just below the top, port side of the air silencer.

3. Note the routing and connection points and carefully disconnect the hoses and wires from the valve.

4A. On 40 and 50 hp models remove the screws and pull the valve and bracket from the power head.

4B. On 70 hp models remove the screws and retainer. Pull the valve, flange and rubber gasket from the intake manifold or valve.

5. Use a suitable solvent to clean the mating surfaces.

6. If necessary, locate and remove the round plastic IAC valve air intake silencer:

    a. On 40 and 50 hp models, the silencer is directly under the throttle body at the front of the engine. One hose from the silencer attaches to the IAC valve and the other supplies air from the main air intake silencer housing. Both hoses should already be disconnected at this point in the procedure.

    b. On 70 hp models, the silencer is under the intake runners at the port front of the engine. One hose from the silencer normally attaches to the IAC valve, while the other remains open as a source of intake air. Remove the silencer from the round bracket, disconnecting the hoses from it, as necessary.

7. Installation is the reverse of removal. Note the following:

    a. Securely tighten the mounting screws.

    b. Make sure all hose and wires are connected and routed to avoid interference.

Table 1 FUEL INJECTION SPECIFICATIONS

Component	Specification
Boat fuel supply line	5/16 in. (8 mm) minimum inner diameter
Engine firing and sequential injection order	
40 and 50 hp	1-3-2
70 hp	1-3-4-2
Fuel injector resistance	11.0-16.6 ohms
High pressure fuel pump (minimum	
system pressure)	34 psi (234 kPa)
Idle speed	
40 and 50 hp	800-900 rpm
70 hp	700 rpm
OMC test propeller part No. and rpm	No. 386665 and 5000 rpm

Table 2 ENGINE SENSOR AND SWITCH SPECIFICATIONS FUEL INJECTED ENGINES*

Component	Specification
CTP switch	
Button extended	Infinite resistance (no continuity)
Button depressed	Continuity (0 or very low resistance)
IAC valve	
40 and 50 hp models	21.5-32.3 ohms
70 hp models	4.8-7.2 ohms
	(continued)

Table 2 ENGINE SENSOR AND SWITCH SPECIFICATIONS FUEL INJECTED ENGINES* (continued)

Component	Specification
MAP sensor	
0 in. hg. (0 kPa) vacuum applied to hose	4.0 volts
11.8 in. hg. (40 kPa) vacuum applied to hose	2.42 volts
24 in. hg. (80 kPa) vacuum applied to hose	0.84 volts
Oil pressure switch	
Less than 10-19 psi (70-131 kPa) oil pressure	Continuity (0 or very low resistance)
10-19 psi (70-131 kPa) or more oil pressure	Infinite resistance (no continuity)
Temperature sensors	
CT and IAT	
At 32° F (0° C)	5100-6000 ohms
At 77° F (25° C)	1900-2100 ohms
At 122° F (50° C)	760-900 ohms
At 135° F (57° C)	340-420 ohms
EM	
40 and 50 hp models	See CT and IAT specifications
70 hp models	2318-2562 ohms

*Except for temperature sensors, all resistance specifications are based upon tests conducted at an ambient/component temperature of 68° F (20° C).

Table 3 ENGINE COMPONENT TESTING THROUGH ECU HARNESS 40 AND 50 HP MODELS*

Component	ECU harness terminals Connectors and terminals (wire colors)	Resistance (ohms)
CKP sensor		
No. 1	E4 (R/B) and D1 (B/W)	168-252
No. 2	E3 (W/B) and D1 (B/W)	168-252
No. 3	E1 (R/W) and D1 (B/W)	168-252
CT sensor	D3 (Lg/W) to D1 (B/W)	See Temperature Sensors
EM temperature sensor	C9 (V/W) to D1 (B/W)	See Temperature Sensors
Fuel injector		
No. 1	A4 (O/B) and B5 (Gr)	11.0-16.5
No. 2	A7 (B/Y) and B5 (Gr)	11.0-16.5
No. 3	A8 (R/W) and B5 (Gr)	11.0-16.5
Intake air control (IAC) valve	B4 (B/R) and B5 (Gr)	21.5-32.3 ohms
Intake air temperature (IAT) sensor	D6 (Lg/B) to D1 (B/W)	See Temperature Sensors
Ignition coil primary circuit		
No. 1	A5 (O) and B5 (Gr)	1.9-2.5
No. 2	A1 (Bl) and B5 (Gr)	1.9-2.5
No. 3	A3 (G) and B5 (Gr)	1.9-2.5
Ignition coil secondary circuit		
No. 1	B5 (Gr) to No. 1 spark plug cap	8100-11,100
No. 2	B5 (Gr) to No. 2 spark plug cap	8100-11,100
No. 3	B5 (Gr) to No. 3 spark plug cap	8100-11,100
Starter motor relay	D11 (Y/G) to ground	3.5-5.1
Temperature sensors circuit values		
At 32° F (0° C)	refer to CT, IAT or EM	5300-6600 ohms
At 77° F (25° C)	refer to CT, IAT or EM	1800-2300 ohms
At 122° F (50° C)	refer to CT, IAT or EM	730-960 ohms
At 135° F (57° C)	refer to CT, IAT or EM	330-450 ohms

*Except for temperature sensors, all resistance specifications are based upon tests conducted at an ambient/component temperature of 68° F (20° C).

6

Table 4 EFI FUEL SYSTEM TORQUE SPECIFICATIONS

Component	in.-lb.	ft.-lb.	(N•m)
Low pressure pump			
screws	84	–	9.5
Fuel rail			
40/50 hp			
Tee-connector screws	84-96	–	9.5-11
Screw plugs	–	25-27	34-37
Injector retaining clip			
screws	96-108	–	11-12
70 hp			
End screws	–	28-30	38-41
Mounting screws	–	16-18	22-24
Intake manifold			
40/50 hp			
Large screws/nuts	–	16-18	22-24
Small screws/nuts	96-108	–	11-12
70 hp	–	16-18	22-24

Chapter Seven

Electrical and Ignition Systems

This chapter provides service procedures for the battery, starter, charging and ignition systems, as well as for the warning system. Fundamental electrical theories and the basics of electrical component testing are covered in Chapter One. Specific electrical troubleshooting procedures are described in Chapter Two. Wiring diagrams are at the end of the manual. **Tables 1-11** at the end of the chapter provide electrical system specifications.

BATTERY

Marine batteries are subjected to far more vibration and pounding than most automotive applications. Always use a battery that is designated specifically for marine appli-

cations (**Figure 1**). These batteries are constructed with thicker cases and plates than typical automotive batteries. This construction allows them to better withstand the marine environment.

Use a battery that meets or exceeds the cold cranking amperage requirements for the engine. Refer to **Table 1** for recommended battery specifications. Many marine batteries list Marine/Deep Cycle on the label. Deep-cycle batteries are constructed to allow repeated discharge and charge cycles. These batteries are excellent for powering accessories such as trolling motors and for marine engines that are used at irregular intervals. Always charge deep-cycle batteries at a low amperage rate. They are generally not designed for charging or discharging at a rapid rate. **Table 2** provides the usage hours (capacity) for typical 80 and 105 ampere-hour batteries. Deep cycle batteries can be used as the starting battery providing they meet the cold cranking amperage requirements for the engine.

NOTE
Because output is non-regulated on models equipped with a 4- or 6-amp charging system, using a maintenance free battery is typically not recommended. Using standard vented batteries, that allow checking and refilling of electrolyte that has evaporated due to excessive charging will allow for a longer service life. Maintenance free batteries may

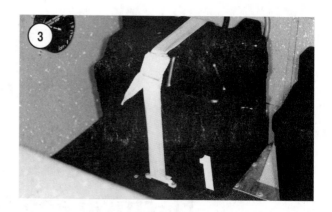

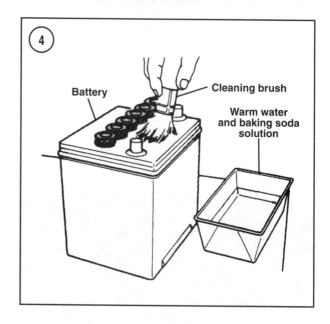

be used however on carbureted models equipped with a 12-amp regulated charging system and all fuel injected models.

Cable Connections

Insufficient or dirty cable connections cause many problems in marine applications. Use cable connectors that are securely crimped or molded to the cable. Avoid temporary or emergency clamps for normal usage. They are prone to corrosion and do not meet U.S. Coast Guard requirements for terminal connections.

For safety, use a cover on the positive terminal post (**Figure 2**). They are available at marine dealerships. The cover helps prevent the possibility of dangerous sparks should a tool or other piece of metal contact a grounded part of the boat or engine and the positive terminal.

Battery Mounting Requirements

Make sure the battery is securely mounted in the boat to avoid a dangerous acid spill or electrical arcing that can cause a fire. The most common types of battery mounting include the bracket mounted to the floor of the boat and the support across the top of the battery (**Figure 1**). The other common type of battery mounting is the battery case and cover that encloses the battery and secures it to the boat structure (**Figure 3**). When properly installed, either of these provides secure mounting and protection for the terminals.

Mount the battery in a location that allows easy access for maintenance. Make sure the battery terminals cannot contact any component in the mounting area. Rigorous marine usage can cause considerable battery shifting.

WARNING
When mounting a battery in a boat constructed of aluminum, mount the battery securely to eliminate the possibility of the

battery contacting metal components. Batteries produce explosive gasses that can ignite if arcing occurs.

Battery Case

Inspect the battery case for cracks, leaks, abrasions and other damage anytime the battery is removed for charging. Replace the battery if any questionable conditions exist. During normal usage, a corrosive deposit forms on top of the battery. These deposits may allow the battery to discharge at a rapid rate.

Make sure the battery caps are properly installed. Remove the battery from the boat and carefully wash loose material from the top of the battery with clean water. Use a solution of warm water and baking soda and a soft-bristled brush to clean the deposits from the battery (**Figure 4**). Rinse the battery with clean water to remove all the baking soda solution from the battery case.

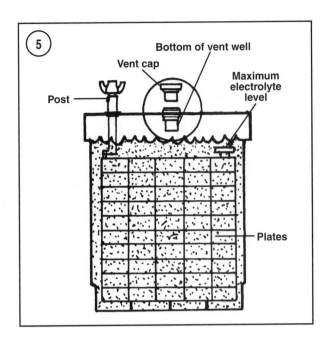

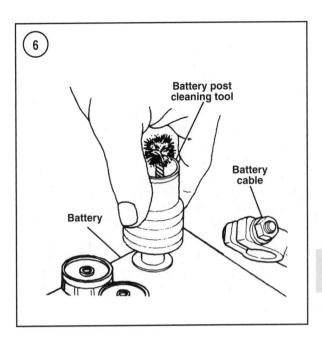

CAUTION
Baking soda will weaken or destroy the battery if the solution is allowed to enter the case. Make sure any caps are closed and keep the solution away from the battery vent as much as possible.

Electrolyte Level

Check the battery electrolyte level on a regular basis. Heavy use or use in warm climates increases evaporation. Carefully remove the vent caps (**Figure 5**) and inspect the electrolyte level in each cell. The electrolyte level should be about 3/16 in. (4.8 mm) above the plates but below the bottom of the vent well (**Figure 5**). Use only distilled water to fill the cells to the proper level. Never use battery acid to correct the electrolyte level. Tap water or other water sources may contain harmful additives or minerals that promote plate deterioration within the battery and shorten battery life.

WARNING
Use care when lifting or transporting the battery. With age, the carry strap can become weak or brittle and break. If the battery is dropped, the case may break and spray or leak a dangerous acid solution.

WARNING
Never overfill the battery. The electrolyte may expand with the heat created from charging and overflow from the battery. A

blocked vent during this condition could cause the battery case to crack or rupture under pressure, spraying or leaking a dangerous acid solution.

Battery Terminals

Clean the battery terminals at regular intervals and whenever the terminal has been removed. Use a battery-cleaning tool, available at most automotive or marine supply stores, to remove stubborn corrosion and deposits quickly. Remove the terminal and clean the post (**Figure 6**). Rotate the tool on the post until the post is clean. Avoid removing too much material from the post or the terminal may not attach securely to it.

Use the other end of the tool to clean the cable end terminal (**Figure 7**). Clean flat spade-type connectors and the attaching nuts with the wire brush end of the tool.

Apply a coat of dielectric grease, petroleum jelly or other corrosion prevention compound to the battery post and cable terminal. Tighten the fasteners securely. Avoid using excessive force when tightening these terminals. The battery and terminals can sustain considerable damage if excessive force is applied.

Battery Testing

Perform the *Cranking Voltage Test* in this section to check the battery condition.

Use a hydrometer to check the specific gravity of the battery electrolyte. This step gives an accurate reading of the charge level of the battery. Hydrometers are available at most automotive and marine supply stores.

To use the hydrometer, insert the tip into the cell and use the ball to draw some of the electrolyte from the cell into the hydrometer (**Figure 8**). Read the specific gravity in all cells. When using a temperature compensating hydrometer, take several readings in each cell to allow the hydrometer to adjust to the electrolyte temperature. Always return the electrolyte to the cell from which it was drawn. With the hydrometer in a vertical position, determine the specific gravity by reading the level of the float (**Figure 9** shows a typical hydrometer, though types vary). A specific gravity reading of about 1.260 points or higher indicates a fully charged battery. Compare the hydrometer readings with the information provided in **Table 3** to determine the condition charge. Always charge the battery if the specific gravity varies more than 0.050 points from one cell to another.

NOTE
Add 0.004 points to the reading for every 10° above 80° F (27° C) if the hydrometer is not a temperature compensating model. Subtract 0.004 points from the reading for every 10° below 80° F (27° C).

NOTE
An inaccurate reading can result if the specific gravity is checked immediately after adding water to the battery. To ensure accuracy, charge the battery at a high rate for 15-20 minutes prior to testing.

Cranking Voltage Test

Measuring the voltage at the battery while cranking the engine is a quick check for battery condition. Connect the positive meter test lead to the positive battery terminal. Connect the negative test lead to an engine ground (preferable) or across the terminals to the negative terminal (acceptable based on battery location). Measure the voltage (**Figure 10**) while cranking the engine without starting for 15 seconds. Charge the battery if the voltage drops below 9.6 volts while cranking. Test the cranking voltage again. Replace the battery if the cranking voltage is not 9.6 or above after a complete charge.

Battery Storage

Batteries lose some charge during storage. The rate of discharge increases in a warm environment. Store the battery in a cool, dry location to minimize the loss of charge. Check the specific gravity every 30 days of storage and

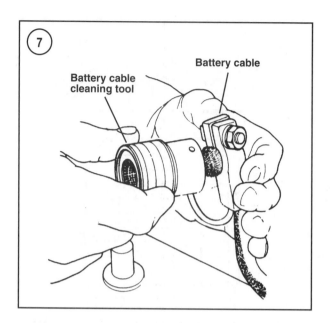

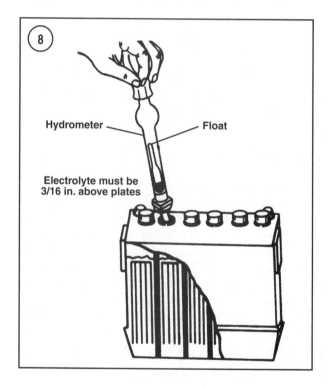

charge the battery as required. Refer to *Battery Charging* in this section for battery charging times.

Battery Charging

WARNING
Batteries produce explosive hydrogen gas. Charge the battery in a well-ventilated area.

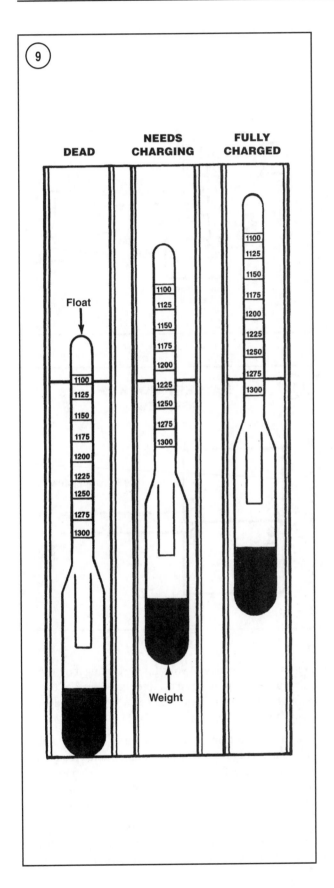

9

| DEAD | NEEDS CHARGING | FULLY CHARGED |

Float

Weight

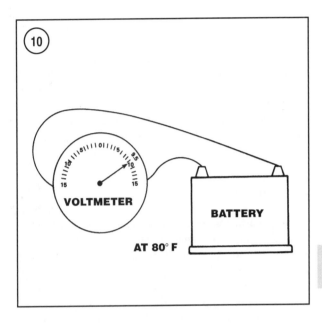

10

VOLTMETER

BATTERY

AT 80° F

7

Wear protective eyewear and suitable gloves when working around batteries. Never smoke or allow any source of ignition in the area where batteries are stored or charged. Never allow non-insulated components to contact the battery terminals, as arcing can occur and ignite the hydrogen gas.

WARNING
Use extreme caution when connecting any wires to the battery terminals. Avoid making the last connection at the battery terminal. Explosive hydrogen gas in and around the battery may ignite and lead to an explosion.

Always remove the battery from the boat to charge it. Because most boats provide limited ventilation, the explosive gasses the battery gives out may remain in the area for a fair amount of time. The gasses may also cause accelerated corrosion of components in the battery compartment. Removing the battery also allows for inspection of the case for damage and cleaning and maintenance of the battery terminals.

Make the connections to the battery *before* plugging in or switching on the charger to avoid arcing at the terminals (sparks could detonate explosive hydrogen gases). Connect the battery charger cables to the proper terminals on the battery. Plug the charger into its power supply and select the 12-volt battery setting.

Charging the battery at a lower amperage results in a more sufficient charge and helps prolong the life of the battery. With a severely discharged battery, it may be necessary to charge the battery at a higher amperage rate for a

few minutes before starting the lower rate charge. A severely discharged battery does not allow the charging process to begin without first charging at the high rate.

Check the specific gravity often and halt the charging
process when the battery is fully charged. Severely discharged batteries may require as long as 8 hours to re-
charge. Check the temperature of the electrolyte during
the charging process. Halt the charging process if the electrolyte temperature reaches or exceeds 125° F (52° C).

Jump Starting

Jump-starting starts an engine that has a severely discharged battery. Jump-starting can be dangerous if correct
instructions are not followed. Never attempt to jump-start
a frozen battery. Always check and correct the electrolyte
level in each battery before making any connection. A significant risk of explosion exists if the electrolyte level is at
or below the top of the plates. Always use a good pair of
jumper cables with clean connector clamps. Keep all
clamps totally separated from any metallic or conductive
material. Never allow the clamps to contact other clamps.

1. Connect a jumper cable to the positive terminal of the
discharged battery (1, **Figure 11**).
2. Connect the other end of the same jumper cable to the
positive terminal of the fully charged battery (2, **Figure
11**).
3. Connect the second jumper cable to the negative terminal of the fully charged battery (3, **Figure 11**).
4. Connect the other end of the second jumper cable to a
good engine ground, such as the starter ground cable (4,
Figure 11).

> *WARNING*
> ***Never*** *connect the final jumper directly to
> the discharged battery as arcing could
> happen as the connection is made. This
> could easily cause an explosion by igniting
> the hydrogen gasses that are normally pres-
> ent in and around a discharged battery.*

5. Make sure the cables and clamps are positioned so they
will not become trapped or interfere with moving components.
6. Start the engine, then remove the cables in exactly the
reverse of the connection order.

Wiring for 12- and 24-Volt Electric Trolling Motors

Many boats are provided with an electric trolling motor
that requires 24 volts to operate. Two or more batteries are
necessary with this application. A series battery hookup

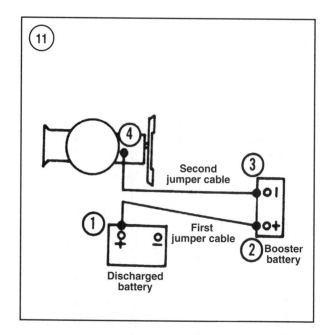

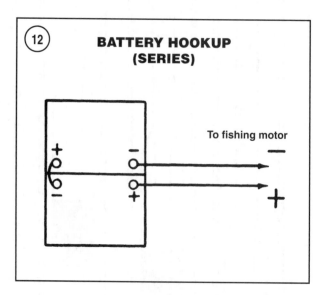

(**Figure 12**) provides 24 volts for the trolling motor. A series connection provides the approximate total of the two
batteries (24 volts). The amperage provided is the approximate average of one battery.

Connect the trolling motor batteries in a parallel arrangement (**Figure 13**) if the trolling motor requires 12
volts to operate. The voltage provided is the approximate
average of the two batteries (12 volt). The amperage provided is the approximate total of the two batteries.

Follow the manufacturer's battery connection instructions for special quick-connect plugs at the trolling motor.
Dedicate a battery for the engine if possible. This avoids

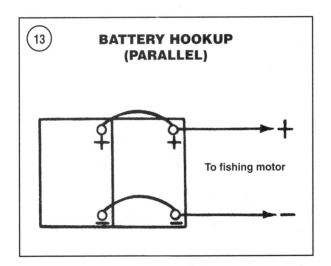

**BATTERY HOOKUP
(PARALLEL)**

To fishing motor

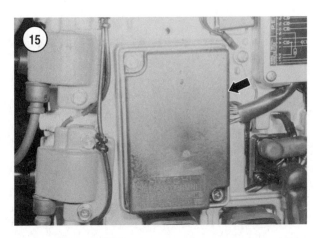

more than 10 seconds. Allow the starter to cool for at least two minutes before further operation.

If the starter does not crank the engine, check the battery and all related wiring for loose or corroded connections, shorted or open circuits or other defects. If this inspection does not determine the problem, test the starting system as described in Chapter Two.

Starter Relay/Solenoid Removal/Installation

This section covers removal and installation of the starter relay/solenoid (**Figure 14**, carbureted models shown). On fuel injected models, remove the electrical component cover (**Figure 15**) from the power head for access to the relay (**Figure 16**).

1. Disconnect the negative battery cable.

2. Locate the starter relay by following the large red battery cable from the battery to the relay.

NOTE
On 40-70 hp models, the starter relay is mounted on the bottom, right side of the electrical component holder, just below two other relays. On 9.9/15 hp (305 cc) models, the relay is mounted to the port side of the power head between the starter and oil filter. On 8/9.9 hp (211 cc) models, the relay is mounted to the rear, starboard side of the power head.

3. Tag and disconnect the wiring from the relay (**Figure 17**). If necessary, refer to the wiring diagrams at the back of the manual for help identifying the wires.

NOTE
Tiller models typically have three connections, one from the start switch, one from the battery and one to the starter, though some

the possibility of having a discharged battery from using the trolling motor or other electrical accessories and no means to start the engine.

STARTING SYSTEM

On models equipped with an electric starter, battery power is supplied to the starter through a remote mounted relay or solenoid. An engine mounted start switch (tiller models) or a boat mounted remote key switch (remote models) activates the relay/solenoid when the circuit is closed allowing fused battery power to the actuator switch side of the relay. On remote models, a neutral safety switch is also incorporated into the key side of the starter circuit. For safety, the switch will remain open (preventing the key switch from activating the relay) unless the gearcase is placed in neutral prior to starting the engine.

The starter is capable of producing very high torque, but only for a brief time due to rapid heat buildup. To prevent overheating, never operate the starter continuously for

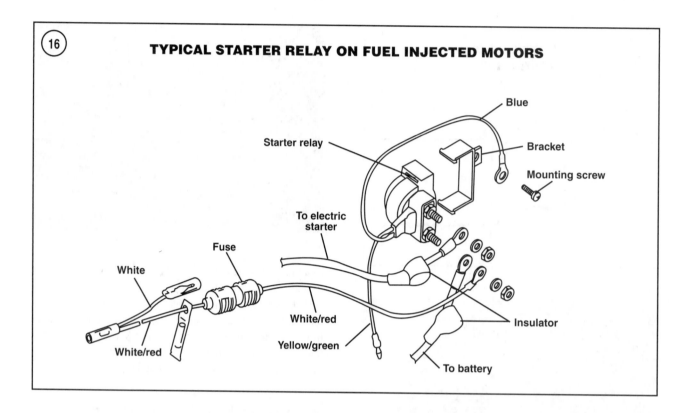

16

TYPICAL STARTER RELAY ON FUEL INJECTED MOTORS

Blue

Starter relay

Bracket

Mounting screw

To electric
starter

Fuse

White

White/red

Yellow/green

Insulator

White/red

To battery

*models may also have a ground wire at-
tached to the relay.*

NOTE
*Remote models will typically have five con-
nections, one from the key switch, one from
the neutral safety switch (which may be
fused), one from the battery, and one to the
starter. In addition, the relay has a wire connected to ground (except 40-70 hp models)
or a fused wire to the rectifier/regulator and
ECU main relay (40-70 hp models).*

4. Remove the mounting screw or screws and lift the
bracket with the starter relay from the power head.

NOTE
*The mounting screws on some models are
Torx head screws and require using a prop-
erly sized Torx driver.*

5. If applicable, pull the starter relay from the arms of the
bracket.

6. Installation is the reverse of removal. Note the following:

  a. Make sure all terminals and fasteners are clean and
     free of corrosion.

  b. Make sure all wire terminals are positioned to pre-
     vent contact with each other or with other engine

components. Position the insulator over the large
wire terminals.

  c. Securely tighten all fasteners.

  d. Route all wires to prevent interference with other
     engine components.

  e. Check for proper starter relay operation.

Neutral Safety Switch

Remote electric start models use a neutral safety switch
to prevent engine starting while in gear. The appearance
and mounting location for the neutral safety switch varies.
Some models may be equipped with a remote mounted
switch. For those models, the service procedure varies depending on the type of remote. Refer to a reputable marine
dealership for information and parts for aftermarket controls. Other models (including the 40-70 hp models) are
equipped with an engine-mounted switch.

The switch used on carbureted models is part of the key
switch-to-starter relay circuit, and is designed to remain
open when the engine is in gear and to close (completing
the circuit) only when the shift linkage is in neutral. For
more details, refer to the wiring diagrams at the back of
the manual.

The engine mounted neutral safety switch used on fuel
injected models prevents ignition and fuel injector operation during attempts to start the engine while in gear. On

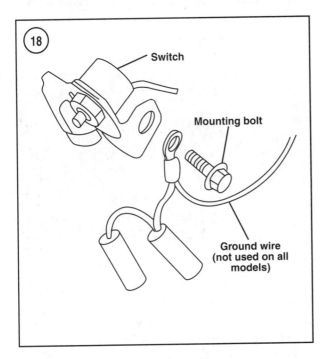

40 and 50 hp models, it also prevents operation of the electric starter.

Engine mounted switch (fuel injected models)

On all fuel injected models, the neutral safety switch is on the side of the engine, near the oil filter. On 40 and 50 hp models, the switch is on the port side of the engine, just above and slightly in front of the oil filter. On 70 hp models, the switch is on the starboard side of the engine, just slightly in front and below the oil filter.

In all cases, the switch has a plunger that completes the switch circuit when it is depressed (in neutral) or opens the circuit when released (linkage in forward or reverse). A defective switch could cause the engine to stall when shifting into gear. Also, a switch that fails in the on or closed circuit position will cause the engine speed to be limited by the ECU to 3000 rpm and the timing to remain in a fixed position.

1. Disconnect the negative battery cable, then shift the engine into forward gear to remove linkage pressure from the switch button.
2. If necessary, refer to the wiring diagrams at the back of the manual and identify the wire colors leading to the switch.
3. Carefully disconnect the brown and yellow/green wires from the engine wire harness.
4. Remove the mounting bolt (**Figure 18**) and ground wire (if used). Slip the switch from its mounting bracket.
5. To install, place the switch onto the mounting bracket with the spring or plunger side facing the shift linkage. Install the ground wire (if used) and mounting bolt. Securely tighten the mounting bolt.
6. Connect the switch wiring. Route the harness carefully to avoid interference.
7. Check and adjust the shift cables and linkage as described in Chapter Four.
8. Connect the negative battery cable. Verify correct operation of the switch before returning the engine to service.

Starter Motor Removal and Installation

1. Disconnect the negative battery cable.
2. Remove the top engine cover and, if necessary one or both of the lower covers. For carbureted models, remove the lower port side cover.
3. For fuel injected models, remove the air intake silencer from the throttle body and engine.
4. If necessary, remove the manual starter as described in Chapter Ten or the flywheel cover as described in Chapter Eight, as applicable, to ensure all starter mounting bolts and nuts (**Figure 19**) are accessible.
5. For carbureted models, proceed as follows:
   a. Disconnect the power lead (**Figure 20**) from the bottom of the starter by loosening the retaining nut.
   b. Remove the bolt (**Figure 21**) retaining the bracket at the bottom of the starter to the power head.
   c. Using a suitable open-end wrench, loosen the starter screw mounted vertically (A, **Figure 22**), just under the lip of the flywheel.
   d. Support the starter assembly and loosen the side bolt (B, **Figure 22**) retaining the starter to the power head, then carefully remove the starter assembly.
6. For fuel injected models, proceed as follows:
   a. Tag the positive and negative wiring connections to ensure proper installation. Remove the terminal in-

7

sulator (A, **Figure 23**) and nut from the positive starter relay-to-electric starter cable connection. Remove the starter negative ground wire (B, **Figure 23**) from the starter motor. Mark the bracket and bolts to ensure proper starter installation.

b. Remove the band clamp retaining the starter.

c. Support the starter while removing the two mounting bolts from the top of the assembly.

d. Carefully remove the starter from the mounting bracket.

7. Use a solvent to clean all corrosion, oil residue or other contaminants from the starter mounting surfaces. Inspect rubber cushions for worn or damaged areas and replace as necessary.

8. Installation is the reverse of removal. Note the following:

a. Clean the bolt threads, then apply a light coating of OMC Nut Lock or an equivalent threadlocking compound to the threads of the starter retaining bolts.

b. Carefully place the starter into position, then install and tighten the mounting bolts to the specification in **Table 11**.

c. On fuel injected models, install and tighten the band clamp securely.

d. Make sure all cables are routed to prevent interference, then install the cable(s) and tighten the retaining nut(s). On fuel injected motors, tighten the nuts to the specification in **Table 11**.

e. On fuel injected engines install the terminal insulator (A, **Figure 23**). On carbureted engines coat the connectors with OMC Black Neoprene Dip.

f. Check for proper starter and neutral safety switch operation.

NOTE
Replace all O-rings, seals and gaskets if removed or disturbed. Apply weather-strip adhesive to the mating surfaces of all terminal insulators-to-starter housings during assembly.

CAUTION
Never drop or strike the frame of the starter. The permanent magnets can crack or break, resulting in starter failure.

Starter Disassembly and Assembly (Carbureted Models)

Refer to **Figure 24** for component identification and orientation throughout this procedure.

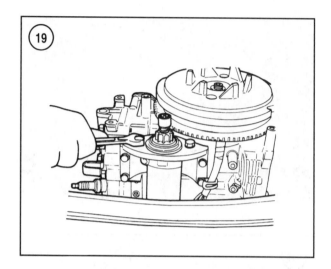

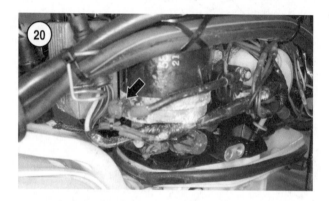

1. Remove the starter (**Figure 25**) as described in this chapter and mount it in a soft-jawed vise.

2. With the starter mounted in a vise, carefully pry the protective cap (1) from the groove spacer (5).

3. Push the cupped spacer (3) downward on the armature (9) shaft until the C-clip (2) is exposed, then carefully remove the clip using a pair of snap ring pliers.

4. Pull the cupped spacer (3), spring (4) and grooved spacer from the armature shaft.

5. Remove the pinion gear (6) and drive base (7) from the armature (9) shaft.

6. Remove the screw(s) retaining the bracket (**Figure 26**) to the bottom of the lower end cap (16).

7. Matchmark the drive end cap (8), starter housing (10) and lower end cap for assembly purposes.

8. Remove the two throughbolts (20). Then separate the end caps and withdraw the armature.

NOTE
*Note the correct orientation of the positive (14) and negative (12) brush sets (**Figure 27**) prior to removal, as reversing the*

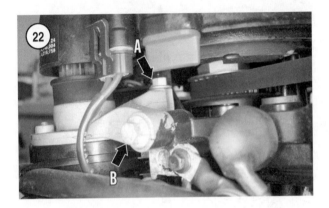

brushes during assembly will cause the starter to run backwards. It is easier to remove the negative brush sets first, then reposition the positive brushes and remove the brush plate (13) before removing the positive brush set. Installation is easiest in the reverse of this order.

9. If necessary, disassemble the brush and terminal sets (12 and 14) from the brush plate (13) and lower end cap. Matchmark the brush plate and the lower end cap before removing the screws and washers holding the brush sets to the plate, and the brush plate to the lower end cap.

10. Use compressed air to remove all brush material from the armature and lower cover.

11. Use a mild solvent to clean the components, except the brush plate and brushes. Clean the brush plate and brushes with electrical contact cleaner.

12. Refer to *Starter Inspection* in this chapter prior to assembling the starter.

13. Use one drop of SAE No. 10 oil to lubricate the armature shaft bearing surface.

14. Use OMC Starter Bendix Lube to lubricate the armature shaft pinion helix.

15. If removed, install the thrust washer on the armature shaft, then place the drive end cap over the armature shaft.

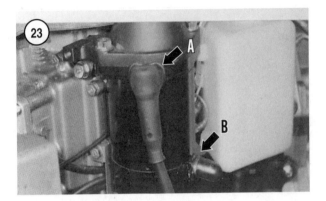

16. Insert the armature into the starter housing aligning the matchmarks made on the drive end cap and housing during removal.

17. If removed, install the brush plate to the lower end cap. Install the positive and negative brush sets (**Figure 27**) as noted during removal. Place each brush spring into the bore in the brush plate and position each brush above its spring.

18. Use a putty knife modified as shown in **Figure 28** to hold the brushes down against their springs during assembly (**Figure 29**).

19. Install the armature, drive end cap and starter housing assembly to the lower end cap, using the putty knife to hold the brushes in place. Once the matchmarks on the lower end cap and housing are aligned, withdraw the putty knife as the components are gently pressed together.

20. Apply a drop of oil to the starter throughbolts, then insert them through the lower end cap and housing assembly. Tighten the bolts to the specification in **Table 11**. Seal the bolt heads using OMC Black Neoprene Dip.

21. Install the bracket to the lower end cap and tighten the retaining screw to the same specification as the throughbolts.

22. Slide the drive base and pinion gear over the armature shaft.

23. Slide the grooved spacer, spring and cupped spacer onto the armature shaft.

24. Push downward on the cupped spacer and install the C-clip, then pull the cup upward over the clip to verify that the clip seats in both the shaft and cup grooves to allow proper Bendix travel. If there is interference, use a small prytool to gently compress and seat the ring.

25. Install the protective cap.

26. Install the starter motor and verify proper operation.

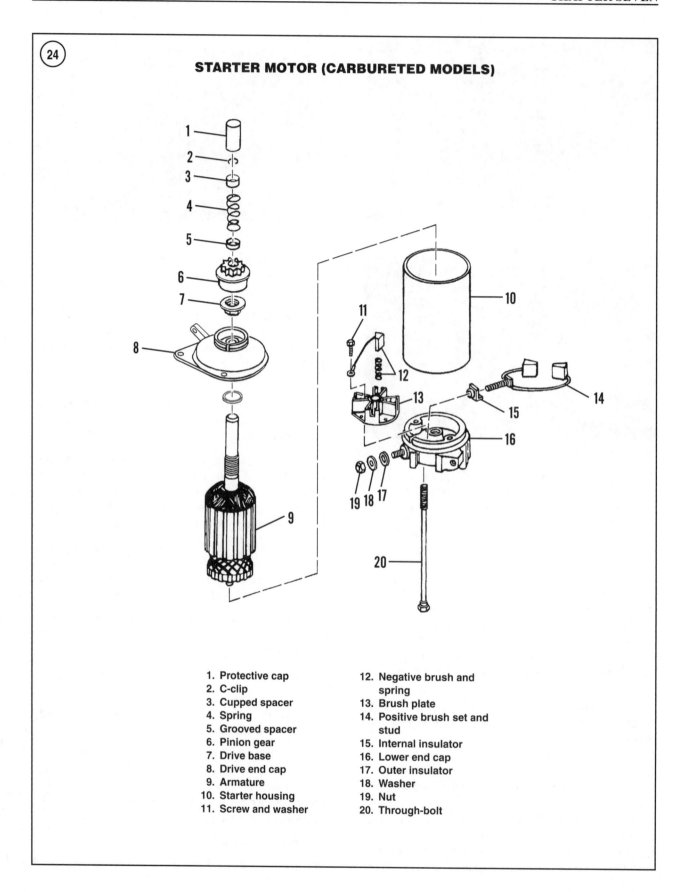

(24)

STARTER MOTOR (CARBURETED MODELS)

1. Protective cap
2. C-clip
3. Cupped spacer
4. Spring
5. Grooved spacer
6. Pinion gear
7. Drive base
8. Drive end cap
9. Armature
10. Starter housing
11. Screw and washer
12. Negative brush and spring
13. Brush plate
14. Positive brush set and stud
15. Internal insulator
16. Lower end cap
17. Outer insulator
18. Washer
19. Nut
20. Through-bolt

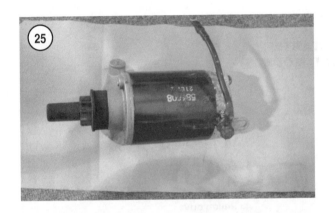

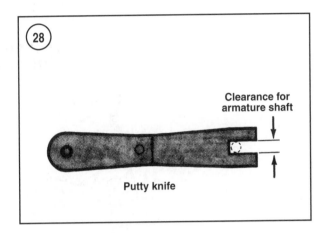

Clearance for armature shaft

Putty knife

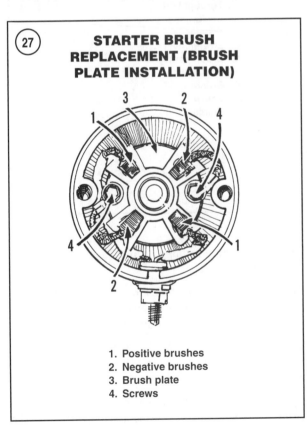

STARTER BRUSH
REPLACEMENT (BRUSH
PLATE INSTALLATION)

1. Positive brushes
2. Negative brushes
3. Brush plate
4. Screws

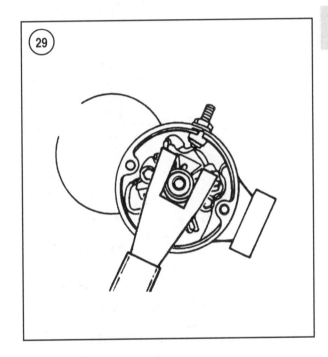

**Starter Disassembly and Assembly
(Fuel Injected Models)**

Refer to **Figure 30** for component identification and orientation during this procedure.

1. Remove the starter as described in this chapter and mount it carefully in a soft-jawed vise.

2. With the starter mounted in a vise, grasp the stopper (**Figure 31**) and push it toward the pinion drive to expose the locking clip. Carefully pry the locking clip from the armature shaft. Pull the stopper and spring from the armature shaft.

3. Turn the pinion drive (4) counterclockwise to unthread it from the helical splines (10) on the armature.

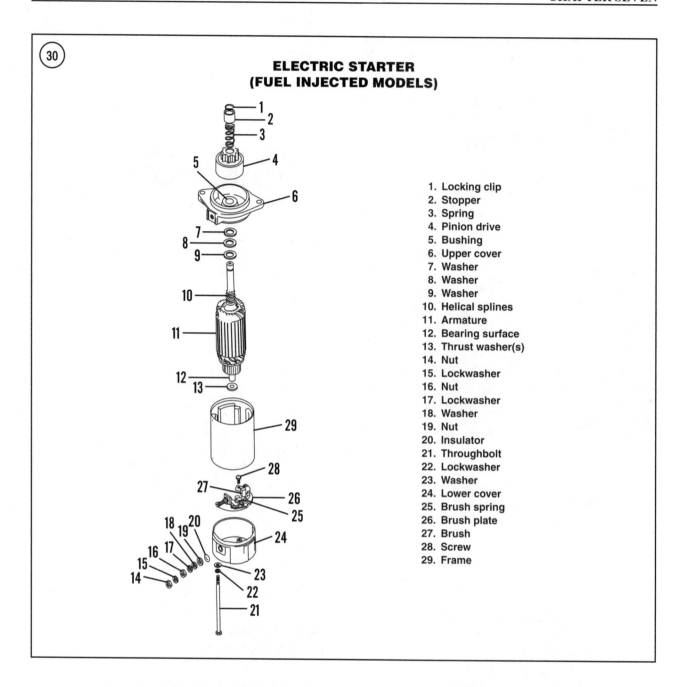

**ELECTRIC STARTER
(FUEL INJECTED MODELS)**

1. Locking clip
2. Stopper
3. Spring
4. Pinion drive
5. Bushing
6. Upper cover
7. Washer
8. Washer
9. Washer
10. Helical splines
11. Armature
12. Bearing surface
13. Thrust washer(s)
14. Nut
15. Lockwasher
16. Nut
17. Lockwasher
18. Washer
19. Nut
20. Insulator
21. Throughbolt
22. Lockwasher
23. Washer
24. Lower cover
25. Brush spring
26. Brush plate
27. Brush
28. Screw
29. Frame

4. Mark the end covers and frame with a permanent marker for reference during assembly (**Figure 32**). Support the starter motor and remove both throughbolts (**Figure 33**).

5. Hold the armature in the frame assembly and carefully pull the lower cover from the frame assembly (**Figure 34**). If necessary, lightly tap on the cover with a rubber mallet. Remove the thrust washer(s) (13) from the armature shaft or lower cover.

6. With the frame assembly placed on its side, lightly tap the exposed end of the armature shaft with a mallet to re-

move the armature and upper cover (6 and 11) from the frame (29).

7. Note the orientation of the thrust washers (7-9) before removing them. Wire them together to ensure they are installed correctly on the armature shaft.

8. Remove the nut from the large terminal (**Figure 35**). Slip the washers and insulators (18 and 20) from the terminal.

9. Mark the brush plate and lower cover (24 and 26) to ensure correct orientation during assembly. Remove the

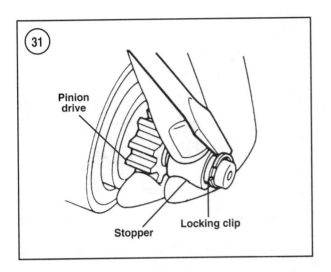

(31)

Pinion drive

Stopper

Locking clip

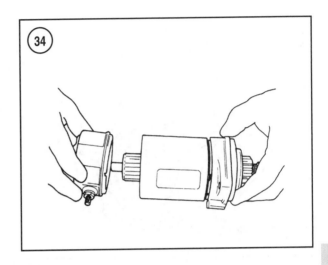

(34)

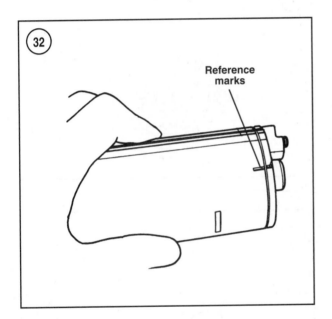

(32)

Reference marks

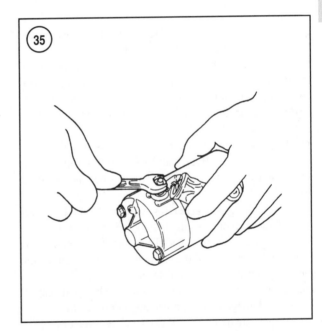

(35)

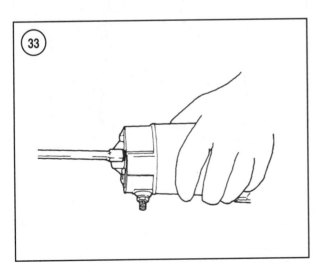

(33)

screws that retain the brush plate to the lower cover (**Figure 36**).

10. Use compressed air to remove all brush material from the armature and lower cover.

11. Use a mild solvent to clean the components, except the brush plate and brushes. Clean the brush plate and brushes with electrical contact cleaner.

12. Refer to *Starter Inspection* in this chapter prior to assembling the starter.

13. Apply a light coat of OMC Moly Lube or equivalent water-resistant grease to the bushing contact surfaces in the upper and lower covers. Also, lubricate the threaded helical splines at the top base of the armature shaft using

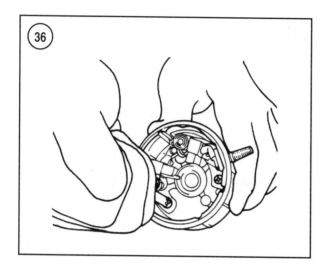

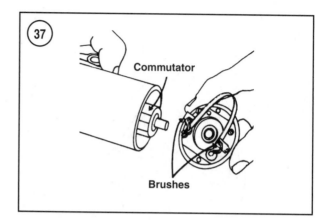

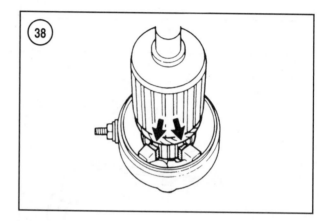

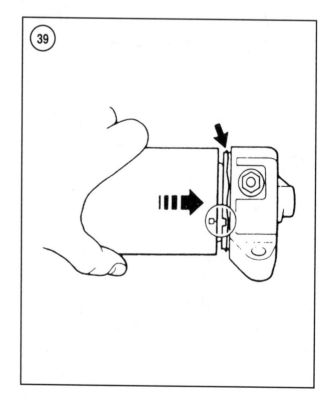

OMC Starter Pinion Lube. Do not apply grease to the brushes or near the brush contact surfaces.

14. To assemble the starter, align the matchmarks made earlier and install the brush plate into the lower starter cover. Tighten all fasteners securely. Make sure the large terminal and insulator fit properly into the opening in the lower cover.

15. Fabricate a brush-retaining tool to assist with the armature installation. Bend a stiff piece of thin rod into a U shape and position it between the brushes as shown in **Figure 37**.

16. Place the thrust washer, if so equipped, onto the lower end of the armature shaft. Install the armature into the bushing in the lower cover. Then carefully remove the tool. If possible, install the armature without using a tool. Manually hold the brushes away and carefully slide the armature into the cover. Release the brushes and inspect them for damage before proceeding (**Figure 38**).

17. Wipe a small amount of OMC Moly Lube or equivalent water-resistant grease onto the upper cover bushing. While holding the armature firmly in position in the lower cover install the frame assembly over the armature. Align the marks (**Figure 32**) and/or anti-rotation structures (**Figure 39**). Install the thrust washers over the upper end of the armature shaft in exactly the same orientation as removed.

18. Without pulling the armature from the frame or lower cover, place the upper cover over the armature shaft and onto the frame. Align the mark on the upper cover with the mark on the frame (**Figure 32**).

19. Install both throughbolts and tighten them to the specification in **Table 11**.

20. Apply a light coating of OMC Starter Pinion Lube or equivalent grease to the helical spline section and thread the pinion drive onto the armature shaft. Install the spring

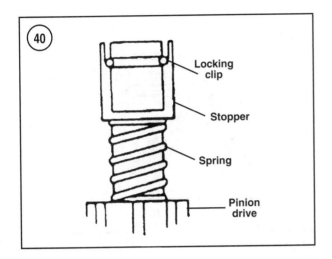

Locking clip

Stopper

Spring

Pinion drive

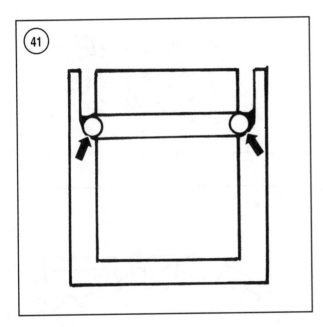

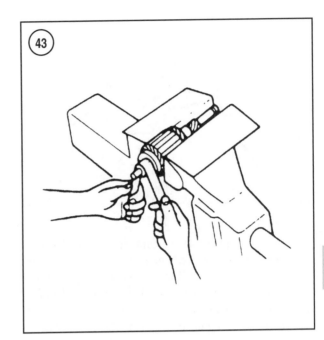

7

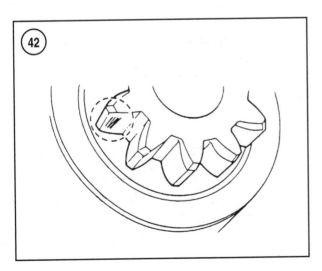

and pinion stopper (**Figure 40**) onto the armature shaft. Push the pinion stopper toward the pinion drive and position the locking clip (**Figure 40**) in the groove. Release the pinion stopper and inspect the locking clip. The clip must be positioned into the groove with the pinion stopper fully over the clip as shown in **Figure 41**. Use pliers to reform the locking clip if it was distorted during installation or replace it.

21. Install the starter as described in this chapter and verify proper operation.

Starter Inspection

1. Inspect the pinion drive teeth (**Figure 42**) for chipped, cracked or worn areas and replace it if needed. Inspect the helical splines (10, **Figure 30**) 25 at the pinion end of the armature fuel injected model, same on carbureted models). Replace the armature if corroded, damaged or worn.

2. Thread the pinion drive onto and off the armature shaft. Replace the pinion drive and/or armature if the pinion drive does not thread smoothly onto the shaft.

3. Carefully secure the armature in a vise with soft jaws (**Figure 43**). Tighten the vise only enough to secure the armature. Carefully polish the commutator using 300-grit emery cloth (**Figure 43**). Rotate the armature often to polish the commutator evenly and be careful not to remove too much material.

4. Set an ohmmeter to the resistance scale.

    a. Connect an ohmmeter between the commutator segments and the laminated section (core) of the ar-

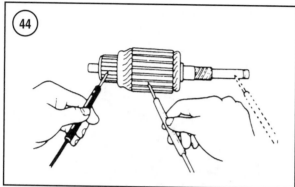

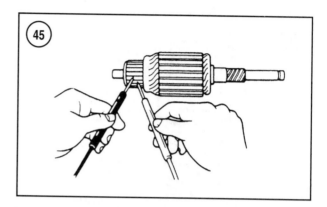

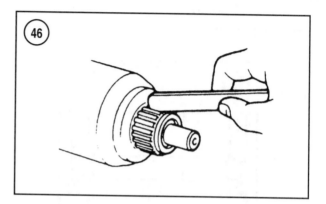

mature (**Figure 44**). No continuity should be present between any commutator segment and any laminated section. If there is continuity, the armature has a shorted winding and must be replaced.

b. Connect the ohmmeter between the armature shaft and each commutator segment. There should be no continuity between each commutator segment and the armature shaft. If there is continuity, the armature has a shorted winding and must be replaced.

c. Connect the ohmmeter between each commutator segment (**Figure 45**). Continuity should be present between pairs of segments. If there is no continuity, the armature has an open winding and must be replaced.

5. Use a small file (**Figure 46**) to undercut the mica between the commutator segments. Blow away any particles with compressed air.

6. On fuel injected models, note the following:

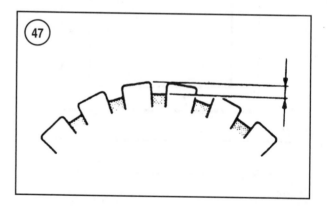

a. Use a depth micrometer to measure the depth of the undercut (**Figure 47**). Compare the measurement with the specifications listed in **Table 4**.

b. Measure the diameter of the armature (**Figure 48**) at several locations. Compare the lowest measurement with the specification in **Table 4**. Replace the armature if the diameter is less than the minimum specification.

c. Measure the brush length as shown in **Figure 49**. Compare the measurements with the brush length specification in **Table 4**. Replace all brushes if any of them are worn beyond the specification.

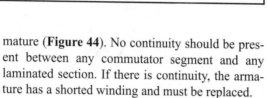

> *NOTE*
> *On all starters, replace the brushes or complete brush plate if there are corroded, contaminated, chipped or broken surfaces. Inspect the brush springs for damage or weak spring tension. Replace the springs if there are any defects.*

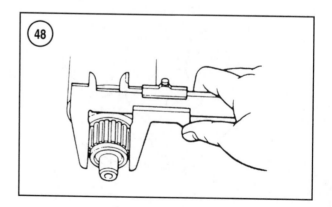

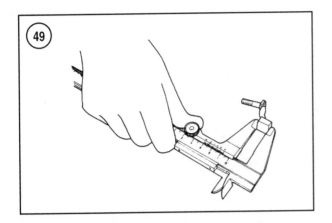

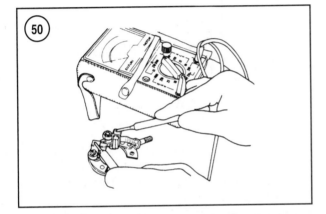

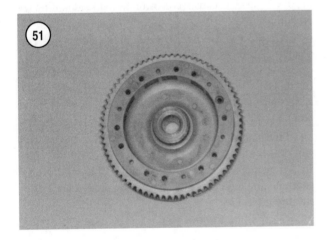

Replace any questionable bearings/bushings using a suitable puller and driver. Replace the armature if rough or uneven surfaces are present on bearing surfaces.

9. On fuel injected models, connect an ohmmeter between the brass-colored brush retainers (**Figure 50**). Replace the brush holder if there is continuity.

10. Assemble the starter as described in this chapter.

CHARGING SYSTEM

All electric start models use a power head mounted stator and a flywheel (**Figure 51**, typical) equipped with permanent magnets to produce electric alternating current. The alternating current is converted to direct current either through a rectifier (**Figure 52**, typical) or through a rectifier/regulator (**Figure 53**, typical) to charge to the battery and operate the engine electrical systems. A rectifier is used on the 4- or 6-amp, non-regulated charging system found on most carbureted engines, while a rectifier/regulator is used on models that are equipped with a 12- or 17-amp charging system.

This section provides removal and installation instructions for the stator (battery charging coil), rectifier and the rectifier/regulator.

7. Inspect the magnets in the frame assembly for corrosion or other contamination and clean as required. Inspect the frame assembly for cracked or loose magnets. Replace the frame assembly if it cannot be adequately cleaned or if damaged magnets are noted.

8. Inspect the bearing surfaces on the armature and the bushings for discoloration and excessive or uneven wear.

Rectifier Replacement

A rectifier (**Figure 52**, typical) component is used on 6-amp charging systems. The rectifier is a series of diodes built into a round metal casing. The diodes are used to convert alternating current from the stator into direct current. Damage to one or more of the diodes could result in a grounded system, a no charge condition or an incorrect charging rate.

Replace the rectifier as follows:

1. Disconnect the negative battery cable.

2. Locate the small round metal cased rectifier on the power head. If necessary, use the wiring diagrams at the back of this manual to identify the wire colors used for the rectifier. Trace the wires out from under the flywheel (from the stator) and follow them back to the rectifier.

3. Disconnect the harness connector and/or bullets connecting the rectifier to the stator (battery charge coil), engine fuse and gray tachometer wire (if connected).

4. Remove the mounting screws from the mounting base.

5. Clean, inspect and repair, if necessary, the threads in the mounting base. Clean all corrosion from the mounting location.

6. Carefully route the wires and position the rectifier to the mounting base. Install the mounting screws and tighten securely.

7. Connect the rectifier wiring.

8. Connect the negative battery cable. Check for proper charging and ignition system operation immediately after starting the engine.

Rectifier/Regulator Replacement

Some carbureted models (such as the 9.9 hp High Thrust) and all fuel injected models are equipped with a rectifier/regulator assembly. On carbureted models, it is mounted to the front of the engine, just below the manual starter. For fuel injected models the rectifier/regulator is mounted on the starboard side of the engine. On 40 and 50 hp models, it is mounted to the rear starboard side of the power head directly above the low pressure fuel filter. On 70 hp models it is mounted to the starboard side of the power head beneath the electrical component cover. Remove the cover on these models to access the regulator wire terminals.

1. Disconnect the negative battery cable.

2. Use the wiring diagrams at the back of this manual to identify the wire colors used for the rectifier/regulator (**Figure 53**).

3. Disconnect the stator harness and any rectifier/regulator wiring bullets. For fuel injected models, trace then dis-

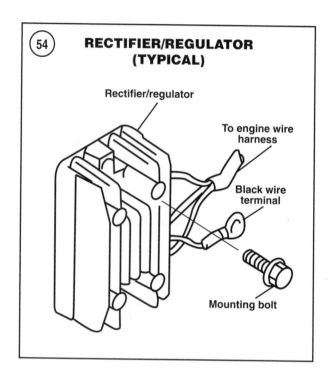

54 **RECTIFIER/REGULATOR (TYPICAL)**

Rectifier/regulator

To engine wire harness

Black wire terminal

Mounting bolt

connect the black wire terminal (**Figure 54**) from its connection to the engine wire harness or power head.

4. Remove both mounting bolts and lift the rectifier/regulator from the power head.

5. Clean, inspect and repair, if necessary, the threads in the power head. Clean all corrosion from the mounting location.

6. Carefully route the rectifier/regulator unit wires and position the rectifier to the power head. Install and securely tighten the mounting bolts, mounting screw and, for fuel injected engines, the black wire terminal. Route and connect the black wire terminal to its connection point.

7. Connect the remaining leads to the engine wire harness and/or battery charge coil.

8. Connect the negative battery cable. Check for proper charging and ignition system operation immediately after starting the engine.

Stator (Battery Charge Coil)

On all fuel injected models and on the 9.9/15 hp (305 cc) models, the stator incorporates the battery charge coil and the ignition power/charge coils. It is mounted to the power head, directly underneath the flywheel, which must be removed for access.

On smaller electric start models (such as the 9.9 hp [211 cc] engine), a separate battery charge coil is mounted im-

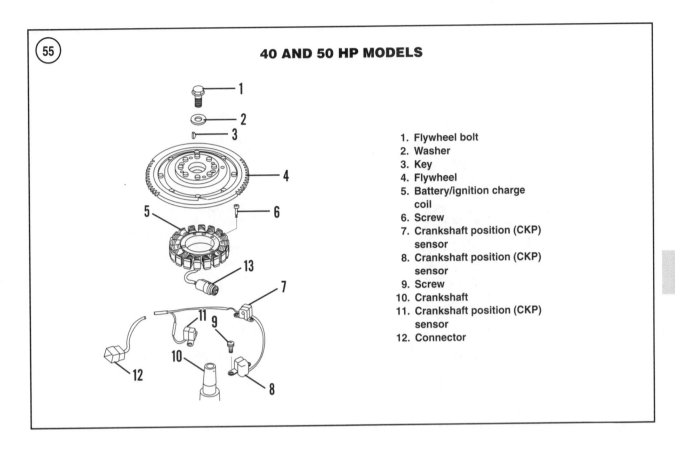

40 AND 50 HP MODELS

1. Flywheel bolt
2. Washer
3. Key
4. Flywheel
5. Battery/ignition charge coil
6. Screw
7. Crankshaft position (CKP) sensor
8. Crankshaft position (CKP) sensor
9. Screw
10. Crankshaft
11. Crankshaft position (CKP) sensor
12. Connector

mediately adjacent to the ignition power/charge coils, but removal and installation is essentially the same, as the flywheel must still be removed for access.

For service, refer to the *Ignition Charge/Power Coil* procedure found under *Ignition System* in this chapter.

IGNITION SYSTEM

The ignition system provides spark for engine combustion by converting low voltage alternating current produced by the stator into high voltage DC current from the primary circuit of the ignition coil. Power is conducted from the ignition coil primary circuit, through a secondary circuit to the spark plugs. All models, except the 40 and 50 hp models, use spark plug leads between the ignition coil and the plugs. The 40 and 50 hp models use a coil mounted directly on top of each spark plug, eliminating the need for separate plug leads. This section provides instructions for removing ignition system components.

Ignition Charge/Power Coil

All fuel injected models, as well as the 9.9/15 hp (305 cc) models use a combination stator/ignition charge/power

coil assembly. Smaller models such as the 5/6 hp (128 cc) and 8/9.9 hp (211 cc) models use an ignition charge/power coil assembly and, if they are equipped with an electric starter, a separate stator.

The stator and/or power/charge coils are mounted to the power head, directly underneath the flywheel, which must be removed for access.

Removal and installation procedures are similar for all models. Refer to **Figure 55** for 40 and 50 hp models and **Figure 56** for 70 hp models. Mounting on 5-15 hp models is similar, though the component shape varies on rope start models.

Prior to removal, make a sketch or take a photograph of the wire routing for reference during installation. During installation, route all wires to prevent interference with moving parts.

CAUTION
It may be necessary to use an impact driver to remove the stator mounting screws. Work carefully and avoid using excessive force that may damage the cylinder block.

1. Disconnect the negative battery cable (if so equipped).
2. Remove the flywheel as described in Chapter Eight.

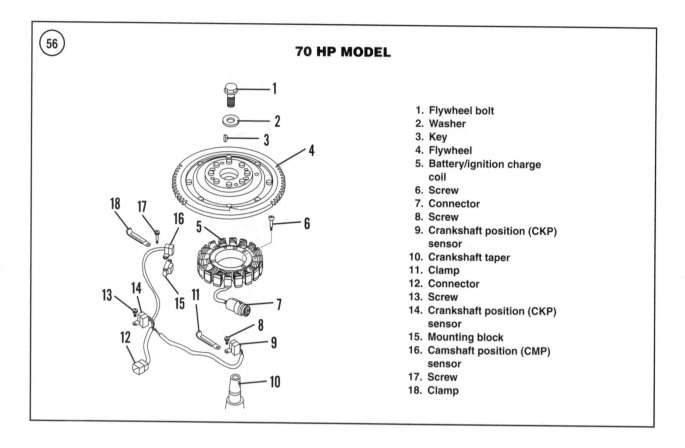

70 HP MODEL

1. Flywheel bolt
2. Washer
3. Key
4. Flywheel
5. Battery/ignition charge coil
6. Screw
7. Connector
8. Screw
9. Crankshaft position (CKP) sensor
10. Crankshaft taper
11. Clamp
12. Connector
13. Screw
14. Crankshaft position (CKP) sensor
15. Mounting block
16. Camshaft position (CMP) sensor
17. Screw
18. Clamp

3. Refer to the wiring diagrams at the end of the manual to assist with wire connection points. Disconnect the stator coil and/or ignition power/charge coil wires, as applicable and necessary.

4. Mark the orientation of the stator/coil relative to the mounting base. Remove the mounting screws and the coil. Carefully guide the coil wires during removal to prevent damage.

5. Clean the coil mounting location, the threads or the mounting screws.

6. To install the coil, reverse the removal sequence, carefully route the wires and lower the coil onto the mounting base.

7. For 5/6 hp (128 cc) and 8/9.9 hp (211 cc) models, align and install the power/charge coil as follows:

   a. Place the coil in position on the power head and apply a coating of OMC Nut Lock to the screws, but do not fully tighten them at this time.

   b. Assemble the guide bridge from the stator alignment kit (OMC part No. 342670) and locating ring (part No. 334994). Position the bridge on the locating ring (**Figure 57**), then secure them using the screws on either end of the bridge.

   c. Install the correct end of the guide bushing (from the alignment kit) to the crankshaft. Align the

keyway and then place the bridge and ring assembly over the bushing.

   d. Move the stator until the guide bushing contacts the locating ring, then tighten the stator mounting screws to the specification in **Table 11**.

8. For all other models, fully seat the coil onto the mounting base. Apply a coating of OMC Nut Lock to the threads and install the stator mounting screws. Securely tighten the screws. For carbureted models, tighten the screws to the specification in **Table 11**.

Ignition Timing Sensor (5/6 and 8/9.9 hp Models)

On 5/6 hp (128 cc) and 8/9.9 hp (211 cc) models, the pulses necessary for the power pack to control ignition timing are generated by a separate ignition timing sensor (**Figure 58**) mounted to the power head. The manual starter assembly must be removed for access to the sensor. Anytime the sensor is removed, the gap between the sensor and flywheel must be adjusted during installation to ensure proper ignition control operation.

1. Remove the manual starter assembly.

2. Remove the sensor mounting screw(s).

3. Disconnect the sensor wiring at the bullet connector.

4. Remove the sensor from the power head.

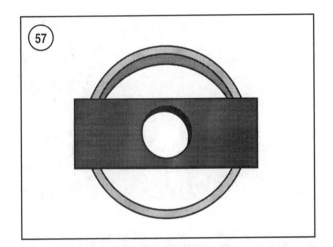

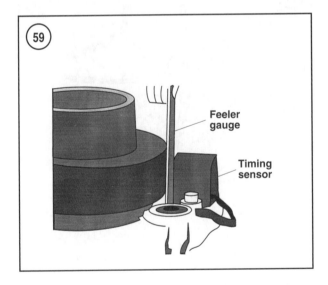

a. Apply a coating of OMC Nut Lock or an equivalent threadlocking compound to the threads of the mounting screw(s).

b. Install the sensor and thread, but do not tighten the retaining screw(s).

c. Turn the flywheel clockwise until the sensing plate protruding from the side of the flywheel faces the sensor.

d. Use a feeler gauge to set the gap (**Figure 59**) to 0.009-0.011 in. (0.23-0.28 mm) for 5/6 hp models or to 0.03-0.05 in. (0.8-1.3 mm) for 8/9.9 hp models.

e. Tighten the screws to 36-60 in.-lb. (4-7 N•m), then recheck the gap to ensure it did not change while tightening the fasteners.

Ignition Module/Power Pack (Carbureted Models)

Carbureted engines covered use an electronic ignition module or power pack to control spark and timing. For 9.9/15 hp (305 cc) models, the module (**Figure 60**) is mounted under the flywheel at the front of the engine directly underneath the rope start handle. On these models, spark timing functions are controlled based on input from a timing sensor that is built into the ignition module. On 5/6 hp (128 cc) and 8/9.9 hp (211 cc) models, the power pack (**Figure 61**) is mounted at the front, starboard side of the engine. For these models, the power for spark comes from the ignition power/charge coils mounted under the flywheel, while the pulses necessary for ignition timing come from a separately mounted timing sensor.

The ignition module performs additional functions besides basic engine timing and spark delivery. The ignition module is also used as a rev limiter to prevent engine over-revving in case of incorrect installation or propeller selection/condition. The ignition module also contains the speed limiting operational warning (S.L.O.W.) system

5. Clean the sensor mounting surface as well as the threads of the mounting screw(s) and in the cylinder head.

6. Installation is the reverse of the removal procedure plus the following:

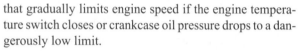

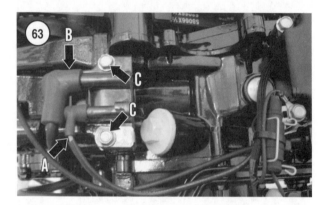

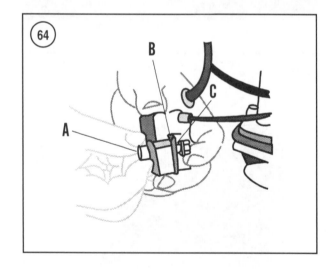

that gradually limits engine speed if the engine temperature switch closes or crankcase oil pressure drops to a dangerously low limit.

The ignition module is a solid state electronic component. No direct testing is possible to ensure proper operation. Make certain to eliminate all other possible causes before replacing a suspect ignition module. On most models, replacement is possible without removing the flywheel, though access is easier on 9.9/15 hp (305 cc) models if the flywheel and/or manual starter cover is removed. To replace the module proceed as follows:

1. Disconnect the negative battery cable.

2. For 9/15 hp (305 cc) models do the following:

   a. Remove the manual starter as described in Chapter Ten and the flywheel as described in Chapter Eight.

   b. Turn the crankshaft to position the lower belt guide opening over the ignition module sensors. This step allows the sensors to clear the wheel during removal.

3. Tag and disconnect the ignition module/power pack wiring (A, **Figure 60**).

4. Remove the retaining screws (B, **Figure 60** or **Figure 61**) and then carefully remove the ignition module/power pack from the power head.

5. Installation is the reverse of the removal procedure. On 9.9/15 hp (305 cc) models, make sure that the crankshaft and belt guide is positioned correctly. Apply a coating of OMC Nut Lock or an equivalent threadlocking compound to the screw threads, then install and tighten the screws to the specification in **Table 11**.

Ignition Coil

Coil mounting location and replacement instructions vary by model. Refer to the wire diagrams at the end of the manual to identify the wire colors and connection points for the ignition coil and then follow the instructions for the selected model.

5-15 hp models

For all carbureted engines, the ignition coil (**Figure 62**) is located on the rear, starboard side of the power head. If there is any question as to the location, follow a secondary ignition wire (spark plug lead) back from a spark plug mounted in the cylinder head to the ignition coil.

1. Disconnect the negative battery cable.

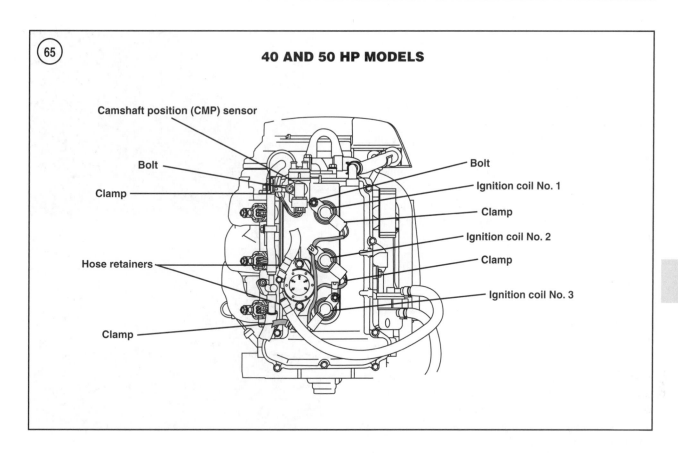

65 **40 AND 50 HP MODELS**

Camshaft position (CMP) sensor

Bolt

Clamp

Hose retainers

Clamp

Bolt

Ignition coil No. 1

Clamp

Ignition coil No. 2

Clamp

Ignition coil No. 3

7

NOTE
Before disconnecting any wires from the ignition coil, take note as to how they are routed for installation purposes.

2. Disconnect the primary circuit wire (A, **Figure 63**, 5/6 hp model shown) from the coil.

3. Tag (except for 5/6 hp models, which only use one lead) and disconnect the secondary spark plug leads (B, **Figure 63**) from the ignition coil.

4. Remove the two mounting bolts (C, **Figure 63**) and lift the coil from the power head, checking for spacers that may be used underneath the coil on some models. Clean the mounting location and threads of the mounting screws.

NOTE
Pay close attention to the ignition coil mounting. If spacers and/or ground wires are used to mount the coil, they must be installed in the proper order during installation.

5. Installation is the reverse of the removal procedure. Note the following:

a. Make sure the wires are properly routed as noted during removal. Make sure all wiring connections are clean and tight.

b. Apply a coating of OMC Nut Lock or an equivalent threadlocking compound to the screw threads, then install and tighten the bolts to the specification in **Table 11**. On 5/6 hp models, make sure to insert the lower retaining bolt through the star washer first (C, **Figure 64**), then the ground strap (B), the ignition coil next and finally the spacer (A).

c. Connect the negative battery cable and check for proper ignition system operation as described in Chapter Two.

40 and 50 hp models

The ignition coils attach directly to the spark plug on these models. The coils are mounted to the rocker arm cover on the rear of the cylinder head.

1. Disconnect the negative battery cable.

2. Release the clamps (**Figure 65**) from the No. 2 and No. 3 ignition coil wires, as necessary.

3. Remove the bolt that retains the selected ignition coil to the rocker arm cover. Pull the ignition coils from the spark plug and rocker cover. Carefully unplug the harness

connector from the ignition coil. If more than one coil is being removed, mark the coil number on the connector to ensure proper connections upon installation.

4. Repeat Step 3 for the remaining coils, as desired. Clean the spark plug terminal in the coil as well as the threads of the bolt and the coil mounting location(s).

5. Carefully snap the coil onto the selected spark plug. Align the coil and install the bolt. Tighten the bolt securely. Clean the terminals and plug the harness connector onto the coil. Install the remaining coils as needed.

6. Connect the negative battery cable, then check for proper ignition system operation as described in Chapter Two.

70 hp model

Locate both ignition coils on the rear, starboard side of the cylinder head (**Figure 66**).

1. Disconnect the negative battery cable.

2. Carefully unplug the primary circuit wiring connector from the coil. If more than one coil is being removed, mark the coil mounting location (top or bottom) on the connector to ensure proper installation.

3. Remove both mounting bolts (**Figure 66**) and lift the coil from the cylinder head.

4. Clean the mounting location and the mounting bolt threads.

5. Repeat Steps 2-4 for the remaining coil.

6. Install the coil onto the cylinder head as shown in **Figure 66**. Install and securely tighten the mounting bolts. Clean the terminals and carefully plug the connector to the ignition coil. Install the remaining coil in the same manner.

7. Connect the negative battery cable and verify proper ignition system operation.

Electronic Control Unit (Fuel Injected Models)

All ignition system functions, as well as all fuel delivery and injection functions are controlled by the engine control unit (ECU). The ECU (**Figure 67**, 70 hp model) is mounted on the starboard side of the power head in a rubber mounted electrical holder.

The ECU is a solid state electronic component. No direct testing is available to ensure proper operation. Make sure to eliminate all other possible causes of a problem through proper troubleshooting before deciding to replace this expensive and usually non-returnable component.

1. Disconnect the negative battery cable to prevent possible damage to the ECU during replacement.

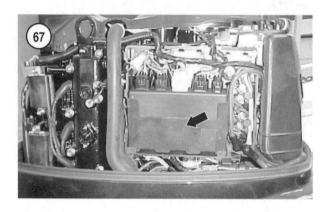

CAUTION
Static electricity can damage the ECU. Always ground yourself by touching another metal part of the engine immediately prior to touching the ECU.

2. If equipped, remove the electrical component cover to access the ECU and harness connectors.

3. Tag and disconnect all wires fastened to the ECU.

4. Remove the screws that retain the ECU to the engine. Note any ground wires connected at these points. To prevent a repeat failure of the unit, make sure they are properly connected on assembly.

5. Lift the ECU from the power head. Clean any corrosion or contamination from the mounting location.

6. Install the ECU and tighten all fasteners securely. Check all ground wires for proper connection. Take care when routing all wires. They must not interfere with other components.

7. Attach all wires to the correct terminal connection.

8. If equipped, install the electrical component cover.

9. Connect the negative battery cable, then check for proper engine operation.

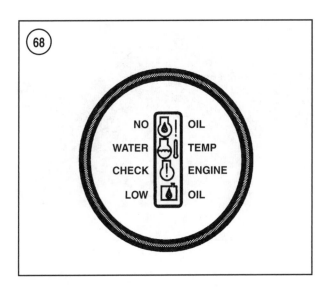

WARNING SYSTEM

All models are equipped with one or more warning systems to alert the boat operator in the event of potential trouble or malfunction in engine operation. Most models are equipped with a version of the speed limited operational warning (S.L.O.W.) system that monitors engine temperature (on remote control models) and/or oil pressure in order to warn the operator if either function exceeds normal operation parameters. A more complex version of the system is used by fuel injected models that monitors engine speed as well as both coolant and exhaust component temperatures.

When the S.L.O.W. system is activated on carbureted models, the ignition module gradually reduces and limits the engine speed to 2000 rpm. This occurs if oil pressure drops to a dangerously low level. On remote control models, it also occurs if the engine temperature exceeds approximately 240° F (116° C). In order for normal operation to resume, engine speed must drop below 1500 rpm and the condition that caused system activation must cease. Normal operation can resume if either the engine temperature (on remote models) drops below 207° F (97° C) or oil pressure is restored.

On fuel injected engines, the ECU monitors input from various sensors to determine if the S.L.O.W. operational mode should be activated. It activates the mode if oil pressure drops below or temperature (coolant or exhaust) rises above predetermined levels. It also activates the system if engine speed exceeds 3000 rpm in neutral or 6500 rpm (40 and 70 hp models)/7000 rpm (50 hp models) in gear for more than 10 seconds. In S.L.O.W. operational mode, the ECU supplies an intermittent signal to the fuel injectors while gradually reducing engine speed to 3000 rpm.

Once engine speed drops to or below 3000 rpm, the engine will operate normally. Once the condition that activated the S.L.O.W. system ceases, normal engine operation will begin again after the engine speed is manually reduced to idle.

Fuel injected and most remote control engines are also equipped with either a stand-alone System Check engine monitor gauge (**Figure 68**) or a tachometer with the same four trouble-lights incorporated into it. The System Check monitor is a dash mounted gauge and horn designed to alert the operator in the event of potentially damaging operating conditions. The gauge is designed to alert the operator if problems exist with engine operation. Monitored conditions include a lack of oil, excessive water temperature, or electronic fault detection (check engine light condition) In addition to the information on oil and water provided by sensors mounted on the power head, the gauge Check Engine light on fuel injected motors is designed to work with the ECU to alert the operator of electronic engine control system faults.

If the ECU detects a fuel injection/engine control fault, it will store a Service Code, sound the horn for 10 seconds and illuminate the gauge LED for a minimum of 30 seconds. The light will go out if the fault does not remain present, otherwise the LED will remain lit until the fault goes away or the key is turned off. If the fault is still present the next time the engine is started, the LED will illuminate again. If a service code is stored in ECU memory, the System Check gauge can be used to read the code. Refer to Chapter Two for code retrieval.

This section provides removal and installation instructions for the oil pressure switch/sensor and engine temperature switch (carbureted engines). Refer to Chapter Six for temperature sensors on fuel injected engines.

Oil Pressure Switch

The oil pressure switch mounting location (**Figure 69**, typical) varies by model. For help in locating the switch, refer to the wiring diagrams at the end of the manual to identify the wire color connected to the switch.

On 5/6 hp (128 cc) models, the switch (**Figure 70**) is mounted under a rubber boot on the upper port side of the power head, directly in front of the carburetor air intake.

On 8/9.9 hp (211 cc) models, the switch is mounted under a rubber boot on the upper port side of the power head, directly behind the carburetor and just in front of the oil dipstick.

On 9.9/15 hp (305 cc) models, the switch (**Figure 71**) is mounted under a rubber boot on the upper port side of the power head, directly above the oil filter and just in front of the oil fill.

7

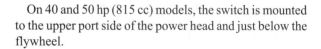

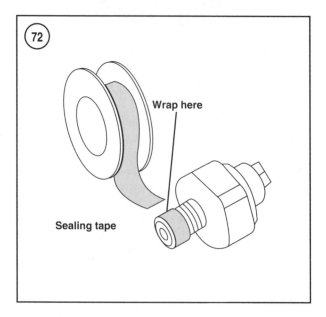

On 40 and 50 hp (815 cc) models, the switch is mounted to the upper port side of the power head and just below the flywheel.

On the 70 hp (1298 cc) model, the switch is mounted on the starboard side of the power head. On these models, remove the electric component holder and electronic control unit to access the switch.

1. If equipped, disconnect the negative battery cable.

2. Disconnect wire from the oil pressure switch.

3. Unthread the switch from the cylinder block. Carefully clean all sealant residues from the switch threads.

4. Wrap a layer of Teflon sealing tape (**Figure 72**) around the threads of the switch. Thread the switch into the opening by hand and tighten until snug.

5. Connect the switch wiring, making sure to route the wire so as to avoid interference with any moving components.

6. Connect the negative battery cable, then start the engine and immediately check for oil leakage. Correct oil leakage before operating the engine.

Temperature Sensors (Fuel Injected Engines)

Refer to Chapter Six for removal and installation procedures.

Temperature Switch (Carbureted Engines)

All remote models are equipped with a temperature switch that is used by the S.L.O.W. system to protect the engine against overheating conditions. The mounting location varies slightly from model to model, but it is usually found in the cylinder head. If necessary, refer to the wiring diagrams at the end of the manual to identify the wire color used for the temperature sensor. Trace the wire to the sensor mounted to the power head. For most models, the switch is located on the upper port side of the power head. On 9.9/15 hp (305 cc) models, it is mounted between the fuel pump and oil filter.

1. Disconnect the negative battery cable.

2. Unplug the temperature sensor connector from the engine wire harness. Unthread the sensor from the power head. Clean the mounting opening and sensor threads.

3. Thread the sensor into the opening by hand and then tighten securely. Do not overtighten it. Plug the sensor wire to the engine wire harness. Route the wires to avoid interference.

4. Connect the negative battery cable.

5. Start the engine and, for sensors threaded into a water jacket, immediately check for water leakage. Correct leakage before returning the engine to service.

Table 1 GENERAL ELECTRICAL SYSTEM SPECIFICATIONS

Component	Specification
Alternator output	
9.9 hp (211 cc)	4-amp, non-regulated
9.9 hp (305 cc)	12-amp, fully-regulated
15 hp (305 cc)	6-amp, non-regulated
40/50 hp (815 cc) and 70 hp (1298 cc)	17 amp, fully-regulated
Battery recommendations	
8-15 hp models	12-volt, 360 CCA (465 MCA) w/ 90 minutes reserve or 50 AH
40-70 hp models	12-volt, 500 CCA (620 MCA) w/ 90 minutes reserve or 60 AH
Engine fuse	
8-15 hp models	One 20 amp fuse
40-70 hp models	One 15 amp fuse and one 30 amp fuse

Table 2 BATTERY CAPACITY (HOURS OF USE)

Amperage draw	Hours of usage	Recharge time (approximate)
With 80 amp-hour battery:		
5 amps	13.5 hours	16 hours
15 amps	3.5 hours	13 hours
25 amps	1.8 hours	12 hours
With 105 amp-hour battery:		
5 amps	15.8 hours	16 hours
15 amps	4.2 hours	13 hours
25 amps	2.4 hours	12 hours

Table 3 BATTERY STATE OF CHARGE (SPECIFIC GRAVITY)

Specific gravity reading	Percentage of charge remaining
1.120-1.140	0
1.135-1.155	10
1.150-1.170	20
1.160-1.180	30
1.175-1.195	40
1.190-1.210	50
1.205-1.255	60
1.215-1.235	70
1.230-1.250	80
1.245-1.265	90
1.260-1.280	100

7

Table 4 STARTING SYSTEM COMPONENT SPECIFICATIONS FUEL INJECTED ENGINES*

Component	Specification
Engine neutral switch	
Button extended (in FORWARD or REVERSE)	Infinite resistance (no continuity)
Button depressed (in NEUTRAL)	Continuity (0 or very low resistance)
Starter motor relay	3.5-5.1 ohms
Start motor	
Armature coil	
Between commutator segments	Continuity (0 or very low resistance)
Between commutator and core	Infinite resistance (no continuity)
Between commutator and shaft	Infinite resistance (no continuity)
Brush holder	
Between positive and negative	Infinite resistance (no continuity)
Between positive and base plate ground	Infinite resistance (no continuity)
Brush length	
Standard	0.49 in. (12.5 mm)
Minimum service limit	0.35 in. (9.0 mm)
Commutator diameter	
Standard	1.30 in. (33 mm)
Minimum service limit	1.26 in. (32 mm)
Commutator mica depth	
Standard	0.02-0.03 in. (0.5-0.8 mm)
Minimum service limit	0.008 in. (0.2mm)
Stop switch	
Key ON	Continuity (0 or very low resistance)
Key OFF	Infinite resistance (no continuity)

*Resistance specifications are based upon tests conducted at an ambient/component temperature of 68° F (20° C).

Table 5 CHARGING SYSTEM COMPONENT SPECIFICATIONS*

Component	Resistance (ohms)
20 amp main power relay (fuel injected engines)	
Between B+ and L terminals (no power applied)	Infinite (no continuity)
Between B+ and L terminals (12 volts across B- and S terminals)	Continuity (0 or very low resistance)
Between B- and S terminals	80-120
Stator (battery charge coil)	
Carbureted engines (6 amp winding)	1.38-1.68
Carbureted engines (12 amp winding)	0.45-0.54
Fuel injected engines (12 volt winding)	0.56-0.84

*Resistance specifications are based upon tests conducted at an ambient/component temperature of 68° F (20° C).

Table 6 IGNITION POWER AND CHARGE COIL SPECIFICATIONS CARBURETED ENGINES*

Engine model	Engine size cu. in. (cc)	Power coil ohms	Cranking voltage	Charge coil ohms	Cranking voltage
5 and 6 hp	7.8 (128)	82-102	100	800-1000	200
8 and 9.9 hp	12.87 (211)	82-102	100	800-1000	200

(continued)

Table 6 IGNITION POWER AND CHARGE COIL SPECIFICATIONS CARBURETED ENGINES* (continued)

Engine model	Engine size cu. in. (cc)	Power coil ohms	Cranking voltage	Charge coil ohms	Cranking voltage
9.9 and 15 hp	18.61 (305)				
1995-1996 manual start		76-92	100	1010-1230	300
1995-1996 electric start		52-62	100	720-880	300
1997 manual start		76-92	70	1010-1230	220
1997 electric start		52-62	70	720-880	220
1998 all		52-62	70	720-880	220
1999-2001 all		52-62	30	720-880	220

*Resistance specifications are based upon tests conducted at an ambient/component temperature of 68° F (20° C).

7

Table 7 IGNITION SYSTEM COMPONENT SPECIFICATIONS CARBURETED ENGINES*

Engine model	Engine size cu. in. (cc)	Ignition coil primary ohms	Secondary ohms	Ignition module/power pack cranking volt./running volt.	Timing sensor ohms
5 and 6 hp	7.8 (128)	0.23-0.33	225-325	50/220	132-162
8 and 9.9 hp	12.87 (211)				
1995-1996		0.23-0.33	2000-2600	100/240	132-162
1997-2001		0.23-0.33	2000-2600	50/240	132-162
9.9 and 15 hp	18.61 (305)	0.23-0.33	2000-2600	100/240	–

*Resistance specifications are based upon tests conducted at an ambient/component temperature of 68° F (20° C).

Table 8 IGNITION SYSTEM COMPONENT SPECIFICATIONS FUEL INJECTED ENGINES*

Component	Resistance (ohms)
CKP and CMP sensors	168-252
Ignition coil primary circuit	1.9-2.5
Ignition coil secondary circuit	
40 and 50 hp models (tested without leads connected)	8100-11,100
70 hp models (tested with leads connected)	15,000-28,000
High tension leads (70 hp models only)	2500-4100

*Resistance specifications are based upon tests conducted at an ambient/component temperature of 68° F (20° C).

Table 9 ENGINE SENSOR AND SWITCH SPECIFICATIONS FUEL INJECTED ENGINES*

Component	Specification
CTP switch	
Button extended	Infinite resistance (no continuity)
Button depressed	Continuity (0 or very low resistance)
IAC valve	
40 and 50 hp models	21.5-32.3 ohms
70 hp models	4.8-7.2 ohms
	(continued)

Table 9 ENGINE SENSOR AND SWITCH SPECIFICATIONS FUEL INJECTED ENGINES* (continued)

Component	Specification
MAP sensor	
0 in. hg. (0 kPa) vacuum applied to hose	4.0 volts
11.8 in. hg. (40 kPa) vacuum applied to hose	2.42 volts
24 in. hg. (80 kPa) vacuum applied to hose	0.84 volts
Oil pressure switch	
Less than 10-19 psi (70-131 kPa) oil pressure	Continuity (0 or very low resistance)
10-19 psi (70-131 kPa) or more oil pressure	Infinite resistance (no continuity)
Temperature sensors	
CT and IAT	
At 32° F (0° C)	5100-6000 ohms
At 77° F (25° C)	1900-2100 ohms
At 122° F (50° C)	760-900 ohms
At 135° F (57° C)	340-420 ohms
Exhaust manifold (EM)	
40 and 50 hp models	See CT and IAT specifications
70 hp models	2318-2562 ohms

*Except for temperature sensors, resistance specifications are based upon tests conducted at an ambient/component temperature of 68° F (20° C).

Table 10 ENGINE COMPONENT TESTING THROUGH ECU HARNESS 40 AND 50 HP MODELS

Component	ECU harness terminals connectors and terminals (wire colors)	Resistance (ohms)
CKP sensor		
No. 1	E4 (R/B) and D1 (B/W)	168-252
No. 2	E3 (W/B) and D1 (B/W)	168-252
No. 3	E1 (R/W) and D1 (B/W)	168-252
CT sensor	D3 (Lg/W) to D1 (B/W)	see Temperature Sensors
EM temperature sensor	C9 (V/W) to D1 (B/W)	see Temperature Sensors
Fuel injector		
No. 1	A4 (O/B) and B5 (Gr)	11.0-16.5
No. 2	A7 (B/Y) and B5 (Gr)	11.0-16.5
No. 3	A8 (R/W) and B5 (Gr)	11.0-16.5
IAC valve	B4 (B/R) and B5 (Gr)	21.5-32.3 ohms
IAT sensor	D6 (Lg/B) to D1 (B/W)	see Temperature Sensors
Ignition coil primary circuit		
No. 1	A5 (O) and B5 (Gr)	1.9-2.5
No. 2	A1 (L) and B5 (Gr)	1.9-2.5
No. 3	A3 (G) and B5 (Gr)	1.9-2.5
Ignition coil secondary circuit		
No. 1	B5 (Gr) to No. 1 spark plug cap	8100-11,100
No. 2	B5 (Gr) to No. 2 spark plug cap	8100-11,100
No. 3	B5 (Gr) to No. 3 spark plug cap	8100-11,100
Starter motor relay	D11 (Y/G) to ground	3.5-5.1
Temperature sensors circuit values		
At 32° F (0° C)	Refer to CT, IAT or EM	5300-6600 ohms
At 77° F (25° C)	Refer to CT, IAT or EM	1800-2300 ohms
At 122° F (50° C)	Refer to CT, IAT or EM	730-960 ohms
At 135° F (57° C)	Refer to CT, IAT or EM	330-450 ohms

*Except for temperature sensors, resistance specifications are based upon tests conducted at an ambient/component temperature of 68° F (20° C).

Table 11 ELECTRICAL COMPONENT TORQUE SPECIFICATIONS

Component	in.-lb.	ft.-lb.	N•m
Ignition coil bolts			
Carbureted engines			
5/6 hp (128 cc) and 8/9.9 hp			
(211 cc) models	84-106	–	9-12
9.9/15 hp (305 cc) models	48-96	–	5-11
Ignition module/power pack			
mounting bolts			
Carbureted engines			
5/6 hp (128 cc) and 8/9.9 hp			
(211 cc) models	84-106	–	9-12
9.9/15 hp (305 cc) models	60-84	–	7-9
Starter cables (fuel injected			
engines)	–	8-10	11-14
Starter bracket screws			
(carbureted engines)	–	14-16	19-22
Starter bolts			
Carbureted engines	–	14-16	19-22
Fuel injected engines	–	15-18	20-24
Starter motor assembly			
throughbolts			
Carbureted engines	95-100	–	11-12
Fuel injected engines	27	–	3
Stator (charge/power coil)			
mounting screws			
Carbureted engines			
5/6 hp (128 cc) and 8/9.9 hp			
(211 cc) models	48-96	–	5-11
9.9/15 hp (305 cc) models	84-106	–	9-12

7

Chapter Eight

Power Head

This chapter provides removal and installation instructions for the power head and flywheel. Complete power head repair instructions are also included. Removal and installation instructions for components like the water jackets, exhaust covers, thermostats and water pressure relief valve are included in the cylinder block section of this chapter.

Since this chapter covers a large range of power heads, engines with similar service procedures are grouped together. The components shown are generally from the most common models. While it is possible that the components shown in the illustrations may not be identical to those being serviced, the step-by-step instructions cover the models in this manual.

Tables 1-14 are at the end of this chapter. The first twelve tables provide service specifications for the power head, while **Table 13** contains torque specifications and **Table 14** is for replacement bearing selection on 40-70 hp models.

FLYWHEEL

This section provides removal and installation instructions for the flywheel and flywheel cover. If the power head has been removed before the flywheel, bolt the power head to a sturdy workbench before removing the

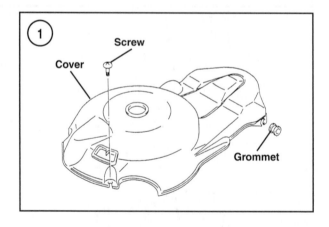

flywheel. Use the mounting bolt holes or mounting studs at the base of the power head to attach the power head to the workbench. Make sure that at least four bolts are attached to the workbench surface.

Flywheel Cover Removal/Installation

This section provides removal and installation instructions for the flywheel cover on fuel injected engines. For removal and installation instructions of the manual starter cover used on carbureted engines, refer to Chapter Ten.

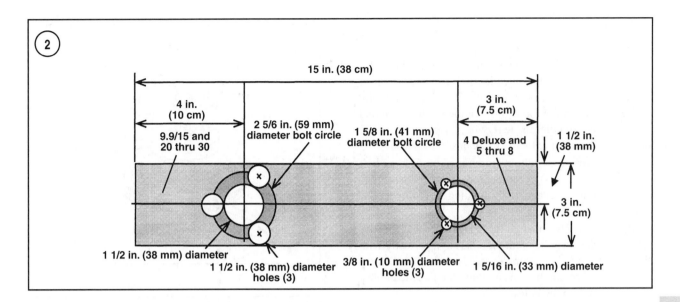

4 in.
(10 cm)

15 in. (38 cm)

3 in.
(7.5 cm)

9.9/15 and
20 thru 30

2 5/6 in. (59 mm)
diameter bolt circle

1 5/8 in. (41 mm)
diameter bolt circle

4 Deluxe and
5 thru 8

1 1/2 in.
(38 mm)

3 in.
(7.5 cm)

1 1/2 in. (38 mm) diameter

1 1/2 in. (38 mm) diameter
holes (3)

3/8 in. (10 mm) diameter
holes (3)

1 5/16 in. (33 mm) diameter

8

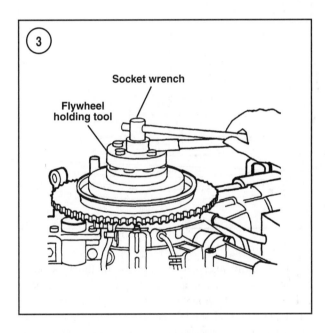

Socket wrench

Flywheel
holding tool

a. Install all bushings, grommets and spacers.

b. Check for interference between the cover and moving engine components. Correct improper installation or replace missing components (such as bushings, grommets and spacers) if interference occurs.

c. Securely tighten all fasteners.

Flywheel Removal/Installation

Use the following special tools to remove the flywheel.

To remove the flywheel nut on 5-15 hp models use the dimensions in **Figure 2** and a piece of 1/4 in. (6 mm) cold roll steel at least 15 in. (38 cm) in length to fabricate a flywheel holding tool.

OMC does not specify a holding tool for the 40-70 hp models. Although it is possible to use a prybar across the teeth of the flywheel, using break flywheel teeth. A generic holding tool (**Figure 3**) may be used, as long as the tool does not damage the flywheel assembly.

Once the flywheel nut is removed, a puller set, such as OMC part No. 378103, must be used to safely withdraw the flywheel from the end of the crankshaft.

CAUTION
Use only the appropriate tools and procedures to remove the flywheel. Never strike the flywheel with a hard object; the magnets may break and result in poor ignition system performance or potentially damage other engine components.

1. Disconnect the negative battery cable.

2. On 40 and 50 hp models remove the two bolts from the front starboard side of the flywheel cover. Remove the bolt at the rear of the flywheel cover.

3. On 70 hp models remove the single screw (**Figure 1**) from the front side of the flywheel cover. Carefully pry the cover loose from the grommets at the rear of the cover.

4. Carefully lift the cover from the power head. Use compressed air to remove belt material and other debris from the power head and cover.

5. Installation is the reverse of removal. Note the following:

1A. On manual start models remove the manual starter as described in Chapter Ten.

1B. On electric start models remove the flywheel cover as described in this section.

2. Place the flywheel holding tool onto the flywheel. Position the tool until the threaded holes in the flywheel align perfectly with the slots or drilled holes in the holding tool. Install the puller bolts through the holding tool and into the threaded holes in the flywheel. Tighten the puller bolts until the holding tool seats against the flywheel.

3. Remove the flywheel nut (carbureted models) or bolt (fuel injected models) by turning it counterclockwise. Remove the puller bolts and lift the holding tool from the flywheel.

4. Position the flywheel puller (**Figure 4**) onto the flywheel. Rotate the puller until the slots align perfectly with the three threaded holes in the flywheel. Install all three puller bolts through the slots and into the threaded holes. Thread them into the holes.

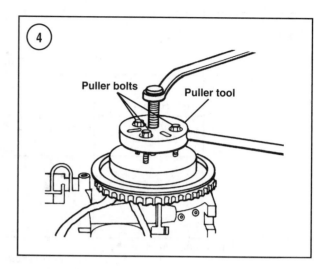

CAUTION
The puller screws must be installed completely to prevent the possibility of damage to the flywheel. Also, when using the OMC puller tool, make sure to install it with the body flat side positioned upwards.

5. Maintain adequate bolt engagement into the flywheel during the entire removal process. Adjust the puller by threading the puller bolts into the flywheel until the flat surfaces of the puller are parallel with the flywheel (**Figure 5**).

6. Turn the puller center bolt inward until it contacts the top of the crankshaft. The center puller bolt must contact the center of the crankshaft. Make sure the flywheel and flat surfaces of the puller are parallel. Adjust the puller bolts as necessary.

7. Use the handle on the flywheel-holding tool to prevent the flywheel from rotating while turning the center puller bolt clockwise. Turn the center puller bolt until it becomes tight.

8. Provide support for the flywheel, then lightly tap the center puller bolt (**Figure 6**) with a small hammer. Repeat Step 7 and Step 8 until the flywheel pops free from the crankshaft.

9. Remove the puller bolts and lift the flywheel puller from the flywheel. If equipped, remove the washer (**Figure 7**, fuel injected model shown) from the flywheel.

10. Carefully lift the flywheel from the crankshaft. Remove the Woodruff key from the slot in the crankshaft (**Figure 7**). Inspect the ignition coils or flywheel magnets if the key is not found in the slot. Inspect the key for corrosion, bent or marked surfaces. Replace the key if it is not in excellent condition.

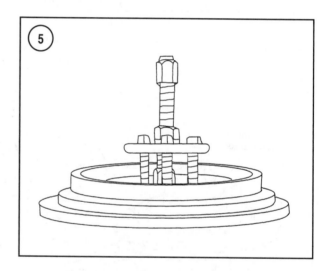

11. Using solvent, clean the crankshaft thread section, key slot and tapered area. Use compressed air to remove debris from the flywheel magnets and other surfaces. Inspect the flywheel for cracked or damaged magnets or other defects. Replace any component if there are defects.

12. Place a new Woodruff key into the key slot with the rounded side toward the crankshaft. Position the flywheel onto the crankshaft. Slowly rotate the flywheel to align the slot in the flywheel with the Woodruff key. When the flywheel drops onto the taper, rotate it while observing the threaded end of the crankshaft. If the crankshaft does not rotate along with the flywheel, remove the flywheel and check for the proper position of the Woodruff key.

13. If equipped, place the flat washer over the crankshaft on the flywheel. For carbureted models, apply a coating of OMC Gasket Sealing Compound to the flywheel nut threads, then thread the flywheel nut onto the crankshaft.

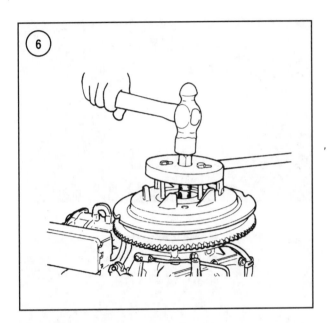

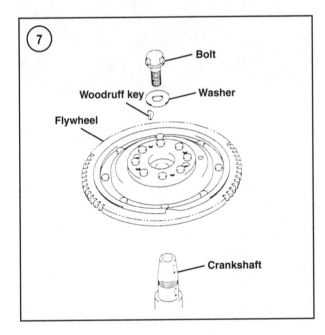

POWER HEAD

WARNING
The power head may abruptly separate from the midsection during removal and drop from the hoist and/or strike other objects. Avoid using excessive force when lifting the power head. Use pry bars to separate the power head from its mounting surface before lifting it with an overhead hoist. A complete power head can weigh several hundred pounds. Obtain the proper lifting equipment before removing the power head. Large engines (25 hp and greater) generally require an overhead hoist to safely lift the power head.

CAUTION
Lift the power head slowly and maintain support to lift the power head straight off the midsection. The drive shaft and other components may be damaged if the power head is lifted or lowered at an angle.

CAUTION
Check for overlooked fasteners before prying the power head from the midsection. Corrosion may prevent easy removal of the power head. Apply penetrating oil to the mating surface and allow it to soak in for a few hours before attempting power head removal. To prevent damage to the mounting surfaces, avoid using any sharp object to pry the components apart.

Make sure the workbench is an appropriate size and strength for the power head.

Use a power head workstand and holding fixture (**Figure 8**). Using these supports greatly reduces the chance of dropping the power head, as well as allowing easier access to the power head components.

Take photographs and make notes of all hose, cable and wire connections **before** removing the power head. Mark all hoses, wires and cables with a permanent marker and tags before disconnection. In many cases, these hoses, cables and wires are much more accessible after the power head is lifted from the mounting surfaces.

Removal (5-15 hp Models)

1. On electric start or battery charging models disconnect the negative battery cable. On manual start only models, disconnect the spark plug wire(s).

2. Remove the manual start starter as described in Chapter Ten.

For fuel injected models, make sure the threads are clean and dry, then thread the flywheel bolt onto the crankshaft.

14. Install the flywheel-holding tool and handle as described in Step 2. Use the handle on the flywheel-holding tool to hold the flywheel while tightening the flywheel nut. Tighten the flywheel nut to the specification in **Table 13**.

15. Remove the holding tool bolts and lift the flywheel holding tool from the flywheel. Install the manual starter (Chapter Ten) or flywheel cover.

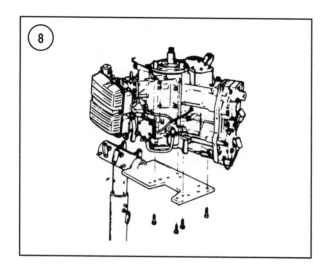

3. Remove the lower engine covers as detailed under the *Oil Filter Cleaning or Replacement*, in Chapter Three. Include the following steps to remove the covers completely:

a. For 9.9/15 hp models, remove the bolt (A, **Figure 9**) securing the choke cable clamp to the power head and then disconnect the cable from the choke link (B).

b. For 5/6 hp and 8/9.9 hp models, disconnect the choke knob from the manual choke link.

c. For 9.9/15 hp models, remove the clip retaining the shift rod clevis to the shift rod link just inside the lower case at the front of the engine and then slide the clevis off the link. Just on the outside of the case at the base of the shifter arm, remove the shoulder screw and wave washer retaining the shift lever to the tiller.

d. Remove the cover retaining screws as detailed in Chapter Three.

e. For 5/6 hp models, separate the covers, then remove the spring clip (A, **Figure 10**) from the slot in the shift lever. Once the spring clip is removed, lift the shift rod (B, **Figure 10**) from the shift lever. Remove the cotter pin from the starter lockout lever (C, **Figure 10**), then remove the lever from the pin and disconnect the lever from the lockout cable. To disconnect the lockout cable, press inward on the sides of the cable tangs.

f. For 8/9.9 hp models, separate the covers, then remove the cotter pin from the shift handle rod-to-shift link pin assembly and remove the pin.

g. Either remove the fuel hose from the cover connector (5/6 and 8/9.9 hp models) or the fuel pump inlet (9.9/15 hp models).

h. Remove the covers completely from the engine.

4. If necessary for power head servicing or replacement, remove the applicable components from the following:

a. Electrical components as detailed in Chapter Seven.

b. Fuel system components as detailed in Chapter Five.

5. For 5/6 and 8/9.9 hp models, disconnect the valve cover oil mist-to-carburetor recirculation hose and the overboard coolant indicator hose. For 8/9.9 hp models, remove the thermostat to oil pump hose. For 5/6 hp models, remove the exhaust tube to oil pump hose.

6. If equipped with a tiller control assembly, remove the tiller retaining bolts (A, **Figure 11**, 5/6 hp shown). There are usually four. Also, disconnect any necessary components, then remove the assembly.

7. Remove the nuts or bolts retaining the power head and oil pump to the midsection exhaust housing or exhaust housing and swivel bracket, as applicable. The 5/6 and 8/9.9 hp models use four nuts (B, **Figure 11**) to hold the pump to the midsection, while the 9.9/15 hp models use six screws (**Figure 12**).

8. Inspect the power head for cables, wires or hoses that may interfere with removal.

9. Use a rubber or plastic mallet to carefully loosen the gasket mating surfaces.

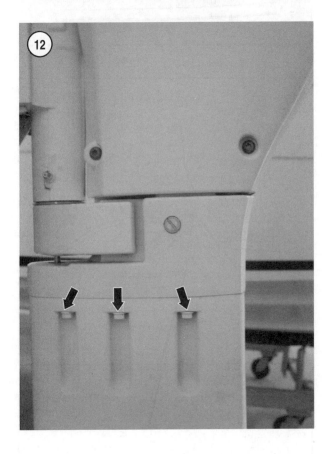

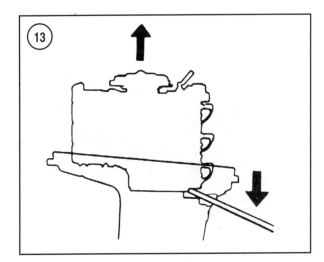

13. Remove the power head mounting gasket. Clean and inspect the power head mounting surfaces for deep pits or extensive corrosion. On models so equipped, replace the adapter if it is defective.

14. Inspect the power head and adapter plate mounting surfaces for missing, bent or damaged alignment pins. Replace any missing or damaged pins.

15. Inspect the locating pin holes in the power head and its mounting surface for elongation or cracked areas. Replace any components with defective pin holes. Remove the locating pins from the power head and install them into their corresponding holes in the midsection.

16. Note the mounting location and seal lip directions, then remove any seals or O-rings from the oil pan or power head adapter. Never reuse gaskets, seals or O-rings.

17. Refer to *Cylinder Head, Removal and Installation* in this chapter for more information on power head component disassembly.

Removal (40-70 hp Models)

1. Properly relieve the fuel system pressure as described in Chapter Six.

2. Disconnect the battery, control cables and trim motor wires as applicable.

    a. On electric start or battery charging models disconnect the negative battery cable.

    b. Remove the ECU cover for access (as necessary), then disconnect the large diameter blue and green wires from the trim relays. Disconnect the trim/tilt sender connector.

    c. On manual start models remove the manual starter as described in Chapter Ten.

    d. On remote control models remove the fasteners and lift the remote control throttle and shift cables from

10. Work carefully to avoid damaging the mounting surfaces. Carefully pry the power head loose from the power head adapter or exhaust housing (**Figure 13**). Check for overlooked mounting bolts or nuts if the power head cannot be separated from the midsection.

11. Provide enough lifting force to slightly lift the power head away from its mount. If necessary, use a pry bar to keep the power head level while slowly lifting it from the midsection.

12. Mount the power head in a holding fixture.

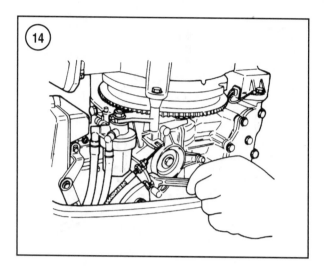

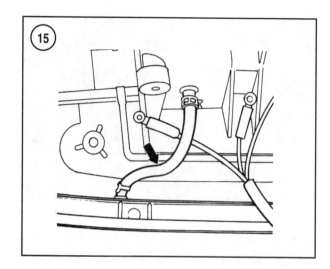

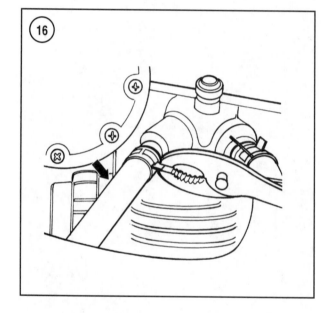

the power head. Lift both cables from their retainer at the front and starboard side of the lower engine cover. Route the cables to a location that prevents them from entangling with other components. Do not place them near the battery. Disconnect the main engine harness from the remote control harness.

e. On models with accessory tiller controls disconnect the throttle cables from the throttle arm (**Figure 14**). Disconnect the shift cable from the shift linkage. At the front of 40 and 50 hp models, remove the screws retaining the shift linkage and the front panel, then move the panel for access and slide back from the linkage. Remove the shift arm from the rod. For 70 hp models, loosen the shift lever shaft nut sufficiently to disengage the rod from the lever.

3. Disconnect the negative battery cable from the cylinder block. Disconnect the positive battery cable from the starter relay. Route the disconnected wires to a location that prevents them from entangling with other components while lifting the power head.

4. Disconnect the hose that connects the cylinder block to the water stream fitting at the rear of the lower engine cover (**Figure 15**).

5. Disconnect the fuel supply hose (**Figure 16**) from the fuel filter or the hose connector at the front of the lower engine cover. Place a container suitable for fuel under the hose clamp and disconnect the fuel supply hose from the fitting just inside the lower engine cover. Drain all fuel from the disconnected hose.

6. Remove the lower engine covers and drain the engine oil as described under the *Oil Filter Cleaning or Replacement* in Chapter Three.

7. For 40 and 50 hp models, remove the thermostat-to-adapter hose.

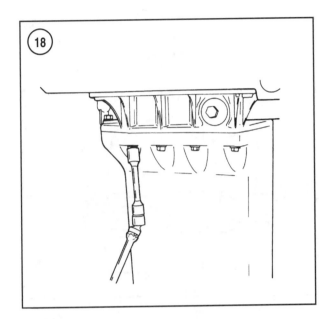

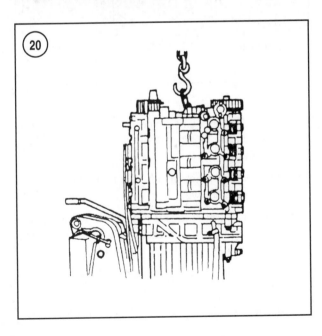

8. For 70 hp models, remove the screws and nuts retaining the exhaust manifold. Remove hoses to the thermostat, adapter and the oil pump along with the manifold assembly. Remove the old gasket. Also on 70 hp models, remove the adapter-to-intake manifold and the vapor separator/crankcase-to-port sump hoses.

9. If necessary, remove the gearcase as described in Chapter Nine.

10. On 40 and 50 hp models remove the three small bolts, five large bolts and the nut retaining the power head and oil pump case (**Figure 17**).

11. On 70 hp models remove the ten power head-to-adapter bolts and washer from the base of the power head (**Figure 18**). Also, remove the two cylinder head-to-adapter nuts and washers.

12. If necessary, remove the oil dipstick from the power head.

13. Inspect the power head for cables, wires or hoses that may interfere with removal.

14. Work carefully to avoid damaging the mounting surfaces. Carefully pry the power head loose from the power head adapter or drive shaft housing (**Figure 13**). Check for overlooked mounting bolts or nuts if the power head cannot be separated from the midsection.

15. The power head assembly is quite heavy and requires an overhead lift for removal. Attach the lift to the power head as follows:

    a. On 40 and 50 hp models, attach the overhead lift to the lifting hook mounted to the top of the cylinder block (**Figure 19**).

    b. On 70 hp models, remove the mounting bolt for the timing belt tensioner. Install a power head lifting hook to the power head using the tensioner bolt opening (**Figure 20**). Securely tighten the lifting hook bolt. Attach the overhead lift to the lifting hook.

16. Provide enough lifting force to slightly lift the power head away from its mount. Use a pry bar to keep the power head level while slowly lifting it from the midsection (**Figure 21**).

17. Mount the power head in a holding fixture.

18. Remove the power head mounting gasket (**Figure 22**) from the oil pan or power head adapter. Clean and inspect the power head mounting surfaces for deep pits or extensive corrosion. Replace the adapter if it is defective.

19. Inspect the power head and adapter plate mounting surfaces for missing, bent or damaged alignment pins (**Figure 22**). Replace any missing or damaged pins.

20. Inspect the locating pin holes in the power head and its mounting surface for elongation or cracked areas. Replace any components with defective pin holes. Remove

8

the locating pins from the power head and install them into their corresponding holes in the midsection.

21. Note the mounting location and seal lip directions, then remove any seals or O-rings from the oil pan or power head adapter. Never reuse gaskets, seals or O-rings.

22. Remove the power head adapter, oil pan and oil pickup tube if the drained oil is contaminated and/or a fault is suspected with the pickup tube. Repair instructions for these components are in Chapter Eleven.

23. On 70 hp models, remove the adapter along with the gasket from the oil pump and steering arm. Inspect and clean the adapter, oil pick-up, pressure relief valve and oil pump. Reinstall the oil pump and related components. Then tighten the retainers to the specifications in **Table 13**.

Installation (5-15 hp Models)

1. Clean the mating surfaces of the power head and the exhaust housing/adapter and/or midsection. Make sure there are no traces of oil, grease, or debris. If used, install a *new* gasket to the mating surface. If used, lubricate O-rings or seals with water resistant grease and install them to the mounting surface

> *NOTE*
> *On 9.9/15 hp models position the power head base gasket with the bead facing the exhaust housing. Once the water seal O-ring and exhaust seal are in place apply a light coating of OMC Gasket Sealing Compound or equivalent.*

2. Slowly lower the power head into position. Make sure all wires, hoses and linkage are clear. Keep the flywheel as level as possible to avoid damaging the drive shaft, gasket or mating surfaces. Align any pin openings in the power head with the pins while lowering the power head into place. Check for proper alignment of all gaskets, seals, O-ring prior to seating the power head.

3. Apply a coating of OMC Nut Lock or an equivalent threadlocking compound to the power head retainers, then install and tighten them to the specifications in **Table 13**.

4. For 9.9/15 hp models, attach the shift rod to the arm.

5. Install the tiller arm and tighten the retainers securely. For 5/6 hp and 8/9.9 hp models, refer to the specification in **Table 13**.

6. Install hoses disconnected during removal. Secure them using wire ties to prevent interference or damage.

7. Install any electrical or fuel components removed during service.

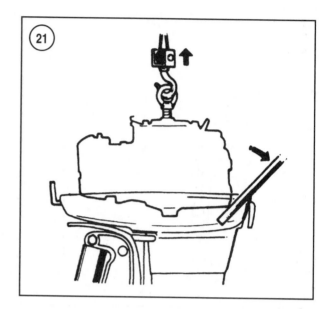

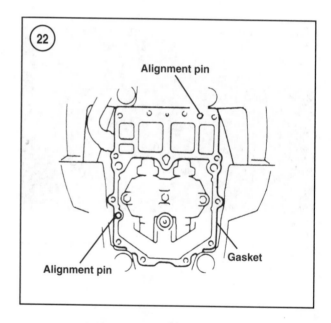

8. Install the lower engine covers along with any remaining components in the reverse of the removal procedure. Note the following:

   a. Connect the water stream hose to the fitting on the lower engine cover.

   b. Connect all throttle and shift cables to the throttle and shift linkage. Connect the fuel supply hose to the fuel filter or the quick connector.

   c. Connect the battery and control cables, as applicable.

9. Install new spark plugs as described in Chapter Three.

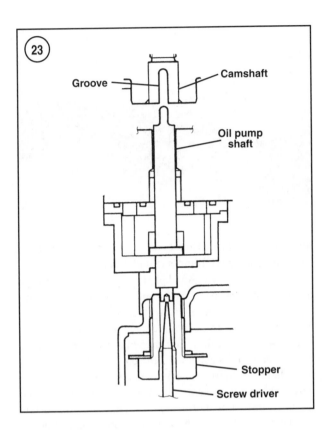

(23)

Groove ─── Camshaft

Oil pump shaft

Stopper

Screw driver

10. Perform all applicable adjustments as described in Chapter Four.

11. If the power head was overhauled or major components were replaced, perform the *Break-in Procedures* described in this chapter.

Installation (40-70 hp Models)

CAUTION
The 70 hp models use an oil pump mounted to the bottom side of the power head adapter. Align the oil pump shaft to the camshaft slot (Figure 23) while mating the power head to the midsection. The oil pump and/or camshaft will be damaged if these components are misaligned.

1. For 70 hp models, prepare the power head for installation:
  a. Install the adapter and *new* gasket onto the oil pump and then tighten the retaining bolts to specifications in **Table 13**.
  b. Apply OMC Nut Lock or equivalent threadlocking compound to the steering arm screws, then install and tighten to specifications in **Table 13**.

  c. Remove the oil pump access screw from the oil pump stopper (**Figure 23**). Bend the tangs from the stopper screw. Then partially back the stopper out from the adapter.

2. For 40 and 50 hp models, if removed, install the oil pan, power head adapter and other midsection components as described in Chapter Eleven.

3. Install a *new* power head mounting gasket onto the power head adapter or midsection mating surfaces. Lubricate O-rings or seals with water resistant grease and install them to the mounting surface. On 40 and 50 hp models, lubricate the crankshaft splines with OMC Moly Lube or equivalent.

4. Slowly lower the power head onto the oil pan or midsection. Make sure all hoses, wires, and linkage are clear. Keep the flywheel as level as possible to avoid damaging the drive shaft, gasket or mating surfaces. Align the pin openings in the power head with the pins while lowering the power head to the midsection. Check for proper alignment of all gaskets, seals, O-ring and the oil pump (if applicable) prior to seating the power head to the midsection.

5. On 70 hp models, proceed as follows:
  a. Insert a screwdriver into the oil pump stopper opening (**Figure 23**) to rotate the oil pump shaft. Rotate the shaft to align the oil pump shaft with the camshaft groove while mating the power head to the adapter.
  b. Once the power head is seated, thread the retainer screw in while holding the pump shaft in position. Tighten the retainer screw to specifications in **Table 13** and align the flats with the tangs. Bend one tang down and one tang upward.
  c. Install the oil pump access screw to the stopper.
  d. Install the two cylinder head-to-adapter nuts and washers, then tighten to the specification in **Table 13**.

6. On 40 and 50 hp models, apply OMC Gel-Seal II to the power head mounting stud and screws.

7. Install the power head mounting fasteners and tighten to the specifications in **Table 13**.

8. For 70 hp models, install the exhaust manifold using a new gasket and tighten the fasteners to the specifications in **Table 13**.

9. If removed, insert the oil dipstick. Fill the oil pan with oil as described in Chapter Three.

10. If removed, install the gearcase as described in Chapter Nine.

11. Attach hoses disconnected during power head removal. For 40 and 50 hp models, install the thermostat-to-adapter hose. For 70 hp models, connect the hoses to the thermostat, adapter and oil pump.

8

12. Install the lower engine covers as described in Chapter Three. Connect the water stream hose to the fitting on the lower engine cover.

13. Connect all throttle and shift cables to the throttle and shift linkage. Connect the fuel supply hose to the fuel filter or the quick connector.

14. Reverse Step 1 of *Removal* to connect the battery, control cables and trim motor wires as applicable.

15. Install new spark plugs as described in Chapter Three.

16. Perform all applicable adjustments as described in Chapter Four.

17. If the power head was overhauled or major components were replaced, perform the *Break-in Procedures* described in this chapter.

Repair (All Models)

A complete power head rebuild requires numerous special tools as well as a considerable amount of mechanical skill. An accurate torque wrench, precision measuring equipment and knowledge of their use is mandatory. Have a reputable marine dealership or machine shop perform the power head rebuild if any of these requirements is lacking.

Much of the repair cost is due to the time required to remove, disassemble and clean the components. Performing these operations ahead of time can save on labor expense. This also eliminates the inconvenience of transporting and storing the boat at the dealership.

Many marine dealerships have a backlog during the boating season. Performing labor-intensive removal, disassembly and cleaning can speed up the repair process. Bear in mind that the dealership may not provide a warranty on their work unless the removal and installation of the power head is performed by the dealership. So discuss the job and intentions before starting any work.

If intending to perform the entire repair without assistance, contact an OMC dealership to purchase the special tools. Secure all tools before rebuilding the power head. Using makeshift tools can result in damage to otherwise good power head components. Often the damage caused by using other tools far exceeds the cost of the special tool.

Bearings and other internal power head components can be removed and reused if they are in good condition. However, it is a good practice to replace all piston rings, seals, rod bolts, gaskets and piston pin lockrings during assembly. The cost of these components is small compared to the damage they can potentially cause if they fail. If reusing bearings, make certain that they are installed in the same location from which they were removed. Piston

rings must be replaced and cylinder bores honed any time a piston is removed from its cylinder bore.

Make notes, drawings and photographs of all externally mounted power head components before beginning power head disassembly. Correct hose and wire routing are important for proper engine operation. An incorrectly routed hose or wire may interfere with linkage movement, causing dangerous lack of throttle control. Hoses or wires may chafe and short or leak if contacting sharp or moving parts. Other components (such as fuel pumps) can be mounted in two or more positions. Note the up and forward direction before removing any component. If possible, remove a section of components that share common wires or hoses. This reduces the time to disassemble and assemble the power head and reduces the chance of improper connections during assembly.

Use muffin tins, egg cartons, or better yet, sealed plastic bags to organize the fasteners as they are removed. Mark their location on the power head.

Never reuse corroded or damaged fasteners. Replace self-locking type fasteners with new ones. If removed, connecting rod bolts or nuts must be replaced.

Timing Belt Removal/Installation (5-15 hp Models)

The timing belt can be removed without removing or disassembling the power head.

CAUTION
Never rotate the crankshaft or camshaft sprockets with the timing belt removed or incorrectly installed. If the valves and pistons contact, they may be damaged.

1. On 5/6 and 8/9.9 hp models, rotate the flywheel clockwise to align the mark on the flywheel with the protrusion on the manual starter boss (between the flywheel and camshaft sprocket). Remove the flywheel as described in this chapter.

NOTE
On most models, once the flywheel is exposed, it is possible to remove the timing belt without removing the flywheel. This is done by sliding the belt off the camshaft sprocket and using the slack to slide it from the crankshaft sprocket teeth and over the flywheel. During installation, the belt would then be positioned over the flywheel and into the teeth of the crankshaft sprocket before sliding it over the camshaft sprocket.

2. On 9.9/15 hp models, remove the flywheel and set the engine at TDC by rotating the camshaft sprocket until the pointer aligns with the raised boss on the cylinder head.

CAUTION
For ease of assembly and prevention of damage to the engine, once the engine is set at TDC, do not disturb the positioning of the sprockets or rotate the camshaft/crankshaft unless specifically instructed in the procedure.

NOTE
*On 5/6 and 8/9.9 hp models the mark on the camshaft sprocket should align with the protrusion on the cylinder head (near the head mating surface split line, between the cam sprocket and crank sprocket). On 9.9/15 hp models a white mark (**Figure 24**) on the lower belt guide should align with the port side crankcase-to-cylinder head split line. In both cases, if both the camshaft and crankshaft sprockets align with the marks described, the engine is at TDC.*

3. If reusing the belt, make a reference mark on the top of the timing belt in the direction of rotation. Pull up on the timing belt to remove it from the camshaft sprocket and then slip the belt from the crankshaft sprocket.

NOTE
If the belt is difficult to remove, remove the camshaft sprocket bolt to free the sprocket and provide the necessary belt slack.

4. Use compressed air to remove belt material and other contaminants from the crankshaft and camshaft sprockets. Inspect the timing belt for worn or damaged surfaces as described in Chapter Three.

5. Make sure the engine is still at TDC. If not, proceed as follows:
   a. For 5/6 and 8/9.9 hp models, place the flywheel back in position (if removed), but do not install the retaining nut, then turn the crankshaft *clockwise* to

align the flywheel mark with the protrusion on the manual starter boss. Then rotate the camshaft sprocket *clockwise* to align the sprocket mark with the cylinder head protrusion.
   b. For 9.9/15 hp models, rotate the camshaft sprocket until the pointer aligns with the raised boss on the cylinder head. Then rotate the crankshaft sprocket *clockwise* until the timing mark (**Figure 24**) aligns with the split line.

6. Align the timing belt teeth with the teeth of the crankshaft sprocket and install the belt around the pulley. If using the original belt, make sure the belt is installed so it rotates in the same direction. If the flywheel is removed at this point, install the upper belt guide and retaining nut to make sure the belt does not move while it is positioned over the camshaft sprocket in the next step.

7. Align the timing belt teeth with the camshaft pulley teeth. Do not rotate either pulley while pushing the timing belt onto the camshaft pulley.

8. Install the flywheel as described in this chapter.

Timing Belt Removal/Installation (70 hp Model)

The timing belt can be removed without removing or disassembling the power head.

CAUTION
Never rotate the crankshaft or camshaft sprockets with the timing belt removed or incorrectly installed. If the valves and pistons contact, they may be damaged.

1. Remove the flywheel as described in this chapter.

2. Remove the bolts retaining the stator and the starter bracket. Remove the stator, then disconnect the MAP sensor and move the wires for better access.

3. Set the engine to TDC. Rotate the camshaft pulley, (**Figure 25**) clockwise until the No. 1 cylinder TDC mark on the camshaft pulley aligns with the raised boss on the cylinder head. At this point the holes in the crankshaft sprocket belt guides should align with the raised boss on the cylinder block.

4. Loosen the two bolts (**Figure 25**) securing the belt tensioner to the cylinder block. Allow the tensioner to move, causing slack in the belt, then retighten the bolts to hold the tensioner in this position. If the tensioner did not move sufficiently under its own spring pressure, force it back by hand before retightening the bolts.

5. Note the orientation of the arrow mark on the side of the timing belt. It should point in a direction of clockwise rotation. Pull up on the timing belt to remove it from the camshaft pulley. Slip the belt from the crankshaft pulley.

8

6. Use compressed air to remove belt material and other contaminants from the crankshaft and camshaft pulleys. Inspect the timing belt for worn or damaged surfaces as described in Chapter Three.

7. Make sure the engine is still at TDC. If one or more pulley only moved very slightly (a couple of teeth) realign them now. If the engine is more than a couple of teeth off on either pulley or completely out of timing due to service, use the valve lash adjusters to close all valves regardless of camshaft position as described below. This will make it possible to rotate the camshaft and crankshaft without of damaging the pistons or valves.

    a. Remove the rocker arm cover as described in *Valve Adjustment* in Chapter Four.

    b. Loosen the lock nuts and fully loosen the valve adjustment screws (**Figure 26**) allowing all of the valves to close under valve spring pressure.

    c. Turn the camshaft or crankshaft pulley as necessary to align the TDC timing marks as noted in Step 3.

    d. Adjust the valves as described in Chapter Four after the belt is reinstalled.

8. Align the timing belt teeth to the crankshaft pulley teeth. Make sure the arrow mark faces the direction indicated in Step 3. Slide the belt over the crankshaft pulley, then onto the camshaft pulley. There should be no slack on the side of the belt opposite the tensioner.

CAUTION
Make sure the directional orientation arrows on the belt cover are pointed in the direction of clockwise rotation as noted during removal.

9. Make sure there is no slack in the belt on the opposite side of the tensioner by turning the crankshaft two full clockwise revolutions. As the timing mark on the crankshaft sprocket comes back to the TDC position, visually inspect the mark on the camshaft sprocket. If it does not align, remove the belt and repeat Step 7.

10. Once the belt-to-pulley and pulley-to-engine timing is verified by the alignment marks in Step 9, loosen the tensioner bolts and allow spring tension to adjust its position against the belt, then tighten the bolts to specifications in **Table 13**.

11. Install the starter bracket and tighten the retainers to specifications in **Table 13**.

12. Apply a coating of OMC Liquid Primer and OMC Nut Lock or an equivalent threadlocking compound to the threads of the retaining bolts, then install the stator and tighten the bolts to specifications in **Table 13**.

13. Install the flywheel as described in this chapter.

14. If necessary, adjust the valve clearance as described in Chapter Four.

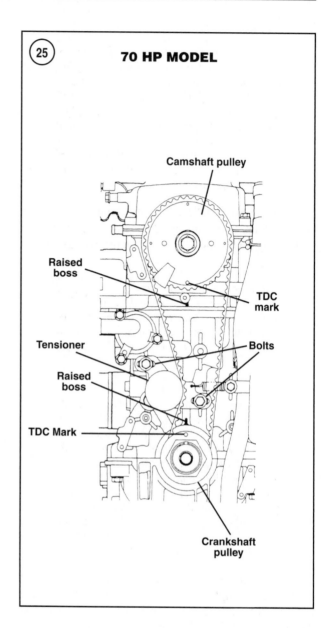

70 HP MODEL

Camshaft pulley

Raised boss

TDC mark

Tensioner

Bolts

Raised boss

TDC Mark

Crankshaft pulley

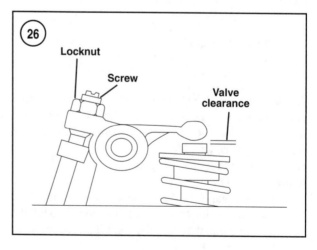

Locknut

Screw

Valve clearance

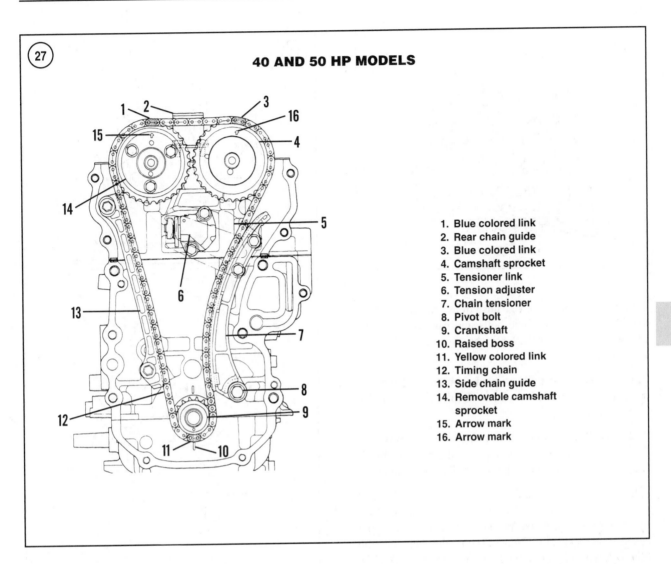

(27) **40 AND 50 HP MODELS**

1. Blue colored link
2. Rear chain guide
3. Blue colored link
4. Camshaft sprocket
5. Tensioner link
6. Tension adjuster
7. Chain tensioner
8. Pivot bolt
9. Crankshaft
10. Raised boss
11. Yellow colored link
12. Timing chain
13. Side chain guide
14. Removable camshaft sprocket
15. Arrow mark
16. Arrow mark

8

Timing Chain Removal and Installation (40 and 50 hp Models)

Removal and partial disassembly of the power head are required for replacement of the timing chain on 40 and 50 hp models.

CAUTION
The 40 and 50 hp models are interference engines, meaning that if either the camshaft or crankshaft is rotated independently (out of timing with the other), the pistons and valves can contact each other, possibly causing engine damage. To rotate one independently of the other, completely back off all valve adjusters, creating sufficient lash at each valve to keep it closed regardless of camshaft position.

1. Remove the power head as described in this chapter.

2. Remove the oil pump housing as described in this chapter.

3. Rotate the crankshaft until the mark on the crankshaft (9, **Figure 27**) aligns with the raised boss (10) on the cylinder block. The colored links (1 and 3, **Figure 27**) of the chain must align with the arrows on the camshaft sprockets (15 and 16). Also, the marks on the camshaft sprockets (which are opposite the arrows) must align with the raised bosses on the cylinder head.

4. Remove the bolts and the tensioner link (5, **Figure 27**). Remove the pivot bolt (8, **Figure 27**), spacer and chain tensioner. Remove both bolts and the tension adjuster (6, **Figure 27**).

5. Remove both bolts and the side chain guide (13, **Figure 27**). Remove both bolts and the rear chain guide (2, **Figure 27**).

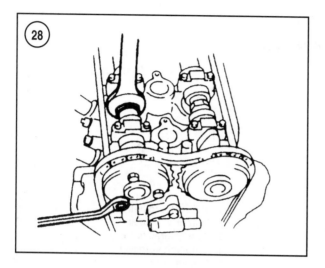

6. Secure the intake valve camshaft as indicated in **Figure 28**. Remove the three bolts and carefully pull the sprocket from the camshaft. Slip the timing chain from the sprockets.

7. Clean and inspect all removed components for worn, damaged or corroded surfaces. Replace questionable components.

8. To install the timing chain, make sure the crankshaft mark aligns with the raised boss on the cylinder block (**Figure 29**). Correct misalignment before continuing.

9. Place the timing chain onto the teeth of the integral crankshaft sprocket with the yellow colored link (11, **Figure 27**) aligned with the raised boss (10). Position the camshaft sprocket (14, **Figure 27**) onto the chain with the blue colored link (1) aligned with the arrow mark (15). Wrap the chain onto the remaining sprocket with the blue colored link (3, **Figure 27**) aligned with the arrow mark on the sprocket.

10. Align the pin opening in the camshaft sprocket with the alignment pin on the camshaft (**Figure 29**) while seating the sprocket (14, **Figure 27**) onto the camshaft. Verify alignment of the arrows and marks with the colored chain links. Correct the alignment as required.

11. Apply clean engine oil to the threads of the camshaft sprocket bolts, then install the three bolts into the sprocket and camshaft. Secure the intake camshaft as indicated in **Figure 29**. Tighten the bolts to the specification in **Table 13**.

12. Position the rear chain guide (2, **Figure 27**) against the timing chain. Secure the guide with the two bolts. Place the side chain guide (13, **Figure 27**) against the chain. Secure the guide with the two bolts.

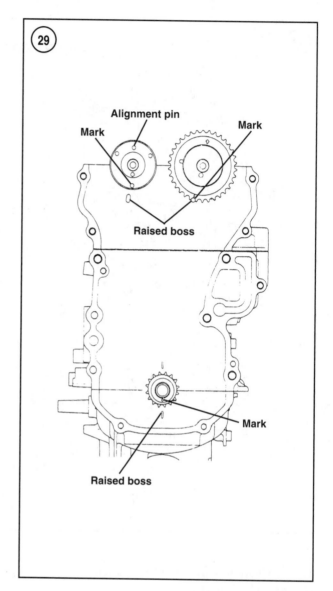

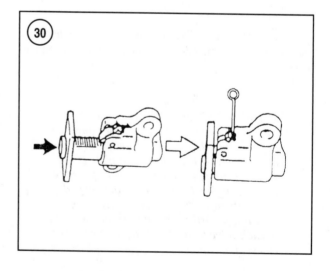

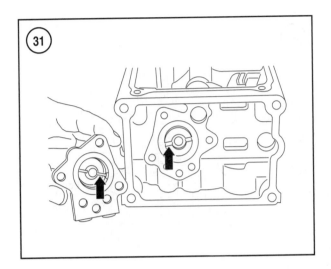

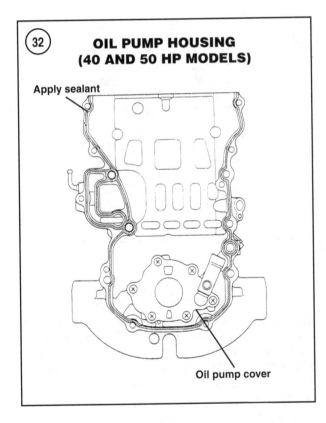

**OIL PUMP HOUSING
(40 AND 50 HP MODELS)**

Apply sealant

Oil pump cover

NOTE
*Apply a light coating of clean engine oil to
each guide tensioner and to the contacting
links of the timing chain while each component.*

13. Position the chain tensioner in contact with the timing
chain as indicated in **Figure 27**. Install the spacer and
pivot bolt (8, **Figure 27**). Secure all tensioner bolts to the
specification in **Table 13**.

14. Move the latch (**Figure 30**) away from the notched
side of the plunger. Push the plunger fully into the tension
adjuster body. Insert a straightened paper clip into the hole
in the latch and body to retain the plunger.

15. Place the tension adjuster (6, **Figure 27**) onto the cylinder block and install the tension adjuster bolts. Tighten
the bolts to the specification in **Table 13**.

16. Engage the tensioner link (5, **Figure 27**) against the
plunger portion of the tension adjuster (6). Install and securely tighten the bolts to secure the link to the tensioner
(7, **Figure 27**).

17. Remove the paper clip from the tension adjuster. Coat
the timing chain and all related components with engine
oil.

18. Rotate the crankshaft two revolutions and verify correct camshaft timing as described in Step 3. Correct improper timing as needed.

19. Install the oil pump housing and the power head as
described in this chapter.

20. If necessary, adjust the valves as described in Chapter
Four.

Oil Pump

Oil pump mounting location varies slightly by model.
Because of the different locations, oil pump replacement
is part of different procedures in this manual, depending
on the location.

On 5-15 hp models, the oil pump is mounted to the bottom of the cylinder head (**Figure 31**, typical) and driven
by the camshaft. For 5/6 and 8/9.9 hp models, the oil filter
housing is part of the oil pump assembly. On these models, refer to the *Cylinder Head Removal* in this chapter for
removal of the oil pump and other power head mounted
components. On 9.9/15 hp models, the pump assembly is
contained within a cylindrical housing bolted to the bottom of the cylinder head. A separate oil filter adapter is
mounted to the side of the power head on these engines.
For oil pump removal on the 9.9/15 hp models, please refer to *Cylinder Head Disassembly* in this chapter.

On 40 and 50 hp models, the oil pump is mounted to a
housing attached to the bottom of the power head (**Figure
32**). The removal and installation procedure is provided in
the next section.

On 70 hp models, the pump is mounted in the power
head adapter (also known as the drive shaft housing/oil
pan assembly) mounted under the power head. For these
models, oil pump removal, as well as cleaning and visual
inspection of the related components, is considered a routine part of power head service, so it is covered under
Power Head Removal in this chapter. It is also mentioned

8

under *Power Head Adapter* in Chapter Eleven for these models.

Oil pump inspection and measurement instructions are provided for 40 and 50 hp models. On 5-15 hp models, disassemble the pump and visually inspect for contamination, excessive wear or obvious damage. The oil pump on all other models is non-serviceable. On models where exact specifications are not provided or where the pump is otherwise considered non-serviceable, replace the pump if low oil pressure occurs and excessive bearing clearances or other causes are ruled out.

40 and 50 hp models

1. Remove the two bolts and lift the lower seal housing from the bottom of the cylinder block (**Figure 33**). Without damaging the seal bore, carefully pry the oil seal from the housing.
2. Remove the seven bolts and carefully pry the oil pump cover (**Figure 32**) from the bottom of the power head.
3. Remove the six screws and carefully lift the oil pump cover from the oil pump housing. Lift the inner and outer rotor (**Figure 34**) from the oil pump housing.
4. Use a suitable solvent to clean all removed components. Inspect the rotors and the oil pump housing for worn, discolored or damaged surfaces. Replace all suspect components.
5. Place the inner and outer rotor into the oil pump housing as indicated in. Measure the clearance between the outer rotor and the oil pump housing (**Figure 35**). Replace the outer rotor and the oil pump housing if the clearance exceeds 0.0122 in. (0.31 mm).
6. Measure the oil pump side clearance as follows:
   a. Place a straightedge on the oil pump housing (**Figure 36**). Make sure the straightedge spans the housing and both rotors.
   b. Push down on the straightedge and measure the clearance between the straightedge and the outer rotor using a feeler gauge.
   c. Replace the outer rotor and the oil pump housing if the clearance exceeds 0.0059 in. (0.15 mm).
7. Apply engine oil to the inner and outer rotors. Install the oil pump cover to the housing. Install and securely tighten the six screws. Reach into the opening and rotate the inner rotor. The oil pump must turn smoothly. Check the installation if there is binding or roughness.
8. Apply a bead of sealant to the housing and power head mating surfaces (**Figure 32**).
9. Align the pins while installing the oil pump housing to the power head. Rotate the crankshaft to align it with the drive surfaces for the oil pump. The housing seats to the

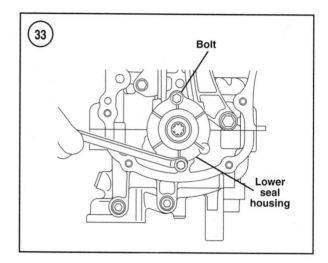

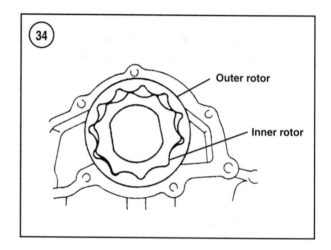

power head as the surfaces align. Install and tighten the seven bolts that retain the housing to the power head.
10. Apply water resistant grease to the seal lip. Place the new seal into the housing with the lip side facing the crankshaft side of the housing. Press the seal fully into the bore with a seal driver or socket that is slightly smaller than the inside diameter of the housing bore.
11. Slide the seal lip over the crankshaft and seat the lower seal housing to the cylinder block. Apply a coating of OMC Nut Lock or equivalent threadlocking compound to the retaining screws, then install and tighten the housing mounting bolts to the specifications in Chapter Thirteen.

CYLINDER HEAD

This section provides removal, disassembly and assembly instructions for the cylinder head. Component mea-

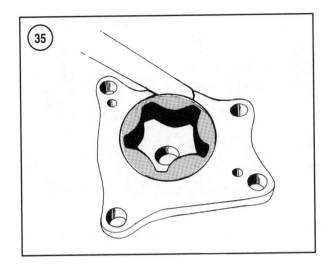

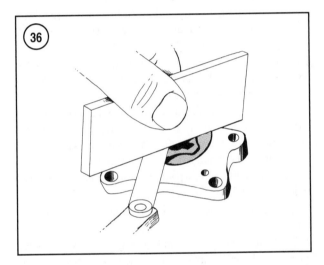

surement requires precision measuring devices. Have a reputable machine shop perform the required measurements if the equipment or experience is not available.

Check the cylinder block and cylinder head for warp before installation. Clean the cylinder block holes with a thread chaser. Make sure the holes are clean and dry. Any debris in the bolt holes may affect bolt torque. Make sure the mating surfaces are clean and dry. Do not apply sealant to the mating surfaces. Always use a new gasket.

Removal and Installation

Most conditions requiring cylinder head removal stem from excessive wear or damage, the removal procedure also provides for the removal and inspection of many power head mounted components. Because not all these steps are necessary strictly for cylinder head service, it is a good idea to take the time now, while the power head is re-

moved from the gearcase, to ensure these other support components are in good condition. Checking items such as the thermostat, oil pump, oil/water/exhaust tubes or passages and breather components may prevent additional repairs after the power head is reassembled.

5/6 hp models

1. Remove the power head and mount it on a suitable workstand as described in this chapter.

2. Remove the bolts securing the upper engine mounts to the oil pump. Inspect the mounts for excessive wear or damage and replace if either is found.

3. Remove the six oil pump-to-power head bolts along with the two exhaust tube-to-cylinder head bolts.

4. Remove the two Philips screws securing the shift linkage assembly. Remove the assembly and inspect all components for wear or damage and replace if either is found.

5. Remove the exhaust tube from the rear of the oil pump assembly, then remove the seal from the tube. Inspect the seal and replace, if necessary. Check the tube for corrosion or damage.

6. Remove the three Philips screws securing the exhaust cover to the side of the oil sump. Remove the cover, then remove and discard the O-ring. Make sure to use a new O-ring during installation. With the cover removed, check the exhaust passages for excessive corrosion or damage.

7. Remove the bushing from the water tube and then remove the three bolts from the exhaust/water tube cover. Remove the cover, discard the gasket and carefully clean all mounting surfaces of any remaining residues.

8. Remove the flange screw retaining the water tube, then remove the tube and grommet. Inspect the tube, grommet and pump passages. Check the hole near the end of the tube for restriction. If necessary, clean it out using some solvent or a piece of wire, but be careful not to elongate the small hole.

9. Remove the three bolts mounting the oil pump and filter assembly, then remove them from the cylinder head. Discard the O-rings, then disassemble the pump for visual inspection as follows:

    a. Remove the two Philips screws and lockwashers from the top of the pump housing.

    b. Lift the cover from the housing, then remove and discard the O-rings.

    c. Mark the gerotor assembly to ensure proper assembly.

    d. Inspect the oil pump components for contamination, excessive wear or obvious damage. Replace the pump or components if there is any.

8

e. Assemble the pump using new O-rings and make sure to use new O-rings when it is mounted back on the cylinder head.

10. Loosen the clamp, then remove the oil pickup tube and filter. Clean the assembly in solvent and check for damage.

11. Remove the four Philips screws mounting the pressure relief valve housing (located adjacent to the oil pickup tube mounting). Remove the housing, then the spring and valve. Remove and discard the gasket, then check the valve housing, spring and valve for excessive wear or damage.

12. Disassemble the thermostat and inspect the components as follows:

a. Remove the two bolts (**Figure 37**) mounting the thermostat housing cover to the top of the power head.

b. Slowly remove the cover and large spring, then discard the gasket and remove all traces of residue from the mating surface.

c. Remove the diaphragm and cup assembly from the thermostat housing along with the large and small washers. Note the locations for installation.

d. Remove the vernatherm, small spring and housing.

13. Remove the four bolts retaining the intake manifold to the power head using multiple passes of a crisscross pattern. Remove the manifold, then remove and discard the gasket.

14. Remove the timing belt.

15. If necessary for further repairs, remove the crankshaft sprocket as follows:

a. Secure the crankshaft from turning using the OMC Crankshaft Pulley Nut removal tool (part No. 342669). It is used to safely hold the crankshaft from turning without damaging the taper or keyway.

b. With a large adjustable wrench on the pulley nut tool and a crowfoot wrench on the crankshaft sprocket nut, slowly loosen the sprocket nut.

c. Remove the key from the keyway and the nut from the shaft.

d. Use a two-jawed puller to carefully remove the pulley and belt guide. Make sure the puller jaws are positioned under the guide for removal.

16. Remove the bolt and washer securing the camshaft sprocket, then remove the sprocket and key from the camshaft.

17. Remove the breather assembly from the valve cover as follows:

a. Remove the four bolts (A, **Figure 38**) securing the breather cover to the valve cover.

b. Remove the cover and discard the O-ring.

c. Remove the screw and lockwasher retaining the reed and reed stop to the breather plate, then remove the reed, stop and plate.

d. Remove the O-ring and mesh breather. Inspect the breather and replace, if necessary. Discard the O-ring.

18. Using the reverse of the torque sequence (4-1, **Figure 38**), loosen the bolts securing the valve cover, then remove the cover and discard the O-ring.

19. Using a crisscross pattern, remove the four bolts securing the cylinder head to the block. Tap on the head using a rubber or plastic mallet to loosen the gasket seal, then remove the head and discard the gasket.

20. Disassemble and inspect the cylinder head and valve train as detailed in this section.

21. Installation is the reverse of removal. Note the following:

a. Replace all gaskets and O-rings. Unless otherwise noted, make sure to coat all new O-rings lightly using OMC Triple-Guard or an equivalent marine grease.

b. Apply OMC Gasket Sealing Compound or an equivalent to both sides of a new cylinder head gasket, then position the cylinder head and gasket. Apply a light coating of clean engine oil to the cylinder head bolt threads, then install and tighten the bolts using two or three passes of a crisscross pattern to the specification **Table 13**.

c. If removed, install the camshaft key with the outer key edge parallel to the camshaft centerline, then install the camshaft sprocket, but do not tighten it fully at this time.

d. If removed, install the crankshaft key. Make sure it is parallel to the shaft centerline. Then install the belt guide and sprocket. Gently tap the sprocket onto the shaft using a socket as a driver to evenly spread the load around the sprocket. Install the outer belt guide and lock plate. Apply a coating of OMC

Nut Lock or equivalent threadlocking compound to the nut, then install the crankshaft sprocket nut and tighten to the specification in **Table 13**.

e. Install the timing belt as detailed in this chapter. Remove the bolt from the camshaft sprocket and apply a coating of OMC Nut Lock or equivalent threadlocking compound, then install and tighten the sprocket bolt to the specification in **Table 13**.

f. Properly adjust the valve lash and install the valve cover as detailed in Chapter Four. Make sure to apply a coating of OMC Triple-Guard or equivalent marine grease to the new O-ring and OMC Gasket Sealing Compound or an equivalent sealant to the bolt threads. Tighten the bolts using the proper torque sequence (1-4, **Figure 38**) to the specification in **Table 13**.

g. Install the breather assembly using new O-rings. Coat the reed stop screw and breather cover screws using OMC Nut Lock or equivalent threadlocking compound. Tighten the stop screw and the breather cover screws to specifications in **Table 13**.

h. Coat the new intake manifold gasket and bolt threads using OMC Gasket Sealing Compound or equivalent sealant. Tighten the bolts using multiple passes of a crisscross pattern to the specification in **Table 13**. If removed, install the flush plug and tighten it to specifications in **Table 13**.

i. Install the thermostat components as noted during removal. Coat the new thermostat housing gasket and bolt threads using OMC Gasket Sealing Compound or an equivalent sealant. Tighten the bolts to the specification in **Table 13**.

j. Install the pressure relief valve spring and cover. Coat the new pressure relief cover gasket using OMC Gasket Sealing Compound or an equivalent sealant. Coat the housing bolts using OMC Nut

Lock or an equivalent threadlocking compound, then install and tighten them to specifications in **Table 13**.

k. Install the oil pickup tube and filter, then secure them using the clamp.

l. If disassembled, install the oil pump components. Note the marks made on the gerotor during removal. Tighten the screws securely. Coat the new O-ring with marine grease and the pump bolts with OMC Gasket Sealing Compound or an equivalent sealant, then install the oil pump and tighten the bolts to specifications in **Table 13**.

m. Install the water tube with the grommet into the oil pump. Apply a coating of OMC Nut Lock or equivalent threadlocking compound to the tube flange screw, then tighten it to specifications in **Table 13**. Install the bushing on the water tube.

n. Apply a coating of OMC Gasket Sealing Compound or equivalent sealant to the new exhaust/water tube cover gasket. Apply a coating of OMC Nut Lock or equivalent threadlocking compound to the cover bolts, then install the cover to the oil pump and tighten the bolts to specifications in **Table 13**.

o. Install the exhaust tube in position on the exhaust/water tube cover using a new seal.

p. Coat the new exhaust passage O-ring with clean engine oil and apply a light coating of OMC Nut Lock or equivalent threadlocking compound to the three exhaust passage Philips screws. Install the passage cover to the side of the oil pump and tighten the screws securely.

q. Coat the shift linkage assembly screw threads with OMC Nut Lock or an equivalent threadlocking compound, then install the linkage assembly and tighten the screws securely.

r. Apply a light coating of OMC Gasket Sealing Compound or an equivalent sealant to the new exhaust tube gasket and sump-to-power head gasket. Apply OMC Ultra Lock or an equivalent high-strength threadlocking compound to the bolts, then install the sump on the power head and tighten the bolts to the specifications in **Table 13** using the sequence shown in **Figure 39**.

s. Apply a light coating of OMC Gasket Sealing Compound or an equivalent sealant to the exhaust tube-to-cylinder head screws, then install and tighten the screws to the specifications in **Table 13**.

t. Apply a light coating of OMC Nut Lock or equivalent threadlocking compound to the threads of the upper mount retainers, then install the mounts and tighten the bolts to the specifications in **Table 13**.

8

u. Install the power head and oil pump assembly to the mid-section as detailed in this chapter.

8/9.9 hp models

1. Remove the power head and mount it on a suitable workstand as described in this chapter.

2. Remove the bolts securing the upper engine mounts to the oil pump. Inspect the mounts for excessive wear or damage and replace if either is found.

3. Remove the five bolts and lockwashers securing the exhaust deflector and water tube to the assembly, then separate the components. Remove and discard the O-ring seal and the water tube/exhaust tube seal.

4. Remove the three bolts mounting the oil pump and filter assembly, then remove the assembly from the cylinder head. Discard the O-ring, then disassemble the pump for visual inspection as follows:

    a. Remove the two bolts securing the filter to the pump and separate them. Remove and discard the O-ring.

    b. Remove the two slotted screws and lockwashers from the pump housing cover. Lift the cover from the housing, then remove and discard the O-rings.

    c. Mark the gerotor assembly to ensure proper assembly.

    d. Inspect the oil pump components for contamination, excessive wear or obvious damage. Replace the pump or components as necessary.

    e. Assemble the pump using new O-rings and make sure to use new O-rings when it is mounted back on the cylinder head.

5. Remove the two bolts securing the exhaust tube to the bottom of the cylinder head, then separate the tube from the head. Remove and discard the gasket.

6. Remove the eight bolts retaining the oil pump to the power head. Separate the pump, then remove and discard the gasket. Inspect the pump for contamination or damage.

7. Remove the oil pan and gasket from the power head.

8. Loosen the clamp, then remove the oil pickup tube and filter. Clean the assembly in solvent and check for damage.

9. Remove the two bolts mounting the pressure relief valve housing (located adjacent to the oil pickup tube mounting). Remove the housing, then the spring and valve. Remove and discard the O-ring, then check the valve housing, spring and valve for excessive wear or damage.

10. Disassemble the thermostat and inspect the components as follows:

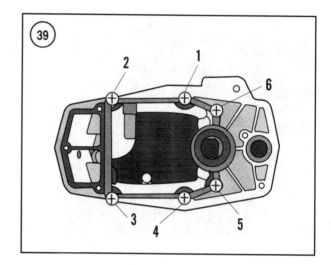

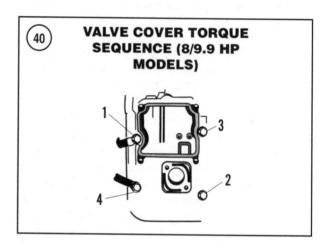

VALVE COVER TORQUE SEQUENCE (8/9.9 HP MODELS)

    a. Remove the two bolts mounting the thermostat housing cover to the side of the power head (just below the camshaft sprocket).

    b. Slowly remove the cover and large spring, then discard the gasket and remove all traces of residue from the mating surface.

    c. Remove the washer along with the diaphragm and cup assembly from the thermostat housing. Note the locations for installation.

    d. Remove the vernatherm, small spring and housing.

11. Remove the seven bolts retaining the intake manifold to the power head using multiple passes of a crisscross pattern starting at the center and working outward. Remove the manifold, then remove and discard the gasket.

12. Remove the timing belt.

13. If necessary for further repairs, remove the crankshaft sprocket as follows:

    a. Secure the crankshaft from turning using the OMC Crankshaft Pulley Nut removal tool (part No.

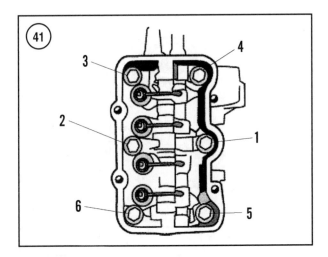

342212). It is used to safely hold the crankshaft from turning without damaging the taper or keyway.

b. With a large adjustable wrench on the pulley nut tool and a crowfoot wrench on the crankshaft sprocket nut, slowly loosen the sprocket nut.

c. Remove the key from the keyway and the nut from the shaft.

d. Remove the three bolts and the starter bracket for access. Check the dowel pins for damage. Remove and replace them, if necessary.

e. Use a two-jawed puller to carefully remove the sprocket and belt guide. Make sure the puller jaws are positioned under the guide for removal. Remove the key.

14. Remove the bolt and washer securing the camshaft sprocket, then remove the sprocket and key from the camshaft.

15. Remove the breather assembly from the valve cover as follows:

a. Remove the four bolts securing the breather cover to the valve cover.

b. Remove the cover and discard the O-ring.

c. Remove the two screws and lockwashers retaining the reed and reed stop to the breather plate, then remove the reed, stop and plate.

d. Remove the O-ring and mesh breather. Inspect the breather and replace, if necessary. Discard the O-ring.

16. Using the reverse of the torque sequence (**Figure 40**), loosen the bolts securing the valve cover, then remove cover and discard the O-ring.

17. Using the reverse of the torque sequence (**Figure 41**), remove the six bolts securing the cylinder head to the block. Tap on the head using a rubber or plastic mallet to loosen the gasket seal, then remove the head and discard the gasket.

18. Disassemble and inspect the cylinder head and valve train as detailed in this chapter.

19. Installation is the reverse of removal. Note the following:

a. Replace all gaskets and O-rings. Unless otherwise noted, make sure to coat all new O-rings lightly using OMC Triple-Guard or an equivalent marine grease.

b. Install new O-rings on the cylinder block dowel pins, but **do not** coat these O-rings with grease.

c. Apply OMC Gasket Sealing Compound or an equivalent to both sides of a new cylinder head gasket, then position the cylinder head and gasket. Apply a light coating of clean engine oil to the cylinder head bolt threads, then install and tighten the bolts using two or three passes of the torque sequence (**Figure 41**) to the specification in **Table 13**.

d. If removed, install the camshaft key with the outer key edge parallel to the camshaft centerline, then install the camshaft sprocket, but do not tighten it fully at this time.

e. If removed, install the crankshaft key make sure it is parallel to the shaft centerline. Then install the belt guide and sprocket. Gently tap the sprocket onto the shaft using a socket as a driver to evenly spread the load around the sprocket.

f. Apply a light coating of OMC Gasket Sealing Compound or equivalent sealant to the starter bracket bolts, then install the bolts and tighten to specifications in **Table 13**.

g. Install the outer belt guide and lock plate to the crankshaft sprocket. Apply a coating of OMC Nut Lock or equivalent threadlocking compound to the nut, then install the crankshaft sprocket nut and tighten to the specification in **Table 13**.

h. Install the timing belt as detailed in this chapter. Remove the bolt from the camshaft sprocket and apply a coating of OMC Nut Lock or equivalent threadlocking compound, then install and tighten the sprocket bolt to the specification in **Table 13**.

i. Properly adjust the valve lash and install the valve cover as detailed in Chapter Four. Make sure to apply a coating of OMC Triple-Guard or equivalent marine grease to the new O-ring and OMC Gasket Sealing Compound or an equivalent sealant to the bolt threads. Tighten the bolts using multiple passes of the proper torque sequence (**Figure 40**) to the specification in **Table 13**.

j. Install the breather assembly using new O-rings. Coat the reed stop screw and breather cover screws

8

using OMC Nut Lock or equivalent threadlocking compound. Tighten the stop screw and the breather cover screws to specifications in **Table 13**.

k. Coat the new intake manifold gasket and bolt threads using OMC Gasket Sealing Compound or an equivalent sealant. Install the manifold and gasket, using multiple passes of the torque sequence (**Figure 42**) to tighten the bolts to the specification in **Table 13**. If removed, install the flush plug and tighten it to specifications in **Table 13**.

l. Install the thermostat components as noted during removal. Coat the new thermostat housing gasket and bolt threads using OMC Gasket Sealing Compound or an equivalent sealant. Tighten the bolts to the specification in **Table 13**.

m. Install the pressure relief valve spring and cover using a new O-ring. Coat the threads of the cover bolts using OMC Gasket Sealing Compound or an equivalent sealant, then install and tighten the bolts to specifications in **Table 13**.

n. Install the oil pickup tube and filter, then secure using the clamp.

o. Apply a light coating of OMC Gasket Sealing Compound or an equivalent sealant to the new oil pan gasket, then install the pan to the power head.

p. Apply a light coating of OMC Gasket Sealing Compound or equivalent sealant to the new sump-to-power head gasket and to the power head studs. Install the sump with the gasket, then install the nuts with lockwashers. Tighten the nuts using multiple passes of the torque sequence (**Figure 43**) to the specifications in **Table 13**.

q. Apply a light coating of OMC Gasket Sealing Compound or equivalent sealant to the new exhaust tube gasket and to the screw threads. Install the exhaust tube in position on the cylinder head and tighten the bolts to specifications in **Table 13**.

r. If disassembled, install the oil pump components noting the marks made on the gerotor during removal. Coat the O-rings with clean engine oil and the pump cover screws with OMC Nut Lock or an equivalent threadlocking compound and then install the cover. Tighten the screws securely.

s. Coat the pump-to-filter housing and pump housing-to-power head bolts, as well as the pump-to-power head gasket with OMC Gasket Sealing Compound or an equivalent sealant. Install the filter housing to the pump and tighten the bolts to specifications in **Table 13**, then install the oil pump to the power head (with the new gasket) and tighten the bolts to specifications in **Table 13**.

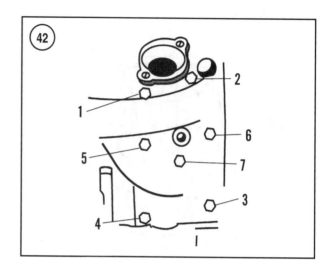

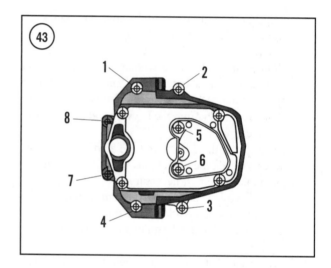

t. Apply a coating of OMC Adhesive M to a new exhaust deflector O-ring seal. Install the O-ring seal, followed by a new water tube/exhaust tube seal on the exhaust tube. Install the exhaust deflector and water tube using the bolts and lockwashers, then tighten the bolts to specifications in **Table 13**.

u. Apply a light coating of OMC Nut Lock or equivalent threadlocking compound to the threads of the upper mount retainers, then install the mounts and tighten the bolts to specifications in **Table 13**.

v. Install the power head assembly to the mid-section as detailed in this chapter.

9.9/15 hp models

1. Remove the power head and mount it on a suitable workstand as described in this chapter.

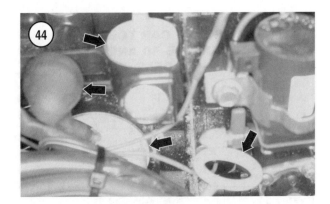

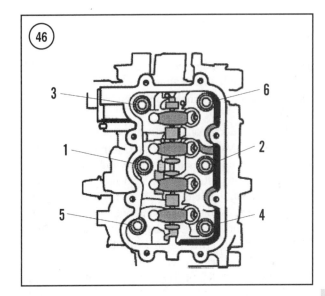

2. Tag and disconnect the overboard indicator, breather and thermostat hoses from the power head.

3. If equipped, remove the emissions testing tube from the power head.

4. From the port side of the engine, remove the oil filter, oil pressure switch, oil fill plug and oil level dipstick (**Figure 44**).

5. From underneath the power head, remove the oil pickup hose and mesh filter. Separate the filter from the hose, then clean the components in solvent and check for damage.

6. Remove the timing belt as detailed in this chapter. If belt removal is difficult, either remove the camshaft sprocket, or if the crankshaft sprocket is being removed for other service, proceed with Step 7.

7. If necessary for further repairs, remove the crankshaft sprocket as follows:

    a. Secure the crankshaft from turning using the OMC Crankshaft Pulley Nut removal tool part (No. 342212). It is used to safely hold the crankshaft from turning without damaging the taper or keyway.

    b. With a large adjustable wrench on the pulley nut tool and a crowfoot wrench on the crankshaft sprocket nut, slowly loosen the sprocket nut.

    c. Remove the nut from the shaft.

    d. Remove the upper belt guide from the crankshaft.

    e. Use a steering wheel type puller along with two 1/4 – 20 × 4 in. screws and two 1/4 in. inner diameter washers, slowly free the sprocket from the crankshaft.

8. If not done in Step 6 to free the timing belt, remove the bolt and washer securing the camshaft sprocket, then remove the sprocket from the shaft.

9. Remove the bolts retaining the intake manifold to the power head. Remove the manifold, then remove and discard the O-ring seals. Inspect the manifold for damage, excessive corrosion or leakage.

10. Remove the bolts securing the exhaust adapter to the underside of the power head, then remove the adapter and O-ring seal. Discard the O-ring and inspect the adapter for corrosion or damage.

11. Remove the three Torx head bolts mounting the pressure relief valve. Remove the valve and discard the gasket, then inspect the valve for corrosion or damage.

12. Using the reverse of the torque sequence (**Figure 45**), loosen the bolts securing the valve cover, then remove the cover and discard the gasket.

13. Using the reverse of the torque sequence (**Figure 46**), remove the six bolts securing the cylinder head to the block. Tap on the head using a rubber or plastic mallet to loosen the gasket seal, then remove the head and discard the gasket.

NOTE
Since the cylinder head bolts are different lengths, note the bolt locations while removing them to ensure proper assembly. Install

the longer bolts on the starboard side of the engine.

14. Disassemble and inspect the cylinder head and valve train as detailed in this section.

15. Installation is the reverse of removal. Note the following:

   a. Replace all gaskets and O-rings.

   b. Apply OMC Gasket Sealing Compound or equivalent to both sides of a new cylinder head gasket, then position the cylinder head and gasket. Apply a light coating of clean engine oil to the cylinder head bolt threads, then install and tighten the bolts using two or three passes of the torque sequence **Figure 46** to the specification in **Table 13**.

   c. Install the pressure relief valve using a new gasket. Prior to installation, coat the gasket with OMC Gasket Sealing Compound and coat the threads of the Torx head bolts with clean engine oil. Install and tighten the bolts to specifications in **Table 13**.

   d. Apply a light coating of OMC Gasket Sealing Compound to the bolt threads and the mating surface of the exhaust adapter. Install a new seal ring to the adapter, then install the adapter and tighten the bolts to specifications in **Table 13**.

   e. Coat the new intake manifold O-rings lightly with clean engine oil, then position them on the manifold assembly. Coat the bolt threads using OMC Gasket Sealing Compound or an equivalent sealant. Install the manifold and tighten the bolts to specifications in **Table 13**.

   f. If removed, install the camshaft key with the outer key edge parallel to the camshaft centerline, then install the camshaft sprocket, but do not tighten it fully at this time.

   g. If removed, begin installing the sprocket over the crankshaft, then position the belt guide on top of the sprocket. Thread the nut onto the crankshaft and install the crankshaft key. Make sure the key is parallel to the shaft centerline. Use the crankshaft pulley nut tool to hold the shaft and tighten the sprocket nut using a crowfoot wrench. The nut will press the sprocket evenly into place. Then remove the nut and belt guide again to ease timing belt installation.

   h. Install the timing belt as detailed in this chapter. Once the belt is installed and the pulleys are properly aligned, install the crankshaft sprocket nut with the belt guide and tighten to the specification in **Table 13**.

   i. If the camshaft sprocket was removed and temporarily positioned to install the timing belt, remove the bolt from the camshaft sprocket and apply a

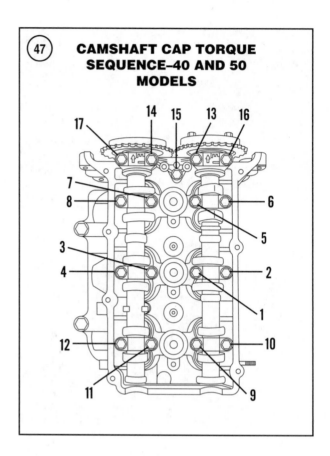

CAMSHAFT CAP TORQUE SEQUENCE–40 AND 50 MODELS

coating of OMC Nut Lock or equivalent threadlocking compound. Install and tighten the sprocket bolt to the specification in **Table 13**.

   j. Properly adjust the valve lash and install the valve cover as detailed in Chapter Four. Make sure to use a new gasket during installation and to apply OMC Gasket Sealing Compound or an equivalent sealant to the bolt threads. Tighten the bolts on the valve cover using multiple passes in the proper torque sequence (**Figure 45**) to the specification in **Table 13**.

   k. Apply OMC Pipe Sealant or an equivalent thread sealant to the oil pressure switch, then install the switch and tighten to specifications in **Table 13**.

   l. Lubricate the seal of a new oil filter using clean engine oil, then install the filter and tighten it by hand an additional 1/4 turn after the seal contacts the filter adapter mating surface.

   m. Install the oil fill plug and dipstick.

   n. If equipped, install the exhaust probe tube and tighten the fitting to specifications in **Table 13**.

   o. Connect the overboard indicator, breather and thermostat hoses to the power head.

   p. Install the oil pump pickup hose and filter to the power head. Secure them using a wire tie.

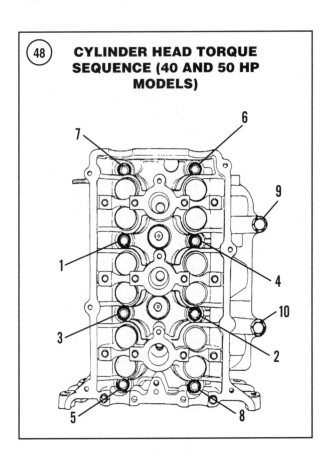

(48) **CYLINDER HEAD TORQUE SEQUENCE (40 AND 50 HP MODELS)**

q. Install the power head assembly to the mid-section as detailed in this chapter.

40 and 50 hp models

1. Remove the timing chain as described in this chapter. Remove the rocker arm cover as described under *Valve Adjustment* in Chapter Four. Remove the intake manifold as described in Chapter Six.

2. Position the power head on a sturdy work surface with the cylinder head facing up. Make reference marks indicating the mounting location and up side for each camshaft cap (**Figure 47**).

3. Loosen the camshaft cap bolts one-quarter turn at a time and in the reverse order of the tightening sequence (**Figure 47**). Support the camshafts while removing the camshaft caps.

4. Lift the camshafts from the cylinder head. Use a 10 mm deep socket to loosen the cylinder head bolts. Loosen them one-quarter turn at a time and in the reverse order of the tightening sequence (**Figure 48**).

5. Without damaging any mating surfaces, pry the cylinder head from the cylinder block. Remove the head gasket from the cylinder head or cylinder block.

6. Inspect the cylinder head components as described in this chapter and perform any needed repairs.

7. Place a *new* head gasket in position on the cylinder block. Make sure the gasket fits over both alignment pins.

8. Align the cylinder head to the alignment pins and seat the cylinder head against the gasket. Apply a light coat of engine oil to the cylinder head bolt threads and install them into the cylinder block.

9. Tighten the head bolts in sequence (**Figure 48**) to specifications in **Table 13**. Fully loosen each bolt in the reverse of the tightening sequence. Again tighten the bolts in sequence to specifications in **Table 13**. Tighten the bolts a third time to the final specification in **Table 13**.

10. Apply engine oil to the camshaft journal and bearing surfaces of the camshaft caps. Carefully place each camshaft into position on the cylinder head with the marks aligned as indicated in **Figure 27**. Install each camshaft cap (**Figure 47**) to its mounting location with the arrow mark facing the flywheel.

11. Tighten the camshaft cap bolts in sequence (**Figure 47**) to one-third the torque in **Table 13**. Tighten the bolts in sequence to two-thirds the torque. Tighten the bolts a third time to the torque specification.

12. Align the marks and install the timing chain (**Figure 47**). Install the intake manifold as described in Chapter Six. Adjust the valves after power head installation as described in Chapter Four.

70 hp model

1. Remove the timing belt as described in this chapter. Remove the rocker arm cover as described under *Valve Adjustment* in Chapter Four. Remove the intake manifold as described in Chapter Six.

2. Loosen the cylinder head bolts one-quarter turn at a time and in the reverse order of the tightening sequence (**Figure 49**).

3. Without damaging any mating surfaces, pry the cylinder head from the cylinder block. Remove the head gasket from the cylinder head or cylinder block.

4. Inspect the cylinder head components as described in this chapter and perform any needed repairs.

5. Place a *new* head gasket in position on the cylinder block. Fit the openings in the gasket over the alignment pins on the cylinder block.

6. Rotate the crankshaft and camshaft to align the marks as indicated in **Figure 25**. Align the pin openings and seat the cylinder head against the gasket. Apply a light coat of engine oil to the cylinder head bolt threads and install them into the cylinder block.

7. Tighten the head bolts in sequence (**Figure 49**) and in three passes to specifications in **Table 13**.

8

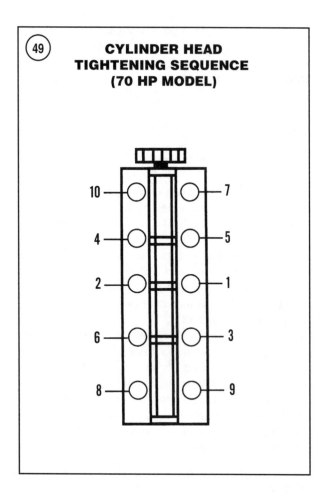

CYLINDER HEAD TIGHTENING SEQUENCE (70 HP MODEL)

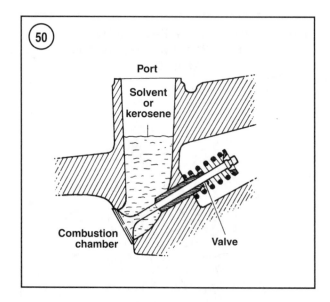

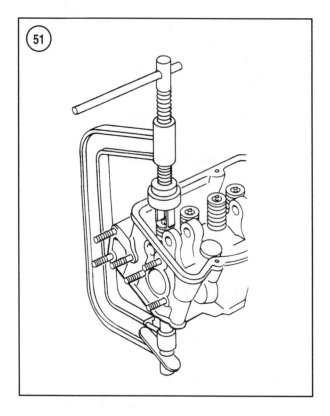

8. Align the pulley marks (**Figure 25**) and install the timing belt as described in this chapter. Install the intake manifold as described in Chapter Six. Adjust the valves as described in Chapter Four.

Disassembly and Assembly

Check the cylinder head for valve leakage as described in this chapter before disassembly. If leakage or an obvious defect is present, disassemble the cylinder head and inspect the valve seating surfaces. Cylinder head disassembly and repair requires special equipment. If this equipment is not available, entrust valve service to a machine shop. Mark or make note of the mounting location and orientation of all cylinder head components prior to removing them. Some engines are equipped with progressive rate valve springs that can only be installed in one direction. Always mark which side faces the cylinder head when removing valve springs. Inspect all applicable components as described in this chapter.

Valve leakage inspection

1. Place the cylinder head on a suitable work surface with the intake manifold ports located above the valves (**Figure 50**).

2. Observe the valves while pouring solvent or kerosene into the intake and exhaust ports.

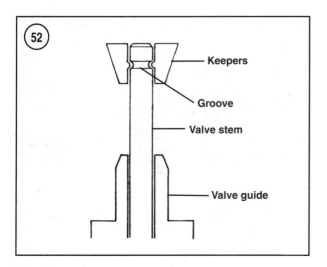

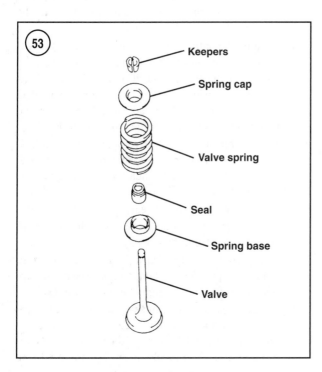

3. Disassemble the cylinder head and inspect the valves and seats if significant leakage occurs.

4. Carefully invert the cylinder head and pour the solvent from the ports.

5-15 hp models

1. Remove the cylinder head from the power head assembly as described in this chapter, then clamp the cylinder head securely into a vice with soft jaws.

2. For 9.9/15 hp models, remove the oil pump from the cylinder head as follows:

    a. Remove the three bolts securing the pump to the end of the head.

    b. Remove the pump cover, then remove and discard the O-ring.

    c. Mark the gerotor for assembly purposes, then remove the housing from the cylinder head with the gerotor and drive pin.

    d. Clean the pump cover, housing, gerotor and drive pin using solvent and inspect for damage or excessive wear. Overhaul the pump if parts are available or replace, if necessary.

3. Mark the rocker arms to ensure installation in their original positions.

4. Install the camshaft pulley bolt and washer into the end of the camshaft, then use the bolt to rotate the camshaft so each rocker arm is resting on the base of the camshaft and not the raised lobe. This is the unloaded position. With the rocker arm in the unloaded position, loosen the valve adjustment nut and back off the tappet screw a couple of turns to create additional valve lash.

NOTE
Use the OMC Tappet Adjustment Tool, (part No. 341444) to quickly and easily rotate the valve tappet screws.

5. Carefully pull the rocker arm shaft from the cylinder head while noting and removing all parts. On some models, especially the 9.9/15 hp models the shaft can be difficult to remove. Gently pry on the shaft ends while rotating the shaft back and forth slightly to loosen it.

6. Remove the camshaft from the cylinder head.

7. Remove the valves from the cylinder head as follows:

    a. Use the OMC Valve Spring Compressor (part No. 341446) or equivalent clamp type universal valve spring compressor to relieve valve spring compression. A screw type compressor (**Figure 51**) may also be used in most instances. Place one clamp of the compressor on the valve face and the other on the valve spring cap, then compress the spring just enough to remove the keepers (**Figure 52**) from the stem. *Do not* compress the spring fully.

    b. Remove the keepers, then release the spring compressor slowly. Remove the valve and valve components from the head. Repeat for each of the valves.

NOTE
*All the individual components for each valve (**Figure 53**, typical) must be kept together if reusing them. Do not intermix value components during assembly.*

8

c. Carefully pry each valve seal (**Figure 54**) from the valve guide. Discard the valve seal and springs, as OMC recommends replacing them after removing them.

d. If replacement is necessary, remove the valve spring base from the cylinder head.

8. If it is being replaced, remove the camshaft seal from the cylinder head using a slide hammer and large jaw puller.

9. Inspect and measure the cylinder head components as described in this chapter.

10. Install the valves to the cylinder head, as follows:

a. If removed, install the new valve spring base to the cylinder head.

b. Lubricate the new valve seal with engine oil and carefully press it onto the valve guide (**Figure 54**). Make sure the seal is properly seated.

c. Lubricate the valve stem with engine oil and slide it into the valve guide. Position the valve fully against the seat.

d. Position the valve spring and spring cap (**Figure 53**) over the valve stem and against the base on the cylinder head, then install the valve spring compressor over the valve and the spring cap.

e. Compress the spring just enough to fully expose the keeper groove on the valve stem (**Figure 52**). Place the keepers onto the valve stem as shown in **Figure 52**. Hold the keepers in position and slowly loosen the compressor. Inspect the keepers for proper positioning. Remove and reinstall the keepers if they are not seated within the spring caps.

f. Repeat to install the remaining valves, springs, caps and keepers.

11. Apply engine oil to the camshaft journals and lobes, then carefully slide the camshaft into the cylinder head.

12. Apply engine oil to the rocker arm shaft, rocker arm bores and rocker arm faces as well as to the tappet adjusting screws and nuts. Carefully slide the shaft into the cylinder head, positioning the rocker arms, springs, spacers and, on 9.9/15 hp models, the caps, as noted during removal. For 5/6 and 8/9.9 hp models, make sure to align the rocker shaft locating pin with the relief in the head.

CAUTION
Leave the valve lash adjusters alone until the cylinder head is installed. The tappets must remain free from contact with the valves to ensure no components are damaged during cylinder head installation and engine timing.

13. On 9.9/15 hp models, install the oil pump to the cylinder head as follows:

a. Coat the gerotor and drive pin with clean engine oil, then position them into the housing as marked during removal.

b. Coat the new O-ring with OMC Triple-Guard or equivalent marine grease, then position it in the housing.

c. Position the pump housing to the cylinder by aligning the pin and slot in the camshaft and pump drive.

d. Apply a light coating of OMC Gasket Sealing Compound or equivalent sealant to a new pump housing gasket and to the bolt threads. Install the cover and tighten to the bolt to specifications in **Table 13**.

14. On 9.9/15 hp models, if the overboard coolant indicator nipple was removed, apply a coating of OMC Gel-Seal II or equivalent to the threads, then install and tighten the nipple to specifications in **Table 13**.

15. Install a new camshaft oil seal as follows:

a. For 9.9/15 hp models, remove the camshaft sprocket key from the keyway.

b. Apply a light coating of OMC Gasket Sealing Compound or equivalent sealant to the seal case, then apply a light coating of engine oil to the seal lips.

c. Start the seal over the camshaft making sure the lips fit properly and the seal is square in the bore. Use a suitably sized seal driver (OMC part No. 342668 for 5/6 and 8/9.9 hp models or 342214 for 9.9/15 hp models) and a hammer to gently tap the seal in place. If using an OMC tool, drive the seal until the installer contacts the cylinder head.

40 and 50 hp models

1. Remove the cylinder head from the power head assembly as described in this chapter. Then place the cylinder head on a sturdy work surface with the valve side facing down.

2. Use a permanent marker to identify the mounting location and lift each tappet (**Figure 55**) from the cylinder head.

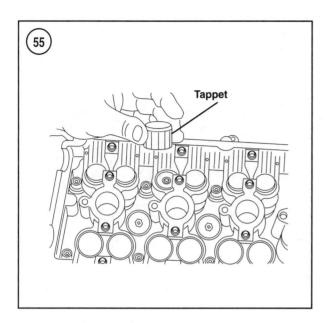

55

Tappet

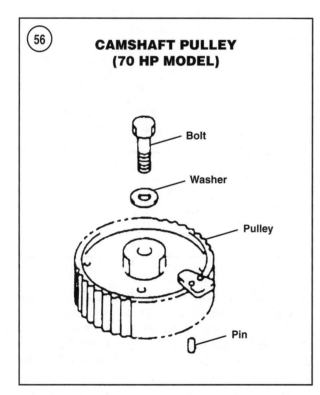

56

**CAMSHAFT PULLEY
(70 HP MODEL)**

Bolt

Washer

Pulley

Pin

3. Install a valve spring compressor over the valve and spring as indicated in **Figure 51**. Tighten the valve spring compressor enough to remove the keepers (**Figure 53**) from the valve stem.

4. Slowly loosen the valve spring compressor. Pull the valve from the cylinder head. Lift the spring cap, valve spring and spring base from the cylinder head.

5. Mark each component as removed. Remove the remaining valves from the cylinder head. Carefully pry the seal (**Figure 53**) from the valve guide.

6. Inspect and measure the cylinder head components as described in this chapter.

7. Lubricate the seal with engine oil and carefully press it onto the valve guide (**Figure 54**). Lubricate the valve stem with engine oil and slide it into the valve guide. Seat the valve against the seat.

NOTE
Make sure to install the narrow valve spring coils facing downward toward the cylinder head.

8. Place the spring base, valve spring and spring cap (**Figure 53**) onto the cylinder head. Install the valve spring compressor over the valve and the spring cap as indicated in **Figure 51**.

9. Compress the spring enough to fully expose the keeper groove on the valve stem (**Figure 52**). Place the keepers onto the valve stem. Hold the keepers in position and slowly loosen the compressor. Inspect the keepers for proper position. Remove the valve if the keepers are not seated within the spring cap. Install the remaining valves, springs, caps and keepers.

10. Lubricate the surfaces of each tappet (**Figure 55**) with engine oil and place them into their original locations in the cylinder head.

70 hp model

1. Remove the cylinder head from the power head assembly, then clamp the cylinder head securely into a vice with soft jaws.

2. Install an adjustable wrench to the hex shaped boss of the camshaft pulley (**Figure 56**) to prevent rotation.

3. Remove the bolt and washer (**Figure 56**) from the pulley. Lift the pulley and pin from the camshaft.

4. Remove the ten screws and lift the rocker arm shaft and retainers from the cylinder head. Mark the rocker arms and springs to identify the mounting locations while removing them from the shafts.

5. Locate the two bolts within the camshaft opening on the pulley side of the cylinder head. Remove the bolts and the camshaft thrust plate from the cylinder head.

6. Remove the seal from the camshaft bore as follows:

   a. Use a pick or scribe to bore a small hole in the oil seal body.

   b. Thread an appropriately sized screw into the hole.

   c. Grip the screw with pliers and pull the seal from the bore.

8

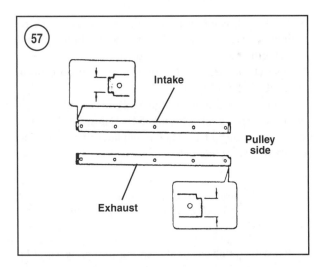

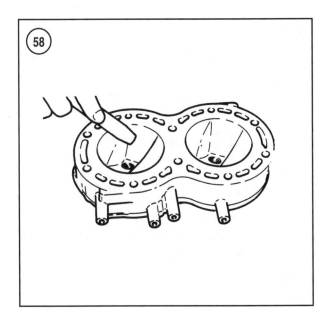

7. Carefully pull the camshaft from the bore on the pulley side of the head.

8. Install a valve spring compressor over the valve and spring as indicated in **Figure 51**. Tighten the valve spring compressor enough to remove the keepers (**Figure 53**) from the valve stem.

9. Slowly loosen the valve spring compressor. Pull the valves from the cylinder head. Lift the spring cap, valve spring and spring base from the cylinder head.

10. Mark each component while removing them. Remove the remaining three valves. Carefully pry the seal (**Figure 53**) from the valve guide.

11. Inspect and measure all cylinder head components as described in this chapter.

12. Lubricate the seal with engine oil and carefully press it onto the valve guide (**Figure 54**). Lubricate the valve stem with engine oil and slide it into the valve guide. Seat the valve against the seat.

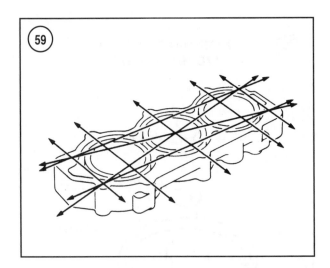

NOTE
Make sure to install the narrow valve spring coils facing downward toward the cylinder head.

13. Place the spring base, valve spring and spring cap (**Figure 53**) onto the cylinder head. Install the valve spring compressor over the valve and the spring cap as indicated in **Figure 51**.

14. Compress the spring enough to fully expose the keeper groove on the valve stem (**Figure 52**). Place the keepers onto the valve stem. Hold the keepers in position and slowly loosen the compressor. Inspect the keepers for proper position. Remove the valve if the keepers are not seated within the spring cap. Install the remaining valves, springs, caps and keepers.

15. Lubricate the camshaft with engine oil and carefully slide it into the bore at the bottom side of the cylinder head. Engage the thrust plate to the groove on the camshaft. Align the bolt opening and install the bolts into the thrust plate and cylinder head. Securely tighten the bolts.

16. Place a *new* camshaft seal into the bore with the lip facing in. Carefully press the seal into the bore with a seal driver or socket that is slightly smaller in diameter than the bore. Press the seal into place until the outer surface of the seal is approximately 0.020 in. (0.5 mm) below the bore opening surface.

17. Apply engine oil to the rocker arm shafts. Slide the rocker arms and springs onto the rocker arm shafts. Orient the notches in the shafts as shown in **Figure 57**. Place the rocker arm shafts onto the cylinder head. Install the five

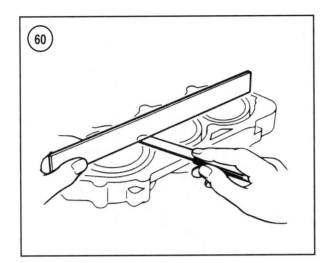

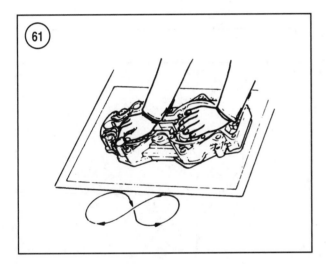

nent closely before and after cleaning as solvent may remove identification marks. Note marks before cleaning and renew marks as required. Measure all components at room temperature and use accurate measuring equipment.

When cleaning internal components, watch for unusual wear patterns, deterioration, or scuffing of components. Also, look for cracks or other damage. On bearing or journal surfaces, look for heat-related discoloration.

Cylinder head

1. Remove the carbon deposits after removing the valves from the cylinder head. See *Cylinder Head, Disassembly and Assembly* in this chapter. Avoid damaging the valve seating surface. Use a blunt tip scraper to remove deposits from the combustion chamber (**Figure 58**). Avoid scraping aluminum material from the surfaces.

2. Inspect water passages for corrosion deposits and debris. Remove debris and clean corrosion as needed.

3. Check for surface warp by placing a straightedge at various points (**Figure 59**) on the cylinder head mating surface. Hold a straightedge firmly against the head. Use a feeler gauge to check the gap at the midpoint in the straightedge. Compare the thickness of the feeler gauge that can be passed under the straightedge (**Figure 60**) with the warp limit in **Table 2**.

4. Measure the intake and exhaust manifold mating surfaces as well. True minor distortion by placing a sheet of 600-grit abrasive paper on a surfacing plate. Use slight downward pressure and move the cylinder head in a figure eight motion as shown in **Figure 61**.

5. Stop periodically and recheck the distortion. Do not remove an excessive amount of material.

6. Thoroughly clean the cylinder head with hot, soapy water and dry with compressed air.

Camshaft

Inspect the camshaft surfaces for worn or damaged surfaces (**Figure 62**). Replace the camshaft if there are defects. Perform all applicable measurements to the camshaft. Replace excessively worn components.

1. Measure the height of the camshaft lobes (**Figure 63**) with a micrometer (**Figure 64**). Record the measurement for each lobe on the camshaft. Compare the measurement with the specification in **Table 3**. Replace the camshaft if any lobe height measurement is less than the minimum specification.

2. On 40-70 hp models measure the bearing surfaces and check oil clearance as follows:

retainers and ten bolts to the rocker arm shafts. Install the shaft assemblies to the cylinder head. Tighten the retainer bolts to the specification in **Table 13**.

18. Place the pin (**Figure 57**) into the opening on the camshaft. Align the opening in the camshaft pulley with the pin while sliding the pulley onto the camshaft.

19. Install the washer and bolt (**Figure 56**) into the camshaft and pulley. Install an adjustable wrench to the hex shaped boss of the camshaft pulley to prevent rotation. Tighten the camshaft pulley bolt to the specification in **Table 13**.

Inspection

This section provides inspection and measurement instructions for the cylinder head components. Clean all components with solvent and dry them with compressed air. Clean one component at a time. Inspect each compo-

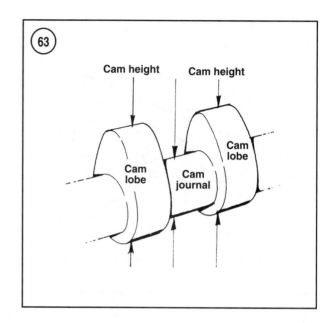

a. Measure the camshaft bearing journals (**Figure 63**) where they contact the cylinder head surface using a micrometer (**Figure 65**). Compare the measurement with the specification in **Table 4** or **Table 5**, as applicable. Replace the camshaft if the measurement is less than the minimum specification.

b. On 40 and 50 hp models install the camshaft caps as described in *Cylinder Head, Removal and Installation*.

c. Measure the camshaft bore within the cylinder head (**Figure 66**) with a micrometer. Measure the bore at each journal contact surface. Compare the measurement with the specification in **Table 4** or **Table 5**, as applicable. Replace the cylinder head if any of the bore measurements exceed the maximum specification.

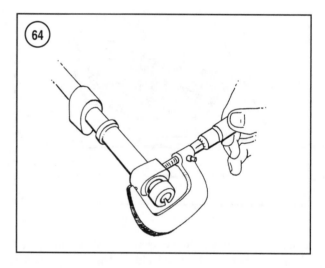

d. Determine the camshaft oil clearance by subtracting the camshaft journal diameter from its corresponding cylinder head bore diameter. Compare the clearance with the specification listed in **Table 3**. Replace the camshaft if the journal diameters are near the minimum diameter. Replace the cylinder head if excessive oil clearance exists and the camshaft diameter is within the specification.

3. On 40-70 hp models, support the camshaft with V-blocks under the top and bottom journals. Align the tip of a dial indicator with one of the middle journals (**Figure 67**). Slowly rotate the camshaft and record the camshaft runout. Replace the camshaft if the camshaft runout exceeds the specification in **Table 3**.

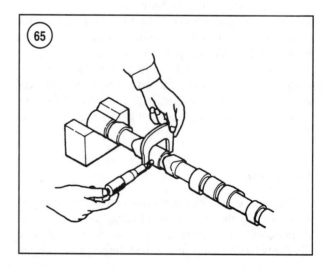

4. On 5/6 and 8/9.9 hp models, locate the compression relief pin on the side, towards the end of the shaft. Use a small, flat-bladed tool to slide the pin. It should move smoothly and without significant effort or sticking, if not, replace the camshaft assembly.

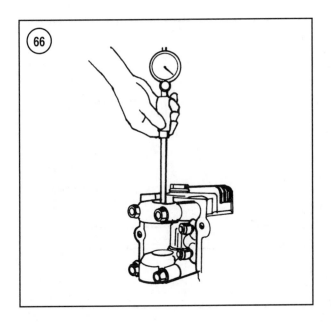

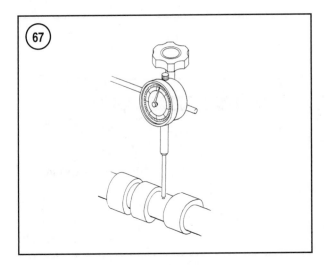

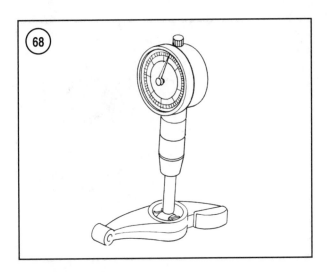

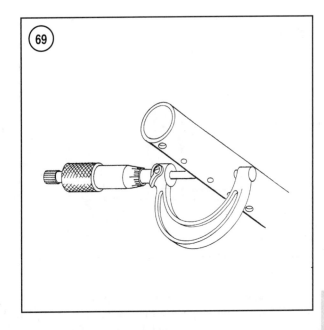

8

Rocker arms, shafts and tappets

1. Thoroughly clean and dry the rocker arm and shaft assemblies. Component usage varies by models.

2. Inspect components for obviously worn, discolored or damaged surfaces. Replace damaged or excessively worn components.

> *NOTE*
> *Some wear on the rocker arm face is normal. However, if the wear is excessive enough to show pitting on the face, replace the rocker arm.*

3. On 70 hp models check the following rocker arm and shaft dimensions:

   a. Measure the rocker arm bore diameter (**Figure 68**) with a micrometer. Replace the rocker arm if its measurement exceeds the specification in **Table 6**.

   b. Measure the rocker arm shaft at the rocker arm contact surfaces (**Figure 69**) with a micrometer. Replace the rocker arm shaft if any measurement is less than the specification in **Table 6**.

   c. Determine the shaft-to-rocker arm clearance by subtracting the rocker arm shaft diameter from the rocker arm bore diameter. Compare the clearance with the specification in **Table 6**. Replace the rocker arm shaft if its diameter is near the minimum specification. Replace the rocker arms if excessive clearance exists and the shaft diameter is within the specification.

d. Support the ends of the rocker arm shaft on V-blocks as indicated in **Figure 70**. Align the tip of a dial indicator to the middle of the shaft and record the shaft runout. Slowly rotate the rocker arm shaft. Replace the shaft if the runout exceeds the specification in **Table 6**.

4. On 40 and 50 hp models, measure the tappet and tappet bore as follows:

a. Use an outside micrometer to measure the outer diameter of the tappets. Record the measurement for each tappet.

b. Measure the tappet bore diameters in the cylinder head. Record the diameter for each tappet.

c. Compare each tappet and tappet bore diameter with the specification in **Table 6**. Replace any tappets with a measurement less than the minimum specification. Replace the cylinder head if any of the bore diameters exceed the maximum specification.

d. Determine the tappet-to-bore clearance by subtracting the tappet diameter from its corresponding bore diameter. Replace the tappet if its diameter is near the minimum specification. Replace the cylinder head if excessive clearances exist and the corresponding tappet is within the specification.

Valve components

Measurement and repairs to valves, seats and guides require specialized equipment and experience. Have a machine shop surface the valves and seats if there are worn or damaged surfaces. Perform all applicable measurements, even if a visual inspection reveals no defects.

1. Visually inspect the valve face (**Figure 71**) and valve seats (**Figure 72**) for pitted, cracked, corroded or damaged surfaces.

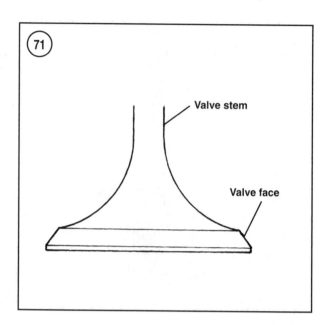

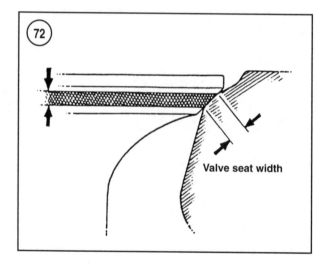

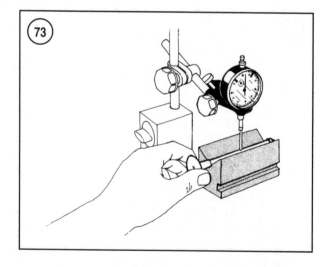

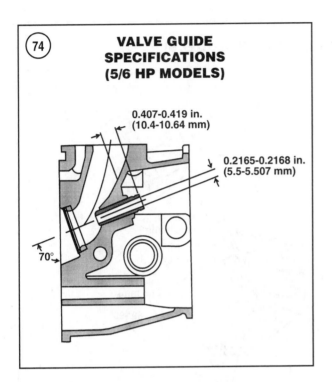

VALVE GUIDE SPECIFICATIONS (5/6 HP MODELS)

0.407-0.419 in.
(10.4-10.64 mm)

0.2165-0.2168 in.
(5.5-5.507 mm)

70°

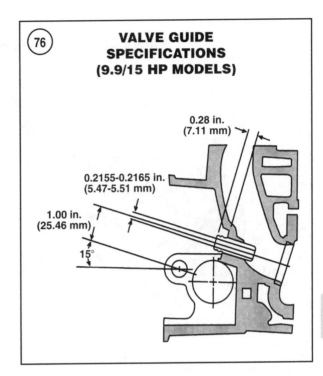

VALVE GUIDE SPECIFICATIONS (9.9/15 HP MODELS)

0.28 in.
(7.11 mm)

0.2155-0.2165 in.
(5.47-5.51 mm)

1.00 in.
(25.46 mm)

15°

8

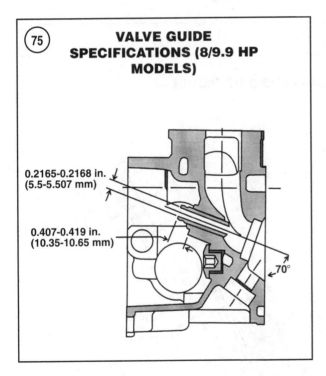

VALVE GUIDE SPECIFICATIONS (8/9.9 HP MODELS)

0.2165-0.2168 in.
(5.5-5.507 mm)

0.407-0.419 in.
(10.35-10.65 mm)

70°

the stems (**Figure 73**), but OMC does not provide a service limit for stem runout so consult a reputable machine shop for advice if runout seems excessive.

b. Make sure all carbon deposits are cleaned from the valve guides, then check the guides for contamination, damage or excessive wear. If guide replacement is necessary, refer the work to a reputable machine shop along with the specifications in **Figure 74** (5/6 hp models), **Figure 75** (8/9.9 hp models) or **Figure 76** (9.9/15 hp models).

c. Have a reputable machine shop check the valve seat concentricity referencing **Figure 77** (5/6 hp models), **Figure 78** (8/9.9 hp models) or **Figure 79** (9.9/15 hp models) and the specifications in **Table 7**.

d. No specifications are provided for the valve springs as OMC recommends replacing them whenever they are removed.

4. For 40-70 hp models proceed as follows:

a. Measure the inside diameter of the valve guides (**Figure 80**). Have a machine shop install new valve guides if the measurement exceeds the specification in **Table 8**.

b. Measure the outer diameter of the valve stems (**Figure 81**) at several locations along the length. Replace any valves with a stem diameter less than the minimum specification in **Table 8**.

2. Inspect the valve stem (**Figure 71**) for worn or damaged surfaces.

3. For 5-15 hp models, proceed as follows:

a. Check the valve stems for obvious signs of warp. V-blocks and a dial indicator can be used to check

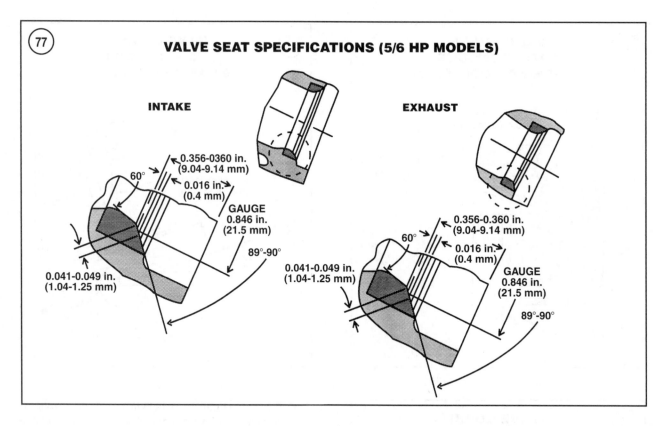

(77)

VALVE SEAT SPECIFICATIONS (5/6 HP MODELS)

INTAKE

EXHAUST

0.356-0360 in.
(9.04-9.14 mm)

60°

0.016 in.
(0.4 mm)

GAUGE
0.846 in.
(21.5 mm)

89°-90°

0.041-0.049 in.
(1.04-1.25 mm)

0.356-0.360 in.
(9.04-9.14 mm)

60°

0.016 in.
(0.4 mm)

GAUGE
0.846 in.
(21.5 mm)

0.041-0.049 in.
(1.04-1.25 mm)

89°-90°

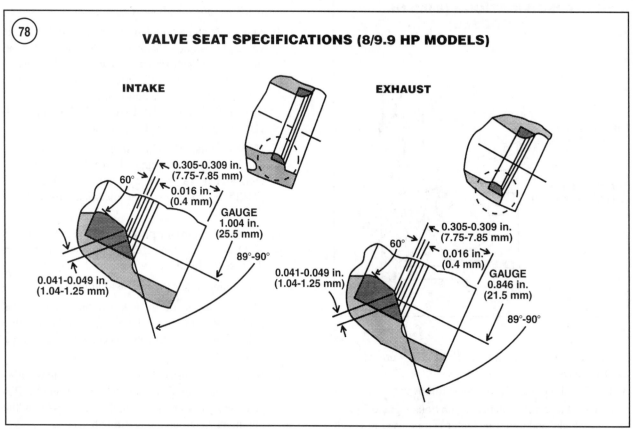

(78)

VALVE SEAT SPECIFICATIONS (8/9.9 HP MODELS)

INTAKE

EXHAUST

0.305-0.309 in.
(7.75-7.85 mm)

60°

0.016 in.
(0.4 mm)

GAUGE
1.004 in.
(25.5 mm)

89°-90°

0.041-0.049 in.
(1.04-1.25 mm)

0.305-0.309 in.
(7.75-7.85 mm)

60°

0.016 in.
(0.4 mm)

GAUGE
0.846 in.
(21.5 mm)

0.041-0.049 in.
(1.04-1.25 mm)

89°-90°

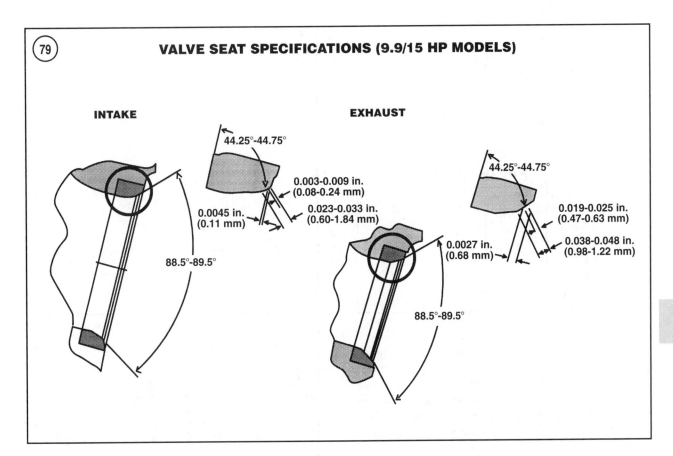

79

VALVE SEAT SPECIFICATIONS (9.9/15 HP MODELS)

INTAKE

EXHAUST

44.25°-44.75°

0.003-0.009 in.
(0.08-0.24 mm)

0.0045 in.
(0.11 mm)

0.023-0.033 in.
(0.60-1.84 mm)

88.5°-89.5°

44.25°-44.75°

0.019-0.025 in.
(0.47-0.63 mm)

0.0027 in.
(0.68 mm)

0.038-0.048 in.
(0.98-1.22 mm)

88.5°-89.5°

8

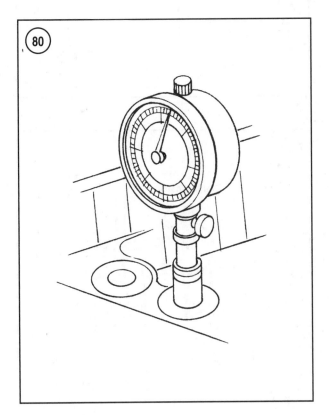

80

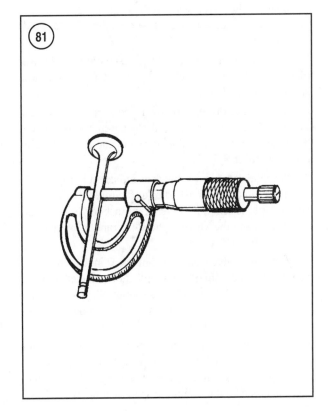

81

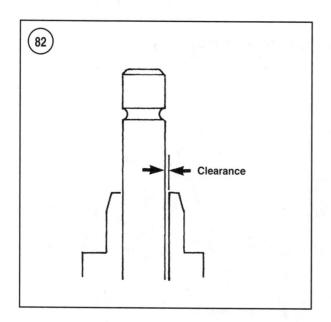

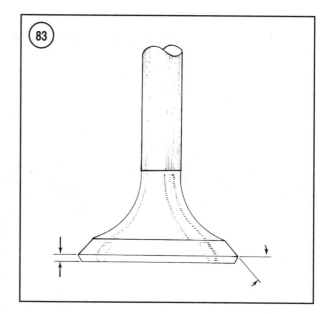

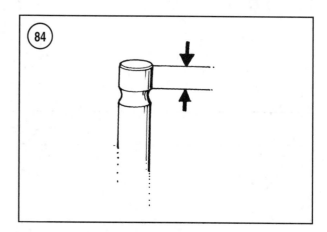

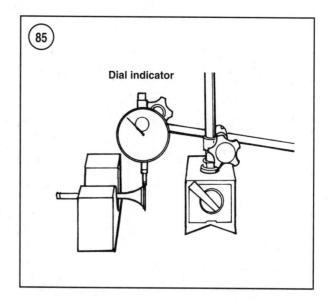

5. Determine the valve stem-to-guide clearance (**Figure 82**) by subtracting the valve stem diameter from the corresponding valve guide diameter. Compare the clearance with the specification in **Table 8**. Replace the corresponding valve if its diameter is near the minimum specification, otherwise have the valve guide replaced at a machine shop.

6. Measure the valve seat width (**Figure 72**). Have the valve seat surfaced at a machine shop if the width exceeds the specification in **Table 8**.

7. Measure the valve head thickness (**Figure 83**). Replace the valve if the thickness is less than the minimum specification in **Table 8**.

8. Measure the distance between the keeper groove and the end of the valve stem (**Figure 84**). Replace the valve if the measurement is less than the stem end length specification in **Table 8**.

9. Place the valve in a V-block as indicated in **Figure 73**. Align the tip of a dial indicator to the middle of the stem and record the amount of stem runout. Slowly rotate the valve. Replace the valve if the stem runout exceeds the specification in **Table 8**.

10. Place the valve stem in a V-block as indicated in **Figure 85**. Align the tip of a dial indicator to the edge of the valve and record the valve head runout. Slowly rotate the valve. Replace the valve if the head radial runout exceeds the specification in **Table 8**.

11. Use a caliper (**Figure 86**) to measure the valve spring free length (**Figure 87**). Do not compress the spring during the measurement. Replace the spring if the measurement is less than the minimum specification in **Table 8**.

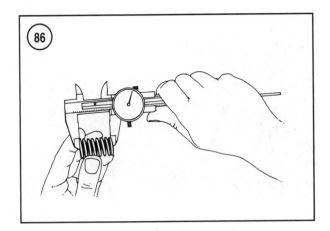

86

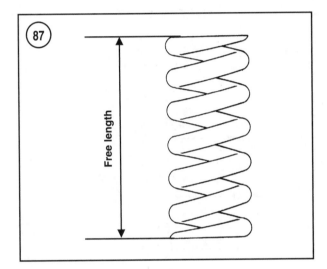

87

Free length

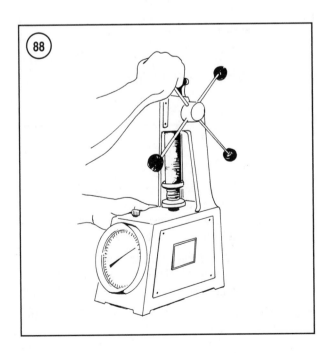

88

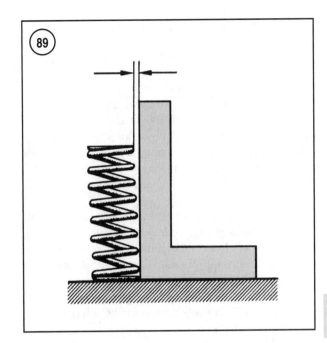

89

12. Measure the valve spring tension (**Figure 88**) or have a machine shop perform the procedure. Compress the spring to the height indicated in **Table 8**. Replace the spring if the spring tension is less than the minimum specification.

13. Place the valve spring on a flat surface. Use a square to measure the amount the spring is out of square (**Figure 89**). Replace the valve spring if the measurement exceeds the specification in **Table 8**.

CYLINDER BLOCK COMPONENT REMOVAL

The number and appearance of the cylinder block mounted components vary by model; however, the repair procedures for many are similar. Model specific instructions are provided when applicable.

To reduce the chance of improper assembly, take photographs or make drawings indicating the hose routing and connection points prior to removing any components from the block.

Take all necessary steps to mark the mounting location and orientation of components before removing them. Bearing, piston and ring sizes can vary from one cylinder to the next. Improper clearances can occur if components from one cylinder are installed in another cylinder.

WARNING
Wear safety glasses when removing or installing the flywheel or other components of the engine. Never use a hammer or other tools without wearing safety glasses.

8

Thermostat Removal and Installation

The mounting location for the thermostat varies by model.

On 5/6 hp models, the thermostat is located beneath a round cover that is secured to the rear, top port side of the cylinder head. Refer to *Cylinder Head, Removal and Installation* for service procedures on the above models.

On 8/9.9 hp models, the thermostat is located beneath a round cover that is secured to the rear port side of the cylinder head, toward the top, immediately above the intake manifold.

On 9.9/15 hp models, the thermostat is located beneath a cover on the upper rear starboard side of the cylinder block, slightly in front of the ignition coil and starboard of the engine lifting bracket along the cylinder block-to-cylinder head split line.

On 40 and 50 hp models, the thermostat is located beneath a cover (**Figure 90**) on the top of the power head behind the lifting hook.

On 70 hp models, the thermostat is located beneath a cover (**Figure 91**) on the upper rear and starboard side of the power head.

1. If necessary, disconnect the hose from the fitting on the thermostat cover.

> *NOTE*
> *On some models the cover may be removed with the hose attached, provided that the cover can be positioned aside without damaging the hose or connected components.*

2. Some covers can be installed in different directions. Note the orientation of the cover hose fitting, then remove the bolts (40-70 hp models) or Torx head screws (9.9/15 hp models) from the cover.

3. Use a plastic mallet to tap the cover loose from the cylinder block.

   a. On 9.9/15 hp models, remove and discard the gasket from the cover or cylinder block, then remove the thermostat assembly from the block housing.

   b. On 40 and 50 hp models, lift the thermostat from the recess in the cylinder block.

   c. On 70 hp models remove the gasket (**Figure 91**) from the cover or cylinder block. Lift the seat, thermostat and seal from the recess in the cylinder block.

4. Test the thermostat as described in Chapter Two. Replace the thermostat if corroded or damaged or if it tests incorrectly. Clean all corrosion from the thermostat cover, bolt threads and the recess in the cylinder block.

5. Installation is the reverse of removal. Note the following:

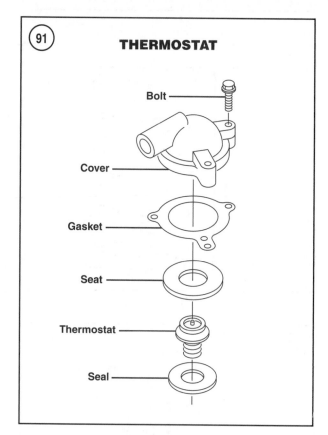

   a. Replace all O-rings, gaskets and seals.

   b. On 9.9/15 hp models, apply a coating of OMC Gasket Sealing Compound or equivalent sealant to both sides of the new thermostat housing gasket and to the threads of the retaining screws.

   c. On 40-70 hp models, place the thermostat into the cylinder block with the spring and copper plug side into the cylinder block.

   d. Tighten the cover bolts to the specification in **Table 13**.

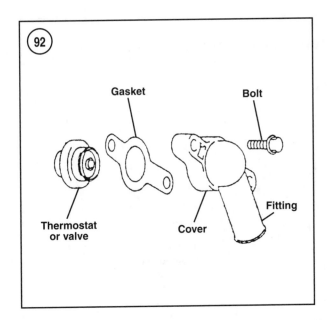

92

Gasket   Bolt

Fitting

Thermostat
or valve   Cover

e. If removed, slip the hose over the fitting and secure the hose with the clamp.
6. Check for proper cooling system operation.

Water Pressure Relief Valve (70 hp Model)

The water pressure relief valve is located beneath a cover (**Figure 92**) on the upper starboard side of the cylinder block and just in front of the exhaust manifold.

Refer to Chapter Eleven for replacement instructions on 40 and 50 hp models.

1. Remove the hose from the fitting on the cover (**Figure 92**). Note the orientation of the hose fitting and remove the bolts from the cover.
2. Use a plastic mallet to tap the cover loose from the cylinder block.
3. Use needlenose pliers to pull the valve from the cylinder block. Clean corrosion or other contaminants from the valve, bolt threads and the recess in the cylinder block.
4. Inspect the valve for corroded, worn or damaged surfaces. Inspect the spring within the valve for corrosion damaged loops or debris. Replace the valve if there are any defects.
5. Place the valve into the recess with the valve oriented as shown in **Figure 92**. Coat the surfaces with OMC Gasket Sealing Compound or an equivalent sealant and place a *new* gasket on the cover. Install the cover with the fitting oriented as noted prior to removal.
6. Install the cover bolts and tighten them to the specification in **Table 13**. Slip the hose onto the fitting and secure it with the clamp. Check for proper cooling system operation.

Exhaust Manifold and Water Jacket (70 hp Model)

The fasteners for these components are often corroded. Corroded fasteners can be quite difficult to remove. Avoid using excessive force if a fastener is seized. Apply a liberal coating of penetrating lubricant such as WD-40 or PB Blaster and allow time for it to penetrate, then use a driver and a hammer to apply a few sharp blows to the bolt heads. Use patience and, if necessary, refer to Chapter One for tips on removing stubborn or broken fasteners.

Loosen bolts 1/4 turn at a time using a crisscross pattern starting at the ends of the manifold/cover assembly and working toward the center. This reduces the chance of cover distortion.

If it is necessary to pry the cover loose from the cylinder block, use a blunt tipped pry bar and pry on the pry bar notches located on the top and bottom mating surfaces. Using excessive force, working with sharp tools, or prying on surfaces other than the provided notches can damage the mating surfaces.

1. Disconnect the water stream hose from the fitting on the bottom of the manifold/cover (12, **Figure 93**). Gradually loosen the eight bolts and four nuts using a crisscross pattern starting at the ends of the manifold and working toward the center.
2. Carefully pry the manifold/cover from the cylinder block. Remove all the gasket material (14, **Figure 93**) from the cover and cylinder block.
3. Remove the plug and gasket (9 and 10, **Figure 93**) from the manifold/cover. Pull the nine plugs (13, **Figure 93**) from the openings in the manifold/cover.
4. Remove the two bolts (4, **Figure 93**) and pull the anode cover (5) and gasket from the manifold/cover.
5. Inspect the anode (7, **Figure 93**) for deep pitting or corrosion. Remove the screw (8, **Figure 93**) and replace the anode as needed.
6. Thoroughly clean the cover-to-cylinder block mating surfaces. Use a thread chaser to clean corrosion from the bolts.
7. Install the nine plugs (13, **Figure 93**) into the corresponding openings in the manifold/cover. Place a *new* gasket (14, **Figure 93**) onto the cover. Slide the cover over the studs and seat it against the cylinder block. Install the bolts and nuts and tighten them gradually in multiple passes using a crisscross pattern starting at the center of the manifold and working toward the ends. On the last pass of the sequence, tighten the bolts to the specification in **Table 13**.
8. Install the gasket and plug (9, **Figure 93**). Place a *new* gasket on the anode cover (5, **Figure 93**) and install it into the manifold/cover (12). Securely tighten the bolts.

8

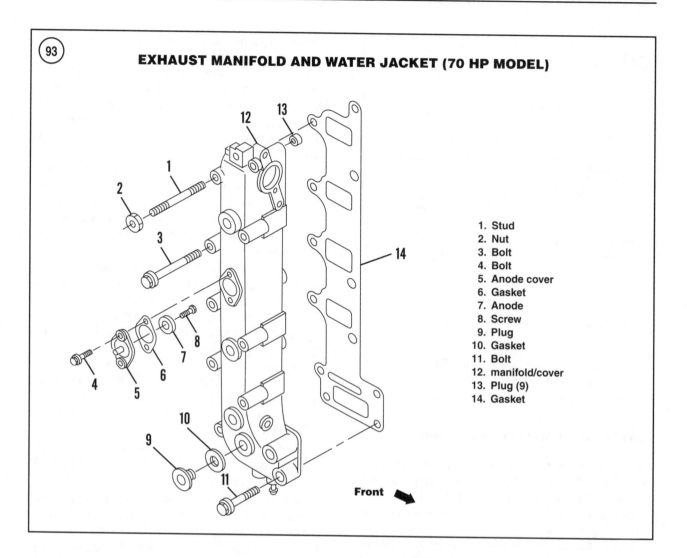

93

EXHAUST MANIFOLD AND WATER JACKET (70 HP MODEL)

1. Stud
2. Nut
3. Bolt
4. Bolt
5. Anode cover
6. Gasket
7. Anode
8. Screw
9. Plug
10. Gasket
11. Bolt
12. manifold/cover
13. Plug (9)
14. Gasket

Front ➤

9. Connect the water stream hose to the fitting on the bottom of the manifold/cover. Secure the hose with the clamp.

Crankshaft Sprocket Pulley Removal and Installation (70 hp Model)

This section provides removal and installation instructions for the crankshaft pulley on 70 hp models. For 5-15 hp models, refer to the *Cylinder Head, Removal and Installation* procedure in this chapter. On 40 and 50 hp models the timing sprocket is integrated into the crankshaft.

CAUTION
Do not allow any crankshaft rotation if removing the crankshaft pulley with the cylinder head installed. Damage to the valves and pistons is likely to occur.

Use an OMC crankshaft holder (part No. 345827) or equivalent tool designed to fit over the crankshaft taper and keyway to hold the crankshaft from turning for this procedure.

1. Remove the flywheel and the timing belt as detailed in this chapter.

2. Place the flywheel key into the slot in the crankshaft. Align the slot in the crankshaft adapter (**Figure 94**) with the key and seat the adapter to the crankshaft taper.

3. Place a wrench on the flywheel nut as shown in **Figure 94**. Hold the crankshaft adapter stationary with a socket and breaker bar and loosen the nut.

4. Remove the nut and washer from the crankshaft. Remove the flywheel key from the crankshaft. Lift the upper guide plate, pulley and lower guide plate (**Figure 95**) from the crankshaft. Remove the pulley key from the crankshaft.

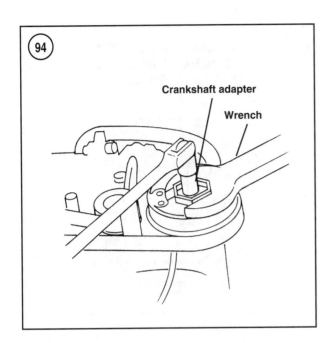

Crankshaft adapter

Wrench

(94)

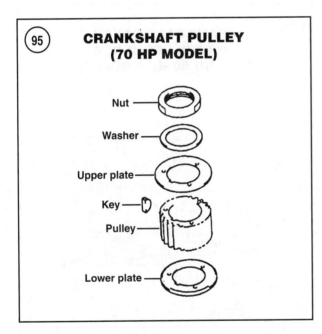

**CRANKSHAFT PULLEY
(70 HP MODEL)**

(95)

Nut

Washer

Upper plate

Key

Pulley

Lower plate

5. Clean all contaminants from the crankshaft taper with a shop towel soaked with oil. Inspect the pulley and plates for worn or damaged surfaces and replace as needed.

6. Place the lower guide plate onto the crankshaft with the curved edge facing the cylinder block. Place the pulley key into the crankshaft slot.

7. Align the slot in the pulley with the key while placing it onto the crankshaft. Rotate the lower guide plate to align the openings with the protrusion on the bottom of the pul-

ley. Seat the pulley and lower guide plate on the crankshaft.

8. Place the upper plate on the pulley with the curved edge facing away from the cylinder block. Rotate the plate to align the openings with the protrusions on the top side of the pulley. Seat the plate against the pulley.

9. Place the washer (**Figure 95**) onto the crankshaft with the concave side facing the upper plate. Thread the nut onto the crankshaft.

10. Place the flywheel key into the slot in the crankshaft. Align the slot in the crankshaft adapter (**Figure 94**) with the key and seat the adapter to the crankshaft taper.

11. Place a wrench on the flywheel nut as shown in **Figure 94**. Hold the crankshaft adapter stationary with a socket and breaker bar. Tighten the nut to the specification in **Table 13**.

12. Install the timing belt and flywheel as described in this chapter.

8

CYLINDER BLOCK DISASSEMBLY

Remove the flywheel and cylinder head as described in this chapter. Remove all fuel, electrical and ignition system components as described in this manual. Remove any remaining brackets or linkage from the cylinder block. Place the cylinder block on a sturdy work surface with the cylinder head side down.

NOTE
Keep components organized by cylinder as they are removed. Use a scratch awl or an ink marker that can withstand solvent cleaning.

Crankcase Cover

5/6 hp models

The design of the single cylinder 5/6 hp engines secures the crankshaft through the crankcase cover. For this reason, remove the piston and connecting rod before the cover is unbolted and separated from the case. Refer to the *Crankshaft, Pistons, Rods and Bearings* procedure.

8-70 hp models

1. On 40 and 50 hp models remove the five bolts and carefully pry the upper seal housing from the top of the crankcase. Note the seal lip direction and carefully pry the seal from the crankshaft.

2. Loosen the crankcase bolts (**Figure 96**) in the reverse of the tightening sequence. Refer to the following:

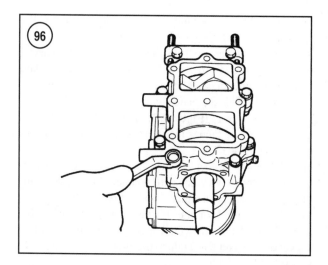

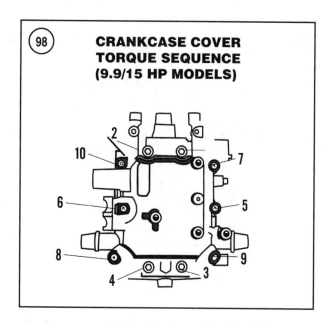

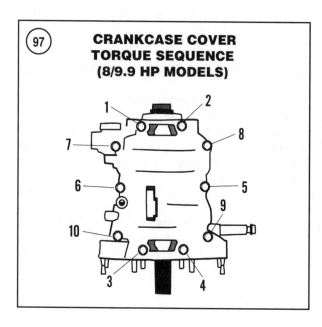

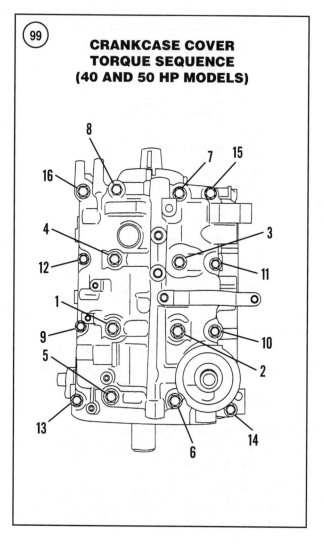

a. **Figure 97** for 8/9.9 hp models.
b. **Figure 98** for 9.9/15 hp models.
c. **Figure 99** for 40 and 50 hp models.
d. **Figure 100** for 70 hp models.

3A. For 8-15 hp models, remove the lower cover rubber mounts (9.9/15 hp models only), then tap on the lower crankcase (use the mounting bosses for the rubber mounts on 9.9/15 hp models) using a rubber or plastic mallet to break the gasket seal. Remove the crankcase cover from the block.

3B. For 40-70 hp models, locate the cast-in notches at the crankcase cover-to-cylinder block mating surfaces. Work carefully to avoid damaging the mating surfaces. Use two blunt pry bars (**Figure 101**) and apply even pressure on each side of the cylinder block and carefully pry the

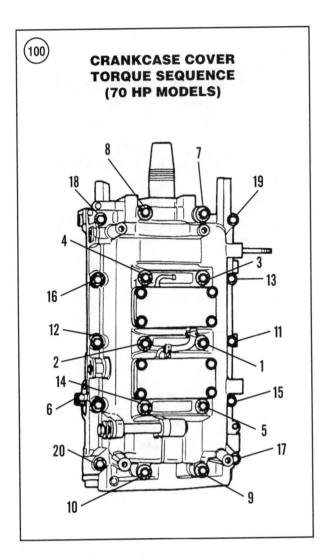

CRANKCASE COVER TORQUE SEQUENCE (70 HP MODELS)

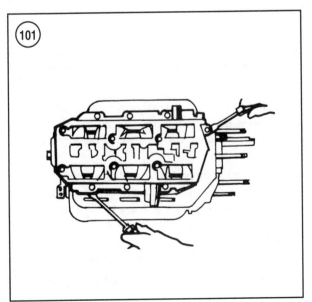

crankcase cover from the cylinder block (**Figure 102**). Note the seal lip direction and pull the oil seal(s) from the crankshaft (**Figure 103**).

Crankshaft, Pistons, Rods and Bearings

5/6 hp models

The design of the single cylinder 5/6 hp models secures the crankshaft through the middle of the crankcase cover. For this reason, remove the piston and connecting rod before the cover is unbolted and separated from the case. This procedure covers piston, crankcase cover and crankshaft removal. If only the piston requires service, follow only the steps specifically dealing with piston removal.

Modify a pair of needlenose pliers as shown in **Figure 104** to use in this procedure when removing the piston wrist pin retaining rings.

8

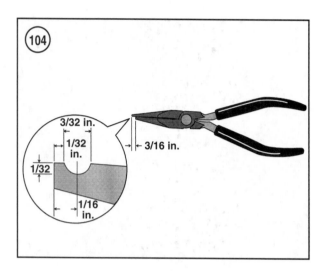

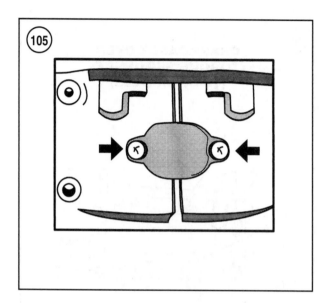

1. If necessary, remove the dowels and the water deflector from the cylinder block mating surface.

2. Remove the two Philips screws (**Figure 105**) securing the cylinder block access plate to the front of the block. Remove the plate, then remove and discard the gasket.

3. Rotate the crankshaft until the rod cap is visible through the access plate. Bend the retainer tabs back and then remove the bolts, washers, retainer and cap. Discard the retainers and cap bolts as they must be replaced any time they are removed.

4. Use a 1/4 in. (6 mm) diameter wooden dowel to gently tap on the rod, pushing the piston and rod up and out of the block. While pushing, *do not* allow the rod to contact and damage the cylinder wall.

CAUTION
The rod end cap is specifically matched to the rod. Do not attempt to replace or use one without using the matched pair.

5. Matchmark the connecting rod to the piston to ensure installation with the same alignment.

6. Use a universal piston ring expander to remove the piston rings. Discard all the rings. Do not reuse them.

7. Use a pair of modified needlenose pliers (**Figure 104**) to remove the wrist pin retaining rings from the piston (**Figure 106**).

8. Use a suitable driver such as the OMC Wrist Pin Removal/Installation tool (part No. 342657) to carefully tap the wrist pin from the piston.

NOTE
The wrist pin-to-piston boss fit is loose on both sides and excessive force should not be necessary to remove the wrist pin.

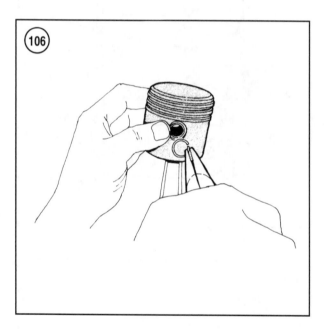

9. Remove the six crankcase cover-to-cylinder block screws using the reverse of the torque sequence (**Figure 107**) and, if not done earlier, remove the key from the crankshaft.

10. Using two small prybars, carefully pry on the bosses located near bolts 3 and 4 (**Figure 107**) Break the gasket seal and separate the cover/crankshaft. If necessary, tap gently on the bottom end of the crankshaft to help separate the assembly from the block.

11. Separate the crankshaft from the cover.

12. If necessary remove the seal and bearing from the cover as follows:

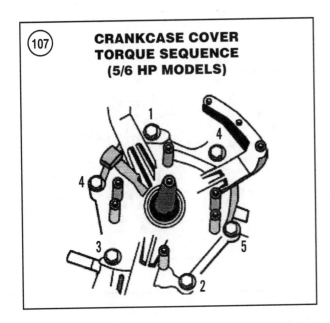

CRANKCASE COVER TORQUE SEQUENCE (5/6 HP MODELS)

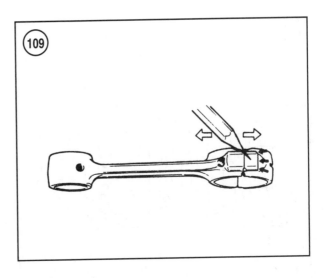

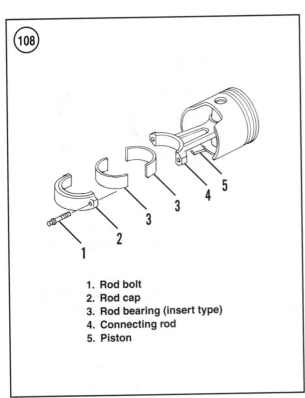

1. Rod bolt
2. Rod cap
3. Rod bearing (insert type)
4. Connecting rod
5. Piston

a. Use a slide hammer and large jaw puller on the seal lips from the front of the cover to remove the seal.

b. Support the outside of the cover facing downward on a 1 3/8 in. (35 mm) socket and use a shoppress and a 13/16 in. (21 mm) socket as a driver to slowly force the bearing out of the cover.

13. Remove the thrust washer from the inside of the center back of the block. If necessary, remove and replace any loose or damaged dowel pins.

14. If necessary, remove the seal and bearing from the block as follows:

    a. Use a slide hammer and large jaw puller on the seal lips from the outside of the block to remove the seal.

    b. Place the block with the cover mating surface facing downward and use a shop press with a 13/16 in. (21 mm) socket as a driver to slowly force the bearing out of the cover.

15. Clean and inspect the cover, block and crankshaft as detailed in this chapter. Pay particular attention to the following:

    a. Check the block mating surface for damage.

    b. Check the bearing surfaces for wear or damage.

    c. Check the oil pressure sender hole from obstructions.

    d. Remove and replace dowel pins that are loose or damaged.

    e. Check the crankshaft sleeve and, if damaged, replace using a slide hammer and a small jawed puller.

8-70 hp models

Use a felt tip marker or paint to mark the cylinder number on each piston, rod and rod cap (**Figure 108**) prior to removal. The rod cap is matched to the connecting rod, so make sure to matchmark the rod to the cap (**Figure 109**) to prevent a mix-up. For further insurance, install the cap onto the rod in the proper position immediately after removing the piston and rod from the cylinder block. Do not intermix components.

8

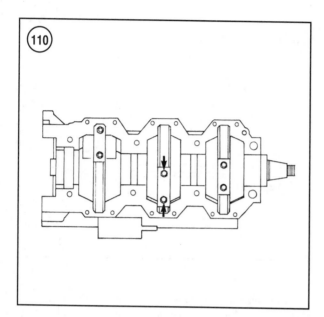

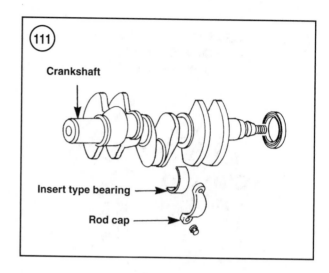

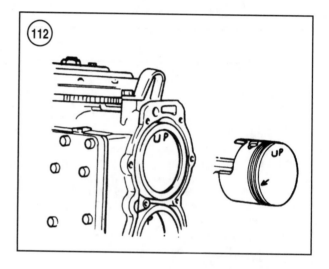

The crankshaft can be removed from the block without withdrawing the pistons. In these circumstances, the block can be placed on a work bench with the cylinder head surface facing downward. If this is attempted, take great care to prevent banging the crankshaft into the connecting rods while removing from the block. If the pistons and the crankshaft are all being removed for a complete overhaul, it is probably safer to mount the block to an engine stand so that both sides are accessible. In this way, each piston can be removed from its bore after the bearing cap is removed, leaving the crankshaft in place until all of the pistons are out of the block.

The block can also be stood on end to access both the cylinder head deck and the crankcase cover surfaces, but make sure that the crankshaft does not fall from the block while the pistons are being removed. The crankshaft could be damaged by such a fall.

1. Matchmark the rod cap-to-connecting rod mating surfaces (**Figure 109**) prior to removing the cap. Provide continuous support for the piston until removed.

2. For 8-15 hp models, bend the tabs on the connecting rod cap bolt retainers out of the way in order to remove bolts.

3. Alternately loosen each rod cap bolt or nut (**Figure 110**) in one-quarter turn increments. Remove the bolts or nuts and gently tap the rod cap loose from the connecting rod.

NOTE
On 8-15 hp models, use the rod cap bolts and retainers to temporarily hold the bearing caps to the connecting rods once the pis-

tons are removed. Replace the bolts/retainers prior to assembly.

4. Remove the rod cap and bearing (**Figure 111**) from the crankshaft. Keep the bearing with the rod cap.

CAUTION
The crankshaft can be removed by following Steps 1-4 for each of the pistons. Then, carefully push the pistons away from the crankshaft in their bores. Do not damage the crankshaft bearing surfaces through contact with the connecting rods during removal.

5. If the cylinder head deck is accessible, then remove the piston at this point. Mark the up (**Figure 112**) or front side on the piston dome prior to removal to ensure easy assembly with the piston facing the proper direction. Use a large

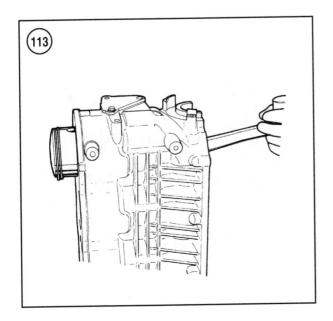

(115) **REMOVING C-TYPE LOCKRINGS**

(114) **REMOVING PISTON RINGS**

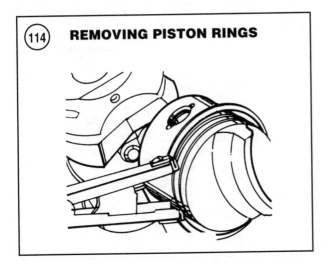

wooden dowel or hammer handle to push the piston and rod assembly from the cylinder block (**Figure 113**). Repeat Steps 1-5 for the remaining pistons.

CAUTION
When removing the pistons take great care to prevent the connecting rods from contacting and damaging the cylinder walls or the crankshaft (if still installed).

6. Carefully pry the bearings from the connecting rod and cap.

7. Carefully remove each piston ring from the piston using a universal piston ring expanding tool (**Figure 114**). Keep the rings arranged so they can be identified as top,

second and bottom rings for possible measurement or diagnostic purposes, but *do not* reuse the rings.

8. Matchmark the pistons to the connecting rods to ensure they are assembled facing the same directions.

9. On 8-15 hp models, disassemble the pistons as follows:

   a. Use a pair of modified needlenose pliers (**Figure 104**) to remove the wrist pin retaining rings from the piston (**Figure 106**).

   b. Use a suitable driver such as the OMC Wrist Pin Removal/Installation tool (part No. 342657) to carefully tap the wrist pin from the piston.

NOTE
The wrist pin-to-piston boss fit is loose on both sides and excessive force should not be necessary to remove the wrist pin.

10. On 40 and 50 hp models, disassemble the pistons and rods as follows:

   a. Use a sharp pick, needle nose pliers or a small screwdriver to remove both c-type lockrings from the pistons (**Figure 115**). Place a shop towel over the lockring and hold a finger or thumb against the lockring opening during removal to prevent the ring from springing free.

   b. Use a socket or section of tubing that is slightly smaller than the piston pin diameter to push the piston pin from the piston and rod. Refer to **Table 10** for the piston pin outer diameter.

11. On 70 hp models, the piston pin is a press fit. Remove the piston only if replacing the piston or conntecting rod. Have a machine shop remove and install the piston pin(s)

8

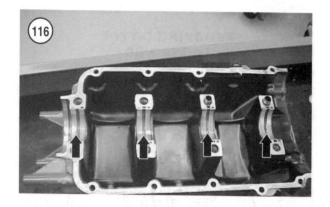

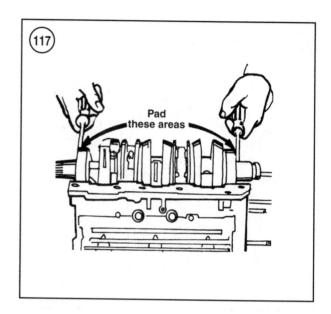

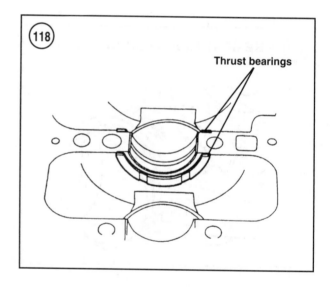

on these models. The piston is easily damaged if improper equipment or procedures are used.

12. If not done before piston removal, remove the crankshaft and bearings as follows:

CAUTION
Avoid using excessive force when removing the crankshaft from the cylinder block. Excessive force may dislodge or damage the main bearings or cause damage to the cylinder block or other components.

a. Carefully push or pry the main bearings from the crankcase cover (**Figure 116**, 40 and 50 hp model shown).

b. Carefully lift the crankshaft from the cylinder block. If necessary, provide padding to prevent damage to the mating surfaces (**Figure 117**) and carefully pry the crankshaft from the cylinder block.

c. Carefully push or pry the main bearings from the cylinder block. Identify and arrange the main bearings in order to install them in their original position.

d. On 8-15 hp models, remove and discard the crankshaft seals. Also, inspect the crankshaft sleeve for wear or damage and replace, if necessary. The sleeve can be removed using a slide hammer and a small jaw puller. Remove and discard the O-ring from the end of the crankshaft on these models.

e. On 40-70 hp models, remove the thrust bearing (**Figure 118**) from the cylinder block.

13. Clean, inspect and measure components as described in this chapter.

CYLINDER BLOCK CLEANING

When reusing any components, make sure they are installed to the same cylinder or position as they were be-

fore removal. Wear patterns form on contact surfaces during use. Maintaining the wear patterns helps ensure a durable and reliable repair.

Use compressed air to blow out all holes and passages, but always wear safety goggles for eye protection. Use the compressed air to blow loose debris from all components. Clean all components one at a time using a suitable solvent. Make sure the marks are present after cleaning or renew the mark on the component right away. Allow the solvent to drain for a few minutes and wash all components, including the cylinder block, with warm, soapy water to remove any remaining traces of solvent or contaminants. Dry the components using compressed air. After drying them, cover the components with clean

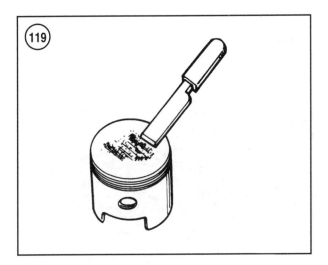

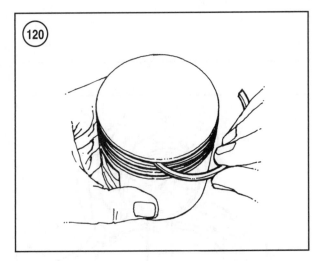

power head components. Delicate surfaces are easily damaged by a wire brush.

Pistons

Remove carbon deposits from the top of the piston with a dull chisel or a blunt scraper (**Figure 119**). Use very light force to prevent gouging or scratching of the piston. Remove any remaining carbon deposits with a Scotchbrite pad and mild solvent.

CAUTION
Never use a wire brush to remove carbon from the piston. Small steel particles may become embedded into the piston surface. These small particles promote pre-ignition or detonation damage.

8

Remove carbon from the ring grooves using a broken piece of the piston ring with an angle ground on the end as a piston groove cleaning tool (**Figure 120**). Use a top ring for the top ring groove and a second ring for the second ring groove. Using the wrong type of piston ring may result in damage to the ring groove. Apply only enough force to remove the carbon. Never allow the ring to scrape aluminum material from the groove. Commercially available tools for ring cleaning can also be used, but, be careful not to damage the grooves. Remove remaining carbon deposits with a brush and solvent. Keep the piston pin and connecting rod identified with the piston at all times.

lint-free towels to protect them from dust or debris contamination.

Cylinder Block and Exhaust Cover

Clean the cylinder block and exhaust cover with hot, soapy water and then rinse with pressurized water. Dry the cylinder block, covers and cylinder heads with compressed air. Apply engine oil to the cylinder walls to prevent corrosion.

Remove corrosion, carbon deposits or gasket material from the exhaust cover and all mating surfaces with a blunt tip scraper.

CAUTION
Never use a wire brush to remove gasket material, carbon or other deposits from the

Crankshaft and Connecting Rods

Thoroughly clean the crankshaft with solvent. Use compressed air to remove all material from the oil holes in the crankshaft. Apply a thin coating of engine oil to the crankshaft to prevent corrosion after cleaning. Wrap the crankshaft with shop towels to prevent dust contamination.

NOTE
Some minor surface corrosion, glaze-like deposits or minor scratches may be cleaned up with crocus cloth or 320-grit carburundum. Polish the surfaces only enough to remove the deposits. Excessive use can remove a considerable amount of material from the surfaces.

CYLINDER BLOCK INSPECTION AND MEASUREMENT

A considerable amount of precision measuring equipment is required for these measurements. If the proper equipment is not available, have a reputable marine machine shop perform these measurements.

All components must be clean and dry before measuring them. To ensure accurate measurements, make sure the components are at room temperature.

Use a bright light when inspecting the components for defects. Use a magnifying glass to help detect small cracks or surface imperfections.

Cylinder Block

Inspect all surfaces of the cylinder bores for cracks or deep grooves. Honing the cylinder cannot usually clean deep grooves in the cylinder bores. If deep grooves are found, either replace the cylinder block, have the cylinder bored to a larger size or have a sleeve installed in the cylinder block (as necessary). Contact a Johnson/Evinrude dealership to verify oversize piston availability prior to having the block bored or sleeved. Contact a marine dealership to locate a source for block boring or sleeving.

Check the cylinder walls for a shiny or mirror-like glazed surface that often occurs due to wear. A glazed cylinder wall prevents proper oil retention and causes some loss of compression. If the clearances are still well within tolerance a hone may be used to restore crosshatching to the cylinder walls. Boring the cylinder will be required if too much material is removed. For more details, refer to *Cylinder Bores* in this chapter.

Inspect the power head, cylinder head, exhaust cover and crankcase cover mating surfaces for cracks or other damage. Replace the cylinder block if cracked or extensively damaged. Check any dowels used on the mating surfaces for damage or looseness and replace, if necessary.

White powder-like deposits in the combustion chamber usually indicate that water is entering the combustion chamber. Inspect the cylinder walls and cylinder head dome thoroughly for cracks if this type of deposit occurs. Crack detection kits that use dies or other diagnostic applications to help find cracks are commercially available.

Inspect all bolt holes for cracks, corrosion or damaged threads. Use the proper sized tap to clean corrosion or sealant from the threads. Most damaged holes can be successfully repaired with threaded inserts. Pay particular attention to the cylinder head bolt holes. Replace the cylinder block if corrosion has extensively damaged the threaded holes. Damaged and subsequently repaired bolt

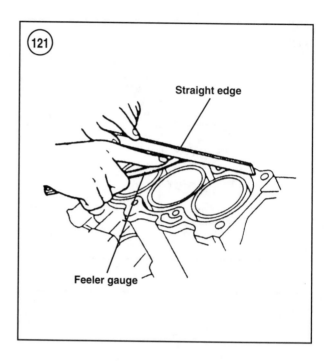

Straight edge

Feeler gauge

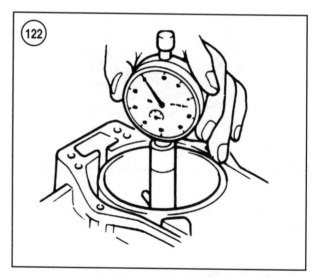

holes may fail, causing water leakage, overheating and extensive damage to other power head components.

NOTE
The cylinder block and crankcase cover are a matched assembly. Replace the assembly if either portion requires replacement.

Mating Surfaces

Measure the amount of warp at the cylinder head (**Figure 121**), cylinder block (40-70 hp models) and intake

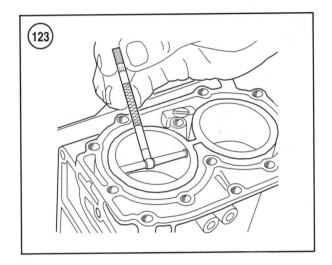

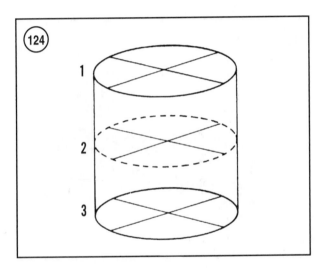

Cylinder Bores

Measure the cylinders with a cylinder bore gauge (**Figure 122**) or telescoping gauges (**Figure 123**). Have a machine shop or marine dealership perform this measurement if the tools are not available. Make certain of all measurements.

1. Lightly hone the cylinder bore to remove any glazing prior to measuring the bore diameter. Clean the cylinder block as described in this chapter.

2. Measure the cylinder bores at a depth of about 1.96 in. (50 mm) below the cylinder head deck. Have the cylinder bored and install an oversize piston if the cylinder bore measurement exceeds maximum bore diameter.

3. Measure the cylinder bore at a depth midway between the indicated measuring depth and the cylinder head mating surface. Measure the bore at a depth midway between the indicated measuring depth and the bottom of the cylinder bore. Take measurements at 90° angles at each depth. Record each measurement.

4. Determine the cylinder taper by subtracting the smallest diameter measured near the bottom of the bore (3, **Figure 124**) from the largest diameter measured near the top of the bore (1).

5. Compare the measurements taken at each depth location. The difference in the measurements taken at each position indicates the out-of-round measurement.

6. Have the cylinder bored and install an oversize piston if the cylinder taper or out–of–round measurement exceeds the specifications in **Table 9**.

7. Oversized pistons are available from a Johnson/Evinrude dealership or from many aftermarket manufacturers. Refer to the specification in **Table 9** for standard oversize piston availability, but always confirm part availability with a dealership and obtain the actual parts prior to boring. Have a reputable machine shop bore the cylinder. Due to manufacturing variances, purchase the oversize pistons and provide them to the machinist prior to boring the cylinder. This allows cylinder boring to a diameter that provides the proper piston–to–cylinder clearance. Specifications are in **Table 9**.

NOTE
The manufacturer does not provide piston clearance specifications for 5-15 hp models. For these models, visually inspect the pistons for obvious wear and replace if necessary. Make sure that the cylinder bore dimensions meet specification or oversize bore specifications, as applicable for the cylinder being used.

manifold (40-50 hp models) mating surfaces. Lay the straightedge across multiple locations on the clean and dry surfaces. Hold the straightedge firmly against the surface and use a feeler gauge to check for a gap at the midpoint of the straightedge. Replace or true components if the distortion exceeds the specification in **Table 2**. True the cylinder head, block or intake manifold, as follows:

1. Place a sheet of 600-grit abrasive paper on a surface plate.

2. Use slight downward pressure and move the component in a figure eight motion.

3. Stop periodically and check the amount of warp. Work slowly and check the work often to avoid removing an excessive amount of material.

4. Thoroughly clean the component with hot, soapy water and dry with compressed air.

5. Have a machine shop perform this operation if a suitable surface plate is not available.

8. Replace the cylinder block or have it sleeved if boring and installing oversized pistons cannot result in a piston–to–cylinder clearance within the specification range listed in **Table 10** for 40-70 hp models. For 5-15 hp models, sleeving may be an option if the bore is worn beyond the specification and oversize limit. Refer to a reputable marine machine shop for options.

Crankshaft

Inspect the crankshaft bearing surfaces for cracks, corrosion etching or discolored surfaces. Also check for rough surfaces or transferred bearing material. Replace the crankshaft if any of these defects occur. Perform the following measurements while noting that not every measurement described is required for 5-15 hp models. Refer to **Table 12** to determine which measurements are required on each model.

1. For 40-70 hp models, support the crankshaft with the upper and lower bearing surfaces resting on V-blocks or in a machine lathe as shown in **Figure 125**. Measure the crankshaft runout as follows:

   a. Mount a dial indicator so its plunger contacts one of the center main bearing journals as shown in **Figure 125**.

   b. Slowly rotate the crankshaft while observing the dial indicator. Record the total amount of dial indicator needle movement. Repeat at the remaining center main bearing.

   c. Replace the crankshaft if the runout exceeds the specification in **Table 12**.

2. Use an outside micrometer to measure the diameter of each crankpin (**Figure 126**). Replace the crankshaft if any measurement is less than the minimum specification in **Table 12**.

3. For 40-70 hp models measure the crankpins, as follows:

   a. Measure the diameter of each crankpin again at various points along the width of the crankpin to determine the taper. Record the measurements for each crankpin, then subtract the smallest measurement from the largest and compare that the to specification in **Table 12** for taper. Replace the crankshaft if taper exceeds the specification for maximum allowable difference in measurements.

   b. Measure the diameter of each crankpin again at 90° intervals around the crankpin. Record all four measurements for each crankpin, then subtract the smallest measurement from the largest and compare that to the specification in **Table 12** for out-of-round. Replace the crankshaft if

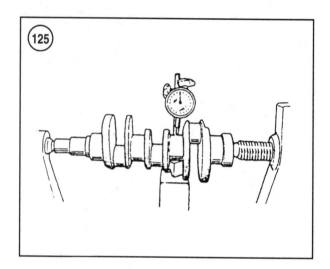

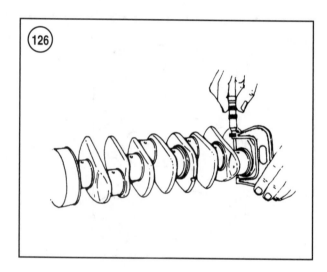

out-of-round exceeds the specification for maximum allowable difference in measurements.

   c. Use a machinist ruler or dial caliper to measure the width of the crankpin. Replace the crankshaft if the journal width is less than the minimum specification in **Table 12**.

4. Use an outside micrometer and measure the diameter of the main bearing journals in the same manner as the crankpin journals.

   a. Replace the crankshaft if any of the measurements are less than the minimum specification in **Table 12**.

   b. On 40-70 hp models, determine the bearing journal taper by subtracting the smallest measurement along the width from the largest measurement.

   c. On 40-70 hp models, determine the bearing journal out-of-round by subtracting the smallest measure-

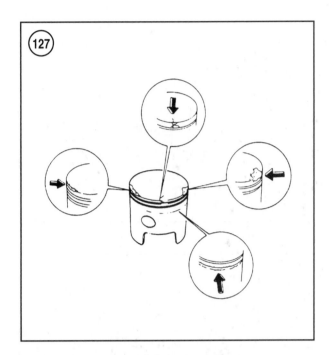

ment of the bearing journal from the largest measurement.

   d. On 40-70 hp models, replace the crankshaft if the bearing journal taper or out-of-round measurement exceeds the maximum specification in **Table 12**.

Piston

   Inspect the pistons for eroded surfaces at the edge of the dome, cracks near the ring grooves and cracks or missing portions in the piston dome (**Figure 127**). Inspect the piston for erosion in the ring groove and scoring or scuffing on the piston skirt (**Figure 128**). Replace the piston if any of these defects occur.

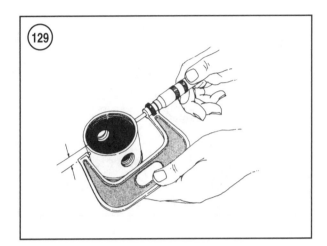

NOTE
The manufacturer does not provide piston specifications for 5-15 hp models. For these models, visually inspect the pistons, wrist pins and connecting rods for obvious wear or damage and replace if necessary. For piston clearance, ensure that the cylinder bore dimensions meet specification or oversize bore specifications, as applicable for the cylinder being used.

40-70 hp models

1. Measure the diameter of the piston at a point 90° from the piston pin bore (**Figure 129**) and at the specified distance from the bottom of the skirt (**Table 10**). Record the measurements for each piston. Replace the piston if the measurement is above or below the specification in **Table 10**. The specification does not apply if using oversize pistons.

2. Measure the piston pin bore diameter at both sides of the piston (**Figure 130**). Replace the piston if the measurements do not fall within the specification in **Table 10**.

3. Measure each piston pin diameter (**Figure 131**). Take the measurements at several locations along the length of the piston pin. Record the maximum and minimum diameters. Replace the piston pin if the measurements do not meet the specification in **Table 10**.

4. Determine the piston pin–to–pin bore clearance by subtracting the largest piston pin diameter measurement from the smallest pin bore measurement. Compare the clearance measurement with the limit specification in **Table 10**. Remeasure the pin and bore if an incorrect clearance exists. Replace the piston and pin if all measurements are correct yet an incorrect clearance exists.

8

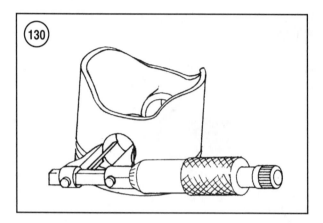

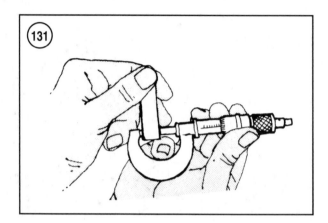

5. Measure the width of the ring grooves (**Figure 132**). Select the feeler gauge thickness that passes in the groove with a slight drag. Replace the piston if the measured groove width exceeds the specification in **Table 10**.

6. Determine the piston-to-cylinder clearance by subtracting the piston diameter from the smallest bore diameter (**Figure 133**). Have the cylinder bored and install an oversize piston if the clearance is not within the specification in **Table 10**.

Piston Rings

Perform all measurements using new piston rings. Keep the rings organized in order to install them in the correct cylinder.

1. For 40-70 hp models, measure the thickness (**Figure 134**) of the top two rings. Verify the part number and the mounting position if the measurements do not meet the specification in **Table 11**. Do not use rings with an incorrect thickness.

2. Measure the installed ring gap for the top two rings on each cylinder after confirming the cylinder bore and piston diameters are correct. Measure the ring gap as follows:

    a. Apply a light coating of oil to the cylinder bore to prevent scuffing.

    b. Carefully compress and install the ring into the top of the bore.

    c. Use a piston without rings (**Figure 135**) and slowly push the new ring to a squared position approximately 1 in. (25.4 mm) from the bottom of the bore.

    d. Measure the ring gap (**Figure 136**) using a feeler gauge. The installed ring gap equals the thickness of the feeler gauge that passes through the gap with a slight drag.

    e. Repeat these steps to measure the gap of each piston ring gap. Measure the cylinder bore again if the gap

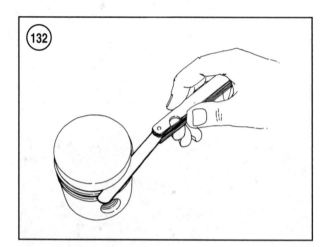

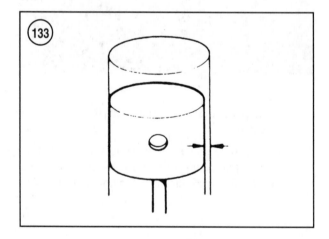

exceeds the specification in **Table 11**. Also try a different ring. Verify that the correct rings are used if an incorrect measurement persists. Do not use rings with an incorrectly installed end gap.

    f. Tag or mark the rings for the cylinder in which they were measured for installation purposes.

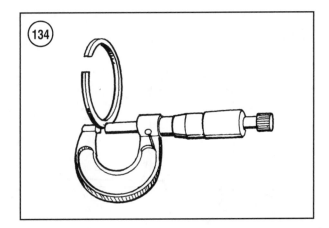

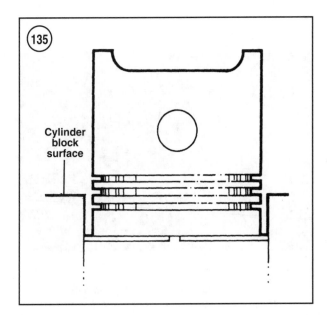

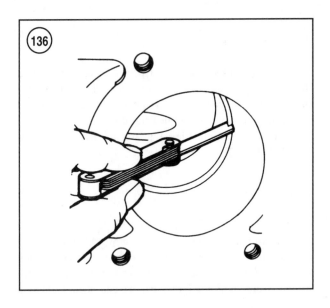

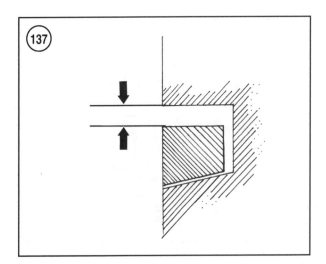

3. Measure the piston compression ring–to–groove clearance as follows:

    a. Temporarily install the top two rings onto the piston as described in *Cylinder Block Assembly*.

    b. Measure the gap between the piston ring and ring groove (**Figure 137**). The ring-to-groove clearance equals the thickness of the feeler gauge that passes through the gap with a slight drag.

    c. Compare the measured clearance with the specification in **Table 11**. Verify the ring part number and mounting position if the clearance is incorrect. Again measure the piston ring thickness and ring groove width to determine the need to replace the piston or ring.

4. For 5-15 hp models, install the rings onto the piston and position a machinist's straight edge along the side of the piston from the skirt to the dome. The rings should not hold the straight edge away from the piston. If they do, remove the rings and clean additional carbon from the grooves or make sure the rings are correct.

Connecting Rods

Visually inspect the connecting rods for bent, twisted, or damaged surfaces. Also inspect the rod for discoloration, rough surfaces or transferred bearing material. Replace the connecting rod if any defects occur.

> *NOTE*
> *The manufacturer does not provide connecting rod specifications for 5-15 hp models other than the connecting rod crankpin specifications covered under Crankshaft inspection. For these models, visually inspect the pistons, wrist pins and connecting rods*

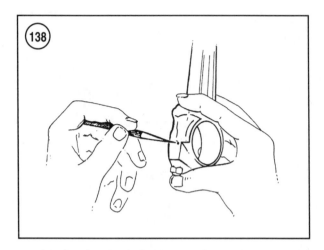

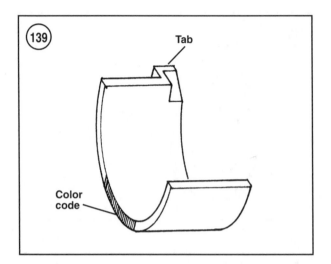

for obvious wear or damage and replace if necessary.

40-70 hp models

1. Place the rod cap onto the rod and align the reference marks (**Figure 138**). Do not install the bearings. Install and securely tighten the rod bolts or nuts. Measure the crankpin big end bore diameter.
2. Measure the width of the connecting rod at the crankpin end.
3. Temporarily install the connecting rod to the crankpin. Use a feeler gauge to check the rod-to-crankshaft side clearance.
4. Compare the measurements with the specifications in **Table 12**. Replace the rod if any of the measurements exceed specification.

Rod and Main Bearings

Inspect the insert type rod and main bearing (**Figure 139**, 40-70 hp model shown) for highly polished, discolored or rough surfaces. Replace the bearings unless in good condition. Bearings are inexpensive compared to the damage caused if they fail.

Unless replacing the crankshaft or cylinder block, purchase main bearings of the same size and type. On 40-70 hp models, purchase one with the same color code mark (**Figure 139**) as the original bearing. Refer to *Bearing Selection* in this chapter for additional instructions.

> *NOTE*
> *Normal bearing surface coloration is silver with very fine lines in the surface. Discolored surfaces occur when excessive heat is applied. Highly polished surfaces or*

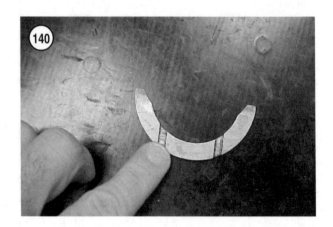

metal transfer occurs from inadequate lubrication, excessive engine speed or excessive bearing wear.

Thrust Bearings

Inspect the thrust bearing surfaces for highly polished, discolored or damaged contact surfaces (**Figure 140**). Replace the thrust bearing if there are any defects. On 40-70 hp models, measure thrust bearing thickness and replace any with a measurement less than the minimum specification in **Table 12**.

Exhaust Covers

There are no specifications available for exhaust cover warp; however, examine the cover for warp that may have resulted from an overheating condition. The cover may also have been distorted by improper installation or removal. Water and/or exhaust leakage can occur if using a

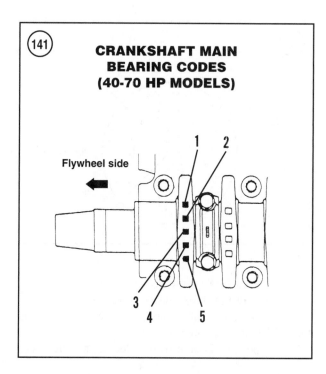

CRANKSHAFT MAIN BEARING CODES (40-70 HP MODELS)

Flywheel side

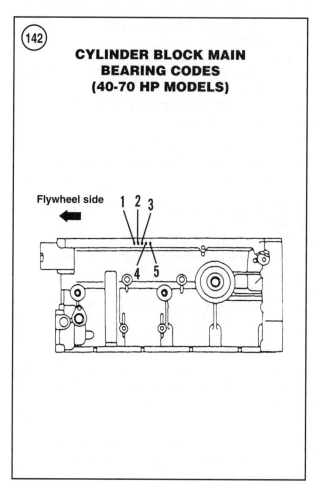

CYLINDER BLOCK MAIN BEARING CODES (40-70 HP MODELS)

Flywheel side

warped exhaust cover. Check the flat surfaces using a straightedge. Replace the exhaust cover if there is warp or if the original gasket indicates leakage.

Bearing Selection

Manufacturing variations requires selecting main bearings that match various crankshaft and cylinder block combinations. Bearing selection is not required for the crankpin bearings. On 5-15 hp models, check the bearings removed from the engine for identification marks or codes and consult a Johnson/Evinrude parts supplier for assistance. Some smaller displacement engines use roller bearings pressed into the cylinder block and cover instead of bearing inserts as described below.

40-70 hp models

Unless the crankshaft was machined, always use the same color code bearing (**Figure 139**) when reinstalling the original crankshaft into the original cylinder block.

1. Locate the number codes (**Figure 141**) stamped on the flyweight nearest the flywheel taper. The numbers indicate the code for the crankshaft main bearing journals. Number 1 identifies the code for the bearing journal closest to the flywheel. On models with only four main bearing to journals, four codes are stamped on the crankshaft. Record the journal number and code for each corresponding main bearing journal.

2. Locate the letter codes (**Figure 142**) stamped into the starboard side of the cylinder block. The letters indicate the code for the cylinder block journal bore. Number 1 identifies the code for the journal closest the flywheel. On models with four main bearings, four codes are stamped into the cylinder block. Record the letter code for each corresponding main bearing journal bore.

3. Match the letter and number codes to the color codes in **Table 14**. Select main bearings with the indicated color code (**Figure 139**) for the individual locations.

CYLINDER BLOCK ASSEMBLY

Clean the cylinder block thoroughly after the boring or honing process to remove any contaminants. Do not use solvent as a cleaning solution; abrasives usually remain in the cylinder block when using solvent alone. Use hot, soapy water to remove all debris from the cylinder block. Use compressed air to thoroughly dry the cylinder block. Wipe the cylinder bores with a clean, white shop towel. The cleaning process is complete if the towel remains clean and white after wiping the cylinder bores. Thor-

8

oughly coat the cylinder bores with engine oil immediately after cleaning to prevent corrosion. Coat all bearing, pistons and cylinder surfaces with engine oil during final assembly.

5/6 hp Models

The design of the single cylinder 5/6 hp engines makes installation of the crankshaft, piston and crankcase cover a single, inter-related procedure. On these models position the piston, then install the crankshaft.

NOTE
The rod end cap is specifically matched to the rod. Do not replace or use one without using the matched pair.

1. Align the matchmarks made on the piston and connecting rod during removal, then assemble the piston as follows:

    a. Coat the wrist pin and bores using clean engine oil or assembly lube, then working by hand insert the wrist pin through the piston and connecting rod bores.

    b. Position the wrist pin retaining ring in the end groove and gently use finger pressure to push it inward fully into position. The ring gap should be 180° opposite of the relief in the piston skirt.

    c. Install the oil control ring assembly by positioning the segmented ring into the bottom groove first. Insert the end of the first scraper ring under the segmented ring, then work around the piston until the scraper ring is seated. Lastly, insert the second scraper ring on top of the segmented ring and work around the piston to seat it.

NOTE
Applying a light coating of fresh engine oil to the rings can help ease installation.

    d. Position the scraper ring end gaps each at 45° (A, **Figure 143**) from each end of the wrist pin (dotted line, **Figure 143**). Position the segmented ring gap (C, **Figure 143**) least 45° from the wrist pin centerline, but on the opposite side from the scraper ring gaps.

    e. Install the middle ring into the middle piston ring groove with the number *2* mark facing up and the white paint to the right side of the gap. Then install the top ring in the top piston groove with the *R* mark facing up and the orange paint to the right side of the gap. Position the gaps directly opposite each other

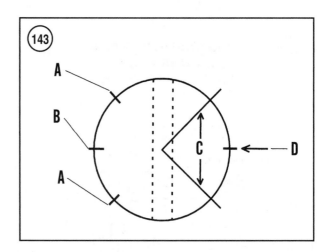

and each 90° from the wrist pin centerline (B middle ring gap and D top ring gap, **Figure 143**).

2. If removed, install the bearing into the bore in the bottom of the block as follows:

    a. Support the bottom of the block flange in a shop press.

    b. Lubricate a new bearing using clean engine oil, then position it into the block aligning the bearing tab with the slot.

    c. Use the OMC Bearing Installer (part No. 115311), or an equivalent sized driver to press the bearing halfway into the bore carefully, then position a 7/8 in. (22 mm) socket and continue pressing until the socket contacts the block.

CAUTION
Do not allow the socket to contact the thrust bearing locating pin.

3. If removed, install the bearing into the cover bore as follows:

    a. Support the cover in a shop press.

    b. Lubricate a new bearing using clean engine oil, then position it into the cover aligning the bearing tab with the slot.

    c. Use the OMC Bearing Installer (part No. 115311), or an equivalent sized driver to press the bearing into the bore carefully until the driver contacts the cover.

4. Lubricate the cylinder wall and an expandable ring compressor with clean engine oil. Position the assembled piston into the ring compressor.

NOTE
*Before installing the ring compressor verify that the ring gaps are still positioned as noted in **Figure 143**.*

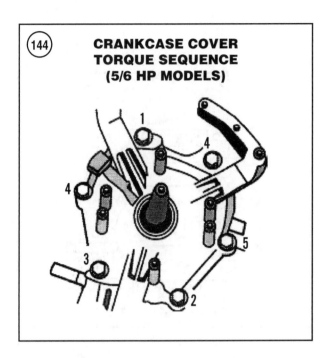

CRANKCASE COVER TORQUE SEQUENCE (5/6 HP MODELS)

5. With the stamped arrow on the piston dome and the raised dot on the bottom end of the connecting rod facing the flywheel side of the engine, position the assembly over the cylinder bore. Carefully tap the piston down out of the compressor and into the bore using a wooden dowel. Make sure the connecting rod does not contact and damage the cylinder wall surface during installation.

6. If removed, install a new crankshaft sleeve to the crankshaft using the OMC Crankshaft Sleeve Installer part No. 342657 or an equivalent sized driver. Make sure to fully seat the sleeve. Apply a coating of OMC Moly Lube or equivalent assembly lube to the seal.

7. Install and seat the thrust washer in the bottom of the block so the bottom slot in the washer aligns with the block locating pin.

8. Make sure the piston crown is slightly above the cylinder deck (but with the rings still in the bore) to allow sufficient clearance for crankshaft installation.

9. Lubricate the thrust washer, bearing as well as the crankshaft main bearing and rod bearing journals with clean engine oil or assembly lube, then carefully position the crankshaft into the block.

CAUTION
Do not overtighten the connecting rod cap bolts as this causes cap distortion and eventual bearing failure.

10. Lubricate the connecting rod and cap bearing surfaces with clean engine oil or assembly lube, then install the cap with the raised dot facing the flywheel. Align any other marks made during removal. Secure the connecting rod cap with a new retainer and rod bolts. Tighten the bolts in stages to the specification in **Table 13** and then bend the retainer tabs to secure the hex bolt heads.

11. Apply a light coating of OMC Gel Seal II or equivalent to the mating surfaces of the cylinder block and cover. Apply a light coating of engine oil to the cover bolt threads, then install the cover and tighten the bolts to the specification in **Table 13** using one or two passes of the torque sequence (**Figure 144**).

12. Apply a light coating of OMC Gasket Sealing Compound or an equivalent sealant to both sides of the new block access plate gasket, then install the plate and gasket. Apply a coating of OMC Nut Lock, or an equivalent threadlocking compound to the threads, then install and securely tighten the two Philips access plate retaining screws (**Figure 105**).

13. If removed, install a new upper crankshaft seal to the crankshaft cover as follows:

a. Apply a light coating of OMC Gasket Sealing Compound or an equivalent sealant to the outer casing of a new upper crankshaft seal, then apply a light coating of clean engine oil to the seal lips.

b. Remove the key(s) from the crankshaft, then start the seal over the crankshaft, making sure the lips fit properly and the seal is square in the cover bore.

c. Use the OMC Seal Installer (part No. 342215) or an equivalent driver along with a 1 in. (25.4 mm) deep well socket to install the seal. The socket and driver fits over the end of the crankshaft allowing the seal to be driven evenly in place without possible damage to the shaft, but keep the driver and socket centered. Tap until the installer contacts the cover.

d. Reposition the keys or place them where they will not be forgotten before sprocket installation.

14. If removed, install a new lower crankshaft seal to the cylinder block as follows:

a. Apply a light coating of OMC Gasket Sealing Compound or an equivalent sealant to the outer casing of a new lower crankshaft seal, then apply a light coating of clean engine oil to the seal lips.

b. Start the seal over the crankshaft, making sure the lips fit properly and the seal is square in the cover bore.

c. Use the OMC Seal Installer (part No. 342215) or equivalent driver along with a 1 in. (25.4 mm) deep well socket to install the seal. The socket and driver fits over the crankshaft allowing the seal to be driven evenly in place without possible damage to the shaft, but keep the driver and socket centered. Tap until the installer contacts the block.

8

15. If removed, install the dowels and the water deflector to the cylinder block mating surface.

16. Follow the *Break-In Procedure* described in this chapter.

8-15 hp Models

The design of the twin cylinder 8-15 hp engine makes installation of the crankshaft, pistons and crankcase cover a single, inter-related procedure. On these models it is easiest to position the pistons in the bore, then install the crankshaft.

> *NOTE*
> *The rod end cap is specifically matched to the rod. Do not replace or use one without using the matched pair.*

1. Align the matchmarks made on the pistons and connecting rods during removal, then assemble the pistons as follows:

   a. Coat the wrist pin and bores with clean engine oil or assembly lube, then working by hand, insert the wrist pin through the piston and connecting rod bores.

   b. Position the wrist pin retaining ring in the end groove and gently use finger pressure to push it fully into position. The retaining ring gap should be 180° opposite of the relief in the piston skirt.

> *NOTE*
> *The retaining ring fit on 9.9/15 hp models may be too tight for installation by hand. If necessary, use OMC Wrist Pin Installer, (part No. 341441) or equivalent shouldered driver to carefully seat the retaining rings.*

   c. Install the oil control ring assembly by positioning the segmented ring into the bottom groove first. Insert the end of the first scraper ring under the segmented ring, then work around the piston until the scraper ring is seated. Lastly, insert the second scraper ring on top of the segmented ring and work around the piston to seat it as well.

   d. Position the scraper ring end gaps each at 45° (A, **Figure 143**) from each end of the wrist pin (dotted line, **Figure 143**). Position the segmented ring gap (C, **Figure 143**) also at least 45° from the wrist pin centerline, but on the opposite side of the piston from the scraper ring gaps.

   e. For 8/9.9 hp models, install the middle ring into the middle piston ring groove with the number *2* mark facing up and the white paint to the right side of the

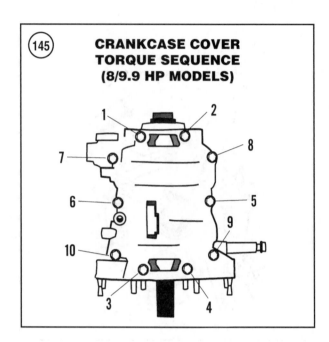

CRANKCASE COVER TORQUE SEQUENCE (8/9.9 HP MODELS)

gap. Then install the top ring in the top piston groove with the *R* mark facing up and/or the orange paint to the right side of the gap. Position the gaps directly opposite each other and each 90° from the wrist pin centerline (B middle ring gap and D top ring gap, **Figure 143**).

   f. For 9.9/15 hp models, install the thicker middle ring into the middle piston ring groove with the stamp facing up and the white paint to the right side of the gap. Then install the top (thinner) ring in the top piston groove with the stamping facing upward with the orange paint to the right side of the gap. Position the gaps directly opposite each other and each 90° from the wrist pin centerline (B middle ring gap and D top ring gap, **Figure 143**).

2. Lubricate the cylinder wall and an expandable ring compressor with clean engine oil. Position the assembled piston into the ring compressor.

> *NOTE*
> *Before installing the ring compressor verify that the ring gaps are still positioned as noted in* **Figure 143**.

3. With the stamped arrow on the piston dome and, on 8/9.9 hp models, the *F* on the connecting rod facing the flywheel side of the engine, position the assembly over the cylinder bore. Carefully tap the piston down out of the compressor and into the bore using a wooden dowel. Make sure the connecting rod does not contact and damage the cylinder wall surface during installation.

4. Repeat Step 2 and Step 3 for the other piston.

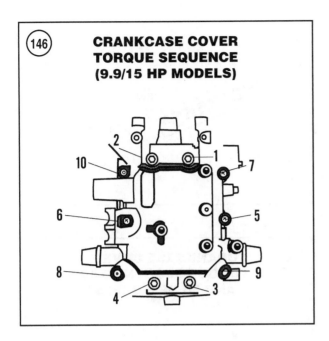

**CRANKCASE COVER
TORQUE SEQUENCE
(9.9/15 HP MODELS)**

threads, then install the cover and tighten the bolts to the specification in **Table 13** using one or two passes of the torque sequence (**Figure 145** for 8/9.9 hp models or **Figure 146** for 9.9/15 hp models).

11. Install a new upper crankshaft seal as follows:

　a. Apply a light coating of OMC Gasket Sealing Compound or an equivalent sealant to the outer casing of a new upper crankshaft seal, then apply a light coating of clean engine oil to the seal lips.

　b. Remove the key(s) from the crankshaft, then start the seal over the crankshaft, with the casing up, making sure the lips fit properly and the seal is square in the cover bore.

　c. Use the OMC Seal Installer (part No. 342661 8/9.9 hp models or No. 342213 9.9/15 hp models) or an equivalent seal installer along with the crankshaft sprocket nut to press the seal into the cylinder block bore. Turn the crankshaft nut until the seal is fully seated, then remove the nut and installer tool.

　d. Reposition the keys or place them where they will not be forgotten before sprocket installation.

12. If removed, install a new lower crankshaft seal to the cylinder block as follows:

　a. Apply a light coating of OMC Gasket Sealing Compound or an equivalent sealant to the outer casing of a new lower crankshaft seal, then apply a light coating of clean engine oil to the seal lips.

　b. Start the seal over the crankshaft, with the casing up, making sure the lips fit properly and the seal is square in the cover bore.

　c. Use the OMC Seal Installer (part No. 342215) or equivalent driver and a hammer, and gently tap the seal into the bore until the installer contacts the block.

13. If removed, install the shift linkage, lifting bracket, thermostat or other block mounted components.

14. Follow the *Break-In Procedure* in this chapter.

5. If removed, install a new crankshaft sleeve to the crankshaft using the OMC Crankshaft Sleeve Installer (part No. 342662 8/9.9 hp models or No. 342210 9.9/15 hp models), or an equivalent sized driver. Make sure to fully seat the sleeve. Apply a coating of OMC Moly Lube or equivalent assembly lube to the O-ring.

6. Thoroughly lubricate the new bearing halves with oil or assembly lube, then position them in the cylinder block and cover flush with the mating surfaces.

7. Thoroughly lubricate the crankshaft main and rod journals as well as the thrust bearing on 9.9/15 hp models with fresh engine oil or assembly lube.

8. Position the pistons at the top of their bores to help ease installation, then carefully lower the crankshaft (and thrust bearing on 9.9/15 hp models, with the reliefs facing the crank) into the cylinder block.

*CAUTION
Do not overtighten the connecting rod cap bolts as this causes cap distortion and eventual bearing failure.*

9. Lubricate the connecting rod and rod cap bearing surfaces with fresh engine oil or assembly lube. Install the cap while aligning any marks made during removal. Secure each connecting rod cap using a new retainer and rod bolts. Tighten the bolts in stages to the specification in **Table 13**, then bend the retainer tabs to secure the hex bolt heads.

10. Apply a light coating of OMC Gel Seal II or equivalent to the mating surfaces of the cylinder block and cover. Apply a light coating of engine oil to the cover bolt

40-70 hp Models

Crankshaft installation

1. Install the selected main bearings to the cylinder block and crankcase cover locations. If used, align the notch in the bearing with the recess in the bore. Ensure the oil groove hole in the bearing aligns with the oil hole in the cylinder block. Carefully place the thrust bearings into the recess provided in the cylinder block as shown in **Figure 118**.

2. Do not apply oil to the bearing surfaces at this time as the oil clearance of the bearings must first be checked using Plastigage or an equivalent. Align the flywheel taper

8

to the top of the cylinder block and temporarily install it to the crankshaft to ease in turning the shaft assembly during later steps of the crankshaft and piston installation.

3. Place a section of Plastigage (**Figure 147**) onto each crankshaft main journal. Position the Plastigage directly in line with the crankshaft.

4. Without rotating the crankshaft, install the crankcase cover to the cylinder block. Do not apply crankcase sealant at this time. Install the bolts and tighten them using three passes of the proper torque sequence (**Figure 148** and **Figure 149**) to the specifications in **Table 13**. Do not rotate the crankshaft or the Plastigage will be damaged.

5. Remove the crankshaft cover as described in this chapter. Gauge the main bearing clearance by comparing the flattened Plastigage with the scale provided with the Plastigage package (**Figure 150**).

6. Compare the main bearing clearance with the crankshaft journal oil clearance specification in **Table 12**. Measure the crankshaft journal diameter if the clearance is incorrect. If the crankshaft measurement is correct, refer to *Bearing Selection*.

7. Use a fingernail to scrape the Plastigage from the main bearing journals. Apply engine oil to the main bearing surfaces.

Piston and connecting rod assembly

Coat the piston pin and piston pin bore with engine oil prior to assembly. Select an appropriately sized section of tubing to use as an installation tool. The tubing must have a diameter slightly smaller than the diameter of the piston pin. Refer to **Table 10** for piston pin diameter specifications.

1. Position the connecting rod within the piston pin bore area at the bottom of the piston. Make sure the marks on the connecting rod face the same direction as the up mark on the piston.

2. Use the installation tool to push the piston pin into the pin bore of the piston and connecting rod.

3. Use needlenose pliers to install the *new* lockrings into their groove in each end of the pin bore (**Figure 151**). Rotate each lockring to position the gap down or toward the crankshaft. Make sure the lockrings are fully seated in their grooves.

4. Refer to the instructions supplied with the new rings to locate the ring to the piston properly. Marks on the rings normally face upward. Install the rings as follows:

NOTE
The markings referenced in these steps are for OE Johnson/Evinrude replacement

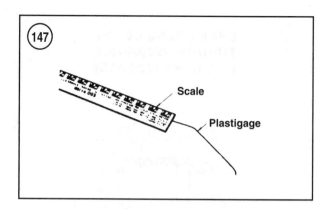

rings. Aftermarket ring identification marks may vary.

a. For 70 hp models, measure the ring thickness if necessary to help identify the top and second rings. Ring thickness specifications are in **Table 11**. On 70 hp models, the thicker compression ring is placed in the middle ring groove.

CAUTION
Use care while spreading the rings for installation. Spread the ends only enough to

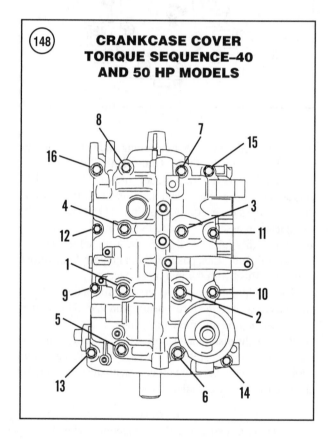

CRANKCASE COVER TORQUE SEQUENCE–40 AND 50 HP MODELS

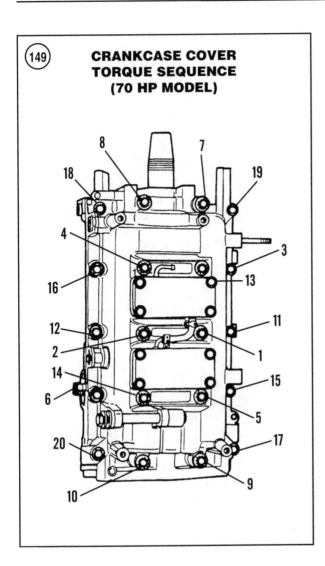

**CRANKCASE COVER
TORQUE SEQUENCE
(70 HP MODEL)**

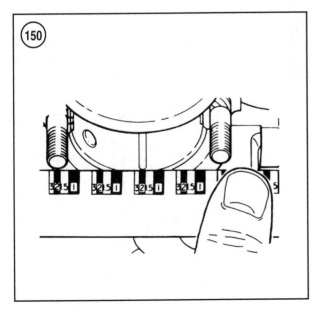

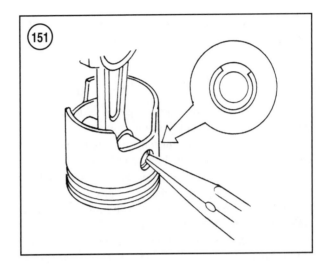

8

allow the rings to slide over the piston. The rings usually break or crack if spread too far. Although some of the rings may be installed by hand (especially the oil control rings), a universal ring expander tool may make installation easier.

b. On 40-50 hp models, the ring marks should help identify the difference between the compression rings. The top ring is normally marked with *N*, while the middle ring is marked with a *2N*.

c. Install the oil control ring assembly by positioning the segmented ring into the bottom groove first. Insert the end of the first scraper ring under the segmented ring, then work around the piston until the scraper ring is seated. Lastly, insert the second scraper ring on top of the segmented ring and work around the piston to seat it as well.

d. Position the scraper ring end gaps each at 45° (A, **Figure 143**) from each end of the wrist pin (dotted line, **Figure 143**). Position the segmented ring gap (C, **Figure 143**) also at least 45° from the wrist pin centerline, but on the opposite side of the piston from the scraper ring gaps.

e. For 40-50 hp models, install the middle ring into the middle piston ring groove with the *2N* facing up. Then install the top ring in the top piston groove with the *N* facing up. Position the gaps directly opposite each other and each 90° from the wrist pin centerline (B middle ring gap and D top ring gap, **Figure 143**).

f. For 70 hp models, install the thicker middle ring into the middle piston ring groove with the *R* facing up. Then install the thinner top ring into the top piston groove. Position the gaps directly opposite each other and each 90° from the wrist pin centerline (B middle ring gap and D top ring gap, **Figure 143**).

Piston and connecting rod installation

1. Lubricate the cylinder bore and piston with engine oil. Install new rod bolts or nuts during assembly.

2. Without disturbing the piston ring alignment, install the piston ring compressor (**Figure 152**) over the piston.

3. Tighten the piston ring compressor just enough to compress the rings into the ring grooves. Do not overtighten the compressor. The piston must be able to slide through the ring compressor.

4. Carefully rotate the crankshaft until the crankpin journal for the selected cylinder is at the bottom of its stroke.

5. Place the piston skirt into the correct cylinder with the *UP* mark (**Figure 153**) or dot on the piston facing the flywheel end of the cylinder block.

6. Using a wooden dowel or hammer handle, carefully push the piston into the bore until the piston top is slightly below the cylinder head mating surface.

> *CAUTION*
> *When inserting the piston make sure the connecting rod does not contact the cylinder wall. Also, if the crankshaft is being installed prevent the connecting rod from damaging the crankshaft journal.*

7. Provide support for the piston and rotate the cylinder block to access the connecting rod.

8. Place the bearing (**Figure 139**) into the connecting rod so the tab engages the notch in the connecting rod.

9. Guide the connecting rod to the crankshaft while pushing the piston into the bore. Place the bearing into the connecting rod cap engaging the tab to the notch in the cap.

10. Place an appropriate length section of Plastigage (**Figure 147**) onto the crankpin journal. Position the Plastigage directly in line with the crankshaft.

11. Make sure the cap is correctly positioned and place the cap onto the connecting rod. Hand-tighten the *new* rod bolts or nuts.

12. Check the alignment of the rod cap and connecting rod by passing a sharpened pencil tip across the mating surfaces. Replace the connecting rod if the pencil tip detects uneven surfaces.

13. Tighten the rod bolts or nuts in alternating steps to the specification in **Table 13**. Do not rotate the crankshaft or the Plastigage application will be damaged.

14. Remove the rod cap. Measure the crankpin oil clearance by comparing the flattened Plastigage with the measurements on the scale (**Figure 150**).

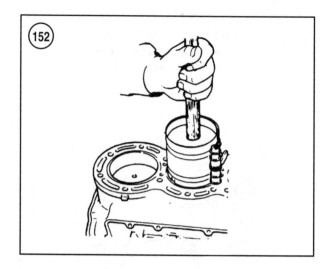

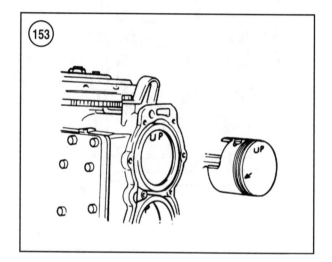

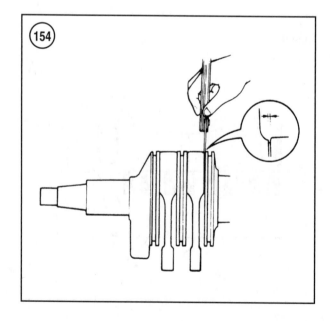

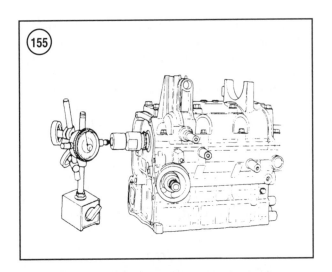

8

15. Compare the clearance with the connecting rod big end oil clearance specification in **Table 12**. Again remeasure the crankpin diameter if an incorrect clearance exists. Replace the bearings and repeat the measurement if the crankpin measurements are correct.

16. Use a fingernail to scrape the Plastigage from the main bearing journals. Apply engine oil to the bearing surfaces and install the rod cap as described in Steps 11-13.

17. If not done earlier during inspection, measure the connecting rod side clearance. The side clearance equals the thickness of the feeler gauge that passes between the connecting rod and the crankshaft (**Figure 154**) with a slight drag. Compare the clearance with the specification in **Table 12**. Replace the connecting rod if the clearance exceeds the maximum specification. Repeat the measurement. Replace the crankshaft if excess clearances persist.

18. Install the remaining piston and rods into the cylinder blocks as described in the previous steps.

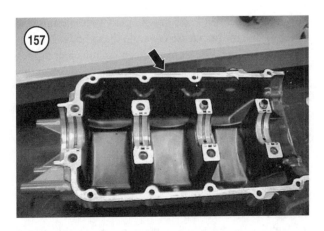

Crankshaft end play (thrust clearance)

1. Install the crankcase cover as described in this chapter. Do not install the seals or apply any sealant at this time.

2. Place the cylinder block on a sturdy work surface with the cylinder head mating surface facing down.

3. Align the plunger of a dial indicator with the lower end of the crankshaft as shown in **Figure 155**.

4. Observe the dial indicator while pushing the crankshaft toward the top and bottom of the cylinder block.

5. Compare the crankshaft end play measurement with the specification in **Table 12**. Replace the thrust bearings if the measurement exceeds the specification. Repeat the measurement. Replace the crankshaft if excess thrust clearances persist and cannot be corrected with suitable thrust bearing.

Crankcase cover installation

1. Thoroughly clean the cylinder block and crankcase mating surfaces with an aerosol parts cleaner. The cylinder block and crankcase surfaces must be absolutely clean.

2A. For 40 and 50 hp models refer to *Upper Seal Housing* in this chapter for seal installation instructions.

2B. For 70 hp models, place the upper seal on the crankshaft with the seal lip facing the connecting rods (**Figure 156**).

3. Apply a light coating of OMC Gel Seal II or equivalent sealant onto the cylinder block-to-crankcase cover mating surfaces (**Figure 157**). Avoid any gap or overlaps of the applied bead. The bead must pass inside all bolt holes or alignment pins.

4. Make sure the alignment pins fit into the recess when placing the crankcase cover onto the cylinder block. Align the seals and thrust rings with their respective grooves in

the crankcase cover. Press down lightly on the crankcase cover to seat the crankcase cover on the cylinder block.

5. Install the crankcase cover attaching bolts and tighten them finger-tight. Do not use any wrench or socket at this time. Make sure the cylinder block and crankcase cover are in contact prior to tightening the bolts.

6. Slowly rotate the crankshaft and note any tight spots, binding or roughness. Remove the cover and inspect the bearing, seal and thrust ring installation if binding or roughness occurs. The surface must be cleaned and a new coating of sealant applied if the cover is removed. Make sure that the cylinder block and crankcase cover mating surfaces are in direct contact.

7. Tighten the bolts using three passes of the proper torque sequence (**Figure 148** and **Figure 149**) to the specifications in **Table 13**.

Upper seal housing

1. Select a socket or section of tubing to use as a seal installation tool. The tool must be large enough in diameter to contact near the outer circumference of the seal, yet not contact the seal bore during installation.

2. Place the new seal into the housing bore with the lip side facing the connecting rod side of the housing.

3. Carefully drive the seal into the bore until firmly seated. Apply a coating of water resistant grease to the seal lips.

4. Carefully slip the seal housing over the tapered end of the crankshaft and seat it against the cylinder block.

5. Rotate the seal housing to align the holes. Install and securely tighten the five bolts.

External Block Component Installation

Install all removed brackets or linkage and position them as noted prior to removal. Install all fuel, electrical and ignition system components as described in the appropriate chapter. Follow the cylinder head, power head and flywheel procedures as described in this chapter.

BREAK-IN PROCEDURE

During the first few hours of operation, many of the engine components need to avoid continuous full load. To ensure a reliable and durable repair, perform the break-in procedure any time internal power head components are replaced.

Increased oil consumption is normal during the break-in period. Oil consumption decreases as the piston rings seat to the cylinder walls.

Check for and correct fuel, water and oil leakage immediately after starting the engine. Check the tightness of all external fasteners after completing the break-in instructions.

To enhance break-in, vary the engine speed during the initial twenty hours. Always allow the engine to reach operating temperature before advancing the throttle. Never exceed the maximum recommended engine speed during the break-in period.

> *CAUTION*
> *Do not run the engine with the engine out of the water. Severe damage to the water pump can occur and the engine may overheat.*

> *CAUTION*
> *During engine break-in, verify proper cooling system operation often by checking the coolant indicator stream. Check for a steady stream of water from the indicator.*

> *CAUTION*
> *Check and add oil before each use, especially during break-in, as increased oil consumption is expected.*

Carbureted Models

During the initial two hours of operation

Run the engine in neutral to allow it to warm up at a slow idle for about five minutes. For the next 15 minutes, run the engine in gear at the lowest speed possible. For the remainder of the two hours, run the engine in gear while changing the throttle setting often. Do not exceed 1/2 throttle. If the first two hours of operation are not continuous, repeat the idle and warm-up procedure each time.

During the third hour of operation

Idle the engine for at least five minutes before advancing the throttle. Do not exceed three-quarter throttle during this period.

During the next seven hours of operation

Idle the engine for at least five minutes before advancing the throttle. Operate the engine at any engine speed, including full throttle operation. Do not exceed the maximum recommended engine speed. Change the throttle position often and do not operate the engine at full throttle for periods exceeding five minutes.

During the final ten hours of operation

Complete break-in by operating the engine under normal use conditions. Following the 20 hour break-in period perform the break-in service. Refer to the *Maintenance Intervals* in Chapter Three.

Fuel Injected Models

During the initial hour of operation

Run the engine at fast idle (but *not* exceeding 1500 rpm) and in gear for the first 20 minutes. For the next 40 minutes, operate the engine in gear at speeds below 1/2 throttle (40 and 50 hp models) or below 3500 rpm (70 hp models). Change the throttle speed every 15 minutes during this period.

During the next nine hours of operation

Idle the engine for at least five minutes before advancing the throttle. For the majority of the nine hours, try to bring the boat onto plane and reduce speed below 3/4 throttle (do not exceed 4500 rpm). Every 30 minutes operate the engine at full throttle for one full minute.

During the final ten hours of operation

Complete break-in by operating the engine under normal use conditions. Following the 20 hour break-in period perform the break-in service. Refer to the *Maintenance Intervals* in Chapter Three.

8

Table 1 GENERAL POWER HEAD SPECIFICATIONS

Engine model	Bore in. (mm)	Stroke in. (mm)	Engine displacement cu. in. (cc)
5 and 6 hp	2.22 (56.6)	2.01 (51.0)	7.8 (128)
8 and 9.9 hp	2.22 (56.6)	1.65 (42.0)	12.87 (211)
9.9 and 15 hp	2.56 (65.02)	1.81 (45.97)	18.61 (305)
40 and 50 hp	2.80 (71.1)	2.70 (68.6)	49.7 (815)
70 hp	2.91 (74.0)	2.97 (75.4)	79.2 (1298)

Table 2 WARP LIMITS

Component	Specification in. (mm)
Cylinder head max warp	
5-15 hp models	
1995-1998	0.004 (0.10)
1999-2001	0.003 (0.08)
40-70 hp models	0.002 (0.05)
Cylinder block max warp	
40-70 hp models	0.0024 (0.06)
Intake manifold max warp (40-50 hp models)	0.004 (0.10)

Table 3 GENERAL CAMSHAFT SPECIFICATIONS

Component	Specification in. (mm)
Camshaft lobe height	
5/6 hp (128 cc) and 8/9.9 hp (211 cc)	
Intake	0.952-0.956 (24.181-24.282)
Exhaust	0.953-0.957 (24.206-24.307)
	(continued)

Table 3 GENERAL CAMSHAFT SPECIFICATIONS (continued)

Component	Specification in. (mm)
Camshaft lobe height (continued)	
9.9/15 hp (305 cc)	
Intake and exhaust	0.959-0.967 (24.360-24.562)
40 hp (815 cc)	
Intake	
Standard	1.4776-1.4839 (37.53-37.69)
Service limit	1.4736 (37.43)
Exhaust	
Standard	1.4858-1.4921 (37.74-37.90)
Service limit	1.4819 (37.64)
50 hp (815 cc)	
Intake	
Standard	1.5051-1.5114 (38.23-38.39)
Service limit	1.5012 (38.13)
Exhaust	
Standard	1.4858-1.4921 (37.74-37.90)
Service limit	1.4819 (37.64)
70 hp (1298 cc)	
Intake	
Standard	1.4815-1.4878 (37.63-37.79)
Service limit	1.4776 (37.531)
Exhaust	
Standard	1.4814-1.4877 (37.628-37.788)
Service limit	1.4775 (37.529)
Camshaft journal oil clearance	
40 and 50 hp models	
Standard	0.0018-0.0034 (0.046-0.086)
Service limit	0.0047 (0.119)
70 hp models	
Standard	0.0020-0.0036 (0.051-0.091)
Service limit	0.0059 (0.150)
Camshaft runout (40-70 hp models)	0.004 (0.10) max

Table 4 CAMSHAFT JOURNAL AND BORE SPECIFICATIONS (40 AND 50 HP MODELS)

	Camshaft journal outer diameter in. (mm)	Camshaft bore inner diameter in. (mm)
Standard	0.9029-0.9037 (22.934-22.940)	0.9055-0.9063 (23.000-23.020)
Limit	0.8970 (22.784)	0.9122 (23.170)

Table 5 CAMSHAFT JOURNAL AND BORE SPECIFICATIONS (70 HP MODEL)

Standard	Camshaft journal outer diameter in. (mm)	Camshaft bore inner diameter in. (mm)
1	1.7687-1.7697 (44.925-44.950)	1.7717-1.7723 (45.001-45.016)
2	1.7608-1.7618 (44.724-44.750)	1.7638-1.7644 (44.800-44.816)
3	1.7530-1.7539 (44.526-44.550)	1.7559-1.7565 (44.600-44.615)
4	1.7451-1.7461 (44.325-44.351)	1.7480-1.7487 (44.400-44.417)
5	1.7372-1.7382 (44.125-44.150)	1.7402-1.7408 (44.201-44.216)

Table 6 ROCKER ARM, SHAFT AND TAPPET SPECIFICATIONS (40-70 HP MODELS)

Component	Specification in. (mm)
Cylinder head bore and tappet dimensions	
(40 and 50 hp models)	
Bore-to-tappet clearance	
Standard	0.0010-0.0024 (0.025-0.061)
Service limit	0.0059 (0.150)
Bore inner diameter (standard)	1.0630-1.0638 (27.000-27.021)
Tappet outer diameter (standard)	1.0614-1.0620 (26.959-26.975)
Rocker arm and shaft dimensions (70 hp models)	
Shaft runout	0.005 (0.13) max
Shaft-to-rocker arm clearance	
Standard	0.0005-0.0018 (0.013-0.046)
Service limit	0.0035 (0.089)
Rocker arm inside diameter (standard)	0.6299-0.6306 (16.0025-16.017)
Rocker arm shaft outside diameter (standard)	0.6289-0.6294 (15.974-15.987)

Table 7 VALVE SPECIFICATIONS (5-15 HP MODELS)

Component	Specification in. (mm)
Valve head-to-seat contact width	
Intake	0.071-0.087 (1.80-2.21)
Exhaust	0.065-0.098 (1.65-2.50)
Valve seat concentricity limit	0.002 (0.05)

Table 8 VALVE SPECIFICATIONS (40-70 HP MODELS)

Component	Specification in. (mm)
Valve guide inner diameter	
40 and 50 hp models	
Intake and exhaust	0.2165-0.2170 (5.500-5.512)
70 hp models	
Intake and exhaust	0.2756-0.2762 (7.000-7.015)
Valve guide-to-stem clearance	
Intake	
Standard	
40 and 50 hp models	0.0008-0.0019 (0.020-0.048)
70 hp models	0.0008-0.0020 (0.020-0.051)
Service limit	0.0028 (0.071)
Exhaust	
Standard	
40 and 50 hp models	0.0018-0.0028 (0.046-0.071)
70 hp models	0.0018-0.0030 (0.045-0.076)
Service limit	0.0035 (0.089)
Valve head maximum radial runout	0.003 (0.08)
Valve head thickness	
Intake	0.028 (0.71)
Exhaust	0.020 (0.51)
Valve head-to-seat contact width	
Intake	0.071-0.087 (1.80-2.21)
Exhaust	0.065-0.098 (1.65-2.50)
Valve seat concentricity limit	0.002 (0.05)

(continued)

8

Table 8 VALVE SPECIFICATIONS (40-70 HP MODELS) (continued)

Component	Specification in. (mm)
Valve spring free length	
40 and 50 hp models	
Standard	1.30 (33.0)
Limit	1.25 (31.8)
70 hp models	
Standard	1.94 (49.3)
Limit	1.89 (48.0)
Valve spring squareness	0.08 (2.0)
Valve spring tension	
40 and 50 hp models	
Standard	21.4-24.9 lb. at 1.12 in. (9.7-11.3 kg at 28.5 mm)
Limit	19.6 lb. at 1.12 in. (8.9 kg at 28.5 mm)
70 hp models	
Standard	54.7-64.3 lb. at 1.63 in. (24.8-29.2 kg at 41.4 mm)
Limit	50.2 lb. at 1.63 in. (22.8 kg at 41.4 mm)
Valve stem minimum end length	
40 and 50 hp models	0.1260 (3.20)
70 hp models	0.2380 (6.05)
Valve stem height above deck	
40 and 50 hp models	0.430 (11.0)
70 hp models	0.550 (14.0)
Valve stem outer diameter	
40 and 50 hp models	
Intake	0.2152-0.2157 (5.466-5.480)
Exhaust	0.2142-0.2148 (5.440-5.456)
70 hp models	
Intake	0.2742-0.2748 (6.965-6.980)
Exhaust	0.2732-0.2738 (6.940-6.955)
Valve stem maximum runout	0.002 (0.05)

Table 9 CYLINDER BLOCK BORE SPECIFICATIONS*

Component	Specification in. (mm)
Cylinder bore diameter	
Standard pistons	
5/6 hp (128 cc) and 8/9.9 hp (211 cc)	2.2244-2.2248 (56.50-56.51)
9.9/15 hp (305 cc)	2.5590-2.5600 (65.00-65.02)
40/50 hp (815 cc)	2.7953-2.7961 (71.00-71.02)
70 hp (1298 cc)	2.9134-2.9142 (74.00-74.02)
Bore oversize service limit (before reboring)	
5-15 hp models	0.002 (0.05)
40-70 hp models	0.004 (0.10)
Oversize pistons	Standard bore + amount oversize
Available oversize pistons	
5-15 hp models	+0.030 (+0.762)
40-70 hp models	+0.0098 (+0.250) or +0.0197 (+0.500)
Cylinder bore out-of-round maximum	
5-15 hp models	0.003 (0.08)
40-70 hp models	0.004 (0.10)
Cylinder bore taper maximum	
5-15 hp models	0.002 (0.05)
40-70 hp models	0.004 (0.10)

Table 10 PISTON SPECIFICATIONS*

Component	Specification in. (mm)
Piston-to-cylinder clearance	
Standard	0.0008-0.0016 (0.020-0.040)
Limit	0.0039 (0.1)
Piston out-of-round limit	0.003 (0.08)
Piston pin bore inner diameter	
40 and 50 hp models	0.7089-0.7092 (18.006-18.014)
70 hp models	0.6694-0.6697 (17.003-17.010)
Piston pin clearance	
Standard	
40 and 50 hp models	0.0002-0.0007 (0.005-0.018)
70 hp models	0.0001-0.0006 (0.003-0.015)
Limit	0.0016 (0.041)
Piston pin outer diameter	
40 and 50 hp models	0.7085-0.7087 (17.996-18.000)
70 hp models	0.6691-0.6693 (16.995-17.000)
Piston ring groove width	
40 and 50 hp models	
Compression ring grooves	0.0398-0.0406 (1.01-1.03)
Oil ring groove	0.0594-0.0602 (1.51-1.53)
70 hp models	
Top compression ring groove	0.048-0.049 (1.22-1.24)
Bottom compression ring groove	0.059-0.060 (1.50-1.52)
Oil ring groove	0.111-0.112 (2.82-2.84)
Piston skirt outer diameter	
40 and 50 hp models, measured 0.75 in (19 mm)	
from bottom	2.7941-2.7949 (70.970-70.990)
70 hp models, measured 0.6 in (15 mm)	
from bottom	2.9122-2.9130 (73.970-73.990)

*The manufacturer does not provide piston clearance specifications for 5-15 hp models. For these models, visually inspect the pistons for obvious wear and replace if necessary. Ensure that the cylinder bore dimensions meet specification or oversize bore specifications, as applicable for the cylinder being used.

Table 11 PISTON RING SPECIFICATIONS

Component	Specification in. (mm)
Ring gap	
5/6 hp (128 cc) and 8/9.9 hp (211 cc)	0.006-0.014 (0.15-0.36)
9.9/15 hp (305 cc)	0.006-0.020 (0.15-0.51)
40/50 hp (815 cc)	
Top ring	0.004-0.010 (0.10-0.25)
Bottom ring	0.010-0.016 (0.25-0.41)
70 hp (1298 cc)	
Top ring	0.006-0.028 (0.15-0.71)
Bottom ring	0.008-0.028 (0.20-0.71)
Ring groove clearance (compression rings)	
5-15 hp models	0.004 (0.10)
40 and 50 hp models	
Standard	
Top ring	0.0008-0.0020 (0.02-0.05)
Bottom ring	0.0008-0.0023 (0.02-0.06)
Limit	0.0039 (0.10)
70 hp models	
Top ring	0.001-0.005 (0.03-0.13)
Bottom ring	0.001-0.004 (0.03-0.10)
	(continued)

8

Table 11 PISTON RING SPECIFICATIONS (continued)

Component	Specification in. (mm)
Ring thickness (compression rings)	
40 and 50 hp models	0.0382-0.0390 (0.97-0.99)
70 hp models	
Top ring	0.046-0.047 (1.17-1.19)
Bottom ring	0.058-0.059 (1.47-1.50)

Table 12 CRANKSHAFT SPECIFICATIONS

Component	Specification in. (mm)
Connecting rod big end oil clearance	
Standard	
40 and 50 hp models	0.0008-0.0016 (0.020-0.041)
70 hp models	0.0008-0.0020 (0.020-0.051)
Limit	
40 and 50 hp models	0.0026 (0.066)
70 hp models	0.0031 (0.079)
Connecting rod big end width (40-70 hp models)	0.864-0.866 (21.95-22.50)
Connecting rod-to-crankshaft side clearance	
(40-70 hp models)	0.004-0.014 (0.10-0.36)
Crankpin big end width (40-70 hp models)	0.870-0.874 (22.10-22.20)
Crankshaft dimensions	
5 and 6 hp (128 cc)	
1997-1998	
Top and bottom journals	1.2200-1.2204 (30.99-31.00)
Rod crankpin	1.1401-1.1398 (28.96-28.95)
1999-2001	
Top and bottom journals	0.9837-0.9842 (24.99-25.00)
Rod crankpin	1.1795-1.1791 (29.96-29.95)
8 and 9.9 hp (211 cc)	
Top and bottom journals	1.2200-1.2204 (30.99-31.00)
Rod crankpin	1.1401-1.1398 (28.96-28.95)
9.9 and 15 hp (305 cc)	
Top and bottom journals	1.2990-1.2994 (32.99-33.00)
Rod crankpin	1.1815-1.1801 (30.01-29.97)
40 and 50 hp models	
Main bearing journal diameter	1.7709-1.7717 (44.9820-45.000)
Crankpin jounral diameter	1.4954-1.4961 (37.983-38.000)
Taper and out-of-round (max difference	
between measurements)	0.0026 (0.066)
70 hp models	
Main bearing journal diameter	2.0465-2.0472 (51.982-51.000)
Crankpin journal diameter	1.6528-1.6535 (41.982-41.000)
Taper and out-of-round (max difference	
between measurements)	0.0016 (0.041)
Crankshaft end play	
Standard	
40/50 hp (815 cc) and 70 hp (1298 cc)	0.0043-0.0122 (0.11-0.31)
Service limit	
40 and 50 hp (815 cc)	0.0138 (0.35)
70 hp (1298 cc)	0.0150 (0.38)
	(continued)

Table 12 CRANKSHAFT SPECIFICATIONS (continued)

Component	Specification in. (mm)
Crankshaft journal oil clearance	
Standard	
40 and 50 hp models	0.0008-0.0016 (0.020-0.041)
70 hp models	0.0006-0.0014 (0.015-0.036)
Limit	
40 and 50 hp models	0.0026 (0.066)
70 hp models	0.0024 (0.061)
Crankshaft runout (measured at center journal)	
40 and 50 hp models	0.0016 (0.04)
70 hp models	0.002 (0.05)
Crankshaft thrust bearing thickness	
(40-70 hp models)	0.097-0.099 (2.46-2.51)
Main bearing case bore size	
40 and 50 hp (815 cc)	1.9291-1.9298 (49.000-49.017)
70 hp (1298 cc)	2.2047-2.2054 (56.000-56.017)

Table 13 POWER HEAD TORQUE SPECIFICATIONS

Component	in.-lb.	ft.-lb.	N•m
Breather cover screws			
5/6 and 8/9.9 hp models	36-60	–	4-6
Camshaft retainer (cap) bolts			
40-50 hp models	88	–	10
Camshaft sprocket/pulley bolts			
5-15 hp models	84-106	–	9.5-12
40-50 hp models	84-90	–	9.5-10.2
70 hp model	–	43-45	58-61
Crankcase cover (main bearing) bolts			
5/6 hp models	–	15-17	20-23
8/9.9 and 9.9/15 hp models			
Small screws	84-106	–	9.5-12
Large screws	–	18-21	24-28
40-70 hp models			
Small screws			
First pass	45	–	5
Second pass	–	14	19
Final pass	–	17-19	23-26
Large screws			
First pass	–	7	9.5
Second pass	–	29	39
Final pass	–	35-37	47-50
Crankshaft sprocket bolts or nuts			
5/6 and 8/9.9 hp models	–	18-20	24-27
9.9/15 hp models	–	17-18	23-24
70 hp model	–	50-52	68-71
		(continued)	

8

Table 13 POWER HEAD TORQUE SPECIFICATIONS (continued)

Component	in.-lb.	ft.-lb.	N•m
Connecting rod cap bolts or nuts			
5/6 hp models	80-96	–	9-11
8/9.9 and 9.9/15 hp models	96-108	–	11-12
40-70 hp models			
First pass	–	13	18
Second pass	–	25-26	34-35
Cylinder head bolts			
5-15 hp models	–	18-20	24-27
40-50 hp models			
First and second pass	–	22	30
Third pass	–	43-44	59-60
70 hp model			
First	84	–	10
Second	–	36	50
Third	–	51-55	69-70
Cylinder head-to-adapter nuts			
70 hp model	–	16-18	22-24
Exhaust adapter bolts			
8/9.9 hp models	84-106	–	10-12
Exhaust deflector to water tube bolts			
8/9.9 hp models	36-60	–	6-8
Exhaust manifold (cover)/water jacket retainers			
70 hp model	–	16-18	22-24
Exhaust-to-cylinder head screws			
5/6 and 8/9.9 hp models	–	15-17	20-32
Exhaust probe fitting retainers			
9.9/15 hp models	–	12-15	16-20
Filter to oil pump bolts			
8/9.9 hp models	84-106	–	10-12
Flush plug			
5/6 and 8/9.9 hp models	60-84	–	8-10
Flywheel nut or bolt			
5-15 hp models	–	45-50	60-70
40-50 hp models	–	145-150	200-205
70 hp model	–	150-160	205-217
Intake manifold bolts			
5-15 hp models	84-106	–	10-12
40/50 hp models			
Large screws/nuts	–	16-18	22-24
Small screws/nuts	96-108	–	11-12
70 hp model		16-18	22-24
Oil pressure switch			
9.9/15 hp models	120	–	13.5-19
Oil pump adapter			
70 hp model	–	16-18	22-24
Oil pump cover bolts			
9.9/15 hp models	84-106	–	10-12
Oil pump fasteners			
70 hp model	72-96	–	8-11
Oil pump housing bolts			
40 and 50 hp models	84-96	–	9.5-11

(continued)

Table 13 POWER HEAD TORQUE SPECIFICATIONS (continued)

Component	in.-lb.	ft.-lb.	N•m
Oil pump mounting bolts			
5/6 hp models	84-106	–	10-12
Oil pump shaft screw			
70 hp model	–	34-38	46-51
Oil pump to powerhead bolts			
8/9.9 hp models	84-106	–	10-12
Overboard coolant indicator nipple			
9.9/15 hp models	20-25	–	2.3-2.8
Power head retainers			
5-15 hp models	–	15-17	20-23
40-50 hp models	–	–	–
Small bolts	–	16-17	22-23
Large bolts and nut	–	35-37	47-50
70 hp model	–	35-37	47-50
Pressure relief valve housing bolts			
5/6 hp models	36-60	–	4-6
8/9 and 9.9/15 hp models	84-106	–	10-12
Reed stop screw			
5/6 and 8/9 hp models	15-22	–	1.7-2.5
Spark plugs			
5-15 hp models	–	14-18	19-24
40-50 hp models	–	11-14	15-19
70 hp model	–	18-21	24-28
Stator botls			
70 hp model	24-36	–	3-4
Starter bracket bolts			
8/9.9 hp models	84-106	–	10-12
Starter sprocket retainers			
70 hp model	–	16-18	22-24
Steering arm screw			
70 hp model	–	40-47	56-64
Sump to power head bolts			
5/6 hp models	36-60	–	4-6
8/9.9 hp models	84-106	–	10-12
Thermostat housing bolts			
5-15 hp models	84-106	–	10-12
40-70 hp models	84-96	–	10-11
Tiller arm bolts			
5/6 hp and 8/9.9 hp models	108-132	–	12-15
Timing belt tentioner bolts			
70 hp model	–	16-18	22-24
Timing chain fasteners			
40-50 hp models	84-90	–	9.5-10.2
Upper mount retainers			
5/6 and 8/9.9 hp models	108-132	–	12-15
Valve (cylinder head or rocker arm) covers			
5-15 hp models	84-106	–	10-12
40-50 hp models	40-54	–	4.5-6.0
70 hp models	84-96	–	10-11

(continued)

8

Table 13 POWER HEAD TORQUE SPECIFICATIONS (continued)

Component	in.-lb.	ft.-lb.	N•m
Water pressure relief valve housing			
70 hp model	84-96	–	10-11
Water tube flange screw			
5/6 hp models	36-60	–	4-6
Water tube cover bolts			
5/6 hp models	84-106	–	10-12

Table 14 BEARING CODE (40-70 HP MODELS)

Crankshaft code	Cylinder block code	Bearing color
1	A	Green
1	B	Black
1	C	No color
2	A	Black
2	B	No color
2	C	Yellow
3	A	No color
3	B	Yellow
3	C	Blue

Chapter Nine

Gearcase

This chapter provides complete gearcase removal, disassembly, inspection, assembly and installation instructions.

A number of special tools are required to remove, position and install many of the components within the gearcase. Using makeshift tools may damage the housing or internal components of the gearcase. OMC part numbers for these tools are included in the repair instructions. **Table 1** at the end of this chapter provides the torque specifications.

When assembled, the gears (**Figure 1**) must be precisely aligned to provide durability and quiet operation. On 40-70 hp models, shims (**Figure 2**) are used to accomplish this precise alignment. The shims are typically located next to the bearing that supports the gears and shafts. Shim selection operations involve using special tools, gauges and meters to measure and determine the required shim thickness. Never compromise this important step. The durability of the gearcase is substantially reduced if the gears are positioned improperly. Shim selection procedures must be performed if replacing gears, bearings, shafts or the housing. For 40-70 hp models, refer to *Shim Selection* in this chapter for instructions.

Gearcase failure is usually caused by impact with underwater objects or lack of gearcase maintenance. Proper maintenance is essential for gearcase operation and dura-bility. Gearcase maintenance instructions are in Chapter Three.

Have a marine repair shop perform the repairs if the required tools or experience is not available. An improper repair can result in extensive damage to the gearcase.

Gearcase Operation

The gearcase transfers the rotation of the vertical drive shaft (**Figure 3**) to the horizontal propeller shaft. The pinion and both driven gears rotate anytime the engine is running. A sliding clutch engages the propeller shaft with either the front or rear mounted gear.

When neutral gear is selected, the propeller shaft is allowed to free wheel or remain stationary, as the gears rotate. No propeller thrust is delivered.

When forward gear is selected, the sliding clutch moves with the shift mechanism to the front mounted gear. The propeller shaft rotates in the direction of the front mounted gear as the clutch dogs (raised bosses) engage with the dogs on the front mounted gear. This provides the clockwise propeller shaft rotation necessary for forward thrust.

When reverse gear is selected (**Figure 3**), the sliding clutch moves with the shift mechanism to the rear mounted driven gear. The propeller shaft rotates in the direction of the rear-mounted gear as the clutch dogs engage

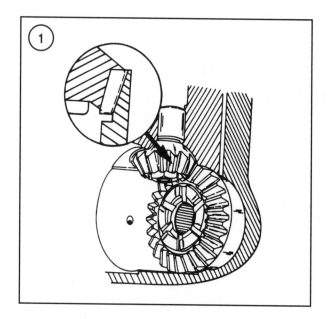

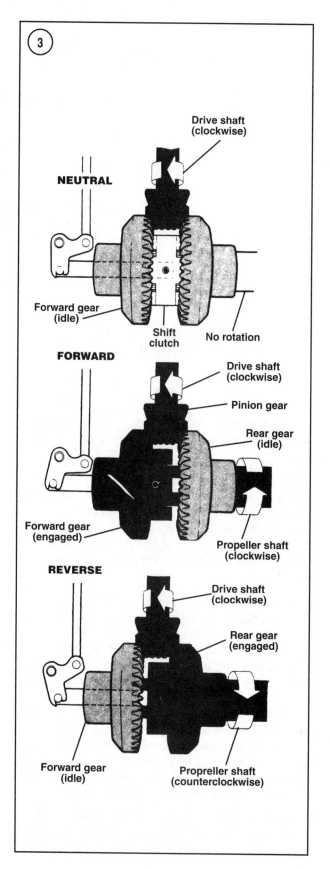

the dogs on the rear-mounted gear. This provides the counterclockwise propeller shaft rotation necessary for reverse thrust.

PROPELLER

The propeller attaches to the propeller shaft either by a drive pin (3, **Figure 4**) on 5/6 hp models or by a castellated hex nut (5, **Figure 5**) on 8-70 hp models.

The propeller is driven by a splined connection to the propeller shaft and the rubber drive hub located within the propeller on most models. The rubber drive hub provides a cushion effect to allow for quieter shifting. It also provides some measure of protection for the gearcase components in the event of an impact. On 5/6 hp models, the propeller is retained by a drive pin. The pin, known as a shear pin, performs the same protective function as the

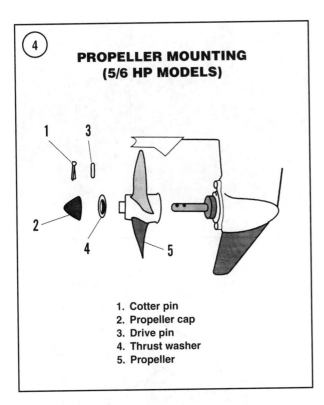

PROPELLER MOUNTING (5/6 HP MODELS)

1. Cotter pin
2. Propeller cap
3. Drive pin
4. Thrust washer
5. Propeller

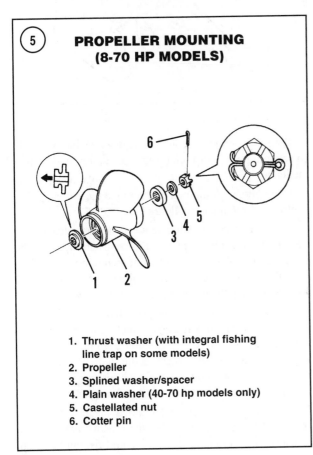

PROPELLER MOUNTING (8-70 HP MODELS)

1. Thrust washer (with integral fishing line trap on some models)
2. Propeller
3. Splined washer/spacer
4. Plain washer (40-70 hp models only)
5. Castellated nut
6. Cotter pin

rubber hub. The pin is designed to shear or break when a predetermined amount of force impacts the propeller.

NOTE
The outboard may be equipped with a Johnson/Evinrude propeller or one from an aftermarket manufacturer. Because of this, the attaching hardware may differ slightly from the illustrations. Contact a propeller repair shop or marine dealership for parts and information on other types of propellers.

CAUTION
Use light force, to remove the propeller from the propeller shaft. Using excessive force will damage the propeller, propeller shaft and, possibly, internal components of the gearcase. Have a marine repair shop or propeller repair shop remove the propeller if the propeller cannot be removed by normal means.

NOTE
Thoroughly clean and lubricate the propeller and shaft splines using OMC Triple-Guard or equivalent marine grease whenever it is removed from the shaft. Lubricating the splines prevents the propeller hub from becoming seized onto the shaft due to corrosion. A seized hub requires special tools to remove without damaging the shaft and gearcase assembly.

Removal and Installation

5/6 hp models

The propeller (5, **Figure 4**) on 5/6 hp models is secured to the propeller shaft using a drive pin (3, **Figure 4**). Although not absolutely necessary, it is advisable to replace the drive pin whenever it has been removed. Keep in mind that sheared drive pin will leave the boat stranded on the water and allow the engine to over-rev. The pin itself is locked in position to the propeller cap (2, **Figure 4**) that is in turn fastened by a cotter pin (1, **Figure 4**). To service the propeller on these models, proceed as follows:

1. Cut the ends of the cotter pin (**Figure 6**) and withdraw the pin by grabbing the head with a pair of needlenose pliers. If necessary, tap on the pliers gently with a hammer to help free the pin from the propeller cap and shaft.

2. Remove the cap for access to the drive pin.

3. Grasp and remove the drive pin using the needlenose pliers. If it is difficult to remove, use a small punch and gently tap the pin from the shaft.

9

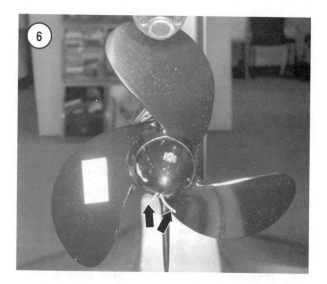

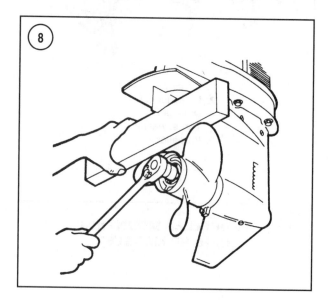

4. After removing the pin, slide the thrust washer and propeller from the propeller shaft and splines.

5. Installation is the reverse of the removal. Note the following:

   a. Clean the propeller and shaft splines, then apply a fresh coating of OMC Triple-Guard or equivalent marine grease.

   b. Align the splines and slide the propeller over the shaft followed by the thrust washer.

   c. Carefully insert a new drive pin to secure the propeller.

   d. Install the propeller cap and install a new cotter pin. Spread the cotter pin ends (**Figure 6**) in order to secure the pin. Do not bend them over too far as the pin will loosen and rattle in the shaft.

8-70 hp models

The propeller is fastened to the shaft by a castellated nut (**Figure 7**), the nut itself is locked in place by a cotter pin that prevents it from loosening in service. The cotter pin (6, **Figure 5**) passes through a hole in the propeller shaft and the notches in the castellated nut. Always install a new cotter pin anytime the propeller is removed. Make sure the cotter pin is for marine use and the correct size.

Inspect the propeller for of black rubber material in the drive hub area. Have the hub inspected or replaced at a propeller repair facility if this material is found. The material normally indicates that the propeller hub has turned inside the propeller bore. Satisfactory performance is not possible with a spun propeller hub. Also, if the propeller has spun on the hub it has already been weakened and is more likely to fail completely in use.

1. For safety, either disconnect the negative battery cable (if so equipped) or disconnect the spark plugs and ground the leads.

2. Use pliers to straighten and remove the cotter pin (6, **Figure 5**) from the propeller nut.

3. Position a block of wood between the propeller and the housing to lock the propeller (**Figure 8**) and remove the propeller nut. Note the orientation, then remove the plain (40-70 hp models only) and/or splined washer (3 and 4, **Figure 5**) from the propeller shaft.

4. Pull the propeller from the propeller shaft (**Figure 9**). If the propeller is sticking, use a block of wood as a cushion and *carefully* drive the propeller from the shaft. If the propeller is completely seized on the shaft, have a reputable marine or propeller shop free it, as excessive force could damage the propeller, shaft and/or gearcase.

5. Note the orientation and remove the thrust washer (**Figure 10**) from the propeller shaft. Most models use a thrust washer equipped with an integral fishing line trap.

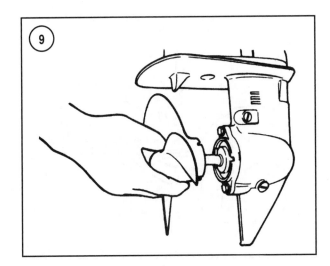

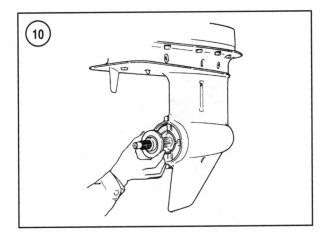

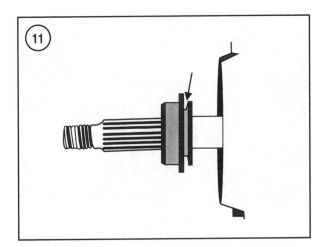

8. Install the propeller onto the propeller shaft. Rotate the propeller to align the splines and slide the propeller fully against the thrust washer. Install the splined and, if equipped, the plain washer onto the propeller shaft.

9. Place a block of wood between the propeller and housing (**Figure 8**) to prevent propeller rotation. Install the castellated propeller nut onto the propeller shaft with the cotter pin slots facing out. For 8-15 hp models, tighten the nut securely. For 40-70 hp models, tighten the propeller nut to the specification in **Table 1**.

10. Install a *new* cotter pin and use pliers to bend the ends over. If the cotter pin hole and the slots in the propeller nut do not align, tighten the nut just enough to align them. Do not loosen the nut to achieve alignment.

11. Connect the spark plug leads or the negative battery cable, as applicable.

GEARCASE REMOVAL AND INSTALLATION

Always remove the propeller prior to removing the gearcase. Refer to *Propeller* in this chapter for instructions.

Disconnect the negative (–) then positive (+) battery cables (if so equipped) prior to removing the gearcase. Remove the spark plugs leads and connect them to an engine ground to prevent accidental starting.

If the gearcase needs repair, drain the gearcase lubricant prior to removal. Refill the gearcase after installation. Refer to Chapter Three for gearcase draining and filling instructions.

Clean any debris or contaminants from the drive shaft, shift shafts and gearcase after removing the gearcase. Inspect the grommet that connects the water tube to the water pump for damage or deterioration. Replace as required. Apply grease to the grommet before installing

The washer must be oriented in the proper direction for it to work correctly. If necessary, *lightly* tap the washer free from the propeller shaft.

6. Thoroughly clean the propeller shaft, then inspect the shaft for twisted splines or excessively worn areas. Rotate the propeller shaft while looking for any shaft deflection. Remove and replace the propeller shaft if there are excessively worn areas, twisted splines or a bent shaft. Refer to gearcase disassembly in this chapter for disassembly instructions.

7. Before installing the propeller, apply a light coat of OMC Triple-Guard or equivalent water-resistant marine grease to all surfaces of the propeller shaft. Clean and install the thrust washer as noted during removal. On 40-70 hp models, the tapered inner diameter of the thrust washer (1, **Figure 5**) and the propeller shaft must contact. On 8-15 hp models, make sure the fishing line trap groove on the thrust washer (**Figure 11**) faces forward.

9

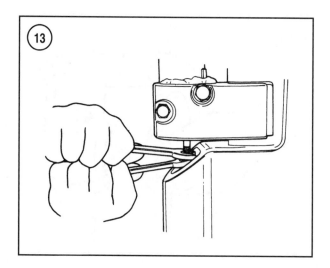

the gearcase. Make sure the dowels or locating pins are properly positioned in the gearcase upon installation.

Apply OMC Moly Lube or equivalent to the splined portion of the drive shaft prior to installing the gearcase.

CAUTION
Never apply lubricant to the top of the drive shaft or fill the crankshaft with grease. The grease may prevent the drive shaft from fully seating in the crankshaft or promote a hydraulic lock on the shaft and cause failure of the power head, gearcase or both. Apply a light coating of OMC Moly Lube or equivalent to only the splined section of the drive shaft during installation.

CAUTION
Work carefully when installing the upper end of the drive shaft into the crankshaft. The lower seal on the crankshaft may be dislodged or damaged by the drive shaft. Never force the drive shaft into the crankshaft. Rotate the drive shaft clockwise as viewed from the top to align the drive shaft and crankshaft splines.

CAUTION
Use caution if using a pry bar to separate the gearcase from the drive shaft housing. Make sure all fasteners are removed before prying the gearcase from the drive shaft housing. Use a blunt tip pry bar and locate a pry point near the front and rear mating surfaces. Apply moderate heat to the gearcase and drive shaft housing mating surfaces if corrosion prevents easy removal.

5-50 hp Models

The gearcase is bolted to the drive shaft housing, though the number of bolts vary by model. Three bolts are

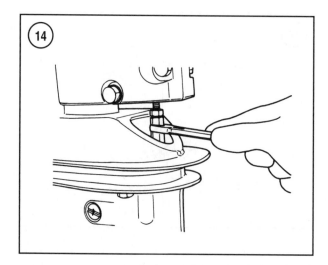

used on 5/6 hp models, and six bolts are used on 8-50 hp models.

1. Remove the propeller as described in this chapter and place the shift selector into *neutral* on all models except the 5/6 hp models. For 5/6 hp models, rotate the propeller shaft slowly and shift into gear to aid installation.

2. If the gearcase is to be overhauled, remove the vent and fill plugs to drain the lubricant from the housing, then loosely install the plugs back into the housing.

3A. For 8/9.9 hp models, locate the shifter linkage at the front of the engine, beneath the manual starter handle and near the electrical bullet junction block. On the opposite side from the electrical block, remove the clip from the clevis on the base of the shift shaft, then tap the shaft toward the electrical block until it just clears the clevis. Remove the snap pin from the pin retaining the clevis to the shift rod, then remove the pin and clevis.

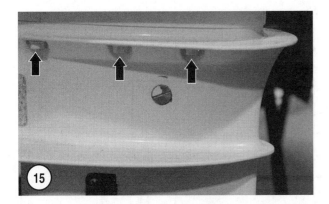

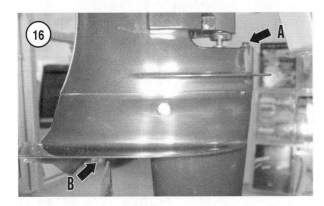

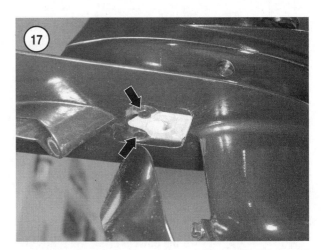

3B. For 9.9/15 hp models, remove the connector clip (**Figure 12**) from the shift lever. Then remove the shift connector from the lever and unscrew the connector from the shift rod.

3C. For 40-50 hp models disconnect the shift linkage as follows:

   a. Locate the shift shaft connector on the forward side of the drive shaft housing. Mark the connector position on the threaded portion of the upper and lower shift shafts. This step saves a great deal of time when adjusting the shift linkage.

   b. Use a wrench to hold the lower connector (**Figure 13**) and loosen the locknut above the connector.

   c. Rotate the lower shift shaft connector (**Figure 14**) and disconnect it from the upper shift shaft.

4. Support the gearcase and remove the bolts that attach it to the drive shaft housing (**Figure 15**, 9.9/15 hp shown, 8-50 hp models similar). For 5/6 hp models, there are three bolts (**Figure 16**) securing the gearcase. One bolt (A, **Figure 16**) is found on the midsection housing, just in front of the pivot, while two bolts (B) are located beneath the antiventilation plate. The two lower bolts (**Figure 17**) on 5/6 hp models are found just in front of the water intake and directly above the propeller.

5. Carefully pull or pry the gearcase from the drive shaft housing.

CAUTION
Never rotate the propeller shaft to align the drive shaft to the crankshaft. The water pump impeller can suffer damage that leads to engine overheating.

6. Thoroughly clean the mating surfaces of the gearcase and drive shaft housing (midsection) of all traces of corrosion, sealant (if used) or other debris.

7. For 5/6 hp models make sure the shift lever is in forward gear. For all other models, make sure the selector is in the neutral position.

8. Apply a light coating of OMC Triple-Guard grease either to the outside diameter of the water tube or on the water pump seal, as applicable.

9. Apply OMC Moly Lube or equivalent to the splines of the drive shaft, but *do not* coat the top surface of the shaft as lubricant may prevent proper seating of the drive shaft in the crankshaft.

10. For 40 and 50 hp models, apply a light coating of RTV silicone sealant to the mating surface of the gearcase. If dowels were removed, coat them with OMC Adhesive M and install the pins.

11. Apply OMC Nut Lock or equivalent threadlocking compound to the threads of the bolts on 5-15 hp models or OMC Gasket Sealing Compound or equivalent sealant to the threads of the bolts on 40-50 hp models.

12. Install the gearcase, taking care to slide the drive shaft into its opening in the drive shaft housing. If applicable, make sure the shift rod passes through the grommet in the housing and/or the water tube enters the impeller housing grommet. Keep the gearcase and drive shaft housing mating surfaces parallel during installation and align the

9

mounting bolt holes in the gearcase with their respective holes in the drive shaft housing. Also note the following:

NOTE
On 40 and 50 hp models, when installing the gearcase, make sure to align the lower shift shaft and the upper shift shaft, but do not thread the connector onto the shift shafts at this time.

13. The gearcase mates to the drive shaft housing if the drive shaft and crankshaft splines align. If the housings do not mate, lower the gearcase slightly. Rotate the drive shaft clockwise, as viewed from the top, until the drive shaft splines engage the crankshaft splines. When properly aligned, the gearcase slips into position.

14. Hold the gearcase in position and thread the mounting bolts into the gearcase and drive shaft housing. Tighten the bolts to the specification in **Table 1**.

15. Connect the shift linkage in the reverse of Step 3. For 40 and 50 hp models, note the following:

   a. Thread the connector onto the lower shift shaft until the reference marks align.

   b. Thread the locknut upward until it contacts the connector. Make sure the chamfered side of the locknut faces the chamfered side of the connector (**Figure 18**).

16. If the gearcase was overhauled or drained, properly refill it with the required lubricant, as detailed in Chapter Three.

17. Refer to Chapter Four to adjust the shift linkage, as necessary.

18. Connect the negative battery cable or spark plug leads. Check for proper cooling system operation *immediately* after starting the engine.

70 hp Model

Seven bolts retain the gearcase to the drive shaft housing. One bolt is located within the trim tab mounting cavity.

1. Remove the propeller as described in this chapter. Place the shift selector into NEUTRAL gear.

2. Locate the shift shaft connector on the forward side of the drive shaft housing. Use needle nose pliers to remove the cotter pin from the connector (**Figure 19**). Pull the connector from the upper and lower shift shaft (**Figure 20**).

3. Use a felt tip marker and mark the trim tab position relative to the gearcase. Remove the bolt (**Figure 21**) and trim tab from the gearcase. Locate the gearcase mounting bolt within the trim tab mounting cavity.

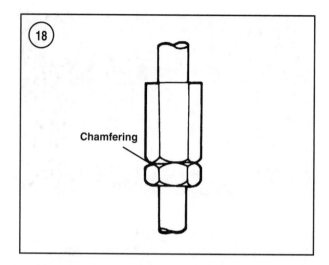

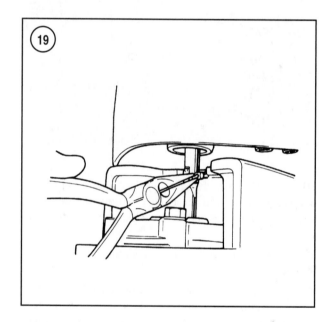

4. Support the gearcase and remove the seven bolts that attach the gearcase to the drive shaft housing (**Figure 15**).

5. Carefully tug or pry the gearcase loose from the drive shaft housing. Lower the gearcase enough to cut the plastic locking type clamp, and remove the speedometer hose from its fitting on the gearcase. Lower the gearcase from the drive shaft housing.

6. Thoroughly clean the mating surfaces of the gearcase and drive shaft housing of all traces of corrosion, sealant or other debris.

7. Make sure the selector is in the neutral position and did not change during overhaul or during other service while the gearcase was removed.

8. Apply OMC Moly Lube or equivalent to the splines of the drive shaft, but *do not* coat the top surface of the shaft

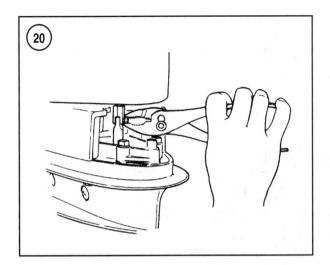

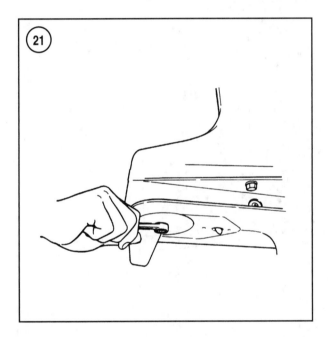

as lubricant there will prevent proper seating of the drive shaft in the crankshaft.

9. Apply a light coating of RTV silicone sealant to the mating surface of the gearcase. If dowels were removed, coat them with OMC Gasket Sealing Compound or equivalent sealant and install the pins.

10. Apply OMC Gasket Sealing Compound or equivalent sealant to the threads of the bolts.

11. Install the gearcase while carefully sliding the drive shaft into its opening in the drive shaft housing. Keep the gearcase and drive shaft housing mating surfaces parallel and align the mounting bolt holes in the gearcase with their respective holes in the drive shaft housing. Also note the following:

a. Make sure the water tube in the drive shaft housing aligns with the water tube sealing grommet on the water pump.

b. Align the lower shift shaft and the upper shift shaft while installing the gearcase. Do not install the connector pin at this time.

c. Slide the speedometer hose onto the gearcase fitting and secure it with a plastic locking type clamp.

12. The gearcase mates to the drive shaft housing if the drive shaft and crankshaft splines align. If the housings do not mate, lower the gearcase slightly. Rotate the drive shaft clockwise, as viewed from the top, until the drive shaft splines engage the crankshaft splines. When properly aligned, the gearcase slips into position.

13. Hold the gearcase in position and thread the mounting bolts into the gearcase and drive shaft housing. Tighten the bolts to the specification in **Table 1**.

14. Install the connector pin into its openings in the upper and lower shift shaft. Install a *new* cotter pin into the hole in the connector pin. Bend over the ends of the cotter pin.

15. Align the marks and install the trim tab to the gearcase. Install and securely tighten the trim tab bolt.

16. If the gearcase was overhauled or drained, properly refill it with the required lubricant, as detailed in Chapter Three.

17. Refer to Chapter Four to adjust the shift linkage, as necessary.

18. Connect the negative battery cable or spark plug leads. Check for proper cooling system operation *immediately* after starting the engine.

WATER PUMP

Always replace the impeller, seals, O-rings and gaskets anytime the water pump is serviced. Never use questionable parts. Doing so may compromise the reliability of this vital component. Water pump components are inexpensive compared to damage that can be caused from their failure. Refer to the instructions for the selected model.

Removal and Installation

5-15 hp models

Refer to **Figure 22** for 5/6 hp models or **Figure 23** for 8-15 hp models.

1. Refer to *Gearcase Removal and Installation* in this chapter and remove the gearcase from the engine. Mount the gearcase on a suitable workstand for easy access to the water pump components.

2. Remove the four bolts from the water pump impeller housing.

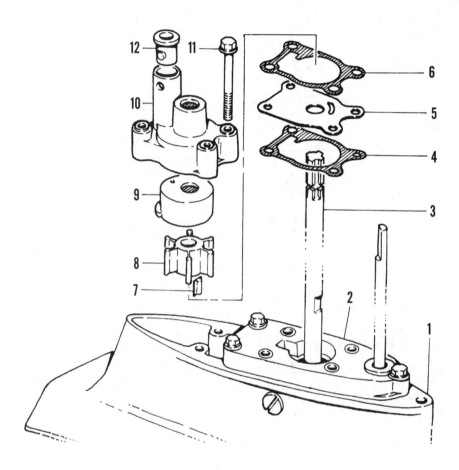

㉒ **WATER PUMP COMPONENTS (5/6 HP MODELS)**

1. Gearcase housing
2. Pump hose
3. Drive shaft
4. Gasket
5. Impeller plate
6. Gasket
7. Impeller key
8. Impeller
9. Impeller liner
10. Pump housing
11. Bolt
12. Water tube grommet

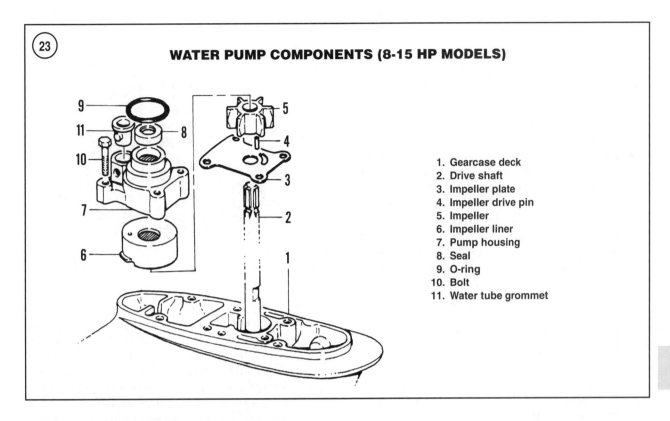

WATER PUMP COMPONENTS (8-15 HP MODELS)

1. Gearcase deck
2. Drive shaft
3. Impeller plate
4. Impeller drive pin
5. Impeller
6. Impeller liner
7. Pump housing
8. Seal
9. O-ring
10. Bolt
11. Water tube grommet

9

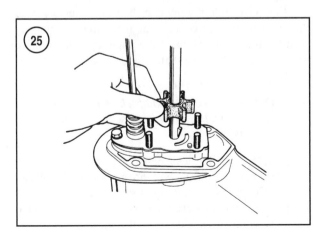

3. Slide the impeller housing and impeller up and off the drive shaft.

> *NOTE*
> *If the impeller remains in the water pump body (**Figure 24**), pry it out with a blunt tip pry bar. If the impeller remains on the drive shaft, gently pry it up with a blunt tip pry bar. Lift the impeller up and over the drive shaft (**Figure 25**).*

4. Remove the impeller drive pin and the impeller plate. On 5/6 hp models there is a gasket used on each side of the impeller plate assembly. Remove and discard these gaskets.

5. Remove and discard the water tube grommet. For 8-15 hp models, also remove and discard the impeller housing O-ring and the drive shaft seal.

6. Clean the impeller plate, gearcase and impeller housing mating surfaces of any remaining sealant or gasket residue.

7. Inspect the water pump housing, impeller and plate for excessive wear or damage. Refer to *Inspection*, in this section.

> *CAUTION*
> *Do not apply excess sealant or adhesive to the impeller plate, housing or gasket (as ap-*

plicable), as it might be pressed out from between the mating surfaces when the impeller housing is installed and, if it dried on an impeller contact surface, could cause premature impeller wear.

8. For 5/6 hp models prep the water pump impeller and housing for installation as follows:

   a. Install the water tube grommet into the tube boss on the end of the impeller housing. Make sure the grommet seats in the housing, then coat the inside of the grommet with OMC Triple-Guard or an equivalent water-resistant marine grease.

   b. Lightly coat the interior of the impeller liner cup with gear oil, then insert the impeller while twisting *counterclockwise*. The impeller blades should bend in a clockwise direction as shown in **Figure 24**.

   c. Lightly coat the outside of the impeller liner cup with OMC Gasket Sealing Compound or an equivalent sealant, then insert the cup into the bottom of the impeller housing.

   d. Lightly coat both sides of both impeller plate gaskets with OMC Gasket Sealing Compound or an equivalent sealant, then position one gasket on top of the impeller plate and one underneath. Slide the impeller plate with the gaskets over the driveshaft and down into position on the gearcase. Make sure the gaskets are properly aligned and that no excess material appears on the upper portion of the impeller plate.

9. For 8-15 hp models prep the water pump impeller and housing for installation as follows:

   a. Apply OMC Gasket Sealing Compound or equivalent sealant to the outside metal casing of the new driveshaft seal, then install the seal into the top of the impeller housing with the lip facing downward into the housing.

   b. Apply a light coating of OMC Adhesive M or equivalent to the impeller housing O-ring, then install it onto the round boss on top of the housing.

   c. Apply a light coating of OMC Adhesive M or equivalent to the outer surface of the water tube grommet, then install it into the water tube boss on the end of the impeller housing. Make sure the grommet bosses seat in the housing. Coat the inside of the grommet with OMC Triple-Guard or equivalent water-resistant marine grease.

   d. Lightly coat the outside of the impeller liner cup with OMC Gasket Sealing Compound or equivalent sealant, then insert the cup into the bottom of the impeller housing with the small bleed hole (if present) facing toward the water tube grommet.

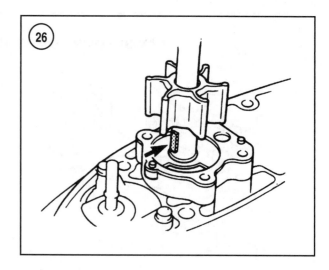

   e. Lightly coat the interior of the impeller liner cup with gear oil, then insert the impeller while twisting *counterclockwise*. The impeller blades should bend in a clockwise direction as shown in **Figure 24**.

   f. Apply a thin bead of OMC Adhesive M or equivalent to the gearcase machined mating surface for the impeller plate and the bottom of the impeller housing, then slide the impeller plate over the driveshaft and down into position on the gearcase.

10. Apply OMC Needle Bearing Assembly grease or equivalent to the impeller drive pin surface, then install it into the drive shaft slot (**Figure 26**).

> *NOTE*
> *Although not specifically called for by the manufacturer, it is a good idea to lubricate the bore of the impeller with a light coating of water-resistant marine grease prior to installing the impeller and housing. This process is especially true if the engine is stored for some time before its next use.*

11. Carefully slide the impeller housing assembly onto the drive shaft. If necessary, align the mpeller housing with the base while aligning the impeller with the drive key by turning the drive shaft slightly *clockwise*.

> *CAUTION*
> *Only rotate the drive shaft **clockwise** when viewed from the top, otherwise the impeller could be damaged.*

12. Seat the impeller housing against the impeller plate. Coat the impeller housing bolt threads with OMC Gasket Sealing Compound for 5/6 hp models or with OMC Nut Lock for 8-15 hp models, then install and finger-tighten the bolts while pressing down on the housing.

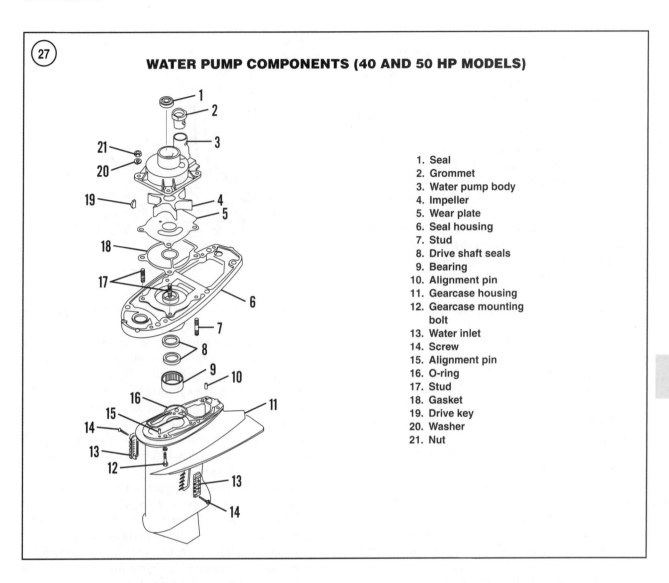

WATER PUMP COMPONENTS (40 AND 50 HP MODELS)

1. Seal
2. Grommet
3. Water pump body
4. Impeller
5. Wear plate
6. Seal housing
7. Stud
8. Drive shaft seals
9. Bearing
10. Alignment pin
11. Gearcase housing
12. Gearcase mounting bolt
13. Water inlet
14. Screw
15. Alignment pin
16. O-ring
17. Stud
18. Gasket
19. Drive key
20. Washer
21. Nut

9

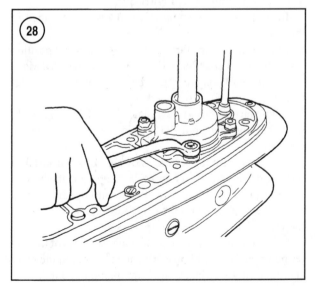

13. Tighten the four water pump impeller housing bolts evenly to the specification in **Table 1**.

14. Install the gearcase as described in this chapter.

40 and 50 hp models

Refer to **Figure 27**.

1. Refer to *Gearcase Removal and Installation* in this chapter and remove the gearcase from the engine. Mount the gearcase on a suitable workstand for easy access to the water pump components.

2. Carefully pry the sealing grommet (2, **Figure 27**) and seal (1) from the water pump body (3).

3. Remove the four nuts and washers from the water pump body (**Figure 28**). Use two pry bars to carefully pry the water pump body free from the drive shaft bearing and

seal housing (6, **Figure 27**). Slip the body over the drive shaft and remove it from the gearcase (**Figure 29**).

4A. If the impeller remains in the water pump body (**Figure 24**), pry it out with a blunt tip pry bar.

4B. If the impeller remains on the drive shaft, gently pry it up with a blunt tip pry bar. Lift the impeller up and over the drive shaft (**Figure 25**).

5. Remove the drive key (**Figure 26**) from the drive shaft. Lift the wear plate and gasket (5 and 18, **Figure 27**) from the seal and bearing housing (6). Thoroughly clean the exposed section of the drive shaft with an aerosol parts cleaner.

6. Remove the bearing and seal housing if these must be removed for further gearcase disassembly or seal replacement. Remove all shafts, gears and bearings to remove the bearing and seal housing. Refer to *Gearcase Overhaul* in this chapter for procedures.

7. Inspect the water pump components as described in this section.

8. Install the gasket and wear plate (18 and 5, **Figure 27**) onto the housing (6).

9. Apply grease to the drive key surfaces and install it into the drive shaft slot (**Figure 26**). Lubricate the bore of the impeller with grease and slide it onto the drive shaft. Align the impeller with the drive key and seat it against the wear plate.

10. Install the *new* seal (1, **Figure 27**) into the drive shaft bore of the water pump body with the seal lip facing out. Use an appropriately sized socket or section of tubing to seat the seal in the bore. Apply water resistant grease to the lip surfaces of the seal.

11. Apply a coat of grease to the inner surfaces of the water pump body (3, **Figure 27**) and slide it onto the drive shaft until it just contacts the water pump impeller (4).

12. Align the water pump body with the base. Lightly push down on the water pump body while rotating the drive shaft clockwise as viewed from the top. Continue until the impeller fully enters the water pump body.

13. Install the four washers and nuts (20 and 21, **Figure 27**). Tighten the nuts evenly to the specification in **Table 1**.

14. Apply grease to the surfaces and install the grommet (2, **Figure 27**) onto the water pump body.

15. Install the gearcase as described in this chapter.

70 hp models

Refer to **Figure 30**.

1. Refer to *Gearcase Removal and Installation* in this chapter and remove the gearcase from the engine. Mount the gearcase on a suitable workstand for easy access to the water pump components.

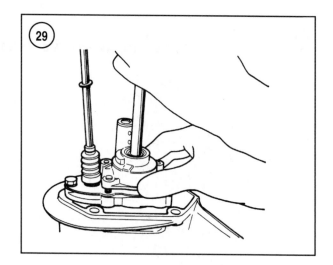

2. Carefully pry the sealing grommet (26, **Figure 30**) from the water pump body (25).

3. Remove the four bolts from the water pump body (**Figure 31**). Use two pry bars to carefully pry the water pump body free from the gearcase (20). Slip the body over the drive shaft and remove it from the gearcase (**Figure 29**).

4A. If the impeller remains in the water pump body (**Figure 24**), pry it out with a blunt tip pry bar.

4B. If the impeller remains on the drive shaft, gently pry it up with a blunt tip pry bar. Lift the impeller up and over the drive shaft (**Figure 25**).

5. Remove the drive key (**Figure 26**) from the drive shaft. Thoroughly clean the exposed section of the drive shaft with an aerosol parts cleaner. Remove the gasket and wear plate (22 and 29, **Figure 30**) from the gearcase.

6. Carefully pull the water tube (28, **Figure 30**) from the bracket and seal (24 and 23, **Figure 30**). Lift the tube out of the rear grommet (27, **Figure 30**).

7. Inspect the water pump components as described in this section.

8. Slip the water tube through the grommets and position it into the bracket and seal (24 and 23, **Figure 30**). Make sure the tube fits securely into the rear grommet (27, **Figure 30**).

9. Align the gasket and wear plate (22 and 23, **Figure 30**) with the alignment pin (24) while seating them on the gearcase.

10. Apply grease to the drive key surfaces and install it into the drive shaft slot (**Figure 26**). Lubricate the bore of the impeller with grease and slide it onto the drive shaft. Align the impeller with the drive key and seat it against the wear plate.

11. Apply a coat of grease to the inner surfaces of the water pump body (25, **Figure 30**) and slide it onto the drive shaft until it just contacts the water pump impeller (3).

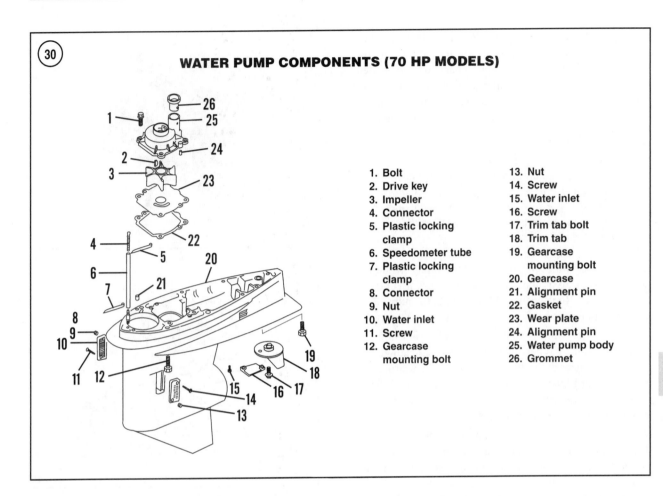

WATER PUMP COMPONENTS (70 HP MODELS)

1. Bolt
2. Drive key
3. Impeller
4. Connector
5. Plastic locking clamp
6. Speedometer tube
7. Plastic locking clamp
8. Connector
9. Nut
10. Water inlet
11. Screw
12. Gearcase mounting bolt
13. Nut
14. Screw
15. Water inlet
16. Screw
17. Trim tab bolt
18. Trim tab
19. Gearcase mounting bolt
20. Gearcase
21. Alignment pin
22. Gasket
23. Wear plate
24. Alignment pin
25. Water pump body
26. Grommet

9

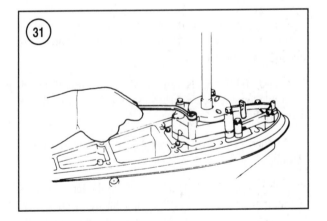

12. Align the water pump body with the base. Lightly push down on the water pump body while rotating the drive shaft clockwise as viewed from the top. Continue until the impeller fully enters the water pump body.

13. Install the four water pump bolts (1, **Figure 30**). Tighten the bolts evenly to the specification listed in **Table 1**.

14. Apply grease to the surfaces and install the grommet (26, **Figure 30**) onto the water pump body.

15. Install the gearcase as described in this chapter.

Inspection (All Models)

1. Clean all metal parts in a mild solvent and dry with compressed air. Make sure to remove all gasket material and sealant residue.

2. Clean all plastic components with OMC cleaning solvent or isopropyl alcohol. Make sure to remove all gasket material and sealant residue.

CAUTION
It is highly recommended that the impeller be replaced anytime it is removed. If reusing the impeller, check the bonding of the rubber to the impeller hub for separation. Check the side seal surfaces and blade ends for cracks, tears, excessive wear or a glazed/melted appearance. If any of these defects appear, do not reuse the original impeller under any circumstances.

3. Inspect the impeller (**Figure 32**) for brittle, missing or burned vanes. Squeeze the vanes toward the hub and release them. The vanes should spring back to the extended position. Replace the impeller if there are damaged, burned, brittle or stiff vanes. Replace the impeller if the vanes are set in a curled position and do not spring back when released.

> *CAUTION*
> *The water pump impeller must be able to float on the drive shaft. Clean the impeller area of the drive shaft thoroughly with emery cloth. Make certain the impeller slides onto the drive shaft easily.*

4. Inspect the water pump body or the lining inside the water pump body, as applicable, for burned, worn or damaged surfaces. Replace the impeller lining, if equipped, or the water pump body if there are any of these defects.

5. Inspect the water pump body/impeller housing for melted plastic or other indications of overheating. Replace the body and, for 40-70 hp models, the bearing and seal housing (**Figure 33**) if any defects are noted. Refer to *Gearcase Overhaul* in this chapter for water pump base/seal carrier replacement instructions.

6. Inspect the water tube, grommets and seals for a burned appearance, cracked surfaces or brittle material. Replace the water tube, grommets and seals if there are any of these defects.

7. Inspect the wear plate (**Figure 34**) for a warped surface, wear grooves, melted plastic or other damaged areas. While some grooving is normal, the grooves must not be deep or sharp. If a groove easily catches a fingernail, replace the part. Replace the impeller liner (or housing) and impeller plate as necessary.

GEARCASE OVERHAUL

General Procedures (All Models)

1. Remove the gearcase from the engine and the water pump components from the gearcase as described in this chapter.

2. Thoroughly clean the external surfaces of the gearcase with pressurized water. Pay particular attention to the bearing carrier area where debris is easily trapped in recesses.

3. Clamp the gearcase skeg in a suitable fixture. Use padded jaws or wooden blocks to protect the gearcase.

4. Perform the necessary removal and disassembly instructions until the required component is accessible.

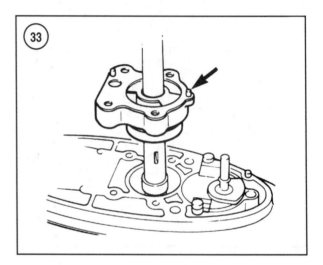

5. Identify and record the location and thickness of all shims and spacers. Store them by wiring them together or placing them in envelopes.

6. On 40-70 hp models, refer to *Shim Selection* if installing replacement gears, bearings, housing, propeller or drive shafts.

7. Replace all seals, O-rings and the pinion nut during assembly.

8. Apply OMC Triple-Guard or an equivalent water-resistant marine grease to all seal lips during assembly, unless otherwise directed. Apply a gear lubricant to the bearings during assembly.

9. Pressure test the gearcase as described in Chapter Two before filling it with lubricant and returning it to service.

10. Refer to the instructions and illustrations that follow for individual models and follow them carefully. Improper assembly can result in improper shift operation, noisy operation, gearcase wear and eventual failure.

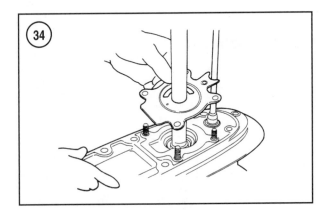

Disassembly (5/6 hp Models)

Refer to **Figure 35** for component identification throughout this procedure. The propshaft bearing carrier and propeller shaft on these models can be removed without removing the gearcase from the outboard motor, if so desired.

1. If not done during removal, drain the gearcase lubricant as described in Chapter Three.

2. Remove the gearcase as described in this chapter.

3. Remove the water pump as described in this chapter.

4. Remove the three screws securing the water pump base to the gearcase deck. See **Figure 36**. Then separate the base from the gearcase and slide it up and off the drive and shift shafts. Remove and discard the gasket.

5. Pull the drive and shift shafts straight up and out of the gearcase.

6. Remove the two screws securing the propshaft bearing carrier to the gearcase housing. Rotate the bearing carrier to break the O-ring seal, then pull the carrier and propeller shaft from the gearcase as an assembly. If necessary, gently tap the carrier mounting screw ears with a soft-faced mallet to assist in rotating the carrier.

7. Make sure the shift cam follower and retainer spring (20, **Figure 35**) comes out with the propshaft. If not, reach into the gearcase bore and remove the cam follower shaft.

8. Slide the propshaft bearing carrier from the propeller shaft. Remove and discard the carrier O-ring (27, **Figure 35**).

NOTE
Use the spring compressor part No. 390766 (or equivalent) to disassemble and assemble the propeller shaft on 1997 and 1998 models. The tool is designed to straddle the clutch dog pin and compress its spring. Once the spring is compressed, the clutch dog pin can be removed or installed.

9. Disassemble the propeller shaft as follows:
   a. Begin by sliding the reverse gear (and its thrust washer) from the shaft.
   b. Pull the shift cam follower from the propshaft bore.
   c. Remove the clutch dog pin's retaining spring with a small screwdriver or awl and discard the spring. Insert the tool under one end of the spring and rotate the propeller shaft to unwind the spring. See **Figure 37**.
   d. Insert the spring compressor (OMC part No. 390766) into the open end of the propeller shaft and depress the clutch dog spring. See **Figure 38**.
   e. While holding the spring compressed, push the clutch dog pin out of the clutch dog with a suitable punch. Slowly release the pressure on the spring, then remove the spring and clutch dog from the propeller shaft. See **Figure 39**.

10. Remove the seal saver and O-ring (not pictured) from the gearcase head.

11. Reach into the gearcase bore and tilt the forward gear out from under the pinion gear. Remove the forward gear.

12. Remove the shift cam from the front of the gearcase bore by tilting the gearcase until the cam falls from the gearcase bore.

13. Remove the pinion gear, upper and lower thrust washers and the thrust bearing. See **Figure 40**.

14. Remove the propeller shaft seal from the shaft bearing carrier as follows:
   a. Position the propeller shaft bearing carrier back into the gearcase and re-install by finger-tightening the two retaining screws (this will hold the carrier in position for seal removal).
   b. Install a suitable small two-jaw puller, and a puller assembly consisting of a puller bridge, threaded rod and support plate (OMC part No. 432127).
   c. Use the puller to carefully withdraw the seal from the carrier. Do not damage the seal bore while removing it. Discard the seal.
   d. Remove the propshaft bearing carrier from the gearcase again.

15. Remove the two drive shaft seals from the bottom of the water pump base in the same manner as the propeller shaft seal. Discard the seals.

16. Remove and discard the shift shaft bushing from the bottom of the water pump base. Pry the bushing from the cover using the shift shaft or a similar sized punch. Then remove and discard the O-ring under the bushing.

NOTE
The forward gear and its bearing may be available separately, but always replace the race when installing a new bearing. When

9

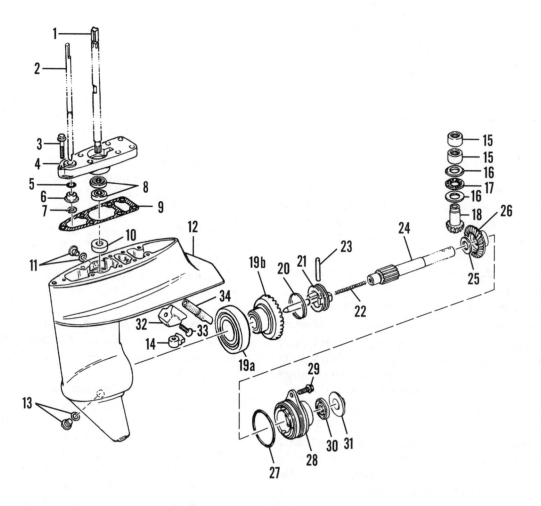

③⑤

GEARCASE ASSEMBLY (5/6 HP MODELS)

1. Drive shaft
2. Shift shaft
3. Bolt
4. Water pump base
5. O-ring
6. Shift shaft bushing
7. Retaining ring
8. Drive shaft seals
9. Gasket
10. Sleeve and bearing assembly
11. Vent plug and seal
12. Gearcase housing
13. Drain/fill plug and seal
14. Shift cam
15. Pinion gear bearings
16. Upper and lower thrust washers
17. Thrust bearing
18. Pinion gear
19a. Roller bearing assembly
19b. Forward gear
20. Shift cam follower and retainer spring
21. Clutch dog
22. Shift spring
23. Clutch dog cross pin
24. Propeller shaft
25. Reverse gear thrust washer
26. Reverse gear
27. O-ring
28. Propshaft bearing carrier
29. Screw
30. Propshaft seal
31. Seal protecting washer
32. Anode
33. Screw
34. Water inlet screen

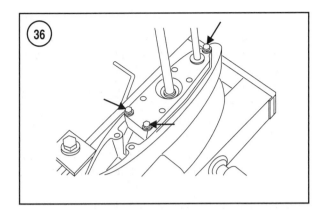

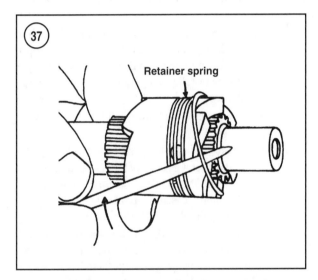

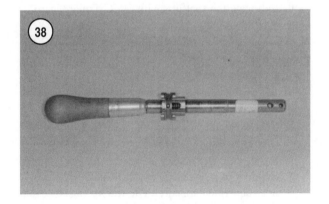

servicing, make sure the puller jaws are positioned in the relief slots behind the bearing race.

17. If the forward gear tapered roller bearing requires replacement, proceed as follows:

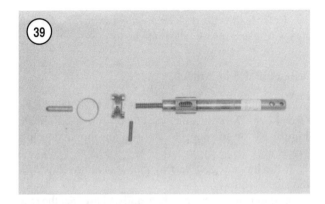

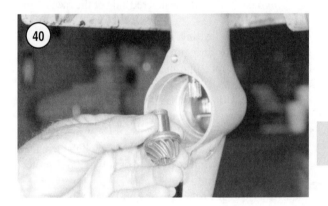

a. Remove the bearing race by pulling it from the gearcase bore with a suitable small jawed puller and a slide hammer.
b. Discard the bearing race.
c. Separate the roller bearing from the forward gear by supporting the bearing in a knife-edged bearing plate. Press on the gear hub with a suitable mandrel until the gear is separated from the bearing.
d. Discard the roller bearing.

18. If the drive shaft upper sleeve and bearing assembly (10, **Figure 35**) requires replacement, pull the bearing and sleeve from the drive shaft bore with a suitable external two-jaw bearing puller. The puller must pull on the outside diameter of the sleeve.

NOTE
The drive shaft upper bearing and sleeve assembly must be removed (and discarded) in order to remove the two lower drive shaft pinion bearings.

19. If the two (lower drive shaft bearings) require replacement, position a shop towel in the gearcase bore directly under the bearings. Drive both bearings into the gearcase bore using a bearing remover (OMC part No. 319880) or an equivalent mandrel. Discard both bearings.

9

20. Refer to *Gearcase Component Cleaning and Inspection*. Clean and inspect all components.

Assembly (5/6 hp Models)

Lubricate all internal components with OMC Ultra HPF Gear Lube. Do *not* assemble components dry. Refer to **Figure 35** for component identification throughout this procedure.

1. If the forward gear bearing race was removed, install the race as follows:
   a. Lubricate the bearing race and its bore. Set the race into the bore with the tapered side of the race facing up (out).
   b. Position a bearing race installer (OMC part No. 326025) or an equivalent mandrel over the race. Drive the race into the gearcase until it seats in its bore.
2. If the forward gear roller bearing was removed from the forward gear, install a new roller bearing onto the forward gear as follows:
   a. Place the gear in a press with the gear hub facing up. Use a suitable piece of wood or soft metal to protect the gear teeth.
   b. Lubricate the roller bearing and gear hub. Then position the bearing over the gear hub with the rollers facing up away from the gear.
   c. Using a suitable mandrel that only contacts the bearing's inner race, press the bearing onto the gear hub until it seats against the hub shoulder.
3. If the drive shaft upper bearing and sleeve assembly was removed, install a new bearing as follows:
   a. Lubricate the new bearing assembly and the drive shaft bore.
   b. Position the bearing assembly into the drive shaft bore. If one side of the bearing is numbered, position that side up.
   c. Drive the bearing assembly into the drive shaft bore using bearing installer (part No. 326575), or an equivalent mandrel that contacts only the sleeve and not the bearing. Drive the sleeve and bearing until the sleeve seats in its bore.
4. If the two lower drive shaft pinion bearings were removed, pull the new bearings into position from the (propshaft) bore, one at a time. To install the new bearings, proceed as follows:
   a. Lubricate the new bearings and the drive shaft bore.
   b. Place a new bearing onto a bearing installer (OMC part No. 319878). The numbered or lettered side of the bearing must face the installer.
   c. Position the bearing and installer into the propshaft bore. Install a 6-1/2 in. long, 3/8 in., coarse-thread bolt (or match the threads of the installer) and a heavy-duty flat washer into the drive shaft bore. The washer must wide enough to cover the upper drive shaft bearing sleeve.
   d. Thread the bolt into the installer. Tighten the bolt to pull the bearing into the drive shaft bore. Tighten the bolt until the installer seats against the gearcase. Then remove the tools.
   e. Place a second new bearing onto the bearing installer. The numbered side of the bearing must face the installer.
   f. Position the bearing and installer in the propshaft bore. Install the bolt and flat washer into the drive shaft bore.
   g. Thread the bolt into the installer. Tighten the bolt to pull the bearing into the drive shaft bore and push the first bearing deeper into the bore. Tighten the bolt until the installer seats against the gearcase. Remove the tools.
5. Install a new seal into the propshaft bearing carrier as follows:
   a. Position the carrier so that its seal bore is facing up.
   b. If the seal is metal cased, coat the outer diameter of the seal with OMC Gasket Sealing Compound. If the seal is rubber cased, lubricate the outer diameter of the seal with OMC DPL Lubricant.
   c. Position the seal into the carrier bore with its numbered or lettered side facing up (out). Press the seal into the carrier using a suitable mandrel or socket until it seats in the bore.
   d. Lubricate the seal lips with OMC Triple-Guard or equivalent marine grease.
6. Lubricate a new O-ring (27, **Figure 35**) with OMC Triple-Guard or equivalent marine grease. Install the O-ring into the propshaft bearing carrier groove.
7. Install two new drive shaft seals into the water pump base as follows:
   a. Coat the outer diameter of each seal with OMC Gasket Sealing Compound or equivalent sealant.
   b. Install the inner seal using the longer, stepped shoulder of a seal installer (OMC part No. 326547) or an equivalent mandrel. The seal lip must face into the pump base (away from the gearcase). Press the seal until the installer contacts the pump base.

NOTE
The two upper drive shaft seals are installed back-to-back. When using a suitable installer tool, such as OMC part No. 326547, they may be positioned back-to-back on the tool and installed together.

c. Install the outer seal using the shorter shoulder of the OMC seal installer or an equivalent mandrel. The seal lip must face out of the pump base (into the gearcase). Press the seal until the installer contacts the pump base. The seal must be flush with the pump base when installed.

d. Lubricate the seal lips and pack the area between the seal lips with OMC Triple-Guard or equivalent marine grease.

8. Lubricate a new shift shaft O-ring with OMC Triple-Guard or equivalent marine grease and install it into the water pump base.

9. Lightly apply OMC Adhesive M or equivalent sealant to the outer diameter of a new shift shaft bushing. Push the bushing into the water pump cover, over the shift shaft O-ring. Make sure the bushing is seated, then allow the adhesive to dry.

10. If the shift shaft retaining ring (7, **Figure 35**) was removed, reinstall it to the shift shaft at this time.

11. Using a pair of mechanical fingers or needlenose pliers, position the shift cam into the gearcase bore. The side marked *UP* must face the gearcase deck (toward the power head) and the cam ramp must face the port side.

12. While holding the shift cam in position, insert the shift shaft into the gearcase bore (retaining ring end first) and engage the shift cam. Rotate the shaft as necessary to align the components, then seat the shaft into the cam. Then rotate the shift shaft as far clockwise as possible.

13. Lightly coat both sides of a new water pump base gasket with OMC Adhesive M or equivalent sealant. Position the gasket to the gearcase deck, then carefully slide the water pump base over the shift shaft and into position against the gasket. Align the base and gasket with the gearcase deck screw holes.

14. Coat the threads of the three water pump base screws with OMC Nut Lock or equivalent threadlocking compound. Install and evenly tighten the bolts to specifications in **Table 1**. See **Figure 36**.

15. Assemble the thrust washers and thrust bearing on the pinion gear. Use OMC Needle Bearing Assembly or equivalent grease to hold the components in position. Position the thrust bearing between the thrust washers as shown in **Figure 40** and 15 and 16 of **Figure 35**.

16. Invert the gearcase and install the pinion gear and bearing assembly into the drive shaft bore.

17. Insert the forward gear and bearing assembly into the gearcase bore. Tilt the gear to get it past the pinion gear, then rotate it into position (meshed with the pinion gear). If it sticks, insert the propeller shaft into the gear to gain additional leverage. Remove the propeller shaft when finished.

NOTE
Use the Spring compressor (OMC part No. 390766) or equivalent to assemble the propshaft on these models. The tool is designed to straddle the clutch dog pin and compress its spring. Once the spring has been compressed, the clutch dog pin can be installed.

18. Assemble the propreller shaft as follows:

a. Align the cross pin holes of the clutch dog with the slot in the propeller shaft. Position the end marked *PROP END* toward the propeller and slide the clutch dog onto the propeller shaft.

b. Install the spring into the propeller shaft. Insert the spring compressor into the open end of the propshaft and depress the spring. See **Figure 38**.

c. With the spring compressed, insert the clutch dog pin into the clutch. The pin must pass in front of the clutch dog spring.

NOTE
When installed correctly, the clutch dog pin retaining spring must lay flat, with no overlapping coils.

d. Secure the pin to the clutch dog with a new retainer spring. Do not open the spring any more than necessary to install it.

e. Coat the shift cam follower with OMC Needle Bearing Assembly or equivalent grease. Then insert the cam follower into the open end of the propreller shaft. The flat end must contact the clutch dog pin so the rounded end is facing outward.

f. Insert the propreller shaft assembly into the gearcase and seat it into the forward gear hub.

g. Coat the reverse gear thrust washer with OMC Needle Bearing Assembly or equivalent grease, then position the washer into its recess in the reverse gear hub. Finally, install the reverse gear assembly over the propreller shaft and engage it to the pinion gear teeth.

19. Apply a light coat of OMC Gasket Sealing Compound or equivalent sealant to the propshaft bearing carrier-to-gearcase mating surfaces. Then install the propshaft bearing carrier. Rotate the carrier to align the screw holes, then seat the carrier on the gearcase.

20. Coat the threads of the two propshaft bearing carrier mounting screws with OMC Gasket Sealing Compound or equivalent sealant. Install and evenly tighten the screws to specifications in **Table 1**.

21. Install the seal protecting washer over the propeller shaft and up against the propreller shaft seals. The stepped side of the washer must face away from the gearcase.

9

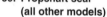

41

GEARCASE ASSEMBLY (8-15 HP MODELS)

1. Drive shaft
2. Drive shaft seals
3. Drive shaft upper
   needle bearing
4. Bearing sleeve
5. Drive shaft lower
   (pinion) needle bearings
6. Screw and washer
7. Shift shaft coupler
8. Shift shaft
9. Shift shaft bushing
10. O-ring
11. Washer
12. Anode
13. Screw and locknut
14. Vent plug and seal
15. Gearcase housing
16. Water inlet screen
17. Screw
18. Drain/fill plug and seal
19. Shift linkage pivot screw
20. O-ring

21. Thrust washers
22. Thrust bearing
23. Pinion gear
24. Roller bearing assembly
25. Forward gear
26. Shift yoke and linkage
27. Clutch dog cradle
28. Clutch dog
29. Detent balls
30. Detent spring
31. Propeller shaft
32. Reverse gear
33. Large needle bearing
34. O-ring
35. Propshaft bearing carrier
36. Screw
37. Small needle bearing
38. Propshaft seals
    (early 1995 models)
39. Propshaft seal
    (all other models)

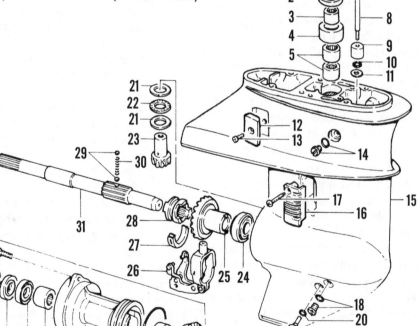

22. Lubricate the lower end of the drive shaft. Install the drive shaft into its bore and rotate the shaft as necessary to engage the pinion gear.

23. Test the integrity of the gearcase seals, gaskets and O-rings as described in Chapter Two before filling the gearcase with lubricant and returning it to service. The drive shaft must be held in position during the pressure tests, or it may be forced out of its bore by the internal pressure.

24. Install the water pump as described in this chapter.

25. Install the gearcase as described in this chapter.

26. Fill the gearcase with the recommended lubricant as described in Chapter Three.

Disassembly (8-15 hp Models)

Early 1995 models may have two propshaft seals installed back-to-back, while all later models use a single double-lipped seal.

It is possible to remove the propshaft bearing carrier and propeller shaft without removing the gearcase from the engine. Refer to **Figure 41**.

1. If not done during removal, drain the gearcase lubricant as described in Chapter Three.

2. Remove the gearcase as described in this chapter.

3. Remove the water pump as described in this chapter.

4. Pull the drive shaft straight up and out of the gearcase.

5. Remove the two screws securing the propshaft bearing carrier to the gearcase.

6. Pull the propshaft bearing carrier from the gearcase. If the carrier sticks, use puller kit (OMC part No. 368631) or an equivalent puller as follows:

   a. Thread two screws from the puller kit into the holes of the screws removed in Step 5.

   b. Place the bridge from the puller kit over the propeller shaft and pilot it on the two puller screws.

   c. Install the propeller nut onto the propeller shaft. Tighten the nut to pull the carrier and the propreller shaft from the gearcase bore. If necessary, add washers under the nut to allow the tool to pull the carrier further from its bore.

   d. Once the carrier is loose, remove the nut, bridge and two screws. Pull the propeller shaft and carrier from the gearcase bore as an assembly.

7. Slide the bearing carrier from the propeller shaft. Remove and discard the carrier O-ring.

8. Slide the reverse gear and its thrust washer from the propeller shaft. Then locate and secure the two clutch dog detent balls and detent spring. The detent balls are most likely in the gearcase bore. If necessary, use a magnetic pickup tool to remove the shift detent balls.

9. Remove the shift linkage pivot screw (19, **Figure 41**) from the starboard side of the gearcase. The screw is easily identified by its *Posidriv* (similar to Phillips) screw head. Remove and discard the O-ring from under the screw head.

10. Fully unthread the shift shaft, then pull the shaft from the gearcase.

11. Using a long pair of needlenose pliers, reach into the gearcase bore and remove the clutch dog.

12. Grasp the shift yoke with a pair of needlenose pliers and remove it and the forward gear as an assembly. Wiggle the components as necessary to allow removal, tilting the shifter lever slightly to free it. Then remove the forward gear roller bearing from the front of the gearcase bore.

13. Remove the pinion gear, both thrust washers and the thrust bearing.

14. The shift shaft bushing must be pulled up and out of its bore to access the shift shaft O-ring. Remove the shift shaft bushing, O-ring and washer as follows:

   a. Position the head of the bushing remover (OMC part No. 327693) into the gearcase bore and under the shift shaft bushing.

   b. Insert a suitable slide hammer (OMC part No. 391008) through the shift shaft bushing and engage the bushing remover.

   c. Unthread the handle from the bushing remover, then pull the bushing up and out the gearcase using the slide hammer.

   d. Locate and secure the washer, then remove and discard the bushing O-ring.

15. Remove the two drive shaft seals from the gearcase by pulling them from their bore with a suitable two-jaw puller, puller bridge, threaded rod and support plate (OMC part No. 432127). See **Figure 42**, typical. Do not damage the seal bore during the removal process. Discard the seals.

NOTE
Inspect the bearings while they are installed. If the driveshaft or pinion bearings are removed for any reason, replace them.

16. Remove the propshaft seal(s) from the propshaft bearing carrier in the same manner as the drive shaft seals. Discard the seal(s).

17. If the forward gear tapered roller bearing requires replacement, remove the bearing race. Pull it from the gearcase bore with a suitable bearing puller and slide hammer. Discard the race and the forward gear roller bearing.

18. If the driveshaft upper bearing and bearing sleeve (3 and 4, **Figure 41**) requires replacement, pull the bearing

9

first, then the sleeve, from the drive shaft bore. Use a suitable bearing puller and puller bridge, threaded rod and support plate (OMC part No. 432127). Assemble the tools as shown in **Figure 42**, typical. Discard the bearing.

NOTE
It is necessary to remove the drive shaft upper bearing and sleeve in order to remove the two lower drive shaft pinion bearings.

19. If the two pinion bearings require replacement, position a shop towel in the gearcase bore directly under the bearings. Drive both bearings into the gearcase bore using a bearing remover (OMC part No. 319880) or an equivalent mandrel. Discard both bearings.

20. If the propshaft bearing carrier small needle bearing (37, **Figure 41**) requires replacement, insert bearing remover (OMC part No. 319880) or an equivalent mandrel into the carrier from the O-ring groove end and press the bearing from the carrier. Discard the bearing.

21. If the large needle bearing (33, **Figure 41**) requires replacement, pull the bearing from the carrier with a suitable bearing puller and puller bridge, threaded rod and support plate (OMC part No. 432127). Discard the bearing.

22. Refer to *Gearcase Component Cleaning and Inspection*.

Assembly (8-15 hp Models)

Lubricate all internal components with OMC Ultra HPF Gear Lube or equivalent. Do *not* assemble components dry. Refer to **Figure 41** for component identification throughout this procedure.

NOTE
The forward gear bearing and race are a matched assembly. Replace them as a set.

1. If the forward gear bearing race was removed, install the new race as follows:

   a. Lubricate the bearing race and its bore. Set the race into the bore with the tapered side of the race facing up (out).

   b. Attach a bearing installer (OMC part No. 319929) to drive handle (OMC part No. 311880).

   c. Position the bearing installer or an equivalent mandrel over the bearing race.

   d. Cushion the leading edge of the gearcase on a suitable block of wood, then drive the race into the gearcase until it seats in its bore.

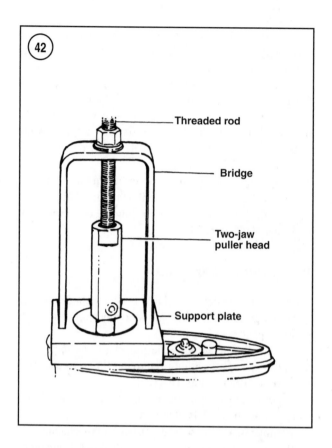

NOTE
Install the driveshaft lower needle bearing (5, Figure 41) before installing the drive shaft upper needle bearing and bearing sleeve (3 and 4).

CAUTION
The screws (1 and 7, Figure 43) must be securely tightened and the flat washer (2) must be perfectly flat or the bearings will not be correctly positioned in the next step.

2. If the two pinion bearings were removed, the new bearings must be pressed into position from the top of the drive shaft bore, one at a time. Several components from the universal pinion bearing remover/installer kit (OMC part No. 391257) and a second longer spacer (OMC part No. 339753) are required to properly locate the bearings. To install the new bearings, refer to **Figure 43** and proceed as follows:

   a. Lubricate two new bearings and the drive shaft bore.

   b. To install the lower bearing, assemble the tool as shown in **Figure 43** using the shorter spacer (OMC part No. 326585). Make sure the screws (1 and 7, **Figure 43**) are securely tightened.

PINION BEARING INSTALLATION (9.9 AND 15 HP)

1. Screw (1/2 in. long)
2. Flat washer (1 in. diameter)
3. Spacer (see text)
4. Plate (part No. 326583)
5. Threaded rod (part No. 326582)
6. Installer (part No. 326578)
7. Screw (1-1/4 in. long)

c. Position the bearing over the installer (6, **Figure 43**) with the numbered side of the bearing against the tool's shoulder.

d. Insert the assembly into the drive shaft bore. Drive against the screw (1, **Figure 43**) with a soft-faced mallet until the flat washer (2) contacts the spacer (3).

e. Replace the short spacer (3, **Figure 43**) with long spacer. After changing the spacer, make sure the screws (1 and 7, **Figure 43**) are securely tightened.

f. Position the second bearing over the installer (6, **Figure 43**) with the numbered side of the bearing against the tool's shoulder.

g. Pilot the assembly into the drive shaft bore. Drive against the screw (1, **Figure 43**) with a soft-faced mallet until the flat washer (2) contacts the spacer (3).

3. If the drive shaft upper bearing and sleeve were removed, assemble a new bearing and sleeve and install the assembly as follows:

a. Lubricate the new bearing, the sleeve and the drive shaft bore.

b. Using a bearing installer (OMC part No. 319931) or a suitable mandrel, press the bearing into the sleeve. Press against the numbered side of the bearing only.

c. Position the sleeve and bearing assembly into the drive shaft bore. Make sure the numbered side of the bearing is facing up.

d. Drive the assembly into the drive shaft bore using a suitable mandrel. The mandrel must only push against the sleeve. Press the assembly into the drive shaft bore until it seats.

4. If the propshaft bearing carrier bearings were removed, install new bearings as follows:

a. Position the carrier in a press with the propeller end facing down.

b. Lubricate a new small needle bearing (37, **Figure 41**) and position it into the carrier's bore with its numbered or lettered side facing up.

c. Press the bearing into position using a suitable mandrel.

d. Lubricate a new large needle bearing (33, **Figure 41**) and position it into the carrier's bore with its numbered or lettered side facing up.

e. Press the bearing into position with the short-stepped side of a bearing installer (OMC part No. 339751) or an equivalent mandrel.

5A. *Double propshaft seal models*—Install two new propshaft seals as follows:

a. Coat the outer diameter of each seal with OMC Gasket Sealing Compound or an equivalent sealant.

b. Install the inner seal with the longer, stepped shoulder of a seal installer (OMC part No. 335822) or an equivalent mandrel. The seal lip must face into the carrier bore. Press the seal until the installer contacts the carrier.

c. Install the outer seal using the shorter shoulder of seal installer (part No. 335822) or an equivalent mandrel. The seal lip must face out from the carrier. Press the seal until the installer contacts the carrier.

9

d. Lubricate the seal lips and pack the area between the seal lips with OMC Triple-Guard or an equivalent marine grease.

5B. *Single propshaft seal models*—Install a new propshaft seal as follows:

a. Lubricate the outer diameter of the seal with OMC DPL or WD-40 Lubricant.

b. Position the seal onto a seal installer (part No. 342663) or an equivalent mandrel. The extended lip of the seal must pilot into the tool's relief. The extended lip must face away from the carrier.

c. Position the installer and seal over the carrier bore. Press the seal into the carrier until the tool contacts the carrier.

d. Lubricate the seal lips with OMC Triple-Guard or an equivalent marine grease.

6. Coat a new O-ring (34, **Figure 41**) with OMC Triple-Guard or equivalent marine grease. Install the O-ring into the propshaft bearing carrier O-ring groove.

7. Install two new drive shaft seals into the drive shaft bore back-to-back as follows:

a. Coat the outer diameter of each seal with OMC Gasket Sealing Compound.

b. Install the inner seal using the longer, stepped shoulder of a seal installer (part No. 326554) or an equivalent mandrel. The seal lip must face into the gearcase. Press the seal until the installer contacts the gearcase deck.

c. Install the outer seal using the shorter shoulder of seal installer (part No. 326554) or an equivalent mandrel. The seal lip (spring side) must face out from the gearcase. Press the seal until the installer contacts the gearcase deck. The seal must be flush with the deck when installed.

d. Lubricate the seal lips and pack the area between the seal lips with OMC Triple-Guard or equivalent marine grease.

8. Install the shift shaft bushing, O-ring and washer as follows:

a. Lubricate a new shift shaft O-ring with OMC Triple-Guard or equivalent marine grease. Install the O-ring into the open end of the shift shaft bushing.

b. Position the shift shaft bushing and O-ring onto a bushing installer (part No. 304515) or an equivalent mandrel. The O-ring end of the bushing must face away from the installer.

c. Position the washer (11, **Figure 41**) over the installer tip, and against the O-ring and bushing.

d. Coat the bushing's outer diameter with OMC Gasket Sealing Compound. Place the bushing assembly into the bore, then drive the bushing into the gearcase until it seats.

9. Lubricate the forward gear roller bearing and position it in the cup at the bottom of the gearcase bore.

10. Use a yoke locating tool (OMC part No. 319991) to install the shift yoke and forward gear assembly. Push the threaded end of the yoke locating tool (part No. 319991) through the shift rod bushing and into the gearcase bore.

11. Position the forward gear hub in the closed end of the yoke. Hold the assembly near the gearcase bore and thread the yoke locating tool into the closed end of the yoke.

12. Slowly pull on the yoke locating tool to pull the gear and yoke assembly into the gearcase bore. Guide the assembly into the bore until the gear seats against its roller bearing and the shift yoke drops into its relief at the bottom of the gearcase bore. Do not remove the locating tool at this time.

13. Assemble the thrust washers and thrust bearing to the pinion gear. Use OMC Needle Bearing Assembly Grease to hold the components in position. Position the thrust bearing between the thrust washers (21, **Figure 41**).

NOTE
If binding occurs when installing the pinion gear, make sure the forward bearing cup is properly seated.

14. Install the pinion gear assembly into its bore. It may be necessary to momentarily push the top of the forward gear away from the pinion gear using a screwdriver to allow the pinion gear to enter its bore. Make sure the pinion gear is seated in its bore and properly meshed with the forward gear.

15. Install a new O-ring on the shift linkage pivot screw. Coat the threads of the screw and the O-ring with OMC Nut Lock or an equivalent threadlocking compound.

16. Using the yoke locating tool, move the shift linkage until it aligns with the hole for the shift linkage pivot screw. Then install and tighten the shift linkage pivot screw to specifications in **Table 1**.

17. Remove the yoke locating tool. Lubricate the lower end of the shift shaft with OMC Triple-Guard or equivalent grease, then carefully thread the rod through the shift shaft bushing to prevent damaging the O-ring. Then align the yoke with the shaft and thread the shaft into the yoke until it seats.

18. Unthread the shift shaft to position the bend at the top of the shaft straight forward. Do not unthread the shaft any more than necessary to position the shaft as specified. The shaft must not be unthreaded more than one full turn.

19. Using a pair of needlenose pliers, install the saddle over the open arms of the shift yoke.

20. Coat the forward gear thrust washer with OMC Needle Bearing Assembly or equivalent grease. Position the washer into the recess of the forward gear hub.

21. Install the clutch dog over the shift saddle and engage it with the forward gear. The grooved end of the clutch dog must face the forward gear. Move the shift shaft up or down as necessary to align the components. Make sure the saddle is not displaced from the shift yoke arms.

22. Coat the reverse gear thrust washer with OMC Needle Bearing Assembly or equivalent grease. Slide the washer over the propeller end of the propreller shaft and up against the shaft shoulder.

23. Coat the detent spring, the two detent balls and their hole in the propshaft with OMC Needle Bearing Assembly or equivalent grease. Install the spring into the propshaft hole, then position a ball over each end of the spring.

24. Carefully insert the propeller shaft assembly into the clutch dog and forward gear. The detent balls must be aligned with the recesses in the clutch dog's internal splines. Use a long screwdriver to compress the detent balls and help guide them into the clutch dog. Push the shaft into the gearcase until it passes through the clutch dog, forward gear and forward gear bearing and seats in the gearcase.

25. Hold the propeller shaft in place, and move the shift rod up into the neutral position. Slide the reverse gear over the propeller shaft and engage it with the pinion gear.

26. Apply OMC Gasket Sealing Compound or equivalent sealant to the propshaft bearing carrier rear flange-to-gearcase mating surfaces. Then coat the forward flange and O-ring with the same sealant. Install the propshaft bearing carrier over the propeller shaft. Rotate the carrier to align the screw holes, then seat the carrier to the gearcase.

27. Coat the threads of the propshaft bearing carrier mounting screws with OMC Gasket Sealing Compound or equivalent sealant. Install and evenly tighten the screws to 60-84 in.-lb. (7-9 N•m).

28. Lubricate the lower end of the drive shaft. Install the drive shaft into its bore and rotate the shaft as necessary to engage the pinion gear.

29. Test the integrity of the gearcase seals, gaskets and O-rings as described in Chapter Two before filling the gearcase with lubricant and returning it to service. The drive shaft must be held in position during the pressure tests, or it may be forced out of its bore by the internal pressure.

30. Install the water pump as described in this chapter.

31. Install the gearcase as described in this chapter.

32. Fill the gearcase with the recommended lubricant as described in Chapter Three.

Bearing Carrier Removal and Disassembly (40 and 50 hp Models)

Refer to **Figure 44**.

1. Remove both carrier mounting bolts and washers (**Figure 45**).

2. Thread a slide hammer adapter such as OMC Propeller shaft retainer remover, (part No. 345831) onto the end of the propeller shaft (**Figure 46**).

3. Thread a slide hammer into the adapter. Use short strokes to pull the carrier slightly away from the gearcase. Remove the slide hammer and adapter. Grasp the end of propeller shaft and pull the carrier from the gearcase. Remove the O-ring (31, **Figure 44**) from the carrier. If necessary, use a torch to apply heat to the gearcase near the gearcase to carrier mating surfaces.

CAUTION
When using heat, make sure to keep the flame away from the seals and/or O-rings. Never heat the housing to the point that the finish is burned. Continually move the flame around the mating surface to apply even heating. Too much heat can distort or melt the gearcase.

4. Pull the propeller shaft (25, **Figure 44**) from the carrier. Lift the shim, reverse gear and thrust washer (32-34, **Figure 44**) from the bearing carrier.

5. Remove the reverse gear bearing (30, **Figure 44**) only if it needs replacing. Refer to *Gearcase Component Cleaning and Inspection* in this chapter to determine the need for replacement. Remove the bearing as follows:

   a. Clamp the bearing carrier into a vice equipped with soft jaws.

   b. Engage the jaws of a slide hammer into the bearing as indicated in **Figure 47**.

   c. Use short hammer strokes to remove the bearing.

6. Engage the jaws of a slide hammer to the propeller shaft seals as indicated in **Figure 48**. Use short hammer strokes to remove the seals from the carrier.

7. Remove the needle bearings (28, **Figure 44**) only if they need replacing. Remove the bearing as follows:

   a. Select an appropriately sized socket or section of tubing to use as a bearing installation tool. The tool must be large enough in diameter to contact the bearing cage yet not contact the bearing carrier during removal.

   b. Place the bearing carrier on a sturdy work surface with the seal bore facing down.

   c. Hold the tool in firm contact with the inner bearing and lightly tap on the tool. Continue until the outer

9

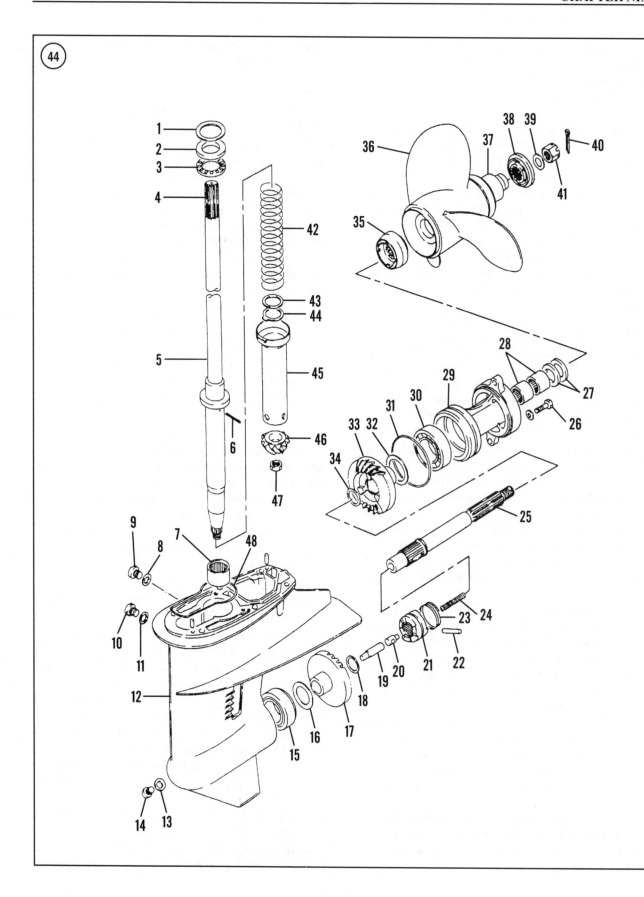

GEARCASE ASSEMBLY
(40 AND 50 MODELS)

1. Shim
2. Washer
3. Thrust bearing
4. Splined section
5. Drive shaft
6. Pin
7. Lower drive shaft bearing
8. Sealing washer
9. Level/vent plug
10. Level/vent plug
11. Sealing washer
12. Gearcase housing
13. Sealing washer
14. Drain/fill plug
15. Forward gear bearing
16. Shim
17. Forward gear
18. Thrust washer
19. Cam follower
20. Cross pin connector
21. Clutch
22. Cross pin
23. Clutch spring
24. Spring
25. Propeller shaft
26. Bolt
27. Propeller shaft seals
28. Needle bearings
29. Bearing carrier
30. Reverse gear bearing
31. O-ring
32. Shim
33. Reverse gear
34. Thrust washer
35. Thrust bushing
36. Propeller
37. Propeller hub
38. Splined washer
39. Plain washer
40. Cotter pin
41. Propeller nut
42. Preload spring
43. Washer
44. Tab washer
45. Collar
46. Pinion gear
47. Pinion nut
48. O-ring

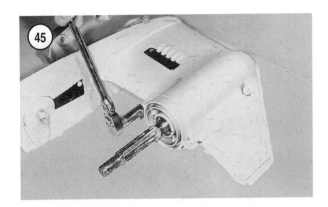

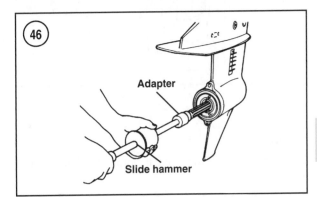

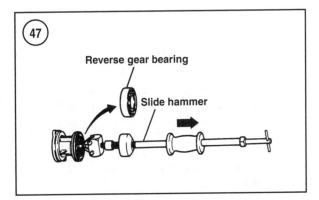

9

bearing is free from the carrier. Repeat the process to remove the inner bearing.

8. Use a suitable solvent and soft bristle brush to clean corrosion and other contaminants from the carrier.

9. Inspect the carrier for cracked, pitted or damaged surfaces. Replace the carrier if there are defects.

Propeller Shaft Disassembly (40 and 50 hp Models)

Refer to **Figure 44**.

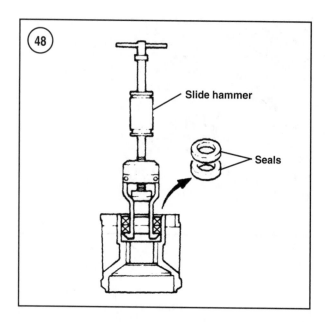

1. Use a screwdriver to unwind the spring from the clutch (**Figure 49**).

2. Pull the cam follower from the propeller shaft (**Figure 50**).

3. Use a pin punch to push the cross pin from the clutch and propeller shaft (**Figure 51**).

4. Remove the cross pin connector (20, **Figure 44**) and spring (24) from the propeller shaft.

5. Remove the forward thrust washer (18, **Figure 44**) from the propeller shaft or forward gear (17).

6. Refer to *Gearcase Component Cleaning and Inspection* in this chapter and inspect the propeller shaft components for excessive wear or defects.

Drive Shaft Removal and Disassembly (40 and 50 hp Models)

Refer to **Figure 44**.

> *NOTE*
> *A driveshaft holding tool can be fabricated using the splined end of a discarded crankshaft with flats machined into the shaft.*

1. Engage a splined adapter (such as the OMC driveshaft holding socket part No. 345834) onto the upper end of the drive shaft (**Figure 52**). Hold the pinion nut (47, **Figure 44**) with a breaker bar and socket. Rotate the adapter counterclockwise until the pinion nut is free from the drive shaft.

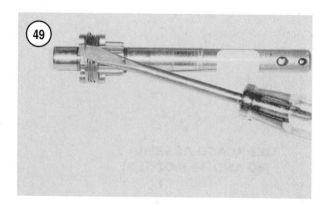

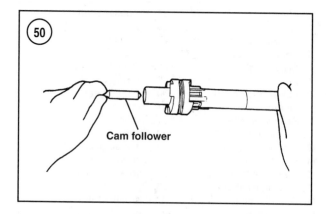

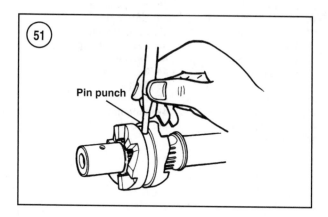

2. Thread two 8 mm bolts into the bearing and seal housing as indicated in **Figure 53**. Evenly tighten the bolts to push the housing away from the gearcase.

3. Carefully pull the bearing and seal housing along with the drive shaft and shift shaft from the gearcase (**Figure 54**). Remove the O-ring (48, **Figure 44**) from the bearing and seal housing or the gearcase.

4. Slide the drive shaft (5, **Figure 44**) from the bearing and seal housing.

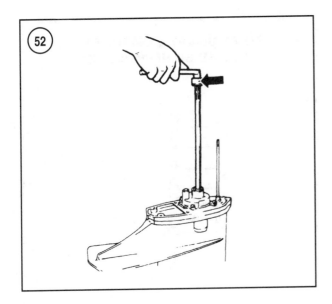

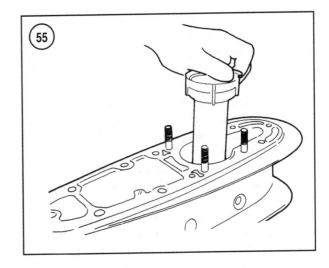

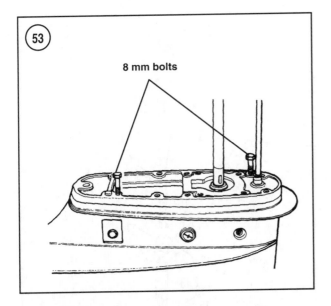

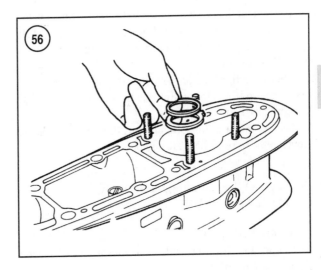

8 mm bolts

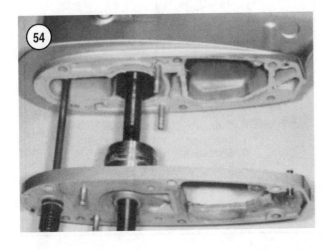

5. Remove the shims, washer and thrust bearing (1-3, **Figure 44**) from the drive shaft (5).

6. Use a pin punch to drive the pin (6, **Figure 44**) from the drive shaft (5). Remove the preload spring (42, **Figure 44**) from the drive shaft.

7. Lift the spring collar from the drive shaft bore (**Figure 55**). Remove the washer and tab washer from the drive shaft bore (**Figure 56**).

Shift Shaft Removal and Disassembly (40 and 50 hp Models)

Refer to **Figure 57**.

1. Remove the coupler and nut (1 and 2, **Figure 57**) from the shift shaft (8).

2. Slide the shift shaft assembly out of the bearing and seal housing.

9

3. Remove the snap ring (7, **Figure 57**) and carefully push the bushing (4, **Figure 57**) from the bearing and seal housing. Pull the boot (3, **Figure 57**) from the bushing. Remove the O-rings (5 and 6, **Figure 57**) from the bushing.

4. Remove the shift cam only if it must be replaced. Refer to *Gearcase Component Cleaning and Inspection* in this chapter to determine the need for replacements. Remove the cam as follows:

    a. Make a reference mark on the shift shaft, guide and shift cam prior to removing the cam.

    b. Use a pin punch to drive the pin (12, **Figure 57**) from the shift shaft (8) and shift cam (13). Pull the shift cam from the shift shaft.

    c. Drive the pin (11, **Figure 57**) from the shift shaft (8) and guide (17). Pull the guide from the shift shaft.

    d. Transfer the reference mark to the replacement cam.

5. Remove the magnet (10, **Figure 57**) from the shift shaft. Use a pin punch to drive the pin (9, **Figure 57**) from the shift shaft (8).

6. Check the fit of the pin to the shift shaft and cam. Replace the pin if it is loose. Replace the cam and/or shaft if the new pin is loose.

7. Inspect the boot for torn, cracked or suspect surfaces. Replace the boot if there are any defects.

Bearing and Seal Housing Disassembly (40 and 50 hp Models)

Refer to **Figure 44**.

1. Clamp the bearing and seal housing into a vice equipped with soft jaws.

2. Engage a two-jawed puller to the inside edge of the needle bearing (**Figure 58**).

3. Thread a slide hammer onto the bearing remover. Use short hammer strokes to remove the bearing from the housing.

4. Working from the upper side of the housing, carefully drive both seals (8, **Figure 27**) from the housing.

5. Use a suitable solvent to clean contaminants from the housing.

Gear and Bearing Removal (40 and 50 hp Models)

Refer to **Figure 44**.

1. Remove the pinion gear (46, **Figure 44**) from the gearcase.

2. Pull the forward gear and shim (17 and 16, **Figure 44**) from the gearcase. Remove the tapered roller bearing from the gearcase or forward gear.

(57) **SHIFT SHAFT COMPONETS (40 AND 50 HP MODELS)**

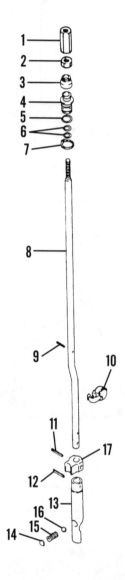

1. Coupler	10. Magnet
2. Nut	11. Pin
3. Boot	12. Pin
4. Bushing	13. Shift cam
5. O-ring	14. Spacer
6. O-rings	15. Spring
7. Snap ring	16. Detent ball
8. Shift shaft	17. Guide
9. Pin	

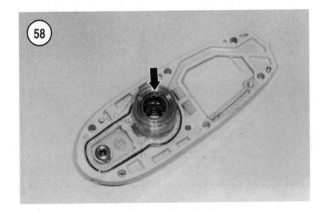

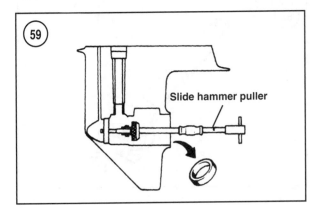

Slide hammer puller

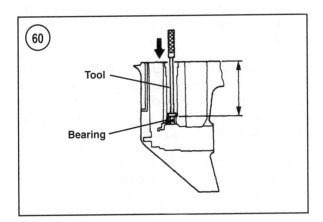

Tool

Bearing

3. Remove the forward bearing (15, **Figure 44**) only if the bearing must be replaced. Refer to *Gearcase Component Cleaning and Inspection* in this chapter to determine the need for replacement. Remove the bearing as follows:

a. Engage the jaws of a slide hammer to the bearing as indicated in **Figure 59**.

b. Use short hammer strokes to remove the bearing from the housing.

4. Remove the lower drive shaft bearing (7, **Figure 44**) only if it must be replaced. Refer to *Gearcase Component Cleaning and Inspection* in this chapter to determine the need for replacement. Remove the bearing as follows:

a. Measure the distance from the top of the gearcase to the lower drive shaft bearing (**Figure 60**). Record the measurement for gearcase assembly.

b. Select an appropriately sized socket and extension or section of tubing to use as a bearing removal tool. The tool must be of a diameter that contacts the top of the bearing yet does not contact the drive shaft bore.

c. Hold the tool in firm contact with the bearing (**Figure 60**) and carefully drive the bearing from the gearcase. Remove the bearing.

5. Remove the spacer, spring, detent ball (14-16, **Figure 57**) from the gearcase.

6. Use a suitable solvent to clean all grease, metal filings or other contaminants from the gearcase.

7. Refer to *Gearcase Component Cleaning and Inspection* in this chapter and inspect all components for defects. Replace defective or questionable components.

**Gear and Bearing Installation
(40 and 50 hp Models)**

Refer to **Figure 44**.

1. Position the *new* lower drive shaft bearing (7, **Figure 44**) into the drive shaft bore with the number stamped side facing up.

2. Using the removal tool, slowly drive the bearing into the bore. Stop frequently and measure the depth. Continue until the bearing just reaches the depth recorded prior to removal.

3. Lubricate the forward gear bearing (15, **Figure 44**) with gearcase lubricant. Position the race into the gearcase with the number tapered side facing out.

4. Select an appropriately sized socket and extension or section of tubing to use as a bearing installation tool. The tool must be of a diameter to contact near the outer circumference of the race yet not contact the housing during installation. Slowly drive the race into the housing until it fully seats (**Figure 61**). Place the tapered roller bearing into the race.

5. Place the spacer (14, **Figure 57**) and spring (15) into the opening at the front of the gearcase. The opening is directly in line with the shift shaft bore. Apply OMC Triple-Guard or equivalent marine grease to the surface and place the detent ball (16, **Figure 57**) into the bore.

6. Place the shim (16, **Figure 44**) onto the hub of the forward gear (17). Push the gear and shim into the bore of the bearing until firmly seated.

9

7. Align the splined bore of the pinion gear (46, **Figure 44**) with the drive shaft bore while installing it into the gearcase. Make sure the pinion gear teeth mesh with the forward gear teeth.

Bearing and Seal Housing Assembly (40 and 50 hp Models)

Refer to **Figure 44**.

1. Select an appropriately sized socket or section of tubing to use as a seal installation tool. The tool must be of a diameter to contact near the outer circumference of the seal yet not contact the housing during installation.

2. Place the bearing and seal housing on a sturdy work surface with the bottom side facing up.

3. Position the new inner seal into the bore opening with the lip side facing down. Position the seal installation tool firmly against the seal. Gently drive the seal into the bore until its surface is just below the bore opening.

4. Position the outer seal into the bore opening with the lip side facing down. Position the seal installation tool firmly against the seal. Drive both seals into the bore until the inner seal contacts the bore seat.

5. Select an appropriately sized socket or section of tubing to use as a bearing installation tool. The tool must be of a diameter to contact near the outer circumference of the needle bearing (**Figure 58**) yet not contact the bearing bore.

6. Position the needle bearing into the bore opening with the numbered side facing out. Place the installation tool firmly against the bearing. Gently drive the bearing into the bore until firmly seated.

7. Apply a bead of OMC Adhesive M or equivalent to the groove for the O-ring (48, **Figure 44**). Place the O-ring into the groove.

8. Apply a bead of OMC Triple-Guard or equivalent marine grease to the lips of both seals. Lubricate the needle bearing with gearcase lubricant.

Shift Shaft Assembly and Installation (40 and 50 hp Models)

Refer to **Figure 57** for component identification throughout this procedure.

1. Lubricate the surfaces with OMC Triple-Guard or equivalent marine grease and install the O-rings (5 and 6, **Figure 57**) onto the bushing (4). Lubricate the surfaces with gearcase lubricant and slide the boot (3, **Figure 57**) onto the bushing.

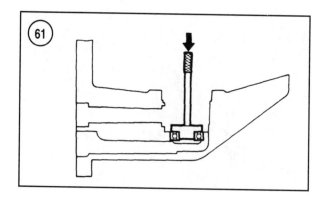

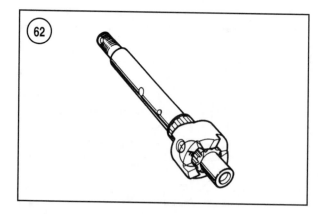

2. Slide the bushing into its opening in the top side of the bearing and seal housing. Install the snap ring (7, **Figure 57**) into the groove to secure the bushing.

3. Install the guide (17, **Figure 57**) onto the shift shaft. Rotate the guide until the reference marks made prior to removal align with the mark on the shift shaft. Drive the pin (11, **Figure 57**) through the guide and shift shaft. The pin must be centered in the guide.

4. Install the shift cam (13, **Figure 57**) onto the shift shaft. Rotate the cam until the reference marks made prior to removal align with the mark on the guide. Drive the pin (12, **Figure 57**) through the cam and shift shaft. The pin must be centered in the cam.

5. Drive the pin (9, **Figure 57**) into the hole in the shift shaft until it protrudes with the same amount on each side.

6. Snap the magnet onto the shift shaft. Position the magnet directly below the bend in the shaft.

7. Carefully slide the shift shaft assembly into the bottom side of the bushing. Rotate the shift shaft to position the detent ball recess in the cam facing the forward side of the bearing and seal housing.

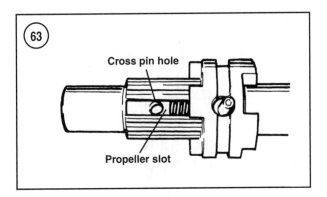

63

Cross pin hole

Propeller slot

Drive Shaft Assembly and Installation
(40 and 50 hp Models)

Refer to **Figure 44**.

1. Place the tab washer (44, **Figure 44**) into the drive shaft bore. Align the tab with the recess in the bore. Place the washer (43, **Figure 44**) directly on top of the tab washer.

2. Carefully slide the collar (45, **Figure 44**) into the drive shaft bore. Rotate the collar to align the protrusion on the collar with the recess in the housing. Seat the collar into the bore.

3. Slide the preload spring (42, **Figure 44**) onto the pinion end of the drive shaft (5). Drive the pin (6, **Figure 44**) into its opening in the drive shaft to secure the spring.

4. Lubricate the surfaces with gearcase lubricant and install the thrust bearing (3, **Figure 44**), washer (2) and shims (1) onto the upper end of the drive shaft (5).

5. Carefully slide the drive shaft into the bearing and seal housing.

6. Align the drive shaft and shift shaft with their respective openings while lowering the bearing and seal housing onto the gearcase. Rotate the drive shaft clockwise to align the drive shaft splines with the pinion gear splines. The drive shaft drops into the pinion gear as the splines align.

7. Press down to seat the bearing and seal housing against the gearcase. Move the shift up and down to verify correct orientation of the detent notch. A distinct detent is felt when the shaft reaches the neutral position. Remove and re-install the shift shaft and/or detent ball as needed.

8. Thread the pinion nut (47, **Figure 44**) onto the drive shaft.

9. Engage a splined adapter such as the OMC drive shaft holding socket part No. 345834 onto the upper end of the drive shaft (**Figure 52**). Hold the pinion nut with a breaker bar and socket. Tighten the pinion nut to the specification in **Table 1**.

Propeller Shaft Assembly and Installation
(40 and 50 hp Models)

Refer to **Figure 44**.

1. Insert the spring (24, **Figure 44**) into the opening in the forward side of the propeller shaft.

2. Place the cross pin connector (20, **Figure 44**) into the opening and seat it against the spring. Insert the cam follower into the opening with the smaller diameter side facing out (**Figure 50**).

3. Slide the clutch over the propeller shaft with the *F* mark facing the forward gear side of the shaft (**Figure 62**).

4. Align the cross pin opening in the clutch with the slot in the propeller shaft (**Figure 63**). Remove and reposition the clutch as needed.

5. Push in and rotate the cam follower (19, **Figure 44**) to align the hole in the cross pin connector (**Figure 63**) with the cross pin hole in the clutch. Push the cross pin (22, **Figure 44**) through both holes and release the cam follower.

6. Make sure the ends of the cross pin are flush with the clutch surfaces. Carefully wind the spring onto the clutch (**Figure 49**). Make sure the spring spans both ends of the cross pin. Reposition the spring as needed.

7. Apply OMC Triple-Guard or equivalent marine grease to the surfaces and install the thrust washer (8, **Figure 44**) onto the forward gear side of the propeller shaft.

8. Install the propeller shaft assembly along with the bearing carrier as described in this chapter.

Bearing Carrier Assembly and Installation
(40 and 50 hp Models)

Refer to **Figure 44**.

1. Place the inner needle bearing (28, **Figure 44**) into the bore opening with the numbered side facing out. Use the bearing removal tool to carefully drive the bearing into the carrier. Seat the bearing against the step at the bottom of the bore. Install the outer bearing into the bore with the numbered side out until it seats against inner bearing.

2. Select an appropriately sized socket or section of tubing to use as a seal installation tool. The tool must be of a diameter large enough to contact near the outer circumference of the seal yet not contact the seal bore during installation.

3. Place one of the seals into the bore in the propeller side of the carrier with the lip side facing out. Slowly drive the seal into the bore until it rests just below the bore opening.

4. Place the remaining seal into the bore with the lip side facing out. Slowly drive the seal into the bore until it contacts the inner seal.

9

5. Carefully drive both seals into the bore until the inner seal fully seats in the bore. Apply a bead of OMC Triple-Guard or equivalent marine grease to the lip surfaces of both seals.

6. Install the reverse gear bearing as follows:

a. Select an appropriately sized socket or section of tubing to use as a bearing installation tool. The tool must be of a diameter to contact the outer race of the bearing yet not contact the bearing bore during installation.

b. Lubricate the bearing with gearcase lubricant. Position the bearing into the bore opening with the numbered side facing out. Place the bearing carrier seal side down on a sturdy work surface.

c. Hold the installation tool firmly against the bearing and tap the bearing into the bore (**Figure 64**). The bearing must seat against the step within the bore.

7. Position the shim (32, **Figure 44**) onto the hub of the reverse gear (33). Lubricate the reverse gear with gearcase lubricant. Slide the reverse gear hub into the bore of the reverse gear bearing until it seats against the shim and bearing (32 and 30, **Figure 44**).

8. Lubricate the O-ring (31, **Figure 44**) with OMC Triple-Guard or equivalent marine grease and position it onto the groove of the bearing carrier. Lubricate the surfaces with grease and slide the thrust washer (34, **Figure 44**) onto the rear side of the propeller shaft. Seat the washer against the step near the clutch.

9. Carefully slide the splined end of the propeller shaft through the opening in the reverse gear. Seat the propeller shaft against the reverse gear. Lubricate the gearcase opening with gearcase lubricant.

10. Position the gearcase with the drive shaft facing up. Grasp the splined section of the propeller shaft to retain the shaft in the carrier. Align the forward side of the propeller shaft with the opening in the forward gear while sliding the carrier into the housing. Rotate the drive shaft clockwise to align the reverse and pinion gear teeth while seating the carrier into the gearcase.

11. Lightly tap on the carrier until it fully seats against the gearcase. Rotate the carrier until the bolt holes align. Apply a light coating of OMC Gasket Sealing compound or equivalent to the bolt threads, then install the bolts and washers (26, **Figure 44**) into the gearcase. Tighten the bolts to the specification in **Table 1**.

12. Refer to *Shim Selection* in this chapter to determine if the gear alignment is correct. Install the water pump components and gearcase as described in this chapter.

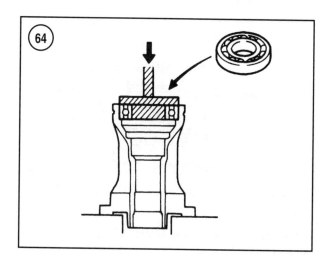

Bearing Carrier Removal and Disassembly (70 hp Model)

Refer to **Figure 65**.

1. Bend the tab(s) away from the cover nut (**Figure 66**).

NOTE
*The propeller shaft bearing carrier is secured using a cover nut or retainer tightened to 115 ft.-lb. (160 N•m). A special cover nut tool (**Figure 67**, OMC part No. 342688) is required.*

2. Slide the cover nut tool over the propeller shaft. Engage the tool to the cover nut as indicated in **Figure 67**. Turn the cover nut counterclockwise and remove the cover nut and tab washer.

3. Engage the arms of a hook equipped puller adapter (OMC part No.5000004) and a universal puller assembly (OMC part No. 378103) to the carrier and propeller shaft as indicated in **Figure 68**. Turn the puller bolt to free the carrier from the gearcase. Grasp the end of the propeller shaft and pull the carrier from the gearcase (**Figure 69**). Remove the key (41, **Figure 65**) from the bearing carrier or groove in the gearcase opening. If necessary, use a torch to heat the gearcase–to–carrier mating surfaces.

CAUTION
When using heat, make sure to keep the flame away from the seals or O-rings. Never heat the housing to the point that the finish is burned. Continually move the flame around the mating surface to apply even heating. Excessive heat can distort or melt the gearcase.

4. Pull the spacer (38, **Figure 65**) from the bearing carrier or gearcase opening. Remove the O-ring (39, **Figure 65**) from the carrier.

5. Pull the propeller shaft (29, **Figure 65**) from the carrier. Place the carrier on a sturdy work surface with the gear side up. Lift the thrust washer, reverse gear and shim (30, 33 and 34, **Figure 65**) from the bearing carrier (40).

6. Remove the reverse gear bearing (35, **Figure 65**) only if it must be replaced. Refer to *Gearcase Component Cleaning and Inspection* in this chapter to determine the need for replacement. Remove the bearing as follows:

   a. Clamp the bearing carrier into a vice with soft jaws.

   b. Engage the jaws of a slide hammer into the bearing as indicated in **Figure 47**.

   c. Use short hammer strokes to remove the bearing. Discard the bearing after removal.

7. Engage the jaws of a slide hammer to the propeller shaft seals as indicated in **Figure 48**. Use short hammer strokes to remove the seals from the carrier.

8. Remove the needle bearings (36, **Figure 65**) only if they must be replaced. Remove the bearing as follows:

   a. Select an appropriately sized socket or section of tubing to use as a bearing installation tool. The tool must be large enough in diameter to contact the bearing cage yet not contact the bearing carrier during removal.

   b. Place the bearing carrier on a sturdy word surface with the seal bore facing down.

   c. Hold the tool in firm contact with the inner bearing and lightly tap on the tool (**Figure 70**). Continue until the outer bearing is free from the carrier. Repeat the process to remove the inner bearing.

9. Use a suitable solvent and soft bristle brush to clean corrosion and other contaminants from the carrier.

10. Inspect the carrier for cracked, pitted or damaged surfaces. Replace the carrier if defects are noted.

Propeller Shaft Disassembly (70 hp Models)

Refer to **Figure 65**.

1. Use a screwdriver to unwind the spring from the clutch (**Figure 49**).

2. Pull the cam follower from the propeller shaft (**Figure 50**).

3. Use a pin punch to push the cross pin from the clutch and propeller shaft (**Figure 51**).

4. Remove the cross pin connector (24, **Figure 65**) and spring (28) from the propeller shaft.

5. Remove the forward thrust washer (22, **Figure 65**) from the propeller shaft or forward gear (21).

6. Refer to *Gearcase Component Cleaning and Inspection* in this chapter and inspect the propeller shaft components for excessive wear or defects.

Drive Shaft Removal and Disassembly (70 hp Models)

Refer to **Figure 65**.

1. Remove the four bolts from the bearing and seal housing (**Figure 71**).

NOTE
A driveshaft holding tool can be fabricated using the splined end of a discarded crankshaft with flats machined into the shaft.

2. Engage a splined adapter such as the OMC driveshaft holding socket (part No. 311875) onto the upper end of the drive shaft (**Figure 52**). Hold the pinion nut (31, **Figure 65**) with a breaker bar and socket. Rotate the adapter counterclockwise until the pinion nut is free from the drive shaft.

3. Carefully pull the drive shaft (8, **Figure 65**) along with the bearing and seal housing (2) from the gearcase. Slide the drive shaft, bearing race (6, **Figure 65**) and shim (5) from the bearing and seal housing (2).

4. Pull the thrust washers (A and B, **Figure 72**) and collar (C) from the gearcase. Slide the spring (9, **Figure 65**) from the drive shaft.

5. Remove the tapered roller bearing from the drive shaft only if it must be replaced. Refer to *Gearcase Component Cleaning and Inspection* in this chapter. Replace the bearing as follows:

   a. Position a bearing separator onto the open jaws of a vice as indicated in **Figure 73**.

   b. Open the separator enough to allow the shaft to just slide through.

   c. Slide the drive shaft into the separator with the pinion gear side facing down. Rest the drive shaft bearing against the separator.

   d. Use a block of wood to protect the splined end of the drive shaft and carefully drive the shaft from the bearing.

6. Place the bearing and seal housing (2, **Figure 65**) on a sturdy work surface right side up. Use a blunt tip pry bar to push both seals from the housing.

Shift Shaft Removal and Disassembly (70 hp Models)

Refer to **Figure 74**.

9

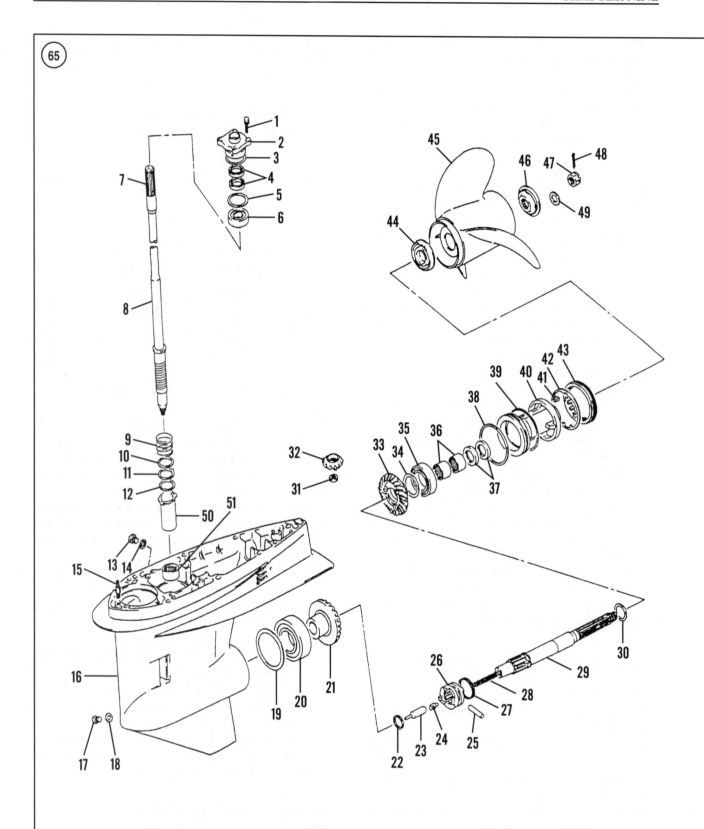

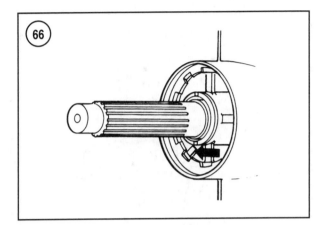

GEAR CASE ASSEMBLY
(70 HP MODEL)

1. Bolt
2. Bearing and seal housing
3. O-ring
4. Seals
5. Shim
6. Bearing
7. Splined section
8. Drive shaft
9. Spring
10. Shim
11. Tab washer
12. Washer
13. Level/vent plug
14. Sealing washer
15. Speedometer connector
16. Gearcase housing
17. Drain/fill plug
18. Sealing
19. Shim
20. Forward gear bearing
21. Forward gear
22. Forward thrust washer
23. Cam follower
24. Cross pin connector
25. Cross pin
26. Clutch

27. Clutch spring
28. Spring
29. Propeller shaft
30. Thrust washer
31. Pinion nut
32. Pinion gear
33. Reverse gear
34. Shim
35. Reverse gear bearing
36. Needle bearing
37. Propeller shaft seals
38. Spacer
39. O-ring
40. Bearing carrier
41. Key
42. Tab washer
43. Cover nut
44. Thrust washer
45. Propeller
46. Splined washer
47. Propeller nut
48. Cotter pin
49. Plain washer
50. Collar
51. Lower drive shaft bearing

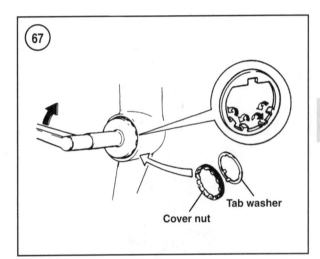

Cover nut

Tab washer

9

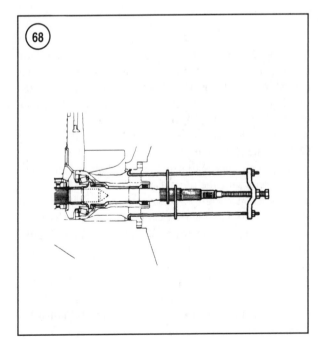

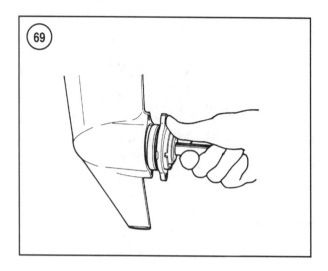

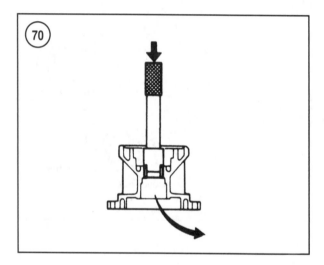

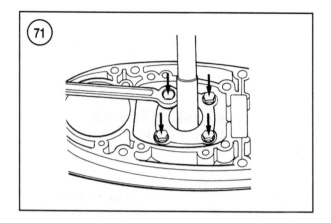

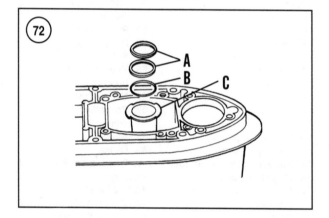

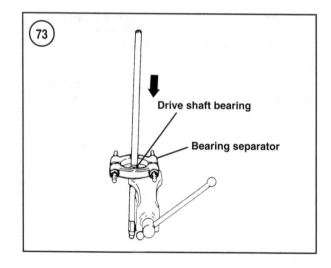

1. Remove the three bolts (**Figure 75**) from the shift shaft cover. Grip the top of the shift shaft with pliers and lift the assembly from the gearcase. Remove the O-ring (3, **Figure 74**) from the cover or gearcase. Remove the alignment pin (24, **Figure 74**) from the cover (2).

2. Remove the snap ring (8, **Figure 74**) and pull the cover (2) from the shift shaft.

3. Make reference marks on the shift shaft and shift cam prior to removing the cam. Use a pin punch to drive both pins (14 and 15, **Figure 74**) from the shift shaft (10) and shift cam (16). Pull the shift cam from the shift shaft.

4. Use a pin punch and carefully drive the pin (9, **Figure 74**) from the shift shaft. Remove the spring, spacer and collar (11-13, **Figure 74**) from the shift shaft.

5. Remove the seal (4, **Figure 74**), washers (5 and 22), sleeve (6) and O-rings (23) from the cover (2).

6. Remove the magnet and clamp (20 and 21, **Figure 74**) from the shift shaft.

7. Check the fit of the pins (14 and 15, **Figure 74**) to the shift shaft (10) and cam (16). Replace the pin if a loose fit occurs. Replace the cam and/or shaft if a loose fit occurs with a new pin installed.

8. Install new O-rings and seals in all locations during assembly.

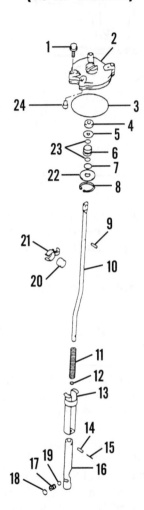

SHIFT SHAFT COMPONENTS (70 HP MODEL)

1. Bolt
2. Cover
3. O-ring
4. Seal
5. Washer
6. Sleeve
7. O-ring
8. Snap ring
9. Pin
10. Shift shaft
11. Spring
12. Spacer
13. Collar
14. Large diameter pin
15. Small diameter pin
16. Shift cam
17. Spring
18. Spacer
19. Detent ball
20. Magnet
21. Clamp
22. Washer
23. O-rings
24. Alignment pin

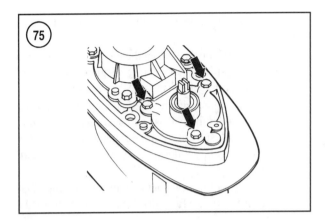

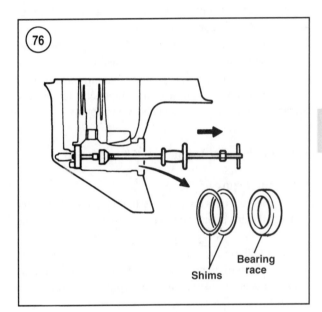

Shims   Bearing race

Gear and Bearing Removal (70 hp Model)

Refer to **Figure 65**.

1. Remove the pinion gear (32, **Figure 65**) from the gearcase.

2. Pull the forward gear and shim (21 and 22, **Figure 65**) from the gearcase. Remove the tapered roller bearing from the gearcase or forward gear.

3. Remove the forward bearing race and shims (20 and 19, **Figure 65**) only if the bearing must be replaced. Refer to *Gearcase Component Cleaning and Inspection* in this chapter. Remove the bearing race as follows:

    a. Engage the jaws of a slide hammer to the race as indicated in **Figure 76**.

    b. Use short hammer strokes to remove the race and shims from the housing.

4. Remove the lower drive shaft bearing (51, **Figure 65**) only if it must be replaced. Refer to *Gearcase Component*

9

Cleaning and Inspection in this chapter. Remove the bearing as follows:

   a. Measure the distance from the top of the gearcase to the lower drive shaft bearing (**Figure 60**). Record the measurement to use in gearcase assembly.

   b. Select an appropriately sized socket and extension or section of tubing to use as a bearing removal tool. The tool must be of a diameter that contacts the top of the bearing yet does not contact the drive shaft bore.

   c. Hold the tool in firm contact with the bearing (**Figure 60**) and carefully drive the bearing from the gearcase.

5. Remove the detent ball, spring and spacer (17-19, **Figure 74**) from the gearcase.

6. Use a suitable solvent to clean all grease, metal filings or other contaminants from the gearcase.

7. Refer to *Gearcase Component Cleaning and Inspection* in this chapter and inspect all components for defects. Replace defective or questionable components.

Gear and Bearing Installation (70 hp Model)

Refer to **Figure 65**.

1. Position the new lower drive shaft bearing (51, **Figure 65**) into the drive shaft bore with the numbered side facing up.

2. Using the removal tool, slowly drive the bearing into the bore. Stop frequently and measure the depth. Continue until the bearing just reaches the depth recorded prior to removal.

3. Lubricate the forward bearing race (20, **Figure 65**) with gearcase lubricant. Place the shims (19, **Figure 65**) and race into the gearcase bore with the tapered side facing out.

4. Select an appropriately sized socket and extension or section of tubing to use as an installation tool. The tool must be of a diameter to contact near the outer circumference of the race yet not contact the housing during installation. Slowly drive the race and shims into the housing until it fully seats (**Figure 77**). Place the tapered roller bearing into the race.

5. Lubricate the surfaces with OMC Triple-Guard or equivalent marine grease and place the spacer, spring and detent ball (17-19, **Figure 74**) into their opening. The opening is located at the front of the gearcase and directly in line with the shift shaft bore.

6. Place the tapered roller bearing into the bearing race. Install the hub of the gear into the bore of the bearing. Make sure the gear seats against the bearing.

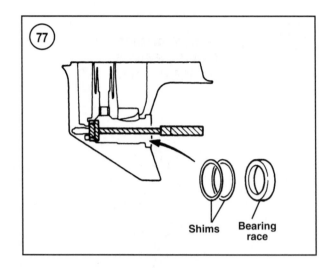

Shims   Bearing race

7. Install the pinion gear into the gearcase. Align the splined opening in the gear with the drive shaft bore and engage the pinion gear teeth to the forward gear teeth.

Shift Shaft Assembly and Installation (70 hp Model)

Refer to **Figure 74**.

1. Snap the magnet and clamp (20 and 21, **Figure 74**) onto the shift shaft. Position the magnet just above the bend in the shaft.

2. Lubricate the surfaces with OMC Triple-Guard or equivalent marine grease and install the seal (4, **Figure 74**), washers (5 and 22), sleeve (6) and O-rings (23) into the cover (2).

3. Place the spring, spacer and collar (11-13, **Figure 74**) onto the shift shaft.

4. Slide the shift cam (16, **Figure 74**) onto the shift shaft (10). Rotate the shift cam to align the reference mark made prior to removal. Use a pin punch to drive the larger diameter pin (14, **Figure 74**) through the shift cam and shift shaft. Drive the smaller diameter pin into the larger diameter pin. Make sure both pins are centered in the shift cam.

5. Use a pin punch to drive the pin (9, **Figure 74**) into its opening in the shift shaft. Make sure the pin protrudes the same amount on each side of the shift shaft.

6. Carefully slide the shift shaft into the opening of the cover (2, **Figure 74**). Push in on the shaft to compress the spring (11, **Figure 74**) and install the snap ring (8). Make sure the snap ring fully engages the groove in the bottom of the cover.

7. Lubricate the surfaces with OMC Triple-Guard or equivalent marine grease and install a new O-ring (3, **Figure 74**) onto the cover (2). Insert the alignment pin (24, **Figure 74**) into the opening in the cover.

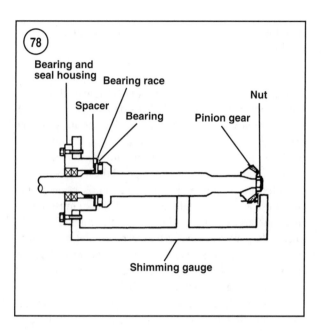

**Bearing and
seal housing** **Bearing race**
Nut
Spacer
Bearing **Pinion gear**

Shimming gauge

8. Rotate the shift shaft to align the detent ball notch and the cover with the forward side of the gearcase.

9. Carefully lower the shift shaft into the gearcase. Align the pin of the cover with its respective opening in the gearcase and seat the cover against the gearcase. Move the shift shaft up and down to verify correct orientation of the detent notch. A distinct detent is felt when the shaft reaches the neutral position. Remove and re-install the shift shaft and/or detent ball as needed.

10. Thread the three bolts into the shift shaft cover (**Figure 75**). Securely tighten the bolts.

**Drive Shaft Assembly and Installation
(70 hp Model)**

Refer to **Figure 65**.

1. Select a section of tubing to use as a drive shaft bearing installation tool. The inner diameter of the tubing must be slightly larger than the drive shaft. Clamp the pinion gear end of the drive shaft into a vice with soft jaws.

2. Slide the tapered roller bearing (6, **Figure 65**) over the upper end of the drive shaft with the tapered side facing away from the pinion gear end.

3. Slide the installation tool over the drive shaft and seat it against the bearing. Carefully tap on the upper end of the tool until the bearing seats against the step on the shaft.

4. If replacing the drive shaft (8, **Figure 65**), bearing (6) or pinion gear (32), use the shim gauge fixture (OMC part No. 342687) to determine the correct drive shaft shim thickness as follows:

   a. Assemble the pinion gear, bearing and seal housing, bearing race and spacers on the drive shaft as shown in **Figure 78**. Do not install the shims (5, **Figure 65**) at this time.

   b. Attach the drive shaft bearing housing to the shim gauge. Securely tighten the bolts that retain the bearing housing on the shim gauge. Make sure the drive shaft rests on the support (**Figure 78**) during the measurement.

   c. Lightly pull the drive shaft to seat the bearing against the housing and measure the gap between the pinion gear and the gauge with a feeler gauge.

   d. Use a shim with the same thickness as the feeler gauge. Assemble the drive shaft to the shimming gauge with the shim installed.

   e. Repeat the measurement. If the correct shim is installed, there will be no gap at the measurement point, but the drive shaft will be able to rotate in the shim gauge. Use a thinner or thicker shim to achieve the desired measurement. Remove the pinion gear, bearing race, spacers and seal housing from the drive shaft.

5. Select an appropriately sized socket or section of tubing to use as a seal installation tool. The tool must contact near the outer circumference of the seal yet not contact the housing during installation. Install the drive shaft seals as follows:

   a. Place the bearing and seal housing on a sturdy work surface with the open side facing up.

   b. Place the inner seal into the bore opening with the lip side facing up. Use the seal installation tool to push the seal into the bore. Stop when the seal surface is just below the bore opening.

   c. Place the outer seal into the bore opening with the lip side facing up. Push the outer seal into the bore until the inner seal seats in the bore.

   d. Apply a bead of OMC Triple-Guard or equivalent marine grease to the lip of both seals.

6. Slide the spring (9, **Figure 65**) onto the pinion end of the drive shaft (8). Seat the spring against the step on the drive shaft.

7. Install the collar (C, **Figure 72**) into the drive shaft bore. Rotate the collar to align the tab with the recess in the housing during installation. Align the opening in the thrust washers (A and B, **Figure 72**) with the drive shaft bore and seat them against the bottom of the collar.

8. Carefully insert the drive shaft into the collar. Rotate the drive shaft clockwise to align the pinion gear and drive shaft splines. The drive shaft drops into position as the splines align.

9. Apply OMC Triple-Guard or equivalent marine grease to the surfaces and place a new O-ring (3, **Figure 65**) onto

9

the bearing and seal housing (2). Slide the bearing race (6, **Figure 65**), shim (5) and bearing and seal housing (2) onto the upper end of the drive shaft.

10. Rotate the bearing and seal housing until the *F* mark on the housing faces the shift shaft. Seat the housing against the gearcase and install the four bolts (1, **Figure 65**). Tighten the bolts to the specification in **Table 1**.

11. Apply OMC Nut Lock or an equivalent threadlocking compound to the threads of the drive shaft and pinion nut (31, **Figure 65**). Thread the pinion nut onto the drive shaft.

12. Engage a splined adapter such as the OMC driveshaft holding socket (part No. 311875) onto the upper end of the drive shaft (**Figure 52**). Hold the pinion nut with a breaker bar and socket, then use a torque wrench and the adapter to tighten the pinion nut to the specification in **Table 1**.

Propeller Shaft Assembly and Installation (70 hp Model)

Refer to **Figure 65**.

1. Insert the spring (28, **Figure 65**) into the opening in the forward side of the propeller shaft.

2. Place the cross pin connector (24, **Figure 65**) into the opening and seat it against the spring. Insert the cam follower into the opening with the smaller diameter side facing out (**Figure 50**).

3. Slide the clutch over the propeller shaft with the *F* marking facing the forward gear side of the shaft (**Figure 62**).

4. Align the cross pin opening in the clutch with the slot in the propeller shaft (**Figure 63**). Remove and reposition the clutch as needed.

5. Push in and rotate the cam follower (23, **Figure 65**) to align the hole in the cross pin connector (**Figure 63**) with the cross pin hole in the clutch. Push the cross pin (25, **Figure 65**) through both holes and release the cam follower.

6. Make sure the ends of the cross pin are flush with the clutch surfaces. Carefully wind the spring onto the clutch (**Figure 49**). Make sure the spring spans both ends of the cross pin. Reposition the spring as needed.

7. Apply OMC Triple-Guard or equivalent marine grease to the surfaces and install the forward thrust washer (22, **Figure 65**) onto the forward gear side of the propeller shaft.

8. Install the propeller shaft assembly along with the bearing carrier as described in this chapter.

Bearing Carrier Assembly and Installation (70 hp Model)

Refer to **Figure 65**.

1. Place the inner needle bearing (36, **Figure 65**) into the bore opening with the numbered side facing out. Use the bearing removal tool to drive the bearing carefully into the carrier. Seat the bearing against the step at the bottom of the bore. Install the outer bearing into the bore with the numbered side out until it seats against the inner bearing.

2. Select an appropriately sized socket or section of tubing to use as a seal installation tool. The tool must be of a diameter large enough to contact near the outer circumference of the seal yet not contact the seal bore during installation.

3. Place one of the seals into the bore in the propeller side of the carrier with the lip side facing out. Slowly drive the seal into the bore until it rests just below the bore opening.

4. Place the remaining seal into the bore with the lip side facing out. Slowly drive the seal into the bore until it contacts the inner seal.

5. Carefully drive both seals into the bore until the inner seal fully seats in the bore. Apply a bead of OMC Triple-Guard or equivalent marine grease to the lip surfaces of both seals.

6. Install the reverse gear bearing as follows:
    a. Select an appropriately sized socket or section of tubing to use as a bearing installation tool. The tool must be of a large enough diameter to contact the outer race of the bearing yet not contact the bearing bore during installation.
    b. Lubricate the bearing with gearcase lubricant. Position the bearing into the bore opening with the numbered side facing out. Place the bearing carrier with the seal side down on a sturdy work surface.
    c. Hold the installation tool firmly against the bearing and tap the bearing into the bore (**Figure 64**). The bearing must seat against the step within the bore.

7. Position the shim (34, **Figure 65**) onto the hub of the reverse gear (33). Lubricate the reverse gear with gearcase lubricant. Slide the reverse gear hub into the bore of the reverse gear bearing until it seats against the shim and bearing (34 and 35, **Figure 65**).

8. Lubricate the O-ring (39, **Figure 65**) with OMC Triple-Guard or equivalent marine grease and position it onto the groove of the bearing carrier. Lubricate the surfaces with grease and slide the thrust washer (30, **Figure 65**) onto the rear side of the propeller shaft. Seat the washer against the step near the clutch.

9. Carefully slide the splined end of the propeller shaft through the opening in the reverse gear. Seat the propeller shaft against the reverse gear. Install the spacer (38, **Figure 65**) into the gearcase opening and seat it against the

step in the housing. Lubricate the gearcase opening with gearcase lubricant.

10. Position the gearcase with the drive shaft facing up. Grasp the splined section of the propeller shaft to retain the shaft into the carrier. Align the forward side of the propeller shaft with the opening in the forward gear while sliding the carrier into the housing. Rotate the drive shaft clockwise to align the reverse and pinion gear teeth while seating the carrier into the gearcase.

11. Lightly tap on the carrier until it fully seats against the gearcase. Rotate the carrier until the key slot in the carrier and gearcase align. Use needle nose pliers to install the key (41, **Figure 65**).

12. Place the tab washer (42, **Figure 65**) into the gearcase opening and align the protrusion on the bearing carrier with the notch in the washer and seat the washer against the carrier.

13. Apply OMC Gasket Sealing Compound or equivalent sealant to the threads of the cover nut (43, **Figure 65**). Place the cover nut into the gearcase opening with the *OFF* mark facing out and carefully thread the cover into the gearcase opening.

14. Slide the cover nut tool (OMC part No. 342688) over the propeller shaft. Engage the tool to the cover nut as indicated in **Figure 42**. Tighten the proeller shaft cover nut to the specification in **Table 1**. Bend one or more of the tabs against the cover nut to retain the nut. If necessary, tighten the cover nut *slightly* to align the tabs with the nut.

15. Refer to *Shim Selection* in this chapter to determine if the gear alignment is correct. Install the water pump components and gearcase as described in this chapter.

GEARCASE COMPONENT CLEANING AND INSPECTION

This section provides instructions for cleaning and inspecting the internal gearcase components in order to determine if they should be replaced during an overhaul. Never use damaged, worn or questionable components. The cost of the new component is usually far less than the cost to repair the gearcase if it fails.

NOTE
Do not remove any pressed-on roller or ball bearing, pressed-in needle bearing, ball bearing or bushing unless they must be replaced. A tapered roller bearing consists of the roller assembly and a bearing race. The roller and race are a matched assembly and must be replaced as such.

1. Discard all seals, gaskets and O-rings removed during disassembly.

2. Clean all parts in a mild solvent and dry with compressed air. Lightly lubricate all internal components to prevent rust.

CAUTION
Metric and U.S. standard fasteners may be used on Evinrude/Johnson gearcases. Always match a replacement fastener to the original. Do not use a tap or thread chaser with out first verifying the thread size and pitch. Check all threaded holes for Heli-Coil stainless steel locking thread inserts. Never use a tap or thread chaser on a Heli-Coil equipped hole. Heli-Coil inserts are replaceable, if damaged.

3. Inspect all screws, bolts, nuts and other fasteners for damaged, galled or distorted threads. Replace any elastic locknuts that can be installed without the aid of a wrench. Clean all sealing compound, RTV sealant and threadlocking compound from the threaded areas. Minor thread imperfections can be corrected with an appropriate thread chaser.

4. Clean all gasket and sealant material from the gearcase housing. Make certain that all water and lubricant passages are clean and unobstructed. Make sure all threaded holes are free of corrosion, gasket sealant or threadlocking adhesive. Damaged or distorted threads may be repaired with stainless steel threaded inserts.

5. On models with hydrostatic seal rings cast into the very rear of the gearcase bore, inspect the rings for wear, damage, debris or excessive corrosion. The rings trap water between the propeller hub and gearcase, sealing the gearcase to the propeller hub. This prevents exhaust gases from leaking into the propeller blade area, causing ventilation. If the seal rings can no longer retain water, the propeller will ventilate excessively. If so, replace the gearcase housing.

6. Inspect all castings for cracks, porosity, wear, distortion and mechanical damage. Replace any housing that shows evidence of having a bearing spun in its bore.

7. Inspect all anodes as described at the beginning of this chapter. Replace any anode that is deteriorated to 2/3 of its original size.

8. Inspect the water inlet screen(s) for damage or obstructions. Clean or replace the screen(s) as necessary.

9. Inspect the drive shaft and propeller shaft as detailed in this chapter for worn, damaged or twisted splines. Excessively worn drive shaft splines are usually the result of shaft misalignment caused by a distorted drive shaft housing or lower gearcase housing, due to impact with an underwater object. Distorted housings must be replaced.

9

10. Check each gear for excessive wear, corrosion or rust and mechanical damage as detailed in this chapter.

11. Inspect all shift components and shift linkage for excessive wear, grooving, metal transfer and discoloration from overheating. Inspect shift shafts for corrosion, wear, distortion or other damage. Inspect all pivot points and pivot pins for wear and elongated holes.

    a. *5/6 hp models*—These models use a rotary shift shaft and a shift cam. Inspect the shaft for wear, distortion or twisting. Replace the shift shaft if it is twisted, damaged or worn. Inspect the shift cam for wear, grooving or other damage.

    b. *All other models*—Inspect the shift bellcrank and pivot pin or shift linkage pivot screw for excessive wear, distortion and elongated holes. Inspect the shift cradle or shift actuator rod (as equipped) for excessive wear, grooving, metal transfer and discoloration from overheating.

12. Inspect all bearings as detailed below for water damage, pitting, and discoloration from overheating and metal transfer. Make sure to locate and inspect all internal needle bearings. On models with bushings, inspect each bushing for excessive wear. Replace any bushing that is noticeably out of round or elongated.

13. Check the propeller for nicks, cracks or damaged blades. Minor nicks can be removed with a file, taking care to retain the original shape and contour of the blade. Replace the propeller or repair it if any of the blades are bent, cracked or badly chipped. If the propeller is excessively corroded, replace it.

Shift Shaft

1. Inspect the bore in the propeller shaft for debris and damaged or worn areas. Clean debris from the bore.

2. Inspect the clutch spring for damage, corrosion or weak spring tension. Replace it if necessary.

3. Inspect the cross pin for damaged, rough or worn surfaces. Replace as required. Inspect the cam follower and spring for damage or corrosion and replace them as required.

4. Inspect the cam follower for cracked, broken or worn areas. Replace any worn or defective components.

5. Inspect the shift cam (**Figure 79**, 40-70 hp shown), located at the lower end of the shift shaft, for worn, chipped, cracked or corroded surfaces. Replace the shift cam and follower if there are defects or worn surfaces.

6. Inspect the shift shaft for worn areas or a bent or twisted condition. Inspect the shift shaft bushing for cracks or a worn shift shaft bore. Replace the housing or shift shaft if there are defects.

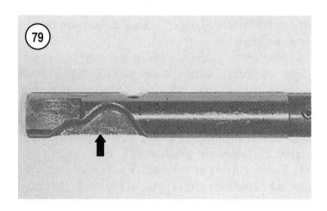

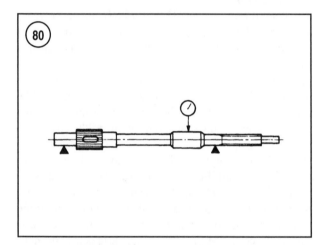

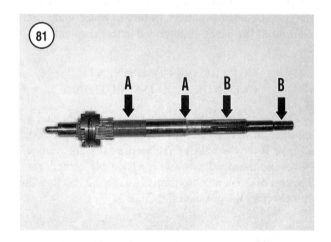

Propeller Shaft

1. Check for a bent propeller shaft by supporting the shaft with V-blocks at its bearing surfaces (**Figure 80**). Mount a dial indicator on a smooth machined area just forward of the shear pin hole or the propeller splines (as equipped). Rotate the propeller shaft while observing the dial indica-

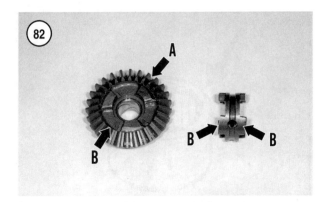

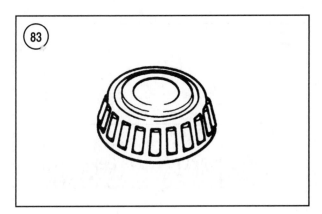

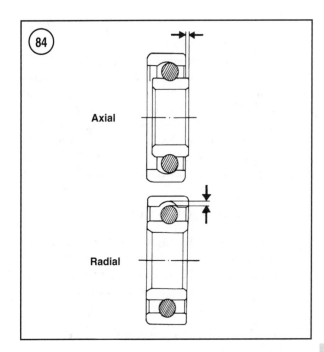

9

tor. Any noticeable wobble or a deflection reading of more than 0.006 in. (0.15 mm) indicates excessive shaft runout or wobble is present. Replace the propeller shaft if there is visible deflection or wobble.

2. Inspect the propeller shaft surfaces (A, **Figure 81**) for corrosion, damaged or worn areas.

3. Inspect the propeller shaft splines and threaded area (B, **Figure 81**) for twisted splines or damaged threads.

4. Inspect the bearing contact areas at the front and mid-point of the propeller shaft. Replace the propeller if there are discolored areas, rough surfaces, transferred bearing material or other defects.

5. Inspect the propeller shaft at the seal contact areas. Replace the propeller shaft if deep grooves are present in the surface.

Clutch, Gears and Bearings

1. Inspect the clutch (B, **Figure 82**) and gear surfaces for cracked, chipped, damaged, worn or rounded over surfaces. Replace the clutch and gears if any of these conditions are found on either component.

2. Inspect the gears for worn, broken or damaged teeth (A, **Figure 82**). Check the pinion gear and clutch dog splines for wear, distortion or mechanical damage.

3. Note the presence of discolored, corroded, pitted, rough or excessively worn (highly polished) surfaces. Replace all the gears if any of these conditions is found. This is especially important on engines with high operating hours.

CAUTION
Replace all gears if any one gear requires replacement. A wear pattern forms on each gear after a few hours of operation. If a new gear is used along with used gears, the wear pattern will be disturbed and premature wear will occur.

4. Thoroughly clean all bearings in solvent and air dry prior to inspection.

5. Replace all bearings if the gear lubricant drained from the gearcase was heavily contaminated with metal particles. The particles tend to collect inside the bearing assembly.

6. Inspect the roller bearing (**Figure 83**) and bearing race surfaces for pitted, rusted, discoloration or rough surfaces.

7. Inspect the bearing race for highly polished or unevenly worn surfaces. Replace the bearing assembly if there are defects.

8. Rotate the ball bearings and note any rough operation. Move the bearing in the directions shown in **Figure 84**.

Note any axial or radial play. Replace the bearing if there is rough operation or excessive play.

9. Inspect the needle bearings (**Figure 85**) located in the bearing carrier, gearcase and drive shaft seal and bearing housing. Replace the bearing if flattened rollers, discoloration, rusting, rough surfaces or pitting is noted.

10. Inspect the propeller shaft and drive shaft at the bearing contact area. Replace the drive shaft and/or propeller shaft along with the needle bearing if any discoloration, pits, transferred bearing material or rough surfaces exist.

Spring Measurement (40-70 hp Models)

Measure the spring that fits within the bore of the propeller shaft at the points indicated in **Figure 86**. Do not compress the spring during the measurement. Compare the measurement to the specifications in **Table 2**.

Shims, Spacers, Thrust Washers and Fasteners

1. Inspect all shims for bent, rusted or damaged surfaces. Replace any shim that is not in like-new condition.

2. Spacers are used in various locations within the gearcase. Some function as thrust bearings or thrust surfaces. Replace them if there are worn areas or if they are bent, corroded or damaged. Use only the correct part to replace them. In most cases, they are of a certain dimension and made of a specific material.

3. Replace any self-locking nut that is not in excellent condition. Replace the pinion nut anytime it is removed from the drive shaft.

4. Replace any worn or damaged washers located on the pinion gear. These washers are sometimes used as a thrust loaded surface and are subject to wear. On 40-70 hp models, they are available in various thickness. Refer to *Shim Selection* to determine the proper thickness.

GEARCASE SHIM SELECTION (40-70 HP MODELS)

Shim selection is required if replacing major internal components including gears, bearings, drive shaft or the gearcase housing.

On most models, shim selection involves using precise measuring equipment. If the measuring equipment and experience is not available, contact a marine repair shop with Johnson/Evinrude outboard repair experience.

Always use the same shim thickness as removed from each shim location during the initial assembly. Assemble the gearcase and measure drive shaft thrust play and gear backlash and propeller shaft thrust play. Refer to *Gear*

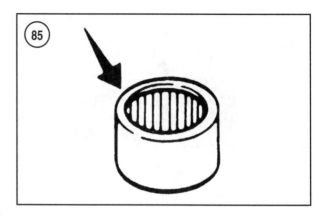

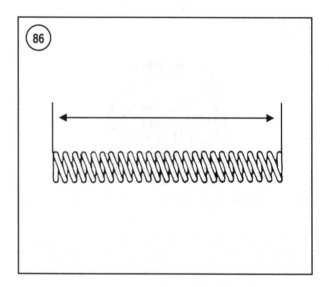

Pattern Inspection in this chapter. If adjustment is necessary, refer to *Gearcase Shim Adjustments*.

Drive Shaft Thrust Play

Use a suitable dial indicator and clamp for accurate measurement of the shaft movement. This measurement determines reverse gear position within the housing.

1. Place the dial indicator and clamp over the drive shaft and align the tip of the dial indictor over a flat and stable gearcase surface as shown in **Figure 87**. Do not tighten the wing nut clamp or otherwise lock the gauge in position yet.

2. Hold the drive shaft in the down position, toward the gearcase.

3. Carefully slide the clamp and dial indicator down until the needle moves about 0.079 in. (2.0 mm) on the meter face.

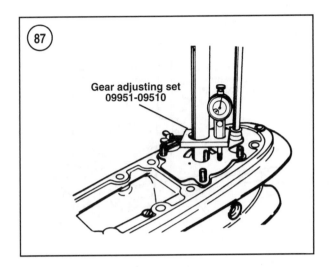

87

Gear adjusting set
09951-09510

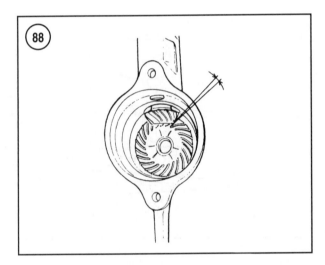

88

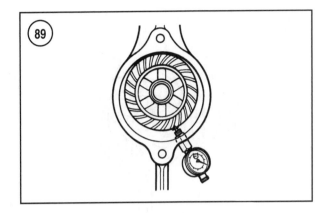

89

4. Hold the drive shaft down and securely tighten the wing nut onto the clamp. While holding the drive shaft down, rotate the meter face until the needle aligns with the 0 mark.

5. Observe the dial indicator reading and pull up on the drive shaft. Repeat the measurement several times and record the reading as drive shaft thrust play. Note that this measurement is with the bearing carrier installed.

6. Remove the bearing carrier and propeller shaft as described in this chapter. Repeat the drive shaft thrust play measurement. Record the average measurement. Note that this measurement is with the bearing carrier removed.

7. The reverse gear is correctly positioned if the measurements in Step 5 and Step 6 are equal. Refer to *Gearcase Shim Adjustments* in this chapter if the measurements differ.

8A. On 70 hp models install the propeller shaft and bearing carrier as described in this chapter.

8B. On all other models, do not install the propeller shaft and bearing carrier at this time.

Gear Backlash Measurement

Gear backlash measurement indicates the amount of free play between the teeth of the pinion and forward gear (**Figure 88**). This free play allows room for heat expansion, gear deflection and the lubricant. Improper backlash results in noisy operation, increased wear and/or gear failure.

Use a suitable dial indicator and clamp for accurate measurement of the shaft or gear tooth movement. For 70 hp models, a backlash indicator arm (OMC part No. 345825) and gear holder (OMC part No. 342689) are also required.

Gear backlash measurement instructions vary by model. Refer to the instructions for the selected model.

CAUTION
Make sure that all gearcase lubricant is drained from the gearcase prior to measuring the gear backlash. An inaccurate reading will result from the cushion effect of the lubricant on the gear teeth.

CAUTION
Remove all water pump components prior to measuring gear backlash. The drag caused by the water pump components prevents accurate backlash measurement.

40 and 50 hp models

1. Remove the drain/fill plug from the gearcase.
2. Securely hold the drive shaft to prevent rotation of the pinion gear.
3. Attach a suitable dial indicator to the gearcase using the drain/fill plug opening (**Figure 89**). Align the tip of

9

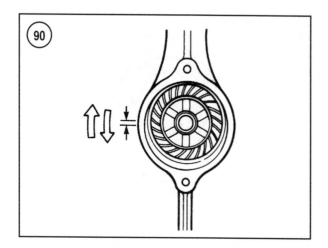

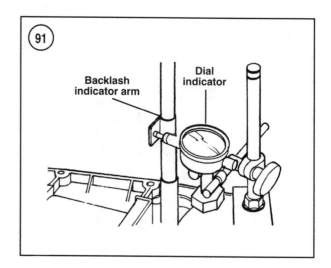

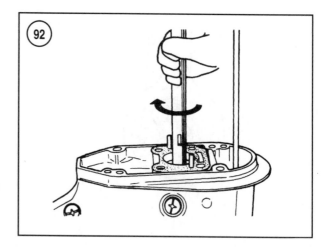

the dial indicator so it contacts the outside edge of one of the forward gear teeth.

4. Make sure the tip of the dial indicator is pushed in slightly and making contact with the convex side of a single tooth at all times during the measurement.

5. Observe the amount of needle movement on the dial indicator while reaching into the gearcase and gently rocking the forward gear (**Figure 90**). Do not move the pinion gear with the forward gear.

6. Record the amount of needle movement as forward gear backlash. Remove the dial indicator.

7. Compare the backlash measurement with the specification in **Table 3**.

8. Refer to *Shim Changes* in this section if the backlash is incorrect.

70 hp models

> *NOTE*
> *The propeller shaft and bearing carrier must be installed during gear backlash measurement.*

1. Install a gear holder (OMC part No. 342689) or equivalent shaft to the propeller shaft to lock it into position. The base of the OMC tool threads into the gearcase and the bolt on the end of the tool turns a collar that threads onto the propeller shaft. Engage the tool bolt and tighten to 35-45 in.-lb.(4-5 N•m).

2. Snap the backlash indicator arm (OMC part No. 345825) onto the drive shaft as indicated in **Figure 91**.

3. Securely mount a dial indicator to the gearcase. Align the tip of the dial indicator with the line on the backlash indicator arm. The dial indicator must be perpendicular to the arm for accurate measurement.

4. Observe the amount of needle movement while gently rotating the drive shaft back and forth (**Figure 92**).

5. Remove the backlash indicator arm and rotate the drive shaft clockwise approximately 90°.

6. Reattach the indicator arm and repeat Step 4 and Step 5. Continue until four measurements are taken.

7. Remove the dial indicator, backlash indicator arm and gear holder.

8. Determine the average of the four backlash measurements. Compare the average with the specification in **Table 3**.

9. Refer to *Shim Changes* in this section if the backlash is incorrect.

Propeller Shaft Thrust Play Measurement

Use a suitable dial indicator and clamp (**Figure 93**) for this measurement. A flat piece of steel is also required. In-

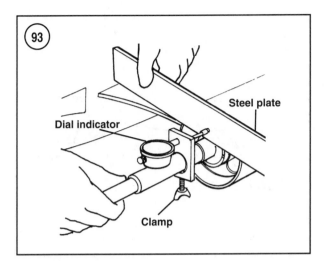

7. While holding the propeller shaft and steel plate in position, rotate the meter face until the needle aligns with the 0 mark.

8. Observe the dial indicator reading and pull on the propeller shaft (**Figure 95**). Keep the steel plate held firmly against the gearcase during this measurement.

9. Repeat the measurement several times and record the reading.

10. Compare the propeller shaft thrust play measurements with the specification of 0.008-0.016 in. (0.2-0.4 mm).

11. Refer to *Gearcase Shim Adjustments* in this chapter if the thrust play is incorrect.

Gear Pattern Inspection

Use Prussian Blue or other suitable marking compound during this inspection. These can be purchased from an automotive parts store or machine tool supply facility.

1. Remove the bearing carrier and propeller shaft from the gearcase as described in this chapter.

2. Apply a light coat of marking compound to the gear tooth surfaces of the forward gear.

3. Install the propeller shaft and bearing carrier as described in this chapter.

4. Firmly push the propeller shaft toward the gearcase. Rotate the drive shaft five complete revolutions clockwise while maintaining pressure on the propeller shaft.

5. Remove the bearing carrier and propeller shaft as described in this chapter.

6. Compare the pattern mark on the forward gear teeth with the mark in **Figure 96**. Ideal tooth contact patterns are about one-third as long as the gear tooth and are located on the toe side of the gear tooth. The pattern should start about 0.040 in. (1.0 mm) below the tooth top.

stall the propeller shaft and bearing carrier as described in this chapter prior to measuring the thrust play.

1. Pull up on the shift shaft and shift the gearcase into forward. Maintain the shift shaft in this position.

2. Place the steel plate against the gearcase as shown in **Figure 93**.

3. Place the dial indicator and clamp over the propeller shaft and align the tip of the dial indictor with the steel plate (**Figure 93**). Do not tighten the wing nut on the clamp at this time.

4. Push the propeller shaft forward toward the gearcase.

5. Carefully slide the clamp and dial indicator toward the gearcase until the needle moves about 0.078 in. (2.0 mm) on the meter face (**Figure 94**).

6. Hold the propeller shaft forward and the steel plate against the gearcase and securely tighten the wing nut on the clamp.

9

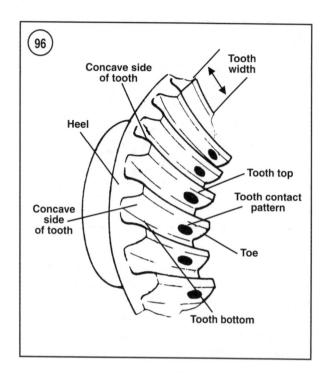

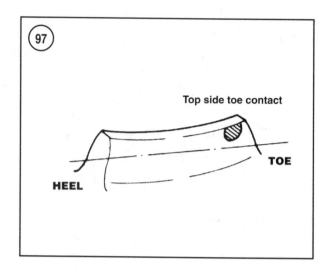

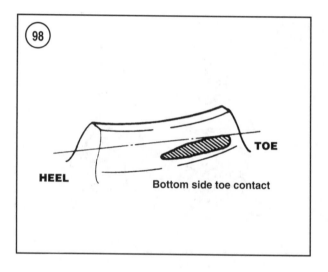

7. Operating the engine with a top of toe contact pattern (**Figure 97**) or bottom side of toe contact pattern (**Figure 98**) causes chipping of the pinion and forward gear teeth.

8. To move the pattern toward the heel and bottom of the gear tooth, refer to the instructions for the selected model:

    a. On 40 and 50 hp models select a thicker pinion gear shim (1, **Figure 44**) and a thinner forward gear shim (16, **Figure 44**).

    b. On 70 hp models select a thicker pinion gear shim (10, **Figure 65**) and a thinner forward gear shim (19, **Figure 65**).

9. Move the pattern toward the top and heel of the tooth as follows:

    a. On 40 and 50 hp models select a thinner pinion gear shim (1, **Figure 44**) and a thicker forward gear shim (16, **Figure 44**).

    b. On 70 hp models select a thinner pinion gear shim (10, **Figure 65**) and a thicker forward gear shim (19, **Figure 65**).

10. Disassemble the gearcase and make the indicated shim changes. Change the shim thickness in small increments. Reassemble the gearcase and repeat this procedure. Continue until the pattern is correct.

GEARCASE SHIM ADJUSTMENTS (40-70 HP MODELS)

This section provides instructions on how to correct drive shaft thrust play, propeller shaft thrust play, and gear backlash measurements.

Shims or thrust washers are available in varying thicknesses.

Drive Shaft Thrust Play Adjustment

Decrease the reverse gear shim thickness if the drive shaft thrust play measurement increases with the bearing carrier removed. The reverse gear shim (5, **Figure 99**) is located between the reverse gear and the reverse gear bearing. Remove the bearing carrier and propeller shaft and install the next thinner size shim in this location. Install the propeller shaft and bearing carrier. Measure the

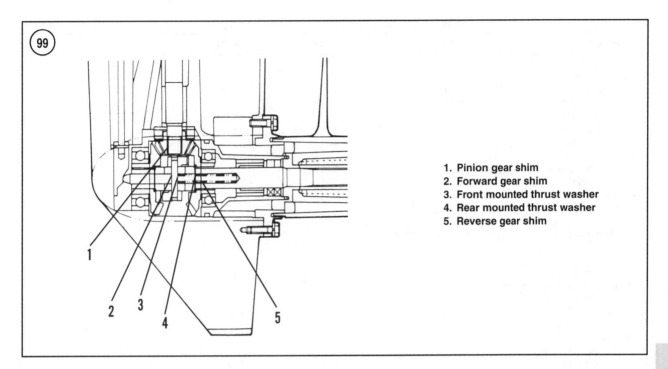

1. Pinion gear shim
2. Forward gear shim
3. Front mounted thrust washer
4. Rear mounted thrust washer
5. Reverse gear shim

9

drive shaft thrust play as described in this chapter. Install a progressively thinner shim until the drive shaft thrust play is equal with or without the carrier installed. Do not use a thinner shim than necessary to achieve equal measurements.

Propeller Shaft Thrust Play Adjustment

Correct the propeller shaft thrust play by changing the thickness of the rear mounted thrust washer (4, **Figure 99**). This washer is located on the propeller shaft between the clutch and the reverse gear. Alternate rear mounted thrust washers are available in sizes that change in 0.004 in. (0.1 mm) increments. The front mounted thrust washer (3, **Figure 99**) is located on the propeller shaft, between the clutch and the forward gear. The manufacturer does not supply this washer in an alternate thickness.

Subtract the measured propeller shaft thrust play from the specification of 0.008-0.016 in. (0.2-0.4 mm) to determine the amount of change required. Select a thinner rear mounted thrust washer to increase the propeller shaft thrust play. Select a thicker rear mounted thrust washer to decrease the propeller shaft thrust play.

Remove the bearing carrier and propeller shaft as described in this chapter and install the selected thrust washer. Re-install the propeller shaft and bearing carrier and measure the thrust play. Perform additional changes as needed.

Gear Backlash Adjustment

Correct the gear backlash by changing the thickness of the shim(s) next to the forward gear bearing. Shim locations in the gearcase vary by model.

On 70 hp models, the forward gear bearing shims (19, **Figure 65**) are located between the forward gear bearing race and the gearcase housing.

On all other models, the forward gear bearing shim (2, **Figure 99**) is located between the forward gear and the forward gear bearing.

Disassemble the gearcase until the shims are accessible as described in this chapter. Install thicker shims to decrease the backlash. Install thinner shims to increase the gear backlash. Change the shim thickness in the smallest possible increments. Reassemble the gearcase and measure the gear backlash. Make additional shim changes as needed.

Perform a gear pattern inspection as described in this section to verify correct gear alignment. Make additional shim changes to correct the gear pattern.

Tables 1-3 are on the following page.

Table 1 GEARCASE TORQUE SPECIFICATIONS

Component	in.-lb.	ft.-lb.	(N•m)
Gearcase bolts			
5/6 hp models			
Upper bolt	120-144	–	14-16
Lower bolts	60-84	–	7-9
8-15 hp models	96-120	–	11-14
40-50 hp models	–	16	23
70 hp models	–	40	55
Pinion nut			
40-50 hp models	–	36	50
70 hp models	–	50	70
Propeller nut			
5/6 hp models	Not applicable (drive pin)		
8-15 hp models	No specification (tighten the nut securely)		
40-70 hp models	120	–	14
Propeller shaft bearing/seal carrier bolts			
5-15 hp models	60-84	–	7-9
40-50 hp models	–	12	17
Propeller shaft bearing/seal cover nut (retainer)			
70 hp models	–	115	160
Shift linkage pivot screw			
8-15 hp models	48-84	–	5-9
Shift shaft bearing and seal housing			
70 hp model	–	4	20
Water pump impeller housing bolts or nuts			
5-15 hp models	60-84	–	7-9
40-50 hp models	70-80	–	8-9
70 hp models	–	14	20

Table 2 SPRING SPECIFICATIONS

Model	in.-lb. (mm)
40-50 hp models	2.362-2.440 (60-62)
70 hp model	2.520-2.637 (64-67)

Table 3 GEAR BACKLASH SPECIFICATIONS

Model	in.-lb.
40-50 hp models	0.004-0.008 (0.1-0.2)
70 hp model	0.008-0.016 (0.2-0.4)

Chapter Ten

Manual Starter

Carbureted models are equipped with a manual rope-operated rewind starter assembly. The starter assembly is mounted directly above the flywheel on all models. Pulling the rope handle causes the starter rope pulley to rotate, engage the flywheel (or flywheel cup) and rotate the engine.

Manual starters are relatively trouble free, but need to be handled appropriately to keep it operating. For instance, if the rope is repeatedly pulled until it can go no further, the rope will quickly fail and pull free from the starter pulley. When operating an engine for the first time, pull the starter rope slowly until it is fully extended; note this position. Then start the engine and make sure to stop pulling before the rope is fully extended. The operator should also make an effort not to jerk the starter rope from the fully retracted position. The starter pawl(s) will jam into the flywheel or starter cup, which will cause premature failure of these parts. Pull the rope slowly until the starter pawl(s) firmly engage and then smoothly pull the rope with enough effort to start the engine.

MANUAL (ROPE) STARTER

WARNING
Wear suitable hand and eye protection during starter service.

NOTE
To help facilitate the removal and installation of the manual rope starter obtain an OMC starter spring installer kit (part No. 342682). The kit contains a mandrel that can be inserted through a hole in the bottom of the pulley and into the manual starter cover to hold the pulley with the rope fully extended against the spring tension. A strong metal driver or mandrel of the same size can be used.

Removal/Installation (5/6 [128cc] and 8/9.9 hp [211 cc] Models)

1. Disconnect and ground the spark plug leads to the power head to prevent accidental starting.

NOTE
For assembly purposes, note the starter lockout cable routing. During installation, make sure the cable is routed properly to avoid damage to or interference with other components.

2. Follow the starter lockout cable (A, **Figure 1**) from the top rear of the manual starter assembly to the other end of the cable where it attaches to the housing on the shift

detent assembly. Disconnect the cable from the shift detent by squeezing the tabs and gently pulling the cable end from the housing.

3. Remove the three screws (B, **Figure 1**) securing the starter assembly to the power head. Lift the starter assembly off the power head.

4. If necessary, after cutting the tie-strap and/or squeezing the tabs to withdraw the cable end from the manual starter housing, disconnect the starter lockout cable from the manual starter and/or disassemble the starter for inspection or repair.

5. To install the starter, place the starter assembly onto the power head and align the mounting screw holes.

6. Install the starter mounting screws. Tighten the screws *finger-tight* at this time.

7. Slowly pull the starter rope to rotate the engine through several revolutions. Then tighten the three mounting screws to the specification in **Table 1**.

8. Route the starter lockout cable as noted during removal, then connect the starter lockout cable to the manual starter and/or the shift detent, as applicable. Connect the cable at the cable end(s) by pushing it firmly into the housing until the locking tabs engage. Gently tug back on the cable to ensure it is locked in position.

NOTE
If the cable was secured by a wire tie either at the manual starter end or elsewhere along the length of the cable, replace the tie at this time.

9. Reconnect the spark plug leads when finished.

10. Verify proper starter operation. The starter should operate smoothly when the shifter is in neutral. When the shifter is in forward or reverse the lockout must engage and prevent starter rotation.

Starter Rope Replacement (5/6 [128cc] and 8/9.9 hp [211 cc] Models)

Although it is much easier to perform this procedure with the OMC starter spring installer kit (part No. 342682), the kit is not absolutely necessary. If the kit is available, use the kit to lock the starter so that the rope is completely extended, then detach and replace the rope at both ends, as described. If the kit is not available, follow this entire procedure to replace the rope.

Refer to **Figure 2** for this procedure.

1. Remove the manual starter assembly as described in this chapter.

2. Extend the starter rope and tie a slipknot close to the housing. Allow the rope to retract into the housing up to

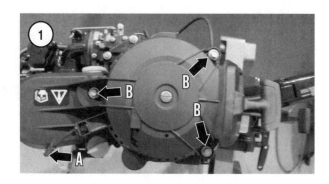

the knot. This will relieve the rope tension from the starter handle.

3. Free the rope anchor (7, **Figure 2**) from the starter handle. Then untie the knot or cut the rope and remove the anchor and handle.

4. Completely extend the rope, hold the rope pulley firmly and remove the slipknot. While firmly holding the rope pulley, grasp the knotted end of the rope with a pair of needlenose pliers and pull the rope from the rope pulley.

5. After removing the rope, carefully allow the pulley to slowly unwind, relieving the rewind spring tension.

6. Prepare a new starter rope as follows:
   a. The starter rope must be 59 in. (150 cm) long.
   b. Heat the last 1/2 in. (13 mm) of both ends of the rope with a match or lighter until the ends are fused. This prevents the rope from unraveling.
   c. Tie a knot in one end of the rope as shown in **Figure 3**. Leave 1/4 -1/2 in. (6-13 mm) reserve length at the end of the rope.

7. Preload the rewind spring by turning the rope pulley counterclockwise until it is fully tensioned and stops. Then carefully allow the rope pulley to unwind 1/4 to 1-1/4 turns, as necessary to align the rope hole in the pulley with the rope hole in the starter housing.

8. While firmly holding the pulley in place, insert the rope into the hole in the pulley and pass it through the hole in the starter housing. Pull the rope until the knotted end is seated in the relief in the rope pulley.

9. Tie a slip knot in the rope as close to the starter housing as possible. Then carefully release the rope pulley and allow the slip knot to be pulled against the starter housing.

10. Pass the rope through the starter handle and secure it with the knot shown in **Figure 4**. Push the knot into the rope anchor, then pull the anchor and knot securely into the starter handle.

11. Untie the slip knot and allow the rope to retract fully under gentle back pressure caused by holding the rope end.

② **MANUAL (ROPE) STARTER ASSEMBLY**
(TYPICAL 5/6 AND 8/9.9 MODELS)

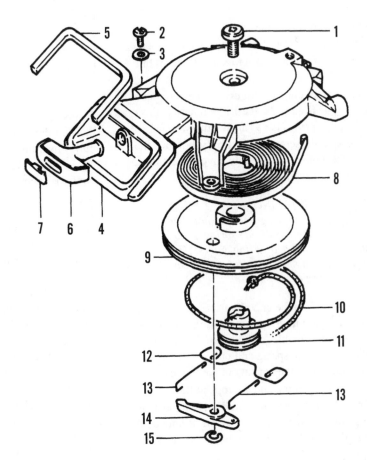

1. Spindle screw
2. Screw
3. Washer
4. Starter housing
5. Housing seal
6. Rope handle
7. Rope anchor
8. Rewind spring
9. Rope pulley
10. Starter rope
11. Spindle
12. Friction spring
13. Friction spring links
14. Starter pawl
15. Retainer clip

10

③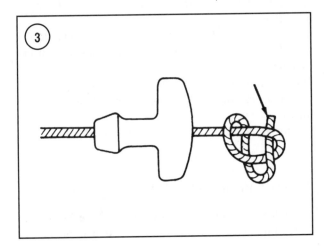

④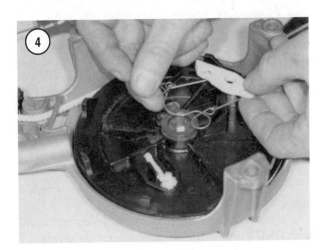

12. Install the starter assembly as described in the previous section.

Disassembly (5/6 [128cc] and 8/9.9 hp [211 cc] Models)

Refer to **Figure 2** for this procedure.

1. Remove the starter as described in this chapter.

2. Remove the rope from the starter as described in this chapter.

3. Remove the retainer clip (15, **Figure 2**). Then remove the starter pawl (14, **Figure 2**), the friction spring links (13) and the friction spring (12) as an assembly.

4. Remove the spindle screw while firmly holding the rope pulley in the housing. Carefully invert the starter housing and lift out the spindle.

> ### WARNING
> ***Do not*** *remove the spring with the housing facing upward.* ***Do not*** *lift the spring out of the housing by hand or using pliers. The spring is under significant tension and can cause injury if released suddenly.*

5. Keep hands away from the uncoiling spring. Place the starter housing upright with the rewind spring and pulley facing down over a suitable bench. Tap the housing against the bench until the spring and pulley fall out and the spring unwinds inside the housing mounting legs.

6. Separate the rewind spring and the rope pulley.

7. Clean all metal components in a mild solvent (such as mineral spirits) and dry with compressed air. Remove all threadlocking adhesive from the spindle screw and the spindle threads.

8. Inspect all components for excessive wear, chips, cracks or other damage. Inspect the rope pulley and starter housing for sharp edges or burrs that could fray the starter rope. If necessary, smooth rough edges with a file or a piece of emery cloth.

9. Take a close look at the rewind spring. Check for cracked or broken end loops.

10. Check the pawl(s) and links for wear.

Reassembly (5/6 [128cc] and 8/9.9 hp [211 cc] Models)

Refer to **Figure 2** for this procedure.

1. Set the starter housing onto a workbench with the spring cavity facing up.

2. Lubricate the rewind spring area of the starter housing with OMC Triple-Guard or equivalent marine grease.

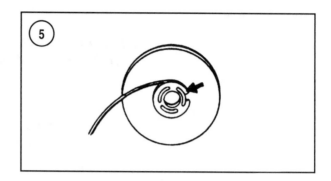

3. Insert the hooked inner end of the rewind spring through the slot in the starter housing. Position the rope pulley over the spring cavity and engage the hooked inner end of the spring into the slot in the rope pulley (**Figure 5**, typical). Then allow the pulley to rest over the spring cavity.

4. Grease the spindle (11, **Figure 2**) with OMC Triple-Guard or equivalent marine grease. Insert the spindle into the rope pulley. Rotate the spindle until the slots are positioned over the raised ribs cast in the starter housing.

5. Coat the spindle screw threads with OMC Nut Lock or equivalent threadlocking adhesive. While holding the spindle slots aligned with the raised ribs in the starter housing, insert the spindle screw into the starter housing and thread it into the spindle. Tighten the spindle screw to the specification in **Table 1**.

6. Rotate the rope pulley counterclockwise to pull the rest of the rewind spring into the starter housing. Continue rotating the pulley until the looped end of the spring is pulled snugly into its recess in the starter housing. Once the looped end is seated, carefully allow the rope pulley to unwind, releasing all tension on the rewind spring.

7. Install a new starter rope as described in this chapter.

8. Install the starter pawl, friction spring and both spring links as an assembly (**Figure 4**, typical). Hook the friction spring into the spindle groove, then push the pawl over its mounting stud.

9. Secure the pawl in place with the retainer clip. Make sure the sharp edge of the clip is facing away from the rope pulley.

10. Check for correct operation of the starter pawl. The pawl must extend when the rope is pulled and retract as the rope rewinds.

11. Install the starter assembly as described in this chapter.

Removal/Installation (9.9/15 hp [305 cc] Models)

The manual rope starter assembly (**Figure 6**) used on 9.9/15 hp models is similar in overall operation and de-

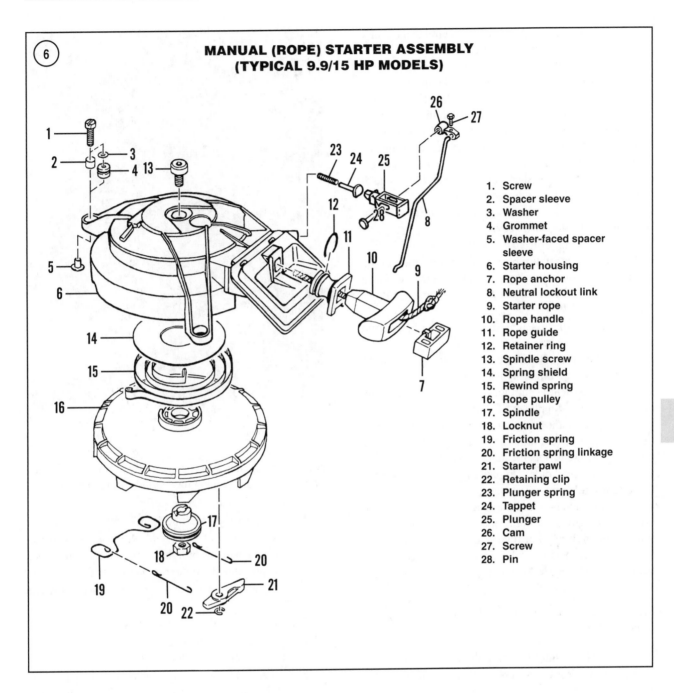

**MANUAL (ROPE) STARTER ASSEMBLY
(TYPICAL 9.9/15 HP MODELS)**

1. Screw
2. Spacer sleeve
3. Washer
4. Grommet
5. Washer-faced spacer sleeve
6. Starter housing
7. Rope anchor
8. Neutral lockout link
9. Starter rope
10. Rope handle
11. Rope guide
12. Retainer ring
13. Spindle screw
14. Spring shield
15. Rewind spring
16. Rope pulley
17. Spindle
18. Locknut
19. Friction spring
20. Friction spring linkage
21. Starter pawl
22. Retaining clip
23. Plunger spring
24. Tappet
25. Plunger
26. Cam
27. Screw
28. Pin

10

sign to the assembly used on the other models. It consists chiefly of a pulley and spring assembly contained within a housing that bolts to the top of the engine over the flywheel. Spring pressure is used to automatically rewind the rope after the engine is started.

The 9.9/15 hp models use a neutral lockout linkage-operated system. The neutral lockout linkage (8, **Figure 6**) is connected to the port end of the power head-mounted shift lever (located below the port side of the carburetor). The neutral lockout link connects to a spring-loaded plunger at the front of the starter housing. See **Figure 6**. The system actuates a spring-loaded plunger in the starter housing that engages the rope pulley (16, **Figure 6**) and prevents it from rotating. In order for the starter to operate, the plunger must be retracted by the linkage.

Refer to **Figure 6** for this procedure.

1. Disconnect and ground the spark plug leads to the power head to prevent accidental starting.

2. Disconnect one end of the neutral lockout link as follows:

a. Disconnect the clevis end of the neutral lockout link from the bellcrank (A, **Figure 7**) or:

b. Disconnect the link from the start housing (B, **Figure 7**) by loosening the screw (27, **Figure 6**) several turns to allow the neutral lockout link (8) to be disconnected from the cam (26). Then disconnect the neutral start lockout link from the lockout cam.

3. Remove the three screws and washers securing the starter housing to the power head. Locate and secure the rubber grommet and washer-faced spacer sleeve (4 and 5, **Figure 6**) on each leg of the starter housing.

4. Pull back gently on the tab and release the fuse holder (**Figure 8**) from the starter cover.

5. Remove the starter from the power head.

6. If removed, install a rubber grommet into each of the starter housing mounting legs, then install a washer-faced spacer sleeve into each rubber grommet (4 and 5, **Figure 6**).

7. Place the starter assembly onto the power head and align the mounting screw holes.

8. Install the three starter mounting screws and washers. Tighten the screws finger-tight at this time.

9. Connect the neutral start lockout link to the bellcrank or lockout cam, as applicable (**Figure 7**).

10. Slowly pull the starter rope to rotate the engine through several revolutions. Then tighten the three mounting screws to specifications in **Table 1**.

11. Snap the fuse holder (**Figure 8**) into position on the starter housing.

12. Operate the starter and check neutral start lockout operation. The starter must only operate in neutral and must not operate in forward or reverse gear. If the starter does not perform as specified, adjust, repair or replace components of the neutral start lockout system as necessary.

Starter Rope Replacement (9.9/15 hp [305 cc] Models)

Refer to **Figure 6** for this procedure.

1. Remove the starter assembly as described in this chapter.

2. Extend the starter rope and tie a slip knot close to the housing. Allow the rope to retract into the housing up to the knot to relieve the rope tension from the starter handle.

3. Pry the rope anchor (7, **Figure 6**) from the starter handle. Then untie the knot or cut the rope and remove the anchor, anchor retainer (if equipped) and rope handle.

4. Completely extend the rope, hold the rope pulley firmly and remove the slip knot. While holding the rope pulley, grasp the knotted end of the rope (with a pair of needlenose pliers) and pull the rope from the rope pulley.

5. After removing the rope, carefully allow the pulley to slowly unwind, relieving the rewind spring tension.

6. Prepare a new starter rope as follows:

a. The starter rope must be 59 in. (150 cm) long.

b. Heat the last 1/2 in. (12 mm) of both ends of the rope with a match or lighter until the ends are fused. This prevents the rope from unraveling.

c. Tie a knot in one end of the rope as shown in **Figure 3**.

7. Preload the rewind spring as follows:

a. Turn the rope pulley counterclockwise until it is fully tensioned and stops.

b. Carefully allow the rope pulley to unwind 1/2 to 1-1/2 turns until the rope hole in the pulley aligns with the hole in the rope guide (11, **Figure 6**).

c. Rotate the rope pulley slightly to align the small round hole in the rope pulley with the small round hole in the starter housing. Then insert a No. 2 Phillips screwdriver or a suitable punch through the holes to lock the pulley in place.

8. With the pulley securely locked in place, insert the rope into the hole in the pulley and pass it through the hole in the rope guide (11, **Figure 6**). Pull the rope until the knotted end is firmly seated in the relief in the rope pulley.

9. Tie a slip knot in the rope as close to the starter housing as possible. Then carefully remove the screwdriver (or punch) while holding the rope pulley in place. Carefully release the rope pulley and allow the slip knot to be pulled up against the starter housing.

10. Pass the rope through the starter handle and secure it with the knot shown in **Figure 3**. Push the knot into the rope anchor (7, **Figure 6**), then pull the anchor and knot into the starter handle.

11. Untie the slip knot and allow the rope to fully retract.

12. Install the starter assembly as described in the previous section.

Disassembly (9.9/15 hp [305 cc] Models)

Refer to **Figure 6** for this procedure.

1. Remove the starter as described in this chapter.

2. Remove the rope from the starter as described in this chapter.

3. Disassemble the neutral start lockout as follows:

   a. Depress the locking tab and remove the retaining pin (28, **Figure 6**).

   b. Remove the screw and cam (27 and 26, **Figure 6**).

   c. Slide the plunger, tappet and spring (25, 24 and 23, **Figure 6**) from the starter housing. After removing them, separate the components.

4. Remove the retainer clip (22, **Figure 6**), then lift the starter pawl (21), friction spring (20) and the friction spring from the rope pulley as an assembly.

5. Remove the retaining clip from the spindle screw (**Figure 9**), then remove the spindle screw locknut (18, **Figure 6**) while holding the rope pulley firmly in the housing. Carefully invert the starter housing and lift out the spindle. Discard the locknut (18, **Figure 6**).

WARNING
Do not *remove the spring with the housing facing upward.* ***Do not*** *lift the spring out of the housing by hand or using pliers. The spring is under significant tension and can cause injury if released suddenly. Keep hands at a safe distance from uncoiling springs.*

6. Place the starter housing upright (rewind spring and pulley facing down) over a suitable bench. Tap the housing against the bench until the spring and pulley fall out and the spring unwinds inside the housing mounting legs.

7. Separate the rewind spring and the rope pulley. If equipped, locate and secure the spring shield (14, **Figure 6**).

8. Clean all metal components in a mild solvent (such as mineral spirits) and dry with compressed air. Remove all threadlocking adhesive from the spindle screw and the spindle threads.

9. Inspect all components for excessive wear, chips, cracks or other damage. Inspect the rope pulley and starter housing for sharp edges or burrs that could fray the starter rope. If necessary, smooth rough edges with a file or a piece of emery cloth.

10. Take a close look at the rewind spring to check for cracked or broken end loops.

11. Check the pawl and links for wear.

12. Inspect the neutral start lockout components for wear or damage. Replace components as necessary.

Reassembly (9.9/15 hp [305 cc] Models)

Refer to **Figure 6** for this procedure.

1. Set the starter housing onto a workbench with the spring cavity facing up.

2. If used, insert the shield (14, **Figure 6**) into the spring cavity.

3. Lubricate the rewind spring area of the starter housing with OMC Triple-Guard or equivalent marine grease.

10

4. Insert the hooked inner end of the rewind spring through the slot in the starter housing. Position the rope pulley over the spring cavity and engage the hooked inner end of the spring with the slot in the rope pulley (**Figure 4**, typical). Then allow the pulley to rest over the spring cavity.

5. Grease the spindle (17, **Figure 6**) with OMC Triple-Guard or equivalent marine grease. Insert the spindle into the rope pulley. Rotate the spindle until the slots are positioned over the raised ribs cast into the starter housing or the raised ribs are positioned into the slots cast into the starter housing.

6. Coat the spindle screw threads with OMC Nut Lock or equivalent threadlocking adhesive. While holding the spindle aligned with the raised ribs or cast slots in the starter housing, insert the spindle screw into the starter housing and through the spindle. Install a new locknut over the spindle screw. Tighten the spindle screw and locknut to specifications in **Table 1**.

7. Rotate the rope pulley counterclockwise to pull the rest of the rewind spring into the starter housing. Continue rotating the pulley until the looped end of the spring is pulled snugly into its recess in the starter housing. Once the looped end is seated, carefully allow the rope pulley to unwind, releasing all tension on the rewind spring.

8. Install a new starter rope as described in this chapter.

9. Install the starter pawl, friction spring and both spring links (as an assembly) as shown in **Figure 4**, typical. Hook the friction spring into the spindle groove, then push the pawl over the mounting stud.

10. Secure the pawl in place with the retainer clip. Make sure the sharp edge of the clip is facing away from the rope pulley.

11. Check for correct operation of the starter pawl. The pawl must extend when the rope is pulled and retract as the rope rewinds.

12. Assemble the neutral start lockout components to the starter housing. Make sure the offset side of the cam (26, **Figure 6**) is facing the retaining plate under the starter housing, then secure the components in place with the retaining pin (28). Make sure the retaining pin locks in place.

13. Install the screw (27, **Figure 6**) into the cam (26), but do not tighten it at this time.

14. Install the starter assembly as described previously in this chapter.

Table 1 TORQUE SPECIFICATIONS

	In.-lb.	N•m
Starter mounting screws	60-84	7-9
Spindle screw		
5/6 hp models	60-84	7-9
9.9 hp models	120-144	14-16

Chapter Eleven

Hydraulic Trim and Midsection

TRIM SYSTEM

This section provides instructions for checking, filling and bleeding air from the power trim system used on 40-70 hp models. Removal and installation of external mounted components and electric trim motor repair instructions are also included.

Repairs to the hydraulic cylinders require special tools and some practical experience in hydraulic system repairs. Have the cylinder(s) repaired at a marine repair facility if these tools and experience are not available.

Work in a clean area and use lint-free towels to wipe components after removal. Cover any openings immediately after removal to prevent contamination of the fluid.

Table 1 provides torque specifications for hydraulic trim and midsection components. **Table 2** provides wear limit specification for the electric trim motor. **Table 1** and **Table 2** are at the end of this chapter.

WARNING
Never work under any part of the engine without providing suitable support. The engine-mounted tilt lock or hydraulic system may collapse and cause the engine to abruptly drop. Support the engine with wooden blocks or an overhead cable before working under the engine.

WARNING
The trim system contains fluid under high pressure. Always wear eye protection and gloves while working with the trim system. Never remove any components or plugs without first bleeding the pressure from the system. Slowly open the manual relief valve and fluid reservoir cap or plug to bleed pressure from the system.

CAUTION
The trim system fluid must be clean. A small amount of contamination can cause damage to the trim system. Thoroughly clean the trim system external surfaces with soapy water. Use compressed air to dry the trim system.

Fluid Level Inspection

Check and correct the trim system fluid level if low fluid level is suspected of causing system malfunction.

Use OMC Power Trim/Tilt and Power Steering Fluid (which is essentially Dexron or Dexron II automatic transmission fluid [ATF]). Before substituting another brand for the OMC fluid, make sure the substitute contains the same properties as the OE fluid, otherwise it may not be compatible with the seals or other components in the system.

Easy access to the fill plug or cap is possible only with the engine in the full up position.

On 40 and 50 hp models, the fill and oil level plug is on the lower and rear side of the fluid reservoir (**Figure 1**). On 70 hp models, the fill cap is on the aft side of the fluid reservoir (**Figure 2**).

1. Operate the trim/tilt system or open the manual relief valve and move the engine to the fully UP position. Securely tighten the manual relief valve, if opened.

2. Secure the engine in position with an overhead cable or blocks (**Figure 3**). Use compressed air to clean all debris from the fill cap or plug area. Place a suitable container under the trim system to catch any spilled fluid.

3. Slowly remove the fill cap or plug from the reservoir.

4. Carefully clean all debris from the cap or plug mounting surface and make sure debris does not enter the fluid reservoir.

5. Note the fluid level.

  a. On 40 and 50 hp models, the fluid level must be even with the bottom of the oil level plug opening.

  b. On 70 hp models, the fluid level must be even with the bottom of the fill plug opening.

6. Add fluid until it is even with the bottom of the fill plug or cap opening (**Figure 4**). Install and securely tighten the fill cap or oil level plug.

7. Remove the overhead cable or supporting blocks and lower the engine. Run the trim system to the fully UP and fully DOWN positions several times to purge air from the system. To ensure the reservoir is properly topped-off, repeat Steps 1-5 if more than 2 oz. (59 ml) of fluid was added to the system.

Fluid Filling

Perform this procedure to correct the fluid level if replacing the manual relief valve, hydraulic pump or fluid reservoir. Use OMC Power Trim/tilt and Power Steering Fluid or Dexron or Dexron II automatic transmission fluid ATF. Before substituting another brand for the OMC fluid, make sure the substitute contains the same properties as the OE fluid, otherwise it may not be compatible with the seals or other components in the system.

1. Use the power trim system or open the manual relief valve and place the engine in the full UP position.

2. Engage the tilt lock level then support the engine with blocks or an overhead cable (**Figure 3**). Locate then remove the fill cap or plug as described in *Fluid Level Inspection*.

3. Fill the fluid reservoir to the lower edge of the cap or plug opening. Install and tighten the fill cap or plug. Close

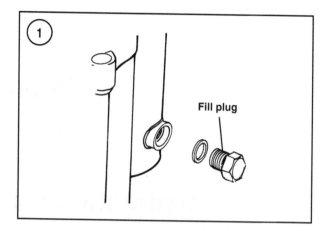

the manual relief valve. Remove the supports and disengage the tilt lock lever.

4. Cycle the trim to the full down position. Note the sound of the system while operating the trim system in the up direction. Stop immediately if the pump ventilates (speeds up). Continued operation results in air in the system.

5. If ventilation occurs, open the manual relief valve and position the engine in the full UP position. Repeat Steps 2-4 until the trim system reaches the full UP position. Check and correct the fluid level as described in *Fluid Level Inspection*.

Bleeding

A spongy feel or inability to hold trim under a load is a common symptom of air in the system. In many cases, the engine tucks under if power is applied and tilts out if the throttle is reduced. Minor amounts of air in the system purge into the fluid reservoir during normal operation. Large amounts of air enter the system when major components are replaced or if the pump is operated with low fluid level.

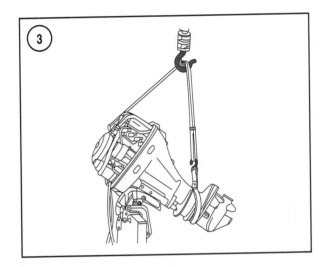

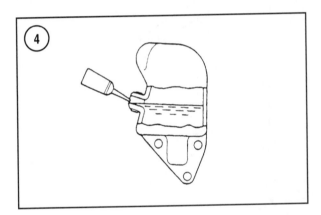

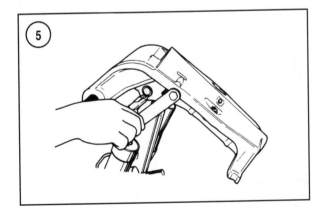

1. Use the power trim system or open the manual relief valve in order to position the engine in the full UP position.

2. Engage the tilt lock level, then support the engine with blocks or an overhead cable (**Figure 3**). Locate then remove the fill cap or plug as described in *Fluid Level Inspection*.

3. Fill the fluid reservoir to the lower edge of the cap or plug opening. Install and tighten the fill cap or plug. Remove the supports and disengage the tilt lock lever. Place the engine in the full DOWN position.

4. Operate the trim system in the UP direction. Stop immediately if the hydraulic pump ventilates (speeds up). Open the manual relief valve and position the engine fully UP. Support the engine and correct the fluid level as described in Step 3.

5. Repeat Step 4 until the engine reaches the full UP position without ventilating the pump. If foam is present in the fluid reservoir, allow the engine to sit for one hour and repeat the process.

6. Cycle the trim system up and down several times to purge any remaining air from the system. Refer to *Fluid Level Inspection* to make the final fluid level correction.

Gas Assisted Tilt System (40 and 50 hp Models) Removal/Installation

Repair to this system is limited to replacing the tilt release lever. The manufacturer provides no parts or overhaul instructions. If the system is defective, replace it.

1. Disconnect the negative battery cable. Place the tilt control level in the RELEASED position. Place the engine in the full UP position.

2. Engage the tilt lock level, then support the engine with blocks or an overhead cable (**Figure 3**).

3. Using appropriate snap ring pliers (**Figure 5**), carefully remove both circlips (3 and 7, **Figure 6**) from the upper cylinder pin (6). Using a section or tubing of steel rod, carefully drive the pin from the cylinder.

4. Remove the nut and washer (13 and 14, **Figure 6**) from the clamp bracket. Support the cylinder while removing the lower mounting bolt (9, **Figure 6**).

5. Refer to *Midsection* to locate the tilt tube nut. Loosen the nut until the clamp brackets separate slightly. Remove both starboard side engine mounting bolts. Spread the brackets apart enough to pull the cylinder, lower pin and bushings from the engine.

6. Remove the lever (2, **Figure 6**) only if replacing it. Loosen the bolt and nut (15 and 16, **Figure 6**) then carefully pull the lever from the valve shaft.

7. Inspect all pins, bushings, bolts and circlips (**Figure 6**) for worn or damaged surfaces. Replace any worn or suspect components.

8. Installation is the reverse of removal including the following:

   a. Align the punch mark on the lever (2, **Figure 6**) with the mark on the valve shaft. Securely tighten the bolt and nut (15 and 16, **Figure 6**).

11

⑥

GAS ASSIST TILT SYSTEMS (40 AND 50 HP MODELS)

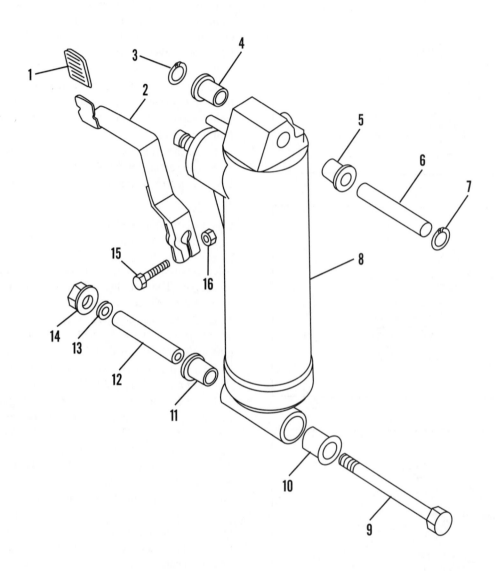

1. Grip
2. Lever
3. Circlip
4. Bushing
5. Bushing
6. Pin
7. Circlip
8. Tilt cylinder
9. Lower mounting bolt
10. Bushing
11. Bushing
12. Pin
13. Washer
14. Nut
15. Bolt
16. Nut

b. Apply a light coating of OMC Triple-Guard or equivalent water resistant marine grease to the pivot points of all pins and bushings during assembly.

c. Apply marine grade silicone sealant to the engine mounting bolt opening in the boat transom. Install then securely tighten the starboard side engine mounting bolts.

d. Tighten the tilt tube nut as described in *Midsection*.

e. Install the circlips (3 and 7, **Figure 6**) into the grooves of the upper pin (6).

9. Remove the overhead support and disengage the tilt lock lever. Place the tilt control level in the RELEASED position. Move the engine to the full UP and DOWN position. Check for improperly installed components if binding occurs.

10. Connect the negative battery cable.

Power Trim System Removal/Installation (40 and 50 hp Models)

1. Turn the manual relief valve 3-4 turns counterclockwise then manually raise the engine to the full UP position. Securely tighten the manual relief valve. Engage the tilt lock lever then support the engine with blocks or an overhead cable (**Figure 3**).

2. Disconnect the negative battery cable. Locate and disconnect the larger diameter blue and green wires from the trim relays (**Figure 7**). Route the disconnected wires out of the lower engine cover.

3. Using appropriate snap ring pliers (**Figure 5**), carefully remove both snap rings from the upper cylinder pin. Using a section of tubing or steel rod, carefully drive the pin from the cylinder and clamp brackets.

4. Turn the manual relief valve 3-4 turns counterclockwise then manually push the cylinder ram down into the cylinder. Securely tighten the manual relief valve. Mark or note the tilt pin mounting holes in the clamp brackets. Loosen the nut then remove the tilt pin.

5. Remove the trim system mounting nut on the lower port side clamp bracket. Support the trim system then pull the lower trim system mounting bolt from the lower starboard side clamp bracket.

6. Refer to *Midsection* and locate the tilt tube nut. Loosen the nut until the clamp brackets separate slightly. Remove the side engine mounting bolts from the clamp brackets. Spread the clamp brackets enough to pull the trim system and lower bushing from the engine.

7. Inspect all trim system mounting pins, bushings, bolts and snap rings for worn or damaged surfaces. Replace any worn or suspect components.

8. Installation is the reverse of removal including the following:

a. Apply a good water resistant grease to the pivot points of all pins and bushings during assembly.

b. Tighten the lower trim motor mounting bolt and nut to the specification in **Table 1**. Install the tilt pin to the clamp bracket holes noted prior to removal. Securely tighten the tilt pin.

c. Apply marine grade silicone sealant to the engine mounting bolt opening in the boat transom. Install, then securely tighten the starboard side engine mounting bolts and nuts.

d. Tighten the tilt tube nut as described in *Midsection*.

e. Open the manual relief valve and manually extend the ram to align the upper pin bores. Push the upper pin into position with an appropriately sized section of tubing or steel rod. Install the snap rings into the grooves of the upper pin.

f. Route the wires to avoid interference then connect the blue and green wires to the relays.

9. Remove the overhead support and disengage the tilt lock lever. Connect the negative battery cable. Check and fill the trim fluid level as described in this chapter.

10. Cycle the trim system to the full UP and DOWN position. Check for improperly installed components if binding occurs.

70 hp model

1. Turn the manual relief valve 3-4 turns counterclockwise then manually raise the engine to the full UP position. Securely tighten the manual relief valve. Engage the tilt lock lever, and then support the engine with blocks or an overhead cable (**Figure 3**).

2. Disconnect the negative battery cable. Remove the electrical components cover from the front and starboard side of the power head. Locate and disconnect the larger diameter blue and green wires from the trim relays (**Figure 7**). Route the disconnected wires out of the lower engine cover.

11

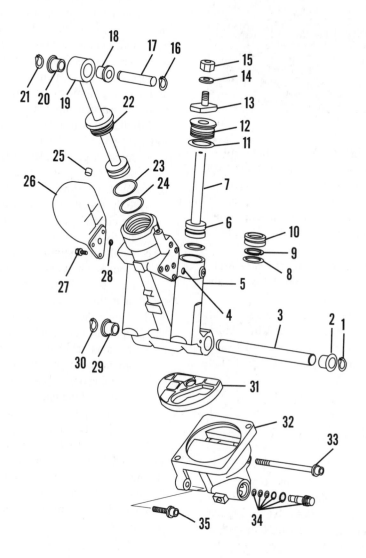

⑧

GAS ASSIST TILT SYSTEMS (70 HP MODEL)

1. Snap ring	10. Floating piston	19. Tilt cylinder ram	29. Snap ring
2. Bushing	11. O-ring	20. Bushing	30. Bushing
3. Lower mounting pin	12. Tilt cylinder cap	21. Snap ring	31. Filter
4. O-ring	13. Striker plate	22. Tilt cylinder cap	32. Hydraulic pump
5. Trim manifold	14. Washer	23. O-ring	33. Bolt
6. O-ring	15. Nut	24. O-ring	34. Manual relief valve
7. Trim tab	16. Snap ring	25. Fill cap	35. Bolt
8. O-ring	17. Upper mounting pin	26. Fluid reservoir	
9. Backing washer	18. Bushing	27. Bolt	
		28. O-ring	

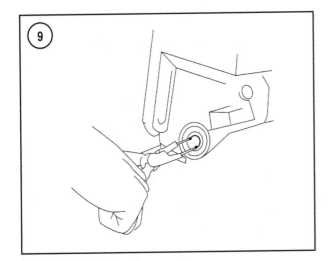

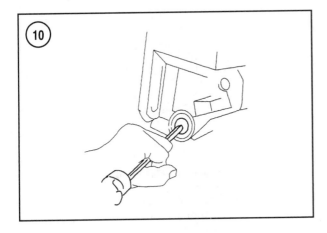

7. Installation is the reverse of removal including the following:

    a. Apply a light coating of OMC Triple-Guard or equivalent water resistant marine grease to the pivot points of all pins and bushings during assembly.

    b. Align the lower mounting pin bores and carefully drive the lower mounting pin into the trim system and clamp brackets. The lower mounting pin must protrude evenly on each side of the clamp brackets.

    c. Open the manual relief valve and manually extend the tilt cylinder ram (19, **Figure 8**) to align the upper pin bores. Push the upper mounting pin into position with an appropriately sized section of tubing or steel rod.

    d. Install the snap rings fully into the grooves of the upper and lower mounting pins.

    e. Route the trim motor wires to avoid interference, then connect the blue and green wires to the relays.

8. Remove the overhead support and disengage the tilt lock lever. Connect the negative battery cable. Check and fill the trim fluid level as described in this chapter.

9. Cycle the trim system to the full UP and DOWN position. Check for improperly installed components if binding occurs.

Manual Relief Valve Removal/Installation

Access to the manual relief valve is through an opening on the port side clamp bracket. Support the engine while replacing the manual relief valve.

1. Operate the trim system or open the manual relief valve to position the engine full UP. Engage the tilt lock lever and support the engine with blocks or an overhead cable (**Figure 3**). Disconnect the negative battery cable.

2. Using needlenose pliers, remove the circlip from the valve opening. Rotate the valve in the open direction until it is free from its bore. Pull the valve from the opening.

3. Use a pick, small screwdriver and/or tweezers to remove all remnants of the valve or O-ring from the opening.

4. Lubricate the valve with OMC Power Trim/Tilt and Power Steering (or equivalent) fluid and carefully slide the O-rings (if removed) onto the valve. Make sure the O-rings fully seat into their respective grooves on the valve.

5. Lubricate the O-rings and valve with OMC Power Trim/Tilt and Power Steering or equivalent fluid and install the valve into the opening. Do not tighten the valve at this time.

6. Rotate the valve in the closed direction until slight resistance is felt. Rotate the valve 1/4 turn in the closed direction, then 1/8 turn in the open direction. Repeat this

3. Using appropriate snap ring pliers (**Figure 5**), carefully remove both snap rings (16 and 21, **Figure 8**) from the upper cylinder pin (17). Using a section of tubing or steel rod, carefully drive the pin from the cylinder and clamp brackets.

4. Turn the manual relief valve 3-4 turns counterclockwise then manually push the tilt cylinder ram (19, **Figure 8**) down into the cylinder. Securely tighten the manual relief valve.

5. Use the appropriate sanp ring pliers (**Figure 9**) and carefully remove both snap rings (1 and 29, **Figure 8**). Support the trim system while removing the lower mounting pin. Using an appropriately sized section of tubing or steel rod (**Figure 10**), carefully drive the lower mounting pin (3, **Figure 8**) from the clamp brackets and trim system.

6. Pull the trim system back and away from the clamp brackets. Inspect all trim system mounting pins, bushings, bolts and snap rings for worn or damaged surfaces. Replace any worn or suspect components.

11

process until the valve fully seats. Tighten the valve to the specification in **Table 1**.

7. Use needlenose pliers to install the circlip into the groove in the valve opening. Disengage the tilt lock lever and remove the overhead support.

8. Connect the negative battery cable. Check and correct the fluid level as described in this chapter.

Trim Motor Removal

Refer to *Trim System* in this chapter and remove the complete trim system. Secure the trim system into a bench vise with padded jaws. Make a sketch of the electric motor wire harness routing before removal. Thoroughly clean the trim system area before removing any components.

40 and 50 hp models

1. Mount the system in the upright position. Mark the mating surfaces of the trim system and electric motor to ensure correct orientation during assembly.

2. Remove the fluid fill plug (**Figure 1**) as described in *Fluid Level Inspection*. Pour the trim fluid from the reservoir.

3. Remove the four screws that retain the trim motor to the trim pump.

4. Lift the trim motor and O-ring from the trim system.

5. Note which side is facing up, then remove the drive coupler from the hydraulic pump shaft.

70 hp model

1. Mount the system in the upright position. Mark the mating surfaces of the trim system and electric motor to ensure correct orientation during assembly.

2. Remove the fluid fill cap (**Figure 2**) as described in *Fluid Level Inspection*. Pour the trim fluid from the reservoir.

3. Remove the four bolts (2, **Figure 11**) that retain the trim motor (3) to the trim pump.

4. Lift the trim motor and O-ring (4, **Figure 11**) from the trim pump.

5. Note the filter (5, **Figure 11**) direction or placement on the pump and carefully pull it from the trim pump opening. Use a mild solvent to clean contaminants from the filter. Use compressed air to dry the filter.

6. Note which side is facing up, then remove the drive coupler (6, **Figure 11**) from the hydraulic pump shaft.

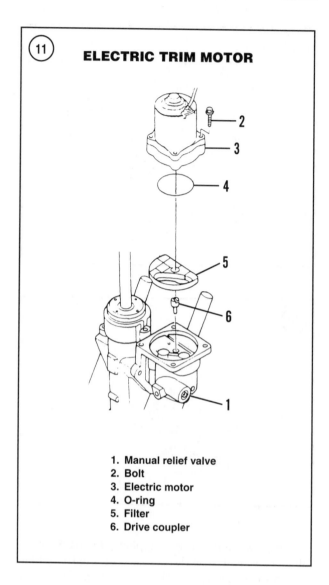

(11) ELECTRIC TRIM MOTOR

1. Manual relief valve
2. Bolt
3. Electric motor
4. O-ring
5. Filter
6. Drive coupler

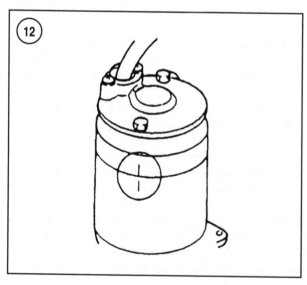

(12)

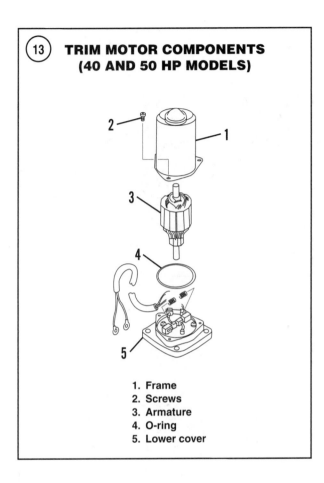

TRIM MOTOR COMPONENTS (40 AND 50 HP MODELS)

1. Frame
2. Screws
3. Armature
4. O-ring
5. Lower cover

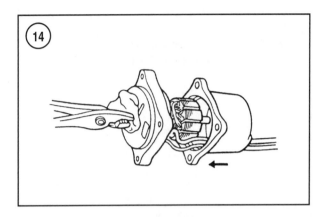

Trim Motor Disassembly

Work in a clean environment to avoid contaminating the internal components of the trim system. Use electrical contact cleaner to clean the electric motor components. Contact cleaner evaporates rapidly and leaves no residue. Avoid touching the brushes and commutator after cleaning. Naturally occurring oils can contaminate these components and shorten their service life. Refer to the instructions for the selected model.

CAUTION
Mark the top cover, frame and lower cover of the electric motor prior to disassembly. Use paint dots or removable tape. Never scratch the components, as it promotes corrosion of metal components.

NOTE
The magnets in the electric motor frame assembly are quite strong. Considerable effort may be required to remove the frame assembly from the armature. Check for remaining fasteners, then carefully pull the frame from the armature.

40 and 50 hp models

1. Mark the frame and upper cover mating surfaces (**Figure 12**) for reference during assembly.

2. Hold the frame (1, **Figure 13**) so it firmly contacts the lower cover (5) and remove all three mounting screws (2).

3. Hold the frame assembly, then grasp the armature shaft with pliers and a shop towel (**Figure 14**). Pull the armature and lower cover from the frame assembly.

4. Use two small screwdrivers to collapse the brush springs and move the brushes away from the commutator. Carefully pull the armature (3, **Figure 13**) from the lower cover. Slowly release the brush springs.

5. Remove the O-ring (4, **Figure 13**) from the lower cover. Mark the orientation of the plate to the lower cover. Remove the screws, then disconnect the terminal connector. Lift the brush and lead assembly and plate from the lower cover.

70 hp model

1. Mark the frame (4, **Figure 15**) and lower cover (10) for reference during assembly.

2. Hold the frame while removing both mounting screws (3, **Figure 15**) from the lower cover.

3. Hold the frame and grasp the armature shaft with pliers and a shop towel as indicated in **Figure 14**. Pull the armature and lower cover away from the frame assembly. Disconnect both leads connected to the cover mounted brushes.

4. Use two small screwdrivers to collapse the brush springs (9, **Figure 15**), then move the brush away from the commutator. Pull the armature (5, **Figure 15**) from the lower cover. Slowly release the brush springs.

5. Remove the thrust washer (13, **Figure 15**) from the armature. Remove the O-ring (14, **Figure 15**) from the lower cover.

11

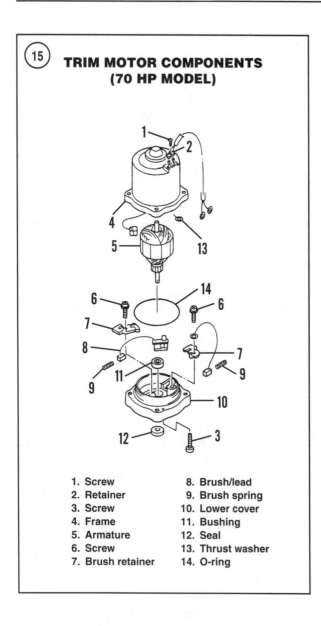

**TRIM MOTOR COMPONENTS
(70 HP MODEL)**

1. Screw
2. Retainer
3. Screw
4. Frame
5. Armature
6. Screw
7. Brush retainer
8. Brush/lead
9. Brush spring
10. Lower cover
11. Bushing
12. Seal
13. Thrust washer
14. O-ring

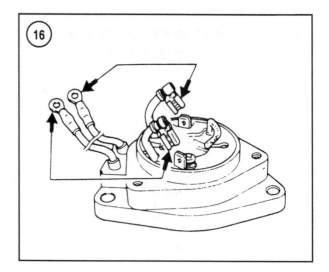

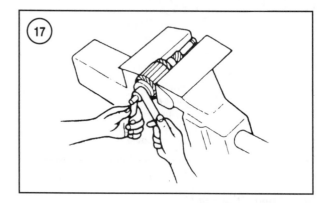

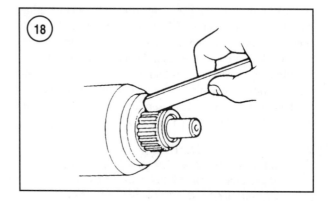

6. Remove both screws (6, **Figure 15**), then lift both brush retainers (7) from the lower cover. Disconnect the wire terminals, then lift the brush lead and breaker and brush assembly (8, **Figure 15**) from the lower cover.

7. Note the seal lip direction, then carefully push or pry the seal and bushing (12 and 11, **Figure 15**) from the lower cover.

Trim Motor Inspection

Thoroughly clean all components prior to testing or measuring. Inspect the magnets in the frame assembly to see if they are broken or loose and replace the frame assembly if it is defective.

1. Connect an ohmmeter between each brush and terminal end of the brush wire (**Figure 16**). Continuity should be present, otherwise replace the brushes and leads.

2. Carefully grip the armature in a vise (**Figure 17**). Use only enough clamping force to retain the armature. Polish the commutator surfaces with 600-grit wet or dry abrasive paper or carburundum. Polish the surface only. Remove

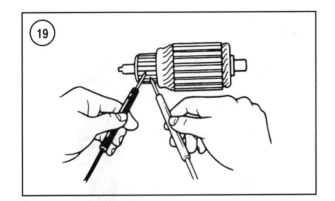

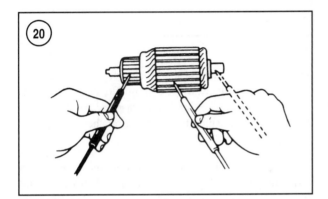

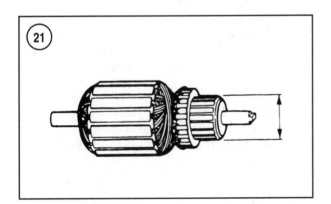

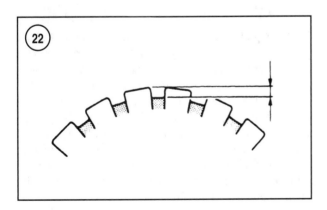

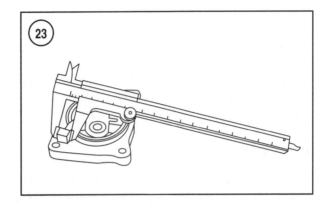

only contamination and glazed surfaces. Periodically rotate the armature to polish evenly. Avoid removing too much material.

3. Use a narrow file to remove the mica and brush material from between the commutator segments (**Figure 18**).

4. Connect an ohmmeter between each commutator segment (**Figure 19**) while noting the meter reading. Continuity should be present between each segment. Otherwise replace the armature.

5. Connect the ohmmeter between each commutator segment and each armature lamination (**Figure 20**), then the armature shaft. No continuity should be present between any commutator segment and armature laminations or shaft. If continuity is present, replace the armature.

6. Using a micrometer or vernier caliper, measure the commutator diameter at the points indicated **Figure 21**. Compare the measurements with the specification in **Table 2**. Replace the armature if the measurements are less than the specification. Inspect the bearing surfaces on the armature for excessive wear or damage and replace as required. Inspect the bushings in the covers or frame assembly. Replace them if worn or damaged.

7. Using a depth micrometer, measure the depth of the undercut between the commutator segments at the points indicated in **Figure 22**. Compare the measurements with the commutator undercut specification in **Table 2**. Replace the armature if the measurements are not within the specification.

8. Inspect the brush springs for damage or corrosion. Replace the brush springs if there is corrosion or lost spring tension. Use a caliper or micrometer to measure the brush length (**Figure 23**). Replace both brushes if the length of either brush is at or below the minimum specification in **Table 2**.

11

Trim Motor Assembly

Clean and dry all components prior to assembly. Apply a light coat of OMC Triple-Guard or equivalent water resistant marine grease to the bushings, O-rings, seals and armature shaft (at the bushing contact surfaces). Do not allow any grease to contact the brushes or commutator.

40 and 50 hp models

1. Insert the brushes and leads into the lower cover (5, **Figure 13**). Connect the wire terminal to the breaker. Place the brush springs into the recesses provided in the lower cover. Place the thrust washer into the lower cover, then install the plate into the lower cover.
2. Install the brush retaining plate and both screws, then securely tighten them. Install a new O-ring (4, **Figure 13**) onto the lower cover.
3. Collapse the brush holder springs. Use two small screwdrivers to position the brushes into the brush holders. Carefully install the commutator end of the armature into the brush holder then release the brushes. Never force the armature into the cover, or the brushes will be damaged.
4. Apply OMC Triple-Guard or equivalent water resistant marine grease to the bushing in the frame assembly. Grasp the armature shaft with pliers and a shop towel (**Figure 14**). Carefully slip the frame assembly (1, **Figure 13**) over the armature while guiding the armature shaft into the bushing in the frame assembly.
5. Position the armature against the lower cover. Position the O-ring on the lower cover. Rotate the frame assembly until the reference marks (**Figure 12**) align. Install all three screws (2, **Figure 13**) then tighten them securely.

70 hp model

1. Insert the breaker/brush lead (8, **Figure 15**) into the lower cover (10). Connect the wire terminal to the breaker and brush retainer.
2. Install the seal into the lower cover with the seal lip facing down or away from the armature. Place the brush springs (9, **Figure 15**) into the recesses provided in the lower cover. Place the thrust washer (13, **Figure 15**) onto the upper portion of the armature shaft.
3. Install the brush retainers (7, **Figure 15**) onto the lower cover. Install the screws (6, **Figure 15**) and securely tighten them. Position the brushes into the brush springs within the lower cover.
4. Apply OMC Triple-Guard or equivalent water resistant marine grease to the bushing in the lower cover. Collapse the brush holder springs. Use two small

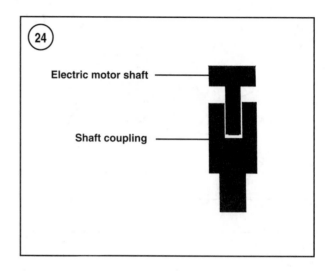

screwdrivers to position the brushes fully into the brush holders. Carefully install the commutator end of the armature into the brush holder then release the brushes. Never force the armature into the cover; the brushes will be damaged.

5. Install a new O-ring onto the lower cover (14, **Figure 15**). Apply OMC Triple-Guard or equivalent water resistant marine grease to the bushing in the frame. Place the thrust washer (13, **Figure 15**) onto the armature shaft. Grasp the armature shaft with pliers and a shop towel (**Figure 14**). Carefully slip the frame assembly (4, **Figure 15**) over the armature while guiding the armature shaft into the bushing in the frame assembly.

6. Position the armature against the lower cover. Position the O-ring onto the lower cover. Rotate the frame assembly until the reference marks align (**Figure 12**). Install the screws (3, **Figure 15**), then securely tighten them.

Trim Motor Installation

Thoroughly clean the trim motor mounting surface prior to installation. Always install a new O-ring onto the trim motor–to–trim system mating surface. Using a deteriorated or damaged O-ring allows water intrusion that will probable damage the internal trim system components. Apply a light coating of OMC Triple-Guard or equivalent water resistant marine grease to the O-ring prior to installation. To allow for easier filling and air bleeding, fill the cavity below the motor mounting surface with OMC Power Trim/Tilt and Power Steering or (equivalent) fluid prior to installing the motor.

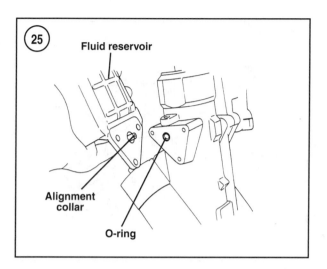

25

Fluid reservoir

Alignment
collar

O-ring

40 and 50 hp models

1. Install a *new* O-ring onto the step of the electric motor mating surface. Place the drive coupler onto the shaft coupling portion of the hydraulic pump. Fill the cavity below the trim motor with trim fluid.

2. Carefully lower the armature shaft onto the coupling. Rotate the electric motor until the shaft and coupling align (**Figure 24**) and the electric motor drops into position. Rotate the electric motor to align the marks made before removal. The wires must exit the trim motor at the point opposite the hydraulic cylinder.

3. Make sure the O-ring remains in position then install the three mounting screws. Tighten the screws to specifications in **Table 1**.

4. Refer to *Trim System* and install the trim system.

70 hp model

1. Place the filter (5, **Figure 11**) onto the trim pump. Seat the filter into its mounting recess. Fill the trim motor mounting cavity with OMC Power Trim/Tilt and Power Steering or equivalent fluid until it is even with the top of the filter.

2. Install a *new* O-ring (4, **Figure 11**) onto the step of the electric motor mating surface. Place the drive coupler (6, **Figure 11**) onto the shaft coupling portion of the hydraulic pump.

3. Carefully lower the armature shaft onto the coupling. Rotate the electric motor until the shaft and coupling align (**Figure 24**) and the electric motor drops into position. Rotate the electric motor to align with the orientation marks made prior to removal. The wires must exit the motor on the front side or opposite of both trim cylinders.

4. Install the mounting bolts (2, **Figure 11**) through the lower cover and into the electric motor mounting pad. Securely tighten the screws to specification in **Table 1**.

5. Refer to *Trim System* and install the complete trim system onto the engine.

Fluid Reservoir Removal/Installation

On 40 and 50 hp models, the fluid reservoir is integrated into the hydraulic cylinder and is not removable. On 70 hp models, the fluid reservoir is located on the starboard side of the trim system.

1. Refer to *Trim System* in this chapter and remove the trim system from the engine. Secure the trim system in a vise with protective jaws or small pieces of wood for padding. Place a container under the hydraulic cylinder(s) to catch any spilled fluid.

2. Clean all debris from the external surfaces in and around the fluid reservoir (**Figure 25**). Support the fluid reservoir while removing the three reservoir mounting screws. Carefully pull the reservoir away from the trim system (**Figure 25**). Remove the O-ring from the trim system or the alignment collar (**Figure 25**).

3. Remove the fluid fill/check cap from the fluid reservoir. Using a solvent, clean the inner and outer surfaces of the reservoir. Use a lint-free shop towel to clean the fluid reservoir mating surface of the trim system.

4. Inspect the fluid reservoir and trim system for deep scratches, cracks, pitting or damage at the reservoir-to-trim system mating surfaces. Replace any defective components.

5. Apply a light coating of OMC Triple-Guard or equivalent water resistant marine grease to the *new* O-ring, then place it in position on the trim system as indicated (**Figure 25**). Without dislodging the O-ring, position the fluid reservoir onto the trim system. Make sure the aligning collar enters its corresponding opening in the trim system.

6. Align the mounting holes in the fluid reservoir with their corresponding threaded holes in the trim system. Install the three mounting bolts and tighten them to the specification in **Table 1**.

7. Fill the reservoir with fluid and install the trim system onto the engine.

Hydraulic Pump Removal/Installation

NOTE
On 70 hp models, the pump is integrated into the pump manifold. If the pump is faulty, replace the pump manifold assembly. On 40 and 50 hp models the pump is integrated into the trim system housing. Do not

11

loosen the pump mounting screws or disturb the pump. The gears in the pump could misalign and cause eventual pump failure. Replace the housing or complete trim system if the pump is faulty.

1. Refer to *Trim Motor Removal* and remove the electric motor and filter from the trim system.

2. Place a suitable container under the trim system to catch any spilled fluid. Refer to *Manual Relief Valve* and remove the manual relief valve from the trim system.

3. Support the pump manifold while removing the three Allen bolts from the port side of the manifold. Carefully pull the manifold from the trim system (**Figure 26**).

4. Note the size and location of the O-rings on the trim system (**Figure 26**). Remove the O-rings.

5. Using lint-free shop towels, clean the manifold mounting surface on the trim system.

6. Carefully press a new filter (**Figure 26**) into the filter opening of the replacement pump manifold.

7. Apply a light coating of OMC Triple-Guard or equivalent water resistant marine grease to all five O-rings. Position the *new* O-rings into position onto the trim system as indicated (**Figure 26**).

8. Without dislodging the O-rings, place the pump manifold onto its mounting surface. Align the collar with the upper hole in the pump manifold.

9. Hold the pump manifold in position and align the Allen bolt holes in the pump manifold with the threaded holes in the trim system.

10. Install the Allen bolts and evenly tighten them.

11. Refer to *Trim Motor Installation* and install the electric motor and filter onto the trim system.

Trim Relay Removal/Installation

1. Disconnect the negative battery cable. Remove the electric component cover.

2. Mark all wire terminal connections and wire routing (**Figure 7**). Carefully disconnect all wire terminals from the relay.

3. Mark the up side of the relay.

4. Remove the two bolts, washers and grommets (if so equipped) that retain the trim relay to the mounting bracket.

5. Place the relay onto the mount with the up mark correctly oriented. Install the bolts, washer and grommets to the relay mounting holes. Securely tighten the bolts.

6. Carefully attach all wires to the relay (**Figure 7**). Route all wires to prevent them from interfering with other components.

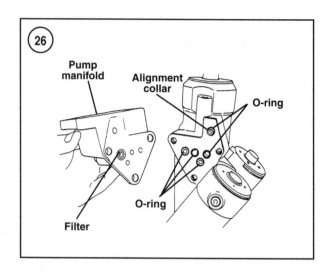

7. Install the electric component cover. Connect the negative battery cable. Check for proper trim system operation.

Trim Position Sender Removal/Installation

The trim sender is located on the inside of the port clamp bracket (**Figure 27**). Note the sender wire routing and connections prior to removal.

Note the size and location of any plastic tie clamps and replace them as required.

1. Position the engine at full-tilt and engage the tilt lock lever. Support the engine with blocks or an overhead cable.

2. Trace the sender wires to the harness connection inside the motor cover and disconnect them. Route the wires out of the motor cover to allow removal of the wire and sender. Remove all clamps prior to removal. Inspect the clamps for corrosion or damage and replace them as required.

3. Use a felt-tip marker to trace the sender outline on the mounting location. Remove both fasteners and the sender (**Figure 27**). Route the wires through the opening in the port clamp bracket and remove the assembly.

4. Clean the mounting location and threaded holes.

5. Installation is the reverse of removal. Align the sender with the outline marks and securely tighten the attaching screws (**Figure 27**). Remove the engine supports or overhead cable. Lower the engine.

6. Refer to Chapter Four to adjust the trim sender. Check for proper operation.

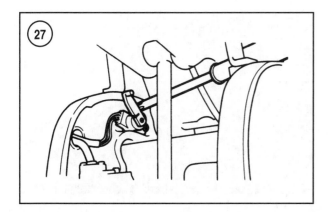

MIDSECTION (5-15 HP MODELS)

Items covered here include the tiller control twist grip, steering handle, exhaust housing and swivel bracket.

Repairs to the midsection typically involve replacing corrosion-damaged components or components damaged because of impact with underwater objects.

Major repair may require removing the power head and gearcase followed by complete disassembly of the midsection. Major repair is required when repairing or replacing the clamp brackets and swivel housing. Components such as the engine mounts are replaced during cylinder head disassembly after power head removal. For details on power head removal or cylinder head disassembly, please refer to Chapter Eight.

Apply OMC Triple-Guard or equivalent water resistant marine grease to all bushings, pins and pivot points during assembly. Tighten the midsection fasteners to the specification in **Table 1**.

Tiller Twist Grip Disassembly/Assembly

The tiller twist grip contains the stop switch, idle control knob and throttle cable connections on these models.

Disassemble the grip in order to replace any of these items.

1. Position the OMC Twist Grip removal tool (part. No. 390767) over the base of the twist grip (where it contacts the steering arm) and tighten the screw to depress the grip detents. With the detents depressed, pull the grip from the steering arm and from over the top of the grip helix halves while turning the idle adjustment knob (**Figure 28**) clockwise.

2. Remove the grip helix halves, rollers and guides. On 5/6 hp models, remove the throttle friction control collar and handle cover.

3. Withdraw the throttle pin from the cable.

4. For 5/6 hp models, proceed as follows:
   a. Remove the clamp screw and washer from the throttle cable/stop switch, then turn the clamp to the side and remove the throttle cable.
   b. If necessary, free the stop switch from the handle by removing the screw. If the switch requires replacement, trace the wiring back and disconnect it from the Amphenol connector using a pin removal tool (part No. 322698).

5. For 8-15 hp models, proceed as follows:
   a. Remove the throttle end cap from the inner handle.
   b. Remove the stop switch cover screws, then separate the cover/switch assembly from the handle.
   c. Remove the throttle control plate, then remove the cable from the steering handle.
   d. If necessary, remove the stop switch assembly along with the throttle cable from the cover. If the switch requires replacement, trace the wiring back and disconnect it from the Amphenol connector using a pin removal tool (part No. 322698).
   e. Remove the throttle cable seal from the inner handle.

6. Inspect the throttle cable for kinks, frayed ends or wear and replace, if necessary.

7. Inspect the steering handle components for damage, cracks or wear and replace, if necessary.

8. If necessary, refer to troubleshooting in Chapter Two for ignition stop switch testing.

9. For 5/6 hp models, begin component assembly as follows:
   a. If removed, install the stop switch to the handle and secure it using the retaining screw.
   b. Position the throttle cable and secure it using the clamp.
   c. Gently insert the throttle cable pin through the end of the cable.

10. For 8-15 hp models, begin component assembly as follows:
    a. Install the throttle cable seal into the inner handle.

11

b. Gently snap the stop switch assembly and throttle cable into the cover, making sure the protective sleeve covers the components.

c. Position the throttle cable into the inner handle while aligning the cover with the handle. Install the throttle control plate onto the outer handle.

d. Position the throttle end cap into the inner handle, making sure the tab is inserted into the inner handle recess.

e. Gently insert the throttle cable pin through the end of the cable.

11. Coat the throttle cable pin along with the grip guides, rollers, helix grooves and inner handle guide slot using OMC Moly Lube or equivalent.

12. Position the grip guides over the roller pin and into the slots of the inner handle, then position the rollers on the ends of the roller pin.

13. Assemble the grip helix halves on the handle, then align and slide the grip over the halves.

NOTE
Make sure during twist grip installation that the speed indicator line is aligned with the speed range symbol on the throttle and not 180° out.

14. Snap the grip into place on the arm.

15. For 5/6 hp models, make sure the throttle friction screw is in the proper position, then install the cover to the handle.

16. For 8-15 hp models, turn the idle speed adjustment knob counterclockwise to the slowest setting, then install the stop switch cover onto the handle.

Steering Handle Removal/Installation

5/6 hp (128 cc) and 8/9.9 hp (211 cc) models

1. Disconnect and ground the spark plug leads to prevent accidental starting.

2. Remove the manual starter assembly as detailed in Chapter Ten.

3. Remove the lower engine covers as detailed in the *Oil Filter Cleaning or Replacement* in Chapter Three.

4. Remove the tie strap and the connector retainer, then disconnect the Amphenol connectors (A, **Figure 29**). Use a pin removal tool (part No. 322698) to remove the stop button black wire from the connector.

5. Remove the lower ignition module screw (B, **Figure 29**) along with the lockwasher, then free the ground black wire.

6. Remove the bolt (A, **Figure 30**) securing the throttle cable anchor.

7. Remove the bolts and washers (B, **Figure 30**) securing the throttle lever, then remove the linkage from the throttle lever (C, **Figure 30**) and unthread the anchor from the cable.

8. Remove the nut, bolt and sleeve from the pivot at the rear of the steering handle, then lift the steering handle and throttle grip assembly from the steering bracket and pull the cable through the grommet.

9. Installation is the reverse of the removal procedure. Note the following:

a. Apply OMC Triple-Guard or equivalent marine grease to the steering handle sleeve, then install it into the bracket.

b. Attach the steering handle to the bracket and route the cable through the grommet, then tighten the nut so the handle can be left in any position. Replace the handle locknut if it cannot hold the handle position.

c. Thread the anchor onto the cable housing until *one* thread is exposed on the end of the anchor. (A, **Figure 30** shows anchor installation on a typical 5/6 hp model, but note that the anchor may face the opposite direction on some models. If so, the one thread should still be exposed just beyond the bent portion

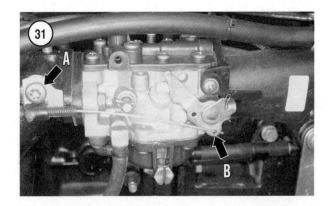

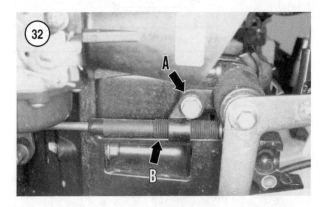

of the anchor where the flat bracket arm attaches to the threaded bore.)

9.9/15 hp (305 cc) models

1. Disconnect and ground the spark plug leads to prevent accidental starting.

2. Remove the Torx head screw (A, **Figure 31**) securing the choke cable clamp to the power head, then carefully disconnect the cable arm from the carburetor linkage (B, **Figure 31**).

3. Remove the nut at the back of the choke cable-to-engine cover mounting, then remove the cable.

4. Remove the lower engine covers as detailed in *Oil Filter Cleaning or Replacement*.

5. Remove the manual starter assembly as detailed in Chapter Ten.

6. Remove the camshaft sprocket cover.

7. Using a small prytool, carefully remove the throttle cable clevis from the linkage throttle arm. Position the blade of the prytool against the air retaining screw.

8. Remove the bolt and washer (A, **Figure 32**) securing the throttle cable anchor to the power head.

9. Remove the back port side mounting screw from the ignition module, then remove the engine stop ground wire from behind the module assembly.

10. Disconnect the three-pin Amphenol connector (**Figure 33**), located just behind a two-pin connector in this case. Use a pin removal tool (part No. 322698) to remove the stop button black wire from the connector.

11. Remove the nut, bolt and sleeve from the pivot at the rear of the steering handle, then lift the steering handle and throttle grip assembly from the steering bracket and pull the cable through the grommet.

12. Installation is the reverse of removal. Note the following:

   a. Apply OMC Triple-Guard or equivalent marine grease to the steering handle sleeve, then install it into the bracket.

   b. Attach the steering handle to the bracket and route the cable through the grommet, then tighten the nut so the handle can be left in any position. Replace the handle locknut if it cannot hold the handle position.

   c. Thread the anchor onto the cable housing until the anchor is 1/8 in. (3 mm) from the aft end of the housing threads, then secure the anchor to the power head using the bolt and washer. Tighten the anchor bolt to the specification in **Table 1**.

   d. Use a pin installation tool such as the OMC pin insert tool (part No. 322697) to safely install the stop button wire to the three-pin Amphenol connector.

Exhaust Housing and Swivel Bracket Service

5/6 hp (128 cc) models

1. Remove the power head as detailed in Chapter Eight.

2. Remove the gearcase as detailed in Chapter Nine.

3. Remove the two bolts at the base of the swivel, then remove the lower mount housings and thrust mount in order to free the exhaust housing from the swivel bracket.

4. Clean and inspect the housing as detailed later in this section.

11

5. Installation is the reverse of removal.

8/9.9 hp (211 cc) models

1. Remove the lower engine covers as detailed in *Oil Filter Cleaning or Replacement* in Chapter Three.
2. Remove the power head as detailed in Chapter Eight.
3. Remove the gearcase as detailed in Chapter Nine.
4. Remove the two bolts at the base of the swivel, then remove the lower mount brackets and separate the exhaust housing from the swivel bracket assembly.
5. Remove the two lower side mounts, the lower front mount and the shift rod grommet from the base of the exhaust housing.
6. Clean and inspect the housing as detailed later in this chapter.
7. If necessary, disassemble the swivel tube assembly as follows:
   a. Remove the three bolts securing the steering bracket, then remove the bracket from the tube.
   b. Remove the lower thrust washer from the tube.
   c. Loosen the steering friction adjustment screw, then lift the pivot tube from the bracket.
   d. Remove the liner and friction block from inside the top of the bracket.
   e. Remove the O-ring and lower bushing from the bottom of the bracket.
   f. Remove the upper thrust washer from the top of the pivot tube.
   g. If necessary, remove and replace any components from the stern brackets. Arrange all parts as they are removed to ensure proper installation. If the tilt bolt is removed, tighten the bolt to the specification in **Table 1**.
8. Installation is the reverse of removal. Note the following:
   a. Make sure to install the liner on the pivot tube with the hole towards the top, then align the protrusion on the friction block with the relief in the bracket.
   b. Make certain to align the opening in the lower bushing with the grease fitting on the swivel bracket.
   c. Coat all metal-to-metal sliding surfaces and O-rings using OMC Triple-Guard or equivalent marine grease.
   d. Coat the steering bracket-to-tube bolt threads using OMC Nut Lock or equivalent threadlocking compound, then install and tighten them to the specification in **Table 1**.
   e. Coat the two lower mount bracket bolt threads using OMC Nut Lock or equivalent threadlocking compound, then install and tighten them to the specification in **Table 1**.

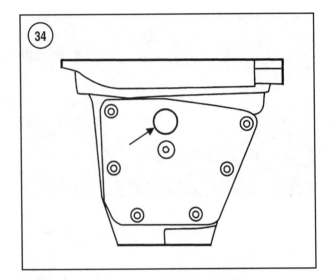

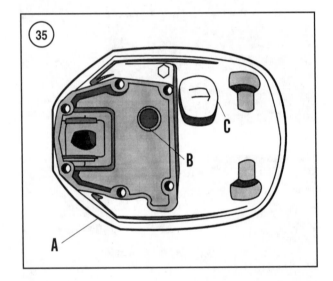

   f. Adjust the steering friction screw as detailed in Chapter Four.

9.9/15 hp (305 cc) models

1. Remove the lower engine covers as detailed in *Oil Filter Cleaning or Replacement* in Chapter Three.

2. Remove the power head as detailed in Chapter Eight.

3. Remove the gearcase as detailed in Chapter Nine.

4. Remove the noise suppressor (**Figure 34**) for cleaning and inspection or replacement.

5. Remove the exhaust housing cover and gasket, then remove the cover seal (A, **Figure 35**), water seal (B) and the exhaust seal (C).

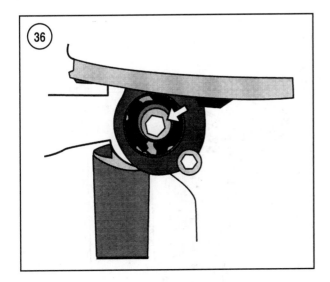

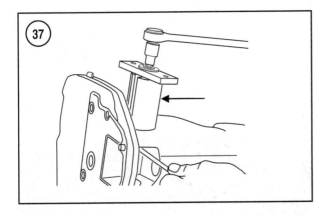

6. On each side of the housing remove the upper mount retaining bracket, then remove the upper mount-to-swivel bracket bolt (**Figure 36**) and nut.

7. Remove the two bolts at the base of the swivel, then remove the lower mount brackets and separate the exhaust housing from the swivel bracket assembly.

8. Remove the two lower side mounts, the lower front mount and the shift rod grommet from the base of the exhaust housing.

9. If necessary, remove the upper and lower mounts by fabricating a tool from a 3 in. (7.6 cm) long piece of pipe (**Figure 37**). Along with the pipe, use either a piece of stock that is longer than the pipe is wide with a hole drilled through the center or use a bridge from universal puller, and a couple washers and a nut.

    a. Position the fabricated pipe over the mount with the bridge (or piece of stock) on top of the pipe.

    b. Insert the mount bolt through a washer, the bridge, the tool and finally the mount (**Figure 37**). Position a small washer and a nut under the mount.

    c. Slowly tighten the screw to draw the mount from the housing.

10. Clean and inspect the housing as detailed later in this chapter.

11. If necessary, disassemble the swivel tube bracket.

    a. Arrange all parts as they are removed to ensure proper installation. Loosen the steering friction adjustment screw, and then lift the pivot tube/steering bracket from the swivel bracket.

NOTE
Do not separate the pivot tube from the steering bracket, as these components are non-serviceable and, if damaged, must be replaced as an assembly.

    b. Remove the friction block from the top of the swivel bracket, then remove the lower bushing from the bottom.

    c. Remove the lower thrust washer, O-ring and liner from the pivot tube.

    d. Remove the upper thrust washer from the top of the pivot tube.

    e. If necessary, remove and replace any components from the stern brackets. If the tilt bolt is removed, tighten the bolt to the specification in **Table 1**.

    f. Upon assembly, make sure to install the liner on the pivot tube with the hole towards the top, then align the protrusion on the friction block with the relief in the bracket.

    g. Make certain to align the opening in the lower bushing with the grease fitting on the swivel bracket.

12. Installation is the reverse of removal. Note the following:

    a. Coat all metal-to-metal sliding surfaces and O-rings using OMC *Triple-Guard* or equivalent marine grease.

    b. If removed, use the fabricated tool (**Figure 38**) to install new upper mounts. Before installation, coat the mounts with OMC Wheel Bearing Grease or equivalent. Make sure to install the mounts with the indentation aligning with the small point on the housing bore (the off-center hole in the mount is positioned toward the rear).

    c. Coat the two lower mount bracket bolt threads using OMC Nut Lock or equivalent threadlocking compound, then install and tighten them to the specification in **Table 1**.

    d. Apply a light coating of OMC Gasket Sealing Compound or equivalent sealant to a new housing cover gasket.

    e. Coat the housing cover screw threads using OMC Nut Lock or equivalent threadlocking compound,

11

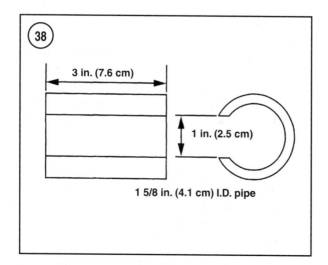

then install and tighten them to the specification in **Table 1**.

f. Adjust the steering friction screw as detailed in Chapter Four.

Exhaust Housing Cleaning and Inspection

1. Remove the exhaust housing as detailed in this chapter.

2. Visually inspect the clamp screw assembly. Replace the swivel plate and retainer if the components are bent or loose. When installing a new plate apply OMC Locquic Primer to the screw threads and let it dry for 4-5 minutes, then apply a coating of OMC Ultra Lock or equivalent to the threads. Install a new swivel plate with a screw and tighten securely.

3. Clean all metal parts with solvent and dry using compressed air. Carefully clean all bolts and nuts of any remaining threadlocking compound. If available, use OMC Screw Lock, OMC Nut Lock, or an equivalent threadlocking compound on those same bolts and nuts during assembly. Prime the threads using OMC Locquic Primer as detailed in Step 2.

4. Remove and discard all oil seals, O-rings and gaskets.

5. Check the rubber mounts for wear, deterioration, excessive cracking or flaking or damage and replace them, if necessary.

6. Carefully clean all traces of sealant and corrosion from the top and bottom mating surfaces of the exhaust housing.

7. Place the housing on a surfacing plate, then use a dial indicator to check the runout around the circumference of the housing (**Figure 39**). *Replace* any housing that shows more than 0.009 in. (0.229 mm) of distortion.

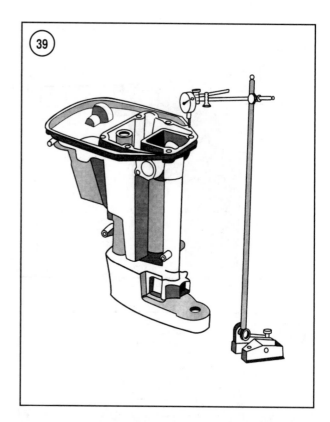

NOTE
Do not *attempt to machine or straighten the surface of a distorted housing. Make sure the runout reading is from distortion and not corrosion or debris before replacing the housing.*

8. Visually check the water tube for restrictions or kinks that could hinder water flow.

9. Check the shift components for wear and replace if damaged, worn or corroded.

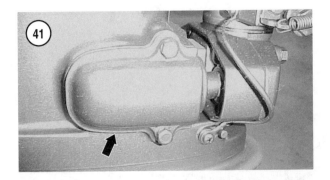

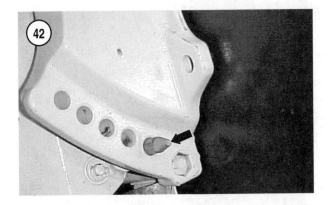

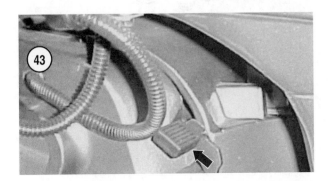

MIDSECTION (40-70 HP MODELS)

Minor repair to the midsection involves replacing easily accessible components such as the anode (**Figure 40**), lower engine mounts (**Figure 41**), tilt pin (**Figure 42**), tilt lock lever (**Figure 43**) or reverse lock mechanism.

Major repair may require removing of the power head and gearcase, followed by complete disassembly of the midsection. Major repair is required when repairing or replacing the clamp brackets, upper engine mounts, tilt tube, swivel housing, drive shaft housing, power head adapter or oil pan.

Refer to *Trim System* if it is necessary to remove the trim system components to access the midsection component(s).

Apply OMC Triple-Guard or equivalent water resistant marine grease to all bushings, pins and pivot points during assembly. Tighten the midsection fasteners to the specification in **Table 1**. If a specif torque specification is not in **Table 1**, refer to *General Torque Specifications* in Chapter One.

> *WARNING*
> *Never work under any part of the engine without first providing suitable support. The engine-mounted tilt lock or hydraulic system may collapse and cause the engine to drop. Support the engine with blocks or an overhead cable before working under the engine.*

> *CAUTION*
> *Do not use excessive amounts of sealer on the anode bolt threads. The anodes cannot protect the engine without maintaining electrical continuity to the engine ground. Check for electrical continuity after installation. Remove the anode and clean the bolts and bolt heads if no continuity or high resistance is measured.*

Anodes Inspection/Replacement

For information regarding the inspection and replacement of the midsection anode, please refer to Chapter Three.

Lower Engine Mounts Removal/Installation

1. Place the engine in the full UP position.
2. Use an overhead hoist to support the engine. Disconnect the negative battery cable.
3. Refer to **Figure 44** and **Figure 45** to locate the lower mounts. Access the lower mounts as follows:
   a. On 40 and 50 hp models, remove the bolts (36, **Figure 44**) and carefully pull the lower mount covers (35) from the drive shaft housing (20).
   b. On 70 hp models, remove the screws (31, **Figure 45**) and push the cover forward enough to disengage the pins (28) and springs (29). Lift the lower covers (30, **Figure 45**) from the drive shaft housing (18). Pull the pins and spring from the lower mount bracket (33, **Figure 45**).
4. Remove the mounts from the drive shaft housing as follows:
   a. On 40 and 50 hp models, remove the rear nuts (37, **Figure 44**), washer (38) and cushion (39) from the mount bolts (41). Remove the nuts and washers (29

11

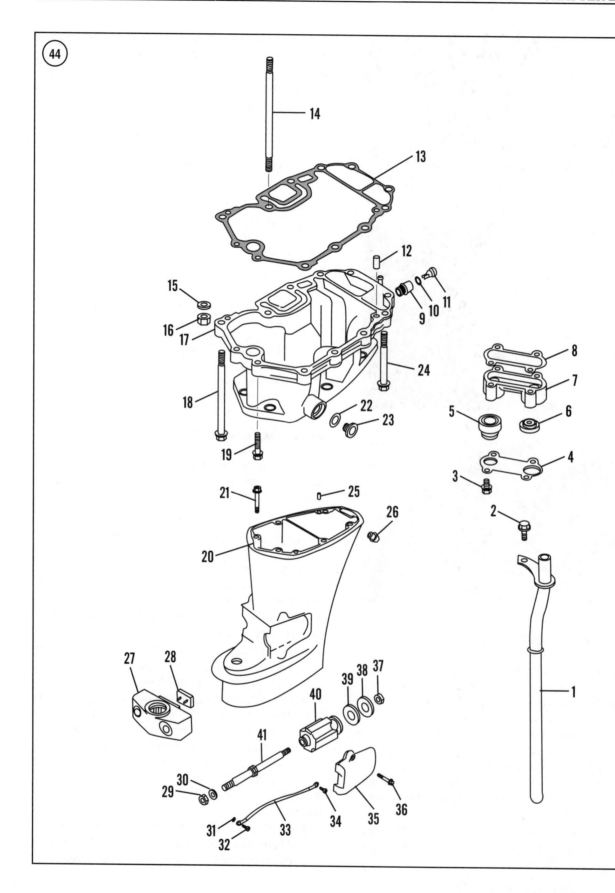

OIL PAN AND DRIVE SHAFT HOUSING (40 AND 50 HP MODELS)

1. Water pump tube
2. Bolt
3. Bolt
4. Cover
5. Grommet
6. Water pressure relief valve
7. Relief valve housing
8. Gasket
9. Water stream fitting
10. O-ring
11. Plug
12. Alignment pin
13. Gasket
14. Power mounting stud
15. Washer
16. Nut
17. Oil pan
18. Bolt
19. Bolt
20. Drive shaft housing
21. Bolt
22. Gasket
23. Oil drain plug
24. Bolt
25. Alignment pin
26. Exhaust grommet
27. Lower mount/swivel tube bracket
28. Cushion
29. Nut
30. Washer
31. Insulating washer
32. Screw
33. Ground wire
34. Screw
35. Lower mount cover
36. Bolt
37. Rear nut
38. Washer
39. Cushion
40. Lower mount
41. Mount bolt

and 30, **Figure 44**) and carefully pry the lower mounts (40) and bolts (41) away from the drive shaft housing (20). Slide the mounts from the bolts.

b. On 70 hp models, remove the bolts (32, **Figure 45**) and carefully pry the lower mount brackets (33) from the drive shaft housing. Remove the rear nuts (34, **Figure 45**), washer (35) and cushion (36) from the mount bolts (39). Remove the nuts and washers (21 and 22, **Figure 45**) and carefully pry the lower mounts (37) and bolts (39) away from the drive shaft housing (18). Slide the mounts and washer (38, **Figure 45**) from the bolts.

5. Clean the mounting bolts, threaded bolt holes and mount contact surfaces.

6. Inspect all fasteners for wear, corrosion or damage. Replace any questionable or defective fasteners. Inspect the mounts for wear or damage. Replace any mount if defective.

7. Inspect the mount contact surfaces in the drive shaft housing for cracked or damaged areas. Replace the drive shaft housing if there are cracks or excessively worn areas.

8. To install apply OMC Nut Lock or equivalent threadlocking compound to the threads of all mount and mount cover bolts. Install the mounts and all applicable fasteners. Tighten the mount fasteners to the specification in **Table 1**.

9. Install all removed mount covers, ground wires, cushions and brackets. Securely tighten all fasteners.

10. Carefully remove the overhead support from the engine. Connect the negative battery cable.

Tilt Pin Removal/Installation

The tilt pin (**Figure 42**) passes through the tilt pin holes in the port and starboard clamp brackets. It is important that the pin be installed into the same hole as removed. Moving the pin to the upper positions can cause excessive bow lift and propeller ventilation problems during acceleration. Moving the pin to the lower positions can cause boat handling problems under certain conditions. Using the lower positions can cause poor idling if the exhaust relief hole in the drive shaft housing is under the water.

1. Place the engine in the full UP position. Disconnect the negative battery cable.

2. Use an overhead hoist to support the engine.

3. Mark or note which hole in the clamp bracket the pin passes through.

4. Grip the clamp on the port side of the tilt pin. Squeeze the clamp to release the pin from the port clamp bracket.

5. Pull the tilt pin from the clamp brackets. Clean the tilt pin and the tilt pin holes in the clamp brackets.

11

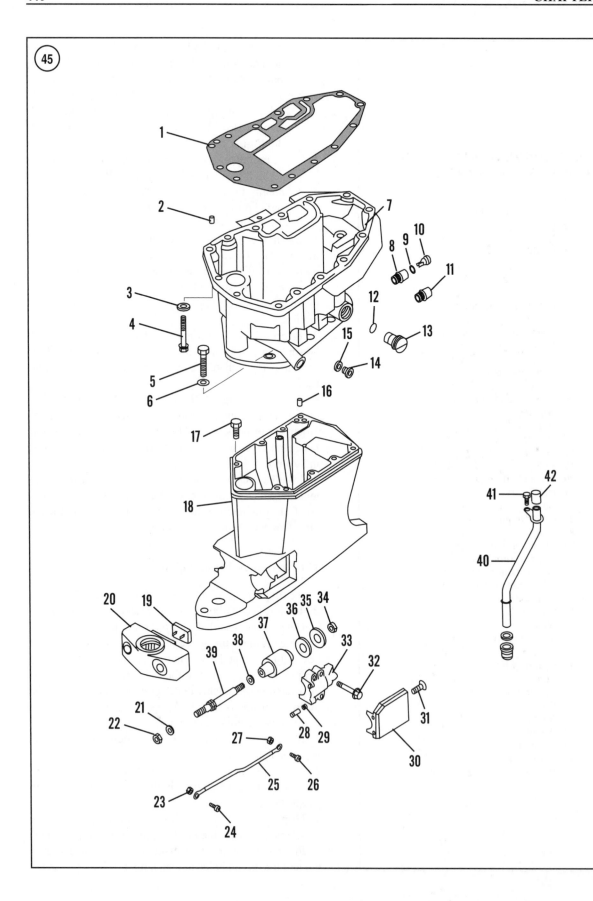

OIL PAN AND DRIVE SHAFT HOUSING (70 HP MODELS)

1. Gasket
2. Alignment pin
3. Washer
4. Bolt
5. Bolt
6. Washer
7. Oil pan
8. Water stream fitting
9. O-ring
10. Plug
11. Exhaust grommet
12. O-ring
13. Flush fitting
14. Oil drain plug
15. Gasket
16. Alignment pin
17. Bolt
18. Drive shaft housing
19. Cushion
20. Lower mount/swivel
    tube bracket
21. Washer
22. Nut
23. Insulating washer
24. Screw
25. Ground wire
26. Screw
27. Insulating washer
28. Pin
29. Spring
30. Lower mount cover
31. Screw
32. Bolt
33. Lower mount bracket
34. Rear nut
35. Washer
36. Cushion
37. Lower mount
38. Washer
39. Mount bolt
40. Water pump tube
41. Bolt
42. Grommet

6. Inspect the tilt pin for bent or damaged areas. Replace the tilt pin if bent, worn or damaged. Replace the drive pin and/or tilt pin if they fit loosely.

7. To install, apply a light coating of OMC Triple-Guard or equivalent water resistant marine grease to the tilt pin and its hole in the clamp bracket.

8. Place the tilt pin into the correct hole in the clamp. Carefully guide the pin through the port then the starboard clamp bracket.

9. Squeeze the clamp on the port side of the tilt pin. Engage the clamp onto the clamp bracket and release the clamp.

10. Carefully remove the overhead support from the engine. Connect the negative battery cable.

Tilt Lock Lever Removal/Installation

Refer to **Figure 46** during tilt lock lever replacement.

1. Place the engine in the full UP position.

2. Use an overhead hoist to support the engine. Disconnect the negative battery cable.

3. Remove all springs, pins, washers and attaching nuts from the tilt lock lever assembly (**Figure 43**).

4. Inspect all pins, levers, bushings and springs for worn, corroded or damaged surfaces. Replace defective components.

5. To install, lubricate all bushings and pivot points with OMC Triple-Guard or equivalent water resistant marine grease prior to assembly. Install all bushings, pins, washers and nuts onto the clamp brackets and swivel housing. Attach the spring(s) to the tilt lock lever mechanism.

6. Make sure the tilt lock lever operates smoothly. Check for improper assembly if rough operation or binding occurs.

7. Carefully remove the overhead support from the engine. Connect the negative battery cable.

Clamp Bracket Removal/Installation

NOTE
Replace all locking-type or tab washers if removed or disturbed.

NOTE
Note the connection points before disconnecting the ground wires. Clean all corrosion or contaminants from the wire contact surface during installation. Securely tighten all ground wire screws during assembly.

1. Place the engine in the full UP position.

2. Use an overhead hoist or some wooden blocks to support the engine. Disconnect the battery.

11

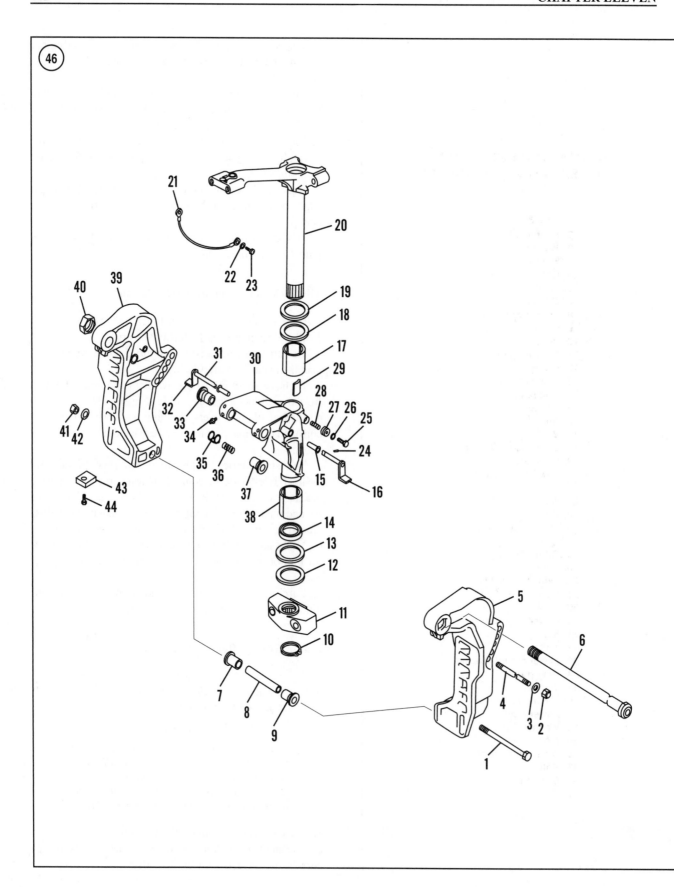

CLAMP BRACKET AND SWIVEL TUBE (40-70 HP MODELS)

1. Lower clamp
   bracket bolt
2. Nut
3. Washer
4. Tilt pin
5. Port clamp bracket
6. Tilt tube
7. Bushing
8. Spacer
9. Bushing
10. Circlip
11. Lower mount/swivel
    tube bracket
12. Washer
13. Washer
14. Seal
15. Bushing
16. Lever
17. Bushing
18. Washer
19. Washer
20. Swivel tube
21. Ground wire
22. Insulating washer
23. Screw
24. Pin
25. Bolt
26. Wave washer
27. Bushing
28. Spring
29. Pad
30. Swivel bracket
31. Bushing
32. Tilt lock lever
33. Bushing
34. Grease fitting
35. Spring
36. Spring
37. Bushing
38. Bushing
39. Starboard clamp
    bracket
40. Tilt tube nut
41. Nut
42. Washer
43. Anode
44. Screw

3. Refer to **Figure 46** to locate the clamp brackets and connected components or fasteners.

4. Remove the trim system (if so equipped) as described in this chapter. Remove the trim position sender (if so equipped) when removing the starboard clamp bracket (39, **Figure 46**).

5. Disconnect and remove the steering linkage and cables from the swivel tube and tilt tube. Remove the engine mounting bolts from the clamp brackets and boat transom.

6. Remove the nuts from the lower pin or spacer (if so equipped). Remove the tilt tube nut (40, **Figure 46**) that retains the tilt tube to the clamp brackets. Carefully pull the clamp bracket from the engine. Clean the mounting bolt holes in the boat transom.

7. Clean the clamp bracket, then inspect the clamp bracket and related fasteners for cracks, wear, or damage. Replace any defective components.

8. To install, place the clamp bracket in position on the midsection. Align all bolts, nuts, spacers and brackets with their respective holes in the clamp bracket.

9. Apply high quality marine-grade sealant to all surfaces of the mounting bolts and the bolt holes. Install the engine mounting bolts through the clamp bracket and boat transom. Securely tighten the mount bolts.

10. Install the trim system (if so equipped) as described in this chapter.

11. Apply OMC Triple-Guard or equivalent water resistant marine grease to the steering cable and tilt tube. Attach the steering cable and linkage to the tilt tube (6, **Figure 46**) and swivel tube (20). Securely tighten all fasteners, then engage any fastener locking devices.

12. Refer to Chapter Twelve and install the trim position sender (if so equipped).

13. Carefully remove the support from the engine. Clean the terminals and connect the battery cables to the battery.

14. Operate the trim and steering system through their entire operating range. Inspect the midsection for improperly installed components if unusual noises or binding occurs. Repair as required.

Upper Engine Mount Removal/Installation

1. On all other models, refer to Chapter Eight and remove the power head.

2. Remove the upper engine mounts as follows:
   a. On 40 and 50 hp models, support the drive shaft housing while removing the nut and washer (29 and 30, **Figure 44**) from the lower engine mount. Remove the nuts, washers and cushions (9-11, **Figure 47**), then pull the drive shaft housing (20, **Figure 44**) from the swivel bracket. Remove the bolts (14 and 15, **Figure 47**), mount covers (12) and mounts

11

47

POWER HEAD ADAPTER (40-70 HP MODELS)

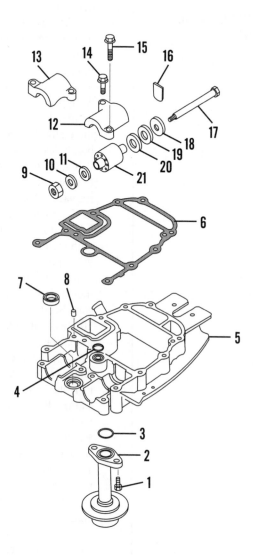

1. Bolt
2. Oil pickup tube
3. O-ring
4. O-ring
5. Power head adapter
6. Gasket
7. Oil seal
8. Alignment pin
9. Nut
10. Washer
11. Cushion
12. Mount cover
13. Mount cover
14. Bolt
15. Bolt
16. Cushion
17. Mount bolt
18. Cushion
19. Washer
20. Washer
21. Upper mount

(21) from the power head adapter (5). Slide the bolts, washers and cushions (18-20, **Figure 47**) and bolt (17) from the mount.

b. On 70 hp models, support the drive shaft housing while removing the nut and washer (21 and 22, **Figure 45**) from the lower engine mount. Remove the nuts, washers and cushions (9-11, **Figure 47**), then pull the drive shaft housing (18, **Figure 45**) from the swivel bracket. Remove the bolts (14 and 15, **Figure 47**), mount covers (12) and mounts (21) from the power head adapter (5). Slide the bolts, washers and cushions (18-20, **Figure 47**) and bolt (17) from the mount.

3. Clean the mount bolts, bolt holes and mount contact surfaces.

4. Inspect all mount fasteners for excessive wear, corrosion or damage. Replace any questionable fasteners. Inspect the rubber portion of the mounts for worn surfaces or damage. Replace defective mounts.

5. Inspect the mount contact surfaces in the power head adapter or oil pan for cracks or damage. Replace a cracked or excessively worn adapter.

6. Installation is the reverse of removal. Note the following:

a. Apply OMC *Nut Lock* or equivalent threadlocking compound to the threads of all mount, mount cover and mount bracket bolts.

b. Tighten the mount fasteners to the specification in **Table 1**.

c. Install all ground wires.

Tilt Tube Removal/Installation

1. Place the engine in the full UP position.

2. Use an overhead hoist or some wooden blocks to support the engine. Disconnect the negative battery cable.

3. Refer to **Figure 46** to locate the clamp brackets and connected components or fasteners.

4. Disconnect the steering linkage and cables from the swivel tube and tilt tube.

5. Remove the nut (40, **Figure 46**), that secures the tilt tube to the starboard clamp bracket.

6. Use a one-foot section of pipe or tubing to drive the tilt tube through the clamp brackets and swivel tube. The selected tool must be slightly smaller in diameter than the tilt tube.

7. Provide overhead support to keep the tube from binding during removal. Do not use excessive force to remove the tube. Excessive force can cause the end of the tube to flare out preventing its removal from the swivel housing and port clamp bracket.

8. Support the engine, then slowly remove the driver tool. Retain the washers as they drop from the clamp brackets and swivel housing. Remove the sealing boot and bushing from the port side of the tilt tube.

9. Thoroughly clean the tilt tube. Inspect the tilt tube for excessive wear, corrosion, cracking or damage. Replace a damaged or worn tilt tube.

10. Thoroughly clean all surfaces of the swivel housing and clamp brackets. Inspect the tilt tube bushings in the swivel housing for excessive wear, corrosion, or damage. If there are defects, remove the grease fittings and replace the bushings. Make sure the holes in the bushing bore align with the grease fitting openings.

11. Apply OMC Triple-Guard or equivalent water resistant marine grease to the tilt tube bore in the swivel bracket and clamp brackets.

12. Place the washer (if so equipped) between the clamp brackets and swivel housing and align with the tilt tube bore.

13. To install, apply a coat of OMC Triple-Guard or equivalent water resistant marine grease to the external surfaces of the tilt tube. Place the tilt tube into its opening in the port clamp bracket with the grooved end facing the port side. Align the tilt tube bores in the clamp brackets, washers and swivel housing during installation of the swivel tube.

14. Using a wooden block for a cushion, carefully tap the tilt tube through the port clamp bracket, swivel bracket and starboard clamp bracket until the threaded end fully extends from the starboard clamp bracket.

15. Install the large nuts, bushing and washers onto the clamp brackets. Tighten the tilt tube nuts to the specification in **Table 1**.

16. Apply OMC Triple-Guard or equivalent water resistant marine grease to the steering cable and tilt tube. Attach the steering cable and linkage to the tilt tube and swivel tube. Securely tighten all fasteners and engage any fastener locking devices.

17. Carefully remove the overhead support from the engine. Connect the negative battery cable.

18. Operate the trim and steering system through the entire operating range. Inspect the midsection for improperly installed components if unusual noise or binding occurs. Repair as required.

Swivel Housing Removal/Installation

Refer to **Figure 46** to identify the swivel housing components and their orientation.

1. Remove the trim system (if so equipped) as described in this chapter.

2. Support the engine with an overhead cable.

11

3. Disconnect the engine from the swivel housing as follows:

   a. On 40 and 50 hp models, support the drive shaft housing while removing the nut and washer (29 and 30, **Figure 44**) from the lower engine mount. Remove the nuts, washers and cushions (9-11, **Figure 47**), and then pull the drive shaft housing (20, **Figure 44**) from the swivel bracket.

   b. On 70 hp models, support the drive shaft housing while removing the nut and washer (21 and 22, **Figure 45**) from the lower engine mount. Remove the nuts, washers and cushions (9-11, **Figure 47**), and then pull the drive shaft housing (18, **Figure 45**) from the swivel bracket.

4. While supported with an overhead cable, pull the engine away from the swivel housing.

5. Remove the clamp brackets, tilt lock lever and reverse lock mechanism as described in this chapter.

6. Clean the swivel housing. Inspect the housing for wear or damage. Replace the swivel housing if it is defective.

7. Move the swivel tube through its full range of motion. Remove the swivel tube as described in this chapter if it binds or feels loose.

8. Installation is the reverse of removal. Note the following:

   a. Carefully slide the engine mount bolts into their openings while positioning the engine to the swivel bracket.

   b. Apply OMC Nut Lock or equivalent threadlocking compound to the threads of all mount, mount cover and mount bracket bolts.

   c. Tighten all fasteners to the specification in **Table 1**.

   d. Apply OMC Triple-Guard or equivalent water resistant marine grease to all bushings, sliding surfaces and pivot points.

   e. Tilt the engine and operate the steering through the entire operating range. Inspect the midsection for improperly installed components if unusual noise or binding occurs. Repair as required.

Swivel tube removal/installation

1. Remove the swivel housing as described in this chapter.

2. Refer to **Figures 44-47** to identify the swivel housing components and their orientation.

3. Remove the circlip (10, **Figure 46**) from its groove on the lower end of the swivel tube. Inspect the circlip for corrosion, cracks or lost spring tension. Replace damaged circlips.

4. Support the lower mount bracket while pulling the swivel tube up and out of the swivel bracket.

5. Remove the lower mount bracket, spacers and washers from the lower end of the swivel bracket in the swivel tube bore. Remove the washers from the upper side of the swivel tube or swivel tube bore.

6. Inspect the bushings at the upper end of the swivel tube bore in the swivel housing. Remove and replace both bushings if worn or damaged.

7. Inspect the swivel tube for cracks, wear or corrosion. Replace as required.

8. Installation is the reverse of removal. Note the following:

   a. Apply OMC Triple-Guard or equivalent water resistant marine grease to the swivel tube bushings and swivel tube.

   b. Install all washers, bushings and spacers as shown in **Figure 46**.

   c. Position the lower seal with the seal lip facing up and the upper seal with the lip facing down.

   d. Make sure the splines in the lower mount bracket (11, **Figure 46**) properly align with the splines of the swivel tube (20).

   e. Fit the circlip into the groove at the lower end of the swivel tube.

Drive Shaft Housing Removal/Installation

Refer to **Figure 44** and **Figure 45** to identify the drive shaft housing components and their orientation.

1. Remove the power head as described in Chapter Eight.

2. Remove the upper and lower engine mounts as described in this chapter.

3. Remove the drive shaft housing as follows:

   a. On 40 and 50 hp models, remove the oil pan (17, **Figure 44**) as described in this chapter. Remove the bolt (2, **Figure 44**) and lift the water pump tube (1) from the drive shaft housing.

   b. On 70 hp models, remove the oil pan (7, **Figure 45**) as described in this chapter. Remove the bolt (41, **Figure 45**) and lift the water pump tube (40) from the drive shaft housing. Remove the grommet (42, **Figure 45**) from the water tube or its opening in the oil pan.

4. Inspect the drive shaft housing for worn areas, cracking or corrosion. Replace the housing if it is defective.

5. Inspect all alignment pins and their bores for worn or damaged pins or elongated holes. Replace any defective components.

6. Installation is the reverse of removal. Note the following:

   a. Install the oil pan as described in this chapter. Install *new* gaskets, O-ring and seals.

b. Apply OMC Nut Lock or equivalent threadlocking compound to the threads of all exhaust tube, engine mount and adapter plate attaching bolts.

c. Install the grommet onto the upper and lower ends of the water tube. Slide the water tube into the drive shaft housing.

d. Install and securely tighten the water tube attaching bolt.

e. Tighten all fasteners to the specification in **Table 1**.

Oil Pan Removal/Installation

40 and 50 hp models

Refer to **Figure 44**.

1. Remove the power head as described in Chapter Eight.

2. Remove the upper and lower engine mounts as described in this chapter.

3. Remove the power head adapter as described in this chapter. Remove the gasket (13, **Figure 44**) from the mating surface.

4. Remove the six bolts (21, **Figure 44**) and carefully lift the oil pan from the drive shaft housing.

5. Remove the four bolts (3, **Figure 44**) and lift the cover (4), water pressure relief valve (6) and grommet (5) from the housing (7). Tap the housing to remove it from the oil pan. Carefully scrape the gasket (8, **Figure 44**) from the mating surfaces.

6. Thread the water stream fitting (9, **Figure 44**) from the oil pan. Pull the cover and O-ring (10 and 11, **Figure 44**) from the fitting. Replace the O-ring during installation.

7. Use a suitable solvent to clean all contaminants from the oil pan. Inspect the oil pan for cracked or corrosion damaged surfaces. Replace the oil pan if it is defective.

8. Installation is the reverse of removal. Note the following:

a. Install a *new* gasket (8, **Figure 44**) to the relief valve housing (7). Install the water pressure relief valve with the cupped plate side facing out or away from the oil pan.

b. Install *new* O-rings at all locations during assembly.

c. Coat all O-rings, grommets and seals with OMC Triple-Guard or equivalent water resistant marine grease during assembly.

d. Apply silicone seal to the oil pan and drive shaft housing mating surfaces.

e. Align the water tube and grommets with the opening in the oil pan during installation.

f. Tighten all fasteners to the specification in **Table 1**.

g. Align the pin opening with the alignment pin (25, **Figure 44**) while mating the oil pan to the drive shaft housing.

70 hp model

Refer to **Figure 45**.

1. Remove the power head as described in Chapter Eight.

2. Remove the upper and lower engine mounts as described in this chapter.

3. Remove the power head adapter as described in this chapter. Remove the gasket (1, **Figure 45**) from the mating surface.

4. Remove the eight bolts and washers (5 and 6, **Figure 45**) and carefully lift the oil pan from the drive shaft housing.

5. Unthread the water stream fitting (8, **Figure 45**) from the oil pan. Pull the plug and O-ring (9 and 10, **Figure 45**) from the fitting.

6. Carefully pry the exhaust grommet (11, **Figure 45**) from the oil pan. Remove the flush fitting (13, **Figure 45**) from the oil pan.

7. Use a suitable solvent to clean all contaminants from the oil pan. Inspect the oil pan for cracked or corrosion damaged surfaces. Replace the oil pan if it is defective.

8. Installation is the reverse of removal. Note the following:

a. Install *new* O-rings and gaskets at all locations during assembly.

b. Coat all O-rings, grommets and seals with OMC Triple-Guard or equivalent water resistant marine grease during assembly.

c. Apply silicone seal to the oil pan and drive shaft housing mating surfaces.

d. Align the water tube and grommets with the opening in the oil pan.

e. Tighten all fasteners to the specification in **Table 1**.

f. Align the pin opening with the alignment pin (16, **Figure 45**) while mating the oil pan to the drive shaft housing.

Power Head Adapter Removal/Installation

1. Remove the drive shaft housing as described in this chapter.

2. Remove the power head as described in Chapter Eight.

3. Remove the upper and lower engine mounts as described in this chapter.

4. Remove the six bolts and washers (3 and 4, **Figure 45**) and carefully pry the power head adapter from the oil pan.

5A. On 40-50 hp models, remove the two bolts (1, **Figure 47**) and pull the oil pickup tube (2) from the adapter.

5B. On 70 hp models, remove the three oil pump bolts and lift the oil pump from the adapter. Replace the O-ring during installation.

11

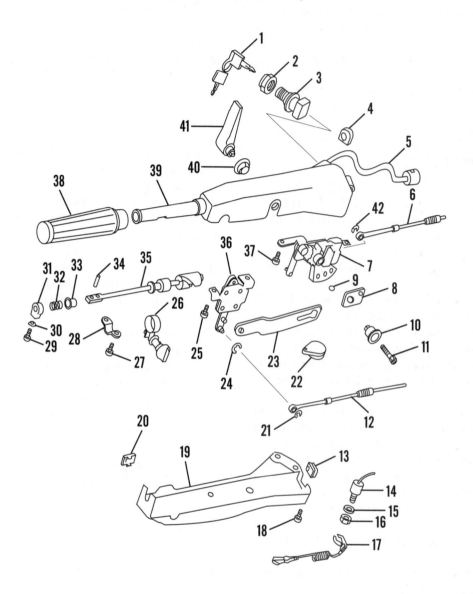

48

OPTIONAL TILLER CONTROL COMPONENTS
(40-70 HP MODELS)

1. Ignition key
2. Plastic nut
3. Ignition key switch
4. Wire grommet
5. Tiller control harness
6. Shift cable
7. Shift linkage
8. Plate
9. Detent ball
10. Bushing
11. Bolt
12. Throttle cable
13. Grommet
14. Lanyard switch
15. Washer
16. Nut
17. Lanyard cord
18. Screw
19. Lower access cover
20. Cover
21. E-clip
22. Warning buzzer
23. Plate
24. E-clip
25. Screw
26. Friction assembly
27. Screw
28. Support
29. Screw
30. Washer
31. Stop
32. Spring
33. Bushing
34. Pin
35. Throttle rod
36. Throttle linkage
37. Screw
38. Grip
39. Tiller arm
40. Bushing
41. Shift selector
42. E-clip

6. Remove the oil pressure relief valve from the adapter. Replace the sealing washer during assembly.

7. Remove all plugs, fittings, gaskets and seals from the adapter.

8. Use a suitable solvent to thoroughly clean the power head adapter.

9. Disassemble and inspect the oil pump as described in Chapter Eight.

10. Installation is the reverse of removal. Note the following:

    a. Fill the oil pump with engine oil prior to installation.

    b. Install *new* O-rings, gaskets and seals if removed.

    c. Apply OMC Triple-Guard or equivalent water resistant marine grease to all seal and O-rings during assembly.

    d. Tighten all fasteners to the specification in **Table 1**.

Tiller Control Removal/Installation (Optional Tiller Kit 40-70 hp Models)

1. Refer **Figure 48** during removal to determine which components need to be removed to access the defective component(s).

2. Inspect all components and fasteners for wear or damage. Never reuse a questionable component.

3. Inspect the throttle and/or shift cables, especially where they pass through the opening in the tiller handle bracket. Make sure the cable moves smoothly in the housing. Replace any damaged or worn cables.

4. Inspect all bushings and pivot bolts or tubes. Replace any that are damaged.

5. To install, use OMC Triple-Guard or equivalent water resistant marine grease on all bushings, pins, rods and pivot surfaces. Apply this grease to the throttle rod assembly.

6. Route all wires to avoid interference during installation and tighten all bolts securely.

7. Check for proper steering and tilting when installation is complete.

Table 1 MIDSECTION AND POWER TRIM TORQUE SPECIFICATIONS (40-70 HP MODELS)

Component	in.-lb.	ft.-lb.	(N•m)
Fluid reservoir mounting bolts			
70 hp models	44	–	5
Housing cover	60-84	–	7-9
Hydraulic pump mounting bolts			
40-70 hp models	71	–	8
Lower engine mount nut			
40-70 hp models			
Front nut	–	44	60
Rear nut	–	29	40
Lower engine mount covet bolt			
40-50 hp models	108-132	–	12-15
Lower mount bracket bolt	60-84	–	7-9
Manual relief valve			
40-70 hp models	30	–	4
Oil pan-to-engine adapter			
40-50 hp models	108-132	–	12-15
Oil pan-to-screw exhaust bolts			
40-70 hp models	60-84	–	7-9
Oil pressure relief valve			
40-70 hp models	–	20	27
Oil pump stopper			
40-70 hp models	–	37	50
Oil pump stopper plug			
40-70 hp models	–	17	23
(continued)			

11

Table 1 MIDSECTION AND POWER TRIM TORQUE SPECIFICATIONS 40-70 HP MODELS (continued)

Component	in.-lb.	ft.-lb.	(N•m)
Shock piston nut			
40-70 hp models	–	74	100
Steering bracket bolt	–	18-20	24-27
Tilt cylinder cap			
70 hp models	–	81	110
Trim cylinder cap			
40-70 hp models	–	59	80
Tilt tube nut	–		
40-70 hp models		32	43
Trim motor mounting screws			
40-70 hp models	53	–	6
Trim system check valve plug			
40-50 hp models	–	15	20
Upper engine mount bolt/nut			
40-70 hp models	–	52	70
Upper engine mount cover			
40-70 hp models	–	17	23
Water pressure reief valve bolt			
40-50 hp models	60-84	–	7-9
Water pump tube bolt			
40-50 hp models	80-90	–	9-10

Table 2 TRIM MOTOR SPECIFICATIONS 40-70 HP MODELS

Component	Specification
Commutator diameter	0.827-0.866 in. (21.0-22.0 mm)
Commutator undercut	0.020-0.031 in. (0.5-0.8 mm)
Brush length	
40-50 hp models	0.189-0.386 in. (4.8-9.8 mm)
70 hp models	0.354-0.492 in. (9.0-12.5 mm)

Chapter Twelve

Remote Controls

This chapter provides illustrations and instructions for removal, repair and installation of the OMC remote control and control cables.

Many different brands, types and styles of remote controls are available to use on OMC outboards. This chapter provides exploded views used to repair the standard side, concealed and binnacle-mount remote control. Contact a marine dealership for parts and information if the engine is equipped with a different brand or type of remote control.

Refer to **Table 1** at the end of this chapter for torque specifications. If a specific torque is not in **Table 1**, refer to Chapter One for general torque specifications. Refer to Chapter Four for cable adjustments procedures.

> *CAUTION*
> *Always refer to the owner's manual for specific operating instructions regarding the remote control. Become familiar with all control functions before operating the engine.*

> *WARNING*
> *A malfunctioning remote control can result in a lack of shift and throttle control. Never operate an outboard with any control system malfunction. Check for proper control system operation before operating the en-*

gine or after performing any service or repair to the control system(s).

CONTROL CABLE RIGGING

Replace the cables if they show any signs of wear, fraying or damage at the exposed ends. Check cable operation and replace any that are hard to move or if there is excessive play. Replace both cables if either cable requires replacement. Mark the cable mounting points with a felt-tip marker before removing them from the remote control. To avoid confusion, remove and install one cable at a time.

When rigging an engine to a new boat, determine cable length by measuring from the centerpoint of the motor (C, **Figure 1**) along the intended cable route to the side-mount (A, **Figure 1**) or center-console (B, **Figure 1**) remote location. Add 3 ft. 4 in. (1.02 M) to the measurement and purchase a cable at or slightly longer than the measurement. OMC replacement cables are available in one foot increments from 5-20 ft. and in two foot increments to 50 ft.

> *WARNING*
> *To prevent the possibility of cable binding or other damage that could cause a loss of steering control under power, always route cables with gentle bends. No bend should have a radius of **less** than 6 in. (15 cm).*

Refer to the procedures in this section for remote service. Refer to the adjustment in Chapter Four when removing, installing and adjusting the throttle and shift cables.

REMOTE CONTROLS

Always mark the orientation of all components prior to removing them. This important step helps ensure proper remote control operation after assembly. Improper assembly can cause internal binding or reversed cable movement.

If complete disassembly is not required to access the faulty component(s), perform the disassembly steps until the desired component is accessible.

Use compressed air to blow debris from the external surfaces prior to disassembling the remote control. Clean all metallic components (except electric switches and the warning buzzer) in a suitable solvent and blow them dry with compressed air. Clean all plastic components with a shop towel. Inspect all components for wear or damage. Replace any defective components. Apply OMC Moly Lube or equivalent to wear surfaces as noted in the figures accompanying the remote *Disassembly and Assembly* procedures. Test all electric components when they have been removed to ensure proper operation after assembly. Refer to Chapter Three to test electrical components.

Refer to Chapter Four for remote control adjustments procedures. Wear safety glasses during remote control service.

Prewired Standard Surface Mount Remote Control

Disassembly and assembly

Refer to **Figure 2**.
1. Disconnect the battery cables.
2. Remove the remote from the boat with the cable attached.
3. Support the control with the housing cover (**Figure 2**, 5) facing downward on small wooden blocks at each end of the housing (4).
4. Loosen the Allen head screw retaining the remote handle (6) with three complete turns. The screw is located at the base of the handle, in the center of a bore at the back of the housing (4). Use a soft-faced mallet with a punch placed inside the head of the Allen screw to gently dislodge the control handle splines from the hub splines, then remove the Allen screw and the remote handle.
5. Remove the three housing–to–housing cover (5) retaining screws (5) from the perimeter of the housing, then separate the halves.

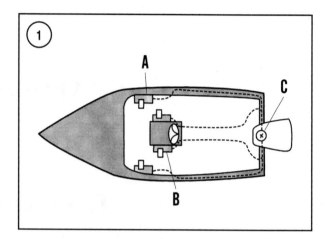

6. Free the shift cable pin from the shift control clevis on the bottom of the shift lever assembly (8), then remove the shift cable from the housing.
7. Lift the throttle cable trunnion from the housing pocket, then pull the cable back to expose the cable pin. Remove the cable and pin from the throttle lever assembly (9).
8. Remove the screw and retainer plate from the top of the shift and throttle plate assembly (10).
9. Remove the friction adjustment knob/screw assembly (12).
10. Loosen the two screws, then remove the neutral switch (2).
11. Carefully lift the shift and throttle plate assembly from the housing, then remove the detent roller, shoe and spring components as well.
12. Lift the shift lever assembly from the housing.
13. Remove and discard the slotted-head screw from the center of the throttle lever assembly, then lift the throttle lever assembly and spacer from the housing.
14. Remove the screw and locknut securing the shift lockout cam to the fast idle lever (11). Discard the locknut. Remove the keeper screw at the top of the housing, above the lever, then lift the shift lockout cam and lever from the housing. Remove the spring washer and fast idle lever from the housing.
15. If necessary, remove the ignition key/lanyard (3) for replacement.
16. If necessary, disassemble the control handle for access to the trim/tilt switch.
17. Clean and inspect the housing components as follows:
   a. Check the shift lockout cam flange bosses and replace the cam if there is rounding at the edges.
   b. Check the slots in the fast idle lever and replace the lever if they are worn.

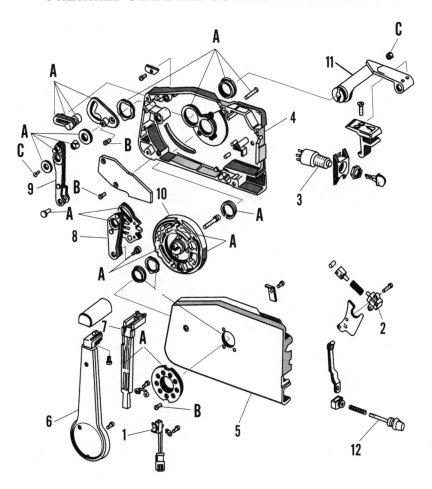

② **PREWIRED STANDARD SURFACE MOUNT REMOTE**

1. Trim/tilt switch
2. Neutral switch
3. Ignition key/lanyard switch
4. Housing
5. Housing cover
6. Remote handle
7. Neutral lock slide
8. Shift lever assembly
9. Throttle lever assembly
10. Shift and throttle plate
    assembly
11. Fast idle lever
12. Friction adjustment
    screw/knob assembly

A-OMC Moly Lube grease
B-OMC Screw Lock
C-Replace this component when removed

12

c. Check all other mechanical parts for excessive wear, cracks or other damage and replace, as necessary.

18. Assembly is the reverse of disassembly. Note the following:

a. Lubricate all pivot points and sliding surfaces with OMC Moly Lube or equivalent, as noted in **Figure 2**.

b. Apply OMC Screw Lock or equivalent threadlocking compound to retainers as noted in **Figure 2**.

c. Make sure the wire harness and connections are routed and installed in a manner that prevents them from contacting any moving components.

d. Connect all wires to the harness at the points noted prior to removal. Make sure no wires become pinched between the back cover during assembly.

e. Securely tighten all fasteners using torque specifications supplied in **Table 1**.

f. Operate the remote handle through its entire range of motion (**Figure 3**) while checking for smooth shifting and throttle movement. Use the friction adjustment screw/knob assembly to adjust remote handle friction to keep the throttle from changing position due to engine vibration during operation. Turn the knob clockwise to increase friction or counterclockwise to decrease it. Do not overtighten the screw to lock the throttle in position.

Small Motor Standard Surface Mount Remote Control

Disassembly and assembly

Refer to **Figure 4**.

1. Disconnect the battery cables.

2. Remove the remote from the boat with the cable attached.

3. Loosen the screws and remove the back plate from the control housing (4).

4. Position the remote handle (6) in NEUTRAL, then remove the shift and throttle cable trunnion plates securing the cable housings to the end of the remote housing.

5. Remove the cotter pins, then remove the shift and throttle cables from the remote assembly.

6. If equipped, remove the cotter pin from the screw in the throttle friction adjustment assembly (1), then remove the screws and the assembly.

7. If equipped, remove the neutral switch (2).

8. Gently pry the cover from the base of the remote handle and then remove the handle retaining screw. Remove the neutral lock plate (5).

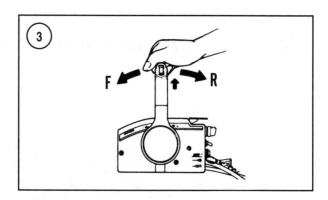

9. Loosen the screw securing the throttle lever (9), then remove the assembly (including the screw, washer, spring and arm). Remove the drive shaft (3).

10. Remove the internal drive components from the housing as follows:

a. Remove the friction adjustment plug, then carefully separate the decal from the handle side of the remote housing.

b. Hold the shift and throttle support plate (10) and other drive components in position while removing the housing three retaining screws on the outside of the cover under the decal mounting surface.

c. Remove the shift and throttle support plate, followed by the shift lever assembly (8), drive gear (11), neutral lock ball, detent roller and leaf springs.

11. Clean and inspect the housing components as follows:

a. Clean all metallic components using a suitable solvent, then wipe dry using a shop rag.

b. Check all mechanical parts for excessive wear, cracks or other damage and replace, as necessary.

12. Assembly is the reverse of disassembly. Note the following:

a. Lubricate all pivot points and sliding surfaces with OMC Moly Lube or equivalent.

b. Replace any of the nuts retaining the shift and throttle support plate if they have lost their locking action.

c. Replace the patch lock screw used to retain the throttle lever if it has lost its locking action.

d. Install the decal using a small amount of OMC Adhesive M or equivalent sealant.

e. When installing the neutral lock plate, turn the thread-forming screws backwards (counterclockwise) until they drop into the original threads, then tighten them by turning clockwise.

f. Make sure the wire harness and connections are routed and installed in a manner that prevents them from contacting any moving components.

④ **SMALL MOTOR STANDARD SURFACE MOUNT REMOTE**

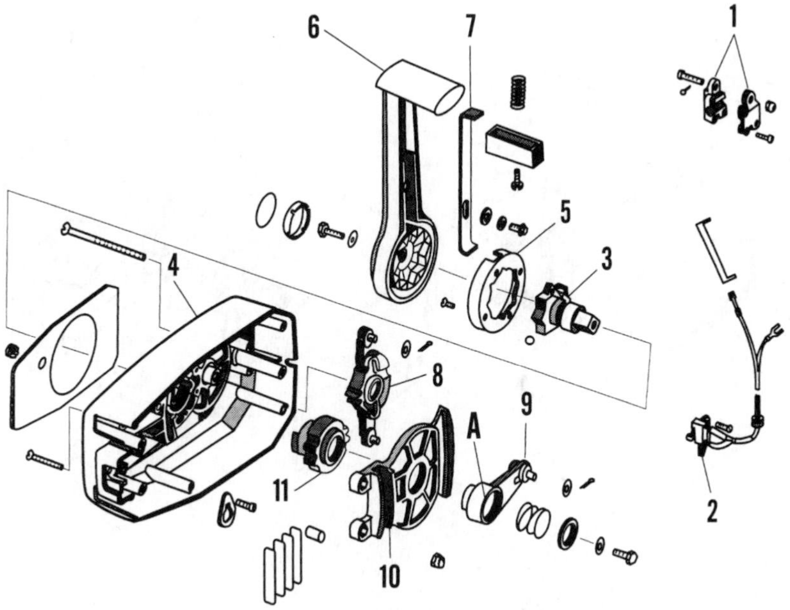

1. Throttle friction adjustment assembly
2. Neutral switch
3. Drive shaft
4. Housing
5. Neutral lock plate
6. Remote handle
7. Neutral lock rod (slide)
8. Shift lever (gear and pin assembly)
9. Throttle lever (arm)
10. Shift and throttle support plate
11. Drive gear

A-OMC Moly Lube grease

g. Connect all wires to the harness at the points noted prior to removal. Make sure no wires become pinched between the back cover during assembly.

h. Securely tighten all fasteners to the specifications in **Table 1**.

i. Operate the remote handle (6) through its entire range of motion (**Figure 3**) while checking for smooth shifting and throttle movement. Use the friction adjustment screw to adjust remote handle friction to keep the throttle from changing position due to engine vibration during operation. The screw is found under the small cover on the housing just in front of the remote handle on starboard installations or just behind the remote handle on port installations. Turn the screw clockwise to increase friction or counterclockwise to decrease it. Do not overtighten the screw to lock the throttle in position.

Dual Handle Surface Mount Remote Control

Disassembly and assembly

Refer to **Figure 5**.

1. Disconnect the battery cables.

12

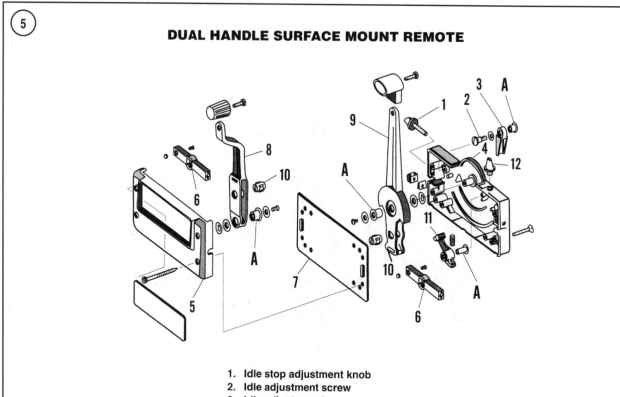

DUAL HANDLE SURFACE MOUNT REMOTE

1. Idle stop adjustment knob
2. Idle adjustment screw
3. Idle adjustment lever
4. Housing
5. Housing cover
6. Casing guide
7. Control housing spacer
8. Shift lever assembly
9. Throttle lever assembly
10. Casing guide insert
11. Throttle friction detent arm and housing
12. Throttle friction adjustment knob

A-OMC Moly Lube grease

2. Remove the remote from the boat with the cable attached.

3. From the two lower corners of the housing (4), remove the two screws that secure the housing and cover (5). Separate the cover and housing, removing the control housing spacer (7).

4. Remove the screw and washer securing the shift lever assembly (8), then lift the lever from the cover. Remove the bushing from the lever and remove the plastic spring and washer from the lever hub.

5. Remove the screw and locknut securing the shift cable to the casing guide (6), then remove the cable. If necessary, push the guide casting insert (10) out and separate the casing guide from the shift lever.

6. Loosen the throttle friction adjustment knob (12), then remove the screw and washer securing the throttle lever assembly (9).

7. Remove the throttle lever from the housing, then remove the bushing from the lever and the two washers from the hub located on the housing.

8. Remove the screw and locknut securing the throttle cable to the casing guide, then remove the cable. If necessary, push the insert out and separate the casing guide from the throttle lever.

9. Completely unscrew the throttle friction adjustment knob, and then pull the throttle friction detent arm (11) with the spring and bushing from the housing.

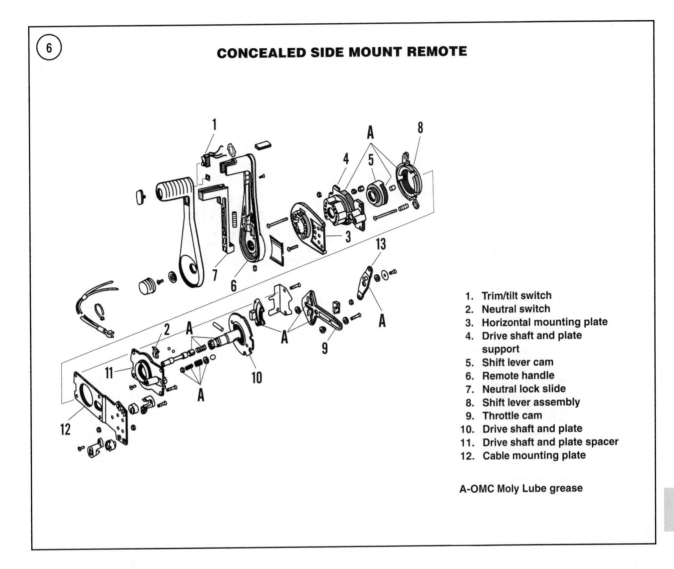

CONCEALED SIDE MOUNT REMOTE

6

1. Trim/tilt switch
2. Neutral switch
3. Horizontal mounting plate
4. Drive shaft and plate support
5. Shift lever cam
6. Remote handle
7. Neutral lock slide
8. Shift lever assembly
9. Throttle cam
10. Drive shaft and plate
11. Drive shaft and plate spacer
12. Cable mounting plate

A-OMC Moly Lube grease

12

10. Remove the idle adjustment screw (2), plastic washer, idle adjustment lever (3) and bushing from the housing.

11. Completely unscrew the idle stop adjustment knob (1), retainer and spring from the housing.

12. Clean and inspect the housing components as follows:

    a. Clean all metallic components using a suitable solvent, then wipe dry using a shop rag.

    b. Check all mechanical parts for excessive wear, cracks or other damage and replace, as necessary.

13. Assembly is the reverse of disassembly. Note the following:

    a. Lubricate all bushings, pivot points and sliding surfaces with OMC Moly Lube.

    b. Operate the remote handle through its entire range of motion (**Figure 3**) while checking for smooth shifting and throttle movement. Use the throttle friction adjustment knob to adjust the throttle handle assembly friction to keep the throttle from changing position due to engine vibration during operation. Turn the screw clockwise to increase friction or counterclockwise to decrease it. Do not overtighten the screw to lock the throttle in position.

14. Idle rpm is set using the idle stop control knob (1). Turn the knob clockwise to increase engine idle or counterclockwise to decrease idle.

Concealed Side Mount Remote Control

Trim/tilt switch removal/installation

Refer to **Figure 6**.

1. Disconnect the battery cables.

2. Cut the wire tie securing the trim switch leads to the lower corner of the control assembly. Note the wire routing for installation purposes.

3. Remove the rubber boot from the warm-up knob at the base of the remote handle (6), then remove the retaining screw and knob.

4. Move the control handle to the full REVERSE position, then insert a 1/8 in. hex-key into the opening at the bottom of the control handle. Use the hex key to loosen the setscrew, then carefully pull the control handle from the shaft. Free the trim switch wires from the mounting plate.

5. Remove the two screws securing the cover, then separate the cover from the remote handle.

6. Remove the neutral lock slide (7) and spring.

7. Remove and discard the retaining clip from the back of the trim/tilt switch (1) and being careful not to scrape or damage the housing in the head of the remote handle. Remove the switch, while carefully pulling the leads from the handle.

8. Installation is the reverse of removal. Note the following:

   a. Use a new retaining clip when installing the trim/tilt switch to the remote handle.

   b. Install the assembled remote handle to the shaft by placing the housing in the full REVERSE throttle position, and carefully pushing it onto the shaft. Make sure the neutral lock slide drops into the slot when shifting the handle up into NEUTRAL, then securely tighten the setscrew.

   c. Route the trim/tilt switch wires as noted during removal and secure them using a new wire tie.

Disassembly and assembly

Refer to **Figure 6**.

1. Remove the remote handle (6) from the control assembly by following **Steps 1-4** of *Trim/tilt switch replacement* in this chapter.

2. Remove the three screws securing the remote assembly to the horizontal mounting plate (3), then remove the control from the boat with the cables still attached.

3. Remove the throttle and shift cables from the control.

4. Temporarily reinstall the remote handle on the control assembly and shift into NEUTRAL for disassembly, then remove the handle again.

5. Remove the screw, washer and throttle arm (13), then remove the spacer.

6. Remove the screw and washer securing the throttle cam (9), then remove the friction control cap and locknut from the other end of the throttle cam. Remove the throttle cam from the assembly, then remove the two spacers.

7. Remove the two screws and locknuts, then remove the shield, shoe and the neutral switch (2).

8. Remove the two remaining screws and nuts, then lift out the drive shaft and plate (10) along with the drive shaft and plate spacer (11) as an assembly.

9. Lift the cable mounting plate (12) off the drive shaft and plate support (4).

10. If necessary, disassemble the drive shaft and plate (10) components as follows:

   a. Press in and hold the neutral warm-up rod on the end of the shaft while withdrawing the shift cam drive pin from the base of the shaft.

   b. Separate the drive shaft from the spacer (11) and remove or catch the detent ball (as it may fall when they are separated).

   c. Withdraw the neutral warm-up rod, drive shaft ball and spring from the end of the shaft.

   d. Loosen the left-hand thread screw and nut by turning them clockwise retaining the detent shoe and springs. Remove the shoe, inner spring and outer spring.

11. If necessary, disassemble the remaining components from the drive shaft and plate support as follows:

   a. Remove the shift lever assembly (8) and the throttle friction screw and spring.

   b. Remove the three shift cam rollers, then remove the shifter lever cam (5) and withdraw the ball from the bore in the side of the cam.

   c. Remove the three hex spacers and locknuts.

12. Clean and inspect the housing components as follows:

   a. Clean all metallic components using a suitable solvent, then wipe dry using a shop rag.

   b. Check all mechanical parts for excessive wear, cracks or other damage and replace, as necessary.

13. Assembly is the reverse of disassembly. Note the following:

   a. Lubricate all pivot points and sliding surfaces with OMC Moly Lube or equivalent.

   b. Remember that the screw and nut securing the shift detent screw and spring assembly to the drive shaft and plate assembly have left-hand threads. They are tightened by being turned counterclockwise.

14. Operate the remote handle through its entire range of motion (**Figure 3**) while checking for smooth shifting and throttle movement. Use the throttle friction adjustment screw through the bore on the horizontal mounting plate located closest to the remote handle. Turn the screw clockwise to increase friction or counterclockwise to decrease it. Do not overtighten the screw to lock the throttle in position.

15. Adjust the shifter detent friction screw through the bore in the horizontal mounting plate (3) located furthest from the remote handle. Turn the screw clockwise to increase friction or counterclockwise to decrease it. Do not overtighten the screw to lock the shifter in position, but adjust while moving the shifter slowly from *forward* through *neutral* to *reverse* and back again, until the desired friction is felt at the handle.

Prewired Binnacle Mount Remote Control

Disassembly and assembly

Refer to **Figure 7**.

1. Disconnect the battery cables.

2. Remove the remote from the boat with the cable attached.

3. Remove the nut securing the ignition key switch (3), then remove the cover.

4. Remove the throttle and shift cables from the control assembly.

5. Place the remote handle (6) in NEUTRAL, then carefully pry the screw cover from the base of the handle. Remove the screw and washer, then carefully pry the remote handle from the drive shaft (12) splines.

6. If necessary, disassemble and inspect the handle assembly. The trim/tilt switch (1) is mounted in the housing at the top of the assembly and can be removed for replacement.

7. Remove the two screws, then lift off the clamp and the neutral switch (2) from the shift lever support (10). Note the routing, then cut the wire tie and remove the screw securing the wire clamp.

8. Remove the warning horn (13) mounting screw, then remove the horn and wiring harness assembly.

9. Remove the housing cover brackets (14).

10. Locate the throttle lever plate (9), then remove the cotter pin from the friction adjustment screw. Loosen the screw and remove it along with the nut and outer friction shoe from over the top of the throttle lever plate. Remove the screw, washer and throttle lever plate.

11. Remove the screw, washer and nut from the throttle cam located just outboard of the drive shaft and support plate(12). Remove the throttle cam, bushing, spacer and throttle pin roller.

12. Using snap ring pliers, remove the snap ring from the splined end of the drive shaft (12).

13. Remove the screws and nuts securing the inner friction shoe, then remove the shoe.

14. Remove the four screws and nuts holding the balance of the assembly together, then carefully pry the outer shaft

support off the drive shaft and from over the top of the neutral warm-up rod (7) and shift lever support (10).

15. Remove the neutral warm-up rod slowly, keeping pressure on the springs at the bottom of the rod until compression is released so as not to lose the springs when withdrawing the rod. Remove the shift lever support.

16. Remove the friction adjustment screw and spring from the shift lever support or the neutral detent plate spacer (11).

17. Remove the housing plate (4) and shift lever cam (8) from the drive shaft and neutral detent plate spacer. Separate the shift lever cam from the plate, then remove the rollers from the lever.

18. If necessary, disassemble the drive shaft and neutral detent plate spacer components as follows:

    a. Push the drive pin tin to the shaft using the neutral warm-up ring, then carefully lift the ring from the cam.

    b. Push the drive pin into the shaft and place a finger over the pin while carefully lifting the cam from the shaft. Slowly release the spring pressure on the pin once the cam is removed.

    c. Remove the pin and spring from the shaft.

    d. Pry the shaft from the detent plate and catch the detent ball located between them.

    e. Remove the ball, shoe, springs, nut and screw from the detent plate.

19. Clean and inspect the housing components as follows:

    a. Clean all metallic components using a suitable solvent, then wipe dry using a shop rag.

    b. Check all mechanical parts for excessive wear, cracks or other damage and replace, as necessary.

20. Assembly is the reverse of disassembly. Note the following:

    a. Lubricate all pivot points and sliding surfaces with OMC Moly Lube or equivalent.

    b. Make sure that both cables attach to the *handle side* of the throttle lever plate. One cable pin is inserted first through the throttle lever, then through the throttle cable. The other pin is inserted first through the shift cable, then through the shift lever.

    c. Make sure the wire harness and connections are routed and installed in a manner that prevents them from contacting any moving components.

    d. Connect all wires to the harness at the points noted prior to removal. Make sure no wires become pinched between the back cover on assembly.

21. Operate the remote handle through its entire range of motion (**Figure 3**) while checking for smooth shifting and throttle movement. Use the friction adjustment screw to adjust remote handle friction to keep the throttle from

12

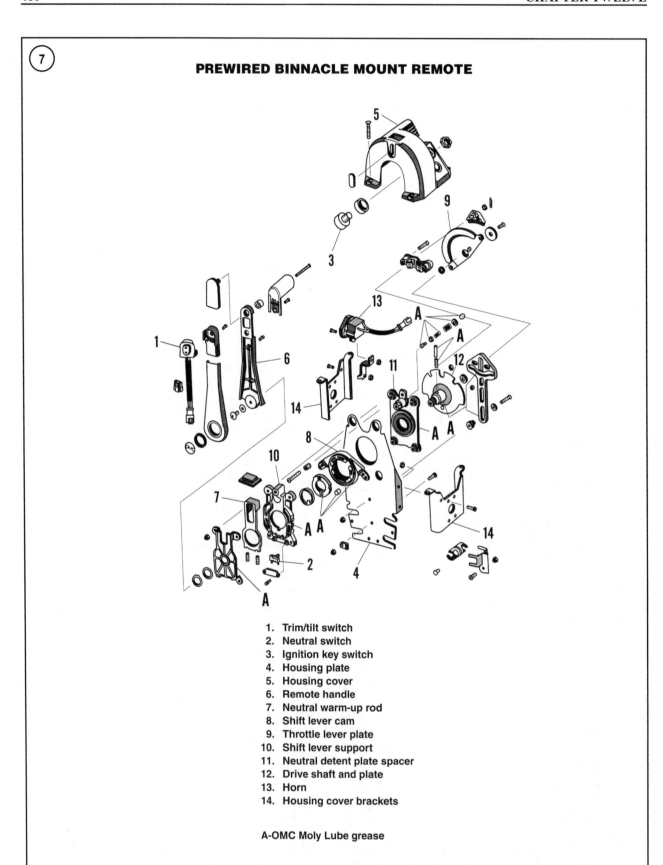

PREWIRED BINNACLE MOUNT REMOTE

1. Trim/tilt switch
2. Neutral switch
3. Ignition key switch
4. Housing plate
5. Housing cover
6. Remote handle
7. Neutral warm-up rod
8. Shift lever cam
9. Throttle lever plate
10. Shift lever support
11. Neutral detent plate spacer
12. Drive shaft and plate
13. Horn
14. Housing cover brackets

A-OMC Moly Lube grease

changing position due to engine vibration during operation. The screw is found under a small cover on the top side of the housing, at the top of the curve on the side of the housing cover. Two adjustment screws are accessible through the oval cutout, the *top* screw is the throttle friction screw. Turn the screw clockwise to increase friction or counterclockwise to decrease it. Do not overtighten the screw to lock the throttle in position.

22. Adjust the shifter detent friction screw through the same oval cutout at the top of the housing cover. The screw is the *bottom* of the two screws accessible through the cutout. Turn the screw clockwise to increase friction or counterclockwise to decrease it. Do not overtighten the screw to lock the shifter in position, but adjust while moving the shifter slowly to the FORWARD detent and then back again to NEUTRAL, until the desired friction is felt at the handle.

Table 1 REMOTE CONTROL TORQUE SPECIFICATIONS

Fasteners	in.-lb.	N•m
Concealed side mount		
All fasteners (except handle cover)	25-35	2.8-4.0
Handle cover screws	15-22	1.7-2.5
Dual handle surface mount		
Cable stop lever screw	25-35	2.8-4.0
Housing and cover screws	60-80	7-9
Shift and throttle lever screw	25-35	2.8-4.0
Shift and throttle cable casting guide screws	60-80	7-9
Prewired Binnacle mount		
All fasteners (except switch-to-lever)	15-35	1.7-4.0
Switch-to-lever screw	7-10	.8-1.2
Prewired standard surface mount		
Control handle cover screw	5-7	.6-.8
Control handle knob screw	20-30	2.3-3.4
Control handle plate screws[2]	25-35	2.8-4.0
Housing-to-housing screws[1]	40-50	4.5-5.6
Keeper screw	10-15	1.1-1.7
Neutral switch screws	15-20	1.7-2.3
Remote handle Allen screw[1]	100-120	11-14
Retainer plate screw*	25-35	2.8-4.0
Safety lanyard/key switch nut	20-30	2.3-3.4
Shift lockout cam screw[2]	25-35	2.8-4.0
Throttle lever screw[1]	25-35	2.8-4.0
Small motor standard surface mount		
Cam plate screws	24-36	3-4
Handle retaining bolt	60-84	7-10
Housing retaining screws	24-36	3-4
Neutral lock plate screw	15-22	1.6-2.4
Neutral lock rod bolt	25-35	2.8-4.0
Neutral switch screw	25-35	2.8-4.0
Throttle adjustment cover screw	15-22	1.6-2.4
Throttle lever bolt	60-84	7-9
Trunnion mounting plate screw	25-35	2.8-4.0

1. OMC Moly Lube grease.
2. OMC Screw Lock.

12

Index

13

13

1997-2001 5/6 HP ROPE START

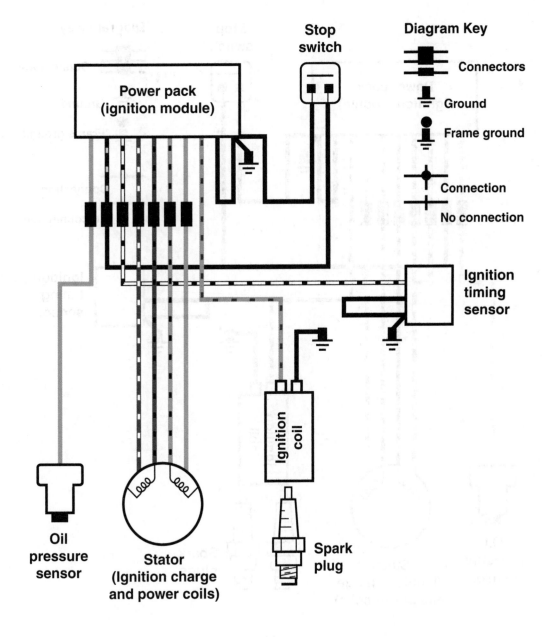

Stop switch

Diagram Key

Connectors

Ground

Frame ground

Connection

No connection

Power pack (ignition module)

Ignition timing sensor

Ignition coil

Oil pressure sensor

Stator (Ignition charge and power coils)

Spark plug

14

1995-2001 8 HP AND 1997-1998 9 HP (211 cc) ROPE START

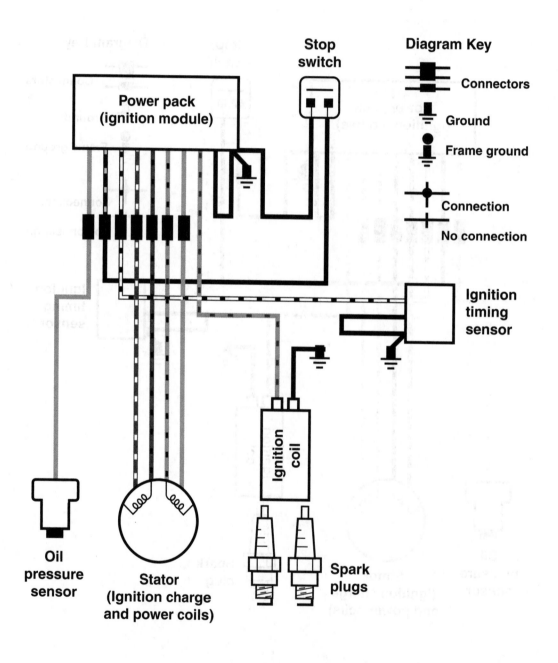

1997-1998 9.9 HP (211 cc) TILLER/ELECTRIC START

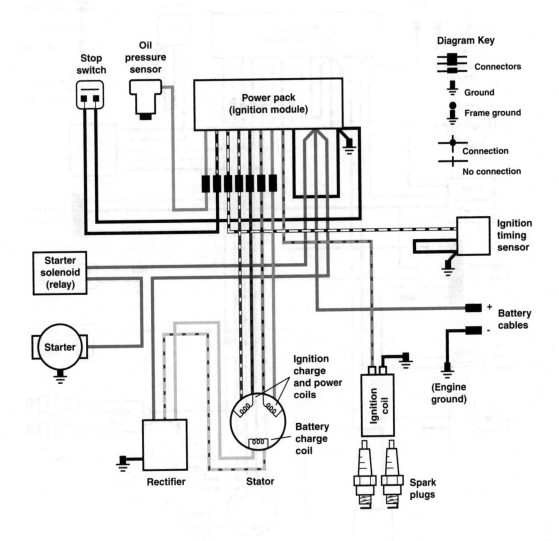

1997-1998 9.9 HP (211 cc) REMOTE

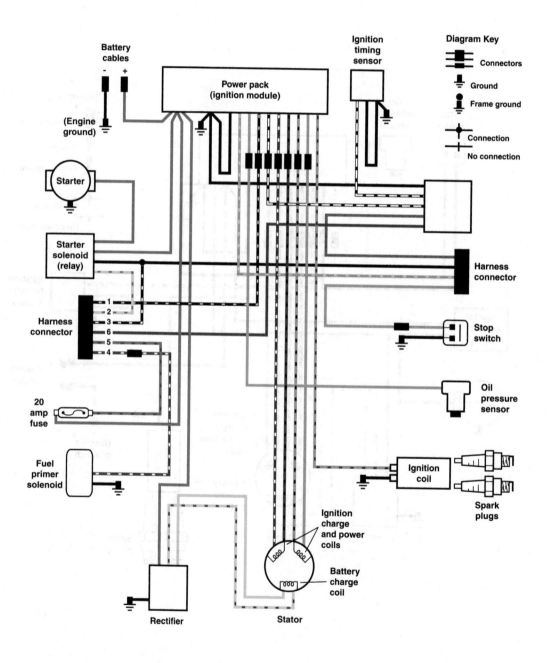

1995-2001 9.9 HP (305 cc) AND 15 HP ROPE START

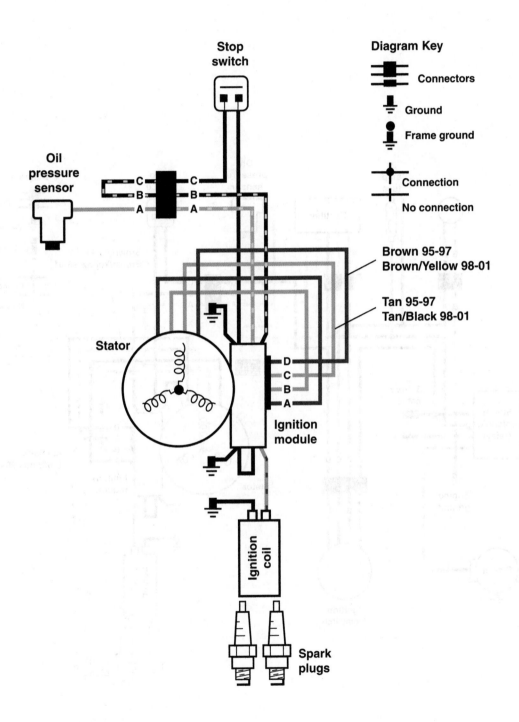

1995-2001 9.9 HP (305 cc) TE HIGH THRUST

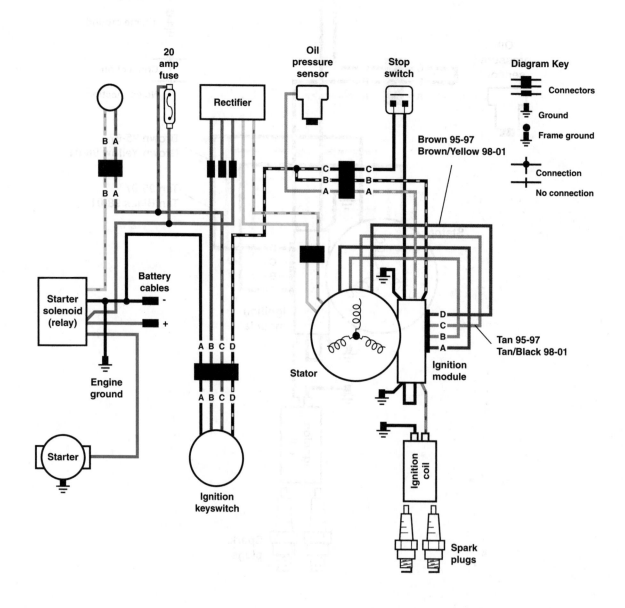

1995 9.9 HP (305 cc) REMOTE HIGH THRUST

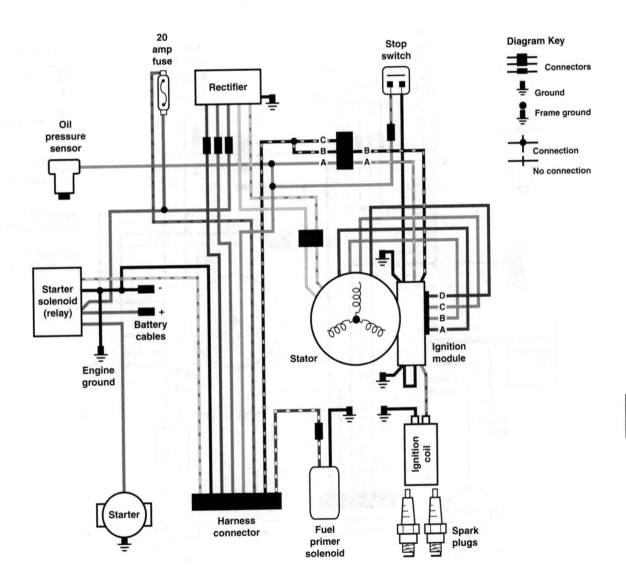

Oil pressure sensor

20 amp fuse

Rectifier

Stop switch

Diagram Key

Connectors

Ground

Frame ground

Connection

No connection

C
B
A

B
A

Starter solenoid (relay)

–
+
Battery cables

Engine ground

D
C
B
A

Stator

Ignition module

Starter

Harness connector

Fuel primer solenoid

Ignition coil

Spark plugs

14

1996-2001 9.9 HP (305 cc) REMOTE HIGH THRUST

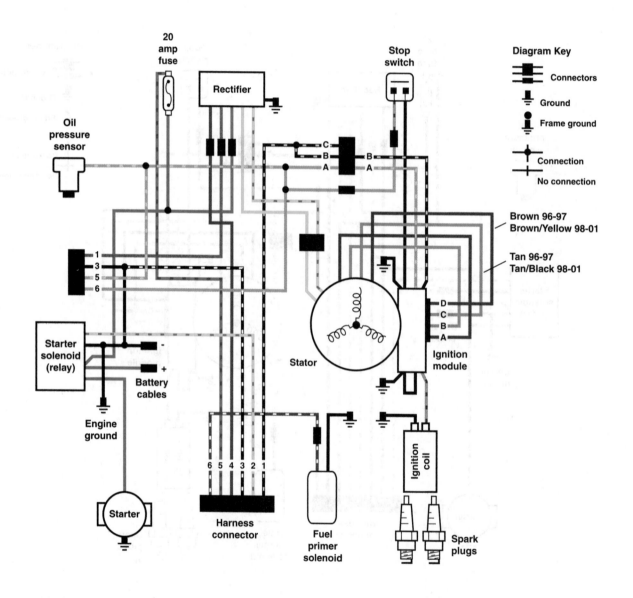

1995 AND 1998 15 HP TE

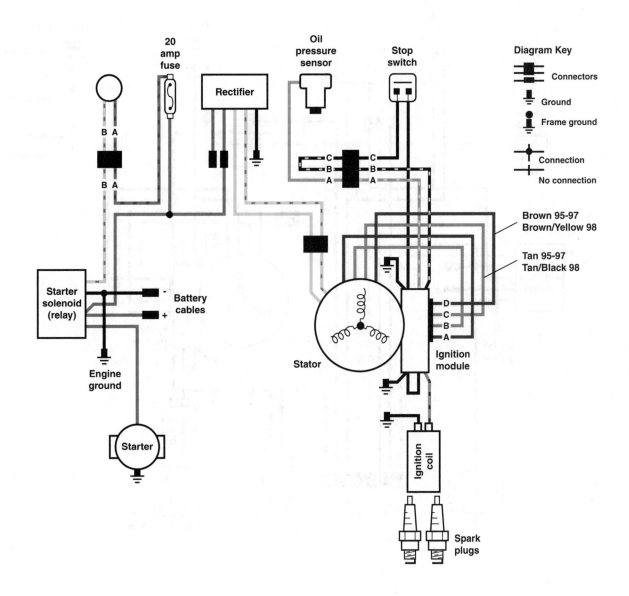

1995 15 HP REMOTE

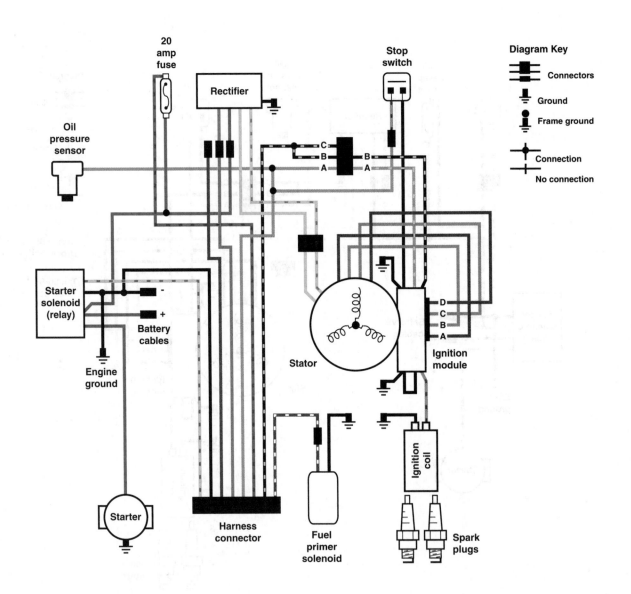

20 amp fuse

Rectifier

Stop switch

Diagram Key

Connectors

Ground

Frame ground

Connection

No connection

Oil pressure sensor

C
B
A

B
A

D
C
B
A

Starter solenoid (relay)

–
+
Battery cables

Engine ground

Stator

Ignition module

Starter

Harness connector

Fuel primer solenoid

Ignition coil

Spark plugs

1996-2001 15 HP REMOTE

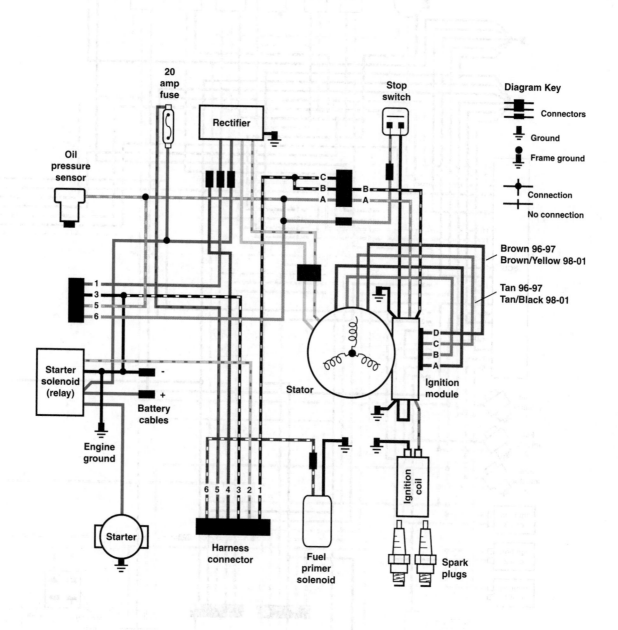

Diagram Key

- Connectors
- Ground
- Frame ground
- Connection
- No connection

Brown 96-97
Brown/Yellow 98-01

Tan 96-97
Tan/Black 98-01

20 amp fuse

Rectifier

Stop switch

Oil pressure sensor

1
3
5
6

Starter solenoid (relay)

Battery cables

Engine ground

Starter

Stator

Ignition module

Harness connector

Fuel primer solenoid

Ignition coil

Spark plugs

D
C
B
A

6 5 4 3 2 1

14

1999-2001 40/50 HP

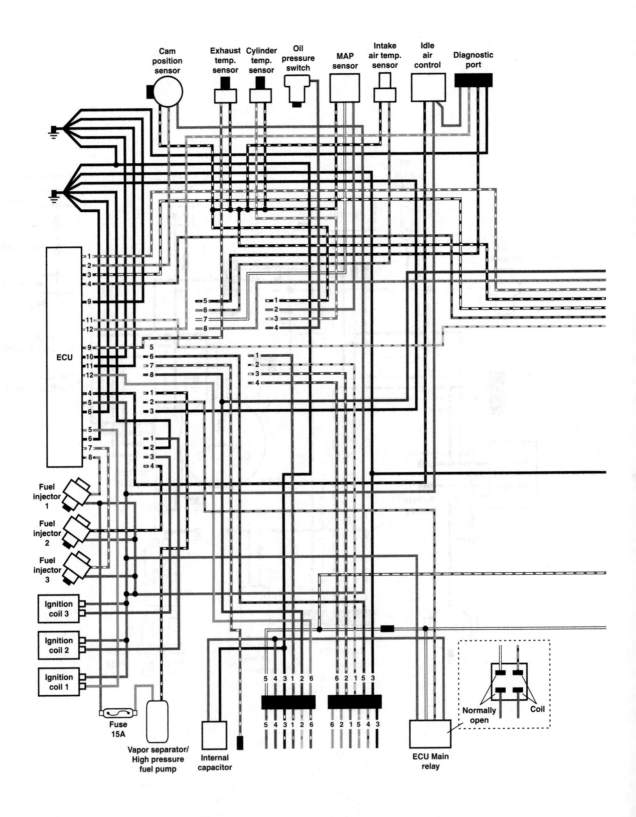

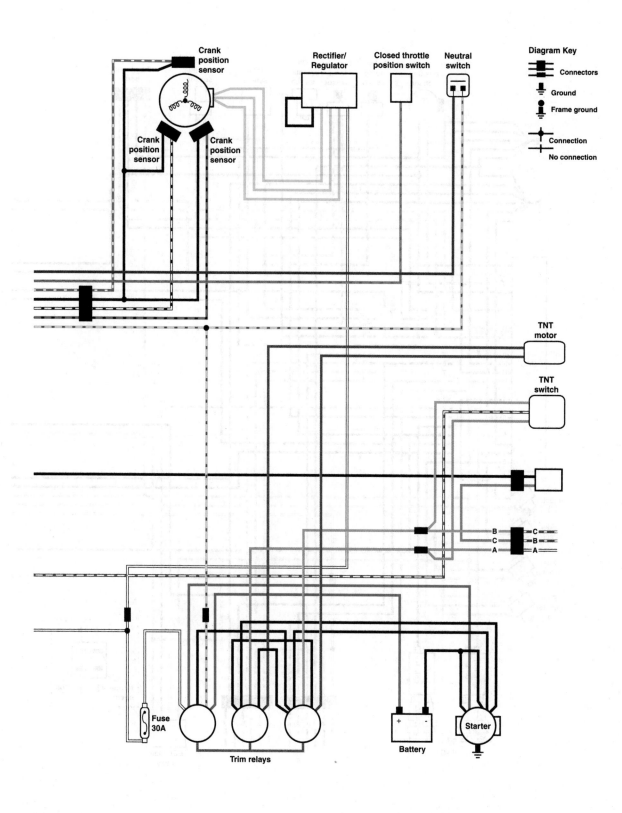

Crank position sensor

Crank position sensor

Crank position sensor

Rectifier/ Regulator

Closed throttle position switch

Neutral switch

Diagram Key

Connectors

Ground

Frame ground

Connection

No connection

TNT motor

TNT switch

B — C
C — B
A — A

Fuse 30A

Trim relays

Battery

+ −

Starter

14

1999-2001 70 HP

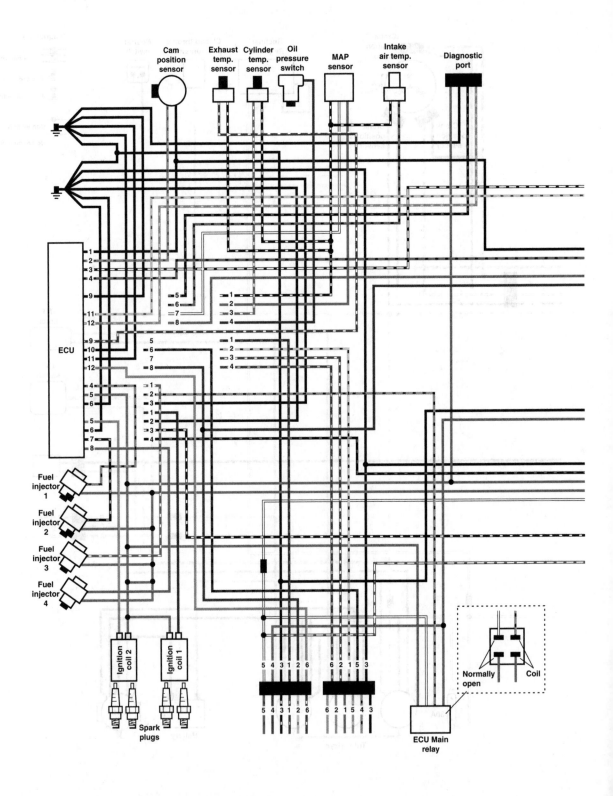

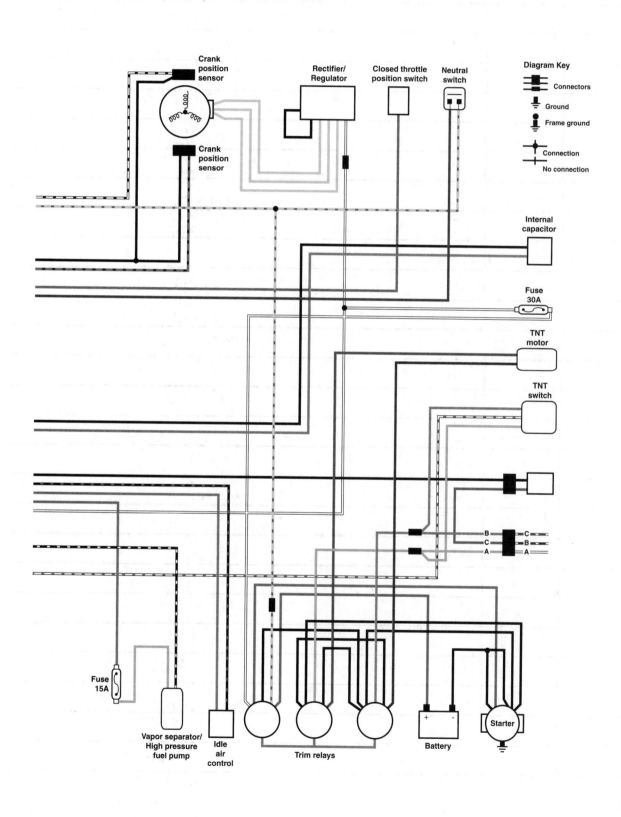

Crank position sensor

Crank position sensor

Rectifier/ Regulator

Closed throttle position switch

Neutral switch

Diagram Key

- Connectors
- Ground
- Frame ground
- Connection
- No connection

Internal capacitor

Fuse 30A

TNT motor

TNT switch

B — C
C — B
A — A

Fuse 15A

Vapor separator/ High pressure fuel pump

Idle air control

Trim relays

Battery

Starter

14

MAINTENANCE LOG

Date	Engine Hours	Type of Service